Marine Mammals: Evolutionary Biology

Marine Mammals: Evolutionary Biology

Annalisa Berta
Department of Biology
San Diego State University
San Diego, California

James L. Sumich
Biology Department
Grossmont College
El Cajon, California

With illustrations by

Pieter Arend Folkens
A Higher Porpoise Design Group
Benecia, California

Peter J. Adam
Department of Biology
San Diego State University
San Diego, California

ACADEMIC PRESS
A Harcourt Science and Technology Company

San Diego San Francisco New York Boston London Sydney Tokyo

Cover photographs: Photographs on front and back cover by Pieter Folkens.

This book is printed on acid-free paper. ♾

Academic Press
An imprint of Elsevier Science
525 B Street, Suite 1900, San Diego, California 92101-4495, USA
http://www.academicpress.com

Academic Press
84 Theobald's Road, London WC1X 8RR, UK
http://www.academicpress.com

Library of Congress Catalog Card Number: 98-86074

International Standard Book Number: 0-12-093225-3

PRINTED IN THE UNITED STATES OF AMERICA
03 04 05 06 07 9 8 7 6 5 4 3

CONTENTS

3. Pinniped Evolution and Systematics

4. Cetacean Evolution and Systematics

5. Sirenians and Other Marine Mammals: Evolution and Systematics

6. Evolutionary Biogeography

Part II: Evolutionary Biology, Ecology, and Behavior

7. Integumentary, Sensory, and Urinary Systems

PREFACE

Marine Mammals: Evolutionary Biology is written for two audiences; as a text for an upper-level undergraduate or graduate-level course on marine mammal biology, and as a sourcebook for marine mammal scientists in research, education, management, and legal/policy development positions. One of our major goals is to introduce the reader to the tremendous breadth of topics that comprise the rapidly expanding interdisciplinary field of marine mammal science today. Our motivation for writing this book was the lack of a comprehensive text on marine mammal biology, particularly one that employs a comparative, phylogenetic approach. We have attempted, where possible, to demonstrate that hypotheses of the evolutionary relationships of marine mammals provide a powerful framework for tracing the evolution of their morphology, behavior, and ecology. This approach has much to offer but is limited, in many cases, by available comparative data. We hope that this book stimulates others to pursue marine mammal research in this exciting new direction.

ACKNOWLEDGMENTS

We thank the following reviewers for reading one or more chapters: Frank Awbrey, Ted Cranford, Daryl Domning, Frank Fish, Burney Le Boeuf, Gina Lento, Clayton E. Ray, Charles A. Repenning, Sam Ridgway, Richard H. Tedford, Hans Thewissen, Bernd Würsig, and Andre R. Wyss. Their critical comments have greatly enhanced the text. We also acknowledge students in the 1997 and 1998 classes of "The Evolution and Ecology of Marine Mammals" at San Diego State University for their bibliographic assistance. Numerous students have evaluated portions of this text and have contributed useful suggestions for its improvement. We owe special thanks to Linda Rhamy and Peter Adam for reading the entire manuscript and providing supportive and constructive feedback. The many colleagues that contributed photographs and line drawings are identified in the captions. The production and editorial staff at Academic Press have been very helpful in preparation of this book; we are especially grateful to Cheryl Uppling, Jackie Garrett, and Charles R. Crumly. Finally, we thank friends and colleagues who provided inspiration by asking "why phylogenies matter?" Although we have relied on existing published literature for information, the interpretations presented here are solely ours. In the spirit of improving this work, we would appreciate notification of any errors, either of omission or of fact.

A. Berta
aberta@sunstroke.sdsu.edu

J. Sumich
jim.sumich@gcccd.net

1

Introduction

1.1. Marine Mammals —"What Are They?"

Some 100 living species of mammals (listed in Appendix 3) depend on the ocean for most or all of their life needs. Living **marine mammals** include a diverse assemblage of species that have representatives in three mammalian orders. Within the order **Carnivora** are the **pinnipeds** (seals, sea lions, walruses), the sea otter, and the polar bear. The order **Cetacea** includes whales, dolphins, and porpoises, and the order **Sirenia** is composed of sea cows (manatees and dugongs). Marine mammals were no less diverse in the past and include extinct groups such as the hippopotamus-like **desmostylians**, the bizarre bear-like carnivore ***Kolponomos***, and the aquatic sloth ***Thalassocnus***.

1.2. Adaptations for Aquatic Life

Marine mammals are well adapted for life in the water though they differ in the degree to which they are adapted to this habitat. Pinnipeds, sea otters, and polar bears are amphibious, spending some time on land to give birth and to molt, whereas cetaceans and sirenians are fully aquatic. A few major aquatic **adaptations** are briefly reviewed below and are covered in greater detail in subsequent chapters. Adaptations of the skin, specifically its increased insulation (through development of **blubber** or a dense fur layer) and circulatory adjustments to minimize heat loss (e.g. increased metabolic rates and **countercurrent heat exchange systems**) help them cope with the cold. Similarly, the eyes, nose, ears, and limbs of marine mammals have changed in association with their ability to live in a variety of aquatic environments, which include salt-, brackish- and freshwater. Most notable among sensory adaptations are the high frequency sounds produced by some whales for use in navigation and foraging. Other marine mammals (e.g. pinnipeds and sea otters) have an acute sense of smell; these same groups also possess well-developed whiskers with sensitive nerve fibers that serve as tactile sense organs. Pinnipeds have modified the front- and hind limbs as flippers which propel them both in the water and on land. In cetaceans and sirenians the hind limbs are virtually absent and locomotion is accomplished by vertical movement of the tail. Most marine mammals cope with living in salt water by conserving water in their heavily lobulated kidneys which are efficient at concentrating urine.

Many marine mammals are capable of prolonged and deep dives. Adaptations of the respiratory system, such as flexible ribs that allow the lungs to collapse and thickened tissue in the middle ear of pinnipeds and cetaceans, enable them to withstand the tremendous pressures encountered at great depths. The long dives of these animals are accomplished by a variety of circulatory changes including a slowed heart rate, reduced oxygen consumption, and shunting blood to essential organs and tissues only.

1.3. Scope and Use of This Book

Marine Mammals: Evolutionary Biology aims to provide an overview of the biology of marine mammals with emphasis on their evolution, anatomy, behavior, and ecology. These topics will be presented and discussed using, in so far as possible, an explicit phylogenetic context. In doing so we consider different ways of incorporating evolutionary history into comparative analyses of marine mammal biology. This approach is different from the two-volume multi-authored review of marine mammal biology by Reynolds and Rommel (1999) which uses an ecological paradigm with an emphasis on conservation. Although the phylogenetic approach advocated in this book is relatively new, we hope that it will promote further research in this area because we believe that this approach to marine mammal science has much to offer.

The book is divided into two major sections: Part I: Evolutionary history (Chapters 2–6) is where the origin and diversity of marine mammals are revealed, and Part II: Evolutionary biology, ecology, and behavior (Chapters 7–15) is where we attempt to explain how this diversity arose by examining patterns of morphological, behavioral and ecologic diversity. We have intended to explain these concepts, wherever possible, by example, and with a minimum of professional jargon. Words and phrases included in the glossary appear in boldface type at their first appearance in the text. "Further reading" sections have been placed at the end of each chapter and are intended to guide the reader to more detailed information about a particular topic.

1.4. Time Scale

A historical discussion of marine mammals requires a standard time framework for relating evolutionary events. Figure 1.1 presents the geologic time scale that will be used throughout this book (based on Harland *et al.,* 1990). Our interest lies in the **Cenozoic Era,** the last 65 million years of earth history, during which time all marine mammals made their first appearance. Whales and sirenians were the first to appear, beginning approximately 50 million years ago (Ma) during the early **Eocene**. Pinnipeds trace their ancestry back between 29 and 23 Ma to the late **Oligocene**. The sea otter lineage goes back approximately 7 Ma to the late **Miocene**, although the modern sea otter is known in the fossil record only as far back as the early **Pleistocene** (1.6 Ma). Polar bears appear even later, during the late Pleistocene (0.5 Ma). The desmostylians, extinct relatives of sirenians, range from the early Oligocene through the late Miocene. The extinct carnivoran *Kolponomos* is known from a brief time interval during the early Miocene and the extinct marine sloth *Thalassocnus* lived during the early **Pliocene** (5.2–3.4 Ma).

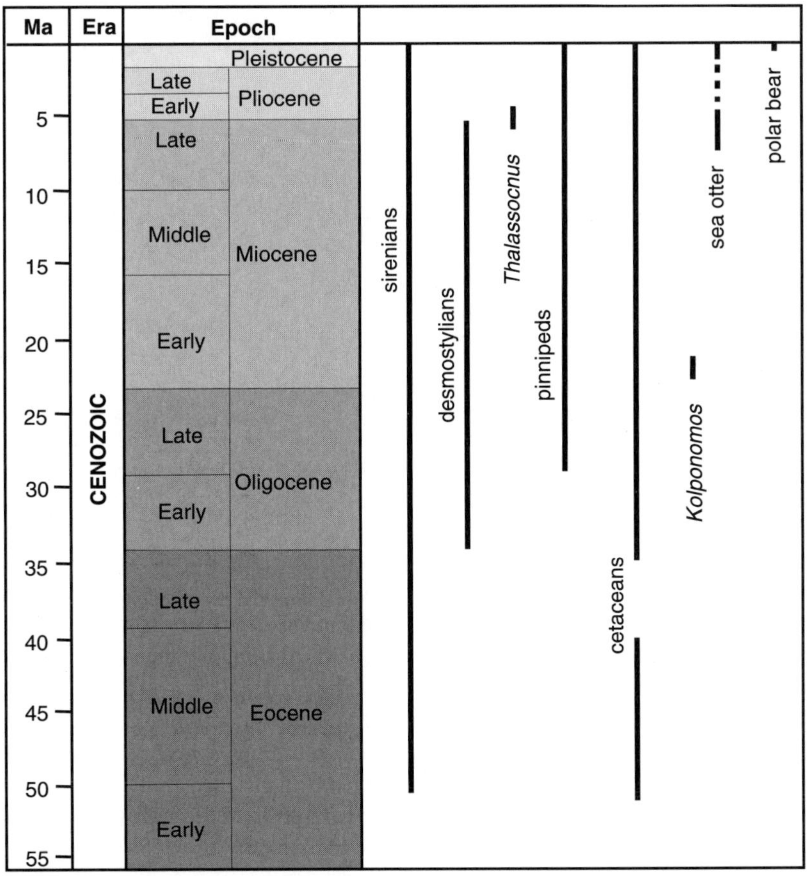

Figure 1.1. Chronologic ranges of marine mammal taxa. Solid bars show reported maximum ranges. Ma = million years ago. (Time scale and correlations are from Harland *et al.,* 1990; Berggren *et al.,* 1995).

1.5. Early Observations of Marine Mammals

The study of marine mammals probably began with casual observations of the appearance and behavior of whales in the fourth century B.C.E. (Before Current Era). Still, the knowledge and history of these animals themselves go much further back. Drawings of seals and dolphins on pieces of reindeer antler and in caves have been found from **Paleolithic** times. The Greek philosopher Aristotle (384–322 B.C.E.) in his *Historia Animalium* describes dolphins, killer whales, and baleen whales, noting that "the [latter] has no teeth but does have hair that resemble hog bristles." Unfortunately, Aristotle's observations were dismissed by many later workers because of his misclassification of dolphins as fish. Following Aristotle, the only other authority on whales in ancient times was Pliny the Elder (24–79 C.E. (Current Era.)) In his 37-volume *Naturalis Historia* he included a book on whales and dolphins in which he provided accounts based on Aristotle's findings and his own observations. Knowledge of marine mammals languished for a thousand years after Aristotle and Pliny during the Dark Ages. During the Renaissance a rapid increase in exploration of the oceans was followed by the publication of scientific reports from various expeditions. The earliest

Figure 1.2. Woodcut by Conrad Gesner, from *Historia Animalium,* first published between 1551 and 1558, shows a whale so large that sailors mistook it for an island.

of these was the *Speculum Regale,* an account of Iceland in the thirteenth century which considered whales the only truly interesting sight the island had to offer. Its author correctly distinguished between northern right whales and bowhead whales, which were still confused by many naturalists five centuries later. In the sixteenth century explorers discovered the rich feeding grounds in the high Arctic and the large whale populations that they supported. In the mid-1500s, Conrad Gesner in his *Historia Animalium* presented illustrations of whales; among them was one so large that sailors mistook it for an island (Fig. 1.2).

A walrus also is illustrated in Gesner's work (Fig. 1.3a). Among the earliest drawings of seals, "*Vitulus marinus*" (Fig. 1.3b) in Pierre Belon's *De Aquatilibus* (1553) is most remarkable for its accuracy, particularly in the detail of the hind limbs. In Guillaume Rondelet's *De Piscibus* (1554), two seals are illustrated, one probably representing the common seal and the other the Mediterranean monk seal (Fig. 1.3c, d; King, 1983). In another book, *The Natural History of Quadrupeds* (1763) by R., Brookes, it is obvious from the illustration and description of the male with a large snout or trunk that the elephant seal is depicted as a cheerful "sea lion" with a "seaweed tail" (Fig. 1.3e; King, 1983).

In 1596 the Dutch navigator Wilhelm Barents discovered Spitzbergen (island north of Norway) and early in the seventeenth century commercial whalers were sent there by Dutch and English companies to establish a whaling town. Although these expeditions were concerned primarily with whale products, they also produced a number of publications which provided reasonably accurate descriptions of the external appearance of the most common kinds of whales. The best of these are found in *Spitzbergische oder Groenlandische Reisen Beschreibung* (1675) by Frederich Martens and *Bloyeyende Opkomst der Oloude en Hedendaagsche Groenlandsche Vischery* (1720) by C. G. Zorgdrager, both of which contained engravings which continued to be reproduced in books until the early 19th century. Georg Wilhem Steller, ship's naturalist and physician for Vitus Bering's second expedition to North America, was among the first Europeans to explore Alaska and the Aleutian and Commander Islands. His notes of marine mammals living in the Bering Sea, *The Beasts of the Sea* (1751), was a natural history of the sea otter, sea lion, fur seal, and the now extinct Steller sea cow, the only first-hand scientific observation of this species.

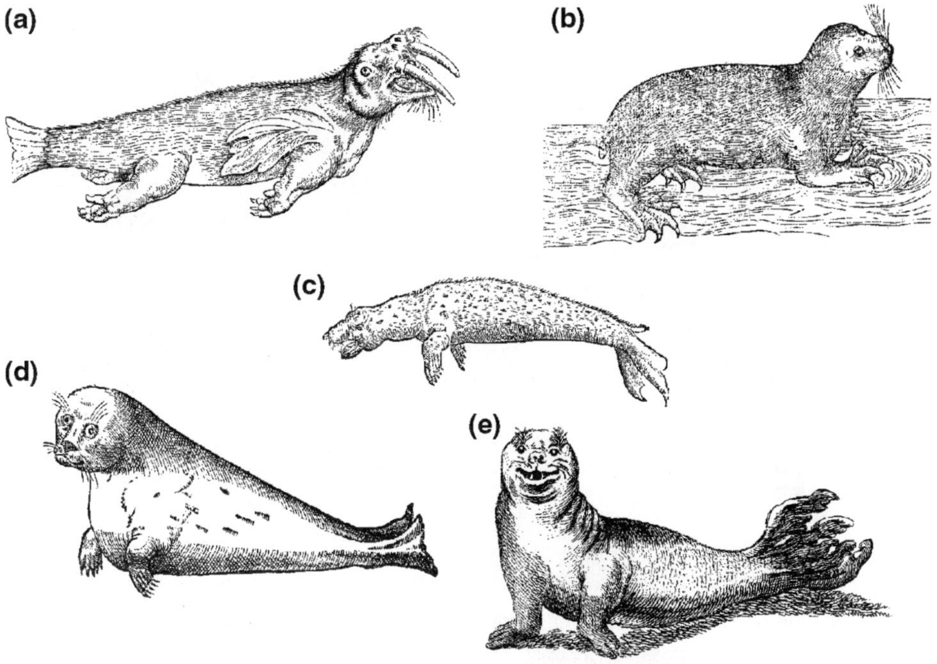

Figure 1.3. Early illustrations of pinnipeds (a) Walrus from Conrad Gesner's *Historia Animalium,* probably taken from a drawing by Albert Dürer, (b) Seal from P. Belon, *De Aquatilibus* (1553), (c) Seal from Guillaume Rondelet, *De Piscibus* (1554), (d) Seal from Guillaume Rondelet, *De Piscibus* (1554), (e) "Sea lion" from R. Brookes, *The Natural History of Quadrupeds* (1763).

Another naturalist, Lacépède, compiled a volume on whales, *Histoire Naturelle de Cétacés* (1804), in which most of the illustrations were copied from previous publications (e.g. Fig. 1.4). Lacépède acknowledged that not having ever seen a whale, he had made his descriptions from those of other naturalists. In the first half of the nineteenth century, additions to the literature included Peter Camper's *Observations Anatomiques sur Plusiers Especes de Cétacés* (1820). The foremost European cetologist of the second half of the nineteenth century was P.-J. Van Beneden, a Belgian zoologist whose many monographs on whales and pinnipeds (including *Histoire Naturelle des Cétacés des Mers d'Europe,* 1889) were published in Brussels between 1867 and 1892. John Edward Gray, who became Keeper of the Zoology Department at the British Museum of Natural History, published his *Catalogue of Seals and Whales in the British Museum* in 1866. John Allen (1880), in his comprehensive monograph of North American pinnipeds, provided keys to the families and genera, described the North American species, and gave accounts of pinniped species in other parts of the world.

Meanwhile, the whaling industries of several countries were making other contributions to the study of whales. Whaling captains such as William Scoresby and Charles Scammon made their own observations in the field or collected those of their colleagues. Scoresby published *An Account of the Arctic Regions* (1820) which is still a valuable source of information on the northern right whale. Scammon's book, *The Marine Mammals of the North-Western Coast of North America,* was published in 1874 and has become a classic, particularly valued for its description of the natural history of the gray whale in California.

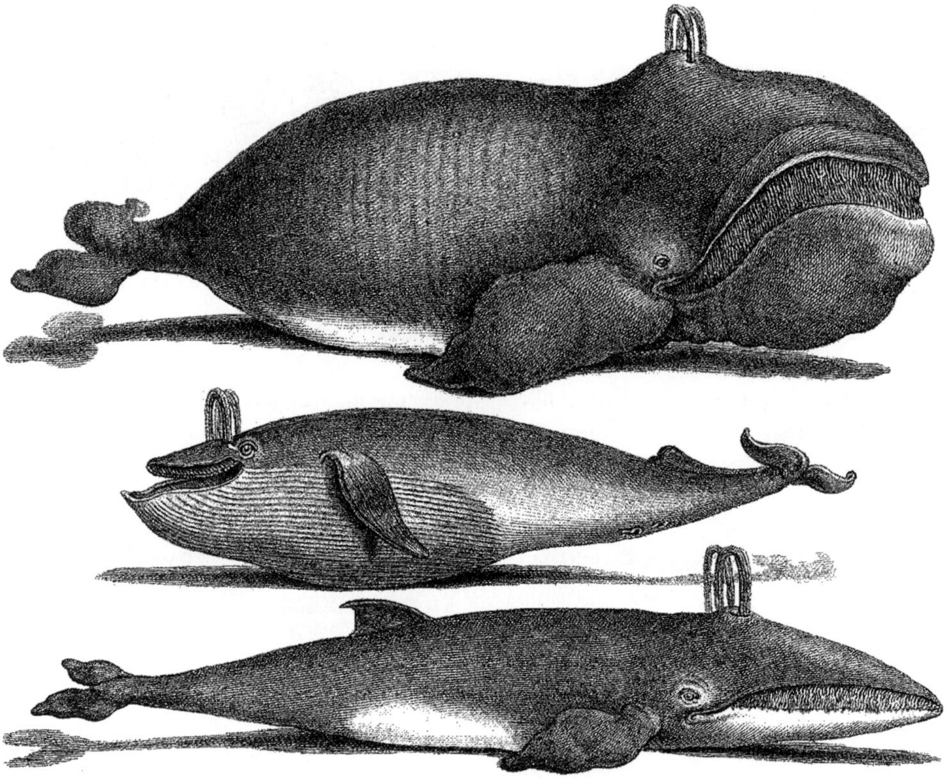

Figure 1.4. Woodcut of baleen whales from Lacépède's *Histoire Naturelle des Cétacés* (1804).

Land-based whaling stations used in more modern whaling provided the material for Frederick True's 1904 monograph *The Whalebone Whales of the Western North Atlantic* and Roy Chapman Andrews's 1906 monograph on the Sei whale in the Pacific.

Apart from whalers, the only people seriously interested in the study of whales (**cetology**) at this time were comparative anatomists (for a more detailed account of the beginnings of cetology see Matthews, 1978). Among their ranks are Rondelet, Bartholin, Camper, Cuvier, Hunter, and Owen. These pioneers in the study of cetacean anatomy made the most of specimens that came their way and the writings that many of them produced show that they made accurate observations. Cuvier in particular made several fundamental advances in cetology. His *Le Règne Animal* (1817) and *Recherches sur les Ossements Fossiles* (1823) contain the original descriptions and illustrations of the three species of cetacean that he named (Cuvier's beaked whale, Risso's dolphin, and the spotted dolphin).

During this time, confusion over the affinities of another marine mammal group, the dugongs, led some to consider them an unusual tropical form of walrus. In a publication from 1800, the manatee is inaccurately shown as hog-nosed (Fig. 1.5a). The earliest illustration of a sirenian to be published, the West Indian manatee from the 1535 edition of *La Historia General de las Indias* by Gonzalo Fernandez de Oviedo y Valdes, is little changed from this depiction more than two centuries later (Fig. 1.5b).

Descriptions of the anatomy of various pinnipeds followed including the walrus (Murie, 1870) and Steller sea lion (Murie, 1872, 1874). Another accomplished anatomist, W. C. S.

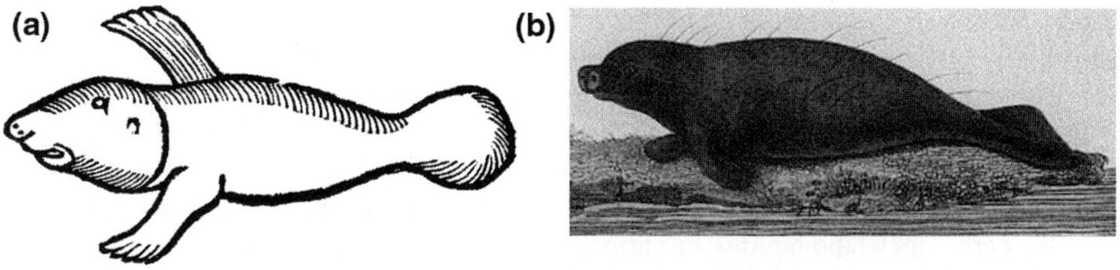

Figure 1.5. Early illustrations of manatees. (a) an "American manatee" (species, unknown) from a lithograph (Reynolds and Odell, 1991), (b) West Indian manatee from the 1535 edition of *La Historia General de las Indias* by Gonzalo Fernandez de Oviedo y Valdes.

Miller (1888), dissected a variety of pinnipeds including the southern fur seal, southern elephant seal, and the harbor seal recovered on the *H.M.S. Challenger* expedition to the Antarctic during the years 1873–1875. Thompson (1915) published the first account of the osteology of antarctic seals including the Ross seal, the Weddell seal, and the leopard seal. Howell (1929) published his well-known comparative study of both phocids and otariids based on the California sea lion and the ringed seal. He followed this with a book on aquatic adaptations in mammals (Howell, 1930).

1.6. Emergence of Marine Mammal Science

Marine mammal science has emerged as a discipline in its own right only in the last 20–30 years. This increasing interest in marine mammals is clearly shown by the expansion of the literature dealing with these animals. J. A. Allen's *Bibliography of the Cetacea and Sirenia* (1882), covering the 350 years from 1495 to 1840, contains 1014 titles, just under three publications per year. In the period from 1845 to 1960, between 3000 and 4000 papers were published, with a conservative estimate of about 28 titles a year (Matthews, 1966). By comparison, c. 24,000 papers on marine mammals were published between 1961 and 1998 according to the *Zoological Record,* a rate of 646 per year. Among the major influences which contributed to the birth of marine mammal science was the growing recognition that marine mammal populations were limited in numbers and that their exploitation had to be regulated (Boyd, 1993). The aim of many early studies was to obtain accurate information about the biology of these animals for use in establishing an effective management policy for sustainable exploitation. Indeed, it is ironic that the decline in whale stocks heralded the beginning of the scientific study of marine mammals. As a result, the *Discovery* investigations (1925–1951) were undertaken to examine the biology of whale stocks in the Southern Ocean. Not only was the biology of whales examined, but also their food supplies and their distributions and abundances in relation to oceanographic conditions. For example, British scientists N. A. Mackintosh and J. F. G. Wheeler examined 1600 carcasses for gut contents in order to produce their report on blue and fin whales in 1929. Leonard Harrison-Matthews had comparable samples in his reports on the humpback whale, sperm whale, and southern right whale in 1938 (Watson, 1981).

In the 1950s the theme of the *Discovery* investigations was continued by the Falkland Islands Dependencies Survey (later known as the British Antarctic Survey) when it established a research program on the southern elephant seal on South Georgia Island under the directorship of R. M. Laws. In parallel with these and other studies, with a focus on population ecology, there also was growing interest in the anatomy and physiology of marine mammals (Slijper, 1962; Norris, 1966; Andersen, 1969; Ridgway, 1972; Harrison, 1972–1977). The establishment of various scientific committees (e.g. the International Whaling Commission's Scientific Committee in 1946 and the U.S. Marine Mammal Commission in 1972) to provide advice about the status of various marine mammal populations also required knowledge and data on the general biology of these animals and thus served to stimulate research. Since the early 1980s, the biology of various marine mammal species has been the subject of many notable books, beginning with Ridgway and Harrison's *Handbook of Marine Mammals* (1981–1998). This has been followed by detailed separate accounts of the biology of the Pacific walrus (Fay, 1982), gray whale (Jones *et al.,* 1984), bowhead whale (Burns *et al.,* 1993), bottlenose dolphin (Leatherwood and Reeves, 1990), Hawaiian spinner dolphin (Norris *et al.,* 1994), harbor porpoise (Read *et al.,* 1997), harp and hooded seals (Lavigne and Kovacs, 1988), elephant seals (Le Boeuf and Laws, 1996) and the northern fur seal (Gentry, 1998). Comprehensive treatments of marine mammal groups are available for pinnipeds (King, 1983; Bonner, 1990; Riedman, 1990; Renouf, 1991), for whales (Evans, 1987; Gaskin, 1982; Matthews, 1978), for manatees and dugongs (Reynolds and Odell, 1991; Hartman, 1979), and for sea otters (Riedman and Estes, 1990; Kenyon, 1969). Invaluable field identification guides for pinnipeds and sirenians are found in Reeves *et al.* (1992) and for whales and dolphins in Leatherwood and Reeves (1983) and Carwardine (1995).

Matthews (1966) wrote "the greatest revolution in the study of the Cetacea . . . has come with the possibility of keeping living cetaceans in oceanariums." However, one of the most significant advances in marine mammal science in recent years has undoubtedly been the move toward studying animals under wild, unrestrained conditions at sea. This is in large part the result of technological advances in microelectronics (e.g. satellite **telemetry** and **time-depth recorders**). For example, the application of microelectronics led to the discovery that elephant seals regularly dive to depths of 1000 m with consistently long dive durations, typically lasting 15 to 45 minutes. This unique feature of elephant seal biology has forced physiologists to reexamine our understanding of the biochemical pathways used by these animals to maximize the efficiency of oxygen utilization.

Technological advances in molecular biology (e.g. analysis of DNA variation) also have provided unparalleled opportunities to examine interactions among populations and the roles of the individuals within those populations. For example, using DNA fingerprinting and other techniques, it is possible to assess paternity and kinship among whales, animals for which this has previously been virtually impossible owing to the difficulty of observing them mating underwater. These techniques have also made it possible to measure effective population sizes and interpret historical events such as population bottlenecks. Molecular techniques also have contributed to our knowledge of the **systematics** and **taxonomy** of various marine mammal groups.

As pointed out by Watkins and Wartzok (1985), information and research about marine mammals range "from intensive to eclectic." Much of the available data is difficult to synthesize because techniques vary widely and sample sizes often are necessarily small. This is not a reflection of poor science but rather the environmental, practical, and legal complications implicit in marine mammal research. It is apparent that the data base must be expanded. Even within a relatively homogeneous group like odontocete whales, one well known species (the bottlenose dolphin, *Tursiops truncatus*) cannot be used reliably to characterize all toothed whales. With this in mind, we hope that as readers of this book you will be able to identify areas in which research must be done. We encourage you to pursue research on marine mammals—there are still many gaps in our knowledge of this diverse and unique assemblage of mammals.

1.7. Further Reading and Resources

There are a large number of internet addresses with information about marine mammal programs and organizations; a few that we consider the most useful are listed below:

http://pegasus.cc.ucf.edu/~smm—Society for Marine Mammalogy (SMM), professional international organization of marine mammal scientists, publishes a journal (quarterly) of original research on marine mammals, *Marine Mammal Science.*

http://web.inter.NL.net/users/J.W.Broekema/ecs/index.htm—European Cetacean Society (ECS), professional biologists and others interested in whales and dolphins.

http://www.earthwatch.org—Earthwatch Institute, offers opportunities for marine mammal enthusiasts to work as volunteers with research scientists.

Also, for career and hobbyist information about marine mammals see the recent book by Glen (1997) *The Dolphin and Whale Career Guide* and the pamphlet *Strategies for Pursuing a Career in Marine Mammal Science* published by SMM.

References

Allen, J. A. (1880). "History of the North American Pinnipeds, a Monograph of the Walruses, Sea-Lions, Sea-Bears and Seals of North America." *U.S. Geol. Geogr. Surv. Terr., Misc. Publ.* **12**: 16+785.

Allen, J. A. (1882). "Preliminary List of Works and Papers Relating to the Mammalian Orders Cete and Sirenia." *Bull. U.S. Geol. Geogr. Surv. Terr.* **6**(3) (Art. 18): 399–562.

Andersen, H. T. (ed.) (1969). "The Biology of Marine Mammals." Academic Press, New York.

Berggren, W. A., D. V. Kent, C. C. Swisher, Jr., and M. P. Aubry (1995). A Revised Cenozoic Geochronology and Chronostratigraphy. *In* "Geochronology, Time Scales and Global Stratigraphic Correlations" (W. A. Berggren *et al.,* eds.). pp. 129–212. SEPM Special Publication, No. 54.

Bonner, W. N. (1990). "The Natural History of Seals." Facts on File, New York.

Boyd, I. L. (1993). Introduction: Trends in marine mammal science. *Symp. Zool. Soc. London* **66**: 1–12.

Burns, J. J., J. J. Montague, and C. J. Cowles (1993). "The Bowhead Whale," Special Publ. No. 2. Soc. Mar. Mammal. Allen Press, Kansas.

Carwardine, M. (1995). "Whales, Dolphins and Porpoises." D. K. Publishing, New York.

Evans, P. G. H. (1987). "The Natural History of Whales and Dolphins." Christopher Helm, London/Facts on File, New York.

Fay, F. H. (1982). Ecology and Biology of the Pacific Walrus, *Odobenus rosmarus divergens* Illiger. U. S. Dept. Int. Fish Wild. Serv. North American Fauna, No. 74, 279 pp.

Gaskin, D. E. (1982). "The Ecology of Whales and Dolphins." Heinemann, London.

Gentry, R. L. (1998). Behavior and Ecology of the Northern Fur Seal. Princeton Univ. Press, New Jersey.

Glen, T. B. (1997). The Dolphin and Whale Career Guide. Omega Publ. Co., Chicago.

Harland, W. B., R. L. Armstrong, A. V. Cox, L. E. Craig, A. G. Smith, and D. G. Smith (1990). "A Geologic Time Scale-1989." Cambridge University Press, New York.

Harrison, R. J. (1972–1977). "Functional Anatomy of Marine Mammals," Vols. 1–3. Academic Press, London.

Hartman, D. S. (1979). Ecology and behavior of the manatee (*Trichechus manatus*) in Florida. *Am. Soc. Mammal. Spec. Publ.,* No. 5, 1–153.

Howell, A. B. (1929). Contributions to the comparative anatomy of the eared and earless seals (Genera *Zalophus* and *Phoca*). *Proc. U. S. Natl. Mus.* **73**: 1–143.

Howell, A. B. (1930). "Aquatic Mammals." Thomas, Springfield, IL.

Jones, M. L., S. L. Swartz, and S. Leatherwood (eds.) (1984). "The Gray Whale." Academic Press, New York.

Kenyon, K. (1969). "The Sea Otter in the Eastern Pacific Ocean," North Am. Fauna No. 68, Bur. Sport Fish. Wild., U.S. Gov. Printing Office, Washington, DC.

King, J. E. (1983). "Seals of the World," 2nd ed. British Museum of Natural History, London, and Cornell University Press, Ithaca, NY.

Lavigne, D., and K. M. Kovacs (1988). "Harps and Hoods." University of Waterloo Press, Ontario, Canada.

Leatherwood, S., and R. R. Reeves (1983). "The Sierra Club Handbook of Whales and Dolphins." Sierra Club Books, San Francisco.

Leatherwood, S., and R. R. Reeves (eds.) (1990). "The Bottlenose Dolphin." Academic Press, San Diego, CA.

Le Boeuf, B., and R. M. Laws (eds.) (1996). "Elephant Seals." University of California Press, Berkeley.

Mackintosh, N. A., and Wheeler, J. F. G. (1929). "Southern Blue and Fin Whales." Discovery Report **1**, 257–540.

Matthews, L. H. (1966). Chairman's introduction to first session of International Symposium on Cetacean Research. *In* "Whales, Dolphins and Porpoises" (K. S. Norris, ed.), pp. 3–6. University of California Press, Berkeley.

Matthews, L. H. (1978). "The Natural History of the Whales." Columbia University Press, New York.

Miller, W. C. G. (1888). The myology of the Pinnipedia. *In* "Report on the Scientific Results of the Voyage of H.M.S. Challenger," Vol. 26, No. 2, pp. 139–240; appendix to Turner's report. Challenger Office, 1880–1895, Edinburgh.

Murie, J. (1870). Researches upon the anatomy of the Pinnipedia. Part I. On the walrus (*Trichechus rosmarus* Linn.). *Trans. Zool. Soc. London* **7**: 411–464.

Murie, J. (1872). Researches upon the anatomy of the Pinnipedia. Part 2. Descriptive anatomy of the sea-lion (*Otaria jubata*). *Trans. Zool. Soc. London* **7**: 527–596.

Murie, J. (1874). Researches upon the anatomy of the Pinnipedia. Part 3. Descriptive anatomy of the sea-lion (*Otaria jubata*). *Trans. Zool. Soc. London* **8**: 501–562.

Norris, K. (1966). "Whales, Dolphins and Porpoises." University of California Press, Berkeley.

Norris, K. S., B. Würsig, R. S. Wells, and M. Würsig (1994). "The Hawaiian Spinner Dolphin." University of California Press, Berkeley.

Read, A. J., P. R. Wiepkema, and P. E. Nachtigall (eds.) (1997). "The Biology of the Harbour Porpoise." De Spil Publishers, Woerden, The Netherlands.

Reeves, R. R., Stewart, B. S., and Leatherwood, S. (1992). "The Sierra Club Handbook of Seals and Sirenians." Sierra Club Books, San Francisco.

Renouf, D. (ed.) (1991). "Behavior of Pinnipeds." Chapman & Hall, New York.

Reynolds, J. E., III and D. K. Odell (1991). "Manatees and Dugongs." Facts on File, New York.

Reynolds, J. E., III, and S. A. Rommel (eds.) (1999). "Biology of Marine Mammals," Smithsonian Institution Press, Washington, DC.

Ridgway, S. H. (ed.) (1972). "Mammals of the Sea." Thomas, Springfield, IL.

Ridgway, S. H., and R. Harrison (ed.) (1981–1998). "Handbook of Marine Mammals," Academic Press, San Diego.

Riedman, M. L. (1990). "The Pinnipeds." University of California Press, Berkeley.

Riedman, M. L., and J. Estes (1990). The sea otter (*Enhydra lutris*): Behavior, ecology, and natural history. *U.S. Dep. Int. Biol. Rep.* **90**(14): 1–126.

Slijper, E. (1962). "Whales." Hutchinson, London.

Thompson, R. B. (1915). Osteology of Antarctic Seals. Rep. Scient. Results Scott. Natn. Antarc. Exped. **4** (3): 17–31.

Watkins, W. A., and D. Wartzok (1985). Sensory biophysics of marine mammals. *Mar. Mamm. Sci.* **1**: 219–260.

Watson, L. (1981). "Whales of the World." Hutchinson, London.

2

Systematics and Classification

2.1. Introduction: Systematics—What Is It and Why Do It?

Systematics is the study of biological diversity that has as its emphasis the reconstruction of **phylogeny**, the evolutionary history of a particular group of organisms (e.g. species). It also includes taxonomy, the description, identification, and classification of species. Although the taxonomy of mammals is relatively well known compared to other groups of organisms, we still are discovering previously unknown species (e.g. two new species of beaked whale were discovered in the early 1990s; Reyes *et al.,* 1991, 1995).

Systematic knowledge provides a framework for interpreting biological diversity. Because it does this in an evolutionary context it is possible to examine the ways in which attributes of organisms change over time, the direction in which attributes change, the relative frequency with which they change, and whether change in one attribute is correlated with change in another. It also is possible to compare the descendants of a single ancestor to look for patterns of origin and extinction or relative size and diversity of these groups. Systematics also can be used to test hypotheses of adaptation. For example, consider the evolution of the ability to hear high frequency sounds, or **echolocation**, in toothed whales. One hypothesis for how toothed whales developed echolocation suggests that the lower jaw evolved as a unique pathway for the transmission of high frequency sounds under water. However, based on a study of the hearing apparatus of archaic whales, Thewissen *et al.* (1996) proposed that the lower jaw of toothed whales may have arisen for a different function, one of transmitting low frequency sounds from the ground, as do several vertebrates including the mole rat. According to this hypothesis, the lower jaw became specialized later for hearing high frequency sound. In this way the lower jaw of toothed whales may be an **exaptation** for hearing high frequency sounds. An exaptation is defined as any adaptation that performs a function different from the function that it originally held. A more complete understanding of the evolution of echolocation requires examination of other characters involved such as the presence of a melon and the morphology of the middle ear and jaw as well as the bony connections between the ear and skull (see Chapter 10).

An understanding of the evolutionary relationships among species can also assist in identifying priorities for conservation (Brooks *et al.,* 1992). For example, the argument for the conservation priority of sperm whales is strengthened by knowing that this lineage, which consists of two extant species, occupies a key phylogenetic position as the basal relative to the other species of toothed whales. These pivotal species are of particular importance in providing baseline comparative data for understanding the evolutionary history of the other 65 species of toothed whales. Sperm whales provide information on the origin of various morphological characters such as suction feeding and the adaptive role of these features in the early evolution of toothed whales.

Perhaps most importantly, systematics predicts properties of organisms. For example, as discussed by Promislow (1996), it has been noted that some toothed whales (e.g. pilot whales and killer whales) which have extended parental care also show signs of reproductive aging (i.e. pregnancy rates decline with increasing age of females), whereas baleen whales (e.g. fin whales) demonstrate neither extended parental care nor reproductive aging (Marsh and Kasuya, 1986). Systematics predicts that these patterns would hold more generally among other whales and that we should expect other toothed whales to show reproductive aging.

Finally, systematics also provides a useful foundation from which to study other biological patterns and processes. Examples of such studies include the coevolution of pinniped parasites and their hosts (Hoberg, 1992, 1995), evolution of locomotion and feeding in pinnipeds (Berta and Deméré, 1993; Adam and Berta, 1997), evolution of body size in phocids (Wyss, 1994), evolution of phocid breeding patterns (Perry *et al.,* 1995), and the evolution of echolocation in toothed whales (Thewissen *et al.,* 1996).

2.2. Some Basic Terminology and Concepts

The discovery and description of species and the recognition of patterns of relationship among them is founded on the concept of evolution. Patterns of relationships among species are based on changes in the features or **characters** of an organism. Characters are diverse, heritable attributes of organisms that include DNA base pairs, anatomical and physiological features, and behavioral traits. Two or more forms of a given character are termed the **character states**. For example, the character "locomotor pattern" might consist of the states "alternate paddling of the four limbs (quadrupedal paddling)," "paddling by the hind limbs only (pelvic paddling)," "lateral undulations of the vertebral column and hind limb (caudal undulation)," and "vertical movements of the tail (caudal oscillation)." Evolution of a character may be recognized as a change from a preexisting, or **ancestral** (also referred to as **plesiomorphic** or **primitive**), character state to a new **derived** (also referred to as **apomorphic**) character state. For example, in the evolution of locomotor patterns in cetaceans, the pattern hypothesized for the earliest whales is one in which they swam by paddling with the hind limbs. Later diverging whales modified this feature and show two derived conditions: 1) lateral undulations of the vertebral column and hind limbs and 2) vertical movements of the tail.

The basic tenet of **phylogenetic systematics**, or **cladistics** (from the Greek word meaning "branch"), is that shared derived character states constitute evidence that the species possessing these features share a common ancestry. In other words, the shared derived fea-

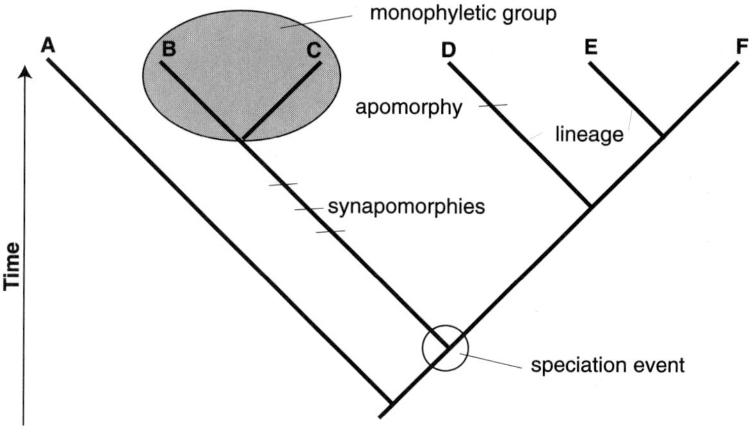

Figure 2.1. A cladogram illustrating general terms discussed in the text.

tures or **synapomorphies** represent unique evolutionary events that may be used to link two or more species together in a common evolutionary history. Thus, by sequentially linking species together based on their common possession of synapomorphies, the evolutionary history of those taxa can be inferred.

Relationships among taxonomic groups (e.g. species) are commonly represented in the form of a **cladogram**, or **phylogenetic tree**, a branching diagram that conceptually represents the best estimate of phylogeny (Fig. 2.1). The lines of the cladogram are known as **lineages** or **clades**. Lineages represent the sequence of ancestor–descendant populations through time. Branching of the lineages at **nodes** on the cladogram represents **speciation events**, a splitting of a lineage resulting in the formation of two species from one common ancestor.

The task in inferring a phylogeny for a group of organisms is to determine which characters are derived and which are ancestral. If the ancestral condition of a character or character state is established, then the direction of evolution, from ancestral to derived, can be inferred, and synapomorphies can be recognized. The methodology for inferring direction of character evolution is critical to cladistic analysis. **Outgroup comparison** is the most widely used procedure. It relies on the argument that a character state found in close relatives of a group (the **outgroup**) is likely also to be the ancestral or primitive state for the group of organisms in question (the **ingroup**). Usually more than one outgroup is used in an analysis, the most important being the first or genealogically closest outgroup to the ingroup, called the **sister group**. In many cases, the primitive state for a taxon can be ambiguous. The primitive state can only be determined if the primitive states for the nearest outgroup are easy to identify and those states are the same for at least the two nearest outgroups (Maddison *et al.*, 1984).

Using the example above, determination of the primitive cetacean locomotor pattern is based on its similarity to that of the sister taxon to the cetaceans, a group of four legged mammals known as the **mesonychids** (i.e. the outgroup), which are thought to have swam by quadrupedal paddling. Locomotion in whales went through several stages. Ancestral whales (i.e. *Ambulocetus*) swam by pelvic paddling propelled by the hind limbs only. Later diverging whales (i.e. *Rodhocetus*) went through a caudal undulation stage propelled by the

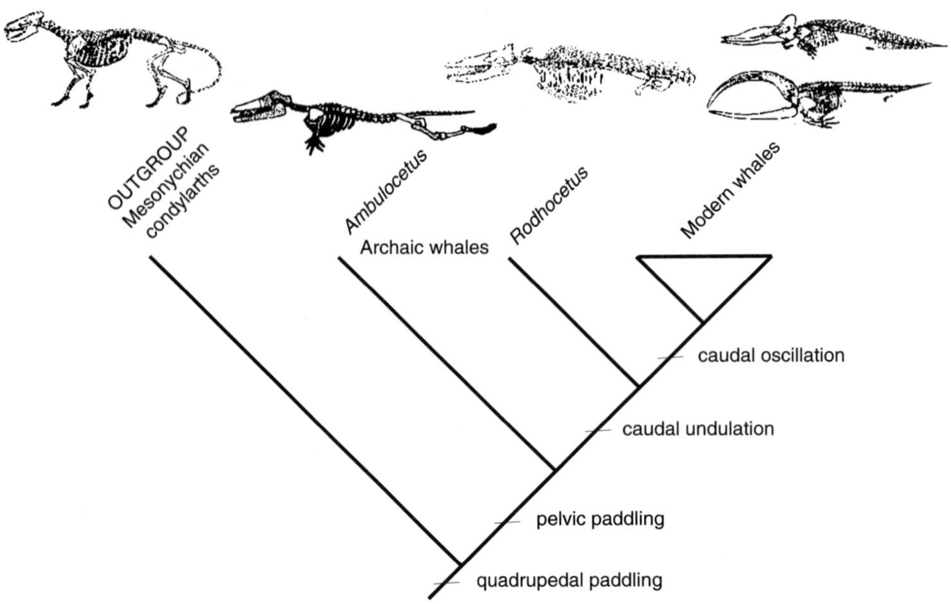

Figure 2.2 Distribution of character states for locomotor pattern among cetaceans. Skeletal reconstructions (mesonychian condylarth, *Mesonyx,* from W. B. Scott (1888); archaic whales, *Ambulocetus natans,* from Thewissen *et al.* (1996) and *Rodhocetus kasrani* from Gingerich *et al.* (1994); modern whales, an odontocete, the sperm whale *Physeter macrocephalus* and a mysticete, the bowhead whale, *Balaena mysticetus* from Oelschläger (1978)).

feet and tail. Finally, modern whales adopted caudal oscillation using vertical movements of the tail as their swimming mode (Fig. 2.2; Fish, 1993).

Derived characters are used to link **monophyletic groups**, groups of taxa that consist of a common ancestor plus all descendants of that ancestor. In contrast to a monophyletic group, a **paraphyletic group** (designated by quotation marks) is one that includes a common ancestor and some, but not all of the descendants of that ancestor. A real example of a paraphyletic group is the recognition of an extinct group of cetaceans known as "**archaeocetes**." A rapidly improving fossil record and phylogenetic knowledge of whales now support the inclusion of "archaeocetes" as the ancestors of both baleen whales and toothed whales rather than as a separate taxonomic category (e.g., Thewissen *et al.,* 1996). It has been suggested that toothed whales may be paraphyletic, a closer relationship being suggested between sperm whales and baleen whales than between sperm whales and other toothed whales (e.g., Fig. 2.3; Milinkovitch *et al.,* 1993).

Monophyletic groups can be characterized in two ways. First, a monophyletic group can be **defined** in terms of ancestry, and second, it can be **diagnosed** in terms of characters (see Appendix 3). For example, whales or cetaceans can be defined as including the common ancestor of *Pakicetus* (an extinct whale) and all of its descendants including both modern toothed and baleen whales. Note that this definition is based on ancestry and does not change because there will always be a common ancestor for whales. On the other hand, cetaceans can be diagnosed by a number of characters (e.g. rotation of the middle ear bones and parallel arrangement of the front teeth; see also Chapter 4). The usefulness of the distinction between definition and diagnosis is that while the definition may not change, the diagnosis can be altered to reflect changes in our knowledge of the distribution of charac-

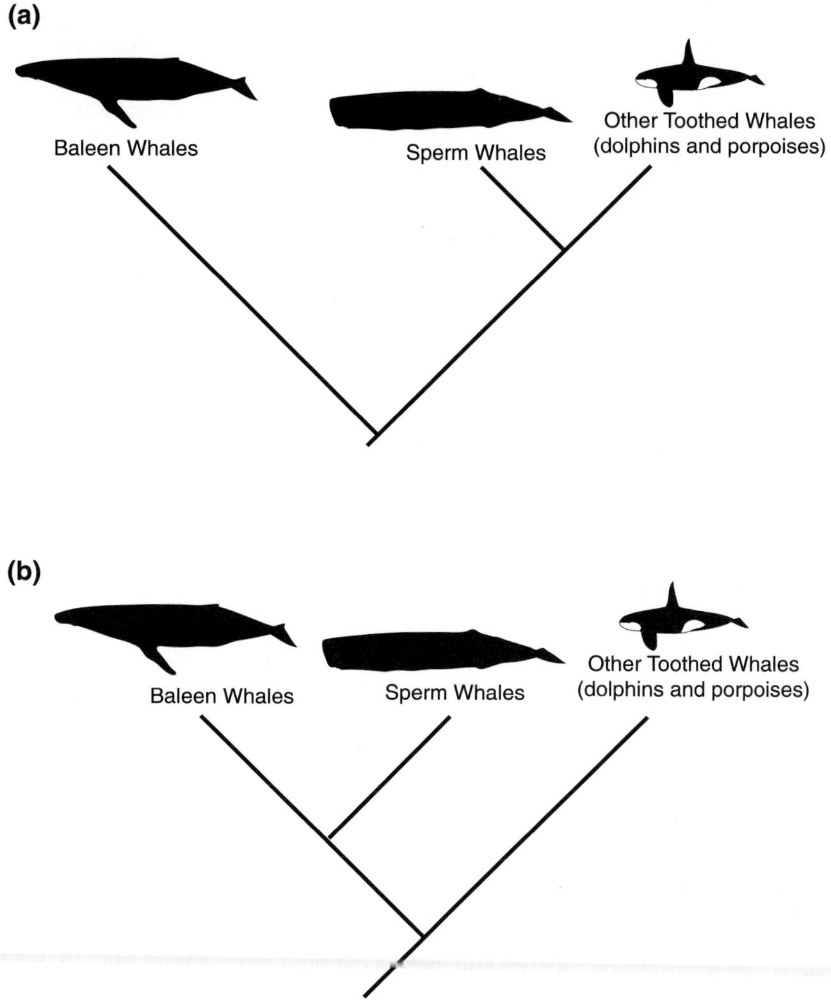

Figure 2.3. Alternative hypotheses for the phylogeny of toothed whales. (a) Traditional view of toothed whale monophyly, (b) Molecular view supporting toothed whale paraphyly.

ters. New data, new characters, or reanalysis of existing characters can modify the diagnosis. For example, in the early 1990s discoveries of new fossil cetaceans (e.g. *Ambulocetus* and *Rodhocetus*) have provided new characters illuminating the transition between whales and their closest ungulate relatives. The definition of Cetacea has not changed, but the diagnosis has been modified according to this new character information. A third term also used in this book, **characterization**, refers to a list of distinguishing features, both shared primitive and shared derived characters, that are particularly useful in field or laboratory identification of various species.

A concept critical to cladistics is that of **homology**. Homology can be defined as the similarity of features resulting from common ancestry. Two or more features are homologous if their common ancestor possessed the same feature. For example, the flipper of a seal and the flipper of a walrus are homologous as flippers because their common ancestor had flippers. In contrast to homology, similarity not due to homology is termed **homoplasy**. The flipper of a seal and the flipper of a whale are homoplasious as flippers because their common ancestor lacked flippers. Homoplasy may arise in one of two ways: **convergence (parallelism)** or **reversal**. Convergence is the independent evolution of a similar feature in two or more lineages. Thus, seal flippers and whale flippers evolved independently as swimming appendages; their similarity is homoplasious by convergent evolution. Reversal is the loss of a derived feature coupled with the reestablishment of an ancestral feature. For example, in phocine seals (e.g. *Erignathus, Cystophora,* and the Phocini) the development of strong claws, lengthening of the third digit of the foot, and deemphasis of the first digit of the hand are character reversals because none of them characterize phocids ancestrally but are present in terrestrial arctoid carnivores.

It is common, but incorrect, practice to refer to taxa as being either primitive or derived. This is deceptive, because individual taxa that have diverged earlier than others may have undergone considerable evolutionary modification on their own relative to taxa that have diverged later in time. For example, otariid seals have many derived characters, although they have diverged earlier than phocid seals. In short, taxa are not primitive, although characters may be.

2.3. How Do You Do Cladistics?

Cladograms are constructed using the following steps:

1. Select a group whose evolutionary relationships interest you. Name and define all taxa for that group. Assume that the taxa are monophyletic.
2. Select and define characters and character states for each taxon.
3. Arrange the characters and their states in a data matrix (see example in Table 2.1).
4. For each character, determine which state is ancestral (primitive) and which is derived. This is done using outgroup comparison. For example, if the distribution of character #1, thick fat layers of the skin, is taken into consideration, two character states are recognized: "absent" and "present". In Table 2.1, the outgroup (bears) have the former condition, which is equivalent to the ancestral state. This same state also is seen in one of the ingroup taxa, the fur seals and sea lions. The other ingroup taxa have thick fat layers "present" which is a synapomorphy that unites walruses and seals to the exclusion of fur seals and sea lions.

Table 2.1 Data Set for Analysis of Recent Pinnipeds Plus an Outgroup Showing Five Characters and Their Character States

	Character/Character states				
Taxon	1 Thick fat layers	2 Locomotor type	3 Pelage	4 Middle ear bones	5 Lacrimal bone
Outgroup	absent	forelimb + hind limb	abundant	small	present
Ingroup:					
Fur seals and Sea lions	absent	forelimb	abundant	small	absent
Walruses	present	hind limb	sparse	large	absent
Seals	present	hind limb	sparse	large	absent

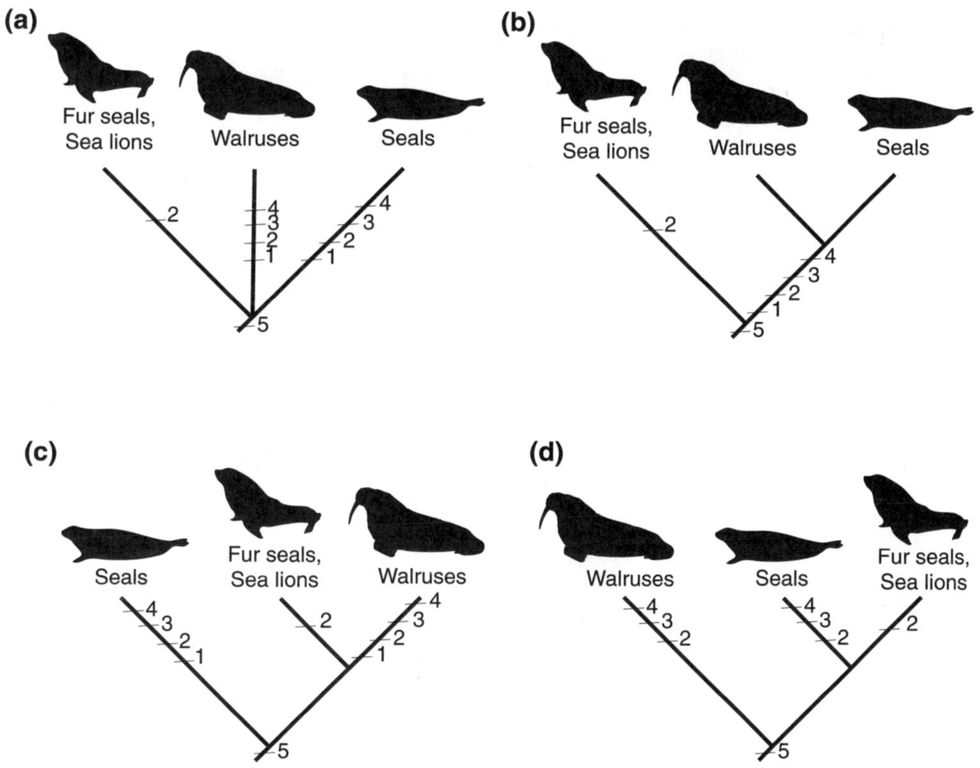

Figure 2.4. Four possible cladograms of relationship and character-state distributions for the three ingroups listed in Table 2.1. B has the most shared derived characters.

5. Construct all possible cladograms by sequentially grouping taxa based on the common possession of one or more shared derived character states (circles around character states in Table 2.1) and choose the one that has the most shared derived character states distributed among monophyletic groups (Fig. 2.4b). Note that the tree in Fig. 2.4a shows no resolution of relationships among taxa, referred to as a **polytomy**, and that the trees in Fig. 2.4c and d show mostly characters that are unique to one taxon and tell us nothing about relationships among different taxa.

2.4. Testing Phylogenetic Hypotheses

An important aspect of the reconstruction of phylogenetic relationships is known as the principle of **parsimony**. The basic tenet of the principle of parsimony is that the cladogram that contains the fewest number of evolutionary steps, or changes between character states of a given character summed for all characters, is accepted as being the best estimate of phylogeny. For example, for all the possible cladograms for the data set of Table 2.1, the one (Fig. 2.4b) illustrated in detail in Fig. 2.5a is the shortest since it contains the fewest number of evolutionary steps.

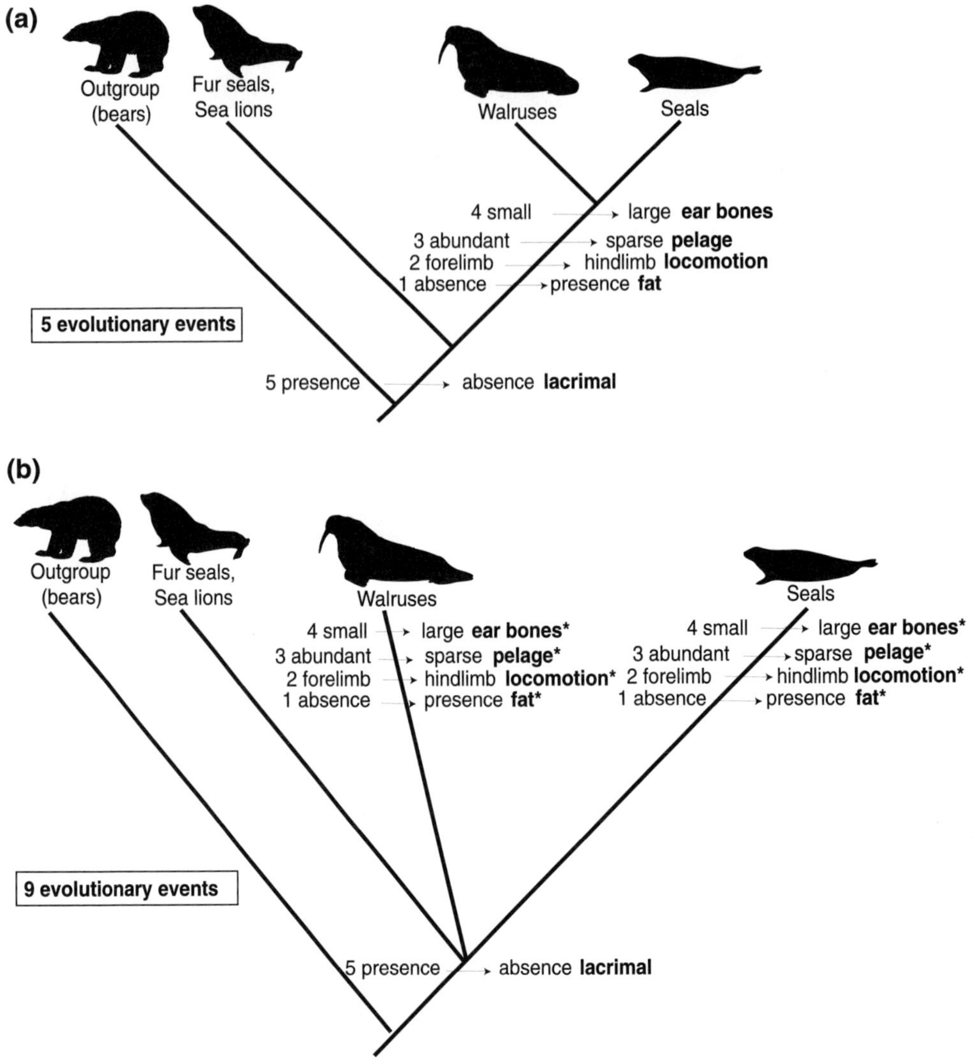

Figure 2.5. Two of the four possible cladograms. (a) Most parsimonious cladogram. Note a total of five evolutionary events. (b) Alternative cladogram showing different relationships for taxa. Note that this cladogram requires nine evolutionary events, four more than the most parsimonious cladogram. Convergences are noted by an asterisk*.

The methods used to search for the most parsimonious tree depend on the size and complexity of the data matrix. These methods are available in several computer programs [e.g. PAUP (Swofford, 1991); HENNIG86 (Farris, 1988); MacClade (Maddison and Maddison, 1992)]. The latter is particularly useful in assessing the evolution of characters. Recently, systematists have become concerned about the relative accuracy of phylogenetic trees (i.e. how much confidence can be placed in a specific phylogenetic reconstruction). Studies indicate that methods of phylogenetic analysis are most accurate if sufficient consideration is given to such parameters as sampling, rigorous analysis, and computer capabilities (Hillis, 1995).

A related issue in systematics is how to evaluate different data sets (e.g. morphology, behavior, and DNA sequences), particularly whether they should be combined (also referred to as a "total evidence" approach) or analyzed separately (Bull *et al.,* 1993). Before data sets can be combined, it is necessary to determine if they are congruent, that is the order of branching is not contradictory. This is done by what is known as the partition homogeneity test which examines data sets as partitions of characters evolving under different sets of rules. If the data sets are significantly incongruent, this suggests that the characters evolved under different models of evolution and that combined analysis would be misleading (Bull *et al.,* 1993; Farris *et al.,* 1995).

2.5. Going Beyond the Phylogenetic Framework: Elucidating Evolutionary and Ecological Patterns

Once a phylogenetic framework is produced, one of its most interesting uses is to elucidate questions which integrate evolution, behavior, and ecology. One technique used in this book to facilitate such evolutionary studies is **optimization**, or **mapping** (Funk and Brooks, 1990; Brooks and McLennan, 1991; Maddison and Maddison, 1992). Once a cladogram has been constructed, a feature or condition is selected to be examined in light of the phylogeny of the group. Examples included in this book include the evolution of body size, host–parasite associations, mating–reproductive behavior, and locomotor behavior. The condition of the terminal taxon (at the ends of branches) is identified and "mapped" onto the cladogram. There are various ways of mapping character changes onto the cladogram as discussed by Maddison and Maddison (1992). Hypothetical states are assigned to the nodes that reflect the most parsimonious arrangement of these conditions at each node. This allows one to determine the evolutionary trend of the condition in question. For example, consider the evolution of body size in phocid seals. One traditional assumption had been that small body size is the ancestral condition among phocids. This view is based on the assumption that seals of large body size represent an evolutionary advancement since they have a decreased surface area which in turn reduces body heat loss, an advantage in cold environments. This assumption, however, lacks historical evidence. When body size is mapped onto a phylogeny for seals and their relatives (walruses and sea lions; Fig. 2.6), there is a more parsimonious explanation for the data (Wyss, 1994). Accordingly, large body size is the ancestral condition for seals. A decrease in body size evolved secondarily among phocine seals (e.g. harbor, ribbon, and spotted seal). This hypothesis led Wyss (1994) to question whether this decrease in size among phocids was correlated with any other pattern of character evolution. He discovered that phocines were characterized by massive character reversals and he hypothesized that these reversals might be related to shifts in timing during development (neoteny). In addition to a decrease in body size, a number of other characters among phocines provided evidence for developmental juvenilization (i.e. failure of certain regions of the skull to ossify, resulting in perforations in the basicranium and the lack of fusion of certain cranial bones). In this example, a phylogenetic approach provided a framework for questions regarding the relationship between the evolution of body size and the pattern of evolution of other characters. A developmental explanation for the observed body size pattern was then proposed and further evidenced by other characters.

Another growing area of interest in the comparative study of phylogenies is how to deal with different types of character change, such as discrete or categorical (e.g. presence or

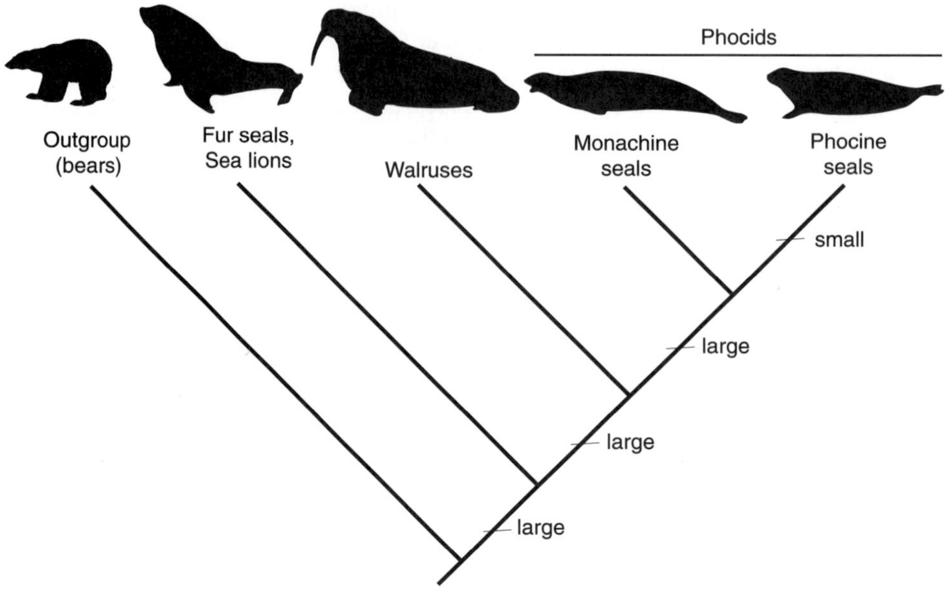

Figure 2.6. Body size mapped onto pinniped phylogeny (based on Wyss, 1994, and Bininda-Emonds and Russell, 1996).

absence of limbs) versus continuously varying characters (e.g. amount of time spent foraging). Several different methods have been proposed to incorporate phylogenetic information into comparative analyses. Examples of these techniques include Felsenstein's (1985) method of independent contrasts and the spatial autocorrelation techniques of Chevrud *et al.* (1985). These methods are designed for use with primarily continuous characters and as such are beyond the scope of this text.

2.6. Taxonomy and Classification

Classification is the arrangement of taxa (e.g. species) into some type of hierarchy. We need a system of classification so that we can more easily communicate about organisms. The taxonomic ranks are hierarchical, meaning that each rank is inclusive of all other ranks beneath it. A **taxon** is a particular taxonomic group at a given rank (plural is taxa). The major taxonomic ranks used in this book are listed below.

Major taxonomic ranks	*Example*
Order	Sirenia
Family	Trichechidae
Genus	*Trichechus*
Species	*manatus*

Nomenclature is the formal system of naming taxa (including the ranks of taxa) according to a standardized scheme, which for animals is the International Code of Zoological Nomenclature. These formal names are known as scientific names. The most important thing to remember about nomenclature is that all species may bear only one scientific name. The scientific name is, by convention, expressed using Latin and Greek words.

Species names are always italicized (or underlined) and always consists of two parts, the genus name (always capitalized, e.g. *Trichechus*) plus the specific epithet (e.g. *manatus*). For this reason, species names are known as binomials and this type of nomenclature is called binomial nomenclature. Species also have common names. In the previous example, *Trichechus manatus* is also known in English by its common name, West Indian manatee.

The two major ways to classify organisms are **phenetic** and **phylogenetic**. Phenetic classification is based on overall similarity of the taxa. Phylogenetic classification is that which is based on evolutionary history, or pattern of descent, which may or may not correspond to overall similarity. Phylogenetic systematists contend that classification should be based on phylogeny and should include only monophyletic groups. We have provided the most recent information on the classification and phylogeny of marine mammals. The classification of many marine mammal groups, however, is in a constant state of change due to new discoveries and information. Indeed, some systematists have offered compelling arguments for the elimination of taxonomic ranks altogether. In general, it is more important to know the names and characteristics of larger taxonomic groups like the Pinnipedia and the Sirenia than it is to memorize their rank.

2.7. Summary and Conclusions

The reconstruction of phylogenetic relationships provides a framework in biology for interpreting patterns of evolution, behavior, and ecology. Relationships are reconstructed based on shared derived similarities between species, whether similarities in morphologic characters or in molecular sequences, that provide evidence that these species share a common ancestry. The direction of evolution of a character is inferred by outgroup comparison. The best estimate (most parsimonious) of phylogeny is the one requiring the fewest number of evolutionary changes. Phylogenetically based comparative analyses have proven to be a powerful tool for generating and testing ideas about the links between behavior and ecology. The classification of species involves their arrangement in a hierarchy. Phylogenetic classification is based on evolutionary history and includes only monophyletic groups.

2.8. Further Reading

Readers are referred to texts by Eldredge and Cracraft (1980), Wiley (1981), Schoch (1986), and Wiley *et al.* (1991) for discussion of the principles and practice of phylogenetic systematics. Treatment of molecular data in phylogeny reconstruction is reviewed by Miyamoto and Cracraft (1991) and Swofford *et al.* (1996). Brooks and McLennan (1991), Harvey and Pagel (1991), Martins (1996), and Krebs and Davies (1997) provide examples of the use of phylogeny in studies of ecology and behavior.

References

Adam, P. J. and A. Berta (1997). Osteo indicators of locomotor type and their utility in determining evolutionary patterns in the Pinnipedimorpha. *Abstr. 57th Ann. Meet. Soc. Vert. Paleo.*, Chicago, p. 28A.

Berta, A., and T. A. Deméré (1993). The evolution of pinniped aquatic locomotor patterns. *Abstr. 10th Bienn. Conf. Biol. Mar. Mamm.*, Galveston, TX, p. 27.

Bininda-Emonds, O. R. P. and A. P. Russell (1996). A morphological perspective on the phylogenetic relationships of the extant phocid seals (Mammalia: Carnivora: Phocidae). Bonner Zoologische Monographien, **41**: 1–256.

Brooks, D. R., and D. A. McLennan (1991). "Phylogeny, Ecology, and Behavior." University of Chicago Press, Chicago.

Brooks, D. R., R. L. Mayden, and D. A. McLennan (1992). Phylogeny and biodiversity; conserving our evolutionary legacy. *Trends Ecol. Evol.* **7**: 55–59.

Bull, J. J., J. P. Hulsenbeck, C. W. Cunningham, D. L. Swofford, and P. J. Waddell (1993). Partitioning and combining data in phylogenetic analyses. *Syst. Biol.* **42**: 384–397.

Chevrud, J. M., M. M. Dow, and W. Leutenegger (1985). The quantitative assessment of phylogenetic constraints in comparative analyses: Sexual dimorphism in body weights among primates. *Evolution* **39**: 1335–1351.

Eldredge, N., and J. Cracraft (1980). "Phylogenetic Patterns and the Evolutionary Process." Columbia University Press, New York.

Farris, J. S. (1988). "HENNIG86, Version 1.5." Distributed by the author, Port Jefferson Station, NY.

Farris, J. S., Källersjö, M., Kluger, A. G., and Bult, C. (1995). Constructing a significance test for incongruence. *Syst. Biol.* **44**: 570–572.

Felsenstein, J. (1985). Confidence limits on phylogenies: An approach using the bootstrap. *Evolution* **39**: 783–791.

Fish, F. (1993). Influence of hydrodynamic design and propulsive mode on mammalian swimming energetics. *Aust. J. Zool.* **42**: 79–101.

Funk, V., and D. R. Brooks (1990). Phylogenetic systematics as the basis of comparative biology. *Smithson. Contrib. Bot.* **73**: 1–45.

Gingerich, P. D., S. Raza, Mahmood, M. Arif, M. Anwar, and X. Zhou (1994). New whale from the Eocene of Pakistan and the origin of cetacean swimming. *Nature* **368**: 844–847.

Harvey, P., and M. D. Pagel (1991). "The Comparative Method in Evolutionary Biology." Oxford University Press, Oxford and New York.

Hillis, D. (1995). Approaches for assessing phylogenetic accuracy. *Syst. Biol.* **44**(1): 3–16.

Hoberg, E. P. (1992). Congruent and synchronic patterns in biogeography and speciation among seabirds, pinnipeds, and cestodes. *J. Parasitol.* **78**(4): 601–615.

Hoberg, E. P. (1995). Historical biogeography and modes of speciation across high latitude seas of the Holarctic: Concepts for host-parasite coevolution among the Phocini (Phocidae) and Tetrabothriidae (Eucestoda). *Can. J. Zool.* **73**: 45–57.

Krebs, J. R., and N. B. Davies (1997). "Behavioral Ecology: An Evolutionary Approach," 4th ed. Blackwell Science, London.

Maddison, W. P., and D. R. Maddison (1992). "Mac Clade: Analysis of Phylogeny and Character Evolution, Version 3.0." Sinauer, Sunderland, MA.

Maddison, W., M. Donoghue, and D. Maddison (1984). Outgroup analysis and parsimony. *Syst. Zool.* **33**: 83–103.

Marsh, H., and T. Kasuya (1986). Evidence for reproductive senescence in female cetaceans. *Rep. Int. Whal. Comm., Spec. Issue* **8**: 57–74.

Martins, E. (ed.) (1996). "Phylogenies and the Comparative Method in Animal Behavior." Oxford University Press, New York.

Milinkovitch, M. C., G. Orti, and A. Meyer (1993). Revised phylogeny of whales suggested by mitochondrial ribosomal DNA sequences, *Nature* **361**: 346–348.

Miyamoto, M. M., and J. Cracraft (eds.) (1991). "Phylogenetic Analysis of DNA Sequences." Oxford University Press, New York.

Oelschläger, H. A. (1978). *Nat. Mus. Frankf.* **108**: 317–333.

Perry, E. A., S. M. Carr, S. E. Bartlett, and W. S. Davidson (1995). A phylogenetic perspective on the evolution of reproductive behavior in pagophilic seals of the Northwest Atlantic as indicated by mitochondrial DNA sequences. *J. Mammal.* **76**(1): 22–31.

Promislow, D. E. L. (1996). Using comparative approaches to integrate behavior and population biology. *In* "Phylogenies and the Comparative Methods in Animal Behavior" (E. Martins, ed.), pp. 288–323. Oxford University Press, New York.

Reeves, R. R., B. S. Stewart, and S. Leatherwood (1992). The Sierra Club Handbook of Seals and Sirenians. Sierra Club Books, San Francisco.

Reyes, J. C., J. G. Mead, and K. Van Waerebeek (1991). A new species of beaked whale *Mesoplodon peruvianus* sp. n. (Cetacea: Ziphiidae) from Peru. *Mar. Mamm. Sci.* **7**(1): 1–24.

Reyes, J. C., K. Van Waerebeek, J. C. Cardenas, and J. L. Yanez (1995). *Mesoplodon bahamondi* sp. n. (Cetacea, Ziphiidae), a new living beaked whale from the Juan Fernandez Archipelago, Chile. *Bol. Mus. Nac. Hist. Nat. Chile* **45**: 31–44.

Schoch, R. M. (1986). "Phylogeny Reconstruction in Paleontology." Van Nostrand-Reinhold, New York.

Scott, W. B. (1888). On some new and little known creodonts. *J. Acad. Nat. Sci* **9**: 155–185, Philadelphia.

Swofford, D. L. (1998). PAUP*: "Phylogenetic Analysis using Parsimony, Version 4." Sinauer Associates, Sunderland, MA.

Swofford, D. L., G. J. Olsen, P. J. Waddell, and D. M. Hillis (1996). Phylogenetic inference. *In* "Molecular Systematics" (D. M. Hillis, C. Moritz, and B. Mable, eds.), 2nd ed., pp. 407–514. Sinauer Assoc., Sunderland, MA.

Thewissen, J. G. M., S. I. Madar, and S. T. Hussain (1996). *Ambulocetus natans,* an Eocene cetacean (Mammalia) from Pakistan. *CFS. Cour. Forschungsinst. Senckenberg* **191**: 1–86.

Wiley, E. O. (1981). "Phylogenetics: The Theory and Practice of Phylogenetic Systematics." Wiley, New York.

Wiley, E. O., D. Siegel-Causey, D. R. Brooks, and V. A. Funk (1991). The Complete Cladist: A primer of phylogenetic procedures. *Univ. Kans. Mus. Nat. Hist., Spec. Publ.,* No. 19.

Wyss, A. R. (1994). The evolution of body size in phocids: Some ontogenetic and phylogenetic observations. *Proc. San Diego Soc. Nat. Hist.* **29**: 69–75.

3

Pinniped Evolution and Systematics

3.1. Introduction

Modern pinnipeds are aquatic members of the mammalian Order Carnivora and comprise three monophyletic families: the Otariidae (eared seals or fur seals and sea lions), the Odobenidae (walruses), and the Phocidae (true or earless seals). Pinnipeds comprise slightly more than one-quarter (28%) of the diversity of marine mammals. Thirty-three different species of pinnipeds are distributed throughout the world: 18 phocids, 14 otariids, and the walrus. Roughly 90% of an estimated 50 million individuals are phocids; the remaining 10% are otariids and odobenids (Riedman, 1990). The fossil record indicates that **extant** pinnipeds represent only a small fraction of what was once a much greater diversity. For example, only a single species of walrus exists today whereas no less than 10 genera and 13 species existed in the past (Deméré, 1994b). The earliest well-documented record of pinnipeds is from the late Oligocene (27 to 25 Ma; Fig. 3.1) although a slightly earlier record (29 Ma) is less well substantiated.

New discoveries of fossil pinnipeds together with comparative studies of living taxa have enabled a more complete understanding of pinniped origin, diversification, and morphology topics explored in this chapter. Characters defining major groups of pinnipeds are also listed for reference. Controversies regarding the relationship of pinnipeds to other carnivores, relationships among pinnipeds, and the alliance of an extinct pinniped group, desmatophocids, also are considered.

3.2. Origin and Evolution

3.2.1. Pinnipeds Defined

The name pinniped comes from the Latin *pinna* and *pedis* meaning "feather-footed," referring to the paddle-like fore- and hind limbs which they use in locomotion on land and in the

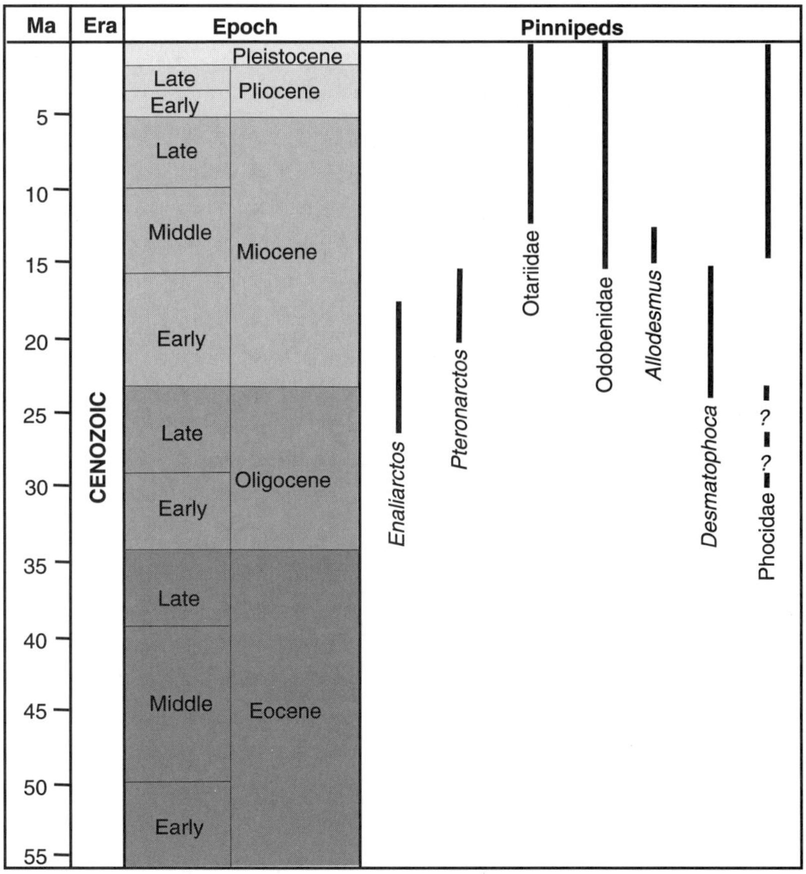

Figure 3.1. Chronologic ranges of extinct and living pinnipeds. Ma = million years ago.

water. Pinnipeds spend considerable amounts of time both in the water and on land or ice, differing from cetaceans and sirenians which are entirely aquatic. In addition to blubber, some pinnipeds have a thick covering of fur.

In seeking the origin of pinnipeds we must first define them. Is the group monophyletic or not? Although this question has been subject to considerable controversy during this century (e.g. see Flynn *et al.,* 1988), the majority of scientists today agree that the Pinnipedia represent a natural, monophyletic group. Pinnipeds are diagnosed by a suite of derived morphological characters (for a complete list see Wyss, 1987, 1988; Berta and Wyss, 1994). All pinnipeds, fossil and recent, possess the characters described below, although some of these characters have been modified or lost secondarily in later diverging taxa.

Some of the well known synapomorphies possessed by pinnipeds (listed in Fig. 3.2 and illustrated in Figs. 3.3–3.5) are defined as follows:

1. *Large infraorbital foramen*—The infraorbital foramen, as the name indicates, is located below the eye orbit and allows passage of blood vessels and nerves. It is large in pinnipeds contrasting with its small size in most terrestrial carnivores.

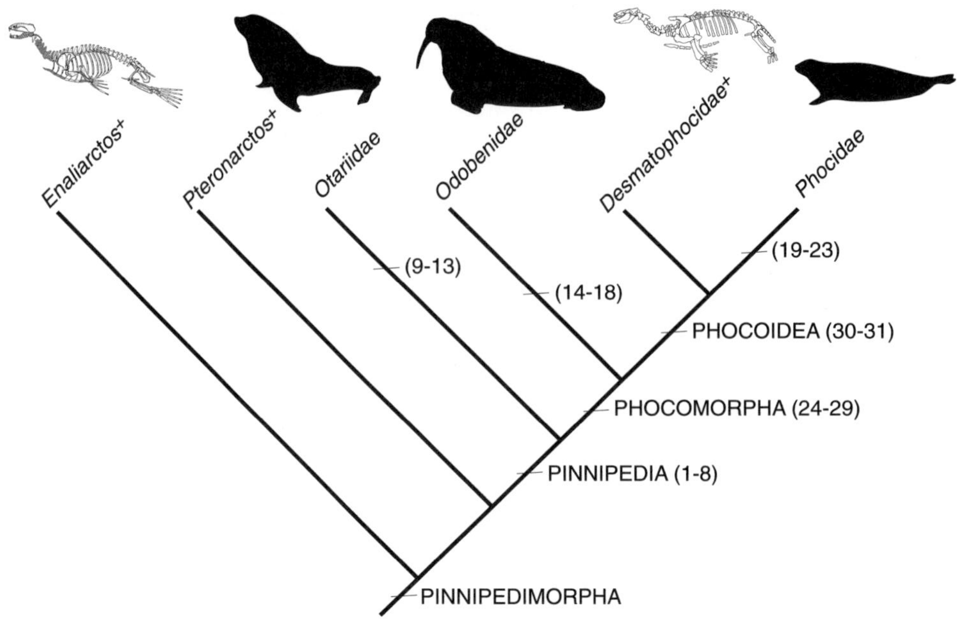

Figure 3.2. A cladogram depicting the relationships of the major clades of pinnipeds. Numbers at nodes refer to synapomorphies listed in the text and +=extinct taxa; see also Figs. 3.3, 3.4, and 3.5. For more detailed cladograms of individual families see Figs. 3.12, 3.19, and 3.20 (Modified from Wyss, 1988; Berta and Wyss, 1994; Deméré, 1994b).

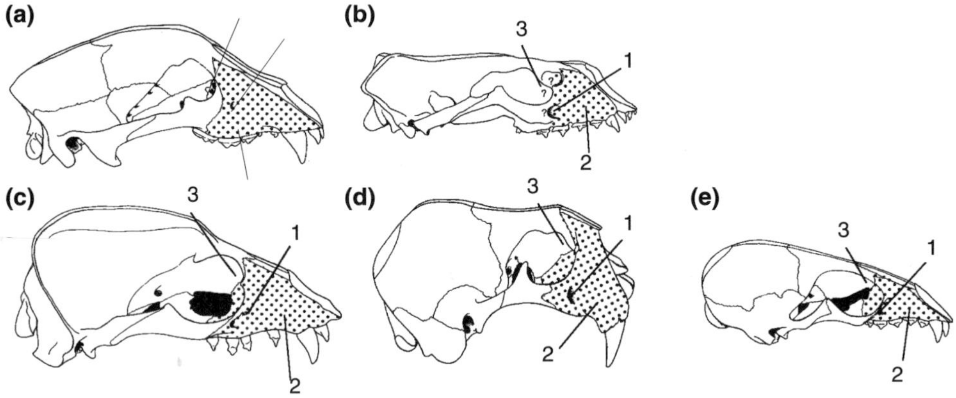

Figure 3.3. Lateral views of the skulls of representative pinnipeds and a generalized terrestrial arctoid (a) Bear, *Ursus americanus,* (b) Fossil pinnipedimorph, *Enaliarctos mealsi,* (c) Otariid, *Zalophus californianus,* (d) Walrus, *Odobenus rosmarus* and (e) Phocid, *Monachus schauinslandi* illustrating pinniped synapomorphies. Character numbers (see text for further description): 1=large infraorbital foramen; 2=maxilla (stippled) makes a significant contribution to the orbital wall; 3=lacrimal absent or fusing early and does not contact jugal (From Berta and Wyss, 1994).

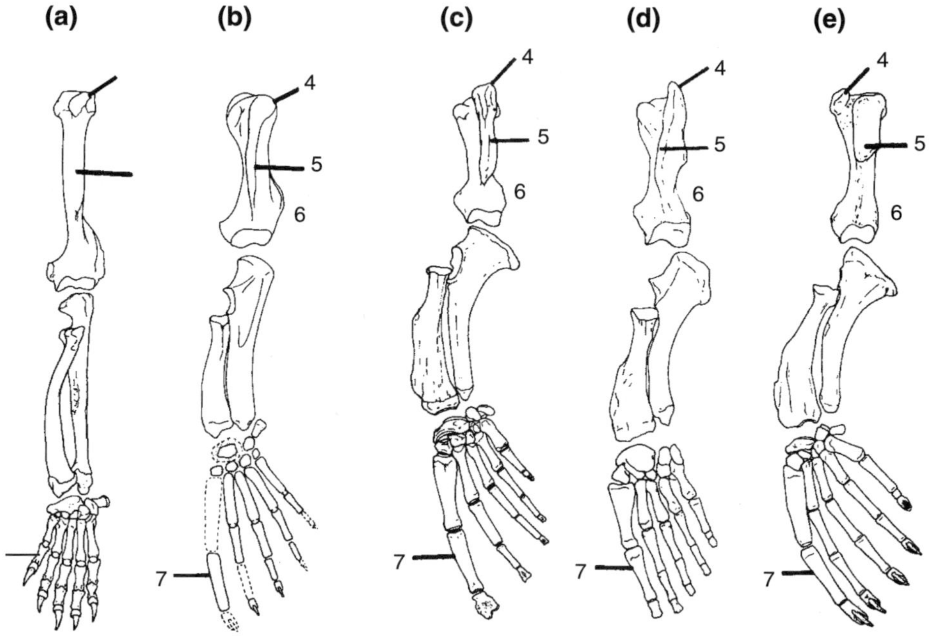

Figure 3.4. Left forelimbs of representative pinnipeds and a generalized terrestrial arctoid in dorsal view illustrating pinniped synapomorphies. Abbreviations as in Fig. 3.3. Character numbers (see text for further description): 4=greater and lesser humeral tuberosities enlarged; 5=deltopectoral crest of humerus strongly developed; 6=short, robust humerus; 7=digit I on manus emphasized (From Berta and Wyss, 1994).

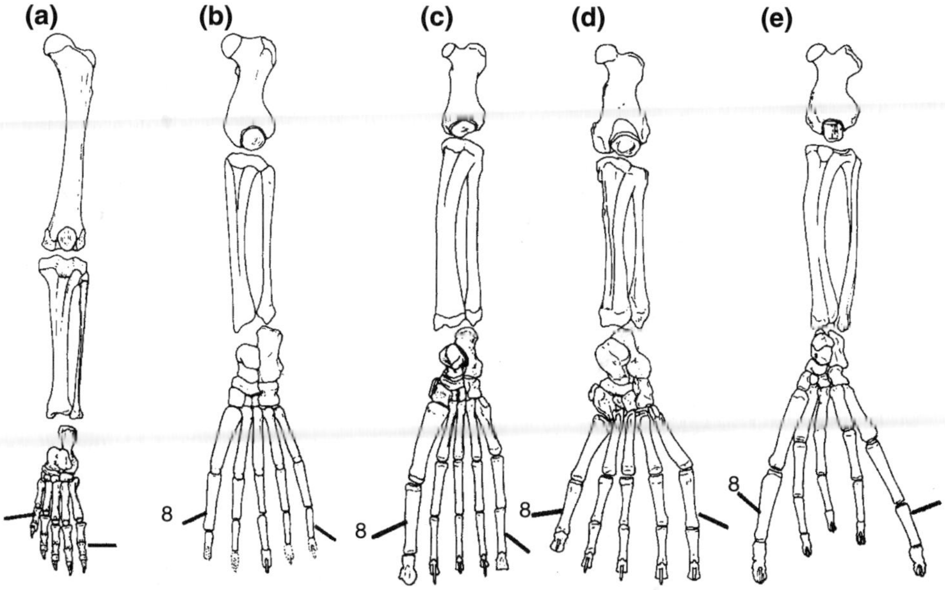

Figure 3.5. Left hind limbs of representative pinnipeds and a generalized terrestrial arctoid in dorsal view illustrating pinniped synapomorphies. Abbreviations as in Fig. 3.3. Character number (see text for further description): 8=digit I and V on the foot emphasized (From Berta and Wyss, 1994).

2. *Maxilla makes a significant contribution to the orbital wall*—Pinnipeds display a unique condition among carnivores in which the maxilla (upper jaw) forms part of the lateral and anterior walls of the orbit of the eye. In terrestrial carnivores, the maxilla is usually limited in its posterior extent by contact of several facial bones (jugal, palatine, and/or lacrimal).

3. *Lacrimal absent or fusing early in ontogeny and does not contact the jugal*—Associated with the pinniped configuration of the maxilla (character 2) is the great reduction or absence of one of the facial bones, the lacrimal. Terrestrial carnivores have a lacrimal that contacts the jugal or is separated from it by a thin sliver of the maxilla, and thus can be distinguished from pinnipeds.

4. *Greater and lesser humeral tuberosities enlarged*—Pinnipeds are distinguished from terrestrial carnivores by having strongly developed tuberosities (rounded prominences) on the proximal end of the humerus (upper arm bone).

5. *Deltopectoral crest of humerus strongly developed*—The crest on the shaft of the humerus for insertion of the deltopectoral muscles in pinnipeds is strongly developed in contrast to the weak development observed in terrestrial carnivores.

6. *Short and robust humerus*—The short and robust humerus of pinnipeds is in contrast to the long, slender humerus of terrestrial carnivores.

7. *Digit I on the hand emphasized*—In the hand of pinnipeds the first digit (thumb equivalent) is elongated, whereas in other carnivores the central digits are the most strongly developed.

8. *Digit I and V on the foot emphasized*—Pinnipeds have elongated the side toes (digits I and V, equivalent to the big toe and little toe) of the foot, whereas in other carnivores the central digits are the most strongly developed.

3.2.2. Pinniped Affinities

Since the name Pinnipedia was first proposed by Illiger in 1811, there has been debate on the relationships of pinnipeds to one another and to other mammals. Two hypotheses have been proposed. The monophyletic hypothesis proposes that the three pinniped families share a single common evolutionary origin (Fig. 3.6a). The **diphyletic** view (also referred to as pinniped diphyly; Fig. 3.6b) calls for the origin of pinnipeds from two carnivore lineages, the alliance of odobenids and otariids being somewhere near ursids (bears) and a separate origin for phocids from the mustelids (weasels, skunks, otters, and kin).

Until recently, morphologic and paleontologic evidence supported pinniped diphyly (McLaren, 1960; Tedford, 1976; Repenning *et al.,* 1979; Muizon, 1982). On the basis of his reevaluation of the morphological evidence, Wyss (1987) argued in favor of a return to the single origin interpretation. This hypothesis of pinniped monophyly has received considerable support from both morphological (Flynn *et al.,* 1988; Berta *et al.,* 1989; Wyss and Flynn, 1993; Berta and Wyss, 1994) and biomolecular studies (Sarich, 1969; Árnason and Widegren, 1986; Vrana *et al.,* 1994; Lento *et al.,* 1995; Árnason *et al.,* 1995; Flynn and Nedbal, 1998).

All recent workers, on the basis of both molecular and morphologic data, agree that the closest relatives of pinnipeds are arctoid carnivores which include procyonids (racoons and their allies) and ursids, although which specific arctoid group forms the closest alliance with pinnipeds is disputed. Most morphologic evidence suggests that pinnipeds are most closely related to the Ursida (including bears and their extinct relatives the Amphicyonidae), with the Musteloidea (Procyonidae and Mustelidae, after Wyss and Flynn, 1993; Berta and Wyss, 1994) forming the next closest outgroup. However, a morphological study

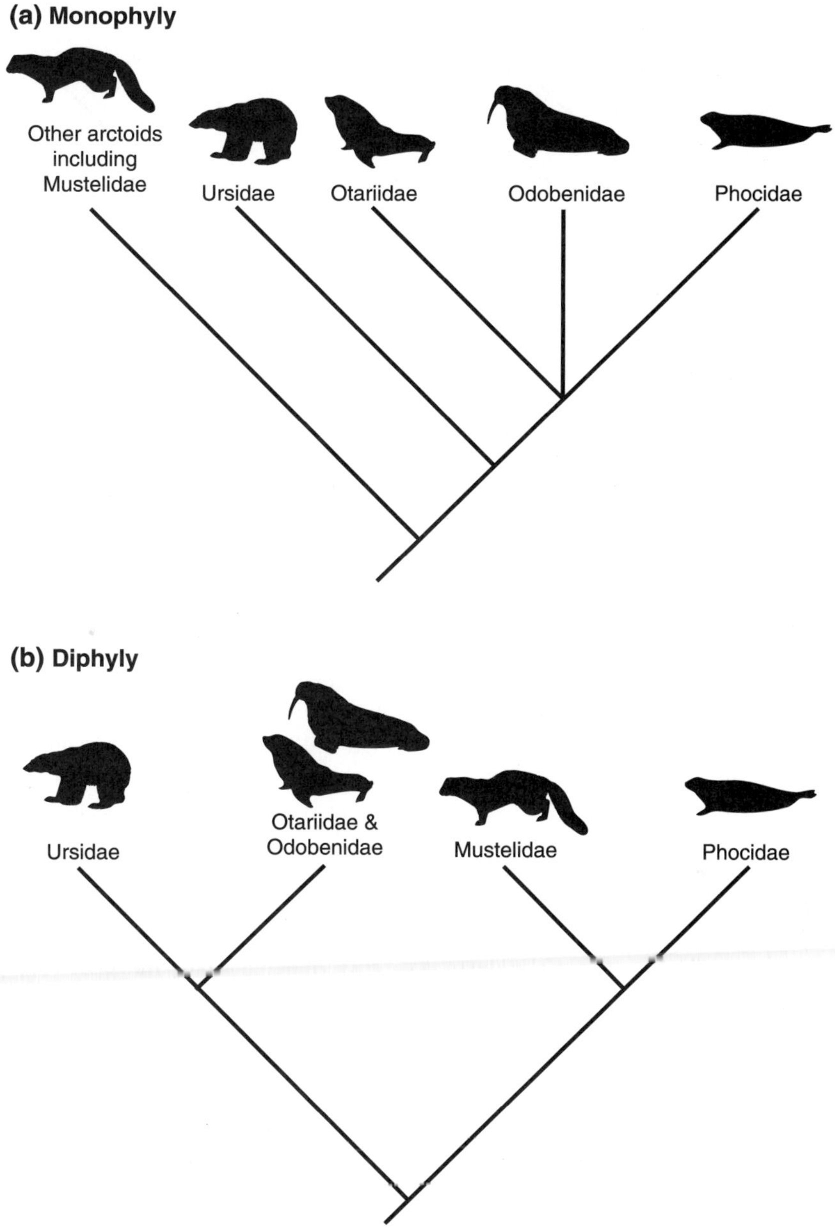

Figure 3.6. Alternative hypotheses for relationships among pinnipeds. (a) Monophyly with ursids as the closest pinniped relatives, (b) Diphyly in which phocids and mustelids are united as sister taxa, as are otariids, odobenids, and ursids.

(Bininda-Emonds and Russell, 1996), while providing support for pinniped monophyly, argues for lutrine (otter) rather than ursid affinities, although the latter result is acknowledged as being weakly supported. Biomolecular studies (e.g. DNA hybridization, karyology, eye lens protein) have supported various arctoids (procyonid, ursid, or mustelid) as being the

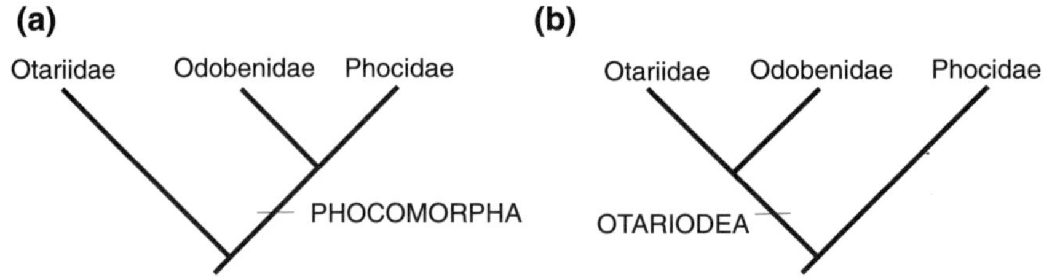

Figure 3.7. Alternative hypotheses for position of the walrus. (a) Phocomorpha clade and (b) "Otarioidea" clade.

closest relatives of the pinnipeds (de Jong, 1982; Árnason and Widegren, 1986; Miyamoto and Goodman, 1986; Árnason and Ledje, 1993; Ledje and Árnason, 1996a,b; Flynn and Nedbal, 1998). Although some molecular sequence studies have supported a pinniped–ursid alliance (Vrana *et al.,* 1994; Árnason *et al.,* 1995), these analyses did not include all species.

Although both morphologic and molecular data support pinniped monophyly there is still disagreement on relationships among pinnipeds. Most of the controversy lies in the debate as to whether the walrus is most closely related to phocids or to otariids. Most recent morphologic evidence for extant pinnipeds unites the walrus and phocids as sister groups (Fig. 3.7a; Wyss, 1987; Wyss and Flynn, 1993; Berta and Wyss, 1994) and is discussed later in this chapter. An alternative view based on molecular data (Vrana *et al.,* 1994; Lento *et al.,* 1995; Árnason *et al.,* 1995) and one morphologic study (Bininda-Emonds and Russell, 1996) supports an alliance between the walrus and otariids (Fig. 3.7b). In the earliest study of mtDNA sequence data from 12S and cytochrome b genes only, one otariid and two closely related phocids were examined (Vrana *et al.,* 1994). A second molecular study using DNA sequence data confirmed this grouping of the walrus with otariids (Lento *et al.,* 1995). This study used a larger sample of phocids and included the basal phocids, the "monachines," the Hawaiian monk seal (*Monachus schauinslandi*), and the Weddell seal (*Leptonychotes weddelli*), as well as later diverging phocine seals, the gray seal (*Halichoerus grypus*) and harbor seal (*Phoca vitulina*). Of two additional molecular studies that focused on phocid interrelationships (Mouchaty *et al.,* 1995; Árnason *et al.,* 1995) the last, more inclusive study confirmed a close relationship between otariids and the walrus. It is significant, however, that in one study (Vrana *et al.,* 1994), a total evidence approach to the data using combined molecular and morphologic data sets supported an alliance between the walrus and phocid seals.

3.2.3. Early "Pinnipeds"

An understanding of the evolution of early "pinnipeds" necessitates a knowledge of certain fossil taxa. The earliest diverging lineage of "pinnipeds" actually are members of the Pinnipedimorpha clade and appear to have originated in the eastern North Pacific (Oregon) during the late Oligocene (27–25 Ma; Fig. 3.1). The earliest known pinnipedimorph, *Enaliarctos,* is represented by five species (Berta, 1991; Mitchell and Tedford, 1973). The ancestral pinnipedimorph dentition, exemplified by *E. barnesi* and *E. mealsi,* is **heterodont**, with large blade-like cusps on the upper cheekteeth well-adapted for shearing (Fig. 3.8). These dental features together with those from the skull (when compared with terrestrial

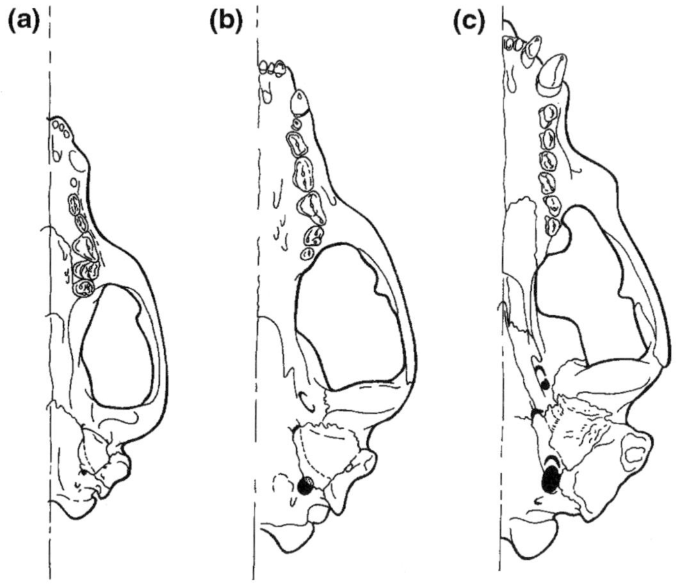

Figure 3.8. Skulls and dentitions of representative pinnipeds and a generalized terrestrial arctoid in ventral view. (a) Archaic bear, *Pachcynodon* (Oligocene, France), (b) Fossil pinnipedimorph, *Enaliarctos mealsi* (early Miocene) and (c) Modern otariid, *Arctocephalus* (Recent, South Atlantic). From Tedford, 1976.

carnivores) indicate closest similarity in terms of derived characters with archaic bears (amphicynodonts; Fig. 3.8).

Other species of the genus *Enaliarctos* show a trend toward the decreasing shearing function of the cheekteeth (e.g. reduction in the number and size of cusps). These dental trends herald the development of the simple peg-like, or **homodont**, dentition characteristic of most living pinnipeds (Berta, 1991). The latest record of *Enaliarctos* is along the Oregon coast from rocks of 25–18 Ma in age. An "enaliarctine" pinniped also has been reported from the western North Pacific (Japan) in rocks of late early Miocene (17.5–17 Ma; Kohno, 1992), although the specimen needs further study before its taxonomic assignment can be confirmed.

The pinnipedimorph *Enaliarctos mealsi* is represented by a nearly complete skeleton collected from the Pyramid Hill Sandstone Member of the Jewett Sand in central California (Fig. 3.9; Berta *et al.,* 1989; Berta and Ray, 1990). The entire animal is estimated at 1.4–1.5 m in length and between 73–88 kg in weight, roughly the weight of a small male harbor seal.

Considerable lateral and vertical movement of the vertebral column was possible in *E. mealsi*. Also, both the fore- and hind limbs were modified as flippers and used in aquatic locomotion. Several features of the hind limb suggest that *E. mealsi* was highly capable of maneuvering on land and probably spent more time near the shore than extant pinnipeds (see also Chapter 8).

A later diverging lineage of fossil pinnipeds more closely allied with pinnipeds than with *Enaliarctos* is *Pteronarctos goedertae* from the late early Miocene (19 to 16 Ma) of coastal Oregon (Berta, 1994; Barnes, 1989, 1992; Fig. 3.1). A striking osteological feature in all pinnipeds is the geometry of bones that comprise the orbital region (Wyss, 1987). In

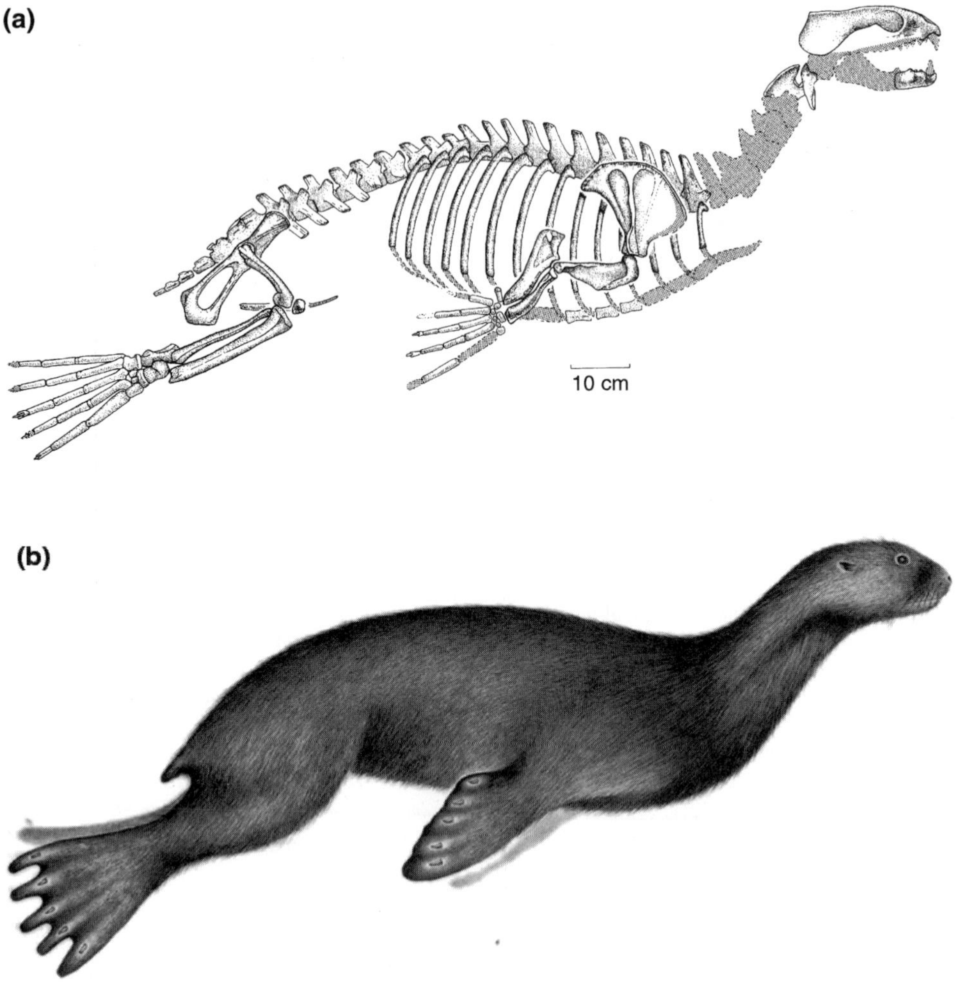

Figure 3.9. The pinnipedimorph, *Enaliarctos mealsi.* (a) Skeletal reconstruction, (b) Life restoration. Total estimated length, snout to tail, 1.4–1.5 m. Shaded areas are unpreserved bones (From Berta and Ray, 1990).

Pteronarctos, the first evidence of the uniquely developed maxilla is seen. Also, in *Pteronarctos* the lacrimal is greatly reduced or absent, as it is in pinnipeds. A shallow pit on the palate between the last premolar and the first molar, seen in *Pteronarctos* and pinnipeds, is indicative of a reduced shearing capability of the teeth and begins a trend toward homodonty.

3.2.4. Modern Pinnipeds

3.2.4.1. Family Otariidae: Sea Lions and Fur Seals

Of the two groups of seals, the otariids are characterized by the presence of external ear flaps, or **pinnae**, and for this reason they are sometimes called eared seals (Fig. 3.10). Another characteristic feature of otariids which can be used to distinguish them from phocids

Figure 3.10. Representative otariids (a) Southern sea lion, *Otaria byronia* and (b) South African fur seal, *Arctocephalus pusillus* illustrating pinna. Note also the thick, dense fur characteristic of fur seals (Illustrations by P. Folkens from Reeves *et al.*, 1992).

is their method of movement on land. Otariids can turn their hindflippers forward and use them to walk (described in more detail in Chapter 8). Otariids generally are smaller than most phocids and are shallow divers targeting fast swimming fish as their major food source. The eared seals and sea lions, Family Otariidae, can be diagnosed as a monophyletic group by several osteological and soft anatomical characters (Figures 3.2, 3.11) as follows:

9. *Frontals extend anteriorly between nasals*—In otariids the suture between the frontal and nasal bones is W-shaped (i.e. the frontals extend between the nasals). In other pinnipeds and terrestrial carnivores, the contact between these bones is either transverse (terrestrial carnivores and walruses) or V-shaped (phocids).

10. *Supraorbital process of the frontal bone is large and shelf-like, especially among adult males*—In otariids, the unique size and shape of the supraorbital process, located above the eye orbit, readily distinguishes them from other pinnipeds. The supraorbital process is absent in phocids and the modern walrus.

11. *Secondary spine subdivides the supraspinous fossa of the scapula*—A ridge subdividing the supraspinous fossa of the scapula (shoulder blade) is present in otariids but not in walruses or phocids.

12. *Uniformly spaced pelage units*—In otariids pelage units (a primary hair and its surrounding secondaries) are spaced uniformly. In odobenids and phocids the units are arranged in groups of two to four or in rows (see Chapter 7, Fig. 7.10).

13. *Trachea has an anterior bifurcation of the bronchi*—In odobenids and phocids the trachea divides into two primary bronchi immediately outside the lung (Fay, 1981; King, 1983b). In otariids, this division occurs more anteriorly, closer to the voicebox and associated structures.

The Otariidae often are divided into two subfamilies, the Otariinae (sea lions) and the Arctocephalinae (fur seals). Five genera and species of sea lions are recognized: *Eumetopias, Neophoca, Otaria, Zalophus,* and *Phocarctos.* Sea lions are characterized and readily distinguished from fur seals by their sparse pelage (Fig. 3.10a). The fur seals, named for their thick dense fur, are divided into two genera. *Arctocephalus* (generic name means bear

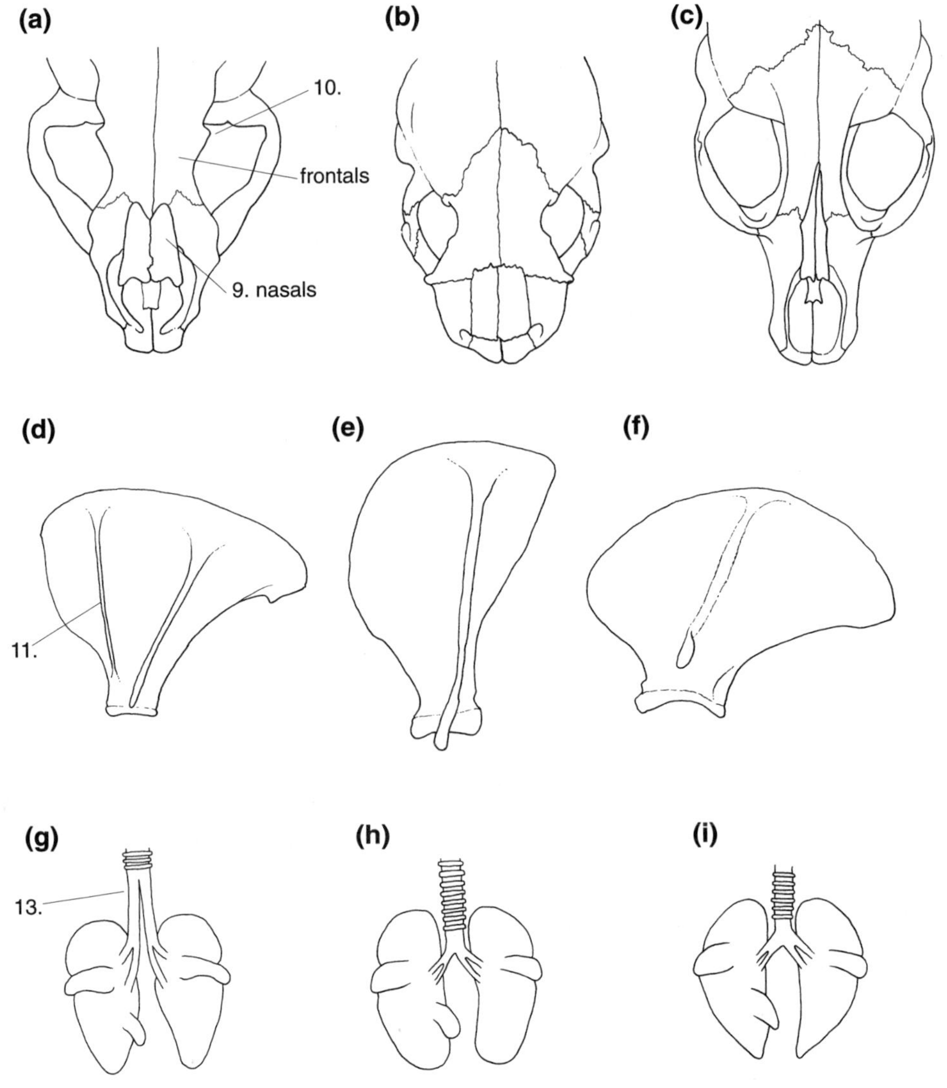

Figure 3.11. Otariid synapomorphies. Skull of an (a) Otariid, (b) Walrus, and (c) Phocid in dorsal view. Illustrations by P. Adam. Character numbers (see text for further description): 9. frontals extend anteriorly between nasals, contact between these bones is transverse (walrus) or V-shaped (phocids); 10. supraorbital process of the frontal bone is large and shelf-like, this process is absent in the modern walrus and phocids. Left scapulae of an otariid (d), walrus (e) and phocid (f); 11. secondary spine subdividing the supraspinous fossa of the scapula, this ridge is absent in the walrus and phocids. Lungs in ventral view of an otariid (g), walrus (h) and phocid (i); 13. trachea has an anterior bifurcation of the bronchi (modified from King, 1983b); this division occurs immediately outside the lungs in the walrus and phocids.

head), or southern fur seals, live mostly in the southern hemisphere and a single species of northern fur seal, *Callorhinus ursinus* (generic name means beautiful nose), inhabits the northern hemisphere (Fig. 3.10b). Relationships among the otariids based on morphology (Berta and Deméré, 1986; Berta and Wyss, 1994) indicate that only the Otariinae are mono-

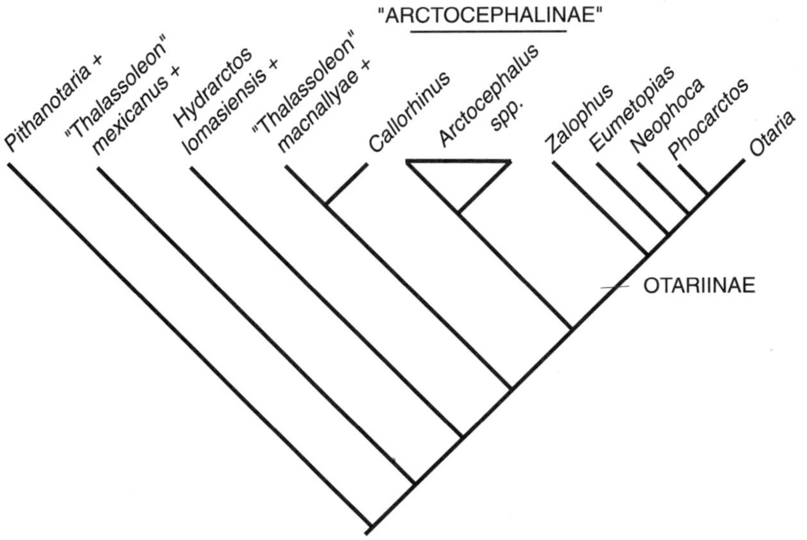

Figure 3.12. Phylogeny of the Otariidae based on morphologic data showing monophyletic Otariinae and paraphyletic "Arctocephalinae" with +=extinct taxa (Berta and Wyss, 1994; Berta and Deméré, 1986).

phyletic with a sister group relationship suggested with *Arctocephalus. Callorhinus* and the extinct taxon *Thalassoleon* are positioned as sequential sister taxa to this clade (Fig. 3.12).

Molecular studies of partial DNA sequence data (cytochrome b and 12S rRNA; Lento *et al.,* 1995 and 1997) revealed paraphyly among both fur seals and sea lions. New Zealand fur seal (*Arctocephalus forsteri*) and the northern fur seal (*Callorhinus ursinus*), both arctocephalines, are separated from each other by two sea lion lineages (Steller's sea lion, *Eumetopias jubatus,* and Hooker's sea lion, *Phocarctos hookeri*) and the two sea lions are no more closely related to each other than they are to other otariid taxa (i.e. the arctocephalines). Work in progress by Lento (personal communication) based on additional sequence data confirms otariid paraphyly. A different arrangement among otariids is suggested by Árnason *et al.* (1995) based on cytochrome b sequence data, but it is weak due to incomplete sampling. Their study supports an alliance between *Arctocephalus forsteri* and the Antarctic fur seal, *Arctocephalus gazella,* and unites Steller's sea lion, *Eumetopias,* and the California sea lion, *Zalophus.* **Hybridization** among different otariid species, based on behavioral observations and skull measurements, has been suggested as a cause for these spurious results (reviewed in Kovacs *et al.,* 1997). Additionally, the violent sexual behavior by male sea lions toward females of different species reported by Miller *et al.* (1996) may have resulted in more hybridization and **introgression** than has been typically recognized for the evolutionary history of otariids.

In addition to the extant fur seal genera *Callorhinus* and *Arctocephalus,* several extinct otariids are known. The earliest otariid is *Pithanotaria starri* from the late Miocene (11 Ma) of California. It is a small animal characterized by double rooted cheek teeth and a postcranial skeleton that allies it with other otariids. A second extinct late Miocene taxon (8–6 Ma), *Thalassoleon* (Fig. 3.13), is represented by three species: *T. mexicanus* from Cedros Island, Baja California, Mexico, *T. macnallyae* from California, and *T. inouei* from central Japan. *Thalassoleon* is distinguished from *Pithanotaria* in its larger size and in lacking a thickened

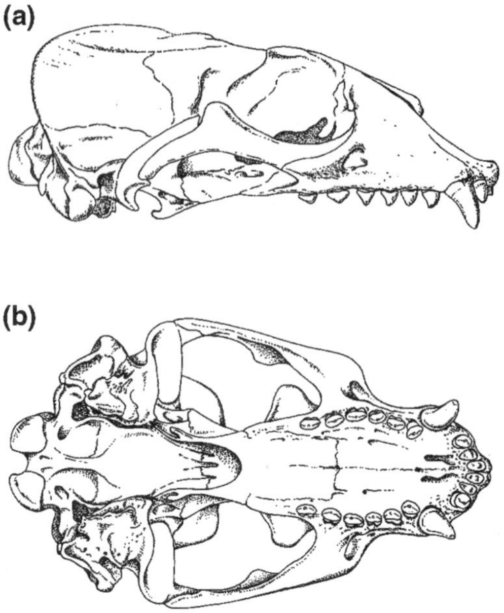

Figure 3.13. Skull of an early otariid, *Thalassoleon mexicanus* from the late Miocene of western North America in (a) lateral and (b) ventral views. Original 25 cm long (From Repenning and Tedford, 1977).

ridge of tooth enamel at the base of the third upper incisor (Berta, 1994). A single extinct species of northern fur seal, *Callorhinus gilmorei,* from the late Pliocene in southern California and Mexico (Berta and Deméré, 1986) and Japan (Kohno and Yanagisawa, 1997) has been described on the basis of a partial mandible, some teeth, and postcranial bones. Several species of the southern fur seal genus *Arctocephalus* are known from the fossil record. The earliest known taxa are *A. pusillus* (South Africa) and *A. townsendi* (California) from the late Pleistocene (Repenning and Tedford, 1977).

The fossil record of sea lions is not well known. Two fossil species have been reported. *Eumetopias* aff. *E. jubatus* is based on isolated postcrania from the early Pliocene of Japan (Miyazai *et al.,* 1995) and *Neophoca palatina* is known from a skull recovered from the middle Pleistocene of New Zealand (King, 1983a).

3.2.4.2. Family Odobenidae: Walruses

Arguably the most characteristic feature of the modern walrus, *Odobenus rosmarus,* is a pair of elongated ever-growing upper canine teeth (**tusks**) found in adults of both sexes (Fig. 3.14). A rapidly improving fossil record indicates that these unique structures evolved in a single lineage of walruses and that "tusks do not a walrus make." The modern walrus is a large-bodied shallow swimmer feeding principally on benthic invertebrates, especially molluscs. Two subspecies of *Odobenus rosmarus* are recognized, *Odobenus r. rosmarus* from the North Atlantic and *Odobenus r. divergens* from the North Pacific (Fig. 3.14). Monophyly of the walrus family, the Odobenidae, is based on five unequivocal synapomorphies (Deméré, 1994b; Figs. 3.2, 3.15).

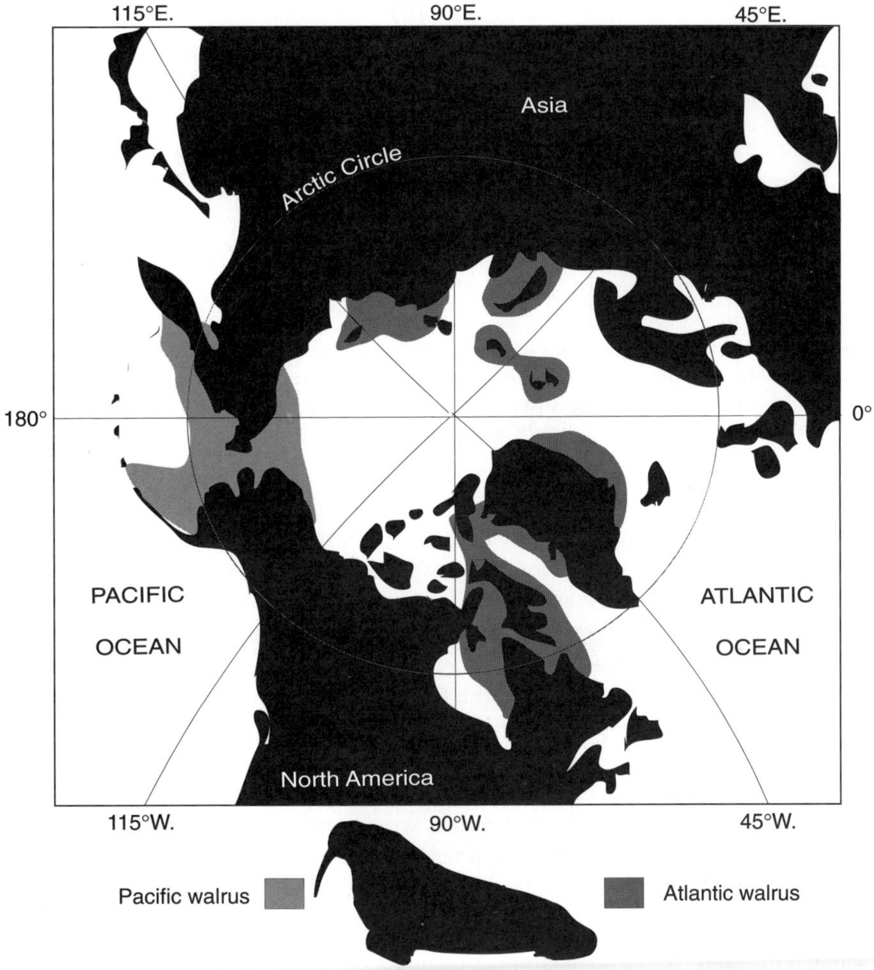

Figure 3.14. Distribution of modern walrus subspecies, *Odobenus rosmarus divergens* (Pacific walrus) and *Odobenus rosmarus rosmarus* (Atlantic walrus).

14. *Antorbital process formed from both the frontal and maxilla*—The walrus has a uniquely developed bony process (protuberance of bone) anterior to the eye orbit, the antorbital process, which is composed of both frontal and maxilla bones. In otariids, the only other pinnipeds with an antorbital process, it is formed entirely from the maxilla.

15. *Distal trochlea of humerus with diameter of medial lip greater than diameter of capitulum*—At the elbow joint the humerus has two articular surfaces, the trochlea (pulley-shaped) for articulation with the ulna (lateral lower arm bone) and the capitulum (head-shaped) for articulation with the radius (medial lower arm bone). In pinnipeds the size of these articular surfaces differs. In the walrus, the trochlea is larger than the capitulum. In *Enaliarctos, Pteronarctos,* otariids, and phocids, the trochlea is smaller than or equal in size to the capitulum.

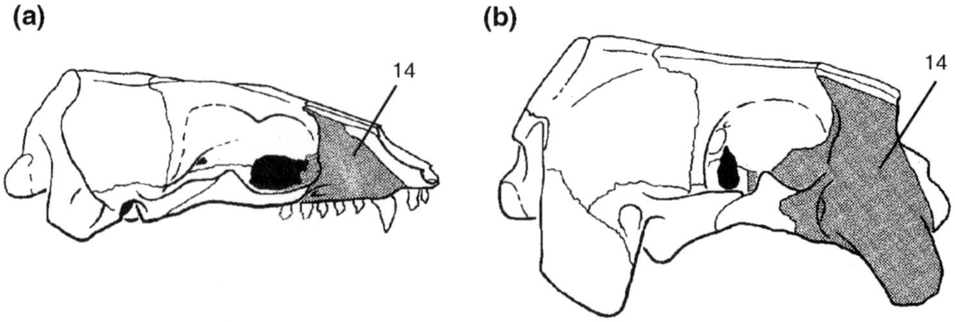

Figure 3.15. A walrus synapomorphy. Skull of an (a) otariid and (b) walrus in lateral view illustrating differences in composition of the orbital region. Character number: 14. antorbital process formed of both frontal and maxillary bones (shaded), in the otariid this process is entirely formed of the maxillary bone (slightly modified from Wyss, 1987).

16. *Distal portion of radius with enlarged radial process*—The condition in walruses (large process) differs from other pinnipedimorphs in which the distal portion of the radius is only slightly expanded with a small radial process.

17. *Insertion for pollicle extensor muscle on first metacarpal developed as a pit or roughened surface*—In otariids and phocids, the proximal surface of the first metacarpal (thumb equivalent) in the hand is smooth. This differs from the condition in walruses in which either a pit or roughened surface is present for insertion of a muscle which extends the thumb.

18. *Scapholunar with a distinct pit for the magnum*—In the walrus the magnum (a wrist bone) articulates with the scapholunar (another wrist bone) in a conspicuous and often deep pocket or pit. The primitive condition is a flat articular surface on the scapholunar for the magnum, also seen in *Allodesmus,* phocids, and the otariids.

Morphologic study of evolutionary relationships among walruses has identified two monophyletic groups. The Dusignathinae includes the extinct genera *Dusignathus, Gomphotaria, Pontolis,* and *Pseudodobenus.* The Odobenidae includes in addition to the modern walrus, *Odobenus,* the extinct genera *Aivukus, Alachtherium, Gingimanducans, Prorosmarus,* and *Valenictus* (Deméré, 1994b). To this latter subfamily can now be added a new genus and species, *Protodobenus japonicus,* from the early Pliocene of central Japan (Horikawa, 1995). Dusignathine walruses developed enlarged upper and lower canines, whereas odobenines evolved only the enlarged upper canines seen in the modern walrus.

At the base of walrus evolution are *Proneotherium, Prototaria, Imagotaria, and Neotherium* from the middle Miocene (16–9 Ma) of the eastern North Pacific (Kohno *et al.,* 1995; Fig. 3.16). These archaic walruses are characterized by unenlarged canines and narrow, multiple rooted premolars with a trend toward molarization, adaptations suggesting retention of the fish diet hypothesized for archaic pinnipeds rather than the evolution of the specialized mollusc diet of the modern walrus. The dusignathine walrus, *Dusignathus santacruzensis,* and the odobenine walrus, *Aivukus cedroensis,* first appeared in the late Miocene of California and Baja California, Mexico. Early diverging odobenine walruses are now known from both sides of the Pacific in the early Pliocene. *Prorosmarus alleni* is known from the eastern U.S. (Virginia) and *Protodobenus japonicus* from Japan. A new species of walrus, possibly the most completely known fossil odobenine walrus, *Valenictus*

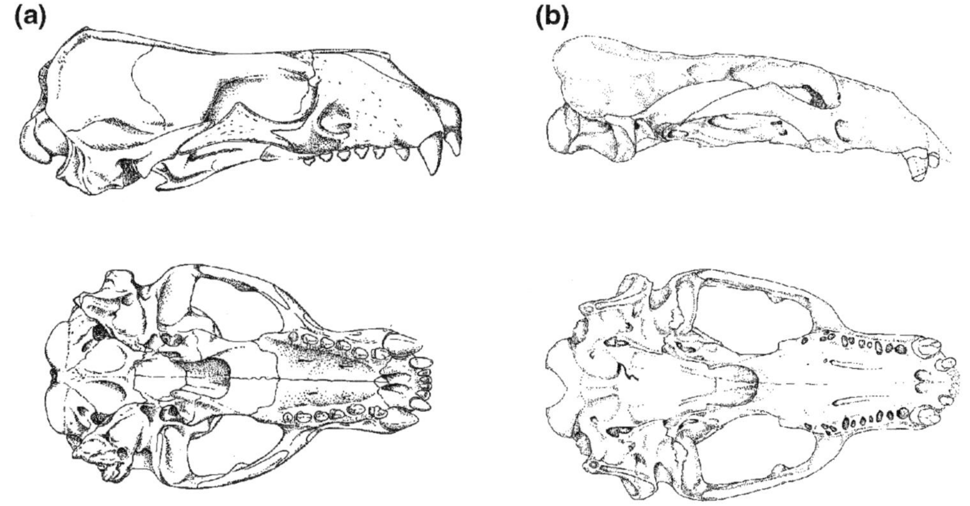

Figure 3.16. Lateral and ventral views of skulls of fossil odobenids (a) *Imagotaria downsi* from the Miocene of western North America. Original 30 cm long (From Repenning and Tedford, 1977) and (b) *Prototaria planicephala* from Miocene of Japan. Original 27 cm (From Kohno *et al.*, 1995).

chulavistensis, was described by Deméré (1994a) as being closely related to modern *Odobenus* but distinguished from it in having no teeth in the lower jaw and lacking all upper postcanine teeth. The toothlessness of *Valenictus* is unique among pinnipeds but parallels the condition seen in modern suction feeding whales and the narwhal.

Remains of the modern walrus *Odobenus* date back to the early Pliocene of Belgium; this taxon appeared approximately 600,000 years ago in the Pacific.

3.2.4.3. Family Phocidae: Seals

The second major grouping of living seals, the phocids, often are referred to as the earless seals for their lack of visible ear pinnae, a characteristic which readily distinguishes them from otariids. Another characteristic phocid feature is their method of movement on land. The phocids are unable to turn their hindflippers forward and progression over land is accomplished by undulations of the body (described in more detail in Chapter 8). Other characteristics of phocids include their larger body size in comparison to otariids, averaging as much as two tons in the northern elephant seal. Several phocids, most notably the elephant seal and the Weddell seal, are spectacular divers which feed on pelagic, vertically migrating squid and fish at depths of 1000 m or more.

Wyss (1988) reviewed the following characters which support monophyly of the Family Phocidae (Figs. 3.2, 3.17):

19. *Lack the ability to draw the hind limbs forward under the body due to a massively developed astragalar process and greatly reduced calcaneal tuber*—The phocid astragalus (ankle bone) is distinguished by a strong posteriorly directed process over which the tendon of the flexor hallucis longus passes. The calcaneum (one of the heel bones) of phocids is correspondingly modified. The calcaneal tuber is shortened and projects only as far as the

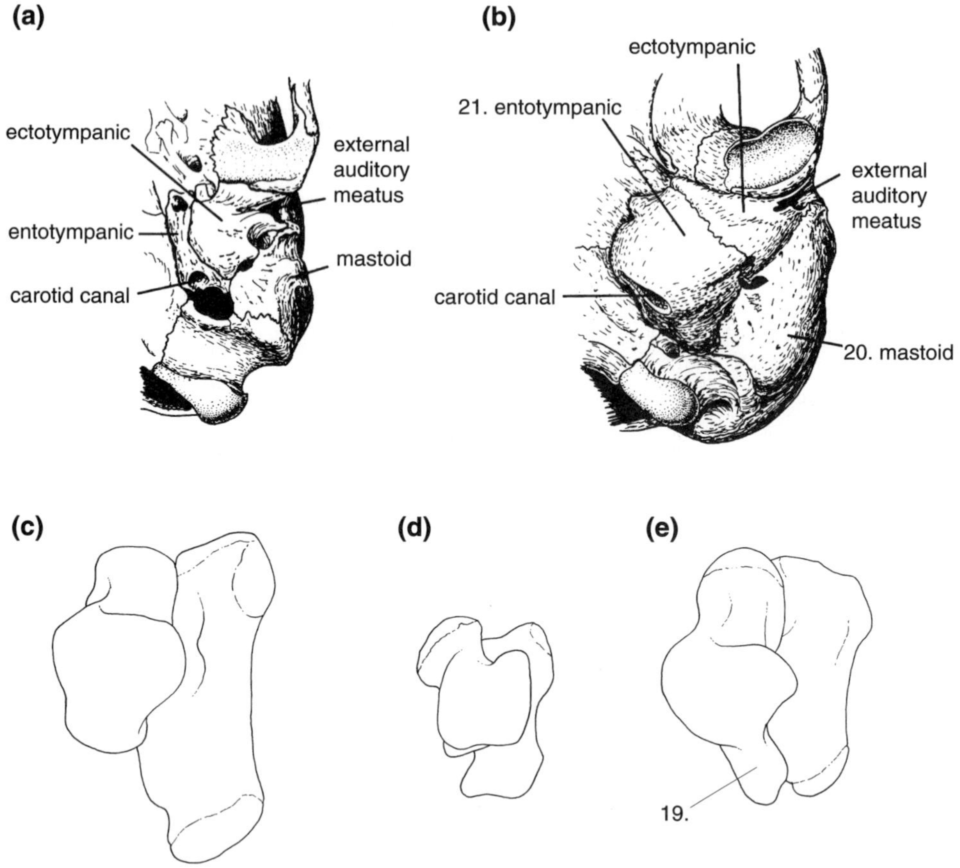

Figure 3.17. Phocid synapomorphies. Ventral view of ear region of an otariid (a) and a phocid (b). Character numbers (see text for further description): 20. pachyostotic mastoid bone; this is not the case in other pinnipeds and 21. greatly inflated entotympanic bone (modified from King, 1983b); in other pinnipeds this bone is flat or slightly inflated. Left astragalus (ankle) and calcaneum (heel) of an otariid (c), walrus (d), and phocid (e). 19. lack the ability to draw the hind limbs under the body due to a massively developed astragalar process and greatly reduced calcaneal tuber; these modifications do not occur in other pinnipeds. Illustrations by P. Adam.

process of the astragalus. This arrangement prevents anterior flexion of the foot, resulting in seals' inability to bring their hind limbs forward during locomotion on land.

20. *Pachyostic mastoid region*—In phocids the mastoid (ear) region is composed of thick, dense bone (**pachyostosis**) which is not the case in otariids or the walrus.

21. *Greatly inflated entotympanic bone*—In phocids the entotympanic bone (one of the bones forming the earbone or tympanic bulla) is inflated. In other pinnipeds the entotympanic bone is either flat or slightly inflated.

22. *Supraorbital processes completely absent*—Phocids differ from other pinnipeds in the complete absence of the supraorbital process of the frontal (Fig. 3.11).

23. *Strongly everted ilia*—Living phocines, except *Erignathus,* are characterized by a lateral eversion (outward bending) of the ilium (one of the pelvic bones) accompanied by a deep lateral excavation (King, 1966). In other pinnipeds and terrestrial carnivores, the anterior termination of the ilium is simple and not everted or excavated.

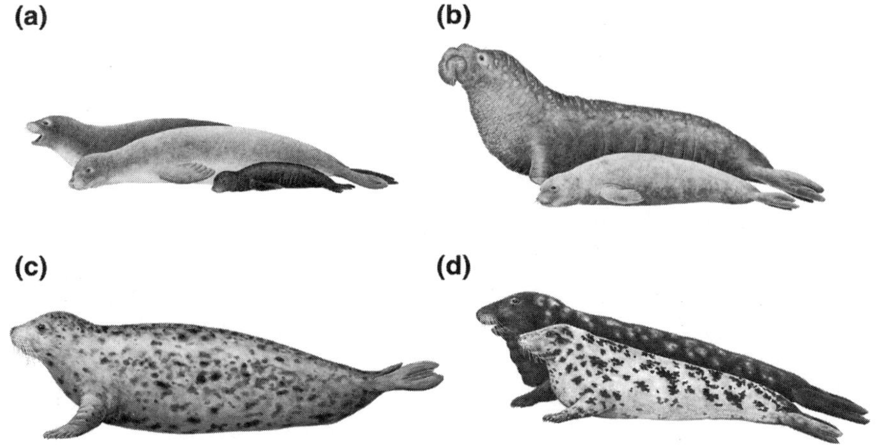

Figure 3.18. Representative "monachines" (a) Hawaiian monk seal, *Monachus schauinslandi,* (b) northern elephant seal, *Mirounga angustirostris* and phocines, (c) Harbor seal, *Phoca vitulina,* and (d) gray seal, *Halichoerus grypus.* Illustrations by P. Folkens from Reeves *et al.,* (1992).

Although traditionally phocids have been divided into two to four major subgroupings, Wyss (1988) argued for the monophyly of only one of these groups, the Phocinae, composed of *Erignathus* and *Cystophora* plus the tribe Phocini, consisting of *Halichoerus, Histriophoca, Pagophilus, Phoca,* and *Pusa.* According to Wyss, both the Monk Seals ("Monachinae") and the genus "*Monachus*" are paraphyletic with "*Monachus,*" in turn representing the outgroup to the elephant seals, *Mirounga,* and the lobodontines (including the Weddell seal, *Leptonychotes,* crabeater seal, *Lobodon,* leopard seal, *Hydrurga,* and the Ross seal, *Ommatophoca;* Figs. 3.18, 3.19). Another study found reasonable support for both traditional phocid subfamilies, although with differing relationships among the taxa within each group (Bininda-Emonds and Russell, 1996). The basal position of *Monachus* and *Erignathus,* in the Monachinae and Phocinae respectively, was not supported. Instead, both taxa were recognized as later diverging members of their respective subfamilies rendering the Lobodontini and Phocini as paraphyletic clades (Bininda-Emonds and Russell, 1996; Fig. 3.18).

Several molecular studies provide data on phocid interrelationships (e.g., Carr and Perry, 1997; Árnason *et al.,* 1995; Mouchaty *et al.,* 1995; see Fig. 3.20). In the more inclusive studies (Carr and Perry, 1997; Árnason *et al.,* 1995), the Hawaiian monk seal, *Monachus schauinslandi,* was identified as sister taxon to all other phocids, in agreement with Wyss (1988). Among the northern phocids, the bearded seal, *Erignathus,* is distinct from the hooded seal, *Cystophora,* and the *Phoca* complex. Árnason *et al.* (1995) support monophyly of [Phocini + *Pagophilus/Histriophoca*] with respect to *Cystophora.* Carr and Perry (1997) found some support for an alternative result [*Cystophora* + Phocini] + *Pagophilus/Histriophoca.* The present state of knowledge based on molecular data is perhaps best represented as an unresolved trichotomy. The gray seal, *Halichoerus grypus,* was placed among species of the genus *Phoca* by Árnason *et al.* (1995), suggesting that generic status of the gray seal is not warranted, a conclusion reached in other molecular (O'Corry-Crowe and Westlake, 1997; Mouchaty *et al.,* 1995; but see Carr and Perry, 1997, for a different view) and morphologic (Burns and Fay, 1970) studies. Included in this redefined *Phoca* complex, in addition to the gray seal, is the ringed seal, *Phoca hispida,* the spotted seal, *Phoca largha,* and the harbor seal, *Phoca vitulina.*

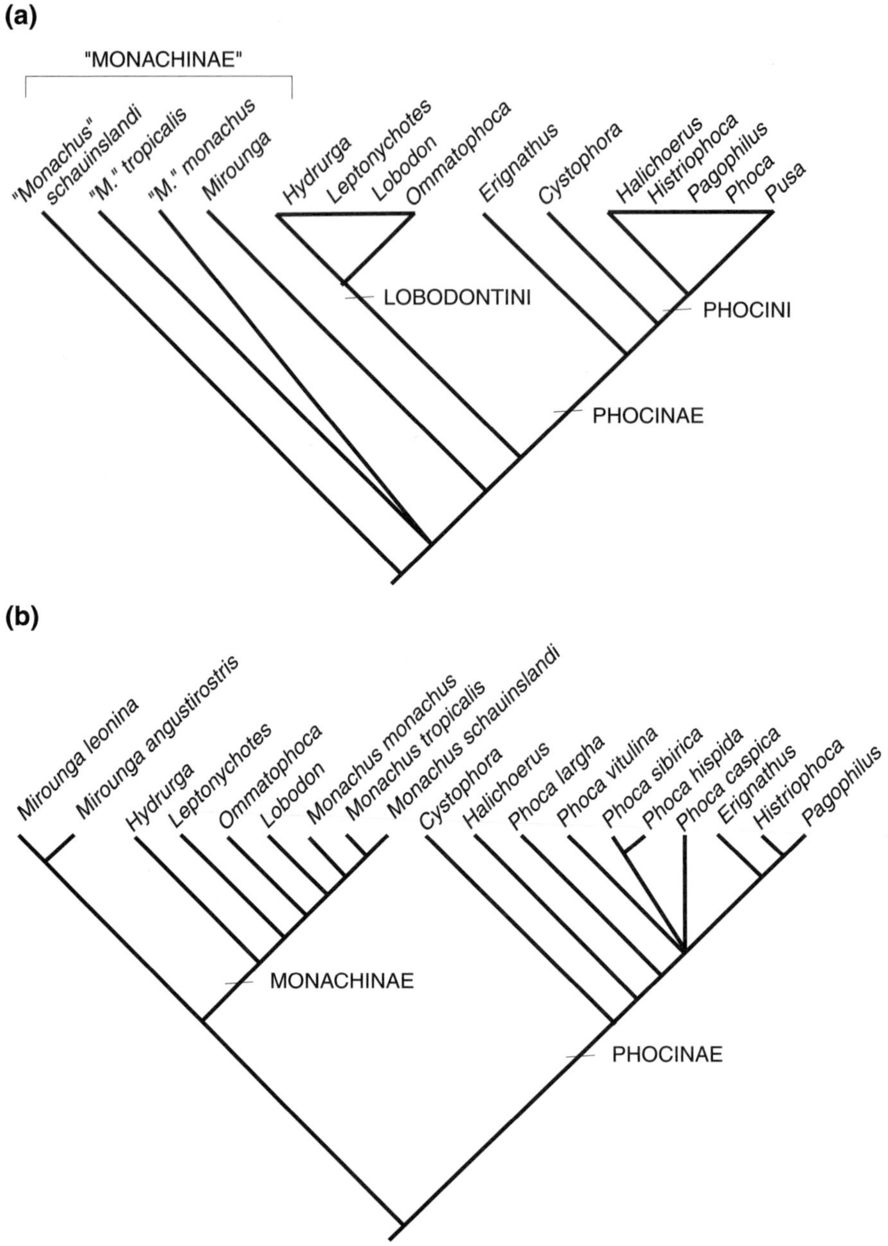

Figure 3.19. Alternative phylogenies for the Phocidae based on morphologic data (a) from Wyss (1988); Berta and Wyss (1994), and (b) from Bininda-Emonds and Russell (1996).

Four subspecies of the harbor seal currently are recognized based on morphologic, molecular, and geographic differences (Stanley *et al.,* 1996): *P. v. vitulina* and *P. v. concolor* (the eastern and western Atlantic Ocean populations, respectively) and *P. v. richardsi* and *P. v. stejnegeri* (the eastern and western Pacific Ocean populations, respectively). A fifth subspecies, *P. v. mellonae,* a freshwater population from the area of Seal Lakes in northern Québec, Canada, is morphologically and behaviorally distinct from the others (Smith and

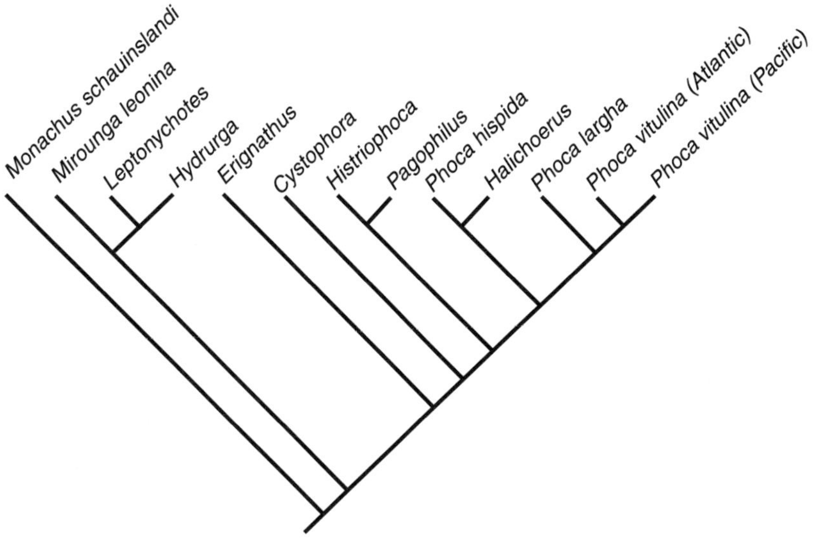

Figure 3.20. Phylogeny of the Phocidae based on molecular data (Árnason *et al.,* 1995).

Lavigne, 1994). Árnason *et al.*'s (1995) data support an alliance between the eastern Pacific harbor seal, *P. v. richardsi* and the Eastern Atlantic harbor seal, *P. v. vitulina,* with the spotted seal, *Phoca largha,* positioned as sister taxon to this clade as well as supporting a sister group relationship between the gray seal, *Halichoerus grypus,* and the ringed seal, *Phoca hispida* (Fig. 3.20).

The confirmation of hybridization among two phocids, the harp seal, *Pagophilus groenlandicus,* and the hooded seal, *Cystophora cristata,* based on molecular data (Kovacs *et al.,* 1997) is intriguing and it suggests further study of species isolating mechanisms and the difficulty of applicability of the biological species concept.

The 1997 report of a fossil phocid from the late Oligocene (29–23 Ma) of South Carolina (Koretsky, 1997) makes it the oldest known phocid and pinniped (Fig. 3.1). Prior to this record, phocids were unknown until the middle Miocene (15 Ma) when both phocine and "monachine" seals became distinct lineages in the North Atlantic. The extinct phocine seal *Leptophoca lenis* and the "monachine" seal *Monotherium? wymani* are known from Maryland and Virginia during this time. *Leptophoca lenis,* or a closely related species under study by Koretsky, also is represented in the eastern Atlantic, from deposits in the Antwerp Basin, Belgium (Ray, 1976). Another addition to the fossil record of phocids is a new genus and species of phocine seal, based on an articulated skeleton (lacking the skull, neck, and part of the hind limbs) reported from the middle Miocene of Argentina (Cozzuol, 1996). Other fossil seals are represented by well preserved skeletal material. For example, *Acrophoca longirostris* (Fig. 3.21) and *Piscophoca pacifica* from the late Miocene and early Pliocene were found in the Pisco Formation of Peru (Muizon, 1981), and *Homiphoca capensis* was discovered in South Africa (Hendey and Repenning, 1972). Although originally considered "monachines" (i.e. lobodontine seals), ongoing study by Cozzuol (1996) indicates that *Acrophoca, Piscophoca,* and new material from the Pliocene of Peru (provisionally referred to two new genera and species) may be closer to phocines. Other phocines evolved in the vast inland Paratethys Sea from 14 to 10 mya (see also Chapter 6) and differentiated mostly in the Pleistocene.

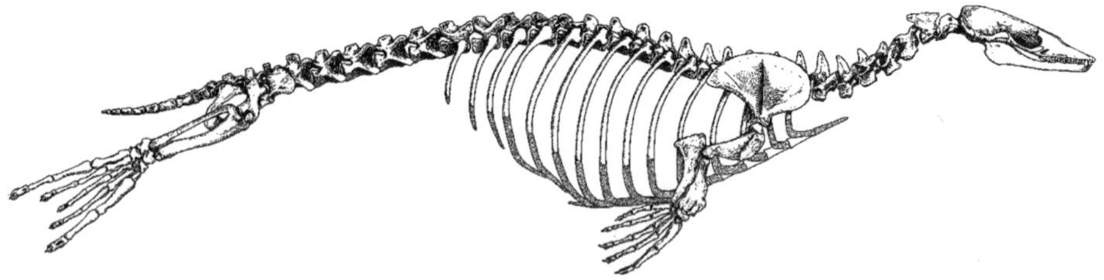

Figure 3.21. Skeleton of an archaic phocid, *Acrophoca longirostris* from the Miocene of Peru (From Muizon, 1981).

3.2.5. Walruses and Phocids Linked?

As noted previously, an alliance between the walrus and phocid seals and their extinct relatives, the Phocomorpha clade, has been proposed based on morphologic data. Among the synapomorphies that unite these pinnipeds are the following (Figure 3.2):

24. *Middle ear bones enlarged*—The middle ear bones of the walrus and phocids are large relative to body size which is not the case in otariids and terrestrial carnivores.
25. *Abdominal testes*—The testes are abdominal (inguinal) in phocids and the walrus. In contrast, the testes of otariids and terrestrial carnivores lie outside the inguinal ring in a scrotal sac.
26. *Primary hair non-medullated*—The outer guard hairs in the walrus and phocids lack a pith or medulla which is present in otariids and other carnivores (see also Chapter 7).
27. *Thick subcutaneous fat*—The walrus and phocids are characterized by thick layers of fat; these layers are less well developed in otariids and terrestrial carnivores.
28. *External ear pinna lacking*—The walrus and phocids lack external ear pinnae, the presence of which characterizes otariids and terrestrial carnivores.
29. *Venous system with inflated hepatic sinus, well-developed caval sphincter, large intervertebral sphincter, duplicate posterior vena cava, and gluteal route for hind limbs*—The walrus and phocids share a specialized venous system that is related, in part, to their exceptional diving capabilities (see Chapter 9). In contrast, otariids and terrestrial carnivores have a less specialized venous system that more closely approximates the typical mammalian pattern.

The question of whether walruses are more closely related to phocids or to otariids involves further exploration of both morphological and molecular data sets. Study of basal walruses will likely provide additional characters at the base of walrus evolution that can then be compared for alliance with either otariids or phocids. The molecular results, which consistently support a link between otariids and the walrus, have been explained as a methodological problem, or a long-branch attraction effect. When dealing with sequence data, branch lengths refer to the expected amounts of evolutionary change along that branch. The walrus lineage is a relatively long branch and it is unlikely that intraspecific variation among the walrus subspecies will aid in bisecting the branch, although this has yet to be examined. Because there is a tendency for longer branches to attract one another and thus give a misleading tree, it is possible that the walrus and otariid alliance may be incorrect. A more conservative interpretation of the molecular data is that the walrus is an early, but not first, independent divergence from the common pinniped ancestor (Lento *et al.*, 1995).

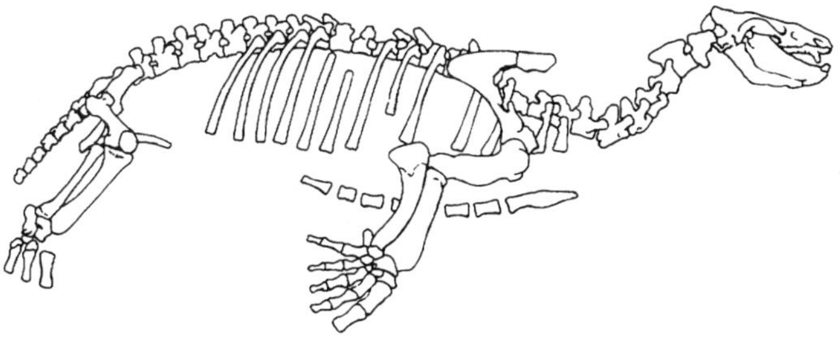

Figure 3.22. Skeleton of the desmatophocid, *Allodesmus kernensis* from the Miocene of western North America. Original 2.2 m long (From Mitchell, 1975).

3.2.6. Desmatophocids: Phocid Relatives or Otarioids?

Study of pinniped evolutionary relationships has identified a group of fossil pinnipeds including *Desmatophoca* and *Allodesmus* (Fig. 3.22) that are positioned as the common ancestors of phocid pinnipeds (Berta and Wyss, 1994). This interpretation differs from previous work that recognized desmatophocids as **otarioid** pinnipeds, a grouping that includes walruses (Barnes, 1989). The question of otarioid monophyly was examined in a comprehensive pinniped data set. The strict consensus tree that resulted by forcing otarioid monophyly was 34 steps longer than the preferred hypothesis (Berta and Wyss, 1994).

Desmatophocids are known from the early middle Miocene (23–15 Ma) of the western U.S. and Japan. Newly reported occurrences of *Desmatophoca* from Oregon confirm the presence of sexual dimorphism and large body size in these pinnipeds (Deméré and Berta, in press). Allodesmids are known from the middle to late Miocene of California and more recently from Japan (Barnes *et al.,* 1995). They are a diverse group characterized, among other characters, by pronounced sexual dimorphism, large eye orbits, bulbous cheek tooth crowns, and deep lower jaws.

A number of features are shared among phocids and their close fossil relatives *Allodesmus* and *Desmatophoca* (identified as the Phocoidea clade) and hence they support a close link between these taxa (Figure 3.2). These synapomorphies include, among others:

30. *Posterior termination of nasals posterior to contact between the frontal and maxilla bones*—In phocids and desmatophocids, the V-shaped contact between the frontal and maxilla bones is the result of the nasals extending posteriorly between these bones (Fig. 3.11).

31. *Squamosal-jugal contact mortised*—A mortised or interlocking contact between the squamosal and jugal (cheekbones) distinguishes phocids and desmatophocids from other pinnipeds in which these bones overlap one another in a splint-like arrangement (Fig. 3.3).

3.3. Summary and Conclusions

Pinniped monophyly is a well-supported hypothesis based on both morphologic and molecular data. The closest relatives of pinnipeds are arctoid carnivores, with most of the evidence supporting a link between pinnipeds and the Ursida (bears and their extinct relatives).

The earliest pinnipedimorphs (i.e. *Enaliarctos*) appear in the fossil record approximately 27–25 Ma in the North Pacific. Modern pinniped lineages diverged shortly thereafter with the first appearance of the phocid seals in the North Atlantic. Phocids usually are divided into two groups, "monachines" and phocines. The monophyly of monachines has been questioned based on morphologic data. Walruses appeared about 10 million years later in the North Pacific. A rapidly improving fossil record indicates that enlarged tusks characteristic of both sexes of the modern walrus were not present ancestrally in walruses. Two monophyletic lineages of walruses are recognized (Dusignathinae and Odobenidae). The last pinniped lineage to appear in the fossil record, the otariids, are only known as far back as 11 Ma in the North Pacific. Morphologic data supports monophyly of the sea lions (Otariinae) but not the fur seals (Arctocephalinae).

A remaining conflict is the position of the walrus. Most morphologic data support a phocid and walrus alliance whereas the molecular data consistently supports uniting otariids and the walrus. Resolution of this conflict will likely benefit from detailed exploration of both morphologic and molecular data sets.

3.4. Further Reading

For a recent comprehensive summary of phylogenetic relationships among pinnipeds see Berta and Wyss (1994). Relationships among various arctoid carnivores and pinnipeds are presented in Wyss and Flynn (1993) and Bininda-Emonds and Russell (1996). For descriptions of the morphology and evolution of fossil pinnipeds see Berta (1991, 1994). See Barnes (1989, 1992) for archaic pinnipeds, Repenning and Tedford (1977) for fossil otariids and walruses, and Muizon (1981) for fossil phocids. Reviews of the evolution and phylogeny of various pinniped lineages include Deméré (1994a,b) and see Kohno *et al.* (1995) for walruses. For alternative views on phocid phylogeny see Wyss (1988), Árnason *et al.* (1995), and Bininda-Emonds and Russell (1996). Lento *et al.* (1995) provides molecular evidence for otariid relationships, but see Berta and Deméré (1986) for a different view based on morphologic data.

References

Árnason, U., and C. Ledje (1993). The use of highly repetitive DNA for resolving cetacean and pinniped phylogenies. *In* "Mammal Phylogeny: Placentals" (F. S. Szalay, M. J. Novacek, and M. C. McKenna, eds.), pp. 74–80. Springer-Verlag, New York.

Árnason, U., and B. Widegren (1986). Pinniped phylogeny enlightened by molecular hybridizations using highly repetitive DNA. *Mol. Biol. Evol.* **3**(4): 356–365.

Árnason, U., K. Bodin, A. Gullberg, C. Ledje, and S. Mouchaty (1995). A molecular view of pinniped relationships with particular emphasis on the true seals. *J. Mol. Evol.* **40**: 78–85.

Barnes, L. G. (1989). A new enaliarctine pinniped from the Astoria Formation, Oregon, and a classification of the Otariidae (Mammalia: Carnivora). *Nat. Hist. Mus. L.A. Cty., Contrib. Sci.* **403**: 1–28.

Barnes, L. G. (1992). A new genus and species of middle Miocene enaliarctine pinniped (Mammalia: Carnivora) from the Astoria Formation in coastal Oregon. *Nat. Hist. Mus. L.A. Cty., Contrib. Sci.* **431**: 1–27.

Barnes, L. G., and K. Hirota. (1995). Miocene pinnipeds of the otariid subfamily Allodesminae in the North Pacific Ocean: Systematics and relationships. *Island Arc* **3**: 329–360.

Berta, A. (1991). New *Enaliarctos* (Pinnipedimorpha) from the Oligocene and Miocene of Oregon and the role of "enaliarctids" in pinniped phylogeny. *Smithson. Contrib. Paleobiol.* **69**: 1–33.

Berta, A. (1994). New specimens of the Pinnipediform *Pteronarctos* from the Miocene of Oregon. *Smithson. Contrib. Paleobiol.* **78**: 1–30.

Berta, A., and T. A. Deméré (1986). *Callorhinus gilmorei* n. sp., (Carnivora: Otariidae) from the San Diego Formation (Blancan) and its implications for otariid phylogeny. *Trans. San Diego Soc. Nat. Hist.* **21**(7): 111–126.

Berta, A., and C. E. Ray (1990). Skeletal morphology and locomotor capabilities of the archaic pinniped *Enaliarctos mealsi*. *J. Vertebr. Paleontol.* **10**(2): 141–157.

Berta, A., and A. R. Wyss (1994). Pinniped phylogeny. *Proc. San Diego Soc. Nat. Hist.* **29**: 33–56.

Berta, A., C. E. Ray, and A. R. Wyss (1989). Skeleton of the oldest known pinniped, *Enaliarctos mealsi. Science* **244**: 60–62.

Bininda-Emonds, O. R. P., and A. P. Russell (1996). A morphological perspective on the phylogenetic relationships of the extant phocid seals (Mammalia: Carnivora: Phocidae). *Bonner Zoologische Monographien* **41**: 1–256.

Burns, J. J., and F. H. Fay (1970). Comparative morphology of the skull of the ribbon seal, *Histriophoca fasciata* with remarks on systematics of Phocidae. *J. Zool.* **161**: 363–394.

Carr, S. M., and E. A. Perry (1997). Intra- and interfamilial systematic relationships of phocid seals as indicated by mitochondrial DNA sequences. *In* "Molecular Genetics of Marine Mammals" (A. E. Dizon, S. J. Chivers, and W. E. Perrin, eds.), Spec. Publ. No. 3, pp. 277–290. Soc. Mar. Mammal. Allen Press, Kansas.

Cozzuol, M. A. (1996). The record of the aquatic mammals in southern South America. *Muench. Geowiss. Abh.* **30**: 321–342.

de Jong, W. W. (1982). Eye lens protein and vertebrate phylogeny. *In* "Macromolecular Sequences in Systematics and Evolutionary Biology" (M. Goodman, ed.), pp. 75–114. Plenum Press, New York.

Deméré, T. A. (1994a). Two new species of fossil walruses (Pinnipedia: Odobenidae) from the Upper Pliocene San Diego Formation, California. *Proc. San Diego Soc. Nat. Hist.* **29**: 77–98.

Deméré, T. A. (1994b). The Family Odobenidae: A phylogenetic analysis of fossil and living taxa. *Proc. San Diego Soc. Nat. Hist.* **29**: 99–123.

Deméré, T. A. and A. Berta. Miocene *Desmatophoca* from the Astoria Formation, Oregon. *Smithson. Contrib. Paleobiol.* (in press).

Fay, F. H. (1981). Walrus: *Odobenus rosmarus. In* "Handbook of Marine Mammals" (S. H. Ridgway and R. J. Harrison, eds.), Vol. 1, pp. 1–23. Academic Press, New York.

Flynn, J. J., and M. A. Nedbal (1998). Phylogeny of the Carnivora (Mammalia): Congruence vs. incompatibility among multiple data sets. *Mol. Phylogenet. Evol.* **9**(3): 414–426.

Flynn, J. J., N. A. Neff, and R. H. Tedford (1988). Phylogeny of the Carnivora. *In* "The Phylogeny and Classification of the Tetrapods" (M. J. Benton, ed.), Vol. 2, pp. 73–116. Clarendon Press, Oxford.

Hendey, Q. B., and C. A. Repenning (1972). A Pliocene phocid from South Africa. *Ann. S. Afr. Mus.* **59**(4): 71–98.

Horikawa, H. (1995). A primitive odobenine walrus of early Pliocene age from Japan. *Island Arc* **3**(4): 309–329.

Illiger, J. C. W. (1811). "Prodromus systematics Mammalium et Avium." C. Salfeld, Berlin.

King, J. E. (1966). Relationships of the hooded and elephant seals (genera *Cystophora* and *Mirounga*). *J. Zool. Soc. London* **148**: 385–398.

King, J. E. (1983a). The Ohope skull—a new species of Pleistocene sea lion from New Zealand. *N. Z. J. Mar. Freshwater Res.* **17**: 105–120.

King, J. E. (1983b). "Seals of the World." Oxford University Press, London.

Kohno, N. (1992). A new Pliocene fur seal (Carnivora: Otariidae) from the Senhata Formation, Boso Peninsula, Japan. *Nat. Hist. Res.* **2**: 15–28.

Kohno, N., and Y. Yanagisawa (1997). The first record of the Pliocene Gilmore fur seal in the western North Pacific Ocean. *Bull. Natl. Sci. Mus. Ser.* C: *Geol. (Tokyo)* **23**(3-4): 119–130.

Kohno, N., L. G. Barnes, and K. Hirota (1995). Miocene fossil pinnipeds of the genera *Prototaria* and *Neotherium* (Carnivora; Otariidae; Imagotariinae) in the North Pacific Ocean: Evolution, relationships and distribution. *Island Arc* **3**: 285–308.

Koretsky, I. (1997). Pinniped bones from the late Oligocene of South Carolina: The oldest known true seal (Carnivora: Phocidae). *Abstr., 57th Ann. Meet. Soc. Vert. Paleo.*, Chicago, p. 58A.

Kovacs, K. M., C. Lydersen, M. O. Hammill, B. N. White, P. J. Wilson, and S. Malik (1997). A harp seal X hooded seal hybrid. *Mar. Mamm. Sci.* **13**(3): 460–468.

Ledje, C., and U. Árnason (1996a). Phylogenetic relationships within caniform carnivores based on analyses of the mitochondrial 12S rRNA gene. *J. Mol. Evol.* **43**: 641–649.

Ledje, C., and U. Árnason (1996b). Phylogenetic analyses of complete cytochrome b genes of the order carnivora with particular emphasis on the caniformia. *J. Mol. Evol.* **42**: 135–144.

Lento, G. M., R. E. Hickson, G. K. Chambers, and D. Penny (1995). Use of spectral analysis to test hypotheses on the origin of pinnipeds. *Mol. Biol. Evol.* **12**(1): 28–52.

Lento, G. M., M. Haddon, G. K. Chambers, and C. S. Baker (1997). Genetic variation, population structure, and species identity of southern hemisphere fur seals, *Arctocephalus* spp. *J. Heredity* **88**: 28–34.

McLaren, I. A. (1960). Are the Pinnipedia biphyletic? *Syst. Zool.* **9**: 18–28.

Miller, E. H., A. Ponce de Leon, and R. L. De Long (1996). Violent interspecific sexual behavior by male sea lions (Otariidae): Evolutionary and phylogenetic implications. *Mar. Mamm. Sci.* **12**(3): 468–476.

Mitchell, E. D. (1975). Parallelism and convergence in the evolution of the Otariidae and Phocidae. Conseil international de l'Exploration de la rev. *Rapports et Proces-Verbaux des Reunions* **169**: 12–26.
Mitchell, E. D., and R. H. Tedford (1973). The Enaliarctinae: A new group of extinct aquatic Carnivora and a consideration of the origin of the Otariidae. *Bull. Am. Mus. Nat. Hist.* **151**(3): 201–284.
Miyamoto, M., and M. Goodman (1986). Biomolecular systematics of eutherian mammals: Phylogenetic patterns and classification. *Syst. Zool.* **35**: 230–240.
Miyazaki, S., H. Horikawa, N. Kohno, K. Hiroto, M. Kimura, Y. Hasegawa, Y. Tomida, L. G. Barnes, and C. E. Ray (1995). Summary of the fossil record of pinnipeds of Japan, and comparisons with that from the eastern North Pacific. *Island Arc* **3**(4): 361–372.
Mouchaty, S., J. A. Cook, and G. F. Shields (1995). Phylogenetic analysis of northern hair seals based on nucleotide sequences of the mitochondrial cytochrome b gene. *J. Mammal.* **76**(4): 1178–1185.
Muizon, C. de (1981). "Les Vertébrés Fossiles de la Formation Pisco (Pérou). Part 1. Recherche sur les Grandes Civilisations," Mem. No. 6. Instituts Français d'Études Andines, Paris.
Muizon, C. de (1982). Phocid phylogeny and dispersal. *Ann. S. Afr. Mus.* **89**(2): 175–213.
O'Corry-Crowe, G. M. and R. L. Westlake (1997). Molecular investigations of spotted seals (*Phoca largha*) and harbor seals (*P. vitulina*), and their relationship in areas of sympatry. *In* "Molecular Genetics of Marine Mammals" (A. E. Dizon, S. J. Chivers, and W. E. Perrin, eds.), Spec. Pub. No. 3, pp. 291–304. Soc. Mar. Mammal. Allen Press, Kansas.
Ray, C. E. (1976). Geography of phocid evolution. *Syst. Zool.* **25**: 391–406.
Reeves, R. R., B. S. Stewart, and S. Leatherwood (1992). The Sierra Club Handbook of Seals and Sirenians. Sierra Club Books, San Francisco.
Repenning, C. A. and R. H. Tedford (1977). Otarioid seals of the Neogene. *Geol. Surv. Prof. Pap. (U.S.)* **992**: 1–93.
Repenning, C. A., C. E. Ray, and D. Grigorescu (1979). Pinniped biogeography. *In* "Historical Biogeography, Plate Tectonics, and Changing Environment" (J. Gray and A. J. Boucot, eds.), pp. 357–369. Oregon State University, Corvallis.
Riedman, M. (1990). "The Pinnipeds. Seals, Sea Lions and Walruses." University of California Press, Berkeley.
Sarich, V. M. (1969). Pinniped phylogeny. *Syst. Zool.* **18**: 416–422.
Smith, R. J., and D. M. Lavigne (1994). Subspecific status of the freshwater harbor seal (*Phoca vitulina mellonae*): A re-assessment. *Mar. Mamm. Sci.* **10**(1): 105–110.
Stanley, H., S. Casey, J. M. Carnahan, S. Goodman, J. Harwood, and R. K. Wayne (1996). Worldwide patterns of mitochondrial DNA differentiation in the harbor seal (*Phoca vitulina*). *Mol. Biol. Evol.* **13**(2): 368–382.
Tedford, R. H. (1976). Relationships of pinnipeds to other carnivores (Mammalia). *Syst. Zool.* **25**: 363–374.
Vrana, P. B., M. C. Milinkovitch, J. R. Powell, and W. C. Wheeler (1994). Higher level relationships of arctoid Carnivora based on sequence data and "total evidence." *Mol. Phylogenet. Evol.* **3**(1): 47–58.
Wyss, A. R. (1987). The walrus auditory region and monophyly of pinnipeds. *Am. Mus. Novit.* **2871**: 1–31.
Wyss, A. R. (1988). On "retrogression" in the evolution of the Phocinae and phylogenetic affinities of the monk seals. *Am. Mus. Novit.* **2924**: 1–38.
Wyss, A. R., and J. Flynn (1993). A phylogenetic analysis and definition of the Carnivora. *In* "Mammal Phylogeny: Placentals" (F. S. Szalay, M. J. Novacek, and M. C. McKenna, eds.), pp. 32–52. Springer-Verlag, New York.

4

Cetacean Evolution and Systematics

4.1. Introduction

The majority of marine mammals belong in the Order Cetacea which includes whales, dolphins, and porpoises. Two major groups of extant whales are recognized: the suborder Mysticeti, or baleen whales, and the suborder Odontoceti, or toothed whales. Toothed whales are more diverse, with approximately 76 species known compared to 11 mysticete species (Leatherwood and Reeves, 1983; Evans, 1987; Rice, 1998).

Cetaceans together with sirenians are the earliest recorded marine mammals, appearing in the Eocene about 53–54 Ma (Fig. 4.1). Cetaceans are also the most diverse mammalian group to adapt to a marine existence. New discoveries of fossil whales provide compelling evidence for both the phylogenetic connections of cetaceans as well as the evolutionary transformation from a terrestrial to a fully aquatic existence.

4.2. Origin and Evolution

4.2.1. Whales Defined

The mammalian order Cetacea comes from the Greek *ketos* meaning whale. Whales and sirenians (see Chapter 5) are the only marine mammals to live their entire lives in water. A thick layer of blubber, rather than hair or fur, insulates them. The hind limbs have been lost and they use the horizontal tail flukes for propulsion. Steering and maintenance of stability when moving is accomplished by a pair of paddle-shaped foreflippers.

Whales have traditionally been defined as a monophyletic group. Thewissen (1994) provided the following derived characters to diagnose the group (Figure 4.2):

1. *Presence of a sigmoid process*—The sigmoid process is an elongated protuberance of the tympanic bone anterior to the external auditory meatus (ear opening). It may serve as a buttress for the malleus (a middle ear bone; Fraser and Purves, 1976) and may have assisted

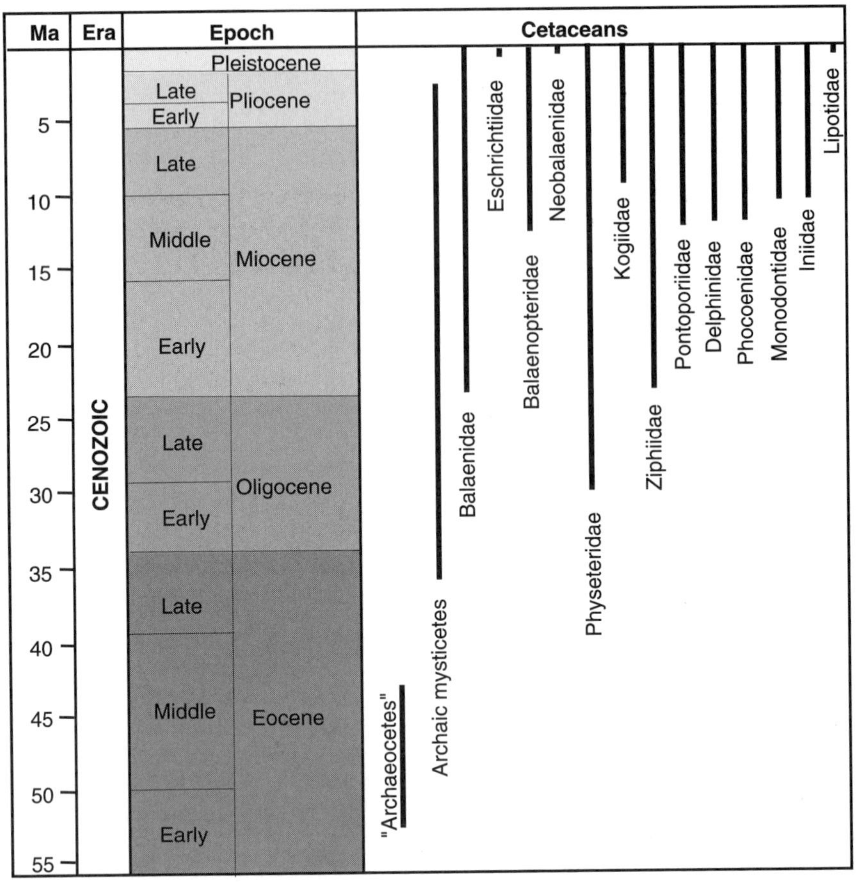

Figure 4.1. Chronologic ranges of extinct and living cetaceans. Ma=million years ago.

in the reorientation of the middle ear that cetaceans underwent (Lancaster, 1990). Subsequently, the sigmoid process has been found to be morphologically variable among archaic cetaceans, and a related feature of the tympanic bone, development of the involucrum (pachyostosis of the medial part of the bulla), is now recognized as an unequivocal cetacean synapomorphy (Luo, 1998).

2. *Pachyosteosclerotic ectotympanic and incus*—The lateral portion of the auditory bulla (ectotympanic bone) and middle ear bone (incus) of cetaceans consists of dense, thick (pachyostotic), and **osteosclerotic** (replacement of spongy bone with compact bone) bone, referred to as pachyosteosclerotic bone. Pachyosteosclerosis occurs in the ear region of all cetaceans. It is absent in known archaic hoofed mammals (e.g. *Diacodexis;* Russell *et al.,* 1983).

3. *Rotation of the middle ear bones*—In cetaceans, the position of the middle ear bones has become rearranged; evolutionarily the ear bones have rotated. This rotation is unique in cetaceans and is only partly developed in the archaic cetacean *Pakicetus* (Thewissen and Hussain, 1993).

4. *Incisors set anteroposteriorly*—In cetaceans the incisors (front teeth) are arranged in parallel with the toothrow (Fig. 4.3). In most fossil relatives of cetaceans (except

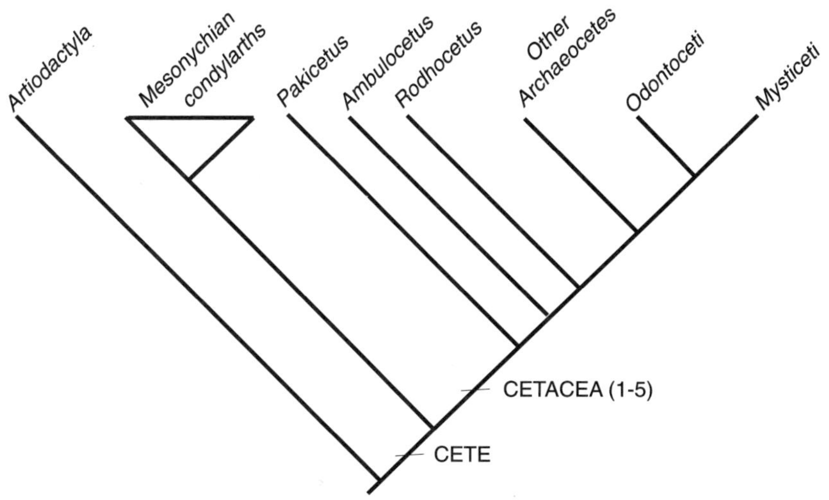

Figure 4.2. A cladogram depicting the relationships for cetaceans and their terrestrial relatives. (Modified from Thewissen, 1994; Thewissen *et al.,* 1996.)

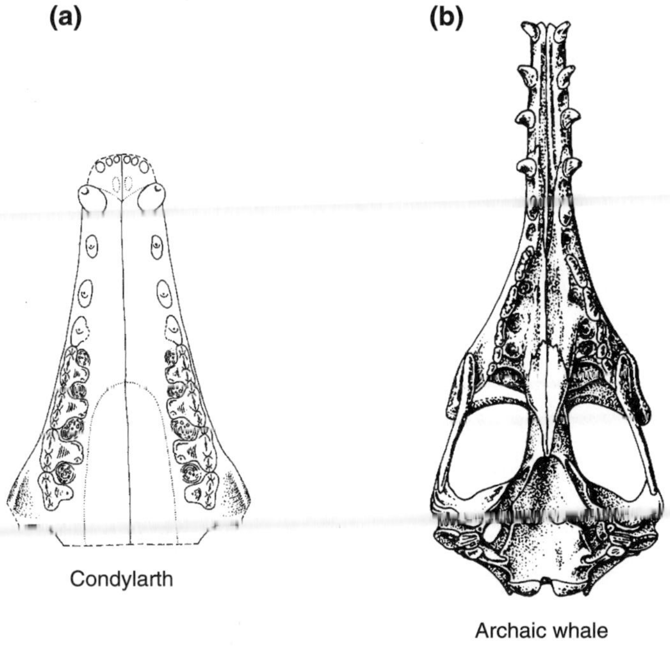

Figure 4.3. Whale synapomorphies. (a) Palate of mesonychian condylarth, *Hapalodectes* (From Szalay, 1969) and (b) Archaic whale, *Zygorhiza* (From Kellogg, 1936) illustrating the difference in incisor arrangement. Character number (see text for further description) 4: incisors are arranged in parallel with the toothrow; in the condylarth the incisors are arranged transversely.

Andrewsarchus, J. G. M. Thewissen, personal communication), the incisors are transversely aligned in front of the canines (e.g., Szalay and Gould, 1966; West, 1981; Ting and Li, 1987).

5. *Fourth upper premolar paracone height twice that of first upper molar*—In archaic cetaceans (e.g. *Pakicetus* and *Ambulocetus*), the upper fourth premolar has an anterior cusp (paracone) that is elevated twice as high as that of the first upper molar. In fossil relatives of cetaceans the paracone is not higher than in the first upper molar.

4.2.2. Cetacean Affinities

4.2.2.1. Relationships of Cetaceans to Other Ungulates

Linneaeus, in an early edition of *Systema Naturae* (1735), included cetaceans among the fishes, but by the tenth edition he had followed Ray (1693) in recognizing them as a distinct group unrelated to fishes. Flower (1883) was the first to propose a close relationship between cetaceans and ungulates, the hoofed mammals. This idea has been endorsed on the basis of dental and other evidence by Van Valen (1966) and Szalay (1969) who argued for a more specific link between cetaceans and an extinct group of ungulates, mesonychian condylarths (Fig. 4.4). Among fossil taxa, mesonychian condylarths are usually recognized as the closest relatives of cetaceans. These animals had wolf-like proportions including long limbs, a **digitigrade** stance (walking on their fingers and toes), and probably had hoofs. In addition, most genera had massive, crushing dentitions. As a group, mesonychians are in need of systematic revision.

A connection between cetaceans and mesonychians (referred to as Cete) comes from the skull and dentition and vestigial hind limbs preserved in several early archaeocete whales, such as *Basilosaurus* and *Ambulocetus.* The hind limbs of these whales distally show a **paraxonic** arrangement, a condition where digits symmetrically extend about a plane located between digits III and IV (Fig. 4.5). This paraxonic arrangement bears striking resemblance to that of mesonychian condylarths as well as that of the artiodactyls (even-toed ungulates including deer, antelope, camels, pigs, giraffes, and hippos). Morphologic evi-

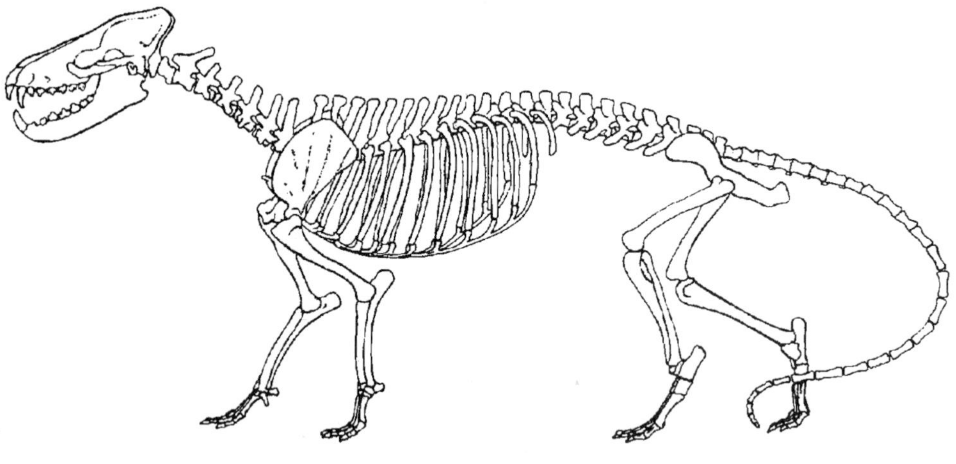

Figure 4.4. Skeleton of *Mesonyx,* a mesonychian condylarth, closely related to whales. (From Scott, 1888.)

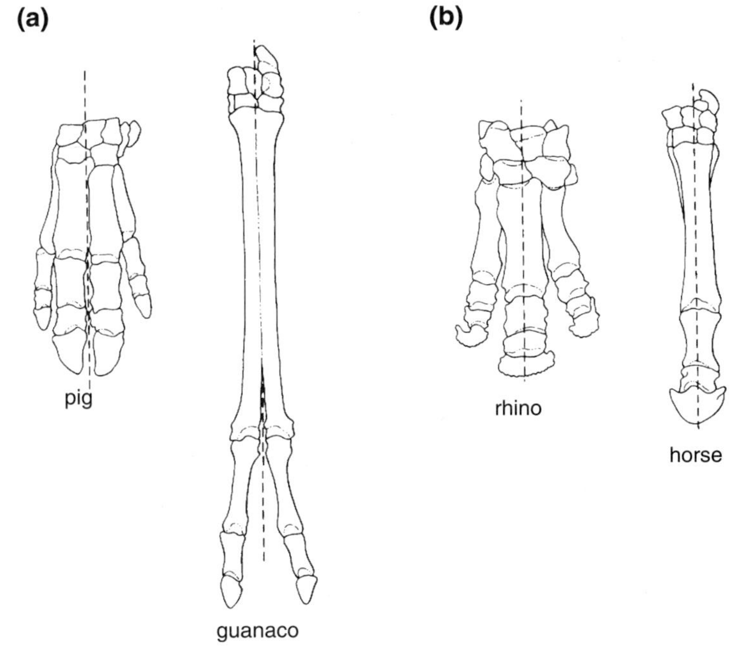

Figure 4.5. Synapomorphy uniting Cete (cetaceans and mesonychian condylarths) + artiodactyls. Paraxonic foot arrangement (a) in which the axis of symmetry runs between digits III and IV (From MacFadden, 1992); in the primitive mesaxonic arrangement (b) the axis of symmetry runs between digit III.

dence in support of mesonychians as the sister group of the cetaceans is reviewed by O'Leary (1998) and O'Leary and Geisler (in press).

Among extant groups, artiodactyls are most commonly cited as the sister group of the Cetacea based on morphologic data (Novacek, 1992). This hypothesis is refuted by the morphological analysis of Thewissen (1994) that supports Cete as most closely related to perissodactyls (odd-toed ungulates; Fig. 4.6) and the extinct phenacodontid condylarths. However, J. G. M. Thewissen (personal communication) suggests that his previous findings of a Perissodactyla link are weak. Close ties between Cete, perissodactyls, and phenacodontids also have been proposed previously by Prothero (1993) and Prothero *et al.* (1988).

Molecular evidence based on analyses of cytochrome b gene sequences (Irwin and Árnason, 1994) and myoglobin acid sequences (Milinkovitch *et al.,* 1993) leaves an unresolved trichotomy of artiodactyls, perissodactyls, and cetaceans (Fig. 4.6). Most molecular data, including immunodiffusion and mitochondrial DNA sequence analyses, suggest that cetaceans are more closely related to artiodactyls than to perissodactyls (Goodman *et al.,* 1985; Irwin *et al.,* 1991; Honeycutt and Adkins, 1993; Milinkovitch *et al.,* 1993; Xu *et al.,* 1996). Other molecular data sets support the derivation of Cetacea from within Artiodactyla, thus rendering the latter group paraphyletic (e.g., Graur and Higgins, 1994; Shimamura *et al.,* 1997). Further combined analyses of DNA sequences from different data sets (including noncoding, protein coding, nuclear, and mtDNA; Irwin and Árnason, 1994; Árnason and Gullberg, 1996; Gatesy *et al.,* 1996, 1999; Gatesy, 1998; Shimamura *et al.,* 1997) suggest that cetaceans and hippopotamid artiodactyls are extant sister taxa. These data support a Hippopotamidae, Cetacea, and Ruminantia (antelope, deer, and kin) clade

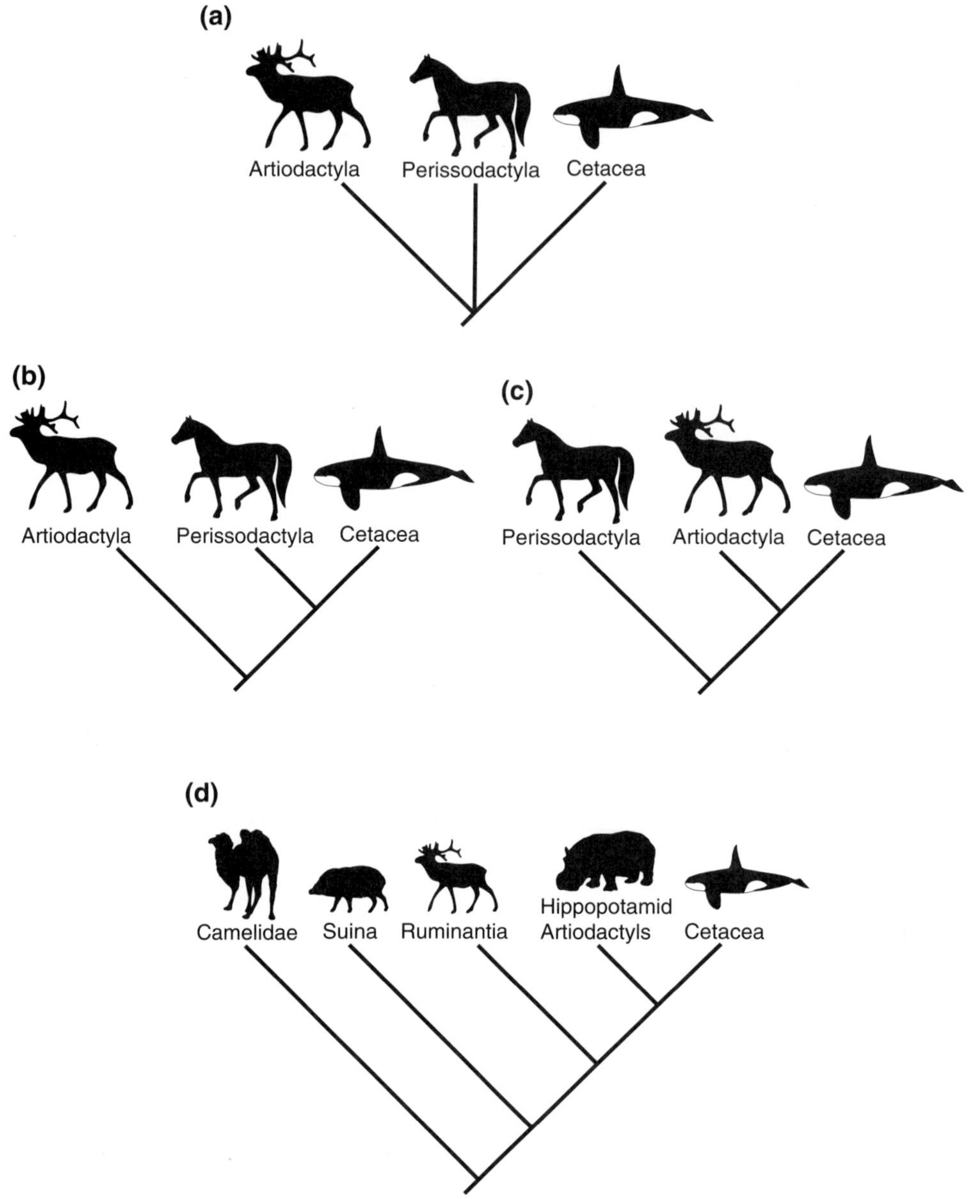

Figure 4.6. Alternative hypotheses for relationships between cetaceans and various extant ungulate groups. (a) Molecular data (Irwin and Árnason, 1994; Milinkovitch *et al.,* 1993), (b) Morphologic data (Thewissen, 1994), (c) Morphologic data (Novacek, 1992), (d) Combined molecular data (Gatesy *et al.,* 1996, 1999; Shimamura *et al.,* 1997).

and a Hippopotamidae, Cetacea, Ruminantia, and Suina (pigs) clade, with the Camelidae (camels and llamas) being more distantly related (Fig. 4.6). The conclusion of Shimamura *et al.* (1997) is especially compelling because it is based on molecular markers, specifically short interspersed elements (SINEs), which mark retropositional events that are inserted at particular loci in the nuclear genome of various artiodactyl and cetacean ancestors. Because the likelihood of these elements being independently inserted at the same locus in different lineages is virtually impossible, these markers may offer a finer degree of phylogenetic resolution than existing molecular sequence data (Milinkovitch and Thewissen, 1997).

Although molecular data support a paraphyletic Artiodactyla morphologic data are in clear conflict (e.g., Geisler and O'Leary, 1997; Prothero, 1993). As discussed by Milinkovitch and Thewissen (1997), if Shimamura *et al.* (1997) are correct, two widely held features supporting artiodactyl monophyly (mobile joint of the heel and three-lobed deciduous lower premolar) have a more complicated phylogenetic history than was previously thought. The development of a trochlea on the distal part of the astragalas (ankle bone) has long been recognized as a unique feature of artiodactyls that enabled rapid locomotion. This bone is not recognizable in the greatly reduced hind limb of modern cetaceans and is lacking in their closest extinct relatives, the mesonychians. If artiodactyls are paraphyletic, then either mesonychians are not closely related to cetaceans (making many dental characters convergent), or the specialized heel morphology has evolved several times independently in artiodactyls or has been lost in the mesonychian/cetacean clade. Morphological data usually have allied pigs, peccaries, and hippos, but this grouping is usually based on uninformative primitive characters that also are present in the ancestral artiodactyls or on features that are subject to convergences, such as certain dental characters (Milinkovitch and Thewissen, 1997). From a morphologic perspective, the issue of artiodactyl monophyly remains unsettled and will require further examination of morphologic data sets with the addition of all fossil taxa (e.g., Geisler and Luo, 1998). Unfortunately, the recently reported discovery of ankle bones from archaic cetaceans does not unambiguously support either mesonychians or hippopotamid artiodactyls as the closest relatives of whales (Thewissen *et al.*, 1998). With regard to the molecular evidence, the power of resolution of molecular markers in the phylogeny reconstruction of these groups is largely untested and will require further corroboration (e.g., see the recent critique by Luckett and Hong, 1998; Buchanan *et al.*, 1999).

4.2.2.2. Relationships among Cetaceans

Several studies have examined phylogenetic relationships among cetaceans using molecular data. According to Milinkovitch *et al.* (1993, 1994, 1996) data from mitochondrial ribosomal RNA and cytochrome b genes indicate that odontocetes are not a monophyletic group (see Fig. 2.3). A closer relationship is suggested between the sperm whales and the mysticetes than between the sperm whales and other toothed whales. Another molecular study (Árnason and Gullberg, 1994) of the cytochrome b gene identified mysticetes as a sister group to non-sperm whale odontocetes, although these results are disputed based on their limited sampling design (Adachi and Hasegawa, 1995) and because they overlooked the saturation of transitions (Milinkovitch *et al.*, 1995). Árnason and Gullberg (1996) concluded from an extended cytochrome b data set that baleen whales were monophyletic but their relationship to a specific odontocete lineage is unclear. From a total evidence approach for molecular data, Hasegawa *et al.* (1997) evaluated 12S and 16S rRNA, cytochrome b, and myoglobin sequence data in order to resolve the relationships among the major groups of cetaceans. Their results provided additional support for the hypothesis that sperm whales are closer to baleen whales and specifically that baleen whales are linked to a clade containing sperm whales and beaked whales.

Most morphologic evidence does not support the molecular view of odontocetes as a nonmonophyletic group (Heyning, 1997). The exception is Klima's (1995) study of cetacean nasal structures which is in agreement with the molecular data supporting an alliance between sperm and baleen whales. However, because some of these similarities are likely shared ancestral characters (J. G. M. Thewissen, personal communication) and none were subjected to phylogenetic analysis, results of this study are inconclusive. Future studies need to address the problem using comprehensive data sets (including both fossil and recent taxa) and rigorous phylogenetic methods (Berta, 1994). One example of such a study is that of Messenger and McGuire (1998) which reevaluates morphologic and molecular data bearing on odontocete phylogeny using separate as well as "total evidence" approaches.

4.2.3. Evolution of Early Whales—"Archaeocetes"

The earliest whales are archaeocetes, a paraphyletic stem group of cetaceans. Archaeocetes evolved from mesonychian condylarths. Archaeocete whales have been found from early to middle Eocene (52–42 Ma) deposits in Africa and North America, but are best known from Pakistan and India. Basal archaeocetes have been divided into four families, the Pakicetidae, Protocetidae, Ambulocetidae, and Remingtonocetidae (Thewissen *et al.,* 1996).

The Pakicetidae are the oldest and most basal archaeocetes and include *Pakicetus, Nalacetus,* and *Icthyolestes* (see Thewissen and Hussain, 1998 and Williams, 1998 for recent taxonomic reviews). It is unclear whether the family forms a monophyletic group because it is characterized by a combination of primitive and derived characters including small mandibular foramina (for passage of blood vessels and nerves), primitive dental morphology, and the lack of **peritympanic sinuses** (air filled sinuses in the ear; Thewissen *et al.,* 1996). One of the oldest pakicetids, *Pakicetus inachus,* is known from skull and teeth fragments from the early Eocene of Pakistan (Gingerich *et al.,* 1983; Thewissen and Hussain, 1998). *Pakicetus* possessed a very dense and inflated auditory bulla that is partially separated from the squamosal (cheekbone), a feature suggesting their ears were adapted for underwater hearing (Gingerich and Russell, 1990; Thewissen and Hussain, 1993). However, pakicetids were predominantly land animals and, except for features of the ear, had few adaptations consistent with aquatic life.

The monophyletic Ambulocetidae include *Ambulocetus* and *Gandakasia.* One of the most significant fossil discoveries is that of a whale with limbs and feet, *Ambulocetus natans,* also from the early Eocene of Pakistan (Thewissen *et al.,* 1994). The well-developed hind limbs and toes that ended as hooves of this so called "walking whale" leave no doubt that they were used in locomotion. Thewissen *et al.* (1994) suggested that *Ambulocetus* swam by undulating the vertebral column and paddling with the hind limbs, combining aspects of modern seals and otters, rather than by vertical movements of the tail fluke, as is the case in modern whales (Fig. 4.7; see also Chapter 8). The frontlimbs and hand of *Ambulocetus* also were well developed, with flexible elbows, wrists, and digits. Body size estimates suggest that *Ambulocetus* weighed between 141 and 235 kg and was similar in size to a female Steller's sea lion (Thewissen *et al.,* 1996). A second genus of ambulocetid whale, *Gandakasia* is distinguished from *Ambulocetus* by its smaller size (Thewissen *et al.,* 1996).

Another newly discovered whale, *Rodhocetus kasrani,* was described from slightly younger rocks (46.5 Ma) in Pakistan (Gingerich *et al.,* 1994). *Rodhocetus* has the distinction of being the first archaeocete with a complete thoracic, lumbar, and sacral vertebral column. The robust tail and high neural spines on the lumbar and caudal vertebrae suggest that it swam using the tail (Fig. 4.8). This new specimen also indicates that early whale habitats were more broadly distributed and included deep offshore waters as well as the more typi-

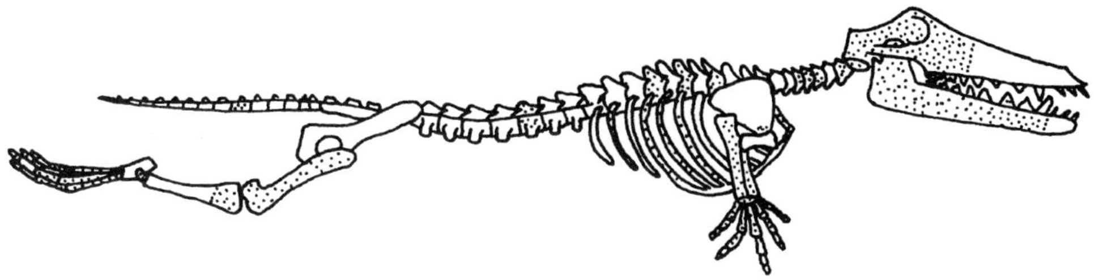

Figure 4.7. Skeletal reconstruction of *Ambulocetus natans*. (From Thewissen *et al.,* 1996.)

cal near shore shallows. *Rodhocetus,* together with *Indocetus, Babicetus,* and *Gaviacetus* from India-Pakistan, *Protocetus* and *Eocetus* from Egypt, *Pappocetus* from Nigeria, West Africa, *Geogiacetus* from Georgia and possibly South Carolina, and *Natchitochia* from Louisiana are included in the family Protocetidae (Thewissen *et al.,* 1996; Uhen, 1998; Hulbert *et al.,* 1998; Uhen, in press). Members of this family are characterized, among other features, by reduction of the hind limbs.

The Remingtonocetidae, a short lived archaeocete clade (middle Eocene of India-Pakistan) containing the genera *Remingtonocetus*, *Dalanistes, Andrewsiphius,* and *Attockicetus* are characterized by long, narrow skulls and jaws. Morphology of the jaws of remingtonocetids suggests a diet of fast-swimming aquatic prey (Thewissen, 1998). The middle ear is large and shows some specializations for underwater hearing (Gingerich, 1998; Bajapl and Thewissen, 1998). Although it has been suggested that remingtonocetids are ancestral to odontocetes, based on the presence of pterygoid sinuses in the orbits (air filled sacs in the pterygoid bone; Kumar and Sahni, 1986), illustrations of the taxa do not support this claim (Fordyce and Barnes, 1994).

The paraphyletic Basilosauridae were late diverging archaeocetes and include one lineage of large species with elongated vertebral bodies, the Basilosaurinae, and the Dorudontinae, a group of species without elongated vertebral bodies (see Uhen, 1998, for a recent taxonomic review). Some basilosaurids were gigantic, approaching 25 m in length, and are known from the middle to late Eocene and probably also from the early Oligocene in the northern hemisphere (Gingerich *et al.,* 1997). The several hundred skeletons of *Basilosaurus isis* known from the middle Eocene of north central Egypt (Wadi Hitan, also known as the Valley of Whales or Zeuglodon Valley) provide evidence of very reduced

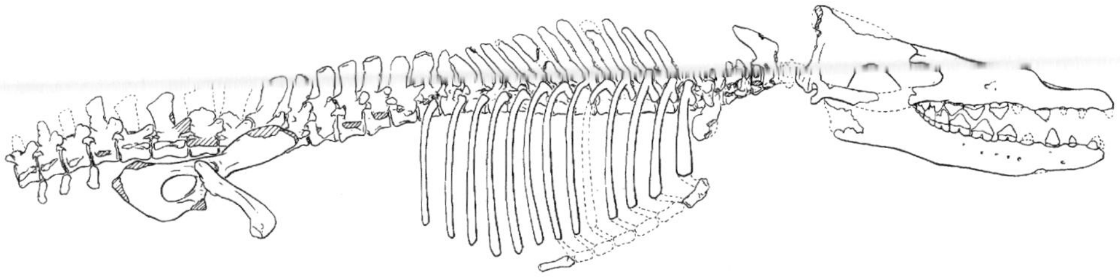

Figure 4.8. Skeleton of *Rodhocetus kasrani.* Dashed lines and crosshatching show reconstructed parts. Original 2 m in length. (From Gingerich *et al.,* 1994.)

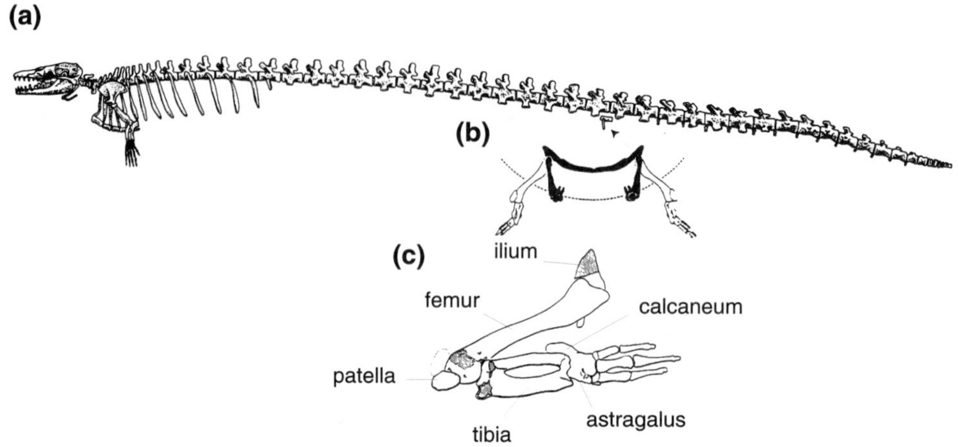

Figure 4.9. Skeleton and hind limb of *Basilosaurus isis.* (From Gingerich *et al.,* 1990.) (a) Skeleton in left lateral view and position of hind limb (arrow), (b) Hypothesized functional pelvic girdle and hind limb in resting posture (solid drawing) and functional extension (open), (c) left hind limb.

hind limbs in this species (Gingerich *et al.,* 1990; Uhen, 1996; Fig. 4.9). Although it was suggested that *Basilosaurus isis* used its tiny limbs to grasp partners during copulation (Gingerich *et al.,* 1990), the limbs could just as easily be interpreted as vestigial structures without function.

The dorudontines were smaller dolphin-like species that were taxonomically and ecologically more diverse than the basilosaurines. They are known from the late Eocene in Egypt, southeastern North America, Europe, and New Zealand (Uhen, 1996). Among the abundant fossil cetaceans from Egypt are the remains of *Dorudon atrox* (Uhen, 1996). Also from this locality is a new genus and species of dorudontine, *Ancalecetes simonsi* (Gingerich and Uhen, 1996), which differs from *Dorudon atrox* in several peculiarities of the forelimb including fused elbows that indicate very limited swimming capability (Fig. 4.10). Modern whales, including both odontocetes and mysticetes, likely diverged from dorudontines (Uhen, 1998).

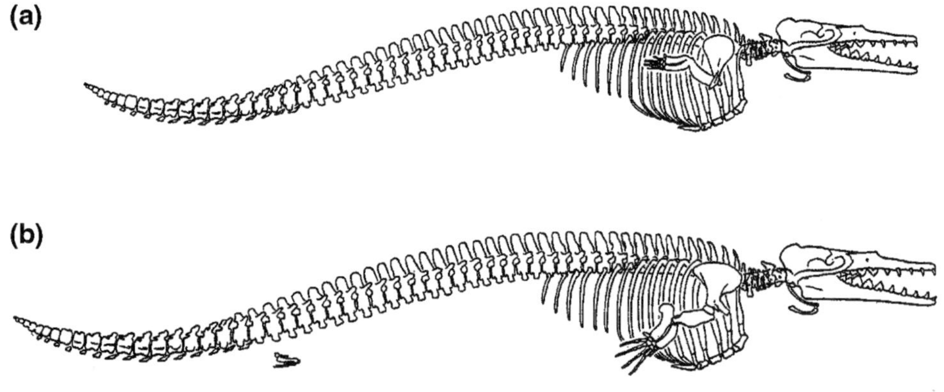

Figure 4.10. Skeletal reconstructions of dorudontines (a) *Ancalectes simonsi* and (b) *Dorudon atrox* from the late Eocene, Egypt. (From Gingerich and Uhen, 1996.)

4.2.4. Modern Whales

Estimates of the divergence time for the mysticete–odontocete split based on gene rates are clearly in conflict with the known fossil record. According to the fossil record, mysticetes and odontocetes diverged from a common archaeocete ancestor about 35 Ma (Barnes *et al.*, 1985; Fordyce, 1980). On the basis of rates of evolution in mitochondrial ribosomal genes of ungulate mammals, Milinkovitch *et al.* (1993) postulated a 10–13 Ma age for the split between sperm whales and baleen whales. This figure has been revised to 25 Ma based on a slower rate of evolution for whale mitochondrial DNA and the recognition that sperm whale and baleen whale fossils are older than 15 Ma (Milinkovitch, 1995).

Modern whales differ from archaeocetes because they possess a number of derived characters not seen in archaeocetes. Arguably one of the most obvious features is the relationship of the bones in the skull to one another in response to the migration of the nasal openings (blowholes) to the top of the skull. Termed **telescoping**, the modern whale skull has premaxillary and maxillary bones that have migrated far posteriorly and presently form most of the skull roof resulting in a long **rostrum** (beak) and dorsal nasal openings. The occipital bone forming the back of the skull and the nasal, frontal, and parietal bones are sandwiched between the other bones (Fig. 4.11).

Another derived feature of modern whales is a fixed elbow joint. The laterally flattened forelimbs are usually short and rigid with an immobile elbow. Archaeocetes have flexible elbow joints, capable of rotation.

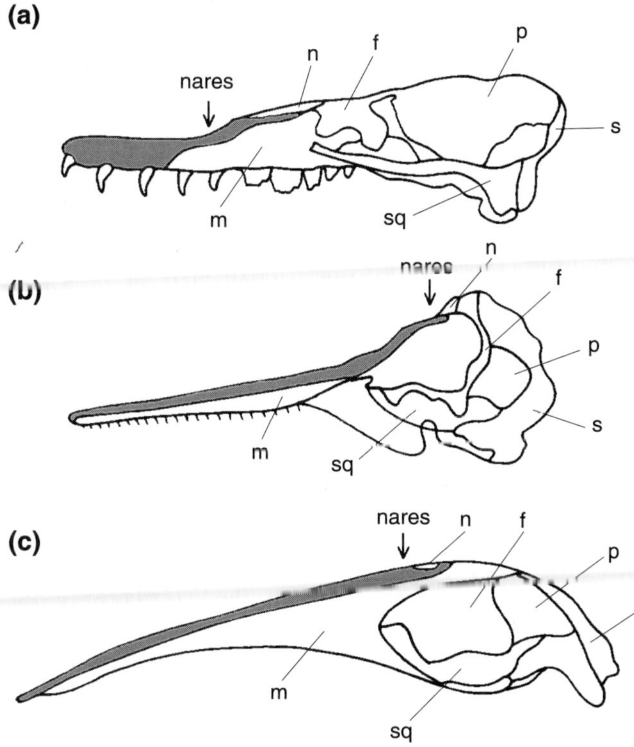

Figure 4.11. Telescoping of the skull in cetaceans. Note the posterior position of the nares and the different arrangement of the cranial bones in an archaic whale (archaeocete) (a), a modern odontocete (b) and mysticete (c). Cranial bones: premaxilla (stippled), frontal (f), maxilla (m), nasals (n), parietal (p), squamosal (sq), supraoccipital (s). (Modified from Evans, 1987.)

4.2.4.1. Mysticetes

The baleen, or whalebone, whales are so named for their feeding apparatus: plates of **baleen** hang from the roof of the mouth and serve to strain planktonic food items. Although extant mysticetes lack teeth (except in embryonic stages) and possess baleen, this is not true for some fossil toothed mysticetes, as discussed below. Major evolutionary trends within the group include the loss of teeth, development of large body size and large heads, shortening of the intertemporal region, and shortening of the neck (Fordyce and Barnes, 1994).

Among characters used to diagnose mysticetes are the following (Fig. 4.11; McLeod *et al.,* 1993).

1. *"Telescoped" skull in which the maxilla extends posteriorly under the orbit to form a plate-like infraorbital process (Miller, 1923)*—Mysticetes display a unique telescoping of the skull in which the maxilla projects under the eye orbit. Odontocetes display a different type of "telescoping" and the maxillae do not project beneath the orbits but spread outward over the expanded supraorbital processes (Fig. 4.11).
2. *Antorbital process of maxilla present*—Mysticetes are distinguished from odontocetes in having developed a bony protuberance on the maxilla anterior to the eye orbit. Archaeocetes and odontocetes lack an antorbital process of the maxilla.
3. *Mandibular symphysis unfused, with only ligamental or connective tissue attachment*—Mysticetes possess a flexible connection between the lower jaws. Archaic cetaceans and odontocetes possess the primitive condition of a bony mandibular symphysis (Fig. 4.12).

4.2.4.1.1. Archaic Mysticetes

Archaic toothed mysticetes have been grouped into four families: the Aetiocetidae, the Llanocetidae, the Mammalodontidae, and the Kekenodontidae. The Aetiocetidae includes four genera: *Aetiocetus* (*A. cotylalvens, A. polydentatus* (Fig. 4.13), *A. tomitai, A. weltoni*), *Chonecetus* (*C. goedertorum, C. sookensis*), *Ashorocetus* (*A. eguchii*), and *Morawanocetus* (*M. yabukli*) (Barnes *et al.*, 1995). *Aetiocetus* and *Chonecetus* possess multicusped teeth and nutrient foramina (openings for blood vessels) for baleen. The oldest described mysticete is the toothed *Llanocetus denticrenatus,* the only member of the family Llanocetidae. It is known only from a fragment of large inflated mandible (Mitchell, 1989) of late Eocene of early Oligocene age (Seymour Island, Antarctica). More complete material of the same species (actually of the same specimen) was recovered and is under study (Fordyce, 1989). The holotype skull and skeleton represent a large individual with a skull length of about 2 m. The multicusped teeth of *Llanocetus denticrenatus* may have functioned in filter feeding, like those of the modern crabeater seal, contrasting with the long pincer-like jaws and teeth typical of other fish-eating archaeocetes (Cozzuol, 1996). Another archaic toothed mysticete, *Mammalodon colliveri,* represents the Mammalodontidae from the late Oligocene or early Miocene in Australia, and has a relatively short rostrum, flat palate, and heterodont teeth. Only the holotype has been described (see Fordyce, 1984) but other late Oligocene specimens occur in the southwest Pacific (Fordyce, 1992). Another archaic mysticete is *Kekenodon onamata* of the family Kekenodontidae. It is known from teeth, earbones, and a few other fragments (Fordyce, 1992).

The Cetotheriidae is a large, diverse, nonmonophyletic assemblage of extinct baleen-bearing, toothless mysticetes that have been grouped together primarily because they lack characters of living mysticetes. "Cetotheres" range in age from the late Oligocene to the late Pliocene of North America, South America, Europe, Japan, Australia, and New Zealand. At least 60 species of "cetotheres" have been named, however many are based on

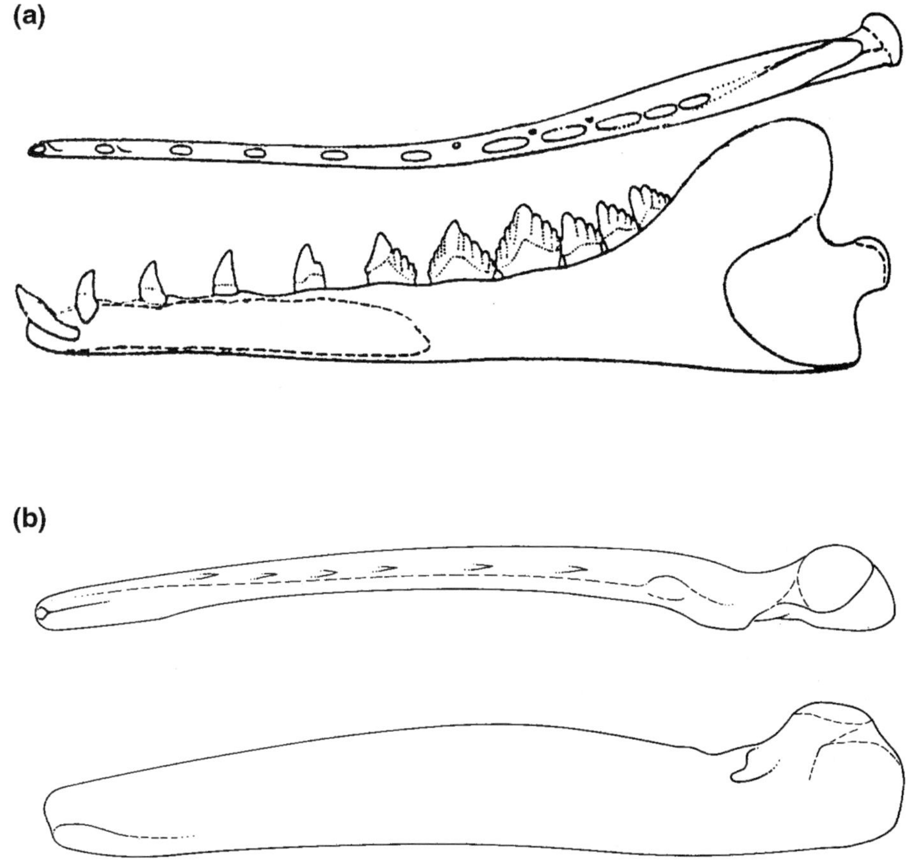

Figure 4.12. Mysticete mandibular symphysis in dorsal and medial views illustrating ancestral (a) *Zygorhiza kochii* and derived conditions (b) Gray whale, *Eschrichtius robustus* (from Deméré, 1986 and unpublished manuscript). Illustrated by M. Emerson.

noncomparable elements and the entire group is in clear need of systematic revision. "Cetotheres" have flat rostra with prominent ventral nutrient foramina for baleen (Miller, 1923). Most "cetotheres" were of moderate size, up to 10 m long, but some were probably as short as 3 m. Some fossil "cetotheres" have actually been found with impressions of baleen

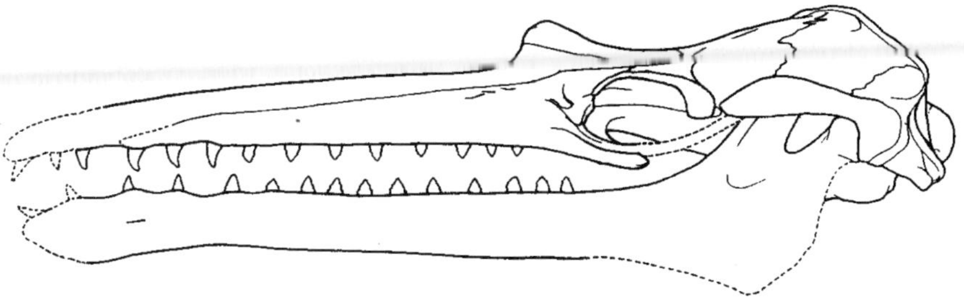

Figure 4.13. Skull and lower jaw restoration of an archaic mysticete whale, *Aetiocetus polydentatus,* from the late Oligocene of Japan. (From Barnes *et al.,* 1995.)

plates (Gascon-Romero *et al.,* 1991) and have been implicated in the ancestry of balaenopterids (McLeod *et al.,* 1993) and balaenids (Geisler and Luo, 1996).

4.2.4.1.2. Later Diverging Mysticetes

There are four families of modern baleen whales: Balaenopteridae (fin whales or **rorquals**), Balaenidae (bowhead and right whales), Eschrichtiidae (gray whale), and Neobalaenidae (pygmy right whale). Molecular studies have produced conflicting phylogenies for baleen whales (Fig. 4.14). According to cladistic analysis of cytochrome b sequence data (Árnason and Gullberg, 1994, 1996), the genus *Balaenoptera* is paraphyletic because the gray whale *Eschrichtius* is positioned within it. Moreover, these molecular data support species distinction for the minke whales, *Balaenoptera acutorostata* (North Atlantic minke whale) and *Balaenoptera bonaerensis* (Antarctic minke whale) (Fig. 4.14). The most recent molecular phylogeny of mysticetes, the total evidence molecular data set of Hasegawa *et al.* (1997), supports an unresolved pattern of relationships at the base of baleen whale divergence between the pygmy right whale, balaenids, and other mysticetes (gray, sei, bryde's, and minke whales) (Fig. 4.14).

Two phylogenetic analyses of mysticetes based on morphology and including fossil and extant taxa are available (McLeod *et al.,* 1993; Geisler and Luo, 1996). The study of Geisler and Luo (1996), based in part on ear characters, agrees with the molecular studies and argues for a sister group relationship among the balaenopterids and eschrictiids. The results of McLeod *et al.* (1993) differ in suggesting that balaenopterid whales occupy a basal position among mysticetes and are most closely allied with the extinct paraphyletic Cetotheriidae. The gray whales are linked with later diverging lineages, the balaenids and pygmy right whale, in their study (Fig. 4.14).

Family Balaenopteridae—The Balaenopteridae, commonly called the rorquals or fin whales, are the most abundant and diverse living baleen whales. They include six species ranging from the small 9 m minke whale, *Balaenoptera acutorostrata,* to the giant blue whale, *Balaenoptera musculus.* The blue whale has the distinction of being the largest mammal ever to have lived, reaching 33 m in length and weighing over 160 tons (Jefferson *et al.,* 1993). The "singing" humpback whale, *Megaptera novaeangliae,* with its long knobby flippers also is a member of this family.

As discussed by Bérubé and Aguilar (1998), hybridization between fin and blue whale DNA occurs at relatively higher frequencies than among other mysticetes and is geographically widespread. Hybrid males may be sterile, while females reach sexual maturity (although their actual capacity to produce viable offspring has not yet been confirmed).

Balaenopterids are characterized by the presence of a dorsal fin, unlike gray whales and balaenids, and by numerous throat grooves that extend past the throat region (Barnes and McLeod, 1984; Fig. 4.15). The fossil record of the group extends from the early late Miocene (10–12 Ma) and fossils are reported from North and South America, Europe, Asia, and Australia (McLeod *et al.,* 1993; Barnes, 1977; Deméré, 1986; Oishi and Hasegawa, 1995; Cozzuol, 1996).

Family Balaenidae—The family Balaenidae includes the right whales, *Eubalaena,* and the bowhead whale, *Balaena.* Some molecular data, however, do not support generic distinction between the two (Árnason and Gullberg, 1994). Two species of right whale are recognized, the North Atlantic right whale (*Eubalaena glacialis*) and the South Atlantic right whale (*Eubalaena australis*). Hunters called them the "right" whales to kill because they inhabited coastal waters and floated when dead.

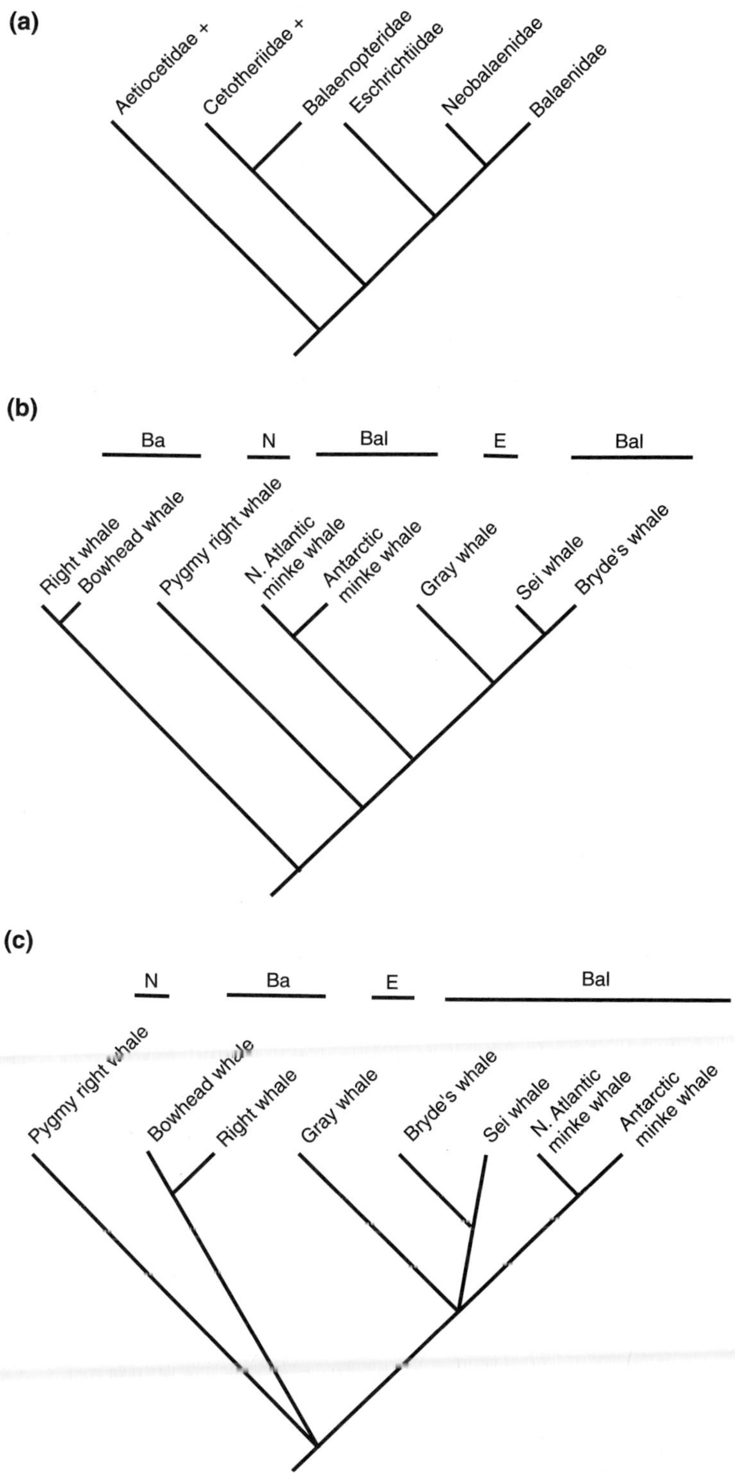

Figure 4.14. Relationships among mysticetes based on molecular and morphologic data. (a) Cladogram of fossil and extant taxa based on morphologic data (McLeod *et al.,* 1993); +=extinct taxa, (b) Cladogram of extant taxa based on cytochrome b sequence data (Árnason and Gullberg, 1994, 1996). Abbreviations: Ba=Balaenidae, Bal=Balaenopteridae, E=Eschrichtiidae, N=Neobalenidae and (c) Cladogram of extant taxa based on a total evidence molecular data set (Hasegawa *et al.,* 1997). Abbreviations as in (b).

Balaenids are characterized by large heads that comprise up to one-third of the body length. The mouth is very strongly arched and accommodates extremely long baleen plates (Fig. 4.16). McLeod *et al.* (1993) provide several cranial characters to diagnose *Eubalena* and *Balaena.*

The oldest fossil balaenid, *Morenocetus parvus,* is from the early Miocene (23 Ma) of South America (Cabrera, 1926). *M. parvus* has an elongated supraorbital process and a triangular occipital shield that extends far anteriorly; both characters are developed to a lesser extent than in later balaenids (McLeod *et al.,* 1993). Relatively abundant fossils of later diverging balaenids are known, especially from Europe.

Figure 4.15. A representative of the Family Balaenopteridae (blue whale, *Balaenoptera musculus*). (a) Dorsal view of the skull, (b) left side of body (illustrated by P. Folkens). Note the dorsal fin and throat grooves (From Barnes and McLeod, 1984). Original skull length 6 m.

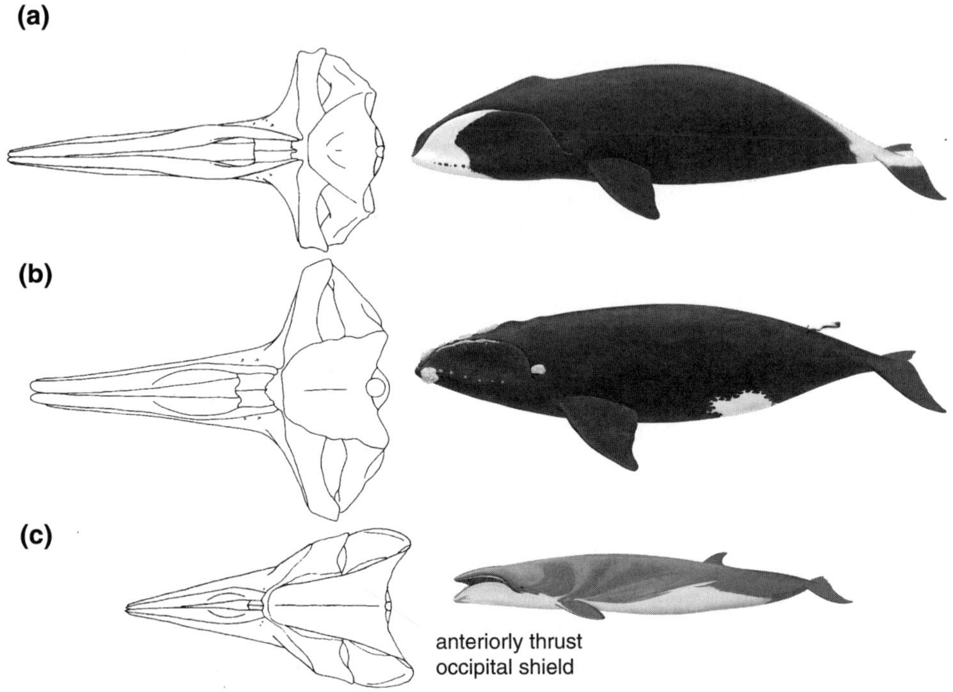

Figure 4.16. Representative balaenid and neobalaenids. Dorsal view of the skull and left side of the body. Note the large head and arched rostra (illustrated by P. Folkens) (a) Bowhead, *Balaena mysticetus,* (b) Northern right whale, *Eubalena glacialis* and (c) Pygmy right whale, *Caperea marginata* (From Barnes and McLeod, 1984). Original skull lengths are 1.97 m, 3.27 m and 1.47 m, respectively.

Family Eschrichtiidae—The family Eschrichtiidae is represented by only one extant species, the gray whale. It has a fossil record that goes back to the Pleistocene (100,000 years bp). The gray whale is now found only in the North Pacific because a North Atlantic population became extinct in historic time (seventeenth or early eighteenth century according to Bryant, 1995). Molecular analyses (Árnason and Gullberg, 1996; Hasegawa *et al.,* 1997) position the gray whale within the balaenopterids (Figure 4.14).

The gray whale lacks a dorsal fin and is characterized by a small dorsal hump followed by a series of dorsal median bumps. Gray whales have two to four throat grooves in comparison to the numerous throat grooves of balaenopterids. The baleen plates differ from those of balaenids by being fewer in number, thicker, and white. A unique feature is the presence of paired occipital tuberosities on the posterior portion of the skull for insertion of muscles which originate in the neck region (Barnes and McLeod, 1984; Fig. 4.17).

Family Neobalaenidae—Traditionally, the small, 4 m long pygmy right whale, *Caperea marginata,* found only in the southern hemisphere, has been included in the Balaenidae (e.g., Leatherwood and Reeves, 1983). Its placement in a separate family, the Neobalaenidae, is supported by anatomical data (Gray, 1873; Mead and Brownell, 1993). In molecular analyses (Árnason and Gullberg, 1996; Hasegawa *et al.,* 1997), the relationship of the pygmy right whale to balaenids and other mysticetes (gray, sei, bryde's, and minke whales) is unresolved (Fig. 4.14).

Caperea has a unique type of cranial architecture, distinguished from other mysticetes by a larger, more anteriorly thrust occipital shield and a shorter, wider, and less arched mouth to accommodate relatively short baleen plates (Fig. 4.16). Other differences in the pygmy right whale in comparison with balaenids include the presence of a dorsal fin, longitudinal furrows on the throat (caused by mandibular ridges that might be homologous with throat grooves), a different type of baleen, smaller head size relative to the body, a proportionally shorter humerus, and four instead of five digits on the hand (Barnes and McLeod, 1984).

The one reported fossil record of a neobalaenid, *Caperea simpsoni* (Philippi, 1887; Donoso-Barros, 1975), from an indeterminate locality and formation in Chile is dubious (Fordyce and Barnes, 1994; Cozzuol, 1996).

4.2.4.2. Odontocetes

The majority of whales are odontocetes, or toothed whales, named for the presence of teeth in adults, a feature distinguishing them from extant mysticetes. Odontocetes encompass a

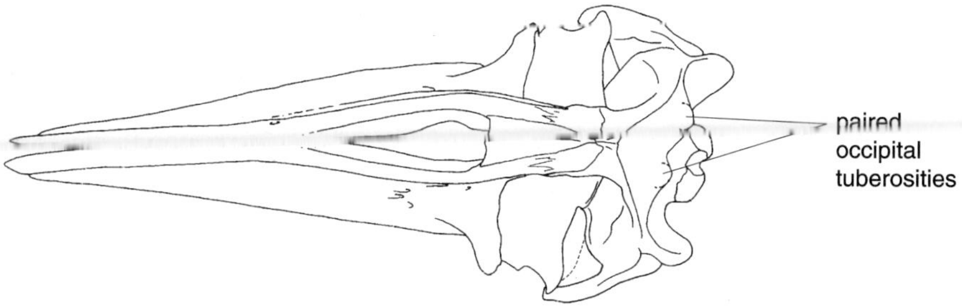

Figure 4.17. The Family Eschrichtiidae (gray whale, *Eschrichtius robustus*) Dorsal view of the skull illustrating the paired occipital tuberosities. (From Barnes and McLeod, 1984). Original skull length 2.33 m.

wide diversity of morphologies ranging from the large, deep-diving sperm whale which has relatively few teeth and captures squid by suction feeding, to the smallest cetaceans, the porpoises, which have many spade-shaped teeth for seizing fish. Another useful distinction of odontocetes is a difference in telescoping of the skull in which the maxilla "telescopes," or extends posteriorly, over the orbit to form an expanded bony supraorbital process of the frontal (Miller, 1923; Fig. 4.11). In living odontocetes, this supraorbital process forms an origin for a facial (maxillonasolabialis) muscle (Mead, 1975a) which inserts around the single blowhole and associated nasal passages. The facial muscle complex and nasal apparatus generate the high frequency sounds used by living odontocetes for echolocation (see Chapter 10). Other characteristic features of toothed whales include the presence of a single blowhole, the development of a melon, and facial asymmetry (see below).

Some of the features traditionally used to diagnose odontocetes have come under scrutiny and reevaluation (Milinkovitch, 1995; Messenger, 1995; Heyning, 1997). For example, the number of blowholes or external nares (nostrils) is one of the most often cited features used to distinguish odontocetes from mysticetes. The derived condition is a single blowhole, seen in odontocetes, whereas in mysticetes the nasal passages are separate tubes (Fig. 4.18). As suggested by Milinkovitch (1995), the blowhole of sperm whales represents the apertures of the right and left nares, and consequently does not constitute a truly singular opening. In his new definition, the character is not simply the number of blowholes but instead the number of nasal passages distal to the bony nares. The character has two character states, "two nasal passages" or "single nasal passage" (Fig. 4.18). The former would be the ancestral state present in mysticetes and in sperm whales and the latter would be a derived character that links all odontocetes, exclusive of sperm whales, in a clade. This interpretation has been criticized (Messenger, 1994; Heyning, 1997). Sperm whales and odontocetes display different derived states of the character "nasal passage morphology," which when subjected to analysis results in the recognition of a multistate character in which baleen whales and the outgroups have separate nasal passages (ancestral condition), sperm whales have separate nasal passages proximal to the blowhole (derived state 1), and the remaining extant toothed whales have confluent nasal passages (derived state 2). Cod-

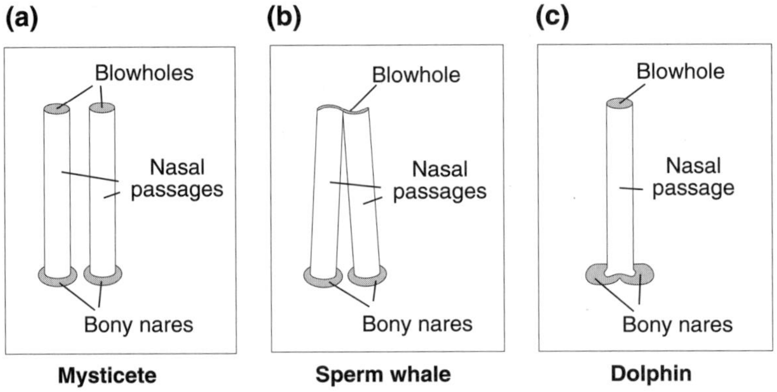

Figure 4.18. Alternate interpretation for homology of the blowholes in whales (modified from Milinkovitch, 1995). According to Milinkovitch's interpretation: Ancestral condition (two nasal passages) (a) present in mysticetes and sperm whales (b) with derived state (single nasal passage) seen in other toothed whales (c). Alternate interpretation: Ancestral condition (a) with two derived conditions (b) and (c).

ing of the character transformations in this way results in a more parsimonious scenario than that proposed by Milinkovitch.

Other purported diagnostic features of odontocetes include two characters that have been specifically related to echolocation abilities: the presence of a **melon**, a region of adipose tissue on top of the skull with varying amounts of connective tissue within it, and **cranial and facial asymmetry**, a condition in which bones (= cranial asymmetry) and soft structures (= facial asymmetry) on the right side of the facial region are larger and more developed than equivalent structures on the left side. Cranial asymmetry is not universal among odontocetes, in either presence or extent. Both cranial and facial asymmetry are found in all modern representatives of the seven extant odontocete families, but fossil evidence indicates that cranial asymmetry is less pronounced in the more basal members of these groups and is totally absent in some extinct taxa. When present, however, the skew is always to the left side. Heyning (1989) argued that it is more likely that cranial asymmetry evolved only once. Milinkovitch (1995) proposed another scenario in which facial asymmetry started to develop in the ancestor of all extant cetaceans and by chance was oriented to the left. It follows from his argument that left-oriented facial asymmetry might be an ancestral character for odontocetes that was lost or greatly reduced in baleen whales. Accordingly, cranial asymmetry would accompany facial asymmetry and would have been developed independently in two (possibly up to four) odontocete lineages. Importantly, what is needed to test this hypothesis is a reevaluation of the degree of development of cranial and facial asymmetry in extant as well as extinct cetaceans.

Regarding the presence of a melon, Milinkovitch (1995) noted that mysticetes possess a fatty structure just anterior to the nasal passages that may be homologous to the melon of odontocetes (Heyning and Mead, 1990). Assuming that the melon of odontocetes and mysticetes is homologous, one might hypothesize that this structure first evolved in archaeocetes. It has been suggested that the vestigial melon of mysticetes might be a hint of more generalized **paedomorphism** of their facial anatomy, seen for example in a fossil delphinoid which has dramatically reversed telescoping of the skull (Muizon, 1993). Milinkovitch (1995) further suggested that presence of a melon (along with facial and cranial asymmetry and echolocation abilities) might be ancestral for all cetaceans and that baleen whales lost or greatly reduced this character. Heyning (1997) disputed this interpretation, arguing that it assumes *a priori* that the melon regressed from a larger melon in the common ancestor, a claim that lacks empirical evidence. In addition, study of the inner ear of an archaic mysticete, which more nearly resembles the nonecholocating modern mysticetes than early fossil toothed whales, offers little support for the suggestion that echolocation was present in ancestral mysticetes and was lost secondarily in extant mysticetes (Geisler and Luo, 1996). In summary, Milinkovitch's alternative interpretations of odontocete morphological synapomorphies are less parsimonious interpretations of character transformations and they lack supporting data.

The traditional monophyletic view of odontocetes is followed here based on a comprehensive reappraisal of both morphologic and molecular data (Messenger, 1995; Messenger and McGuire, 1998). According to this study, odontocete monophyly is supported by at least 20 morphological characters. Some of these synapomorphies are listed below (Fig. 4.19):

1. *Concave facial (sagittal) plane*—The cranium of most odontocetes in lateral view is concave dorsally such that the cranium slopes upward from the rostrum posteriorly to the braincase. In the primitive condition, seen in baleen whales and artiodactyls, the cranium is dorsally convex.

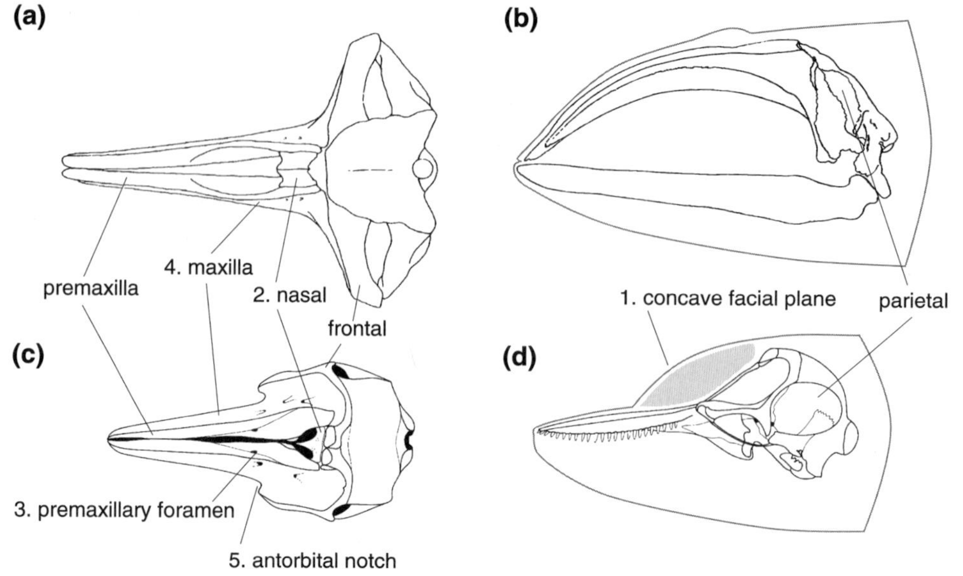

Figure 4.19. Simplified outlines of cetacean skulls in dorsal and lateral views illustrating odontocete synapomorphies. (a) and (b) a mysticete, *Balaena mysticetus* (c) and (d) an odontocete, *Tursiops truncatus* (modified from Fordyce, 1982). Character numbers (see text for further discussion): 1=concave facial plane, 2=asymmetric cranial vertex (shown here as asymmetry of nasals), 3=premaxillary foramen present, 4=maxillae overlay supraorbital process of frontal and 5=antorbital notch present.

2. *Asymmetric cranial vertex*—In most odontocetes (except *Pontoporia*) the cranial vertex (elevated region of the skull posterior to the bony nares) is asymmetrical. Mysticetes have a symmetric cranium.

3. *Premaxillary foramen present*—Odontocetes possess infraorbital or premaxillary foramina of varying shapes and sizes of the premaxillae. Neither mysticetes nor artiodactyls possess foramina in the premaxillary bones.

4. *Maxillae overlay supraorbital process*—"Telescoping" of the skull in odontocetes involves the presence of ascending processes of the maxillae that cover the supraorbital processes of the frontals. This condition is not seen in mysticetes or terrestrial mammals.

5. *Antorbital notch present*—In odontocetes, antorbital notches are located at the base of the rostrum where the maxillae expand laterally to cover the supraorbital process of the frontals. They allow for the passage of the facial nerves.

Evolutionary trends among odontocetes include expansion and increase in size of the face, shortening of the intertemporal region, elevation of the cranial vertex posterior to the nasals, increased facial asymmetry, and isolation of the earbones from the skull. The jaws become either extremely long, narrow, and polydont, or short and blunt, or toothless (Fordyce and Barnes, 1994).

4.2.4.2.1. Archaic Odontocetes

Archaic odontocetes comprise five extinct families: the Agorophiidae, Squalodontidae, Squalodelphidae, Dalpiazinidae, and Waipaitiidae. The extinct Squalodontidae, Squalodelphidae, Waipaitiidae, and perhaps the Dalpiazinidae, together with the extant Platanistidae

(Ganges and Indus river dolphins), have been shown not to be basal odontocetes but are members of the Platanistoidea, an ancient and once speciose clade (Muizon, 1994; Fordyce, 1996). The agorophiids are Oligocene (28–24 Ma) in age. The few known skulls demonstrate that these animals had only a moderate degree of telescoping (the nares were anterior to the orbits) and that the cheekteeth had multiple roots and accessory cusps on the crowns (Barnes, 1984b). Fordyce (1981) suggested that the only certain member of the family is *Agorophius pygmaeus* (late Oligocene, South Carolina) of uncertain phylogenetic relationship.

The squalodonts (Family Squalodontidae), or shark-toothed dolphins, named for the presence of many triangular, denticulate cheekteeth, are known from the late Oligocene to the late Miocene. They have been reported from North America, South America, Europe, Asia, New Zealand, and Australia. Squalodontids include a few species known from well-preserved skulls, complete dentitions, earbones, and mandibles but many nominal species are based only on isolated teeth and probably belong in other families. Most squalodontids were relatively large animals with bodies 3 m or more in length. Their crania were almost fully telescoped, with the nares located on top of the head between the orbits. The dentition was polydont but still heterodont, with long pointed anterior teeth and wide, multiple-rooted cheekteeth (Fig. 4.20). It is likely that the anterior teeth functioned in display rather than in feeding and the robust cheekteeth with worn tips may reflect feeding on prey such as penguins (Fordyce, 1996).

The Squalodelphidae include several early Miocene genera *(Notocetus, Medocinia,* and *Squalodelphis* (Muizon, 1981)) with small, slightly asymmetrical skulls and moderately long rostra and near-homodont teeth (Muizon, 1987).

The family Dalpiazinidae was established by Muizon (1988a) for *Dalpiazina ombonii,* an early Miocene species with a small symmetrical skull and a long rostrum armed with many near-homodont teeth (Fordyce and Barnes, 1994). Fordyce and Sampson (1992) reported an undescribed earliest Miocene species from the southwest Pacific.

The family Waipatiidae was established by Fordyce (1994) for a single described species, *Waipatia maerewhenua,* characterized by a small slightly asymmetrical skull and long rostrum with small heterodont teeth.

4.2.4.2.2. Later Diverging Odontocetes

Modern odontocetes include 10 families: Ziphiidae (beaked whales), Physeteridae (sperm whales), Kogiidae (pygmy sperm whales), Platanistidae (Asiatic river dolphins),

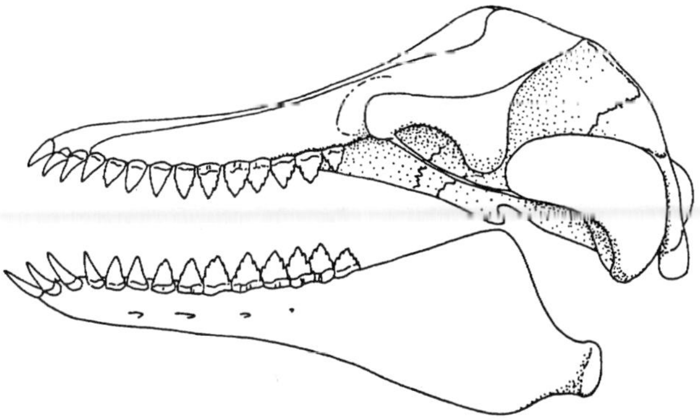

Figure 4.20. Skull and lower jaw of an archaic odontocete, *Prosqualodon davidsi,* from the early Miocene of Tasmania. (From Fordyce *et al.*, 1995.)

Pontoporiidae (franciscana), Iniidae (bouto), Lipotidae (baji), Delphinidae (dolphins, killer whales, and pilot whales), Phocoenidae (porpoises), and Monodontidae (narwhal and beluga). Molecular and morphologic phylogenies for odontocetes are presented in Figures 4.21 and 4.22. Molecular sequence data provide strong support for the monophyly of the Delphinoidea (families Delphinidae plus Phocoenidae plus Monodontidae). This is consistent with morphologically based phylogenies (Heyning, 1989, 1990; Barnes, 1990). The franciscana, *Pontoporia blainvillei* (Pontoporiidae), and the Amazon River dolphin, *Inia geoffrensis* (Iniidae), have been positioned as sequential sister taxa to the superfamily Delphinoidea in the molecular phylogeny. This hypothesis is supported by some morphologic data (Muizon, 1988c, 1991; Heyning, 1989; Heyning and Mead, 1990). Molecular data linking the Physeteridae and Kogiidae in the superfamily Physeteroidea is consistent with morphological data. The most basal odontocete lineage on the basis of molecular data is a clade containing beaked whales and sperm whales (Árnason and Gullberg, 1996; Hasegawa *et al.,* 1997; Fig. 4.21). The placement of beaked whales using morphologic data differs in having them placed as the sister group to sperm whales (Heyning, 1989; Barnes, 1990) or as the basal odontocete lineage including sperm whales and pygmy sperm whales (Muizon, 1988c, 1991; Fordyce, 1994). Finally, in the most controversial arrangement of odontocetes proposed, baleen whales are sister group to the sperm whales on the basis of molecular data (e.g., Milinkovitch *et al.,* 1993).

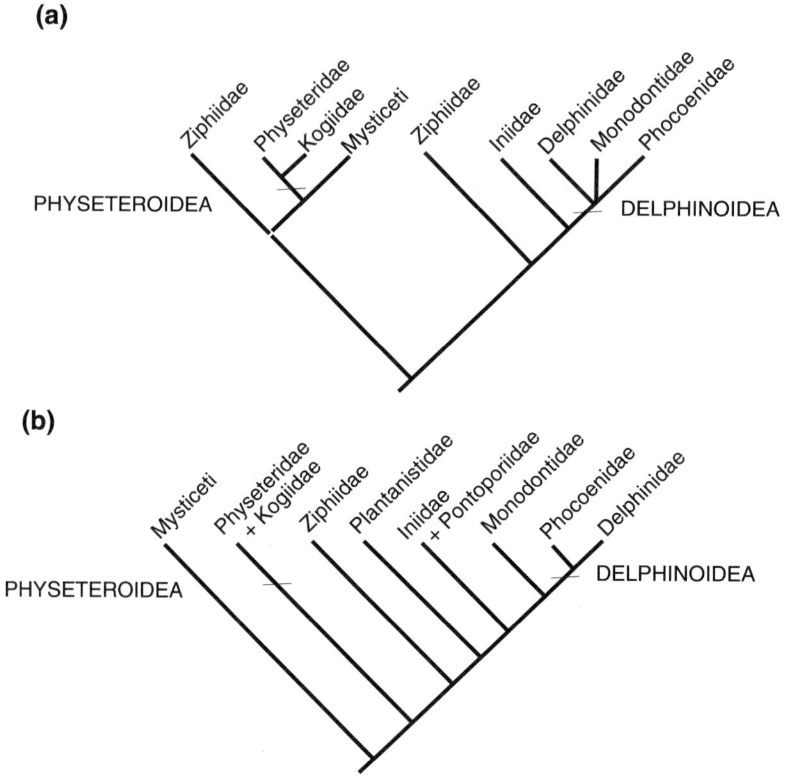

Figure 4.21. Alternative hypotheses for the phylogeny of extant odontocetes. (a) Cladogram based on cytochrome b sequence data (Árnason and Gullberg, 1996; Hasegawa *et al.,* 1997), (b) Cladogram based on morphologic data (Heyning, 1989, 1997; Heyning and Mead, 1990).

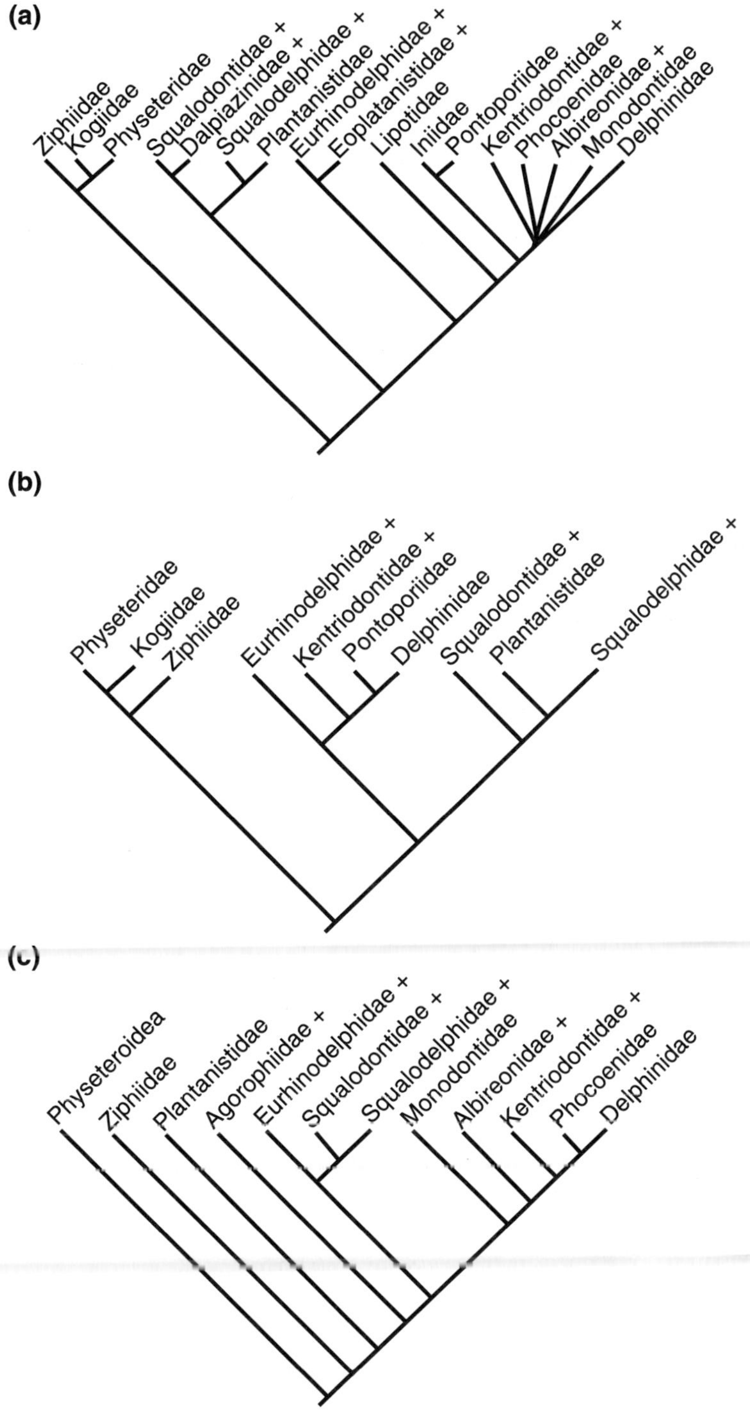

Figure 4.22. Alternate phylogenies for fossil and recent odontocetes based on morphology. +=extinct taxa (a) Muizon, 1988b; 1991, (b) Fordyce, 1994, (c) Barnes, 1990.

Family Ziphiidae—Beaked whales are a relatively poorly known but diverse group of toothed whales composed of at least five genera and 19 extant species. They are characterized by a snout which is frequently drawn out into a beak and from which the group obtains its common name, beaked whales. Ziphiids inhabit deep ocean basins and much of our information about them comes from strandings and whaling activities. One evolutionary trend in ziphiids is toward the loss of all teeth in the rostrum and most in the mandible, with the exception of one or two pairs of teeth at the anterior end of the jaw that become much enlarged (Fig. 4.23). In addition to several features of the ear, premaxilla, and palatal region (e.g., see Fordyce, 1994), extant ziphiids can be distinguished from other odontocetes by possession of one pair of anteriorly converging throat grooves (Fig. 4.23).

Ziphiids have been classified either with sperm whales in the superfamily Physeteroidea or as a sister group to extant odontocetes other than physeterids. Ziphiids are known in the fossil record from the Miocene and Pliocene of Europe, North and South America, Japan, and Australia. A freshwater fossil ziphiid has been reported from the Miocene of Africa (Mead, 1975b).

Family Physeteridae—The physeterids, or sperm whales, have an ancient and diverse fossil record, although only a single species, *Physeter macrocephalus* survives. Derived characters of the skull which unite sperm whales include, among others, a large, deep, supracranial basin which houses the spermaceti organ (Figure 4.24) and loss of one or both nasal bones (Fordyce, 1984). The terms sperm whale and spermaceti organ derive from the

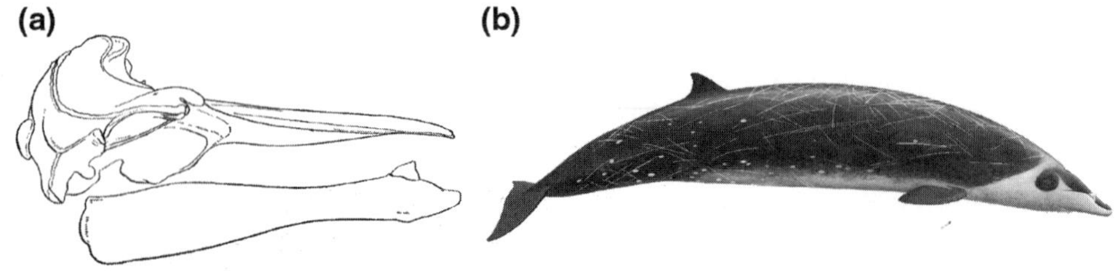

Figure 4.23. A representative of the Family Ziphiidae. (a) Lateral view of the skull and lower jaw of Gervais' beaked whale, *Mesoplodon europaeus*, (b) right side of the body of Stejneger's beaked whale, *Mesoplodon stejnegeri*. llustrating the throat grooves (illustrated by P. Folkens). Note the reduced dentition. (From Van Beneden and Gervais, 1880.)

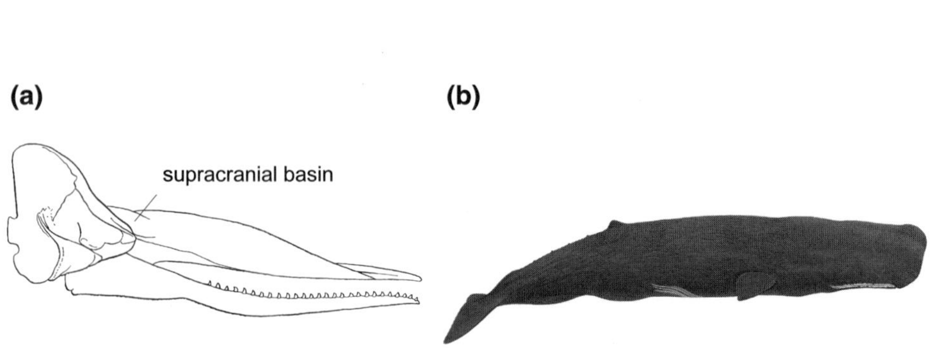

Figure 4.24. The Family Physeteridae (Sperm whale, *Physeter macrocephalus*). (a) Lateral view of the skull and lower jaw, (b) right side of the body (illustrated by P. Folkens). Note the deep supracranial basin. (From Van Beneden and Gervais, 1880.)

curious belief of those who named this whale that it carried its semen in its head. Sperm whales are the largest of the toothed whales, attaining a length of as much as 19 m and weighing 70 tons. They also are the longest and deepest diving vertebrates known (138 min and 3000 m; Clarke, 1976; Watkins *et al.,* 1985). One fictional sperm whale named Moby Dick achieved literary notoriety as the inspiration for Herman Melville's book by that name.

The fossil record of the Physeteridae goes back at least to the Miocene (late early Miocene 21.5–16.3 Ma) and earlier if *Ferecetotherium* from the late Oligocene (29–23 Ma) of Azerbaidjan is included. By middle Miocene time, physeterids were moderately diverse and the family is fairly well-documented from fossils found in South America, eastern North America, western Europe, the Mediterranean region, western North America, Australia, New Zealand, and Japan (Hirota and Barnes, 1995).

Family Kogiidae—The pygmy sperm whale, *Kogia breviceps,* and the dwarf sperm whale, *Kogia simus,* are closely related to the sperm whale family, Physeteridae. The pygmy sperm whale is appropriately named, because males only attain a length of 4 m and females are no more than 3 m long. The dwarf pygmy sperm whale is even smaller, with adults ranging from 2.1 to 2.7 m. As in physeterids, there is a large anterior basin in the skull, but kogiids differ markedly in their small size, short rostrum, and other details of the skull (Fordyce and Barnes, 1994; Fig. 4.25). The oldest kogiids are from the late Miocene (8.8–5.2 Ma) of South America and the early Pliocene (6.7–5 Ma) of Baja California.

"River Dolphins"—Living river dolphins are often treated as a single family, yet they represent four families (Platanistidae, Lipotidae, Iniidae, Pontoporiidae) which have invaded the estuarine and freshwater habitat. Their similarities (e.g. reduced eyes) are the result of convergent evolution, adaptations to the same environment, among animals of different origins.

Family Platanistidae—The extant Asiatic river dolphins, *Platanista* spp. (the blind endangered Ganges and Indus River dolphins), comprise the family Platanistidae. They are char-

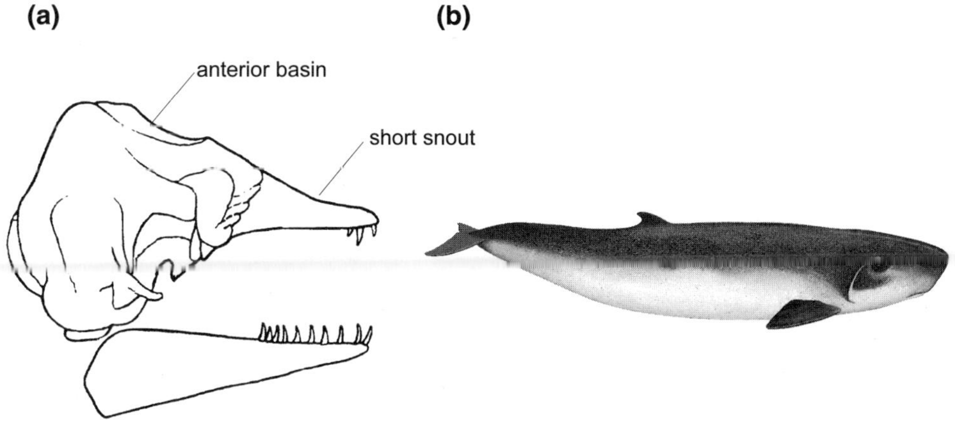

Figure 4.25. The Family Kogiidae (Pygmy sperm whale, *Kogia breviceps*). (a) Lateral view of the skull and lower jaw, (b) right side of the body (illustrated by P. Folkens). (From Bobrinskii *et al.,* 1965: 197.) Note the short snout and anterior basin.

acterized by a long narrow beak, numerous narrow pointed teeth, and broad paddle-like flippers. They have no known fossil record and the time of invasion into fresh water is unknown. Middle to late Miocene marine species of *Zarhachis* and *Pomatodelphis* are closely related to *Platanista,* although they differ in rostral profiles and cranial symmetry and in their development of pneumatized bony facial crests (Fig. 4.26; Fordyce and Barnes, 1994).

The superfamily Platanistoidea, a clade which according to Muizon (1987, 1988a, 1991, 1994) includes the Platanistidae, the Squalodontidae, the Squalodelphidae, and the Dalpiazinidae, has had a long and confusing history and its validity has been questioned (Messenger, 1994; Cozzuol, 1996).

Family Pontoporiidae—The small, long-beaked franciscana, *Pontoporia blainvillei,* lives in coastal waters in the western South Atlantic and is the only extant pontoporiid. All pontoporiids except for the fossil *Parapontoporia* have virtually symmetrical cranial vertices and most have long rostra and many tiny teeth (Fig. 4.27).

Fossil *Pontoporia*-like taxa include species of *Pliopontos* and *Parapontoporia* from temperate to subtropical marine settings in the east Pacific (Barnes, 1976, 1984a; Muizon, 1983, 1988c). Late Miocene *Pontistes* and *Pontoporia* species come from marine sediments of Argentina (Cozzuol, 1985, 1996).

Family Iniidae—The bouto, *Inia geoffrensis,* is a freshwater species with reduced eyes found only in Amazon River drainages. The name comes from the sound of its blow. Ac-

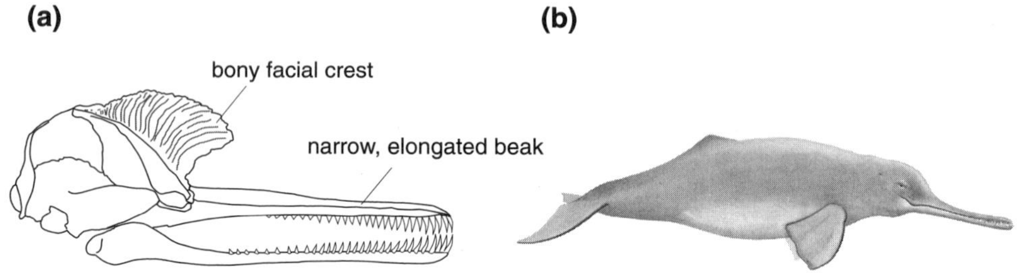

Figure 4.26. A representative of the Family Platanistidae (Ganges river dolphin, *Platanista gangetica*). (a) Lateral views of the skull and lower jaw, (b) right side of the body (illustrated by P. Folkens). (From Duncan 1877–83: 248.) Note the development of bony facial crests.

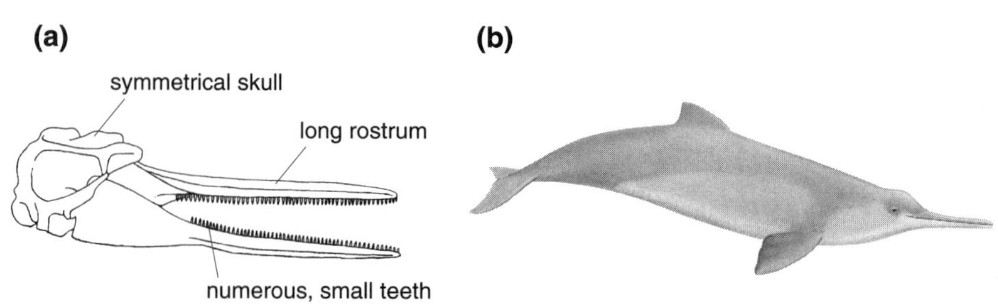

Figure 4.27. The Family Pontoporiidae (franciscana, *Pontoporia blainvillei*). (a) Lateral view of skull and jaws, (b) right side of the body (illustrated by P. Folkens). (From Watson, 1981.) Note the symmetrical skull, long rostrum and numerous small teeth.

cording to Heyning (1989), the monotypic extant taxon *Inia* is diagnosed by having the premaxillae displaced laterally and not in contact with the nasals (Fig. 4.28). Dentally they are diagnosed by conical front teeth and molariform posterior teeth. According to Cozzuol (1996), iniids (including fossil taxa) are characterized by an extremely elongated rostrum and mandible, very narrow supraoccipital, greatly reduced orbital region, and pneumatized maxillae forming a crest.

The fossil record of iniids goes back to the late Miocene of South America (Cozzuol, 1996) and the early Pliocene of North America (Muizon, 1988b; Morgan, 1994). The North American record of iniids, however, is disputed by Cozzuol (1996, and references therein). The phylogenetic history and fossil record of iniids indicates that they originated in South America in the Amazonian basin, entering river systems along the Pacific coast (Cozzuol, 1996).

Family Lipotidae—The endangered baiji, or Chinese river dolphin (*Lipotes vexillifer*), lives in the Yangtze River, China. They are characterized by a long narrow upturned beak, a low triangular dorsal fin, broad rounded flippers, and very small eyes (Zhou *et al.,* 1979; Fig. 4.29).

The only fossil closely related to *Lipotes* is *Prolipotes,* based on a fragment of mandible from China (Zhou *et al.,* 1984).

Archaic "Dolphins"—Archaic dolphins of the Miocene are grouped into one of three extinct families: the Kentriodontidae, the Albeirodontidae, and the Eurhinodelphidae. The earliest diverging lineage, the kentriodontids, were small animals approximately 2 m or less in length and with numerous teeth, elaborate basicranial sinuses, and symmetrical cranial vertices (Barnes, 1978). This group's monophyly has been questioned (Cozzuol, 1996) because of relatively diverse species and widespread distribution ranging from the late Oligocene to late Miocene in both the Atlantic and Pacific Oceans (Ichishima *et al.,* 1995). Barnes (1984a) suggested that the Albeirodontidae, known by only one late Miocene species (Fig. 4.30), was derived from kentriodontids, although Muizon (1988b) placed this taxon as sister group to phocoenids. The long beaked eurhinodelphids were widespread and moderately diverse during the early and middle Miocene and disappeared in the late Miocene (Fig. 4.31). Eurhinodelphid relationships are contentious. They have been either included in a clade with other archaic odontocetes, the squalodontids and squalodelphids (Barnes, 1990), or grouped with another extinct family, the Eoplatanistidae (Muizon, 1988a, 1991).

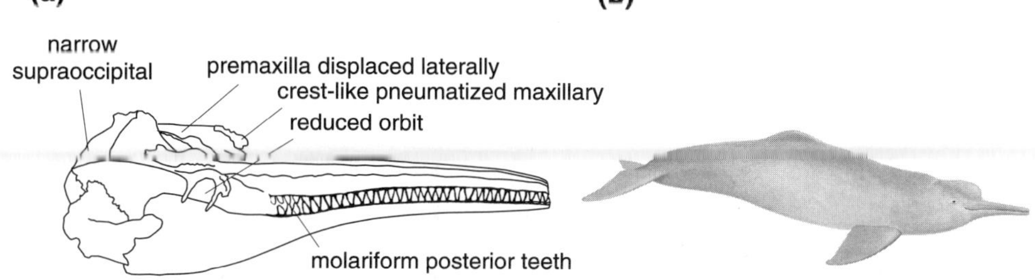

Figure 4.28. The Family Iniidae (bouto, *Inia geoffrensis*). (a) Dorsal view of the skull, (b) right side of the body (illustrated by P. Folkens). (From Geibel, 1859: 498.) Note the premaxillae is displaced laterally and is not in contact with the nasals, narrow supraoccipital, reduced orbit, crest-like pneumatized maxillary, and molariform posterior teeth.

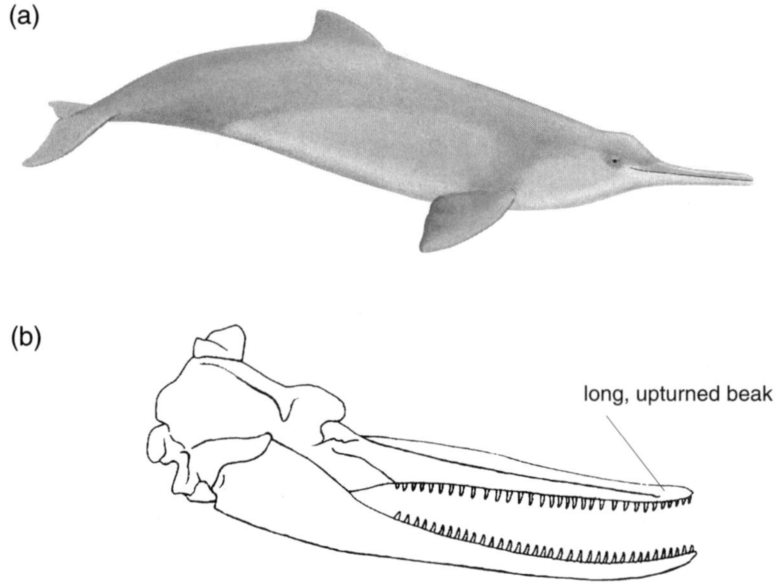

Figure 4.29. The Family Lipotidae (Chinese River dolphin, *Lipotes vexillifer*). (a) Right side of the body, (illustrated by P. Folkens), (b) Lateral view of skull and jaws. (From Watson, 1981.) Note the long, upturned beak.

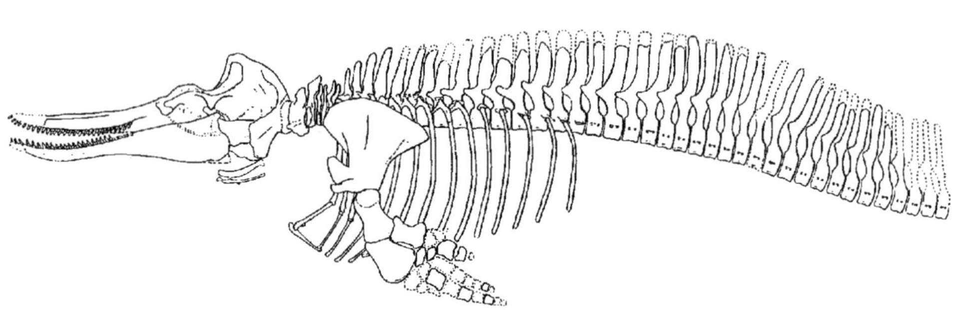

Figure 4.30. Reconstruction of a fossil dolphin, *Albireo whistleri.* (From Fordyce *et al.,* 1995: 376.)

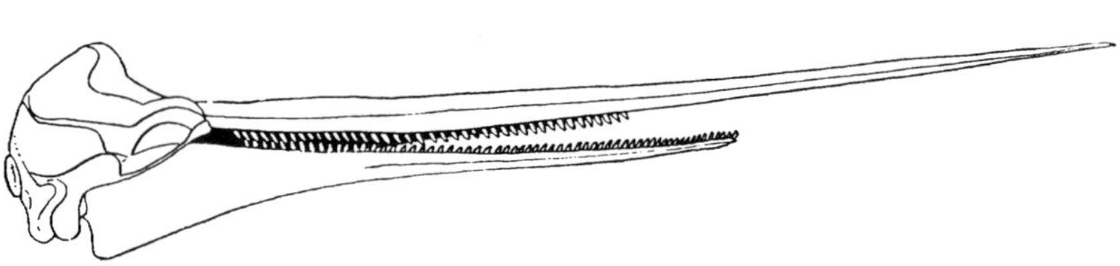

Figure 4.31. An archaic dolphin (*Eurhinodelphis cocheteuxi*) from the late Miocene of Belgium. (From Slijper, 1962.)

Family Delphinidae—Delphinids are the most diverse of the cetacean families and include 17 genera and 36 extant species of dolphins, killer whales, and pilot whales. Most delphinids are small to medium sized, ranging from 1.5 to 4.5 m in length. The giant among them, the killer whale, reaches 9.5 m in length. Although the Irrawaddy dolphin (*Orcaella brevirostris*) found only in the Indo-Pacific has been regarded as a monodontid by some (Kasuya, 1973; Barnes, 1984b), more recent morphologic and molecular work suggests that this species is a delphinid (Muizon, 1988b; Heyning, 1989; Árnason and Gullberg, 1996; Arnold and Heinsohn, 1996; Messenger and McGuire, 1998). Delphinids, including *Orcaella,* are united by the loss of the posterior sac of the nasal passage (Fordyce, 1994). Another distinguishing feature of delphinids is reduction of the posterior end of the left premaxilla so that it does not contact the nasal (Fig. 4.32; Heyning, 1989). The oldest delphinid is of latest Miocene age, possibly 11 Ma (Barnes, 1976).

Family Phocoenidae—Porpoises include six small extant species. One of the most diagnostic features of phocoenids is the presence of raised rounded protuberances on the premaxillae. Additionally, the premaxillae do not extend posteriorly behind the anterior half of the nares. Phocoenids are further distinguished from other odontocetes by having spatulate-shaped rather than conical teeth (Fig. 4.33; Heyning, 1989). Phocoenids and delphinids have been recognized by several workers (e.g., Barnes, 1990) as being more closely related to one another than either is to monodontids (Fig. 4.22). Among derived characters they share but monodontids do not is the presence of a head stripe system, or bridle, consisting of an eye stripe and blowhole stripe (Perrin, 1997).

Phylogenetic relationships among extant species based on mitochondrial cytochrome b sequence data (Rosel *et al.,* 1995; Fig. 4.34) support a close relationship between Burmeister's porpoise, *Phocoena spinipinnis,* and the vaquita, *Phocoena sinus,* and also the association of these two species with the spectacled porpoise, *Australophocoena dioptrica.* The latter result differs from morphological classification (Barnes, 1985) which groups *A. dioptrica* with Dall's porpoise, *Phocoenoides dalli,* in the subfamily Phocoeninae. The molecular analysis found no support for this grouping. Results of Rosel *et al.* (1995) support returning *A. dioptrica* to its original allocation as a member of the genus *Phocoena.* Finally, this molecular study suggests that the finless porpoise, *Neophocoena phocaenoides,* may be the most basal member of the family. Like delphinids, phocoenids have a fossil record that extends back to the late Miocene and Pliocene in North and South America (Barnes, 1976, 1984b; Muizon, 1988a).

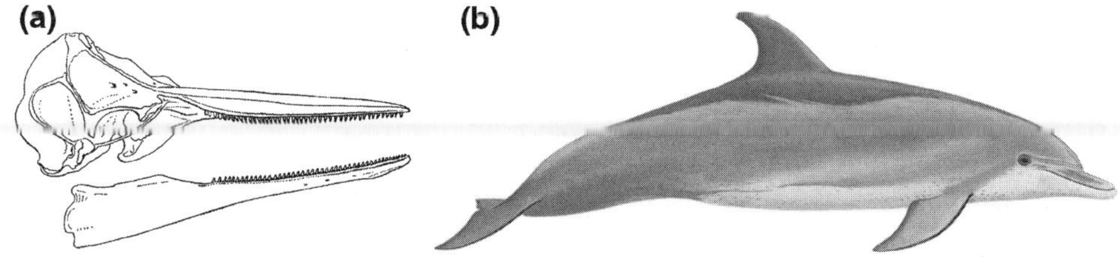

Figure 4.32. Representatives of the Family Delphinidae of common dolphin, *Delphinus delphis.* (a) Lateral view of skull and lower jaw, (b) right side of the body of bottlenose dolphins, *Tursiops trancatus* (illustrated by P. Folkens). (From Van Beneden and Gervais, 1880.)

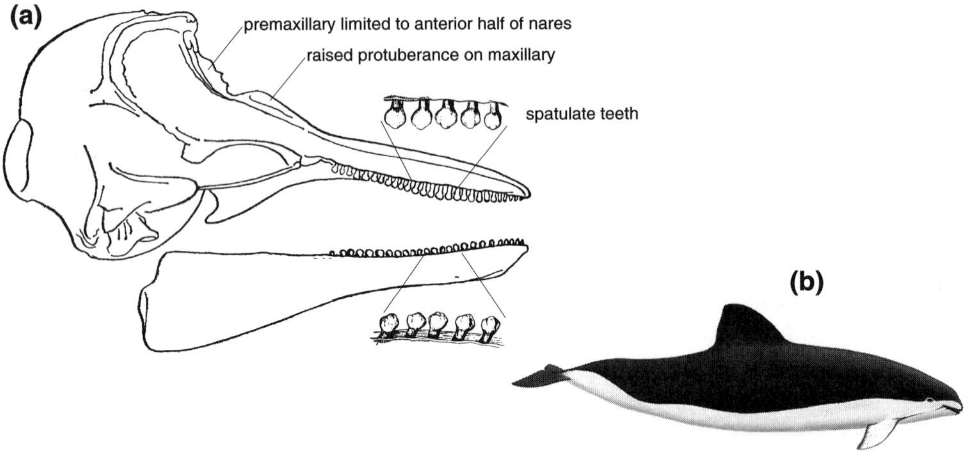

Figure 4.33. Representatives of the Family Phocoenidae (porpoises). (a) Lateral view of the skull and lower jaw of a phocoenid illustrating the raised rounded protuberances on the premaxillae (from Gervais 1855: 327) and spatulate-shaped teeth. (From Flower and Lydekker, 1891: 263.) (b) Right side of the body of spectacled porpoise, *Phocoena dioptrica* (Illustrated by P. Folkens).

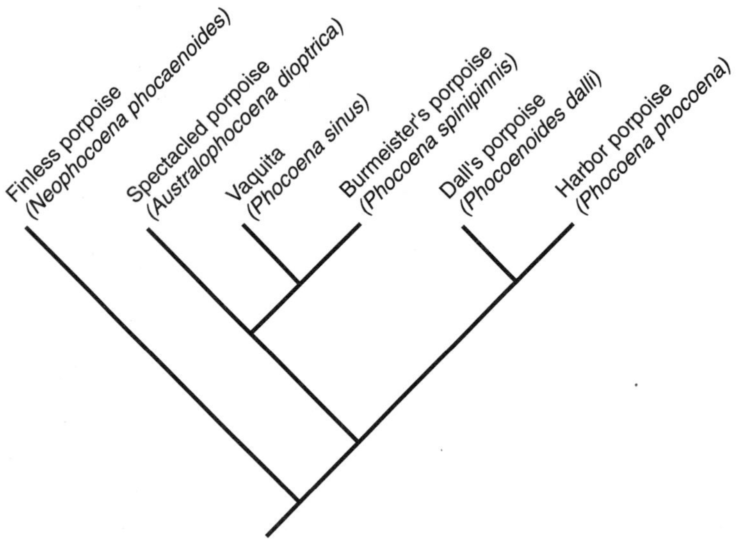

Figure 4.34. Species-level phylogeny of phocoenids (Rosel *et al.* 1995).

Family Monodontidae—Monodontids include two extant species, the narwhal (*Monodon monoceros*) and the beluga (*Delphinapterus leucas*). The narwhal is readily distinguished by the presence of a spiraled incisor tusk in males and occasionally in females (Fig. 4.35). It has been suggested that the narwhal tusk may have been used in creating the legend of the unicorn, a horse with cloven hooves, a lion's tail, and a horn in the middle of its forehead that resembles the narwhal tusk (Slijper, 1962). The living beluga is characterized by its completely white coloration (Fig. 4.35).

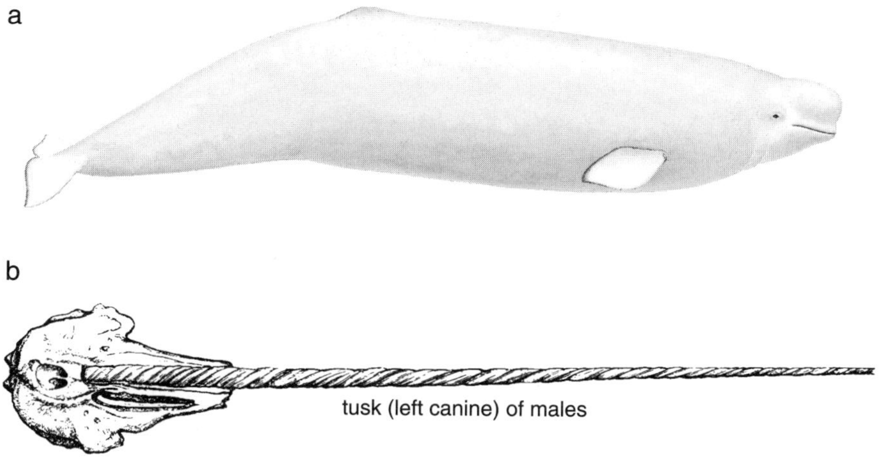

Figure 4.35. Representatives of the Family Monodontidae (narwhal, *Monodon monoceros* and beluga, *Delphinapterus leucas*). (a) Right side of the body of beluga (illustrated by P. Folkens), (b) Dorsal view of the skull of the narwhal. Note the top of the nostrum has been removed to show the root of the large left tusk and the small, unerupted right tusk. (From Flower and Lydekker, 1891: 261.)

The narwhal and beluga have a circumpolar distribution in the Arctic. During the late Miocene and Pliocene, monodontids occupied temperate waters as far south as Baja California (Barnes, 1973, 1976, 1984b; Muizon, 1988a).

4.3. Summary and Conclusions

Although cetacean monophyly is widely accepted there is controversy regarding whether artiodactyls are their closest living relatives (a claim supported by morphologists) or whether some artiodactyls (i.e. hippopotamids) are more closely related to cetaceans than they are to other artiodactyls (as held by some molecular systematists). This issue will require further examination of morphologic data sets with the addition of all fossil taxa as well as further evaluation of the use of molecular markers in phylogeny reconstruction. Another area of controversy is whether toothed whales are monophyletic. Some molecular sequence data support a closer relationship between the sperm whales and the baleen whales than between the sperm whales and other toothed whales. Morphologic data conflicts with this hypothesis, although few studies have addressed the problem using both fossil and recent taxa and rigorous phylogenetic methods.

The earliest whales are archaeocetes, a paraphyletic stem group that first appeared approximately 50 million years ago and are best known from India and Pakistan. New discoveries provide evidence that these early whales had feet. Divergence estimates for baleen and toothed whales from a common archaeocete ancestor range from 25 to 35 Ma depending on whether rates are calibrated using morphologic or molecular data. There is evidence that some archaic mysticetes possessed both teeth and baleen. Later diverging mysticetes lost the teeth but retained baleen. Relationships among modern families of baleen whales conflict based on morphologic vs molecular data. Relationships among odontocetes are no less controversial than the issue of odontocete monophyly. There is, however, general agreement of both molecular and morphologic data that beaked whales and sperm whales are basal odontocetes. Relationships among other odontocete lineages will require comprehensive assessment of both fossil and recent taxa.

4.4. Further Reading

The evolutionary history of fossil whales is summarized in Fordyce *et al.* (1995) and Fordyce and Barnes (1994). See Thewissen (1998) for an account of the early evolution of whales. For a popular treatment of the evolutionary significance of recent whale fossil discoveries see Gould (1994) and Zimmer (1998). The relationship of cetaceans to other ungulates based on morphologic data is reviewed in Thewissen (1994) and see Shimamura *et al.* (1997) and Gatesy (1998) for molecular evidence. The controversy regarding odontocete monophyly is reviewed by Novacek (1993), Milinkovich (1995), Heyning (1997), and Messenger and McGuire (1998).

References

Adachi, J., and M. Hasegawa (1995). Phylogeny of whales: Dependence of the inference on species sampling. *Mol. Biol. Evol.* **12**(1): 177–179.

Árnason, U., and A. Gullberg (1994). Relationship of baleen whales established by cytochrome b gene sequence comparison. *Nature (London)* **367**: 726–727.

Árnason, U., and A. Gullberg (1996). Cytochrome b nucleotide sequences and the identification of five primary lineages of extant cetaceans. *Mol. Biol. Evol.* **13**: 407–417.

Arnold, P. W., and G. E. Heinsohn (1996). Phylogenetic status of the Irrawaddy dolphin (*Orcaella brevirostris* Owen in Gray): A cladistic analysis. *Mem. Queensl. Mus.* **39**(2): 141–204.

Bajpal, S., and J. G. M. Thewissen (1998). Middle Eocene cetaceans from the Harudi and Subathu formations of India, pp. 213–233. *In* "The Emergence of Whales: Patterns in the Origin of Cetacea" (J. G. M. Thewissen, ed.), Plenum Press, New York.

Barnes, L. G. (1973). *Praekogia cedroensis,* a new genus and species of fossil pygmy sperm whale from Isla Cedros, Baja California, Mexico. *Contrib. Sci. Nat. Hist. Mus., Los Angeles Co.* **247**: 1–20.

Barnes, L. G. (1976). Outline of eastern North Pacific fossil cetacean assemblages. *Syst. Zool.* **25**: 321–343.

Barnes, L. G. (1978). A review of *Lophocetus* and *Liolithax* and their relationships to the delphinoid family Kentriodontidae (Cetacea: Odontoceti). *Nat. Hist. Mus.* Los Angeles Cty., *Sci. Bull.* **28**: 1–35.

Barnes, L. G. (1984a). Fossil odontocetes (Mammalia: Cetacea) from the Almejas Formation, Isla Cedros, Mexico. *PaleoBios* **42**: 1–46.

Barnes, L. G. (1984b). Whales, dolphins and porpoises: Origin and evolution of the Cetacea. *In* "Mammals Notes for a Short Course Organized by P. D. Gingerich and C. E. Badgley" (T. W. Broadhead, ed.), pp. 139–153. University of Tennessee, Department of Geological Sciences, Knoxville.

Barnes, L. G. (1985). Evolution, taxonomy and antitropical distributions of the porpoises (Phocoenidae, Mammalia). *Mar. Mamm. Sci.* **1**: 149–165.

Barnes, L. G. (1990). The fossil record and evolutionary relationships of the genus *Tursiops. In* "The Bottlenose Dolphin" (S. Leatherwood and R. R. Reeves, eds.), pp. 3–26. Academic Press, San Diego, CA.

Barnes, L. G., and S. A. McLeod (1984). The fossil record and phyletic relationships of gray whales. *In* "The Gray Whale *Eschrichtius robustus*" (M. L. Jones, S. L. Swartz, and S. Leatherwood, eds.), pp. 3–32. Academic Press, New York.

Barnes, L. G., and E. D. Mitchell (1978). Cetacea. *In* "Evolution of African Mammals" (V. J. Maglio and H. B. S. Cook, eds.), pp. 582–601. Harvard University Press, Cambridge, MA.

Barnes, L. G., D. P. Domning, and C. E. Ray (1985). Status of studies on fossil marine mammals. *Mar. Mamm. Sci.* **1**(1): 15–53.

Barnes, L. G., M. Kimura, H. Furusawa, and H. Sawamura (1995). Classification and distribution of Oligocene Aetiocetidae (Mammalia; Cetacea; Mysticeti) from western North America and Japan. *Island Arc* **3**: 392–431.

Berta, A. (1994). What is a Whale? *Science* **263**: 180–181.

Bérubé, M., and A. Aguilar (1998). A new hybrid between a blue whale, *Balaenoptera musculus,* and a fin whale, *B. physalus:* Frequency and implications of hybridization. *Mar. Mamm. Sci.* **14**(1): 82–98.

Bobrinskii, N. A., B. A. Kuznekov, and A. P. Kuzyakin (1965). Key to the mammals of the USSR, 2nd ed. Moscow, 382 pp (In Russian).

Bryant, P. J. (1995). Dating remains of gray whales from the eastern North Atlantic. *J. Mammal.* **76**(3): 857–861.

Buchanan, F., A. Crawford, C. Strobeck, P. Palsbøll, and Y. Plante (1999). Evolutionary applications of MIRs and SINES. *Animal Genetics* **30**: 47–50.

Cabrera, A. (1926). Cetaceos fosiles del Museo de La Plata. *Rev. Mus. La Plata* **29**: 363–411.

Clarke, M. R. (1976). Observations on sperm whale diving. *J. Mar. Biol. Assoc. U.K.* **56**: 809–810.

Cozzuol, M. A. (1985). The Odontoceti of the 'Mesopotamiense' of the Parana River ravines. Systematic review. *Invest. Cetacea* **7**: 39–53.

Cozzuol, M. A. (1996). The record of the aquatic mammals in southern South America. *Muench. Geowiss. Abh.* **30**: 321–342.

Deméré, T. (1986). The fossil whale *Balaenoptera davidsonii* (Cope 1872), with a review of other Neogene species of *Balaenoptera* (Cetacea: Mysticeti). *Mar. Mamm. Sci.* **2**(4): 277–298.

Donoso-Barros, R. (1975). Contribución al conocimiento de los cetáceos vivientes y fósiles del territorio de Chile. *Gayana (Zool.)* **36**: 1–127.

Duncan, P. M. (1877–83). Cassell's natural history. Cassell and Co., London, 3 vols.

Emlong, D. (1966). A new archaic cetacean from the Oligocene of northwest Oregon. *Bull. Mus. Nat. Hist. Univ. Oregon* **3**: 1–51.

Evans, P. G. H. (1987). "The Natural History of Whales and Dolphins." Helm, London.

Flower, W. H. (1883). On whales, past and present, and their probable origin. *Nat. Proc. R. Inst. G. B.* **10**: 360–376.

Flower, W. H. and R. Lydekker (1891). An introduction to the study of mammals living and extinct. Adam and Charles Black, London, 763 pp.

Fordyce, R. E. (1980). Whale evolution and Oligocene southern ocean environments. *Palaeogeogr., Palaeoclimatol., Palaeoecol.* **31**: 319–336.

Fordyce, R. E. (1981). Systematics of the odontocete *Agorophius pygmeus* and the family Agorophiidae (Mammalia: Cetacea). *J. Paleontol.* **55**: 1028–1045.

Fordyce, R. E. (1982). A review of Australian fossil Cetacea. *Memoirs of the National Museum of Victoria,* **43**: 43–58.

Fordyce, R. E. (1984). Evolution and zoogeography of cetaceans in Australia. *In* "Vertebrate Zoogeography and Evolution in Australasia" (M. Archer and G. Clayton, eds.), pp. 929–948. Hesperian Press, Carlisle, Australia.

Fordyce, R. E. (1989). Origins and evolution of Antarctic marine mammals. *Spec. Publ. Geol. Soc. London* **47**: 269–281.

Fordyce, R. E. (1992). Cetacean evolution and Eocene Oligocene environments. pp. 368–381, *In* D. Prothero, W. Berggren (eds.), Eocene-Oligocene climatic and biotic evolution. Princeton University Press, NJ.

Fordyce, R. E. (1994). *Waipatia maerewhenua,* new genus and species (Waipatiidae, new family), an archaic Late Oligocene dolphin (Cetacea: Platanistidae) from New Zealand. *Proc. San Diego Soc. Nat. Hist.* **29**: 147–176.

Fordyce, R. E. (1996). New Zealand Oligocene fossils and the early radiation of platanistoid dolphins. *In* "Abstracts of the Conference on Secondary Adaptation to Life in the Water" (J.-M. Mazin, P. Vignaud, and V. de Buffrénil, eds.), p. 12. Poitiers, France.

Fordyce, R. E., and L. G. Barnes (1994). The evolutionary history of whales and dolphins. *Annu. Rev. Earth Planet. Sci.* **22**: 419–455.

Fordyce, R. E., and C. R. Sampson (1992). Late Oligocene platanistoid and delphinoid dolphins from the Kokoamu Greensand-Otekaike Limestone, Waitaki Valley region, New Zealand: An expanding record. *Geol. Soc. N.Z., Misc. Publ.* **63a**: 66 (abstr.).

Fordyce, R. E., L. G. Barnes, and N. Miyazaki (1995). General aspects of the evolutionary history of whales and dolphins. *Island Arc* **3**: 373–391.

Fraser, F. C., and P. E. Purves (1976). Anatomy and function of the cetacean ear. *Proc. R. Soc. London* **152**: 62–78.

Gascon-Romero, G. A., F. J. Aranda-Manteca, and L. G. Barnes (1991). Una nueva evidencia de la evolucion de las ballenas barbadas en Baja California (New evidence for the evolution of baleen whales in Baja California). *Programa Resumenes, Reun. Int. Estud. Mamiferos Marinos, 16th,* Nuevo Vallarta, Nayarit, Mexico, 1991; Abstr. No. 4.

Gatesy, J. (1997). More DNA support for a cetacean/Hippopotamidae clade: The blood-clotting protein gene ?-fibrinogen. *Mol. Biol. Evol.* **14**(5): 537–543.

Gatesy, J. (1998). Molecular evidence for the phylogenetic affinities of Cetacea. *In* "The Emergence of Whales: Patterns in the Origin of Cetacea" (J. G. M. Thewissen, ed.), pp. 63–111. Plenum Press, NY.

Gatesy, J., C. Hayashi, M. A. Cronin, and P. Arctander (1996). Evidence from milk casein genes that cetaceans are close relatives of hippopotamid artiodactyls. *Mol. Biol. Evol.* **13**(7): 954–963.

Gatesy, J., M. Milinkovitch, V. Waddell, and M. Stanhope (1999). Stability of cladistic relationships between Cetacea and higher-level Artiodactyla taxa. *Syst. Biol.* **48**(1): 6–20.

Geisler, J. H., and Z. Luo (1996). The petrosal and inner ear of *Herpetocetus* sp. (Mammalia: Cetacea) and their implications for the phylogeny and hearing of archaic mysticetes. *J. Paleontol.* **70**(6): 1045–1066.

Geisler, J. H., and Z. Luo (1998). Relationships of Cetacea to terrestrial ungulates and the evolution of cranial vasculature in Cete. *In* "The Emergence of Whales: Patterns in the Origin of Cetacea" (J. G. M. Thewissen, Ed.), pp. 163–212. Plenum Press, New York.

Geisler, J. H. and M. O'Leary (1997). A phylogeny of Cetacea, Artiodactyla, Perissodactyla, and archaic ungulates: the morphological evidence. Abstracts of Papers of the 57th Annual Meeting of the Society of Vertebrate Paleontology (Chicago, Ill.), p. 48A.

Gervais, M. P. (1855). Histoire naturelle de mammiferes. L. Curmer, Paris, 344 pp.

Giebel, C. G. (1859). Die Naturgeschichte des Thierreichs. Book 1: Die Saugethiere. Verlag von Otto Wigand, Leipzig, 522 pp.

Gingerich, P. D. (1998). Paleobiological perspectives on Mesonychia, Archaeoceti, and the origin of whales. *In* "The Emergence of Whales: Patterns in the Origin of Cetacea" (J. G. M. Thewissen, ed.), pp. 423–449. Plenum Press, New York.

Gingerich, P. D., and D. E. Russell (1990). Dentition of early Eocene *Pakicetus* (Mammalia, Cetacea). *Contrib. Mus. Palaeontol., Univ. Mich.* **28**(1): 1–20.

Gingerich, P. D., and M. Uhen (1996). *Ancalecetus simonsi,* a new dorudontine archaeocete (Mammalia, Cetacea) from the early late Eocene of Wadi Hitan, Egypt. *Contrib. Mus. Paleontol., Univ. Mich.* **29**(13): 359–401.

Gingerich, P. D., N. A. Wells, D. E. Russell, and S. M. Shah (1983). Origin of whales in epicontinental remnant seas: New evidence from the early Eocene of Pakistan. *Science* **220**: 403–406.

Gingerich, P. D., B. H. Smith, and E. L. Simons (1990). Hind limbs of Eocene *Basilosaurus:* Evidence of feet in whales. *Science* **249**: 403–406.

Gingerich, P. D., S. M. Raza, M. Arif, M. Anwar, and X. Zhou (1994). New whale from the Eocene of Pakistan and the origin of cetacean swimming. *Nature* **368**: 844–847.

Gingerich, P. D., M. Arif, M. Akram Bhatti, M. Anwar, and W. J. Sanders (1997). *Basilosaurus drazindai* and *Basiloterus hussaini,* new Archaeoceti (Mammalia, Cetacea) from the middle Eocene Drazinda Formation, with a revised interpretation of ages of whale-bearing strata in the Kirthar Group of the Sulaiman Range, Punjab (Pakistan). Contributions of the Museum of Paleontology, University of Michigan, **30**(2): 55–81.

Goodman, M., J. Czelusniak, and J. E. Beeber (1985). Phylogeny of primates and other eutherian orders: A cladistic analysis using amino acid and nucleotide sequence data. *Cladistics* **1**: 171–185.

Gould, S. J. (1994). Hooking Leviathan by its past. *Nat. Hist.* **5**: 8–15 (artic.).

Graur, D., and D. G. Higgins (1994). Molecular evidence for the inclusion of cetaceans within the Order Artiodactyla. *Mol. Biol. Evol.* **11**(3): 357–364.

Gray, J. E. (1873). Remarks on some of the species in the foregoing paper. *Ann. Mag. Nat. Hist.* (Ser. 4) **11**: 107–112.

Hasegawa, M., J. Adachi, and M. C. Milinkovitch (1997). Novel phylogeny of whales supported by total evidence. *J. Mol. Evol.* **44**(Suppl. 1): S117–S120.

Heyning, J. E. (1989). Comparative facial anatomy of beaked whales (Ziiphidae) and a systematic revision among the families of extant Odontoceti. *Nat. Hist. Mus. Los Angeles Cty., Contrib. Sci.* **405**.

Heyning, J. E. (1990). Comparative facial anatomy of beaked whales (Ziphiidae) and systematic revision among the family of extant Odontoceti. *Nat. Hist. Mus. Los Angeles Cty., Contrib. Sci.* **405**: 1–64.

Heyning, J. E. (1997). Sperm whale phylogeny revisited: Analysis of the morphological evidence. *Mar. Mamm. Sci.* **13**(4): 596–613.

Heyning, J. E., and J. Mead (1990). Evolution of the nasal anatomy of cetaceans. *In* "Sensory Abilities of Cetaceans" (J. Thomas and R. Kastelain, eds.), pp. 67–79. Plenum Press, New York.

Hirota, K., and L. G. Barnes (1995). A new species of middle Miocene sperm whale of the genus *Scaldicetus* (Cetacea; Physeteridae) from Shiga-mura, Japan. *Island Arc* **3**: 453–472.

Honeycutt, R. L., and R. M. Adkins (1993). Higher level systematics of eutherian mammals: An assessment of molecular characters and phylogenetic hypotheses. *Ann. Rev. Ecol. Syst.* **24**: 279–305.

Hulbert, R. C., Jr., R. M. Petkewich, G. A. Bishop, D. Bukry, and D. P. Aleshire (1998). A new middle Eocene protocetid whale (Mammalia: Cetacea: Archaeoceti) and associated biota from Georgia. *J. of Paleontol.* **72**: 907–927.

Ichishima, H., L. G. Barnes, R. E. Fordyce, M. Kimura, and D. J. Bohaska (1995). A review of kentriodontine dolphins (Cetacea; Delphinoidea; Kentriodontidae): Systematics and biogeography. *Island Arc* **3**: 486–492.

Irwin, D. M., T. D. Kocher, and A. C. Wilson (1991). Evolution of the cytochrome b gene of mammals. *J. Mol. Evol.* **32**: 128–144.

Jefferson, T. A., S. Leatherwood, and M. A. Weber (1993). "FAO Species Identification Guide: Marine Mammals of the World." Food and Agriculture Organization, Rome.

Kasuya, T. (1973). Systematic consideration of recent toothed whales based on the morphology of tympano-periotic bone. *Sci. Rep. Whales Res. Inst.* **25**: 1–103.

Kellogg, R. (1936). A review of the Archaeoceti. *Carnegie Inst. Wash. Publ.* **482**: 1–366.

Klima, M. (1995). Cetacean phylogeny and systematics based on the morphogenesis of the nasal skull. *Aqua. Mamm.* **21**(2): 79–89.

Kumar, K., and A. Sahni (1986). *Remingtonocetus harudiensis,* new combination, a middle Eocene archaeocete (Mammalia: Cetacea) from western Kutch, India. *J. Verteb. Paleontol.* **6**(4): 326–349.

Lancaster, W. C. (1990). The middle ear of Archaeoceti. *J. Verteb. Paleontol.* **10**: 117–127.

Leatherwood, S., and R. R. Reeves (1983). "The Sierra Club Handbook of Whales and Dolphins." Sierra Club Books, San Francisco.

Luckett, N. P., and N. Hong (1998). Phylogenetic relationships between the orders Artiodactyla and Cetacea: A combined assessment of morphological and molecular evidence. *Journal of Mammalian Evolution* **5**(2): 127–182.

Luo, Z (1998). Homology and transformation of cetacean ectotympanic structures. *In* "The Emergence of Whales: Patterns in the Origin of Cetacea" (J. G. M. Thewissen, Ed.), pp. 269–301. Plenum Press, New York.

MacFadden, B. J. (1992). Fossil Horses: Systematics, Paleobiology and Evolution of the Family Equidae. Cambridge Univ. Press, Port Chester, NY.

McLeod, S. A., F. C. Whitmore, and L. G. Barnes (1993). Evolutionary relationships and classification. *In* "The Bowhead Whale" (J. J. Burns, J. J. Montague, and C. J. Cowles, eds.), Spec. Publ. No. 2, pp. 45–70. Soc. Mar. Mammal.

Mead, J. (1975a). Anatomy of the external nasal passages and facial complex in the Delphinidae (Mammalia: Cetacea). *Smithson. Contrib. Zool.* **207**: 1–72.

Mead, J. (1975b). A fossil beaked whale (Cetacea: Ziphiidae) from the Miocene of Kenya. *J. Paleontol.* **49**: 745–751.

Mead, J., and R. Brownell (1993). Order Cetacea. *In* "Mammal Species of the World: A taxonomic and geographic reference" (D. E. Wilson and D. M. Reeder, eds.), pp. 349–364. Smithsonian Inst. Press, WDC.

Messenger, S. L. (1994). Phylogenetic relationship of platanistoid river dolphins (Odontoceti, Cetacea): assessing the significance of fossil taxa. *Proc. San Diego Soc. Nat. Hist.* **29**: 125–133.

Messenger, S. L. (1995). Phylogenetic systematics of cetaceans: A morphological perspective. Unpublished MS Thesis, San Diego State University, San Diego, CA.

Messenger, S. L., and J. McGuire (1998). Morphology, molecules and the phylogenetics of cetaceans. *Syst. Biol.* **47**(1): 90–124.

Milinkovitch, M. C. (1995). Molecular phylogeny of cetaceans prompts revision of morphological transformations. *Trends Ecol. Evol.* **10**(8): 328–334.

Milinkovitch, M. C., and J. G. M. Thewissen (1997). Even-toed fingerprints on whale ancestry. *Nature* **388**: 622–623.

Milinkovitch, M. C., G. Orti, and A. Meyer (1993). Revised phylogeny of whales suggested by mitochondrial ribosomal DNA sequences. *Nature* **361**: 346–348.

Milinkovitch, M. C., G. Orti, and A. Meyer (1994). Phylogeny of all major groups of cetaceans based on DNA sequences from three mitochondrial genes. *Mol. Biol. Evol.* **11**: 939–948.

Milinkovitch, M. C., G. Orti, and A. Meyer (1995). Novel phylogeny of whales revisited but not revised. *Mol. Biol. Evol.* **12**(3): 518–520.

Milinkovitch, M. C., R. G. Le Duc, J. Adachi, F. Farnir, M. Georges, and M. Hasegawa (1996). Effects of character weighting and species sampling on phylogeny reconstruction: A case study based on DNA sequence data in cetaceans. *Genetics* **144**: 1817–1883.

Miller, G. S. (1923). The telescoping of the cetacean skull. *Smithson. Misc. Collec.* **76**: 1–71.

Mitchell, E. D. (1989). A new cetacean from the late Eocene La Meseta Formation, Seymour Island, Antarctic Peninsula. *Can. J. Aquat. Sci.* **46**: 2219–2235.

Morgan, G. (1994). Miocene and Pliocene marine mammal faunas from the Bone Valley Formation of central Florida. *Proc. San Diego Soc. Nat. Hist.* **29**: 239–268.

Muizon, C. de (1981). "Les Vértebrés Fossiles de la Formation Pisco (Pérou). Part 1. Recherche sur les Grandes Civilisations," Mém. No. 6. Institut Français d'Études Andines, Paris.

Muizon, C. de (1983). *Pliopontes littoralis* un nouveau Platanistidae Cetacea du Pliocéne de la côte péruvienne. *C. R. Seances Acad. Sci. Ser. 2* **296**: 1101–1104.

Muizon, C. de (1987). "The Affinities of *Notocetus vanbenedeni,* an Early Miocene Platanistoid (Cetacea, Mammalia) du Pliocene Inférieur de Sud-Sacaco," Mém. No. 50. Institut Français d'Études Andines, Paris.

Muizon, C. de (1988a). "Les Vértebrés Fossiles de la Formation Pisco (Pérou). Part 3. Recherche sur les Grandes Civilisations," Mém. No. 78. Institut Français d'Études Andines, Paris.

Muizon, C. de (1988b). Le polyphylétisme des Acrodelphidae, Odontocètes longirostres du Miocène européen. *Bull. Mus. Nat. Hist. Nat.* [4] **10**(1): 31–88.

Muizon, C. de (1988c). Les relations phylogénétiques des Delphinida (Cetacea, Mammalia). *Ann. Paleonto. (Vértebr.-Invértebr.)* **74**(4): 159–257.

Muizon, C. de (1991). A new Ziphiidae from the early Miocene of Washington State (USA) and phylogenetic analysis of the major groups of odontocetes. *Bull. Mus. Nat. Hist. Nat.* [4] **12C**: 279–326.

Muizon, C. de (1994). Are the squalodontids related to the platanistoids? *Proc. San Diego Soc. Nat. Hist.* **29**: 135–146.

Muizon, C. de (1993). Walrus-feeding adaptation in a new cetacean from the Pliocene of Peru. *Nature* **365**: 745–748.

Novacek, M. J. (1992). Mammalian phylogeny: Shaking the tree. *Nature* **356**: 121–125.

Novacek, M. J. (1993). Genes tell a new whale tale. *Nature* **361**: 298–299.

Oishi, M. and Y. Hasegawa (1995). Diversity of Pliocene mysticetes from eastern Japan, *Island Arc* **3**(4): 493–505.

Perrin, W. F. (1997). Development and homologies of head stripes in the delphinoid cetaceans. *Mar. Mamm. Sci.* **13**(1): 1–43.

Philippi, R. A. (1887). "Die tertiären und quartären Versteinerungen Chiles," Quarto 266. Leipzig.

Prothero, D. (1993). Ungulate phylogeny: molecular vs. morphological evidence. *In* "Mammal Phylogeny: Placentals" (F. S. Szaklay, M. J. Novacek, and M. C. McKenna, eds.), pp. 173–181. Springer-Verlag, New York.

Prothero, D. R., E. M. Manning, and M. Fischer (1988). The phylogeny of ungulates. *In* "The Phylogeny and Classification of the Tetrapods" (M. J. Benton, ed.), Vol. 2, pp. 201–234. Clarendon Press, Oxford.

Ray, J. (1693). "Synopsis methodica animalium quadrupedum et serpentini generis." S. Smith and B. Walford, London.

Rice, D. W. (1998). Marine Mammals of the World, *Special Publications 4, Society of Marine Mammalogy,* Allen Press, Kansas.

Rosel, P. E., M. G. Haygood, and W. F. Perrin (1995). Phylogenetic relationships among the true porpoises (Cetacea: Phocoenidae). *Mol. Phylogenet. Evol.* **4**(4): 463–474.

Russell, D. E., J. G. M. Thewissen, and D. Sigoneau-Russell (1983). A new dichobunid artiodactyl (Mammalia) from the Eocene of North-West Pakistan. Part II. Cranial osteology. *Proc. K. Ned. Acad. Wet., Ser. A* **86**: 285–300.

Russell, L. S. (1968). A new cetacean from the Oligocene Sooke Formation of Vancouver Island, British Columbia. *Can. J. Earth Sci.* **5**: 929–933.

Scott, W. B. (1888). On some new and little known creodonts. *J. Acad. Nat. Sci.* Philadelphia, **9**: 155–185.

Shimamura, M., H. Yasue, K. Ohshima, H. Abe, H. Kato, T. Kishiro, N. Goto, I. Munechika, and N. Okada (1997). Molecular evidence from retroposons that whales form a clade with even-toed ungulates. *Nature* **388**: 666–670.

Slijper, E. J. (1962). Whales. Basic Books, New York.

Szalay, F. (1969). The Hapalodectinae and a phylogeny of the Mesonychidae (Mammalia, Condylarthra). *Am. Mus. Novit.* **2361**: 1–26.

Szalay, F., and Gould, S. J. (1966). Asiatic Mesonychidae (Mammalia, Condylarthra). *Bull. Am. Mus. Nat. Hist.* **132**: 129–173.

Thewissen, J. G. M. (1994). Phylogenetic aspects of cetacean origins: A morphological perspective. *J. Mamm. Evol.* **2**(3): 157–183.

Thewissen, J. G. M. (1998). Cetacean origin: evolutionary turmoil during the invasion of the ocean. *In* "The Emergence of Whales: Patterns in the Origin of Cetacea" (J. G. M. Thewissen, ed.), pp. 451–464. Plenum Press, New York.

Thewissen, J. G. M. (ed.) (1998). "The Emergence of Whales: Patterns in the Origin of Cetacea." Plenum Press, New York.

Thewissen, J. G. M., and S. T. Hussain (1993). Origin of underwater hearing in whales. *Nature* **361**: 444–445.

Thewissen, J. G. M., and S. T. Hussain (1998). Systematic review of the Pakicetidae, early and middle Eocene Cetacea (Mammalia) from Pakistan and India. *Bull. Carnegie Mus. Nat. Hist.* **34**: 220–238.

Thewissen, J. G. M., S. I. Madar, and S. T. Hussain (1998). Whale ankles and evolutionary relationships. *Nature* **395**: 452.

Thewissen, J. G. M., S. T. Hussain, and M. Arif (1994). *Ambulocetus natans,* the walking whale. *Science* **263**: 210–212.

Thewissen, J. G. M., S. I. Madar, and S. T. Hussain (1996). *Ambulocetus natans,* an Eocene cetacean (Mammalia) from Pakistan. *CFS, Cour. Forschungsinst. Senckenberg* **191**: 1–86.

Ting, S., and C. Li (1987). The skull of *Hapalodectes* (? Acreodi, Mammalia), with notes on some Chinese Paleocene mesonychids. *Vertebr. PalAsiat.* **25**: 161–186.

Uhen, M. (1996). Composition and characteristics of the subfamily Dorudontinae (Archaeoceti, Cetacea). Abstracts of the sixth North American Paleontological Convention (Smithsonian Institution, WDC), Paleontological Society, Spec. Publ. 18.

Uhen, M. (1996). *Dorudon atrox* (Mammalia, Cetacea): Form, function, and phylogenetic relationships of an archaeocete from the late middle Eocene of Egypt. Ph.D. Dissertation, University of Michigan, Ann Arbor.

Uhen, M. (1998). Middle to late Eocene basilosaurines and dorudontines. *In* "The Emergence of Whales: Patterns in the Origin of Cetacea" (J. G. M. Thewissen, ed.), pp. 29–61. Plenum Press, New York.

Uhen, M. (1998). New protocetid (Mammalia: Cetacea) from the late middle Eocene Cook Mountain Formation of Louisiana. *Journal of Vertebrate Paleontology* **18**(3): 664–668.

Uhen, M. D. (in press). New species of protocetid archaeocete whale, *Eocetus wardii* (Mammalia: Cetacea), from the middle Eocene of North Carolina. *Journal of Paleontology.*

Van Valen, L. (1966). Deltatheridia, a new order of mammals. *Bull. Am. Mus. Nat. Hist.* **132**: 1–126.

Watkins, W. A., K. E. Moore, and P. Tyack (1985). Investigations of sperm whale acoustic behaviors in the southeast Caribbean. *Cetology* **49**: 1–15.

Watson, L. (1981). Whales of the World. Hutchinson, London.

Williams, E. (1998). Synopsis of the earliest cetaceans. *In* "The Emergence of Whales: Patterns in the Origin of Cetacea" (J. G. M. Thewissen, ed.), pp. 1–28. Plenum Press, New York.

West, R. M. (1981). Geology and paleontology of the Bridger Formation, Southern Green River Basin, Southwestern Wyoming, Part 5. *Harpagolestes macrocephalus* and comments on structure, function, and diversity of middle Eocene to early Oligocene large mesonychids. *Contrib. Biol. Geol., Milwaukee Publ. Mus.* **43**: 1–17.

Xu, X., A. Janke, and U. Árnason (1996). The complete mitochondrial DNA sequence of the Greater Indian Rhinoceros, *Rhinoceros unicornis,* and the phylogenetic relationship among Carnivora, Perissodactyla, and Artiodactyla (+Cetacea). *Mol. Biol. Evol.* **13**(9): 1167–1173.

Zhou K., W. Qian, and Y. Li (1979). The osteology and systematic of the baji, *Lipotes vexillifer. Acta Zool. Sin.* **25**: 58–74.

Zhou K., M. Zhou, and Z. Zhao (1984). First discovery of a Tertiary platanistoid fossil from Asia. *Sci. Rep. Whales Res. Inst.* **35**: 173–181.

Zimmer, C. (1998). "At the Water's Edge: Macroevolution and the Transformation of Life." Free Press/Simon and Schuster, New York.

5

Sirenians and Other Marine Mammals: Evolution and Systematics

5.1. Introduction

The mammalian order Sirenia, or sea cows, includes two extant families, the Trichechidae (manatees) and the Dugongidae (the dugong). The name Sirenia comes from mermaids of Greek mythology known as sirens. Sirenians have a fossil record extending from the early Eocene (50 Ma) to the present (Fig. 5.1). Manatees include three living species and are known from the early Miocene (15 Ma) to the Recent in the New World tropics. The dugong is represented by a single extant species, *Dugong dugon,* of the Indopacific. Dugongs were considerably more diverse in the past, with 13 extinct genera described and a fossil record that extends back to the Eocene. A North Pacific lineage of dugongids survived into historic times and had successfully adapted to cold climates. Sirenians are unique among living marine mammals in having a strictly herbivorous diet which is reflected in the morphology of their teeth and digestive system.

The Desmostylia, the only extinct order of marine mammals, are relatives of sirenians and are discussed here, as is the extinct marine bear-like carnivoran, *Kolponomos*. Other marine mammals include members of two extant carnivore families, the Mustelidae (which includes the sea otter, *Enhydra lutris*), the Ursidae (containing the polar bear, *Ursus maritimus*), and the extinct sloth family Megalonychidae (which includes the aquatic sloth *Thalassocnus natans*).

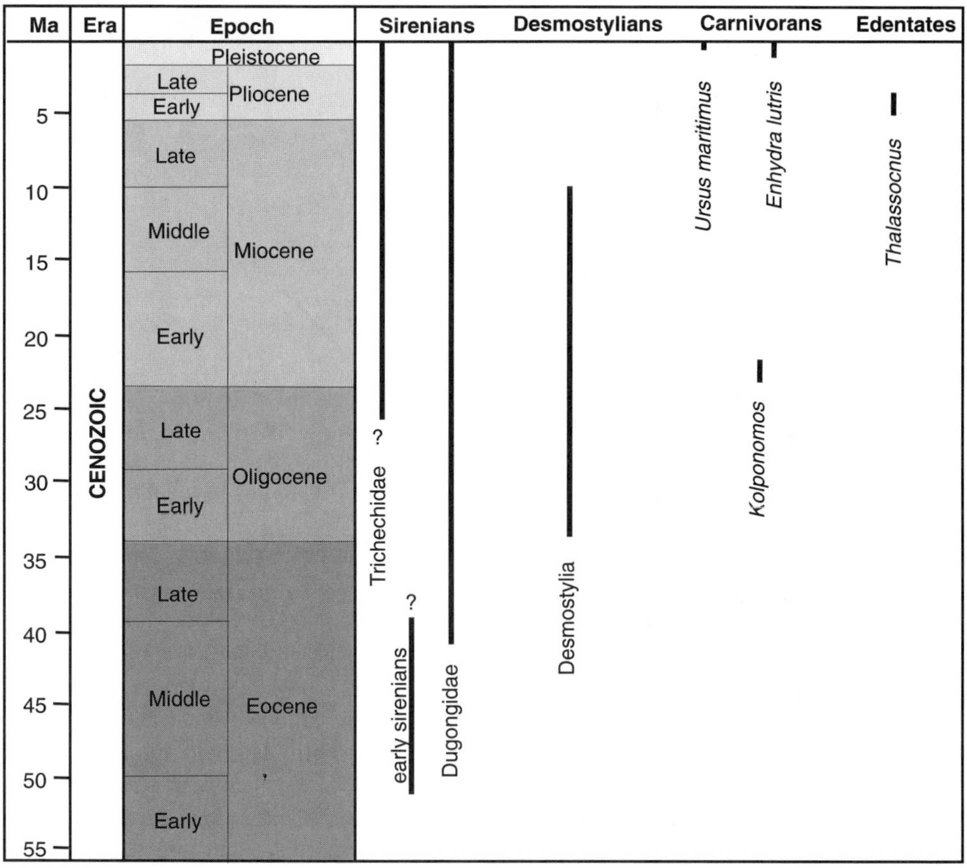

Figure 5.1. Chronologic ranges of living and extinct sirenians and other marine mammals. Ma=million years ago.

5.2. Origin and Evolution of Sirenians

5.2.1. Sirenians Defined

Sirenians possess relatively large stout bodies, downturned snouts, short paddle-like rounded flippers, and a horizontal tail fluke. Manatees can be readily distinguished from dugongs by their smaller size, a rounded rather than notched tail, and a less-pronounced deflection of the snout. The latter feature enables manatees to feed at any level in the water column rather than being obligate bottom feeders, like the dugong with its strongly downturned snout.

The monophyly of sirenians is well established. Sirenians are united by possession of the following synapomorphies (Domning, 1994; Figs. 5.2, 5.3):

1. *External nares retracted and enlarged, reaching to or beyond the level of the anterior margin of the orbit*—In the primitive condition, the external nares (nostrils) are not retracted.
2. *Premaxilla contacts frontal*—All sirenians are characterized by a premaxilla-frontal contact. In the primitive condition, the premaxilla does not contact the frontal; instead it contacts the nasal posteriorly.

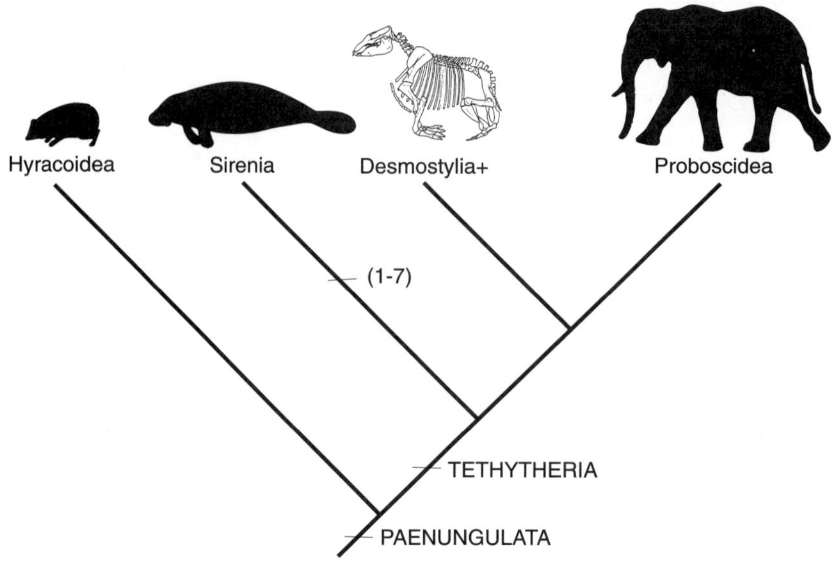

Figure 5.2. A cladogram depicting the relationship of sirenians and their close relatives. Numbers refer to sirenian synapomorphies, several of which are illustrated in Fig. 5.3. +=extinct taxa.

3. *Sagittal crest absent*—The skull of sirenians can be distinguished from other closely related mammals in lacking development of a sagittal crest.

4. *Five premolars, or secondarily reduced from this condition by loss of anterior premolars*—Early sirenians possess five premolars as did ancestral placental mammals (Archibald, 1996). This tendency was later reversed by post-Eocene sirenians, which often reduce the number of premolars. Ungulates show the primitive condition, possession of four premolars (Thewissen and Domning, 1992).

5. *Mastoid inflated and exposed through occipital fenestra*—In sirenians, the mastoid is inflated and fills a large fenestra (window-like opening) in the dorsal occiput. It does not extend around the base of the cranium to form a flange on the ventral occiput (Novacek and Wyss, 1987). In the primitive condition seen in most mammals, there is continuous mastoid exposure between the horizontal basicranium and ventral (vertical) occiput.

6. *Ectotympanic inflated and drop-like*—Sirenians are distinguished by having an inflated ectotympanic (one of the bones forming the auditory bulla) that is drop-like in shape. In the primitive condition, the ectotympanic is uninflated (Tassy and Shoshani, 1988).

7. *Pachyostosis and osteosclerosis present in skeleton*—The skeleton of sirenians displays both pachyostosis and osteosclerosis, modifications involved in hydrostatic regulation (Domning and de Buffrénil, 1991).

5.2.2. Sirenian Affinities

Proboscideans (elephants) are usually considered the closest living relatives of sirenians (e.g., McKenna, 1975; Thewissen and Domning, 1992; Domning *et al.,* 1986). Characters which unite proboscideans and sirenians include rostral displacement of the orbits with associated reorganization of the antorbital region, strongly laterally-flared zygomatic process of the squamosal, and incipiently bilophodont (double crested) teeth (Savage *et al.,* 1994). Sirenians, proboscideans, and the extinct desmostylians are recognized as a monophyletic

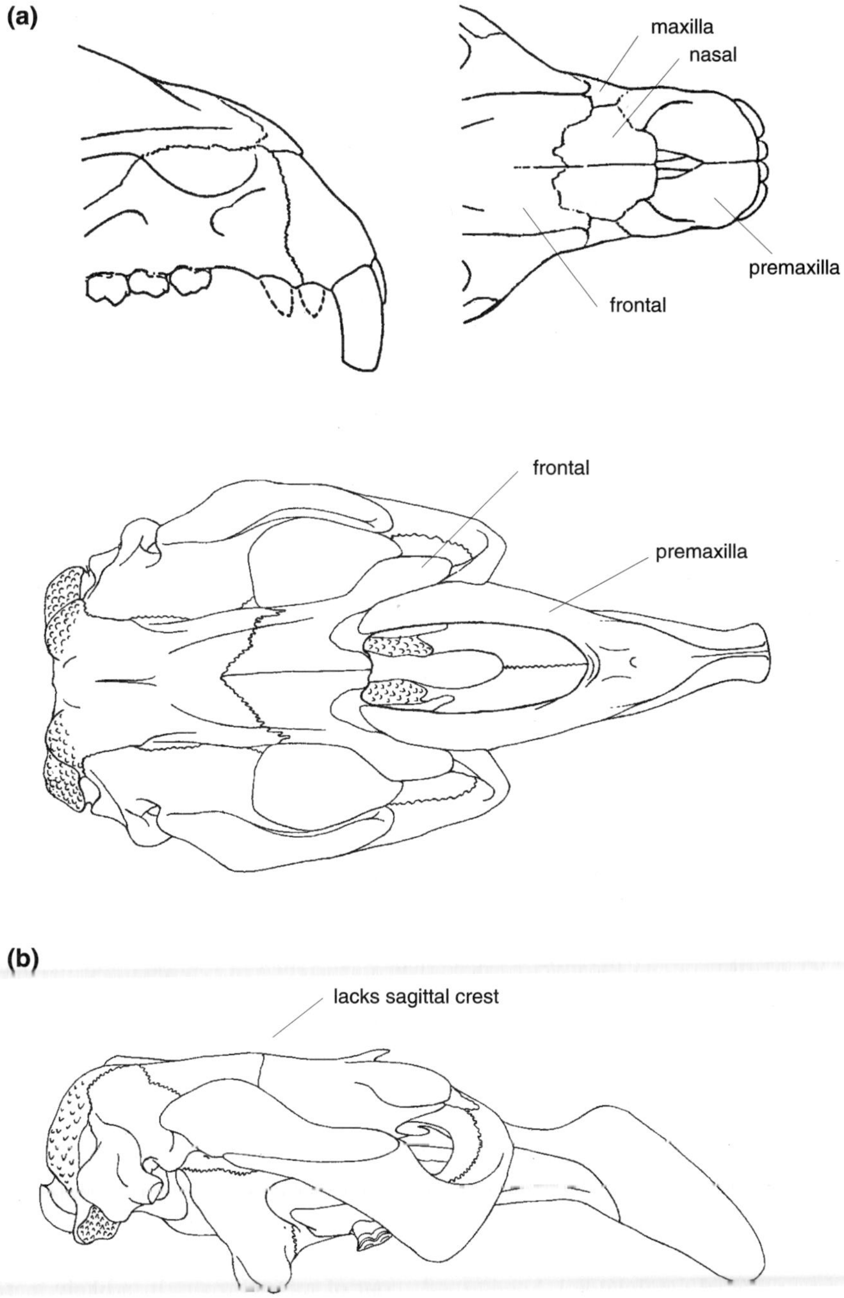

Figure 5.3. Sirenian synapomorphies. (a) Snout of archaic elephant, *Moeritherium,* in dorsal and lateral views illustrating the lack of contact between the premaxilla and the nasals (primitive condition of character 2) (see text for further description) (modified from Tassy and Shoshani, 1988), and (b) Skull of the sirenian *Dusisiren,* in dorsal and lateral views illustrating the derived condition of character 2, premaxilla lies in contact with nasals (modified from Domning, 1978). Also visible are other sirenian synapomorphies, character: 1=external nares retracted and enlarged, reaching to or beyond the anterior margin of the orbit and 3=sagittal crest absent.

clade, termed the **Tethytheria** (named because early members were thought to have inhabited the shores of the ancient Tethys Sea; McKenna, 1975; Fig. 5.2). The phylogenetic relationships within tethytheres are not yet resolved (Thewissen and Domning, 1992). Morphological characters supporting an alliance between tethytheres, the perissodactyls (horses, rhinos, and tapirs), and the hyracoids (hyraxes), referred to as the Pantomesaxonia clade (Prothero *et al.,* 1988), have been refuted (Savage *et al.,* 1994). Molecular data (Lavergne *et al.,* 1996) remove perissodactyls from a relationship with tethytheres and hyracoids.

Recognition of another clade, the Paenungulata, composed of the Tethytheria and hyracoids (Novacek *et al.,* 1988; Shoshani, 1993), is more controversial. Fischer (1986, 1989; Prothero, 1993) maintained that morphological features supporting the Paenungulata can be disallowed as shared primitive characters and therefore are not indicative of relationship. These workers have argued for a closer relationship between hyracoids and perissodactyls. Molecular sequence data, however, strongly support the Paenungulata clade (sirenians, proboscideans, and hyracoids; Springer and Kirsch, 1993; Lavergne *et al.,* 1996).

Several assessments of sirenian phylogeny using molecular data have been made. The study by Rainey *et al.* (1984) based on immunological comparisons among the living sirenians as well as Steller's sea cow and the Indian and African elephants agreed topologically with the morphologic data. However, the inferred ages for major branch points on the cladogram are inconsistent with fossil data (Domning, 1994). Results of a similar study based on mitochondrial cytochrome b sequence data were reported by Ozawa *et al.* (1997), although relationships among the three sirenian lineages (manatees, dugong, and Steller's sea cow) were not well resolved. The data suggested that the sea cow–dugong divergence was likely as ancient as the dugong–manatee split, a conclusion not contradicted by fossil data (Domning, 1994).

5.2.3. Evolution of Early Sirenians

The earliest known sirenian is *Prorastomus sirenoides* from early and middle Eocene age rocks (50 Ma) of Jamaica (Fig. 5.4). *Prorastomus* occupies a basal position close to the ancestry of all other sirenians (Fig. 5.5). The dense and swollen ribs of prorastomids point to at least a partially aquatic lifestyle, as does their occurrence in marine deposits. The hip joint and pelvic bones of these animals indicate that the most primitive known sirenians possessed a functional hind limb.

The presence of well-developed hip and knee articulations in another middle Eocene sirenian, *Protosiren smithae,* described from the middle Eocene of Fayum, Egypt, indicates that this animal was capable of terrestrial locomotion, as was probably the case for earlier diverging sirenians (e.g. *Prorastomus sirenoides;* Domning and Gingerich, 1994). Study of the type skull of *Protosiren fraasi* using CAT scans (Gingerich *et al.,* 1994) reveals small olfactory bulbs, small optic tracts, and large maxillary nerves, consistent with the diminished importance of olfaction and vision in an aquatic environment and consistent with enhanced tactile sensitivity of the enlarged downturned snout of most Sirenia. It is likely that *Prorastomus* and *Protosiren* were amphibious quadrupeds and not as fully aquatic as most later sirenians. The peculiar forceps-like snouts of *Prorastomus* and other early sea cows suggests a selective browsing habit by analogy with extant narrow-muzzled ungulates. Additional morphologic, ecologic, and **taphonomic** data support consideration of prorastomids as fluvatile (river) or estuarine semiaquatic herbivores (Savage *et al.,* 1994). Middle and late Eocene dugongids in need of taxonomic revision include *Eotheroides* and *Eosiren* from Egypt and *Prototherium* from Italy.

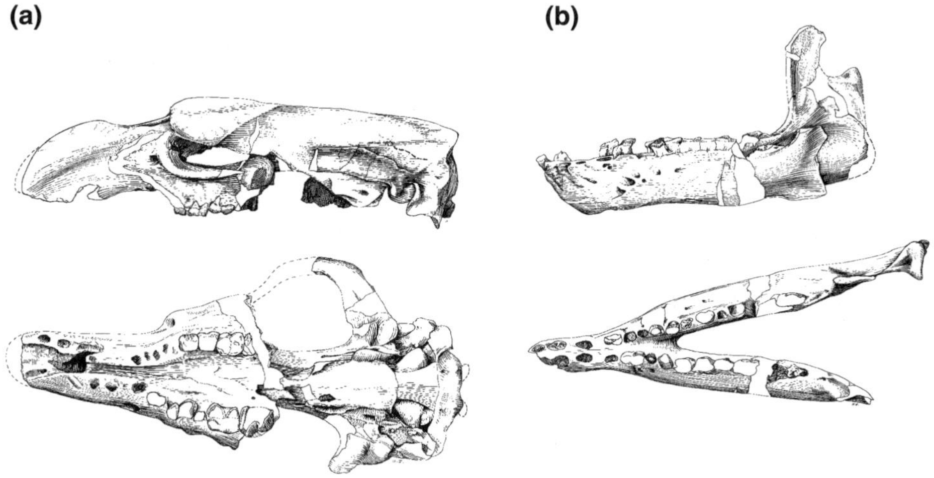

Figure 5.4. An early sirenian, *Prorastomus sirenoides,* from the late early Eocene of Jamaica. (a) Skull in lateral and ventral views and (b) Mandible in lateral and dorsal views. Original 27 cm long. From Savage *et al.,* 1994.

5.2.4. Modern Sirenians

5.2.4.1. Family Trichechidae

Some scientists as recently as the nineteenth century considered the manatee to be an unusual tropical form of walrus; in fact the walrus was once placed in the genus *Trichechus* along with the manatees (Reynolds and Odell, 1991). The family Trichechidae was

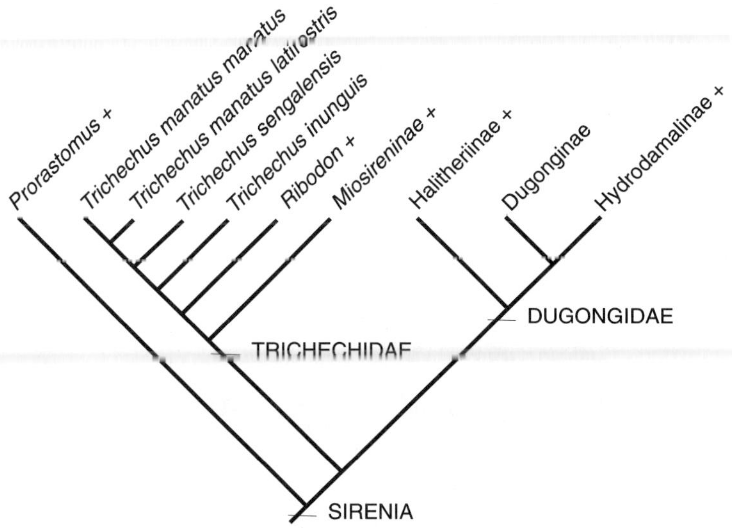

Figure 5.5. Relationships among sirenians based on morphologic data (modified from Domning, 1994). +=extinct taxa.

expanded by Domning (1994) to include not only the manatees (Trichechinae) but also the Miosireninae, a northern European clade composed of two genera, *Anomotherium* and *Miosiren.* The trichechid clade as a whole appears to have been derived from late Eocene or early Oligocene dugongids. The subfamily Trichechinae includes three living species: the West Indian manatee (*Trichechus manatus*), the West African manatee (*Trichechus senegalensis*), and the Amazon manatee (*Trichechus inunguis;* Fig. 5.6). Two subspecies of the West Indian manatee can be distinguished on the basis of morphology and geography, the Antillean manatee, *T. m. manatus,* and the Florida manatee, *T. m. latirostris* (Domning and Hayek, 1986). Manatees are united as a monophyletic clade by features of the skull (e.g. ear region). Other derived characters include reduction of neural spines on the vertebrae, a possible tendency toward enlargement, and, at least in *Trichechus,* anteroposterior elongation of thoracic vertebral centra (Domning, 1994).

According to Domning (1982), the West African manatee and the West Indian manatee share a more recent common ancestor than either does with the Amazon manatee, *Trichechus inunguis.*

5.2.4.2. Family Dugongidae

The Family Dugongidae is paraphyletic as defined by Domning (1994). It includes two monophyletic subfamilies, the Dugonginae and extinct Hydrodamalinae, and the paraphyletic extinct "Halitheriinae."

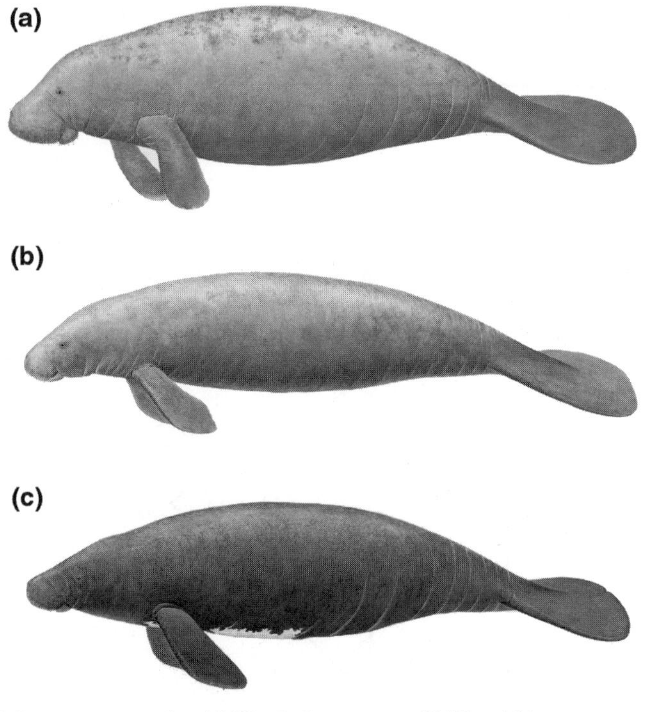

Figure 5.6. Modern manatee species. (a) West Indian manatee, (b) West African manatee, and (c) Amazon manatee (Illustrated by P. Folkens from Reeves *et al.,* 1992).

The "Halitheriinae" includes the paraphyletic genera *Halitherium, Eotheroides, Prototherium, Eosiren, Caribosiren,* and *Metaxytherium.* The best known genus, *Metaxytherium,* was widely distributed in both the Old and New Worlds during the Miocene. *Metaxytherium* had a strongly downturned snout and small upper incisor tusks and members of this lineage were most likely generalized bottom-feeding animals, probably consuming rhizomes (root-like stems) of small to moderate sized sea grasses and sea grass leaves (Domning and Furusawa, 1995). A New World origin for the genus is suggested, specifically in the Caribbean and West Atlantic, with subsequent dispersal to the North Pacific via the Central American Seaway and later dispersal to coastal Peru.

The extinct Hydrodamalinae includes the paraphyletic genus *Dusisiren* and the lineage that led to the recently extinct Steller's sea cow, *Hydrodamalis gigas.* (Fig. 5.7). *Dusisiren* evolved a very large body size, decreased snout deflection, and the loss of tusks, suggesting that these animals may have fed on kelp which grows higher in the water column than do sea grasses (Domning and Furusawa, 1995). Steller's sea cow, named for its discoverer,

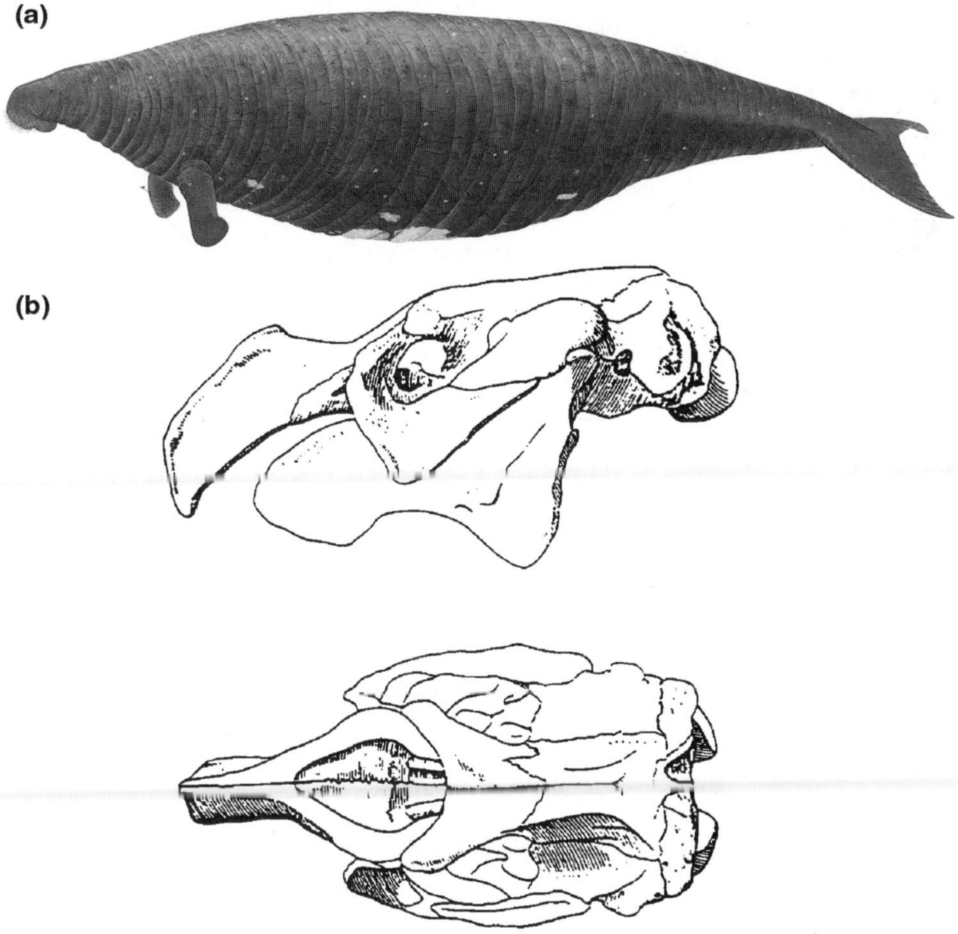

Figure 5.7. Steller's sea cow. (a) Left side of the body (Illustrated by P. Folkens from Reeves *et al.,* 1992), (b) Lateral and dorsal views of the skull and mandible (after Heptner, 1974).

Georg W. Steller, a German naturalist, was a gigantic animal. It measured at least 7.6 m in length and was estimated to weigh between 4 and 10 tons. The sea cow was unusual in lacking teeth and finger bones and in possessing a thick, bark-like skin. Steller's sea cow lived in cold waters near islands in the Bering Sea, in contrast to the distribution of other sirenians in tropical or subtropical waters, and in prehistoric times from Japan to Baja California. The ancestry of this animal involves *Metaxytherium* and *Dusisiren jordani* from the Miocene of California. *Dusisiren dewana,* described from 9 Ma rocks in Japan, makes a good structural intermediate between *Dusisiren jordani* and Steller's sea cow in showing a reduction of teeth and finger bones. A penultimate stage in the evolution of Steller's sea cow is represented by *Hydrodamalis cuestae* from 3 to 8 Ma deposits in California. *Hydrodamalis cuestae* lacked teeth, probably lacked finger bones, and was very large.

Steller unfortunately described the sea cow's blubber, 3–4 inches thick, as tasting something like almond oil. Steller's sea cow quickly became a major food resource for Russian hunters. By 1768, only 27 years after its discovery, the sea cow was extinct. Anderson (1995) proposed that the extinction of sea cows may also have been contributed to by a combination of predation, competition, and decline in food supplies that occurred when aboriginal human populations colonized mainland coastlines and islands along the North Pacific (further discussed in Chapter 11).

The subfamily to which the modern dugong belongs, the Dugonginae, includes in addition to *Dugong* the following extinct genera: *Bharatisiren, Corystosiren, Crenatosiren, Dioplotherium, Rytiodus,* and *Xenosiren.* Fossil remains of this dugongid clade have been found from 15 Ma rocks in the Mediterranean, western Europe, southeastern U.S., Caribbean, Indian Ocean, South America, and the North Pacific. The most elaborate development of tusks in the Sirenia are found in later diverging dugongines such as *Rytiodus, Corystosiren, Xenosiren,* and *Dioplotherium.* These species possessed enlarged, blade-like, self-sharpening tusks that may have been used to dig up sea grasses (Fig. 5.8). The modern

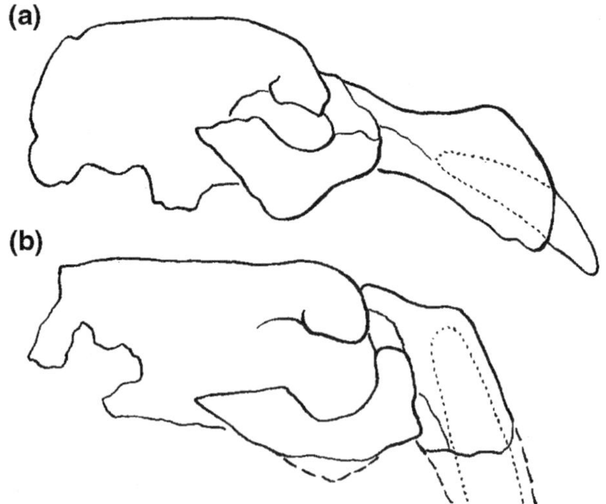

Figure 5.8. Members of the dugong lineage illustrating differential development of the tusks. (a) *Dioplotherium manigaulti,* and (b) *Rytiodus* sp. From Domning, 1994.

dugong may have evolved large tusks for a similar reason, but now appears to use them chiefly for social interactions. The discovery of a fossil dugongine in the Indian Ocean (Bajpai and Domning, 1997) was not unexpected given the presence of living *Dugong* in that region today and it corroborates Domning's earlier (1994) suggestion that the discovery of additional fossils from that region would lend support for an Indo-Pacific origin for the genus.

The modern dugong, *Dugong dugon* (Fig. 5.9), is distinguished by the following derived characters (Domning, 1994): nasals absent, constant presence in juveniles of a deciduous first incisor, frequent presence in adults of vestigial lower incisors, sexual dimorphism in size and eruption of permanent tusks (first incisor), and functional loss of enamel crowns on cheekteeth and persistently open roots of M2-3 and m2-3.

5.3. The Extinct Sirenian Relatives—Desmostylia

5.3.1. Origin and Evolution

First described on the basis of tooth fragments, the Desmostylia bear a name derived from the bundled columnar shape of the cusps of the molar teeth in some taxa (Fig. 5.10). These biazrre animals constitute the only extinct order of marine mammals. They were confined

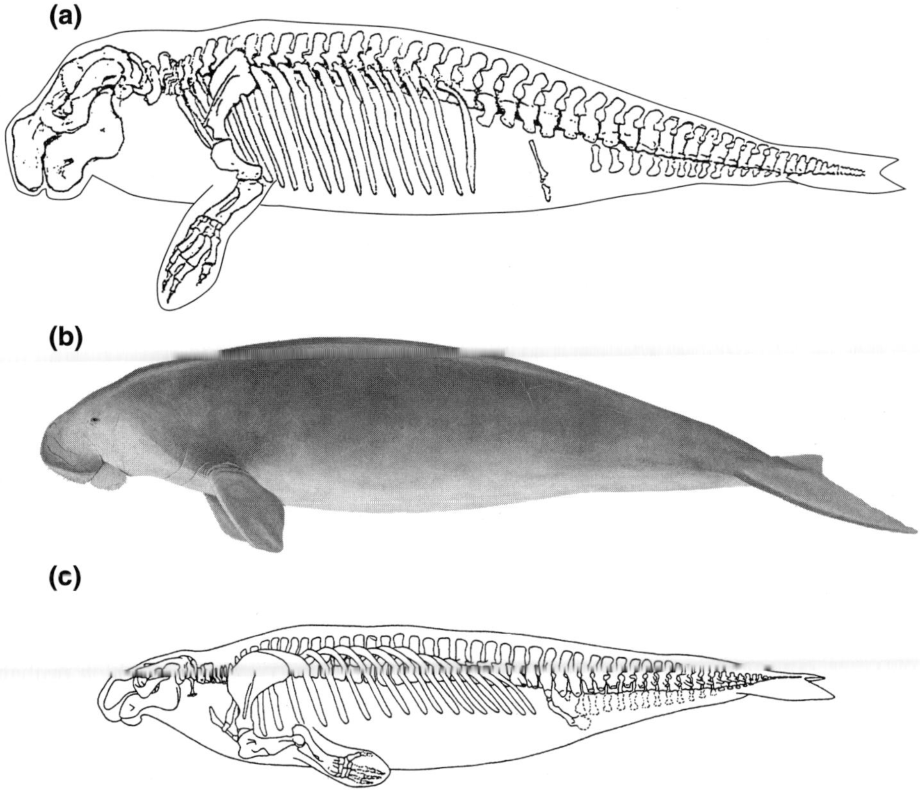

Figure 5.9. Lateral view of skeleton of modern dugong and its fossil relative (a) *Dugong dugon* (modified from Kingdon, 1971) (b) Left side of body (illustrated by P. Folkens from Reeves *et al.*, 1992.), and (c) *Dusisiren jordani* from the late Miocene-early Pliocene of California (from Domning, 1978).

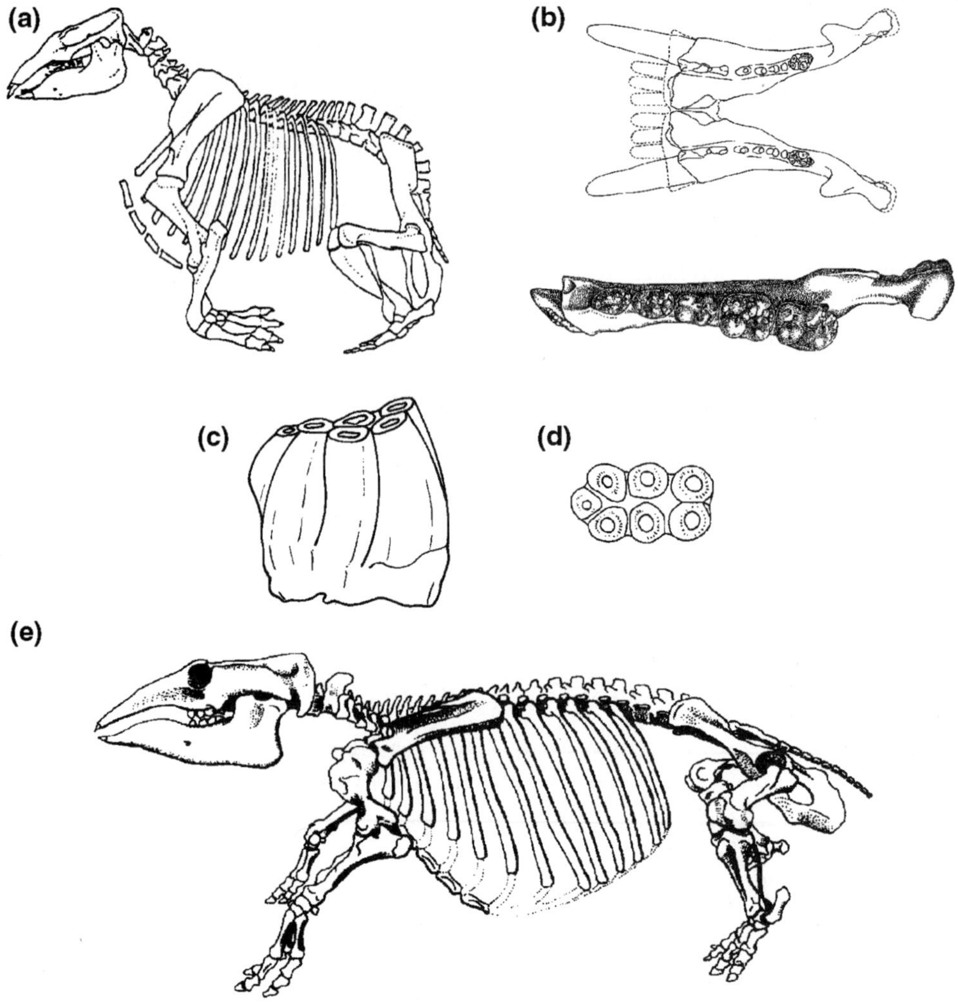

Figure 5.10. Representative desmostylians. (a) Skeleton of *Paleoparadoxia* after Repenning, 1965, (b) Lower jaw of *Behemetops* in occlusal aspect from Domning *et al.,* 1986, (c,d) Lower molar of *Desmostylus* in lateral and occlusal aspect (modified from Vanderhoof, 1937), (e) Restored skeleton of *Desmostylus* from Inuzuka *et al.,* 1995 (see text for discussion of controversial posture).

to the North Pacific area (Japan, Kamchatka, and North America) during the late Oligocene and middle Miocene epochs (approximately 33–10 Ma). Known fossils represent at least six genera and 10 species, all hippopotamus-like amphibious quadrupeds which probably fed on marine algae and sea grasses in subtropical to cool-temperate waters (Fig. 5.10; Inuzuka *et al.,* 1995; Barnes *et al.,* 1985).

Basal desmostylians are represented by *Behemotops* from the middle or late Oligocene of North America and Japan (Domning *et al.,* 1986; Ray *et al.,* 1994). *Cornwallius,* a later diverging genus, is known from several eastern North Pacific late Oligocene localities. *Paleoparadoxia* is a Miocene genus known on both sides of the Pacific. Sexual dimorphism in this species is suggested based on cranial and dental differences (Hasegawa *et al.,* 1995). A skeleton with skull from Point Arena, California was described as a new species, *Paleoparadoxia weltoni* (see Clark, 1991). Another new species of *Paleoparadoxia* has been reported from southern California and Mexico (Barnes and Aranda-Manteca, 1997). *Desmostylus,* the most specialized and best represented genus of the order, is found widely in Miocene coastal deposits of the North Pacific.

A phylogenetic analysis of desmostylians strongly supports a clade comprising *Desmostylus, Cornwallius, Paleoparadoxia,* and *Behemotops* as consecutive sister taxa (Clark, 1991; Ray *et al.,* 1994; Fig. 5.11). Synapomorphies that unite desmostylians include lower incisors transversely aligned, enlarged passage present through squamosal from external auditory meatus to roof of skull, roots of the lower first premolar fused, and paroccipital process elongated. Desmostylians are most closely related to proboscideans (elephants) on the basis of several characters of the lower molars and ear region, with sirenians forming the next closest sister group (Ray *et al.,* 1994).

Reconstructions of the skeleton and inferred locomotion of desmostylians have been controversial (e.g. Inuzuka, 1982, 1984, 1985; Halstead, 1985). In Inuzuka *et al.*'s (1995) proposed reconstruction, desmostylians had a digitigrade posture with an extended wrist, the front toes pointing anteriorly and laterally and the hind toes pointing forward. According to Inuzuka *et al.* (1995), desmostylians had feet positioned well away from a very low center of gravity, a posture that sacrificed mobility for stability which would be advantageous in nearshore marine habitats. Locomotion in the water probably resembled that of polar bears, with the forelimbs providing the principal means of propulsion and the hind limbs used for steering (Inuzuka *et al.,* 1995). The dental morphology is varied, and later diverging species show an adaptation for an abrasive diet, probably one that contained grit mixed with plant material scooped from the sea bottom or shore.

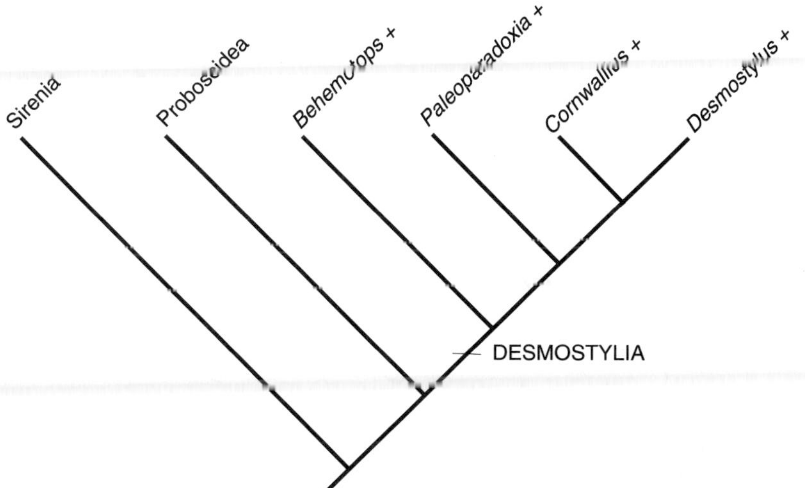

Figure 5.11. Relationships among desmostylians and related taxa (modified from Ray *et al.,* 1994). +=extinct taxa.

5.4. The Extinct Marine Bear-Like Carnivoran, *Kolponomos*

5.4.1. Origin and Evolution

The large extinct carnivoran species *Kolponomos clallamensis* was originally described on the basis of an essentially toothless, incompletely preserved snout of middle Miocene age from Clallam Bay, Washington. Study of this specimen together with new material from coastal Oregon has resulted in the description of a second species, *K. newportensis* (Fig. 5.12; Tedford *et al.,* 1994). *Kolponomos* had a massive skull with a markedly downturned snout and broad, crushing teeth.

The relationship of *Kolponomos* to other carnivores has been problematic. Originally this genus was questionably assigned to the Procyonidae, a family of terrestrial carnivores that includes raccoons and their allies. Study of additional specimens, including a nearly complete skull and jaw with some postcranial elements, has supported recognition of *Kolponomos* as an ursoid most closely related to members of the extinct paraphyletic family Amphicynodontidae, which includes *Amphicynodon, Pachycynodon, Allocyon,* and *Kolponomos* (Tedford *et al.,* 1994). *Kolponomos* and *Allocyon* are hypothesized as the stem group from which the Pinnipedimorpha arose (Fig. 5.13). Shared derived characters which link *Allocyon, Kolponomos,* and the pinnipedimorphs include details of the skull and teeth (Tedford *et al.,* 1994).

Kolponomos was probably coastal in distribution, because all specimens have been discovered in nearshore marine rocks. The crushing teeth would have been suited to a diet of hard-shelled marine invertebrates. *Kolponomos* probably fed on marine invertebrates living

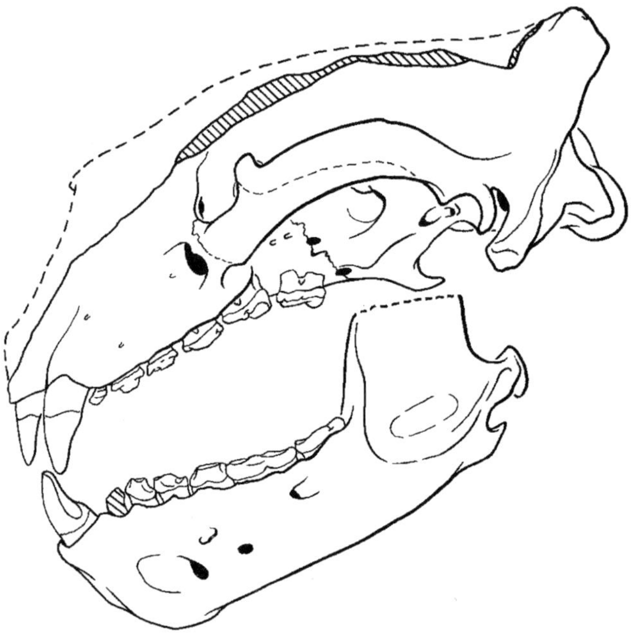

Figure 5.12. Line drawing of the skull and lower jaw of *Kolponomos newportensis* from the early Miocene of Oregon. Original 25 cm. long (From Tedford *et al.,* 1994).

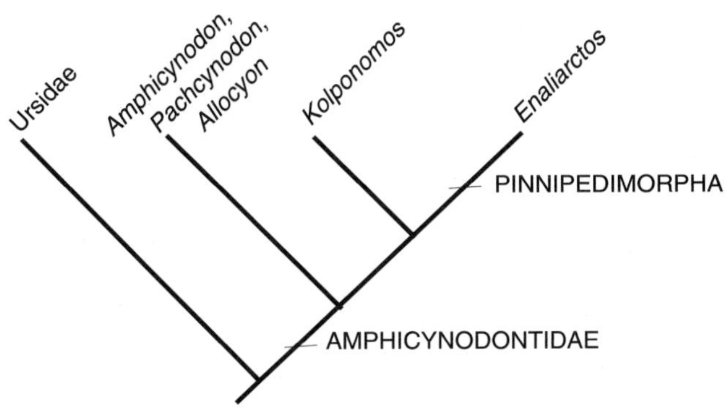

Figure 5.13. Relationships among *Kolponomos* and related taxa (modified from Tedford *et al.,* 1994).

on rocky substrates, prying them off with the incisors and canines, crushing their shells, and consuming the soft parts as sea otters often do. *Kolponomos* represents a unique adaptation for marine carnivores; its mode of living and ecological niche are approached only by the sea otter (Tedford *et al.,* 1994).

5.5. The Extinct Aquatic Sloth, *Thalassocnus natans*

5.5.1. Origin and Evolution

In 1995, an aquatic sloth, *Thalassocnus natans* (Muizon and McDonald, 1995), represented by an abundance of associated complete and partial skeletons, was reported from early Pliocene marine rocks of the southern coast of Peru (Fig. 5.14). *Thalassocnus* is a nothrotheriine ground sloth on the basis of a number of diagnostic cranial, dental, and postcranial features (Muizon and McDonald, 1995; Muizon, 1996).

This discovery adds considerably to our understanding of the range of adaptation of nothrotheriine sloths and indeed, of marine mammals. As previously known these sloths were medium to giant-sized herbivores with terrestrial or arboreal habits. As judged from the paleoenvironment of the locality where these sloths have been recovered and its morphology it is likely that *Thalassocnus* had aquatic or semiaquatic habits and grazed on sea grasses or seaweeds. The tail probably was used for swimming and a ventrally downturned premaxilla expanded at the apex suggests the presence of a well-developed lip for grazing (Muizon and McDonald, 1995; Muizon, 1996).

5.6. The Sea Otter, *Enhydra lutris*

Although sea otters (Fig. 5.15) are the smallest marine mammals, they are the largest members of the Family Mustelidae, which includes 70 species of river otters, skunks, weasels, and badgers, among others. The generic name of the sea otter is from the Greek *enhydris,* for "otter," while the specific epithet is from the Latin *lutra,* for "otter." Three subspecies of sea otter are recognized based on differences in morphology as well as distribution: *Enhydra l. lutris* (Linnaeus, 1758) inhabits the Kuril Islands, the east coast of the Kamchatka

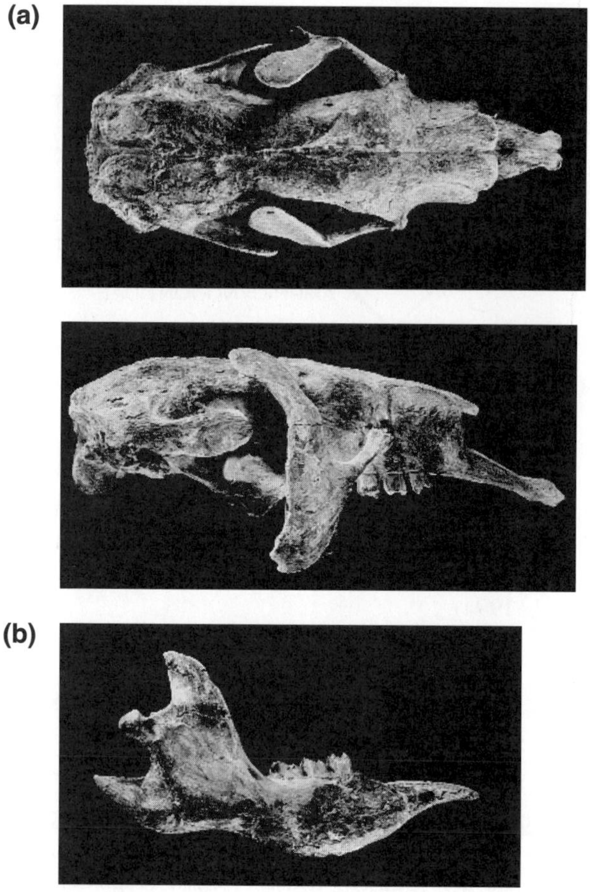

Figure 5.14. Aquatic sloth, *Thalassocnus natans* from the early Pliocene of Peru. (a) Skull in dorsal and lateral view and (b) Lower jaw in lateral view (From Muizon and McDonald, 1995). Courtesy C. de Muizon.

Peninsula, and the Commander Islands; *Enhydra l. kenyoni* (Wilson *et al.,* 1991) ranges from the Aleutian Islands to Oregon; and *Enhydra l. nereis* (Merriam, 1904) ranges from northern California to approximately Punta Abrejos, Baja California.

Based on a cranial morphometric analysis, individuals of *E. l. lutris* are characterized by large wide skulls with short nasal bones. Specimens of *E. l. nereis* have narrow skulls with a long rostrum and small teeth, and usually lack the characteristic notch in the postorbital region found in most specimens of the other two subspecies. Specimens of *E. l. kenyoni* are intermediate to the other two, but do not possess all characters and have longer mandibles than either of the other two subspecies (Wilson *et al.,* 1991).

5.6.1. Origin and Evolution

The modern sea otter *Enhydra* arose in the North Pacific at the beginning of the Pleistocene, about 1 to 3 million years ago, and has not dispersed since this time. There are records of *Enhydra* from the early Pleistocene of Oregon (Leffler, 1964) and California

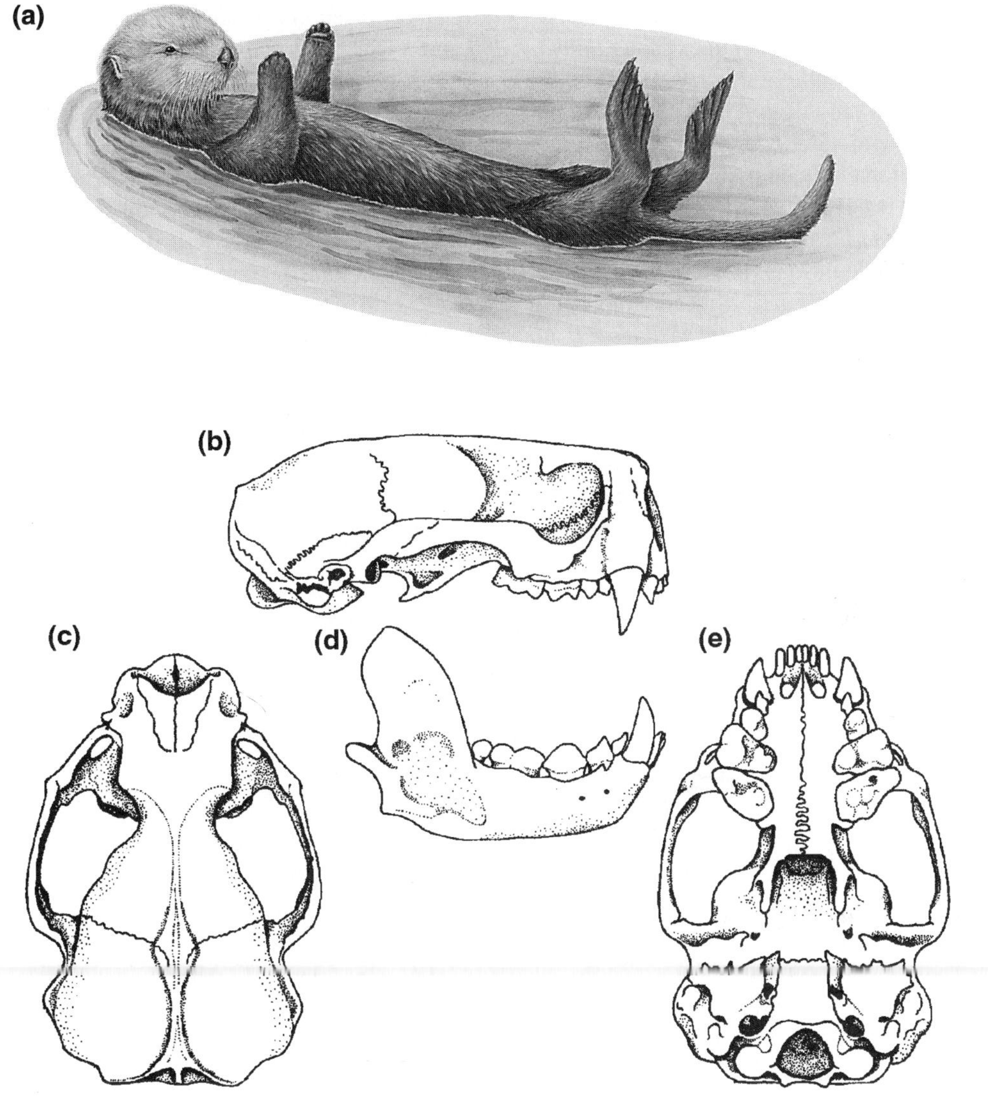

Figure 5.15. Sea otter, *Enhydra lutris.* (a) Ventral view of body (Illustrated by P. Folkens in Reeves *et al.,* 1992), and (b) Skull in dorsal, lateral and ventral views and lower jaw in lateral view (From Lawlor, 1979).

(Repenning, 1976; Mitchell, 1966). One extinct species, *Enhydra macrodonta* (Kilmer, 1972), has been described from the late Pleistocene of California.

The closest living relative of *Enhydra* is the freshwater otter *Lutra* according to both morphologic (Berta and Morgan, 1985) and molecular sequence data (Masuda and Yoshida, 1994). A different hypothesis, however, resulted from a combined analysis of molecular (including 12S and 16S rRNA and cytochrome b sequences) and morphologic data (e.g., Bryant *et al.,* 1993) that placed *Enhydra* as sister taxon to *Lutra* and the short-clawed otter *Aonyx* (Dragoo and Honeycutt, 1997). In a phylogenetic analysis, Berta and

Morgan (1986) proposed that there were two lineages of sea otters: an early diverging lineage that led to the extinct genus *Enhydriodon* and a later diverging lineage that led to the extinct giant otter *Enhydritherium* and the extant sea otter *Enhydra* (Fig. 5.16). *Enhydriodon* is known only from Africa and Eurasia, with three well-described species. In addition, there are several more poorly known specimens from Greece, England, and east Africa that have provisionally been assigned to the genus. All of this material is of late Miocene/Pliocene age. It is not known if *Enhydriodon* lived in marine or fresh water habitats or both. However, they were as large or larger than modern sea otters and had similarly well-developed molariform dentitions (Repenning, 1976). *Enhydritherium* is known from the late Miocene of Europe and the late Miocene/middle Pliocene of North America. Two species of *Enhydritherium* are described: *E. lluecai* from Spain and *E. terraenovae* from Florida and California. *Enhydritherium* is united with *Enhydra* based on dental synapomorphies.

An incomplete articulated skeleton of *Enhydritherium terraenovae* was recently described from northern Florida (Fig. 5.17; Lambert, 1997). The depositional environment of this site which is located a considerable distance from the coast indicates that *Enhydritherium terranovae* frequented large inland rivers and lakes in addition to coastal marine environments. *Enhydritherium* was similar in size to *Enhydra,* with an estimated body mass of approximately 22 kg. The unspecialized distal hind limb elements and heavily developed humeral muscles of *Enhydritherium* strongly suggest that, contrary to *Enhydra,* this animal was primarily a forelimb swimmer. With its more equally

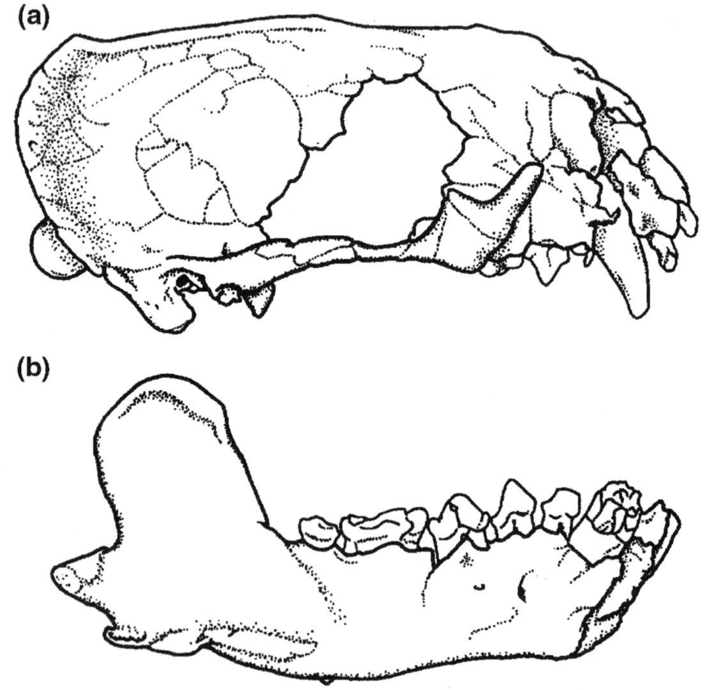

Figure 5.16. Extinct giant otter, *Enhydritherium terranovae* from the late Miocene of Florida, skull and lower jaw in lateral view. Original 16 cm long (From Lambert, 1997).

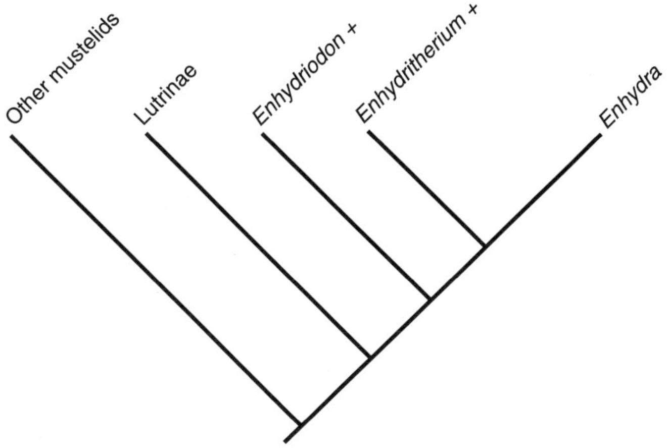

Figure 5.17. Relationships of *Enhydra* and related taxa. +=extinct taxa (Berta and Morgan, 1986).

proportioned forelimbs and hind limbs, *Enhydritherium* was almost certainly more effective at terrestrial locomotion than *Enhydra.* The thickened cusps of the upper fourth premolars of *Enhydritherium terranovae* and their tendency to be heavily worn suggest that these otters, like *Enhydra,* consumed extremely hard food items such as molluscs (Lambert, 1997).

5.7. The Polar Bear, *Ursus maritimus*

5.7.1 Origin and Evolution

Polar bears are the only species of bear that spend a significant portion of their lives in the water. The generic name for the polar bear, *Ursus,* is the Latin word for bear, while its specific epithet, *maritimus,* refers to the maritime habitat of this species. The previous suggestion that the polar bear (Fig. 5.18) might represent a separate genus, *Thalarctos,* because of its adaptation to aquatic conditions and its physical appearance is not supported. *Ursus maritimus* has a fossil record limited to the Pleistocene. Fossil and molecular data support evolution of polar bears from a lineage of brown (or grizzly) bears, *Ursus arctos,* during the middle Pleistocene (300,000–400,000 years ago, Kurtén, 1964, 1968; Talbot and Shields, 1996). A previous hypothesis of a close relationship between the spectacled bear and the polar bear (Zhang and Ryder, 1993) has received no other support. Brown bears are paraphyletic, with brown bears of the islands of southeastern Alaska being most closely related to polar bears (Fig. 5.19). It has further been proposed that separation of the polar bear and brown bear clades probably occurred somewhere in Siberia or Alaska. However, it also is possible that the close affinity of polar bears and brown bears of the southeastern islands could be the result of hybridization between polar bears and brown bears in this region (Talbot and Shields, 1996). Hybridization between brown bears and polar bears has been observed in captivity but not under natural conditions.

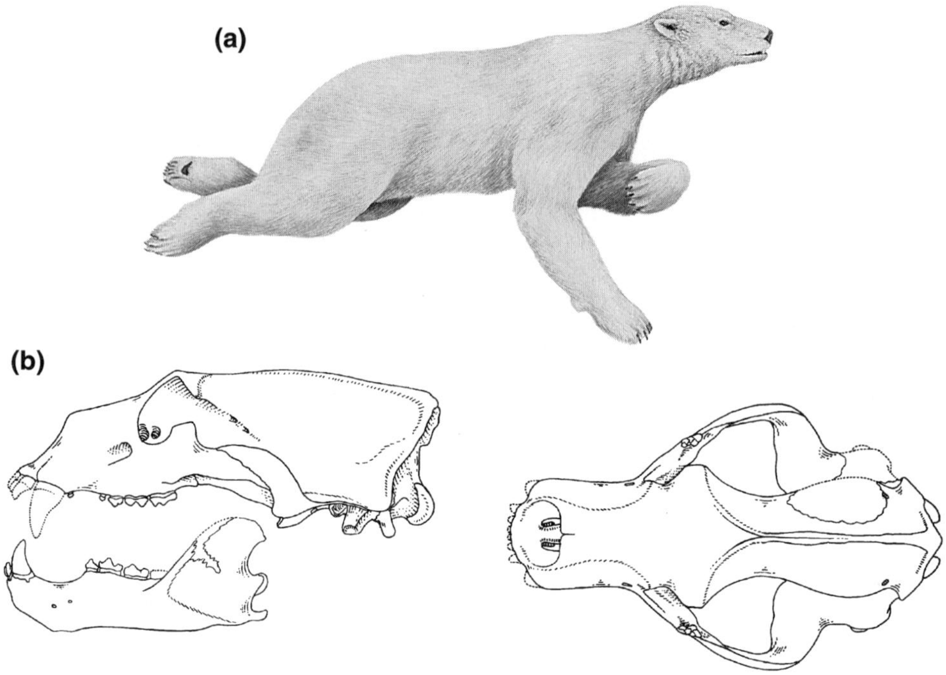

Figure 5.18. Polar bear, *Ursus maritimus.* (a) Right side of body and (b) Lateral and dorsal views of skull and lateral view of lower jaw (From Hall *et al.,* 1959).

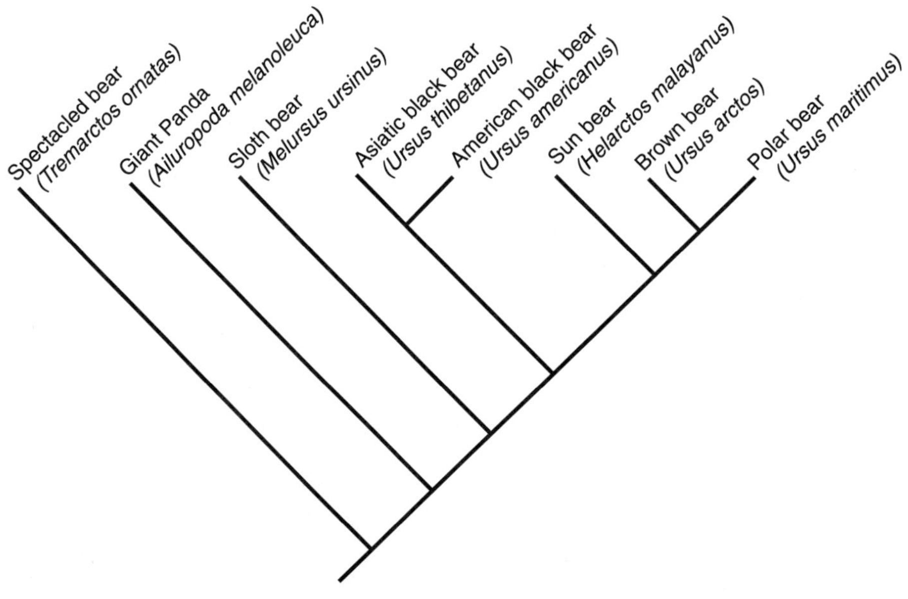

Figure 5.19. Relationships of polar bears and their relatives (From Talbot and Shields, 1996).

5.8. Summary and Conclusions

The monophyly of sirenians is widely accepted and elephants are usually considered their closest living relatives. Sirenians, elephants, and extinct desmostylians form a monophyletic clade, the Tethytheria. Sirenians are known in the fossil record from approximately 50 Ma. Early sirenians were fluvatile or estuarine semiaquatic herbivores with functional hind limbs. Manatees are likely derived from dugongids. An extinct lineage of dugongids led to the recently extinct Steller's sea cow that was cold adapted for life in the Bering Sea, in contrast to other members of this lineage distributed in tropical or subtropical waters. The hippopotamus-like desmostylians (33–10 Ma) have the distinction of comprising the only extinct order of marine mammals. The large extinct bear-like carnivoran *Kolponomos* is now recognized as more closely related to amphicynodontine ursids and pinnipedimorphs rather than its previous allocation to the raccoon family. The range of adaptation of sloths, formerly known to have only terrestrial and arboreal habits, was extended based on discovery of another marine mammal, the aquatic sloth *Thalassocnus*. The modern sea otter appears to have evolved in the North Pacific 1–3 Ma. Among fossil sea otters is *Enhydritherium* which likely frequented large rivers and lakes as well as coastal marine environments. The most recently diverging lineage of marine mammals, the polar bear, appears to have been derived from brown bears as little as 500,000 years ago.

5.9. Further Reading

Sirenian phylogeny is detailed in Domning (1994) and a popular account of the evolution of manatees and dugongs can be found in Reynolds and Odell (1991). For a summary of the evolution and phylogeny of desmostylians see Clark (1991) and Ray *et al.* (1994). An excellent description of the bear-like carnivoran *Kolponomos* is provided in Tedford *et al.* (1994). For description of the aquatic sloth see Muizon and MacDonald (1995). Sea otter evolution is reviewed by Berta and Morgan (1985) and Lambert (1997). Polar bear phylogeny, especially the molecular evidence, is discussed by Talbot and Shields (1996).

References

Anderson, P. K. (1995). Competition, predation, and the evolution and extinction of Steller's sea cow, *Hydrodamalis gigas*. *Mar. Mamm. Sci.* **11**(3): 391–394.

Archibald, J. D. (1996). Fossil evidence for a late Cretaceous origin of "hoofed mammals." *Science* **272**: 1150–1153.

Bajpai, S., and D. P. Domning (1997). A new dugongine sirenian from the early Miocene of India. *J. Vertebr. Paleontol.* **17**(1): 219–228.

Barnes, L. G., and F. Aranda-Manteca (1997). New middle Miocene Paleoparadoxidae (Mammalia, Desmostylia) from Baja California and Mexico. *Abstr., 57th Ann. Meet. Soc. Vert. Paleo.*, Chicago, p. 30A.

Barnes, L. G., D. P. Domning, and C. E. Ray (1985). Status of studies on fossil marine mammals. *Mar. Mamm. Sci.* **1**: 15–53.

Berta, A., and G. S. Morgan (1985). A new sea otter (Carnivora: Mustelidae) from the late Miocene and early Pliocene (Hemphillian) of North America. *J. Paleontol.* **59**: 809–819.

Bryant, H. N., A. P. Russell, and W. D. Fitch (1993). Phylogenetic relationships within the extant Mustelidae (Carnivora): Appraisal of the cladistic status of the Simpsonian subfamilies. *Zool. J. Linn. Soc.* **108**: 301–334.

Clark, J. M. (1991). A new early Miocene species of *Paleoparadoxia* (Mammalia: Desmostylia) from California. *J. Vertebr. Paleontol.* **11**: 490–508.

Domning, D. P. (1978). Sirenian evolution in the North Pacific Ocean. *Univ. Calif. Publ. Geol. Sci.* **118**: 176 pp.

Domning, D. P. (1982). Evolution of manatees: A speculative history. *J. Paleontol.* **56**(3): 599–619.

Domning, D. P. (1994). A phylogenetic analysis of the Sirenia. *Proc. San Diego Soc. Nat. Hist.* **29**: 177–189.

Domning, D. P., and V. de Buffrénil. (1991). Hydrostasis in the Sirenia: Quantitative data and functional interpretations. *Mar. Mamm. Sci.* **7**: 331–368.

Domning, D. P., and H. Furusawa (1995). Summary of taxa and distribution of Sirenia in the North Pacific Ocean. *Island Arc* **3**: 506–512.

Domning, D. P., and P. D. Gingerich (1994). *Protosiren smithae,* new species (Mammalia, Sirenia), from the late middle Eocene of Wadi Hitan, Egypt. *Contrib. Mus. Paleontol. Univ. Mich.* **29**(3): 69–87.

Domning, D. P., and L. Hayek (1986). Interspecific and intraspecific morphological variation in manatees (Sirenia: Trichechidae). *Mar. Mamm. Sci.* **2**(2): 87–141.

Domning, D. P., C. E. Ray, and M. C. McKenna (1986). Two new Oligocene desmostylians and a discussion of tethytherian systematics. *Smithson. Contrib. Paleobiol.* **59**: 1–56.

Dragoo, J. W., and R. L. Honeycutt (1997). Systematics of mustelid-like carnivores. *J. Mammal.* **78**(2): 426–443.

Fischer, M. S. (1986). Die Stellung der Schliefer (Hyracoidea) im phylogenetischen System der Eutheria. *CFS, Cour. Forschungsinst. Senckenberg* **84**: 1–132.

Fischer, M. S. (1989). Hyracoids, the sister-group of perissodactyls. *In* "The Evolution of Perissodactyls" (D. R. Prothero and R. M. Schoch, eds.), pp. 37–56. Clarendon Press, New York.

Gingerich, P. D., D. P. Domning, C. E. Blane, and M. D. Uhen (1994). Cranial morphology of *Protosiren fraasi* (Mammalia, Sirenia) from the middle Eocene of Egypt: A new study using computed tomography. *Contrib. Mus. Paleontol. Univ. Mich.* **29**(2): 41–67.

Hagey, L. R., Crombie, D. L., Espinosa, E., Carey, M. C., Iguimi, H., and Hoffman, A. F. (1993). Ursodeoxycholic acid in the Ursidae: Biliary bile acids of bears, pandas, and related carnivores. *J. Lipid Res.* **34**: 1911–1917.

Hall, E. R. and K. R. Kelson (1959). "The Mammals of North America." Ronald Press, New York.

Halstead, L. B. (1985). On the posture of desmostylians: A discussion of Inuzuka's "herpetiform mammals." *Mem. Fac. Sci., Kyoto Univ., Ser. Biol.* **10**: 137–144.

Hasegawa, Y., Y. Taketani, H. Taru, O. Sakamoto, and M. Manabe (1995). On sexual dimorphism in *Paleoparadoxia tabatai. Island Arc* **3**: 513–521.

Heptner, V. G. (1974). Unterordnung Tricheciformes Hay, 1923, eigentliche Sirenen. *In* Die Saugetier der Sowjetunion (V. G. Heptner and N. P. Naumov, eds.), pp. 30–51. Gustav Fischer Verlag, Jena, **2**: 1–1006.

Inuzuka, N. (1982). Published Reconstructions of Desmostylians. Saitama, (Japan), Association for the Geological Collaboration in Japan, pp. 1–16.

Inuzuka, N. (1984). Skeletal restoration of the desmostylians: Herpetiform mammals. *Mem. Fac. Sci., Kyoto Univ., Ser. Biol.* **9**: 157–253.

Inuzuka, N. (1985). Are "herpetiform mammals" really impossible? A reply to Halstead's discussion. *Mem. Fac. Sci., Kyoto Univ., Ser. Biol.* **10**: 145–150.

Inuzuka, N., D. P. Domning, and C. E. Ray (1995). Summary of taxa and morphological adaptations of Desmostylia. *Island Arc* **3**: 522–537.

Kilmer, F. H. (1972). A new species of sea otter from the late Pleistocene of northwestern California. *Bull. South. Calif. Acad. Sci.* **71**(3): 150–157.

Kingdon, J. (1971). East African mammals, an atlas of evolution in Africa. Academic Press, London.

Kurtén, B. J. (1964). The evolution of the polar bear. *Ursus maritimus* Phipps. *Acta Zool. Fenn.* **108**: 1–26.

Kurtén, B. J. (1968). "Pleistocene Mammals of Europe." Weidenfeld & Nicolson, London.

Lambert, W. D. (1997). The osteology and paleoecology of the giant otter *Enhydritherium terranovae. J. Vertebr. Paleontol.* **17**(4): 738–749.

Lavergne, A., E. Douzery, T. Strichler, F. M. Catzeflis, and M. S. Springer (1996). Interordinal mammalian relationships: Evidence for paenungulate monophyly is provided by complete mitochondrial 12sRNA sequences. *Mol. Phylogenet. Evol.* **6**(2): 245–258.

Lawlor, T. (1979). Handbook to the Order and Families of Living Mammals. Mad River Press, California.

Leffler, S. R. (1964). Fossil mammals from the Elk River Formation, Cape Blanco, Oregon. *J. Mammal.* **45**(1): 53–61.

Linnaeus, C. (1758). "Systema naturae," 10th ed. L. Salvii. Uppsala.

Masuda, R., and M. C. Yoshida (1994). A molecular phylogeny of the Family Mustelidae (Mammalia, Carnivora), based on comparison of mitochondrial cytochrome b nucleotide sequences. *Zool. Sci.* **11**: 605–612.

McKenna, M. C. (1975). Toward a phylogenetic classification of the Mammalia. *In* "Phylogeny of the Primates" (W. P. Luckett and F. S. Szalay, eds.), pp. 21–45. Plenum, New York.

Merriam, C. H. (1904). A new sea otter from southern California. *Proc. Biol. Soc. Wash.* **17**: 159–160.

Mitchell, E. D. (1966). Northeastern Pacific Pleistocene otters. *J. Fish. Res. Board Can.* **23**: 1897–1911.

Muizon, C. de (1996). *Thalassocnus natans,* the marine sloth from Peru. *In* "Abstracts of the Conference on Secondary Adaptation to Life in the Water" (J.-M. Mazin, P. Vignaud, and V. de Buffrénil, eds.), p. 29. Poitiers, France.

Muizon, C. de, and H. G. McDonald (1995). An aquatic sloth from the Pliocene of Peru. *Nature* **375**: 224–227.

Novacek, M., and A. R. Wyss (1987). Selected features of the desmostylian skeleton and their phylogenetic implications. *Am. Mus. Novit.* **2870**: 1–8.

Novacek, M., A. R. Wyss, and M. C. McKenna (1988). The major groups of eutherian mammals. *In* "The Phylogeny and Classification of the Tetrapods" (M. J. Benton, ed.), Vol. 2, pp. 31–71. Clarendon Press, Oxford.

Ozawa, T., S. Hayashi, and V. M. Mikhelson (1997). Phylogenetic position of mammoth and Steller's sea cow within Tethytheria demonstrated by mitochondrial DNA sequences. *J. Mol. Evol.* **44**: 406–413.

Prothero, D. (1993). Ungulate phylogeny: Molecular vs. morphological evidence. *In* "Mammal Phylogeny: Placentals" (F. S. Szalay, M. J. Novacek, and M. C. McKenna, eds.), pp. 173–181. Springer-Verlag, New York.

Prothero, D. R., E. M. Manning, and M. Fischer (1988). The phylogeny of the ungulates. *Syst. Assoc. Spec. Vol.* **35B**: 201–234.

Rainey, W. E., J. M. Lowenstein, V. M. Sarich, and D. M. Magor (1984). Sirenian molecular systematics—including the extinct Steller's sea cow (*Hydrodamalis gigas*). *Naturwissenschaften* **71**: 586–588.

Ray, C. E., D. P. Domning, and M. C. McKenna (1994). A new specimen of *Behemotops proteus* (Order Desmostylia) from the marine Oligocene of Washington. *Proc. San Diego Mus. Nat. Hist.* **29**: 205–222.

Reeves, R. R., B. S. Stewart, and S. Leatherwood (1992). The Sierra Club Handbook of Seals and Sirenians. Sierra Club Books, San Francisco.

Repenning, C. A. (1965). [Drawing of *Paleoparadoxia* skeleton]. *Geotimes* **9**(6): 1.3.

Repenning, C. A. (1976). *Enhydra* and *Enhydriodon* from the Pacific coast of North America. *J. Res. U.S. Geol. Surv.* **4**(2): 305–315.

Reynolds, J. E., III, and D. K. Odell (1991). "Manatees and Dugongs." Facts on File, New York.

Savage, R. G. J., D. P. Domning, and J. G. M. Thewissen (1994). Fossil Sirenia of the West Atlantic and Caribbean region. V. The most primitive known sirenian, *Prorastomus sirenoides* Owen, 1855. *J. Vertebr. Paleontol.* **14**(3): 427–449.

Shoshani, J. (1993). Hyracoidea-Tethytheria affinity based on myological data. *In* "Mammal Phylogeny: Placentals" (F. S. Szalay, M. J. Novacek, and M. C. McKenna, eds.), pp. 235–256. Springer-Verlag, New York.

Springer, M. S., and J. A. W. Kirsch (1993). A molecular perspective on the phylogeny of placental mammals based on mitochondrial 12s rDNA sequences, with special reference to the problem of the Paenungulata. *J. Mamm. Evol.* **1**(2): 149–166.

Talbot, S. L., and G. F. Shields (1996). A phylogeny of bears (Ursidae) inferred from complete sequences of three mitochondrial genes. *Mol. Phylogenet. Evol.* **5**(3): 567–575.

Tassy, P., and J. Shoshani (1988). The Tethytheria: Elephants and their relatives. *Syst. Assoc. Spec. Vol.* **35B**: 283–315.

Tedford, R. H., L. G. Barnes, and C. E. Ray (1994). The early Miocene littoral ursoid carnivoran *Kolponomos:* Systematics and mode of life. *Proc. San Diego Mus. Nat. Hist.* **29**: 11–32.

Thewissen, J. G. M., and D. P. Domning (1992). The role of phenacodontids in the origin of modern orders of ungulate mammals. *J. Vertebr. Paleontol.* **12**: 494–504.

Vanderhoof, V. L. (1937). A study of the Miocene sirenian *Desmostylus.* Univ. Calif. Publ. *Bull. Dept. Geol. Sci.* **24**: 169–262.

Wilson, D. E., M. A. Bogan, R. I. Brownell, Jr., A. M. Burdin, and M. K. Maminov (1991). Geographic variation in sea otters, *Enhydra lutris. J. Mammal.* **72**(1): 22–36.

Zhang, Y.-P., and O. A. Ryder (1993). Phylogenetic relationships of bears (the Ursidae) inferred from mitochondrial DNA sequences. *Mol. Phylogenet. Evol.* **3**(4): 351–359.

6

Evolutionary Biogeography

6.1. Introduction—What Is Biogeography and Why Is It Important?

Biogeography involves the study of the distributions of organisms, both past and present. It attempts to describe and understand patterns in the distributions of species and higher taxonomic groups and interprets aspects of both ecology and evolutionary biology. Understanding marine mammal distributions necessitates knowledge of a species' ecological requirements. These parameters affect biotic factors such as food availability and are discussed in the first part of the chapter. Among evolutionary questions of interest explored later in this chapter are: (1) How did a species come to be confined to its present range?, (2) How have geologic events, such as the opening of the Bering Strait or the Central American Seaway, shaped this distribution?, and (3) Why are some closely related species confined to the same region, while others are widely separated and even found on opposite sides of the world?

6.2. Ecological Factors Affecting Distributions of Marine Mammals

Marine mammals have adapted to several properties of the ocean environment not experienced by their terrestrial ancestors. These include increased buoyancy derived from the relatively high density of sea water, frictional resistance to swimming created by viscous forces between water molecules, poor transmittance of light and high frequency sounds underwater, **osmotic** stresses created by **hyperosmotic** sea water, and substantial heat loss to the cold environment. Each of these are discussed in later chapters. Two additional features of the ecology of marine mammals that vary over oceanic distances appear to strongly influence the present and past distribution patterns of marine mammal species. These are the patterns of geographic and seasonal surface water temperature variations and the spatial and temporal patterns of **primary productivity** and the resulting distribution of food items.

6.2.1. Water Temperature and Sea Ice

For most of their lives, marine mammals exist in direct contact with seawater much colder than their core body temperatures. Even though large body sizes, streamlined body shapes, and the resultant low surface area: body volume ratios characteristic of marine mammals serve to reduce thermal losses, the heat capacity of even temperate latitude sea water is about 25 times as high as air of the same temperature. This means that marine mammals lose considerable heat to their aquatic environment, particularly when they are of small body size. Geographically, surface ocean temperatures tend to be highest near the equator and decrease with increasing latitude toward both the north and south poles. This poleward gradient of surface ocean temperatures has been used to establish several latitudinal marine climatic zones shown (with approximate ranges of sea surface temperatures) in Fig. 6.1.

Sea ice forms only in polar and subpolar zones and reaches its maximum extent in winter (approximate maximum winter limits of ice are also indicated in Fig. 6.1). The seasonal cycles of freezing and melting of sea ice limit access to high latitude by most species of marine mammals to the warmest summer months only. Two forms of ice are found near the poles: **fast ice** (ice attached to land) and **pack ice** (floating ice). Pinnipeds inhabiting pack ice are the walrus, harp, hooded, bearded, ribbon, ross, crabeater, leopard, largha, gray, and harbor seals and the Steller sea lion. Weddell, ringed, southern elephant, Caspian, Baikal, and gray seals occupy fast ice (Riedman, 1990, Table 5). The importance of sea ice and oceanic islands as features critical for pinniped breeding and pupping is discussed in Chapter 12.

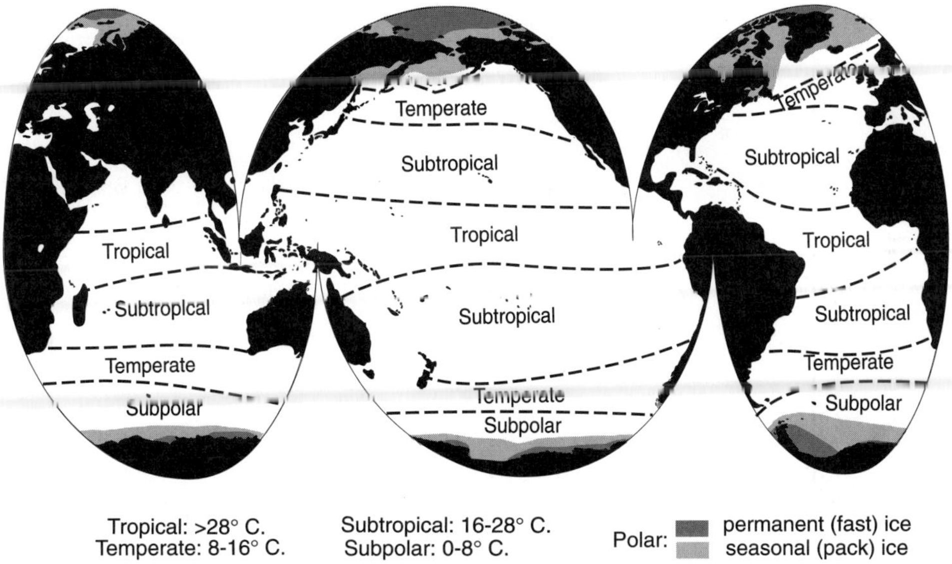

Figure 6.1. Average distribution of marine climatic zones and polar areas of permanent fast ice and seasonal pack ice (Adapted from Bogdanov, 1963).

6.2.2. Distribution of Primary Productivity

The availability of food for marine mammals is established first by patterns of marine primary production and secondly by the number of **trophic levels** between primary production and the marine mammal consumer. **Phytoplankton** cell sizes are quite small, and numerous trophic levels link these extremely small primary producers with larger animals at high trophic levels (Steele, 1974). Sirenians are the only marine mammals to feed directly on primary producers (sea grasses), whereas some pinnipeds and odontocetes consume prey five or more trophic levels removed from the primary producers (Fig. 6.2). Rates of marine primary production can vary by several orders of magnitude over geographic areas and also between seasons. Seasonal and spatial variations in primary production are related to differences in light intensity, nutrient abundance, and grazing pressure. The underlying pulse for these temporal changes, however, is the predictable seasonal variation in the intensity of sunlight reaching the sea surface. This in turn influences seasonal variations in water temperature, density, and the pattern of vertical mixing of water, with the magnitude of these variations becoming more pronounced at higher latitudes between summer and winter.

In tropical and subtropical waters, sunlight is abundant all year long, yet a strong permanent thermocline inhibits vertical mixing of nutrients from deeper waters. Low rates of nutrient return are partially compensated for by a year-round growing season and a deep **photic zone**. Even so, net primary production and standing crops are low, with little seasonal variability (Fig. 6.3, curve a).

A prominent feature in the production cycle of temperate seas is the spring **diatom** bloom. In general, bloom conditions in the open ocean occur as a broad band of primary production that sweeps poleward with the onset of spring (Brown *et al.*, 1985). At this time, the standing crop of diatoms increases quickly to the largest of the year and begins to deplete nutrient concentrations. Grazing zooplankton respond by increasing their numbers;

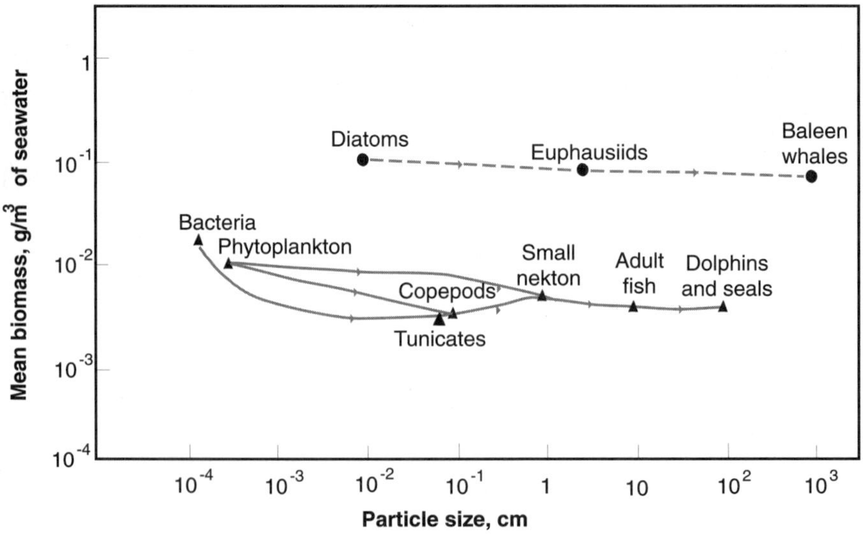

Figure 6.2. Relationship between food particle size and biomass in two pelagic food webs. The biomass in the Antarctic is about 10x higher at all trophic levels than those in subtropical gyres.

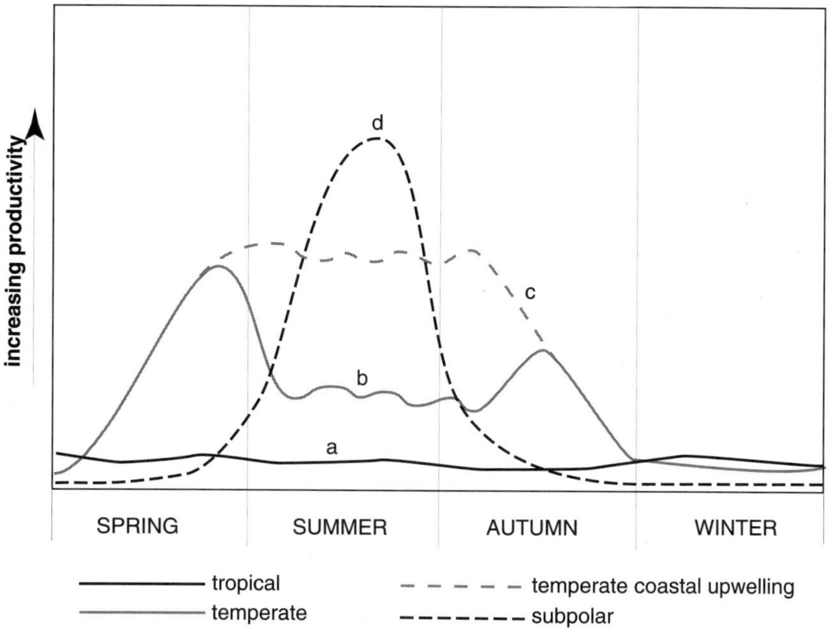

Figure 6.3. General patterns of seasonal variation in marine primary productivity for four different marine production systems.

the diatom population peaks, then declines and remains low throughout the summer (Fig. 6.3, curve b). Autumn air temperatures then begin to cool the water in this zone and allow the mixing of water of different temperatures; this renews nutrient supply to the photic zone. The phytoplankton respond with another period of rapid growth, which, although typically not as remarkable as the spring bloom, is often sufficient to initiate another growth of the zooplankton populations. As winter approaches, the autumn bloom is cut short by decreasing light and reduced temperatures. On average, about 120 $gC/m^2/yr$ are produced in oceanic temperate and subpolar areas, with most of that total occurring during the spring diatom bloom (Falkowski, 1980).

Coastal **upwelling** alters the generalized picture presented for temperate seas (see Fig. 6.3) by replenishing nutrients during the summer when they would otherwise be depleted. As long as light is sufficient and upwelling continues, high phytoplankton production occurs and is reflected in abundant local animal populations. Coastal upwelling zones have average productivity rates of about 300 $gC/m^2/yr$. They are most apparent along the west coasts of Africa and North and South America (Fig. 6.3, curve c).

In polar regions, sea surface temperatures are always low. The thermocline, if one exists at all, is weak and is not an effective barrier to upward mixing of nutrients from deeper waters. Light, or more correctly the lack of it, is the major limiting factor for phytoplankton growth in polar seas. Sufficient light to sustain high primary production lasts for only a few months during the summer, when photosynthesis can continue around the clock during those few months to quickly produce huge phytoplankton populations (Fig. 6.3, curve d). The short summer diatom bloom declines rapidly as light intensity and day length decline. Winter conditions resemble those of temperate regions except that in polar seas these conditions endure for much longer. The complete annual cycle of production consists of a single short period of phytoplankton growth, equivalent to a typical spring bloom, immediately followed by an autumn bloom and then a decline that alternates with an extended winter of reduced net production. The annual average productivity rate for north polar seas is low (about 25 $gC/m^2/yr$) because so much of the year passes in darkness with almost no phytoplankton growth. In northern subpolar seas and around the Antarctic continent, however, upwelling of deep, nutrient-rich water supports very high summertime primary production rates and annual productivity rates of over 100$gC/m^2/yr$ (Falkowski, 1980). Although a few species of pinnipeds and the polar bear remain in these summer-intensive polar and subpolar production systems year-round, mysticete whales exemplify the more common approach of exploiting these high-latitude production systems, with intensive summer feeding followed by long-distance migrations to low latitudes in winter months. The distributions of baleen and sperm whales during their summer feeding, their principal prey, and high phytoplankton biomass were recently shown to coincide with the southern boundary of the Antarctic Circumpolar Current (ACC; Tynan, 1998). The southern boundary was identified as an ecologically important critical trophic structure providing whales and other species a predictably profitable foraging area.

The average annual geographic variation of global marine primary production, as compiled from several years of observations by the satellite-borne Coastal Zone Color Scanner, is shown in Fig. 6.4 (Perry, 1986). Primary production is low (less than 50 $gC/m^2/year$) in the central gyres of ocean basins, moderate (50–100 $gC/m^2/year$) in most coastal regions, and high (greater than 100 $gC/m^2/year$) in coastal upwelling regions. In general, the distribution of marine organisms at higher trophic levels resembles the general geographic patterns of primary productivity shown in Fig. 6.4, with the largest aggregations concentrated in coastal areas and zones of upwelling. However, as the organic material produced by marine primary producers is moved through higher trophic levels, much of it is dispersed out of the near-surface photic zone. Animal populations utilizing this organic material also

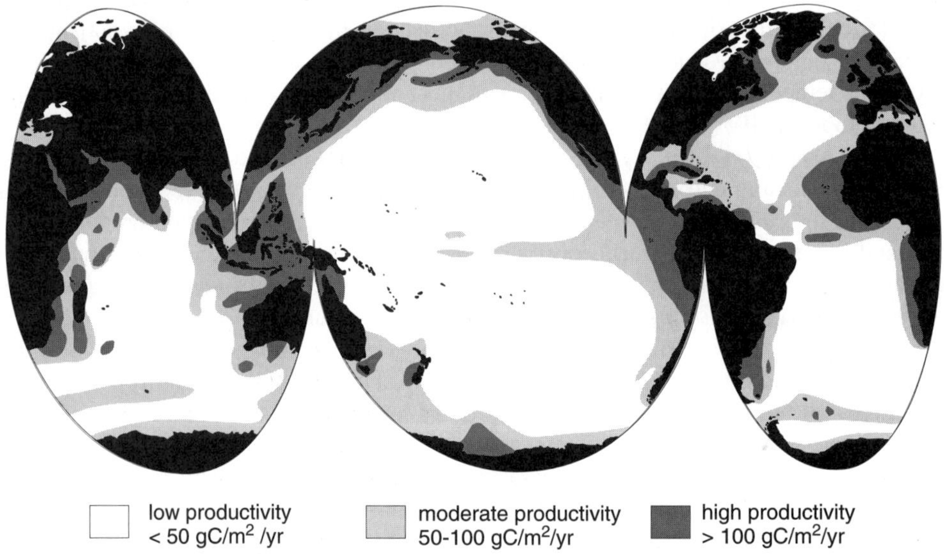

Figure 6.4. Global distribution of areas of low, moderate, and high annual marine primary productivity (Adapted from data from NASA/Space Data Computing Division).

congregate at sharp density interfaces such as current eddies, water mass boundaries, and especially the sea bottom where many marine mammal species focus their feeding efforts. Zooplankton species such as **krill** (small shrimp-like crustaceans of the family Euphausiidae, Fig. 6.5), but also squid, are concentrated in well-defined sound-reflecting layers during daylight at considerable depth. These layers migrate upward to shallower water at night in temperate areas and during the warmer months in high latitudes. Krill are most efficiently captured by marine mammals in shallower water. Baleen whale and seal distributions largely mimic the distribution of krill. Research has confirmed fluctuations in the abundance of krill in the last 30 years and provides evidence of its lower abundance in recent years (Loeb *et al.,* 1997). Decreased krill availability may negatively affect their vertebrate predators, including pinnipeds and whales.

Water temperature has been shown to affect the diving behavior of the southern elephant seal (Boyd and Arnbom, 1991). The majority of dives of a southern elephant seal were spent at a relatively constant depth of 200–400 m, usually in association with the transition to warm water. Given that there was little if any penetration of light to the normal depth of foraging, Boyd and Arnbom (1991) suggested that this seal used other physical characteristics of its environment, such as the temperature discontinuity between water masses, to locate suitable foraging areas.

Water temperature and availability of food resources vary from one year to the next, in some years drastically, because of the effect of El Niño events. **El Niño-Southern Oscillation (ENSO)** is a meteorological and oceanographic phenomenon which occurs at irregular intervals in the eastern tropical Pacific (Fig. 6.6). Its most obvious characteristic is the warming of surface waters, which blocks the upward mixing of deeper, nutrient-rich water from below. During a typical ENSO event, cold water currents in the eastern tropical Pacific slow down and upwelling is reduced. The 1982–1983 and 1997–1998 ENSO were presumably the most intense in the last century.

ENSO events, which heavily affect tropical marine environments where they originate, are propagated poleward. The severity of ENSO impacts on marine organisms declines from low to high latitudes. Both the 1982–1983 and the 1997–1998 ENSO were times of food shortage and increased rate of mortality, especially for temperate and tropical pinnipeds. Severe negative effects on otariids were observed on the Galapagos Islands, where 100% mortality of Galapagos fur seal pups and nearly 100% mortality of California sea lions occurred in 1982. An important long term effect of the 1982–1983 ENSO was increased adult female mortality, in these populations most likely due to decreased primary productivity and reduced availability of prey (Trillmich *et al.,* 1991), and similar effects are anticipated in the aftermath of the 1997–1998 ENSO. Phocid seals, especially those living in tropical/subtropical areas, also have been affected by El Niño events. During the 1982–1983 ENSO for example, at the Farallon Islands (38° N) pup mortality rates were normal, whereas at Año Nuevo (37.5° N) pup mortality rates roughly doubled, and at San

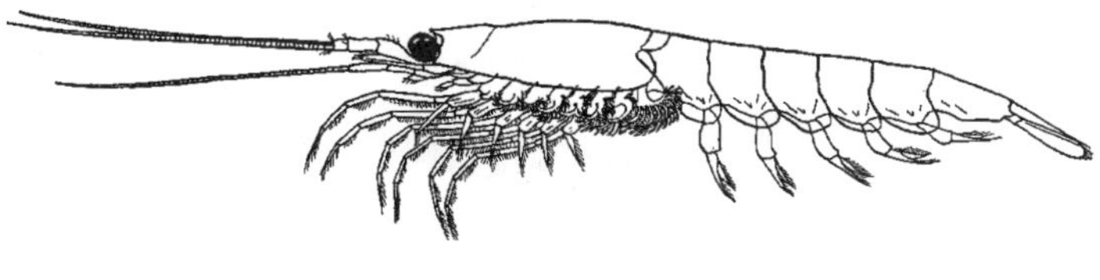

Figure 6.5. Side view of an adult *Euphausia superba,* actual size (From Macintosh and Wheeler, 1929).

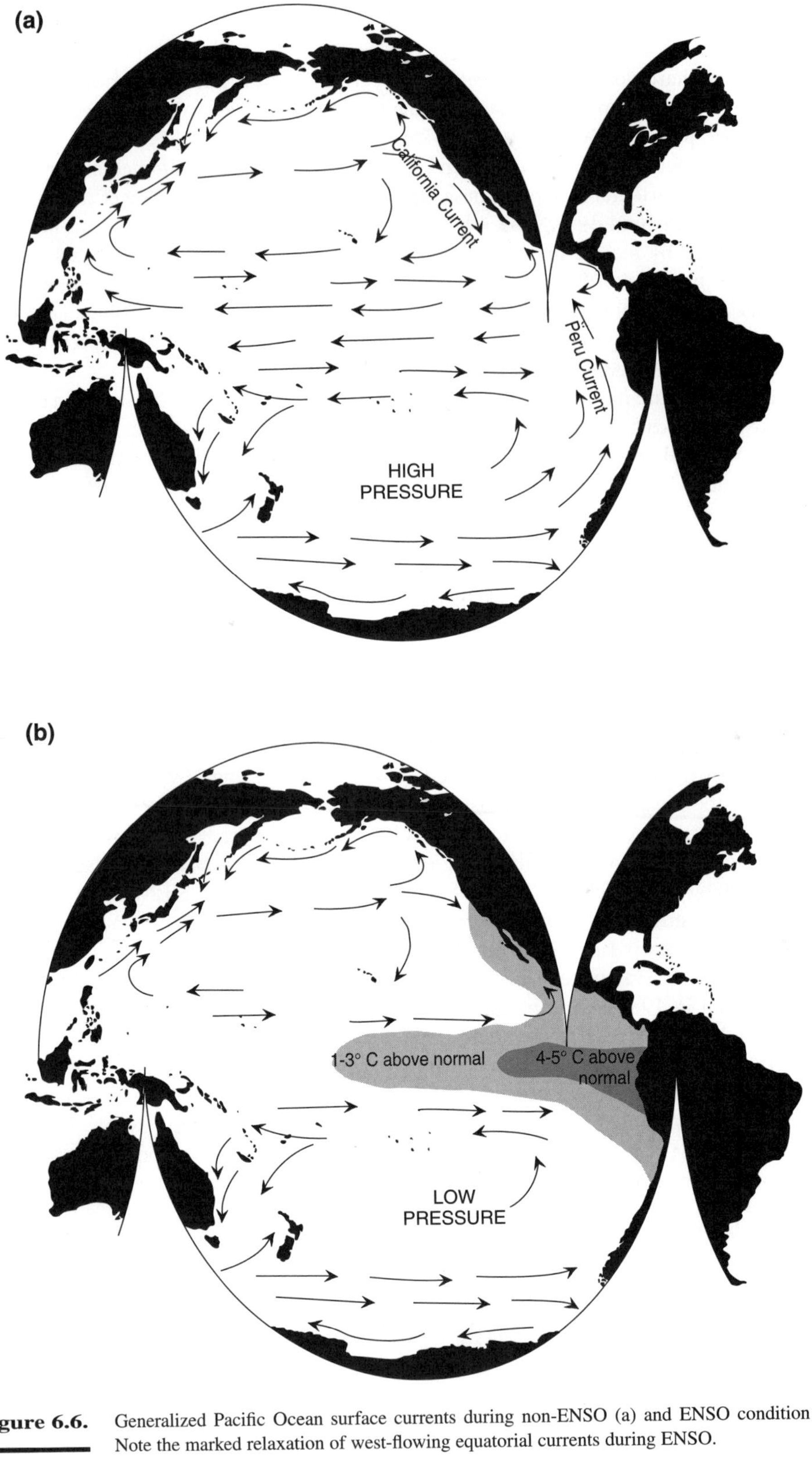

Figure 6.6. Generalized Pacific Ocean surface currents during non-ENSO (a) and ENSO condition (b). Note the marked relaxation of west-flowing equatorial currents during ENSO.

Nicholas Island (33° N) the pup mortality rate was five times above normal (Trillmich *et al.*, 1991).

In addition to short-term climatic fluctuations such as El Niño long-term climate changes have the potential to profoundly effect marine mammals particularly those living in the Arctic. Analyses continue to substantiate trends over the last several decades of decreasing sea ice extent in the Arctic Ocean. Such trends may be indicative of global climate warming in response to increasing atmospheric CO_2. Direct effects of long-term climate change on marine mammals include among others the loss of ice-associated habitat and changes in prey availability (Tynan and DeMaster, 1997). Ice seals (e.g., ringed seals, bearded seals, and walruses) which rely on suitable ice substrate for resting, pupping, and molting may be especially vulnerable to such changes. For example, declines in ringed seal density have been linked with the severity of ice conditions in the Beaufort Sea 1974–1975 and 1982–1985 (Stirling *et al.*, 1977; Harwood and Stirling, 1992). For cetaceans inhabiting the arctic climatic change is more likely to affect their prey availability. For example, the distribution of Arctic cod, an important food source for belugas and narwhals and pelagic amphipods, prey items of northeast Atlantic populations of harp seals vary with ice conditions (references cited in Tynan and DeMaster, 1997). In summary, given the potential for climate-driven changes in the Arctic to affect habitat and prey availability, regional studies and monitoring of marine mammals are essential to document and interpret the effects of these long-term changes on the ecosystem.

6.2.3. Ocean Temperatures and Productivity Fluctuations in the Past

Lipps and Mitchell (1976) proposed that radiations and declines of marine mammal species in the past were due to variations in the availability of resources in ocean environments. These trophic resources were related to upwelling processes. They proposed that increased upwelling intensity, due to climatic or tectonic events, permitted the initial invasions and radiations of pinnipeds and cetaceans. They further postulated that the apparent decline in marine mammal diversity reflects a decrease in thermal gradients, which led to decreased upwelling and primary productivity and thus limited dispersal and speciation in marine mammals.

This general hypothesis has been subsequently examined with respect to the distribution of cetaceans (Orr and Faulhaber, 1975; Gaskin, 1976; Fordyce, 1977, 1980). According to Orr and Faulhaber (1975), cooling during the Oligocene could have led to reduced thermal barriers, and hence to drops in plankton numbers and cetacean diversity. Gaskin (1976) noted that the low diversity might likewise reflect cool conditions. Other workers, noting the origin of mysticetes and odontocetes in the Oligocene, questioned whether the reported low diversity of cetaceans was real (Barnes, 1977; Fordyce, 1977). The late Eocene-early Oligocene (38–31.5 Ma) was marked by many environmental changes across the globe. Major continental glaciation occurred in Antarctica which resulted in a marked drop in temperature. Concomitant with cooling was the development of bottom water currents which increased the turnover and circulation of nutrient rich water. Fordyce (1980) proposed that the establishment of high-productivity areas in the southern hemisphere during the early Oligocene probably triggered odontocete and mysticete radiation. He further suggested that perhaps early odontocetes and mysticetes were restricted to the southern hemisphere because northern trophic resources were not affected enough by upwelling to have allowed exploitation by whales. During the middle Oligocene (31.5–28 Ma), the establishment of the Circum-Antarctic current also known as the Antarctic Circompolar Current between Australia and Antarctica and the effect of glaciations in Antarctica, which induced sea cooling, increased nutrient availability and hence productivity in shallow seas of the southwest Pacific. Fordyce suggested that the diversification of filter feeding mysticetes during the middle Oligocene is related to this increase in primary productivity. Because odontocetes consume prey (e.g. small fish and squid) which concentrate in areas of zooplankton abundance, the increase in odontocete diversity during this time likely also reflects these major water mass features. The persistence of archaic whales in the late Oligocene suggests an environment that supported several types of feeding adapations, including the baleen filter feeding mechanism of mysticetes, the echolocation assisted feeding of odontocetes, as well as the less specialized feeding apparatus of toothed archaeocetes (Fordyce, 1980).

6.3. Present Patterns of Distribution

Two major patterns of modern marine mammal distribution can be identified: 1) **cosmopolitan** and 2) **disjunct**. Many species have wide, or cosmopolitan, distributions, inhabiting most of the world's oceans. Examples of cetaceans having cosmopolitan distributions are the common dolphin (*Delphinus delphis*), the false killer whale (*Pseudorca crassidens*), and Risso's dolphin (*Grampus griseus*). In addition, several widely distributed pinnipeds, such as the harbor seal (*Phoca vitulina*), may live in a wide range of environments including coastal areas, bays, and estuaries, as well as freshwater lakes.

Other marine mammals can be more or less widespread but are limited to a particular area and have either **endemic** or **circumpolar** distributions. Examples of marine mammals with occurrence restricted to southern cool-temperate/Antarctic waters or Arctic waters (i.e. circumpolar distributions) include the pygmy right whale (*Caperea marginata*) in the southern hemisphere, the narwhal (*Monodon monoceros*) confined to the Arctic, and the beluga (*Delphinapterus leucas*) distributed in Arctic and subarctic waters. Occurrences naturally restricted to a particular area are also referred to as endemic distributions. The restricted distributions of "river dolphins" to river drainage systems in South America (Amazon River dolphin, *Inia geoffrensis*), China (Baji, *Lipotes vexillifer*), and India and Pakistan (Indus and Ganges River susus *Platanista minor* and *P. gangetica*) are examples. Among pinnipeds, the Caspian seal (*Phoca caspica*) is endemic to the Caspian Sea and the Baikal seal (*Phoca siberica*) is restricted to Lake Baikal.

Other marine mammals occur in multiple regions that are separated from each other by a geographic barrier. These are **antitropical** or disjunct distributions. Antitropical distributions specifically involve different populations of the same species or sister species living in different hemispheres (Fig. 6.7). For example, in the case of the porpoise genus *Phocoena* (see fig. 4.34), one member of a species pair the vaquita (*P. sinus*) occupies the temperate/subtropical region of northern hemisphere and the other member Burmeister's porpoise (*P. spinipinnis*) occupies a similar southern hemisphere habitat. Another example is the northern right whale dolphin (*Lissodelphis borealis*), which occurs in the North Pacific, and the southern right whale dolphin (*Lissodelphis peronii*) which lives in the southern hemisphere. The ziphiid genus *Berardius* has a distribution pattern similar with Baird's beaked whale (*B. bairdii*) in the temperate North Pacific and Arnonx's beaked whale (*B. arnuxii*) in temperate and polar waters of the Southern Ocean. Among pinnipeds, antitropical distributions are exemplified by the northern and southern elephants seals (*Mirounga* spp.). The northern elephant seal occurs in the Northern Pacific and the southern elephant seal inhabits the Southern Ocean. Examples of disjunct distributions include Pacific and Atlantic populations of the harbor porpoise (*Phocoena phocoena;* see Fig. 6.7), the walrus

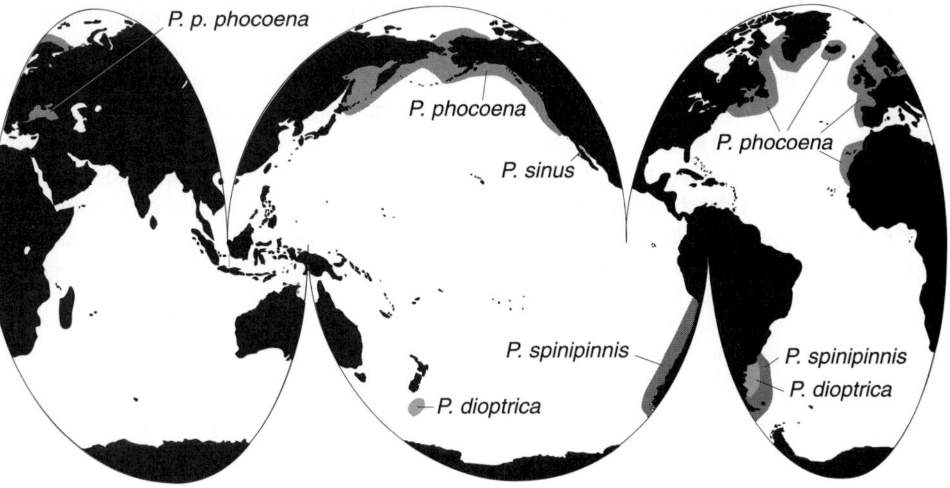

Figure 6.7. Patterns of antitropical distribution of several species of porpoises in the genus *Phocoena* (Adapted from Gaskin, 1982).

(*Odobenus rosmarus;* see Fig. 3.14), fin whale (*Balaenoptera physalus*), and humpback whale (*Megaptera novaengliae*), and West and East Pacific populations of the otter (*Enhydra lutris*) and gray whale (*Eschrichtius robustus*).

The fossil record coupled with reconstructions of the evolutionary relationships among marine mammal species provides evidence that can be used to explain these patterns. For example, the presence of beluga whales in fossil deposits of North Carolina (Whitmore, 1994) as well as Baja California (Barnes, 1984) indicates that this species historically has had a disjunct (Atlantic and Pacific) rather than a circumpolar distribution.

6.4. Reconstructing Biogeographic Patterns

Traditionally, biogeographers, in attempting to interpret the distributions of organisms, have sought to discover a small area (or center) in which species originated and from which they dispersed, known as the **"center of origin/dispersalist explanation."** This "center of origin" was that area showing the greatest species diversity. Recognized as a corollary principle was the notion that the more differentiated taxa would be found at the center of origin, with the most conservative or primitive forms having dispersed farthest from it. A center of origin is usually designated by reference to the occurrence and age of fossils but these may represent a biased record because not all locations and times inhabited by a given organism may be recorded by the fossil record. Rather than starting with an assumption about the center of origin, current workers prefer first to trace the geographic spread and fragmentation of the group through time and do not look for a specific locality for a group's origin. Dispersal explanations are employed in situations in which organisms are assumed to have evolved elsewhere and dispersed into that area. For example, the lineage that led to the modern walrus, *Odobenus,* is hypothesized to have evolved in the North Atlantic and dispersed into the North Pacific across the Arctic corridor in the late Pleistocene. In this case, the pattern of distribution is explained by the merging of two faunal elements (North Pacific and North Atlantic).

An alternative hypothesis, the **vicariance explanation**, argues that organisms occur in an area because they evolved there and were later fragmented (by geographical, behavioral, or other means), with subsequent speciation. Accordingly, the formation of barriers (a process called vicariance) fragmented the ranges of once continuously distributed species. Thus, if related species are found in different areas, it is not necessary to assume that there has been dispersal between these areas, only that a barrier (e.g. mountain range, river, or in the case of marine organisms, a land barrier separating two ocean basins) has appeared between them.

It is likely that most species associations contain both vicariance and dispersalist elements. For example, consider the distribution of species 1–3 in areas A-C (Fig. 6.8). This

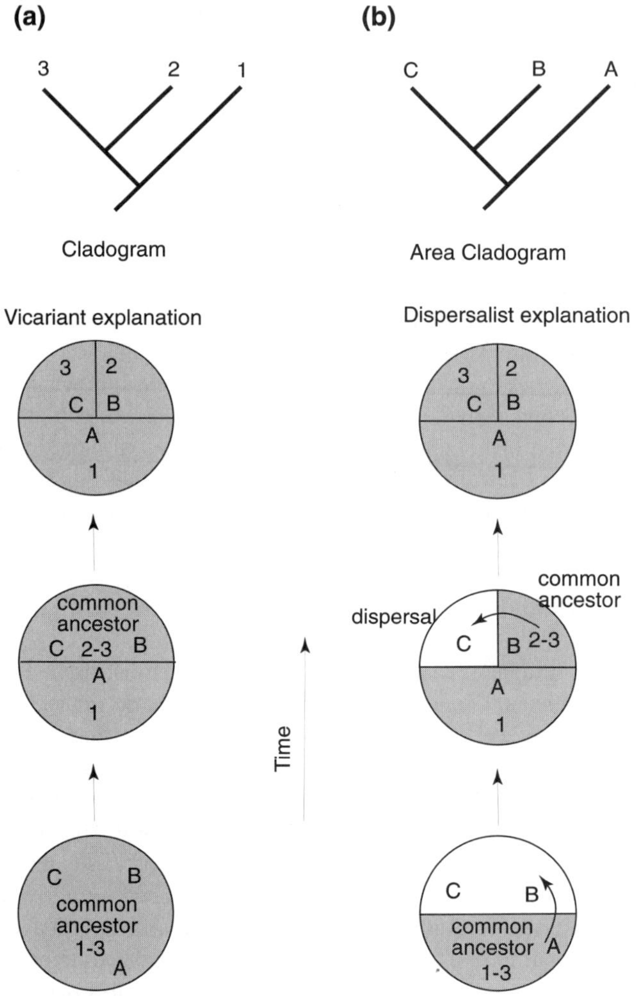

Figure 6.8. Cladogram showing hypothesized phylogenetic relationships among species and corresponding dispersal and vicariant explanations to account for their distributions. Species are identified by numbers, area by letters. (a) In a vicariant explanation, an ancestor occupying A+B+C had a range split first into A and B+C and then the descendant in B+C had its range split, (b) In a dispersal explanation, an ancestral species with a center of origin in area A dispersed first to area B and a descendant from there then dispersed to area C (modified from Ridley, 1993).

hypothesized biogeographic reconstruction is called an **area cladogram** because of its analogy to a phylogenetic cladogram. A vicariant hypothesis would have the common ancestor of species 1–3 occupying area A+B+C. In the case of marine organisms, the emergence of a land barrier would have first separated the oceans into A, occupied by species 1, and B+C, occupied by species 2–3. Subsequently, areas B+C occupied by the common ancestor of species 2 and 3 would have had another barrier divide their range. A dispersalist hypothesis would have the common ancestor of species 1–3 originating in area A. The common ancestor of species 2–3 would disperse to area B, followed by descendant species 3 dispersing into area C. These predictions can be compared with data on the geologic and climatic history of the earth and the distribution of other extinct and extant species that occur in the same area at the same time. If different species tend to speciate when their ranges are fragmented, they should all show similar relationships between phylogeny and biogeography and their area cladograms should match.

A real example of a vicariant explanation comes from a population study of Steller sea lions (Bickham *et al.,* 1996). Analysis of mtDNA haplotypes revealed the presence of two genetically different populations of Steller sea lions, a western population which included sea lions from rookeries in Russia, the Aleutian Islands, and the Gulf of Alaska (Beringia), and an eastern population which included sea lions from southeastern Alaska and Oregon (Pacific Northwest). Bickham *et al.* (1996) suggested that these two populations of Steller sea lion were descended from populations isolated in glacial refugia in Beringia and the Pacific Northwest. In this case, the vicariant event was the onset of glacial periods and fluctuating sea levels which fragmented the ranges of sea lion populations. They further noted that a similar pattern of population differentiation was observed in sockeye salmon and chinook salmon.

6.5. Past Patterns of Distribution

Past arrangements of continents and ocean basins have affected the distribution of marine mammals. The term **corridor** was proposed for a route that permits the spread of many or most taxa from one region to another (Simpson, 1936, 1940). Some of the more important dispersal corridors and their affect on marine mammal distributions are reviewed below (Figs. 6.9–6.11).

The Tethys Sea (from Tethys of greek mythology, a sea goddess who was the wife of Oceanus) was an equatorial sea that once divided the northern and southern continents (Fig. 6.10). The main body of the sea occupied an area now called the Mediterranean with a south arm connected with the Indian Ocean. Tethys lasted more than 500 million years, a remnant of the Mesozoic Tethys seaway, opening in the Eocene-late Oligocene (53 Ma). Restriction of the Tethys seaway occurred (40–45 Ma) when India became sutured to Eurasia. This was important in opening dispersal routes between North and South America from the Atlantic via the Caribbean into the Pacific and around the southern hemisphere via the Southern Ocean. The Paratethys Sea was a northern arm of the Tethys Sea stretching across the area now inhabited by the Black, Caspian, and Aral Seas of Asia (Fig. 6.10). A large scale drying of the Mediterranean occurred between 5–6 Ma and both it and the Tethys seaway were reduced to series of lakes so that the Black, Caspian, and Aral seas became separate bodies of water. Marine mammals with Tethyan or Paratethyan distributions include the oldest whales and sirenians (Fig. 6.9).

The Central American, or Panamanian, Seaway existed between North and South America during the Miocene (12 Ma) until 5 Ma when it began to close. It was completely closed

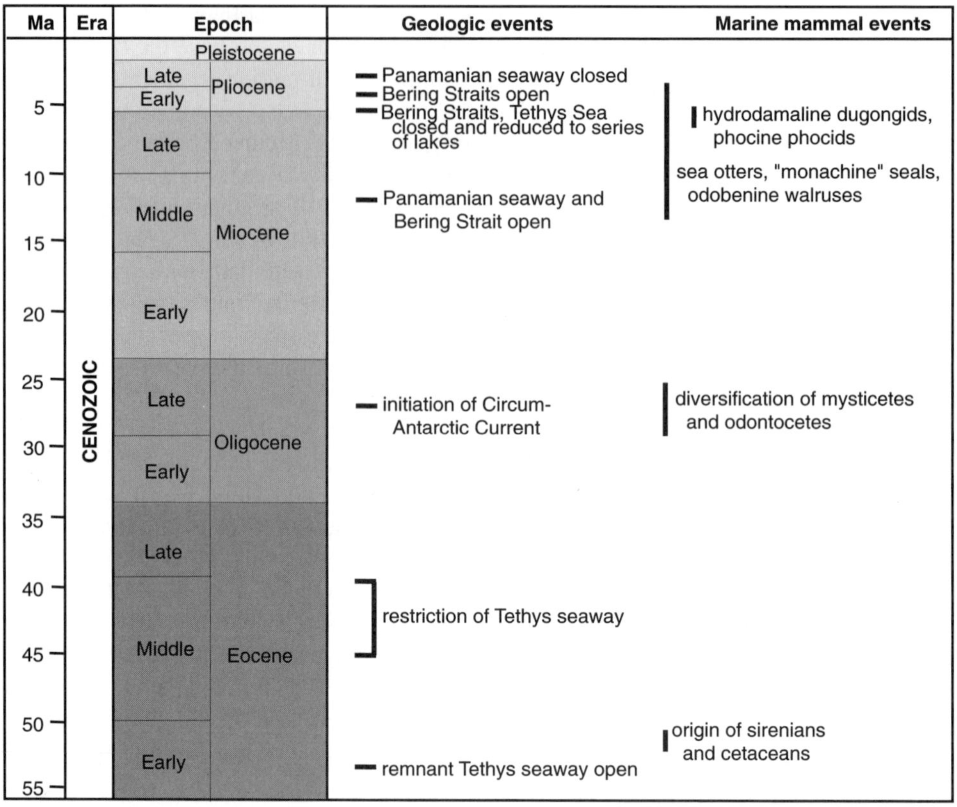

Figure 6.9. Chronology of major geologic events affecting marine mammal distributions.

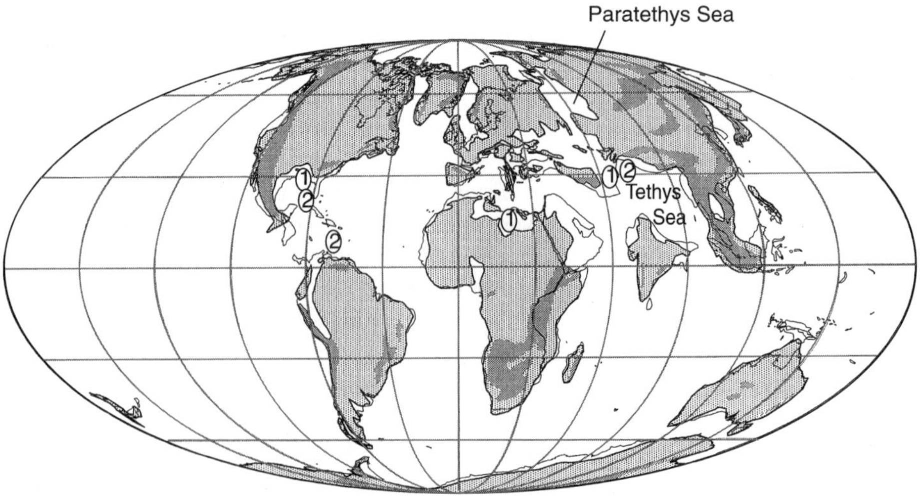

Figure 6.10. Reconstruction of continents, ocean basins, and paleocoastlines in the early Eocene (Base map from Smith *et al.,* 1994). Note extent of Tethys and Paratethys seaways; 1=early records of cetaceans, 2=early records of sirenians.

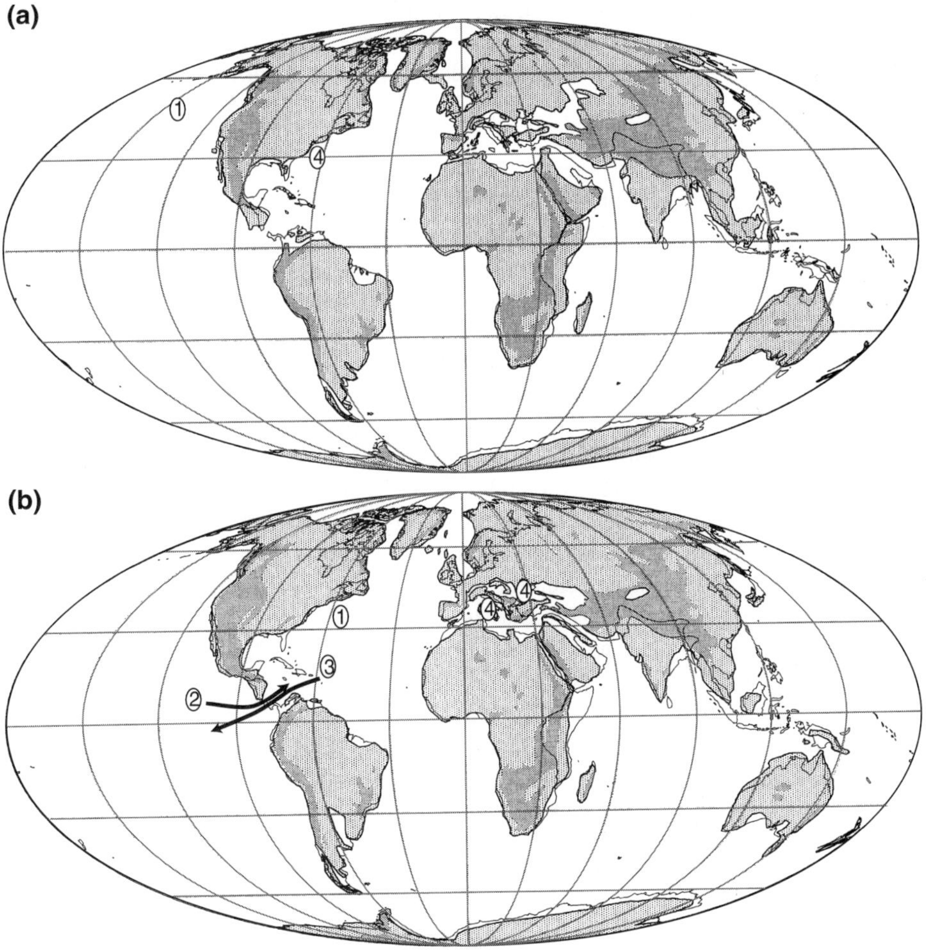

Figure 6.11. Reconstruction of continents, ocean basins, and paleocoastlines in the (a) early Miocene (20 Ma) (1 = early records of archaic pinnipeds, odobenids and desmatophocids), and (b) middle Miocene (12 Ma) (1 = early well documented phocids, 2 = dispersal of "monachines" and odobenids to Atlantic, 3 = dispersal of phocines to South Pacific, 4 = isolation of phocines in remnants of Paratethys Sea and in North Atlantic) (Base map from Smith *et al.,* 1994).

between 3.7 and 3.1 Ma (Duque-Caro, 1990; Fig. 6.11b). This is the route most likely followed by the lineage which led to the modern sea otter *Enhydra* (Berta and Morgan, 1985), odobenine walruses, and "monachine" seals (Fig. 6.9).

The Bering Strait, a seaway between Alaska and Siberia, first opened during the late Miocene (12–10 Ma but see Marincovich and Gladenkov, 1999, for revised dates) and provided a connection between the Pacific and Arctic Oceans. A land bridge established approximately 5.0 Ma disrupted the seaway. The seaway opened again between 4.0–3.0 Ma, at which time the Bering and Chukchi Seas were formed. Marine mammals that used this route include hydrodamaline dugongids and phocine phocids (Fig. 6.9). The Arctic basin, a corridor between the North Pacific and North Atlantic during interglacial periods over the last 3 Ma, was an important dispersal route followed by the modern walrus, the bowhead whale, several phocine seals, and possibly the gray whale.

In discussing the distributions of marine mammals it also is important to recognize the presence of barriers to dispersal, including physical barriers (continents or other landmasses), climatic barriers (the equator or cold temperatures), or biotic factors (low productivity).

6.5.1. Pinnipeds

The oldest walruses are known from the North Pacific during the middle Miocene, approximately 16 Ma (Kohno *et al.,* 1995; Fig. 6.11a). During the late Miocene, odobenids underwent dramatic diversification with later members of this lineage coming from the North Atlantic. It has been proposed that the modern walrus lineage (odobenine walruses) entered the Caribbean from the Pacific via the Central American Seaway (between 5 and 8 Ma) and dispersed northward into the North Atlantic. Less than 1 Ma, the living genus *Odobenus* returned to the North Pacific through the Arctic Ocean (Repenning and Tedford, 1977; Repenning *et al.,* 1979). Alternatively, on the basis of new, earlier (late Pliocene, 3 Ma) fossil records of the modern walrus lineage from Japan, it has been suggested that this lineage may have evolved in the North Pacific and dispersed instead to the North Atlantic through the Arctic Ocean during the late Pleistocene (Kohno *et al.,* 1996). Future discoveries of walrus fossils may allow us to determine which hypothesis is correct.

The earliest recognized otariids are mid-Miocene in age (approximately 11–12 Ma) from the North Pacific (Repenning, 1976; Barnes *et al.,* 1985; Berta and Deméré, 1986; Fig. 6.11a). The sea lions diverged as a distinct lineage by about 3 Ma (or perhaps 5 Ma + as implied by Berta and Deméré, 1986) and represent the most recently derived of the otariids. Although fur seals had dispersed to the southern hemisphere by about 5 Ma, the sea lions crossed the equator within the past 3 Ma. Dispersal of otariids south of the equator occurred presumably at times when a continuum of cold-water habitat existed along the Eastern Pacific rim, as otariids are usually limited to temperate and subtropical temperatures. This pathway was thought by Davies (1958a) to have resulted from gradual southward movements of isotherms in the North Pacific in pre-Pliocene times and perhaps involved the cold north-flowing Peru Current, whose influence at this time reached almost to the equator. The close correlation between high levels of primary productivity and the distribution of otariids happened to occur in colder waters (Costa, 1993). The diversification of otariids in the southern hemisphere also has been explained by island hopping assisted by the West Wind Drift (circumpolar circulation). Sea lion diversification proceeded subsequent to isolation of populations in the northern and southern hemispheres of the Pacific basin, leading to the radiation of the California sea lion (*Zalophus californianus*) and Steller's sea lion (*Eumetopias jubatus*) in the north and the Australian sea lion (*Neophoca cinerea*), southern sea lion (*Otaria byronia*), and the New Zealand sea lion (*Phocarctos hookeri*) in the south. A different hypothesis of otariid relationships such as that proposed by Lento *et al.* (1995 and personal communication) would alter this interpretation.

The biogeographic history of phocids, reviewed by Bininda-Emonds and Russell (1996), is summarized here. Much of the previous biogeographic history of phocids was suggested prior to general acceptance of pinniped monophyly. When pinniped monophyly is taken into account, it is most parsimonious to consider all pinnipeds as having originated in the North Pacific. Traditionally the oldest known phocids, representatives of both "monachine" and phocine lineages, were believed to have appeared during the middle Miocene (15 Ma) in the North Atlantic (North America and Europe; Fig. 6.11b). The discovery of a phocid in the South Atlantic in rocks that may be as old as 29 Ma (Koretsky, 1997) suggests that the common ancestor of phocids had migrated to the North Atlantic, either northward through the Arctic basin or southward through the Central American Seaway. Costa (1993) had suggested such a route (specifically via the southern route) based on the hypothesized sister group relationship of phocids and the extinct desmatophocids. A southern route of dispersal is more likely, as discussed by Bininda-Emonds and Russell (1996), given that the Bering land bridge blocked access to the Arctic through much of the late Oligocene and early Miocene. It may also be that the colder climate through the Arctic basin hindered phocid dispersal along the northern route. The Central American Seaway was open during this time and is in agreement with the warm water affinities of North Atlantic phocids at this time. Desmatophocids, proposed as sister group to the phocids, are likewise known from this time. Species of both *Allodesmus* and *Desmatophoca* extended their ranges from the North Pacific (Japan and the Pacific Northwest) at least to central southern California (Barnes *et al.,* 1995; Deméré and Berta, in press). As mentioned above, the recent discovery of an Oligocene phocid from the Atlantic coast of North America also lends support to a southern route. Thus, it is possible that the phocids may represent an offshoot of one of the lineages that migrated through the Central American Seaway into the North Atlantic. This same route was suggested to have been followed later by ancestors of the modern walrus as noted above (Repenning and Tedford, 1977; Repenning *et al.,* 1979).

The biogeographic history of *Monachus* is conflicting since there are differing hypotheses for its phylogenetic position relative to other phocids. If we accept the hypothesis of *Monachus schauinslandi* as the sister group to the remaining monk seals, as advocated by Repenning and Ray (1977) and Wyss (1988), then a likely dispersal route for this species was through the Central American Seaway. As noted by Costa (1993), however, the relatively young age of the Hawaiian Islands (6 Ma) suggests that *M. schauinslandi* may not have migrated through the Central American Seaway with the ancient phocids in the first place, but that a founder population later reached the Hawaiian islands. According to a previous hypothesis for monk seal diversification, the record of a fossil monachine (*Homiphoca capensis*) from Africa indicated that speciation was the result of a progressive westward dispersal from the northwest coast of Africa (Hendey, 1972; Muizon, 1982; Fig. 6.11b). A second previous hypothesis had speciation occurring as an interruption of the gene flow of a wide-ranging North Atlantic population (giving rise to a Mediterranean and Caribbean populations) followed by dispersal to the Hawaiian islands (Ray, 1976). "Monachines" apparently diversified later in the colder waters of the southern hemisphere to produce the lobodontine seal fauna of the Antarctic today.

The biogeographic pattern for the phocine seals is no less complicated given the different phylogenetic hypotheses proposed (i.e. Wyss, 1988; Bininda-Emonds and Russell, 1996). Until recently, less was known about phocine seals due to their poor fossil record and their previously recognized relatively recent (Plio/Pleistocene) radiation (Ray, 1976). It also was suggested that phocines were high latitude animals and never crossed the Central American Seaway (Repenning *et al.,* 1979), an assertion that is no longer accepted. The discovery of a considerable diversity of phocines (at least five species) from the southern hemisphere (both Atlantic and Pacific coasts) in the Miocene and Pliocene points to the need for a reevaluation of the early biogeographic history of phocids. Phocine seals are apparently known in the southern hemisphere as far back as the middle Miocene where they have been recovered from Argentina (Cozzuol, 1996). Other fossil seals, also apparently phocines, are from the late late Miocene and Pliocene (6.7–5.2 Ma) of Peru. In addition to a diversification in the southern hemisphere, other phocine lineages appear to have been isolated in the Parathethys Sea and the North Atlantic during the late Miocene and Pliocene. One hypothesis evoked two separate dispersal events for phocines (Repenning *et al.,* 1979). The first dispersal involved an initial northward migration from the Paratethys Sea into the Arctic Basin, followed by an eastward migration to give rise to modern *Phoca.* The landlocked Baikal seal (*Phoca sibirica*) gained access to Lake Baikal from the Arctic via large lakes at the southern margin of the Siberian ice sheet. A second land-locked species, the Caspian seal (*Phoca caspica*), remained in the Caspian Sea, an isolated remnant of Paratethys, as judged by the presence of fossils similar to living Caspian seals in this location (Repenning *et al.,* 1979). The second dispersal involved a westward migration of the remaining phocines from the North Atlantic to their current ranges. Phocine seals dispersed to the Arctic and Pacific 2.5–3.0 Ma. A single species, the hooded seal (*Cystophora cristata*), occurs at high latitudes of the Atlantic basin and apparently never successfully dispersed to the Pacific Basin (Davies, 1958b; Ray, 1976). The bearded seal (*Erignathus barbatus*), presently confined to Arctic and subarctic waters around the northern periphery of the North Atlantic, is known from the Pleistocene on both sides of the Atlantic as far south as Portugal (Ray *et al.,* 1982). As discussed by Bininda-Emonds and Russell (1996), a second hypothesis (Davies, 1958b) argued for a North Atlantic origin for all phocines with glacial events causing speciation. The role of glacial events in the speciation of phocines also was discussed by Hoberg (1995). He noted that cylical fluctuations in glacial maxima (with concomitant variations in sea level) through the Pleistocene mediated range expansions and contractions for *Phoca* spp., ultimately leading to the isolation of populations in refugial centers (i.e. Arctic, Okhotsk, Aleutian) and divergence of populations (e.g. ringed seal (*P. hispida*), largha seal (*P. largha*), ribbon seal (*Histriophoca fasciata*), harbor seal (*P. vitulina*), and harp seal (*P. groenlandicus*). Árnason *et al.* (1995) proposed that the separation of the ringed seal, gray seal, and harbor (+spotted) seal lineages was triggered by the onset of the first major northern hemisphere glacial event 2.3 Ma or its predessor 2.5 Ma.

The historical biogeography of pinnipeds and parasites was studied by Hoberg and Adams (1992). They proposed that radiation of seven species of tapeworms (*Anophryocephalus* spp.) among phocine pinnipeds in the Holarctic was driven by isolation in response to habitat disruption (especially variations in sea level) during the late Tertiary and Pleistocene. A minimum of four species of tapeworm is hypothesized to have evolved with ringed seals (*Phoca hispida*) in the Atlantic basin. The diversification of basal species of this tapeworm are associated with isolation of populations of ringed seals in the Atlantic portion of the Arctic basin (e.g. vicariance associated with closure of the Bering Strait) during glacial periods.

6.5.2. Cetaceans

The earliest known cetaceans, the archaeocetes, are known from the middle Eocene (52 Ma) of the southern U.S. (Texas, Georgia), Africa (Nigeria, Egypt), and India. Cetaceans radiated rapidly, becoming diverse in the area encompassing the shallow Tethys Sea. Closure of the Tethys Sea by collision of India with Asia by about 40–45 Ma concomitant with global climatic cooling apparently resulted in a drop of species-level diversity of archaeocetes (Fordyce, 1996).

The earliest known mysticetes and odontocetes are from the southern hemisphere, specifically from Oligocene (30 Ma) deposits of New Zealand. Fordyce (1977) proposed that the advent of filter feeding in the earliest mysticetes known from New Zealand (e.g. *Mauicetus*) was rapidly induced by changes in the productivity of zooplankton associated with initiation of the Circum-Antarctic current. Mysticetes and odontocetes were taxonomically and ecologically diverse and attained worldwide distribution during the late

Oligocene. Odontocete diversification produced the earliest squalodontids, physeterids, waipatiids, squalodelphids, kentriodontids, and possibly eurhinodelphids. Some groups were confined to certain oceanic basins, such as the physeterids and eurhinodelphids (Paratethys), while other groups like the squalodontids had a more cosmopolitan distribution (Parathethys, western North Atlantic, and western North and South Pacific; Deméré, 1994). Odontocete diversity increased during the early Miocene, the warmest interval in cetacean history. In the eastern North Pacific and earliest ziphiids and platanistids appeared and the extinct squalodontids maintained their high diversity concentrated in the Mediterannean and Paratethys regions. Middle Miocene odontocete diversity was also high and included an increased diversity in the above-mentioned groups as well as among physeterids (Deméré, 1994). The early Miocene, was also marked by the high diversity of archaic mysticetes (e.g. "cetotheres"), last recorded during the middle Pliocene. During the middle Miocene, balaenopterids and delphinoids radiated extensively whereas platanistoids progressively declined either because of competition with delphinoids or climatic changes (Fordyce, 1996). The cosmopolitan distribution of mysticetes during the late Miocene suggests a high level of faunal interchange between the Atlantic and the Pacific (Deméré, 1994). Representatives of modern odontocete families are known from the late Miocene of the eastern North Pacific (monodontids and phocoenids) and western South Atlantic (pontoporiids). Phocoenids had dispersed to the western North Pacific and eastern South Pacific by the latest Miocene. At the same time archaic dolphins, the kentriodontids, declined to extinction, the earliest modern dolphins (delphinids) are reported from both sides of the North Pacific. By the Pliocene mysticetes and odontocetes were represented by modern taxa, some of which are placed in extant genera (Deméré, 1994).

The Quaternary (Pleistocene to Recent) record of distribution of cetaceans was influenced by cyclical changes in sea level. Sea-level drops (correlated with cooling) are suggested to have isolated populations resulting in incipient speciation and if extreme, the elimination of some shelf areas and ultimately in the extinction of species with limited ranges. Rises in sea level (warming) are suggested to have increased continental shelf space and led to either mixing of populations or extinction (Fordyce, 1996).

Warm tropical waters also appear to have segregated species in the northern and southern hemisphere creating antitropical distributions (e.g., northern and southern right whales and northern and southern right whale dolphins).

6.5.3. Sirenians

The earliest known sirenians appeared in the early Eocene (50 Ma) and had a Tethyan distribution (Java, India, Europe, and the southeastern U.S.) where they underwent a rather rapid diversification throughout the Tethys Sea during the middle and the late Eocene. During the Oligocene, halitheriine and dugongine sirenians occupied the western North Atlantic, with halitheriines and the earliest trichechids found in the central Tethys (Deméré, 1994).

During the early Miocene, sirenians dispersed into the eastern North Pacific through the Central American Seaway. Dugongines, for the most part, remained confined to the Atlantic. By the Pleistocene a single genus, *Dugong,* had entered the Pacific and remained restricted to tropical latitudes in the Indo-Pacific Basin. In the late Miocene there was a major decline in the diversity of halitheriine sirenians and they disappeared in the late Pliocene (Deméré, 1994). This decline was likely related to progressive climatic cooling which eliminated tropical sea grasses, altering the resource biomass for these large herbivores. At the same time, cool-water kelp flourished during the late Miocene, which probably accounts for adaptive trends observed in hydrodamalines. For example, the lineage that lead to Steller's sea cow (*Hydrodamalis gigas*) had a North Pacific distribution and occupied the Bering Sea during the late Pleistocene until it was hunted to extinction by man.

Domning (1982) attempted to explain the evolution, biogeography, and feeding ecology of manatees using a historical context. By the late Miocene (5 Ma), manatees occurred along coastal rivers and estuaries on both sides of South America. During the Miocene and Pliocene, uplift of the Andes created erosion and runoff of dissolved nutrients into river systems, which greatly increased the abundance of grasses. Manatees adapted to this new food resource by evolving smaller, more numerous teeth that were continually replaced. In addition, enamel ridges that formed the chewing surfaces of the teeth became more complex. During the Pliocene (3 Ma) manatees gained access to the Amazon basin, which at the time was temporarily isolated by the Andean uplift. Cut off from marine waters, the Amazonian Manatee (*T. inunguis*) evolved. Manatees later dispersed to North America (*T. manatus*) and to West Africa (*T. sengalensis;* Fig. 6.12).

6.6. Summary and Conclusions

Understanding the geographic distribution of a species involves a knowledge of both their ecology and evolutionary biology. The ecological requirements of a species limit where it can live. For marine mammals, patterns of water temperature and the distribution of primary productivity influence their past and present distributions. Two major patterns of present day marine mammal distribution can be identified: widespread or cosmopolitan distributions and disjunct or antitropical distributions. Two major historical processes have influenced the geographic distribution of species: dispersal (movement of a species into an area) or vicariance (the formation of a barrier that splits the range of a species). An area cladogram shows the phylogenetic relationships between species inhabiting different areas. If

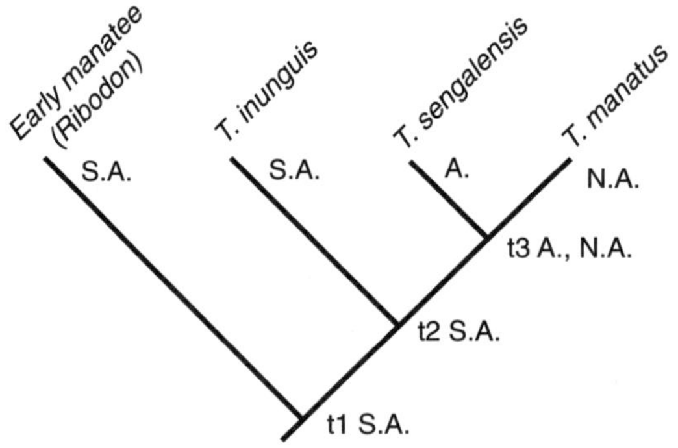

Figure 6.12. Biogeographic history of manatees. A=Africa, N.A.=North America, S.A.=South America (based on Domning, 1982). Timetable of Events: t1, 5 mya—Manatees inhabit rivers and estuaries of S.A. Uplift of Andes, increase in silt and grasses, corresponding changes in dentition ("conveyor belt" tooth replacement, increase in number of teeth, decrease in tooth size, increase in tooth (enamel) complexity. t2, 3 mya—Manatees gain access to Amazon basin, localized speciation of *T. inunguis*. t3, 1-2 mya—Dispersal of manatees-A. (*T. sengalensis*) and N.A. (*T. manatus*).

geographic distributions are determined mainly by vicariant events then the area cladograms of a taxon should match the geologic history of an area. Phylogenies also have been used to study the biogeography of host-parasite relationships, such as between tapeworms and phocine seals, and the evolution, biogeography, and feeding ecology of manatees.

The historical biogeography of pinnipeds suggests the following major patterns. The early evolution of walruses took place in the North Pacific. The modern walrus lineage entered the Carribean from the Pacific via the Central American Seaway between 5 and 8 Ma and dispersed northward into the North Atlantic. Less than 1 Ma the living genus *Odobenus* returned to the North Pacific through the Arctic Ocean. Otariid evolution largely took place in the North Pacific. Fur seals and sea lions crossed into the southern hemisphere by 6 Ma. The evolutionary history of phocids apparently began in the North Atlantic, although earlier the common ancestor of phocids likely migrated there via a southern route through the Central American Seaway. Subsequent climatic deterioration resulted in monachine seals retreating southward while the phocines adapted to colder climates in the north. Monachines apparently diversified later in the colder waters of the southern hemisphere to produce the lobodontine seal fauna present in the Antarctic today. The diversification of phocines occurred in both the southern hemisphere and the North Atlantic; speciation in the latter area was affected by glacial events.

Both cetaceans and sirenians had a Tethyan origin. The earliest baleen and toothed whales are from the southern hemisphere. The evolution of filter feeding in mysticetes has been linked to initiation of the Circum-Antarctic Current and rapidly induced changes in zooplankton productivity. Recent diversification of cetaceans has been related to sea level changes which promoted isolation and speciation in some cases and extinction in other cases. Dugongids were considerably more diverse in the past and were reduced to a single genus confined to a tropical distribution in the Indo-Pacific Basin. The lineage that lead to Steller's sea cow had a North Pacific distribution and occupied the Bering Sea during the late Pleistocene until it was hunted to extinction by man.

6.7. Further Reading

A general introductory text on biogeography is Brown and Lomalino (1998). The ecologic influences on distribution are reviewed in Steele (1974) and Brown *et al.* (1985). The effect of El Niño on marine mammal populations is summarized in Trillmich and Ono (1991). For vicariance biogeography see Humphries and Parenti (1986). A classic introduction to pinniped biogeography is Repenning *et al.* (1979); for other reviews of the topic see Muizon (1982), Bininda-Emonds and Russell (1996), and Kohno *et al.* (1996). Cetacean biogeography is summarized by Gaskin (1976) and Fordyce (1977, 1980). For sirenian biogeography see Domning (1978, 1982) and Domning and Furusawa (1995).

References

Árnason, U., K. Bodin, A. Gullberg, C. Ledje, and S. Mouchaty (1995). A molecular view of pinniped relationships with particular emphasis on the true seals. *J. Mol. Evol.* **40**: 78–85.

Barnes, L. G. (1977). Outline of eastern North Pacific fossil cetacean assemblages. *Syst. Zool.* **25**: 321–343.

Barnes, L. G. (1984). Fossil odontocetes from the Almejas Formation, Isla Cedros, Mexico. *PaleoBios* **42**: 1–46.

Barnes, L. G., D. P. Domning, and C. E. Ray (1985). Status of studies on fossil marine mammals. *Mar. Mamm. Sci.* **1**: 15–53.

Barnes, L. G., and K. Hirota (1995). Miocene pinnipeds of the otariid subfamily Allodesminae in the North Pacific Ocean: systematics and relationships. *Island Arc* **3**: 329–360.

Berta, A., and T. A. Deméré (1986). *Callorhinus gilmorei* n. sp. (Carnivora: Otariidae) from the San Diego Formation (Blancan) and its implications for otariid phylogeny. *Trans. San Diego Soc. Nat. Hist.* **21**(7): 111–126.

Berta, A., and G. S. Morgan (1985). A new sea otter (Carnivora: Mustelidae) from the late Miocene and early Pliocene (Hemphillian) of North America. *J. Paleontol.* **59**: 809–819.

Bickham, J. W., J. C. Patton, and T. R. Loughlin (1996). High variability for control-region sequences in a marine mammal: implications for conservation and biogeography of Steller sea lions. *J. Mammal.* **77**(1): 95–108.

Bininda-Emonds, O. R. P., and A. P. Russell (1996). A morphological perspective on the phylogenetic relationships of the extant phocid seals (Mammalia: Carnivora: Phocidae). Bohner Zoologische Monographien, **41**: 1–256.

Bogdanov, D. V. (1963). Map of the natural zones of the ocean. *Deep-Sea Res.* **10**: 520–523.

Boyd, I. L., and T. Arnbom (1991). Diving behavior in relation to water temperature in the southern elephant seal: Foraging implications. *Polar Biol.* **11**: 259–266.

Brown, J. H., and M. V. Lomalino (1998). "Biogeography." 2nd ed., Sinauer Assoc., Sunderland, MA.

Brown, O. B., R. H. Evans, J. W. Brown, H. R. Gordon, R. C. Smith, and K. S. Baker (1985). Phytoplankton blooming off the U.S. east coast: A satellite description. *Science* **229**: 163–167.

Costa, D. (1993). The relationship between reproductive and foraging energetics and the evolution of the Pinnipedia. *Symp. Zool. Soc. London* **66**: 293–314.

Cozzuol, M. A. (1996). The record of the aquatic mammals in southern South America. *Müench. Geowiss. Abh.* **30**: 321–342.

Davies, J. L. (1958a). The Pinnipedia: An essay in zoogeography. *Geogr. Rev.* **48**: 474–493.

Davies, J. L. (1958b). Pleistocene geography and the distribution of northern pinnipeds. *Ecology* **39**: 97–113.

Deméré, T. A. (1994). Phylogenetic systematics of the Family Odobenidae (Mammalia: Carnivora), with description of two new species from the Pliocene of California and a review of marine mammal paleofaunas of the world. Unpublished Ph.D. Dissertation, University of California, Los Angeles.

Deméré, T. A., and A. Berta (in press). The Miocene pinniped *Desmatophoca oregonensis* Condon, 1906 (Mammalia: Carnivora) from the Astoria Formation, Oregon. *Smithson. Contrib. Paleobiol.*

Domning, D. P. (1978). "Sirenian evolution in the North Pacific Ocean." *Univ. Calif. Publ. Geol. Sci.* 118, 176 pp.

Domning, D. (1982). The evolution of manatees: A speculative history. *J. Paleontol.* **56**(3): 599–619.

Domning, D. P., and H. Furusawa (1995). Summary of taxa and distribution of Sirenia in the North Pacific Ocean. *Island Arc* **3**: 506–512.

Duque-Caro, H. (1990). Neogene stratigraphy, paleoceanography, and paleobiogeography in northwestern South America and the evolution of the Panama seaway. *Paleogeogr. Paleoclimatol. Paleoecol.* **77**: 203–234.

Duxbury, A. C., and A. B. Duxbury (1997). "An Introduction to the World's Oceans." Wm. C. Brown, Dubuque, IA.

Evans, G. H. P. (1987). "The Natural History of Whales and Dolphins." Facts On File, New York.

Falkowski, P. G. (ed.) (1980). "Primary Productivity in the Sea." Plenum, New York.

Fordyce, R. E. (1977). The development of the Circum-Antarctic current and the evolution of the Mysticeti. *Palaeogeogr., Palaeoclimatol., Palaeoecol.* **21**: 265–271.

Fordyce, R. E. (1980). Whale evolution and Oligocene southern ocean environments. *Palaeogeogr. Palaeoclimatol. Palaeoecol.* **31**: 319–336.

Fordyce, R. E. (1996). An evolutionary perspective on cetaceans and climate change. *Abstr., Int. Whal. Comm. Symp. Clim. Change Cetaceans,* Oahu, HI.

Gaskin, D. E. (1976). The evolution, zoogeography and ecology of Cetacea. *Oceanogr. Mar. Biol.* **14**: 247–346.

Gaskin, D. E. (1982). "The Ecology of Whales and Dolphins." Heinemann, London.

Harwood, L. A., and I. Stirling (1992). Distribution of ringed seals in the southeastern Beaufort Sea during the late summer. *Can. J. Zool.* **70**: 891–900.

Hendey, Q. B. (1972). The evolution and dispersal of the Monachinae. *Ann. S. Afr. Mus.* **59**(5): 99–113.

Hoberg, E. P. (1995). Historical biogeography and modes of speciation across high latitude seas of the Holarctic: Concepts for host-parasite co-evolution among the Phocini (Phocidae) and Tetrabothriidae (Eucestoda). *Can. J. Zool.* **73**: 45–57.

Hoberg, E. P., and A. M. Adams (1992). Phylogeny, historical biogeography, and ecology of *Anophryocephalus* spp. (Eucestoda: Tetrabothriidae) among pinnipeds of the Holarctic during the late Tertiary and Pleistocene. *Can. J. Zool.* **70**: 703–719.

Humphries, C. J., and L. Parenti (1986). "Cladistic Biogeography." Oxford University Press, Oxford.

Kohno, N., L. G. Barnes, and K. Hirota (1995). Miocene fossil pinnipeds of the genera *Prototaria* and *Neotherium* (Carnivora: Otariidae; Imagotariinae) in the North Pacific Ocean: Evolution, relationships and distribution. *Island Arc* **3**(4): 285–308.

Kohno, N., Y. Tomida, Y. Hasegawa, and H. Furusawa (1996). Pliocene tusked odobenids (Mammalia: Carnivora) in the western North Pacific, and their paleobiogeography. *Bull. Natal. Sci. Mus. Ser. C: Geol. (Tokyo)* **21**(3–4): 111–131.

Koretsky, I. (1997). Pinniped bones from the late Oligocene of South Carolina: the oldest known true seal (Carnivora: Phocidae). *Abstr., 57th Ann. Meet. Soc. Vert. Paleo.,* Chicago, p. 58A.

Lento, G., R. E. Hickson, G. K. Chambers, and D. Penny (1995). Use of spectral analysis to test hypotheses on the origin of pinnipeds. *Mol. Biol. Evol.* **12**(1): 28–52.

Lipps, J., and E. D. Mitchell (1976). Trophic model for the adaptive radiations and extinctions of pelagic marine mammals. *Paleobiology* **2**: 147–155.

Loeb, V., V. Siegel, O. Holm-Hansen, R. Hewitt, W. Fraser, W. Trivelpiece, and S. Trivelpiece (1997). Effects of sea-ice extent and krill or salp dominance on the Antarctic food web. *Nature (London)* **387**: 897–898.

Marincovich, L. Jr., and A. Yu. Gladenkov. (1999). Evidence for an early opening of the Bering Strait. *Nature* **397**: 149–151.

Muizon, C. de (1982). Phocid phylogeny and dispersal. *Ann. S. Afr. Mus.* **89**: 175–213.

Orr, W. N., and J. Faulhaber (1975). A middle Tertiary cetacean from Oregon. *Northwest Sci.* **49**: 174–181.

Perry, M. J. (1986). Assessing marine primary production from space. *BioScience* **36**: 461–466.

Ray, C. E. (1976). Geography of phocid evolution. *Syst. Zool.* **25**: 391–406.

Ray, C. E., F. Reiner, D. E. Sargeant, and C. N. Quesada (1982). Notes on past and present distribution of the Bearded Seal, *Erignathus barbatus,* around the North Atlantic Ocean. *Mem. Mus. Mar, Ser. Zool.* **2**(23): 1–32.

Repenning, C. A. (1976). Adaptive evolution of sea lions and walruses. *Syst. Zool.* **25**(4): 375–390.

Repenning, C. A., and R. H. Tedford (1977). Otarioid seals of the Neogene. Professional Papers of the United States Geological Survey, **992**: 93 pp.

Repenning, C. A., C. E. Ray, and D. Gigorescu (1979). Pinniped biogeography. *In* "Historical Biogeography, Plate Tectonics, and the Changing Environment" (J. Gray and A. J. Boucot, eds.), pp. 357–369. Oregon State University Press, Corvallis.

Ridley, M. (1993). "Evolution." Blackwell Scientific, London.

Riedman, M. (1990). "The Pinnipeds." University of California Press, Berkeley.

Simpson, G. G. (1936). Data on the relationships of local and continental mammalian faunas. *J. Paleontol.* **10**: 410–414.

Simpson, G. G. (1940). Mammals and land bridges. *J. Wash. Acad. Sci.* **30**: 137–163.

Smith, A. G., D. G. Smith, and B. M. Funnell (1994). "Atlas of Mesozoic and Cenozoic Coastlines." Cambridge Univ. Press, Cambridge.

Steele, J. H. (1974). "The Structure of Marine Ecosystems." Harvard University Press, Cambridge, MA.

Steele, J. H. (1980). Patterns in plankton. *Oceanus* **25**: 3–8.

Stirling, I., H. Cleator, and T. G. Smith (1977). Marine mammals. In Polynas in the Canadian Arctic, Canadian Wildlife Service Occasional Paper No. 45, pp. 45–58.

Sumich, J. (1996). "An Introduction to the Biology of Marine Life." Wm. C. Brown, Dubuque, IA.

Trillmich, F., and Ono, K. (eds.) (1991). "Pinnipeds and El Niño." Ecol. Stud. No. 88. Springer-Verlag, Berlin.

Trillmich, F., K. A. Ono, D. P. Costa, R. L. DeLong, S. D. Feldkamp, J. M. Francis, R. L. Gentry, C. B. Heath, B. J. LeBoeuf, P. Majluf, and A. E. York (1991). The effects of El Niño on pinniped populations in the eastern Pacific. *In* "Pinnipeds and El Niño" (F. Trillmich and K. A. Ono, eds.), Ecol. Stud. No. 88. Springer-Verlag, New York.

Tynan, C. T. (1998). Ecological importance of the southern boundary of the Antarctic Circumpolar Current, *Nature* **392**: 708–710.

Tynan, C. T., and D. P. DeMaster (1997). Observations and predictions of Arctic climate change: potential effects on marine mammals. *Arctic* **50**(4): 308–322.

Whitmore, F. C., Jr. (1994). Neogene climatic change and the emergence of the modern whale fauna of the North Atlantic Ocean. *Proc. San Diego Soc. Nat. Hist.* **29**: 223–227.

Wyss, A. R. (1988). On "retrogression" in the evolution of the Phocinae and phylogenetic affinities of the monk seals. American Museum Novitates, 2924: 1–38.

7

Integumentary, Sensory, and Urinary Systems

7.1. Introduction

Before exploring the behavioral and ecological adaptations of marine mammals to their environment in Part II, it is necessary to discuss how the internal workings of these animals makes possible the diverse ways in which they live. This chapter summarizes the functional anatomy and physiology of the integumentary, sensory, and urinary systems of marine mammals. Review of the integumentary system includes description of components of the system (i.e. skin, hair, glands, vibrissae, and claws) as well as consideration of how most marine mammals cope with heat loss or how those living in warm environments cope with overheating. Discussion of the nervous system highlights how relative brain size is measured and what it means and how enlargements of different segments of the spinal cord are correlated to differing patterns of locomotion. Similarities and differences among marine mammals with respect to development of the visual system and acuity, olfaction, and taste are described later in the chapter. Sound production and reception are discussed in Chapter 10. Finally, the urinary system of marine mammals is reviewed and the maintenance of water balance considered.

7.2. Integumentary System

7.2.1. Skin

As in all mammals, the skin of marine mammals consists of an outer layer (the epidermis), a middle layer (the dermis), and a deep layer, which forms the blubber (the hypodermis). The dermis contains hair follicles, sebaceous and sweat glands, and claws (in pinnipeds, the sea otter, and the polar bear). The skin of cetaceans and sirenians is distinguished by the absence of glands and hair, except for bristle-like hairs especially dense around the mouth.

The structure of the epidermis in marine mammals is multilayered stratified squamous epithelium consisting of at least three of the five layers typical of mammals: stratum basale, stratum spinosum, and stratum corneum (Fig. 7.1). The outermost layer of the epidermis, the stratum corneum, consists of a layer of flattened, solid, keratinized cells. In pinnipeds, these keratinized cells are lubricated by lipids from sebaceous glands which form a pliable waterproof layer. The thickness of the epidermis varies among pinnipeds; it is thickest in the walrus and thinnest in fur seals. The epidermis of phocids is heavily pigmented as discussed below. The epidermis of the walrus is characterized by the presence of transverse projections on the underside, similar to those seen in sirenians.

Cetacean skin is smooth with a rubbery feel. **Cutaneous ridges** have been described on the surface of the skin in many cetaceans. While the function of these structures is unknown, it has been suggested that they may play a role in tactile sensing or in the hydrodynamic characteristics of the animal or both (Shoemaker and Ridgway, 1991). Another distinguishing feature of the cetacean integument is the development of **rete ridges** on the underside of the epidermis which are oriented parallel to the body axis. These ridges form slender flap-like projections between which dermal papillae are located (Fig. 7.1). The epidermis of odontocetes is 10–20 times thicker than in terrestrial mammals (Geraci *et al.,* 1986). Thickness of the epidermis varies over the surface of the animal and changes with age (Harrison and Thurley, 1974).

In a study of skin growth in the bottlenose dolphin, the average turnover rate of germinal cells was 70 days (Geraci *et al.,* 1986). However, the sloughing rate is high due to the large number of cells in the stratum basale. Combining this information with their growth studies, Geraci *et al.* (1986) calculated that the outermost layer of epidermis is renewed

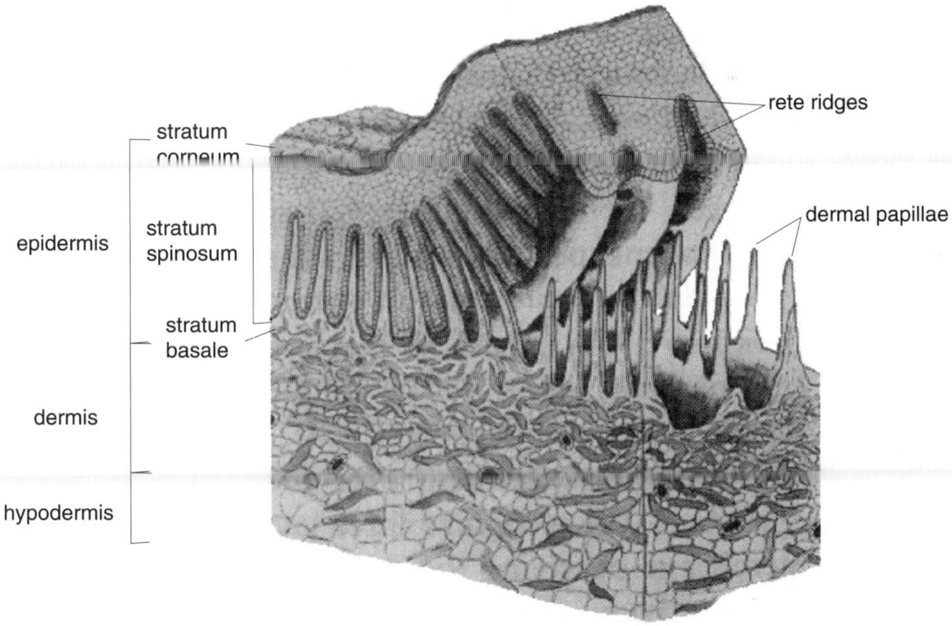

Figure 7.1. Skin of the bottlenose dolphin, *Tursiops truncatus,* illustrating the three layers of the epidermis (stratum basale, stratum spinosum, stratum corneum), the rete ridges between the epidermis and dermis and the hypodermis (from Geraci *et al.,* 1986).

every 2 hours or 12 times/day, which is nine times faster than the sloughing rate in humans (Bergstresser and Taylor, 1977).

An accelerated turnover of superficial layers of the epidermis and an increase in production of germinal cells (stratum basale) in beluga whales provided evidence of a seasonal epidermal molt (St. Aubin *et al.,* 1990). This annual cycle of epidermal growth in belugas is not seen in other whales. Results of a study that modelled heat flux in marine mammals in water during the annual molt suggested that belugas would be able to molt in water. Movement of belugas into warm water estuaries during the molt, would allow them either to save energy or molt more rapidly than if they stayed in colder open waters (Boily, 1995; St. Aubin *et al.,* 1990).

The dermis is composed of dense irregular connective tissue (Fig. 7.1). It is well vascularized and contains an increasing number of fat cells with depth as it becomes continuous with the hypodermis. Hair follicles are located in the dermis of pinnipeds, the sea otter, and the polar bear. The unusual thickness, strength, and durability of walrus skin are functions mainly of the reticular layer of the dermis, in which thick bundles of collagen fibrils form a particularly dense network (Sokolov, 1983). In the walrus the skin attains its greatest thickness on the neck and shoulders of adult males, where it is supplanted by rounded "bosses" or lumps about 1 cm thicker than the surrounding skin. These bosses have generally been regarded as a secondary sexual characteristics that develop as males approach maturity (Fay, 1982).

The most notable features of the cetacean dermis are the absence of hair follicles and sebaceous and sweat glands, its thinness relative to the epidermis, and the elaboration of finger-like projections (dermal papillae; Fig. 7.1) which extend into epidermal ridges (Ling, 1974). In sirenians, a very thick dermis is formed by dermal papillae and a subpapillary layer. Dermal papillae often penetrate the epidermis and may even extend into the horny layer, so that they lie only a few cell rows below the surface. They may therefore have a tactile function (Dosch, 1915).

The hypodermis, or blubber, is loose connective tissue composed of fat cells interlayered with bundles of collagen (Fig. 7.1). It is loosely connected to the underlying muscle layer. In the walrus, phocids, cetaceans, and sirenians the fatty hypodermis substitutes for the absence of hair and functions as insulation. Blubber is of variable thickness and lipid content depending on the age and sex of the animal, as well as individual, and seasonal variations. Blubber thickness varies among pinnipeds and its pattern of distribution optimizes streamlining as well as insulation. In the Atlantic harp seal, blubber was thickest and most variable dorsally along the posterior region of the body, becoming gradually thinner through the neck region and around the flippers (Beck and Smith, 1995). A similar distribution of blubber was reported for ringed seals (Ryg *et al.,* 1988). Blue whales have the thickest blubber of any marine mammal, averaging 23 cm deep, and over some parts of the body it can attain a depth of 50 cm (Slijper, 1979). Blubber is thinner in sirenians than in most other marine mammals, with the exception of the sea otter (Ling, 1974).

7.2.1.1. Color

The outer epithelial portion of the skin and/or pelage of marine mammals may be pigmented. Color patterns in the pelage of pinnipeds occur almost exclusively among phocids (Fig. 7.2). **Pagophilic**, or ice breeding, phocids (e.g. ribbon seal, harp seal, hooded seal, ringed seal, crabeater seal, Weddell seal, and leopard seal) show contrasting dark and light or disruptive color patterns. The unique, striking markings of the ribbon seal and harp seal

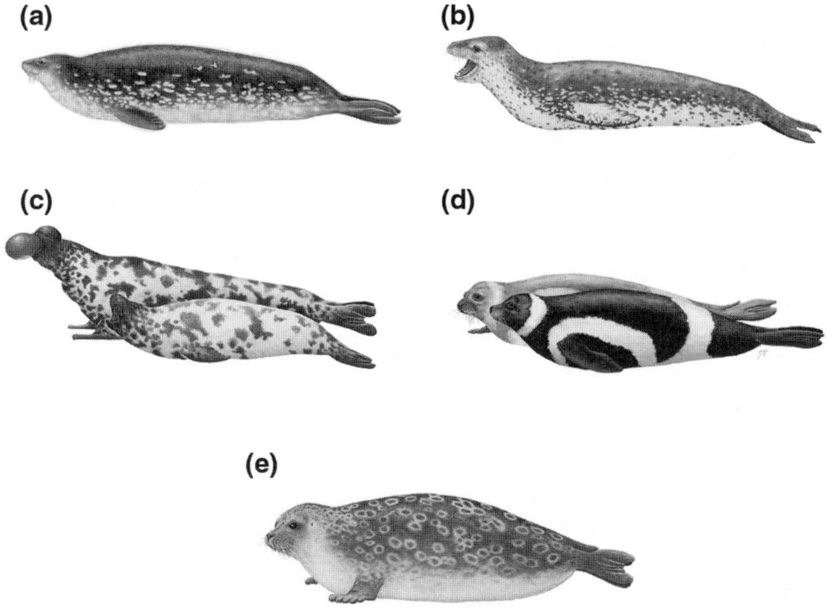

Figure 7.2. Examples of phocid pelage patterns (a) Weddell seal, *Leptonychotes weddellii,* (b) leopard seal, *Hydrurga leptonyx,* (c) hooded seal, *Cystophora cristata,* (d) ribbon seal, *Phoca fasciata,* and (e) ringed seal, *Phoca hispida.* (Illustrated by P. Folkens from Reeves *et al.,* 1992).

are informative about age and gender because they develop with age and are most strongly expressed in males (Fig. 7.3). Other more uniformly colored pinnipeds (e.g. white coloration of harp seal pups) allow them to more readily blend into their arctic environment.

Coloration patterns are determined by regional differences in the concentration of melanocytes in the epidermis. Numerous melanocytes are present throughout the epidermis of phocids, especially in the basal layers of dark regions. Otariid skin possesses only minor amounts of melanin. Walrus skin is darker in younger individuals, becoming less so with age.

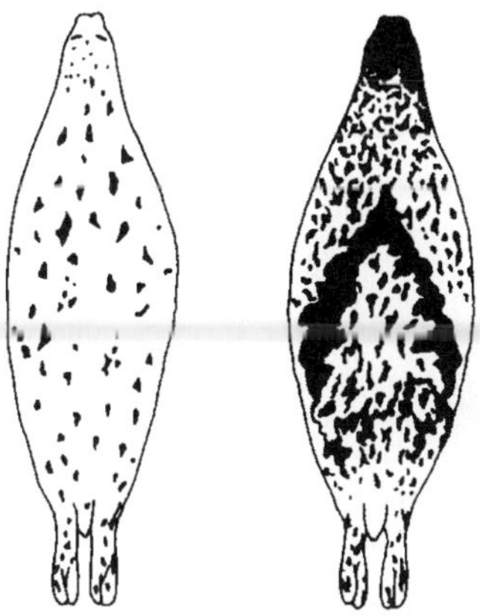

Figure 7.3. Age variation in pelage markings of harp seals, *Pagophilus groenlandica.* Youngest animal is on the left and oldest animal is on the right (from Lavigne and Kovacs, 1988).

The color patterns of cetaceans have been discussed by Yablokov *et al.* (1972) and Mitchell (1970). Three basic color patterns are recognized: 1) uniform pattern (e.g. the completely white coloration of the beluga), 2) spotted or striped pattern with sharp colored areas on the head, side, belly, and flukes (e.g. the killer whale), and 3) saddled or countershading pattern, in which the animal is dark above and light below (e.g. most dolphins; Fig. 7.4). The most common saddled and striped patterns primarily function in concealment. Different coloration patterns also are probably related to the search for food, protection from enemies, and intraspecific communication. For example, signaling between individual Hawaiian spinner dolphins and white-sided dolphins is suggested as being accomplished by their body patterns which are a dark gray cape, lighter gray lateral field, and a white belly (Mitchell, 1970; Perrin, 1972). Norris *et al.* (1994) suggested that these patterns may allow the animal to determine the degree of rotation of an adjacent neighbor. If rotation of the back is toward a neighbor, the dark cape increases in area at the expense of belly exposure. The white belly covers a larger area if the animal rotates the other way (Fig. 7.5).

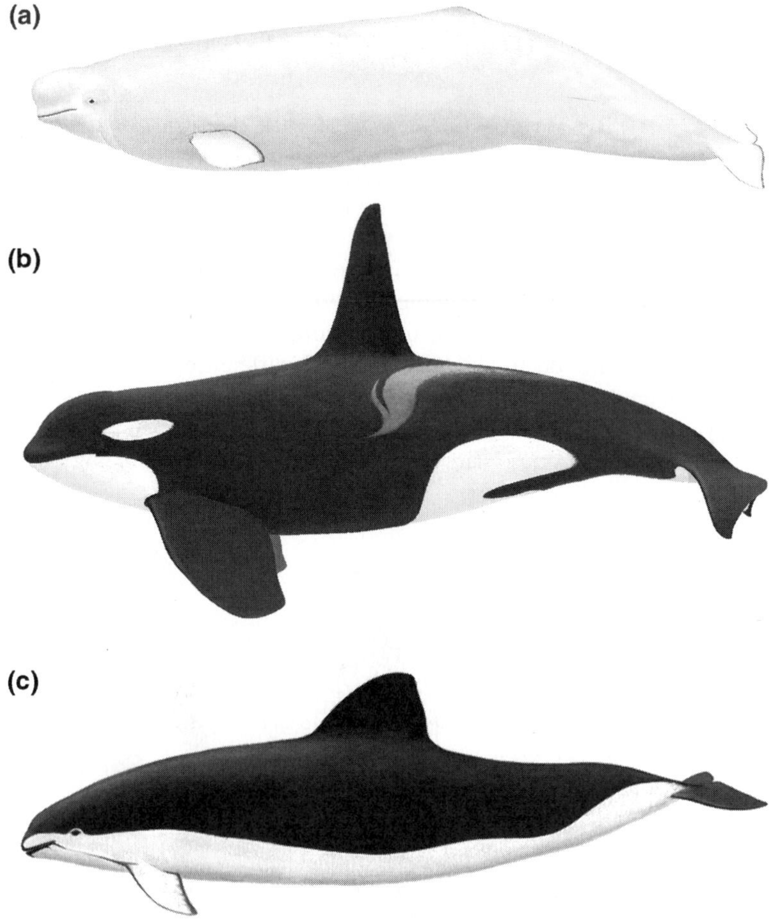

Figure 7.4. Examples of cetacean pigmentation patterns (a) Beluga, *Delphinapterus leucas,* (b) killer whale, *Orcinus orca,* and (c) Spectacled porpoise, *Phocoena dioptrica* (Illustrated by P. Folkens from Leatherwood and Reeves, 1983).

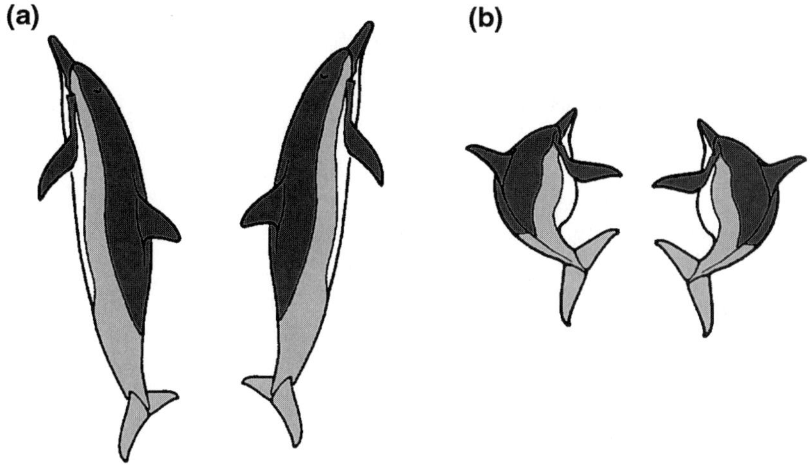

Figure 7.5. Rotating pairs of Hawaiian spinner dolphins illustrating the use of pigment patterns in signaling (a) tilt away and (b) tilt-toward (from Norris *et al.*, 1994).

Such pattern relationship cues may be used as part of the overall system that allows synchrony of animals during dives and turns, especially when schooling.

Pigment granules and dendritic (branching) melanocytes of epidermal origin are present in sirenians. Numerous fibers occur both in and between the cells of the stratum spinosum layer and probably impart considerable elasticity to the epidermis. There are no major differences between the skin structure of manatees and the dugong except that the dugong skin may be less pigmented in the adult (Ling, 1974).

7.2.1.2. External Parasites

Diatoms, **whale lice**, and barnacles often are found attached to the skin in the larger cetaceans and occasionally in the smaller ones. Many baleen whales have a thin yellow-green film of diatoms (e.g. *Cocconeis* on the blue whale) over their skin which is acquired during their summer stay in polar waters. Its presence has helped identify the migration patterns of those species (Nemoto, 1956; Nemoto *et al.,* 1980). Cyamid amphipod crustaceans (species of *Cyamus;* see Leung, 1967, for a review), commonly called whale lice (Fig. 7.6), are found almost exclusively on the larger cetaceans, especially the humpback, gray, and right whales.

There are anatomical and physiological explanations for the occurrence of whale lice on the surface of large cetaceans. Cyamids aggregate in areas of reduced water flow such as the deep longitudinal grooves and prominent ridges covering the throat, chest, and anterior part of the ventral body surface on the margins of the lips, and on **callosities**, the raised patches of roughened skin found only on the head of right whales. Callosities which surround a single sensory hair may have evolved to help the whale sense its environment, although their roughened surfaces also provide good attachment sites for cyamids. The cyamids that blanket a callosity could interfere with sensory reception of a whale by covering, breaking, or bending the sensory hairs. However, it also is possible that cyamids amplify the signal to the whale by sensing a plankton bloom and changing their activity patterns which could signal to a whale that it had entered or left plankton-rich water (Rowntree, 1996). The whale lice

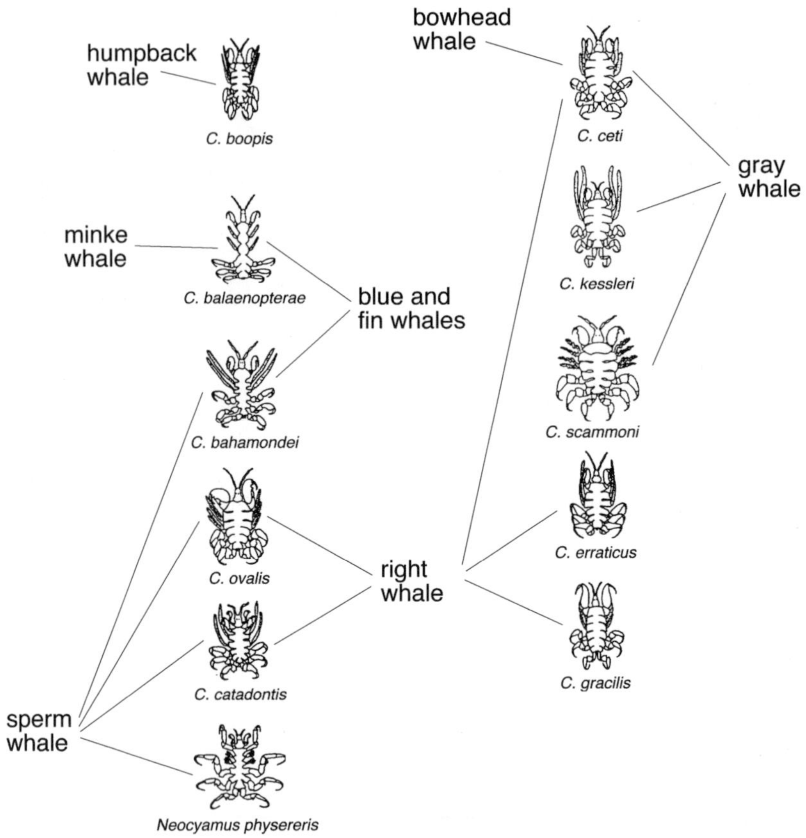

Figure 7.6. Hosts of several species of whale lice, mostly in the genus *Cyamus* (adapted from Rowntree, 1983).

require shelter where they will not be swept off the whale's surface and this is available in the depths of these body grooves. Physiologically, *Cyamus* needs heat and blood and hence it inhabits areas that are well vascularized. Observations indicate that cyamids feed on the epidermal layer of whale skin (Rowntree, 1996). Although the principal diet of cyamids is whale skin, it is possible that they also feed on plankton. Cyamids may be more accurately regarded as **mutualists** rather than parasites. In an association of mutualism, both the whale and cyamids benefit; the whale skin provides food for the cyamids and the cyamids inform the whale of nearby food resources. In gray whales, cyamids also may actively undercut barnacles and increase their rates of detachment.

Barnacles of three main types are found on the surfaces of slow-moving whales: mound-shaped acorn barnacles (*Coronula* and *Cryptolepas*), stalked or ship barnacles (*Conchoderma*), and pseudostalked barnacles (*Xenobalanus* and *Tubicinella;* Fig. 7.7). Because these external parasites do not seem to cause any infection or inflammation, and given the relationship suggested for cyamids, it is possible that they too should be regarded as mutualists or **commensals**; the latter association is distinguished from the former in that only one partner, in this case the barnacles, benefit from the association because they feed on the whale skin.

(a)

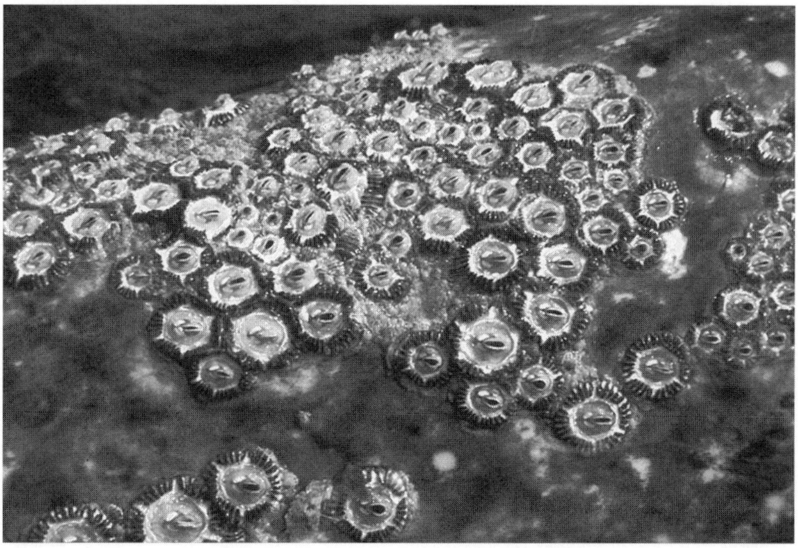

(b)

Figure 7.7. Acorn barnacles on the skin of gray whales (a) and stalked barnacles from humpback whales (b) (photo courtesy of P. Colla).

The callosities on the head in front of the blowhole of right whales are infested with colonies of barnacles, parasitic worms, and whale lice. The largest patch, located on the snout, was called the "bonnet" by old time whalers and is a feature by which the species is easily recognized. The pattern of callosities is individually unique and may facilitate recognition of individuals (Fig. 7.8).

External infestations of pinnipeds are most common in the form of sucking lice. Sucking lice of the family Echinophthiridae are obligate parasites exclusive to marine carnivores, mainly pinnipeds. Their claws may be modified for clinging to the fur or to the skin where they are found commonly on eyelids, nostrils, and the anus (Kim, 1971, 1975). Pups are

Figure 7.8. Bonnet of right whale with prominent callosities (photo courtesy of J. Goodyear).

more prone to infestation than adults and may serve as hosts soon after birth. The evolution of sucking lice and their otariid pinniped hosts is discussed by Kim *et al.* (1975).

Manatees often are covered with algae, barnacles, and other incrustations that obscure their basic pigmentation (Caldwell and Caldwell, 1985).

7.2.1.3. Hair

The hair or pelage of pinnipeds, sea otters, and the polar bear consists of two layers: outer protective **guard hairs** and inner soft **underfur hairs**. The longer, thicker guard hairs lie on top of the shorter, finer underfur hairs (Fig. 7.9). Growth of the pelage is influenced by thyroid, adrenal, and gonadal hormones and by nutrition as well as indirectly by day length, thermal conditions, and reproduction (Ebling and Hale, 1970; Ling, 1970). Among the pinnipeds, monk seals, elephant seals, and the walrus lack underfur (Ling, 1974; Scheffer, 1964; Fay, 1982). The guard hairs have a pith, or medulla (central cavity), in otariids which is lacking in the walrus and phocids (Scheffer, 1964). Since medullated hair has been documented among other carnivores, the nonmedullated condition has been interpreted as a phylogenetically informative feature that unites phocids and the walrus (Wyss, 1987). Hair grows in distinct patterns over the body and among pinnipeds these patterns also are phylogenetically informative. In otariids, the hairs are uniformly arranged; in the walrus and in phocids and other carnivores, the hairs are arranged in clusters of two to four or in rows (Fig. 7.10). As with sea otters, the hair of pinnipeds lack arrector pili muscles which serve to erect the hair. This may enhance the ability of the hairs to lie flat during submersion, further contributing to streamlining of the body.

The natal or first coat of a pinniped differs from the adult pelage. Monk seals and elephant seals are born with black pelage (King, 1966; Ling and Button, 1975) whereas phocines and the walrus have white or gray natal coats (Fay, 1982; King, 1983; Ling and

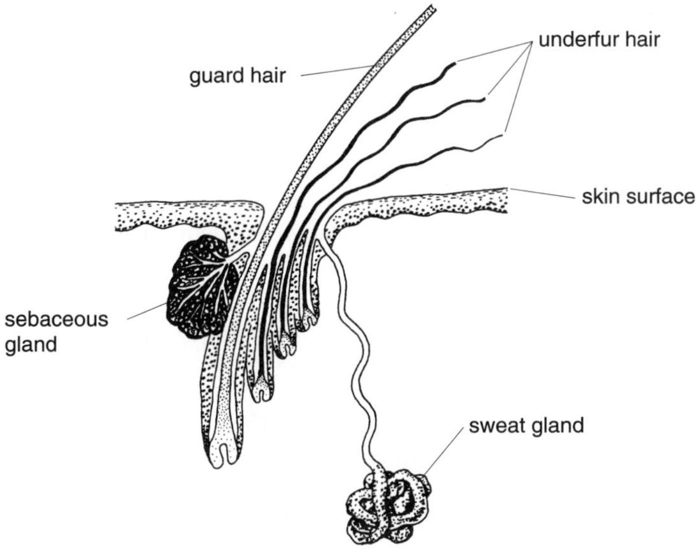

Figure 7.9. Hair and related structures (from Bonner, 1994).

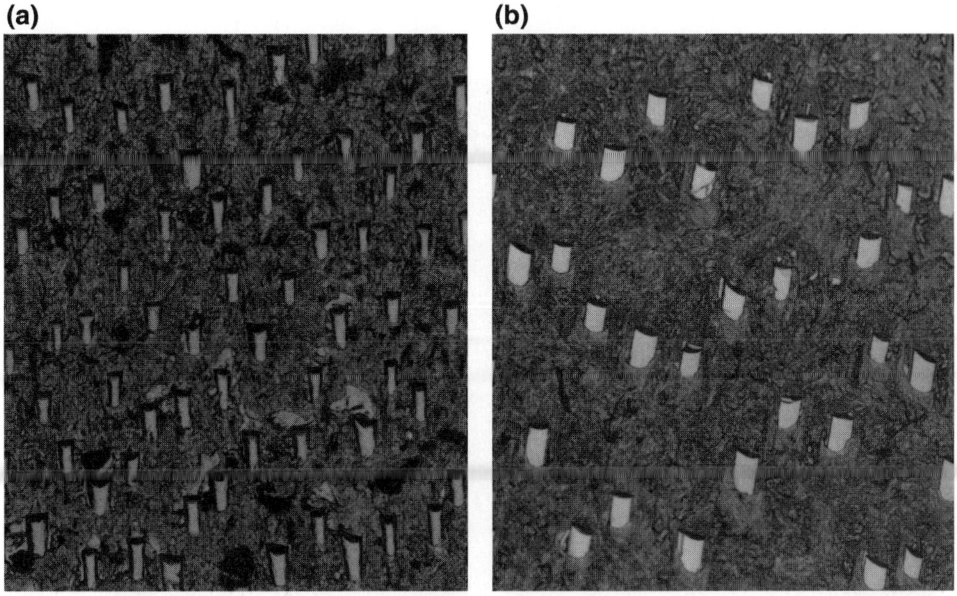

Figure 7.10. Pinniped hair patterns (a) Otariid pattern in which the hairs are uniformly arranged and (b) Pattern seen in the walrus and phocids in which the hairs are arranged in groups of two to four or in rows (from Scheffer, 1964; reprinted courtesy of V. B. Scheffer).

Button, 1975). Natal coats in otariids are dark brown to black (King, 1983; Ling and Button, 1975). Based on these patterns, Wyss (1988) interpreted the light-colored pelage of phocids (exclusive of elephant and monk seals) as a shared derived feature uniting phocines and lobodontines.

The guard hairs of the sea otter, *Enhydra lutris,* are typically medullated; underfur hairs often are medullated at their base (Kenyon, 1969; Williams *et al.,* 1992; Fig. 7.11). The sea otter has the most dense pelage of any mammal, an adaptation against heat loss. The mean hair density in the midback region is about 125,000 hairs/cm^2. This is more than twice that of the northern fur seal (Tarasoff, 1974). The guard hairs are sparse compared to underhairs and probably have little direct insulative value. Their main function may be one of protecting the integrity of the underhairs when the animal is immersed in water. Also, their relatively short shaft and springiness may assist in elevating the underhairs to renew trapped air when the animal emerges from the water (Tarasoff, 1974). The wavy underhairs are shorter and of more uniform diameter than the guard hairs. Their waviness contributes to reducing the size of the air spaces in the longitudinal plane. Thus, when the animal is immersed, the underhairs overlap and interlock to help maintain trapped air.

The hairs of the polar bear are medullated. The pelage of polar bears is not always creamy white. Hair can appear white, yellow, gray, or even brownish according to the season and lighting conditions. Immediately after molting, the fur is nearly pure white, matching the Arctic landscape. In summer, it often takes on a yellowish cast, probably due to oxidation by the sun (Reeves *et al.,* 1992). The green coloration of the pelage is due to algal growth within the hair shaft (Lewin and Robinson, 1979). The claim that polar bear hairs act as optical fibers directing the sun's ultraviolet rays to the skin where it warms the animal has been refuted. Direct measurement of the transmission of light through polar bear hairs reveals a very small optical loss that is of little consequence to the energetics of polar bears (Koon, 1998).

Figure 7.11. Guard hairs and underfur of the sea otter, *Enhydra lutris* (from Williams *et al.,* 1992).

7.2.1.3.1. Molt

All phocid seals, the sea otter, and one cetacean, the beluga whale, are known to undergo an annual molt. Terrestrial mammals molt to generate a new pelt as part of an acclimation process to seasonal changes in the thermal environment. Since many phocids are pelagic for most of the year, except for breeding which occurs on land or ice, the molt likely serves a different purpose: an annual opportunity to repair and renew their pelt and epidermis (Boily, 1995).

The molt pattern varies among pinnipeds. The natal coat is molted in the uterus of some phocids (e.g. hooded seal and harbor seal) before the pups are born. McLaren (1966) proposed that prenatal shedding was related to selection of breeding site. According to McLaren, the natal coat of phocids is an adaptation to breeding on ice. The *in utero* molt of the natal coat of harbor seals reflects a secondary adaptation to breeding on land. However, this does not explain the prenatal molt of hooded seals which are born on pack ice, or the presence of natal pelage in other land-breeding phocids such as elephant seals and monk seals (Bowen, 1991). It has been argued that prenatal molting, like prenatal blubber deposition, is instead an adaptation enabling newborn pups to enter cold water without adverse consequences. This ability allows the use of pupping substrates that are unstable or regularly inundated with water, as illustrated by the breeding habitats of both hooded and harbor seals (Oftedal *et al.,* 1991). In all other pinnipeds the natal coat is molted at varying periods up to a few months of age. After this molt, the adult pelage is shed and replaced annually.

Molting takes place during the summer and autumn (December to April or May) in the southern hemisphere. In the northern hemisphere the timing of the molt is more variable, usually occurring during the spring (April to June). Molting in pinnipeds begins around the face and is followed by the face, abdomen, and finally the back (Stutz, 1967; Ashwell-Erikson *et al.,* 1986). The molt then spreads over the body surface, eventually replacing the entire pelage (Worthy *et al.,* 1987). The molt of phocids can be relatively fast (e.g. for elephant seals, about 25 days; Boyd *et al.,* 1993) or slow and gradual (e.g. for harbor seal, 10–170 days; Ashwell-Erikson *et al.,* 1986). An unusual pattern of molting characterizes the elephant seal and the Hawaiian monk seal: the shed hairs are attached by their roots to larger sheets of molted epidermis (Fig. 7.12; Kenyon and Rice, 1959; Ling and Thomas, 1967; Worthy *et al.,* 1992). In other pinnipeds, hairs are shed individually (Ling, 1970). Fur seals and sea lions do not molt annually but instead renew their pelt gradually all year long. Most of the guard hairs are shed every year, starting about a week after the underfur is shed, so at all times the animal retains a coat (Ling, 1970). Results of the heat flux study of marine mammals mentioned above in the context of the epidermal molt of beluga whales indicated that phocids must become terrestrial during the molt to satisfy the thermal requirements of their epidermis. The model predicted that although phocids should be able to produce enough heat in water to compensate for the heat loss resulting from molting in the water, it would be at a high energetic cost and only possible within a limited range of water temperature (Boily, 1995).

Molting in sea otters takes place gradually throughout the year, although a peak period of molting seems to take place in spring among captive Alaskan otters (Kenyon, 1969).

7.2.1.4. Glands

In pinnipeds, sebaceous glands are associated with each hair canal and their thick secretions primarily function to keep the epidermis pliable (Fig. 7.9). The sweat glands of pinnipeds occur singly with guard hair follicles and their ducts open into the follicle

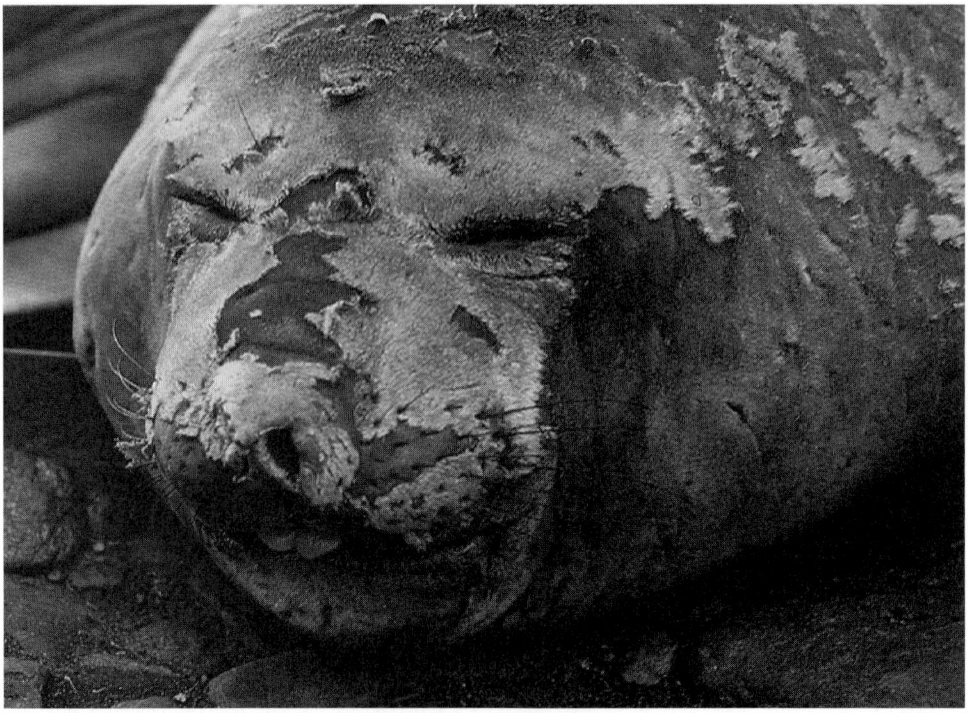

Figure 7.12. Molting pattern of elephant seal (and the Hawaiian monk seal) in which the hairs are shed in large sheets (from MacDonald, 1984).

(Fig. 7.9). The sweat glands vary from large coiled structures in fur seals (related to their need for a large cooling surface, especially on land; Ling, 1965) to simple coiled tubules in phocids. The largest sweat glands of the walrus are located around the mouth and it has been suggested that their odiferous secretions may function in mother and pup recognition (Ling, 1974).

In the sea otter, sebaceous glands are associated with hair follicles and characteristically have a long, thin, tubular shape, but they often are dilated at their base. Sebaceous secretions in the sea otter are predominantly composed of lipids. Removal of lipids from these sebaceous secretions, especially in the sea otter, greatly lessen the water repellency of the fur, reducing its thermoregulatory capability. Apocrine sweat glands are more prominent than the other sebaceous glands (Williams *et al.,* 1992). There are no sebaceous or sweat glands in cetaceans or sirenians (with the exception of rudimentary sebaceous glands associated with snout hairs in sirenians).

7.2.1.5. Vibrissae

Vibrissae, or whiskers, are stiff hairs that in pinnipeds occur only on the face (Fig. 7.13). Differences between the vibrissae of terrestrial mammals and those of pinnipeds include 1) enlargement of whiskers and their sites of innervation among pinnipeds, 2) stiffer hair in pinnipeds, and 3) follicles surrounded by three rather than the two blood sinuses found in

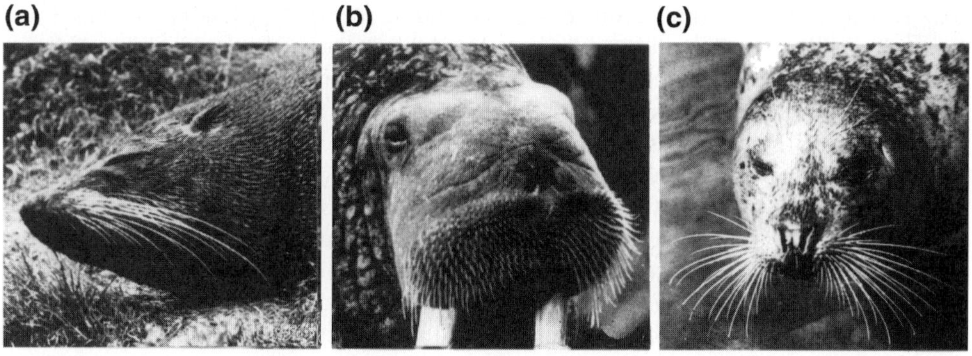

Figure 7.13. Heads of various pinnipeds showing facial vibrissae. (a) New Zealand fur seal, *Arctocephalus forsteri,* (b) walrus, *Odobenus rosmarus,* and (c) Pacific harbor seal, *Phoca vitulina richardsi* (from Ling, 1977; reprinted courtesy of J. K. Ling).

terrestrial mammals. Pinnipeds possess three kinds of facial vibrissae: rhinal, superciliary, and mystacial. The most prominent and numerous vibrissae are mystacial whiskers.

Vibrissae appear early in the embryonic development of pinnipeds, long before pelage hairs appear (Ling, 1977). Vibrissae follicles are similar to hair follicles in development and structure but differ in being controlled by voluntary muscles. Pinniped vibrissae are heavily innervated, with blood vessels in the connective tissue sheath surrounding the follicle and prominent circular (ring) sinuses around the vibrissae. Walruses possess on average 600–700 vibrissae, more than other pinnipeds and most terrestrial carnivores.

Mystacial whiskers are arranged in rows along the sides of the snout and have either a smooth or a beaded outline. Beaded mystacial whiskers diagnose phocids (excluding monk seals). The primitive smooth condition is seen in otariids, the walrus, bearded, Ross, and leopard seals. The functional significance of these differences is not known. Mystacial whiskers range in size from the short stiff bristles of the walrus to the very long whiskers of fur seals. Walruses have the toughest mystacial vibrissae. The upper lip, in which the follicles are implanted, is characterized by small compartments with fibrous septa filled with adipose tissue. This gives the upper lip both strong rigidity and flexibility (Kastelein *et al.,* 1993). The walrus uses its mystacial vibrissae to locate prey in the substrate. As noted earlier by Murie (1871), the walrus can move its vibrissae together as a group or individually.

Superciliary (supraorbital) whiskers, located above the eyes, are usually better developed in phocids than otariids. Rhinal whiskers, one to two on each side just posterior to each nostril are found only in phocids (Ling, 1977).

Vibrissae function as tactile receptors and most research has been conducted on phocids. Renouf (1979) and Mills and Renouf (1986) found that vibrissal sensitivity to sound improved with increasing frequency of stimulation. The best sensitivity to vibrations was found at 100 Hz, with a range up to 2500 Hz, the upper limit of the test equipment. The Baltic ringed seal has exceptionally well-developed vibrissae which appear to help them find their way in the dark and often cloudy waters beneath the ice (Hyvärinen, 1989, 1995). A single vibrissae of the Baltic ringed seal contains 10 times the number of nerve fibers typically found in that of a land mammal. Hyvärinen suggested that the ringed seals can sense compressional waves such as sounds with their vibrissae (specifically by nerve fibers located within the ring sinus). Sound waves could be received by the blood sinuses and by tissue conduction through the vibrissae. In addition, the vibrissae could be used as a speedometer to measure changes in swimming speed and direction, which could be important during navigation in darkness.

The possible use of vibrissae in prey detection also has been investigated. Cutting the vibrissae of a harbor seal disturbes its success in capturing fish (Renouf, 1980). Experimental observations of blindfolded captive ringed seals presented with acoustic cues (tapping on ice with a metal rod) showed that vibrissal sensation helped the seals position themselves within holes in ice-covered ponds, but did not help in locating the hole (Wartzok *et al.,* 1992). Psychophysical studies of the Pacific walrus suggest that they employ their vibrissae to discriminate shape and size of food objects and the substrate (Kastelein and van Gaalen, 1988; Kastelein *et al.,* 1990). Similar studies have shown that the mystacial vibrissae of the California sea lion (Denhardt, 1994) and the Pacific harbor seal (Denhardt and Kaminski, 1995) allow excellent shape, size, and tactile discrimination and as such may be useful in prey detection.

Vibrissae occur only on the head of cetaceans and are distributed along the margins of the upper and lower jaws. The structure and especially the innervation of vibrissae indicate a sensory role and suggest a role in feeding. Baleen whales possess a larger number of vibrissae than odontocetes, and some odontocetes have only vestigial follicles. The Ganges and Indus River dolphins and the bouto are notable exceptions in possessing a large number of well-developed vibrissae which have been related to their murky water bottom-feeding habit (Yablokov *et al.,* 1972; Ling, 1977).

The hair of sirenians is of the sinus type, intermediate in form between pelage hairs and true vibrissae. The hairs are lightly scattered over the body but become denser and very robust on the muzzle and around the mouth. Unlike the body hairs, the facial hair surrounding the mouth contains prominent bristles with a medulla and the follicles are of the true sinus type. Blood vessels and nerves penetrate the follicle. A well-developed dermal papilla extends deep into the hair shaft where it is continuous with the medulla (Reep *et al.,* 1998; Lins, 1977).

In a study of bristle use and feeding in the Florida manatee, Marshall *et al.* (1998) reported that the bristles around the mouth are controlled by various facial muscles and their movements contribute significantly to changes in the shape of the mouth during feeding (see Chapter 11).

The sea otter has mystacial, superciliary, and rhinal vibrissae, with mystacial whiskers being the most numerous (Ling, 1977). In the polar bear, vibrissae are few in number but are very stiff.

7.2.1.6. Claws/Nails

The fore- and hindflippers of phocine seals are characterized by the presence of well-developed claws (Fig. 7.14). In contrast, "monachine" seals claws tend to be poorly developed. Wyss (1988) interpreted the primitive condition in phocids to be the presence of reduced claws. The claws of the hand are reduced to small modules in otariids and the walrus. The fore- and hindflippers of otariids have cartilaginous extensions which project from the distal edge of the flipper border. Short cartilaginous extensions are present in the claws of the walrus (Fig. 7.14).

Cetaceans have lost all trace of claws/nails on their foreflippers. Rudimentary nails are present on the second, third, and fourth digits in manatees, except for the Amazon manatee

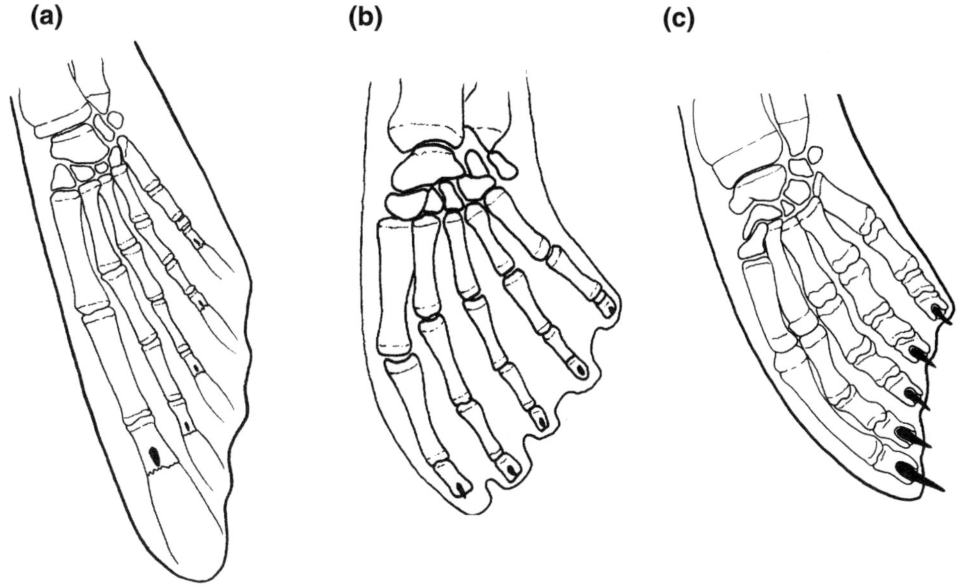

Figure 7.14. Claws and cartilaginous extensions on the fore flippers of pinnipeds. (a) Sea lion, (b) Walrus illustrating the otariid and walrus condition in which there are cartilagenous extensions to the digits and the nails are reduced to small nodules, and (c) Harbor seal illustrating the phocine condition with well-developed claws. (Illustrated by P. Adam; modified from Howell, 1930).

which lacks nails. Polar bears and sea otters possess claws on both fore- and hind digits. The claws are not retractable in the polar bear, and in the sea otter only those on the forefeet are retractile.

7.2.2. Thermoregulation

The aquatic environment is a cold place for mammals to live because water has 25 times the heat capacity of air. Marine mammals may accommodate the potentially immense heat loss imposed by their cold environment in four ways: increased insulation, heat exchange systems, decreased surface-to-volume ratios, and increased metabolic heat production (the latter is discussed in Chapters 9 and 11).

7.2.2.1. Insulation

The dense fur or blubber covering marine mammals minimizes heat loss in the water. Blubber not only insulates the animals from the cold but improves their hydrodynamic shape, stores elastic energy (as discussed in Chapter 8), and also serves as an energy reservoir, providing nourishment during long periods of fasting. Studies show that blubber can also provide information on the nutritional state and diet of marine mammals (e.g., Iverson, 1998). In contrast to the fat reservoirs of adult seals and whales, most pinniped pups are born with very little blubber and must quickly develop a covering of fatty insulation to survive. In Weddell seals, for example, the newborn's hair, or lanugo, is several times longer than the fur of the adult, which helps to conserve heat (Elsner *et al.,* 1977, cited in Riedman,

1990). Harp seal pups born on Arctic ice use the sunlight, which is reflected by the white hairs onto the surface of the skin where the heat is absorbed. The pup's coat traps this warmth between hair and skin, producing a "greenhouse effect" that prevents heat loss (T. Øritsland, 1970; N. A. Øritsland, 1971, cited in Riedman, 1990). In addition, although the newborns lack a layer of blubber and have fur of poor insulative quality, they do possess a layer of **brown fat** in a subcutaneous layer along the back and at several sites internally, around the neck and heart, kidneys, and abdominal walls (Blix *et al.,* 1975). This specialized brown fat, also found in human babies and many hibernating mammals, helps keep the pups warm by means of **nonshivering thermogenesis** (Grav *et al.,* 1974; Grav and Blix, 1975; Blix *et al.,* 1975). Instead of shivering to produce heat, seals metabolize this high energy fat to produce considerable heat. After a few days the thermogenic fat is converted into insulative blubber (Blix *et al.,* 1979) but the internal thermogenic fat stores remain to provide heat at the time pups are weaned and enter water for the first time.

Whales and seals rely on controlled peripheral blood flow from the body core to the skin and appendages for heat conservation or loss. Unlike terrestrial mammals, whose insulation typically overlies vascular circulation to the skin, the insulating blanket of whale and seal blubber is penetrated by vascular beds to the base of the epidermis (Parry, 1949). Consequently, minimum heat flux is achieved when peripheral vasoconstriction is greatest and is independent of maximum heat flux achieved during periods of heat stress.

The thermal conductivity of blubber is the inverse of its insulative value and is a function of both its thickness and its peripheral blood flow. For cetaceans, the thermal conductivity of blubber is mostly a function of its lipid content. Worthy and Edwards (1990) found both higher lipid content and greater thickness in the blubber of temperate-water harbor porpoises when compared to blubber of tropical spotted dolphins, giving the former a fourfold increase in overall insulative value (Fig. 7.15). Williams and Friedl (1990) showed that in bottlenose dolphins the blubber layer thickness adapts to water temperature by changing as quickly as two mm a month. Bryden (1964) has shown that seal blubber is a better insulator than whale blubber, probably because there is very little fibrous tissue present in seal blubber. In addition to blubber conductivity, another important variable with respect to heat loss models is the distribution of blubber around the body core. Kvadsheim *et al.* (1977) demonstrated that heat loss models, which are based on calculations of heat flux across the blubber layer, overestimate heat loss from the body of seals because they fail to take into account that the blubber is distributed asymmetrically, as noted in the previous discussion about the skin.

Research on thermoregulation in harbor seals and gray seals (Hansen *et al.,* 1995; Hansen and Lavigne, 1997a,b) provides evidence that ambient air temperature plays an important role in limiting the distribution of seals. For gray seals, cold air temperatures seem to affect distribution mainly through the breeding season, primarily through their thermoregulatory effects on small, fasting pups before they enter the water. Fasting seals are especially vulnerable because they have a thinner insulative layer and reduced metabolic rates (to conserve energy during a fast). Additional work is necessary to demonstrate whether this is a more general phenomenon among pinnipeds. Specifically, researchers wonder if the distribution of pinnipeds toward the equator is limited by their inability to thermoregulate at elevated temperatures, especially during those periods when they are on land (i.e. during parturition, nursing, and the post weaning fast and for some species during the annual molt) (Hansen *et al.,* 1995). In a study of the effect of water temperature on the thermoregulatory costs of bottlenose dolphins, (Williams *et al.* 1992) found that

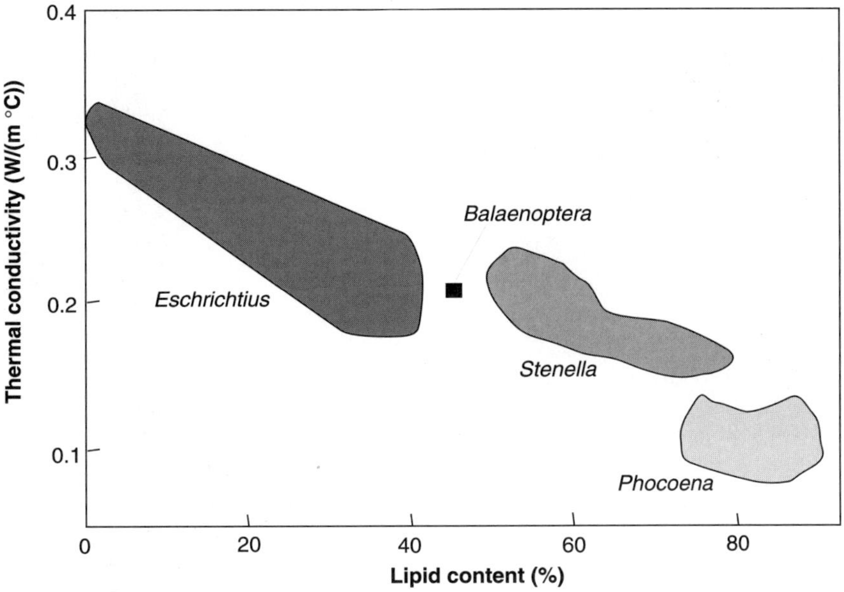

Figure 7.15. The relationship between lipid content and thermal conductivity of the blubber of four genera of cetaceans (adapted from Worthy and Edwards, 1990).

changes in water temperature altered energetic costs. Animals acclimated to 15° C had a basal metabolic rate that was 1.4 times the value measured for dolphins acclimated to 25° C. The lower critical temperature was less than 6° C for the cold acclimated dolphins and 11–16° C for the animals living in warm water.

7.2.2.2. Heat Exchange Systems

A striking feature in the vascular system of all marine mammals is the **rete mirabilia** (miraculous network). Retia mirabilia are massive contorted spirals of blood vessels, mainly arteries but with thin-walled veins among them, that usually form blocks of tissue on the inner dorsal wall of the thoracic cavity and extremities or periphery of the body (Fig. 7.16). The sperm whale has been described as having the most extensively developed retia among cetaceans (Melnikov, 1997). Retia also are found in a wide variety of other animals including sharks, tuna, large billfish, certain wading birds, sloths, anteaters, and lemurs (O'Dea, 1990).

Retia function as **countercurrent heat exchangers** (CCHE; Fig. 7.17). Countercurrent heat exchangers work by maintaining a heat differential between oppositely directed flows, thereby increasing the amount of heat transferred (compared to a concurrent flow). Countercurrent heat exchangers in the flippers, fins, and flukes function to conserve body temperature. So that these tissues may stay alive and functional and not freeze solid, it is necessary to maintain some blood circulation through them. In flippers, fins, and flukes the blood supply is arranged so that the main arteries, carrying blood to cooler extremities, are closely surrounded by veins, bringing the blood back to the body core. Cold blood from the

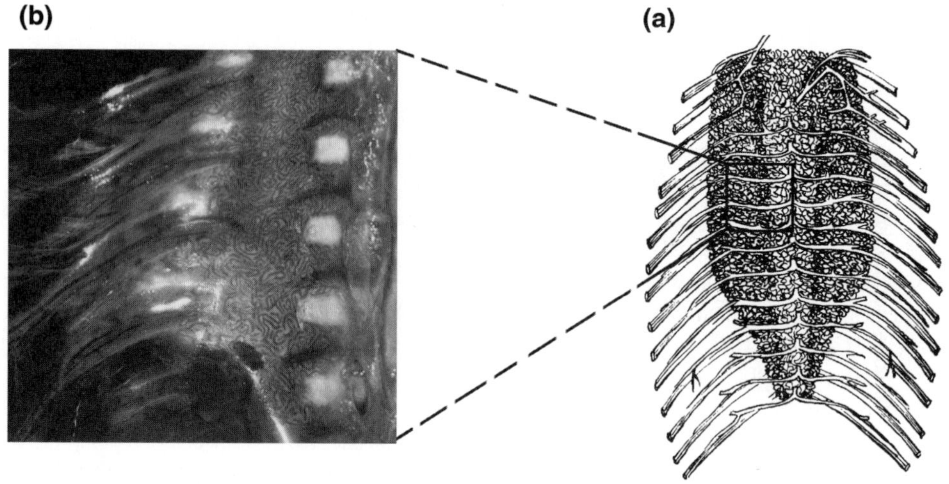

Figure 7.16. Rete mirabilia, their anatomical position within the ribs (a) and the right thoracic rete of a spotted dolphin *Stenella* (b) (adapted in part from Slijper, 1962).

veins extracts heat from the arterial blood coming from the body core so that the blood returning to the body is warmed and heat loss is minimized.

Countercurrent heat exchangers also are associated with reproductive tracts where they prevent overheating in these heat-sensitive organs. Phocid seals and dolphins possess a vascular countercurrent exchanger that functions to cool their testes (Rommel *et al.,* 1995; Pabst *et al.,* 1995; Pabst *et al.,* 1998). In phocids, venous plexuses located between the veins of the distal hind limbs and the pelvis suggest that the testes are cooled directly. Cooled blood from the hindflipper flowing through the inguinal plexus located in the groin would introduce a thermal gradient which could allow local and direct heat transfer from the testes and adjacent muscles. This theory is supported by measurements of testicular temperatures which can be lower than core body temperatures by as much as 6–7° C in elephant seals (Bryden, 1967).

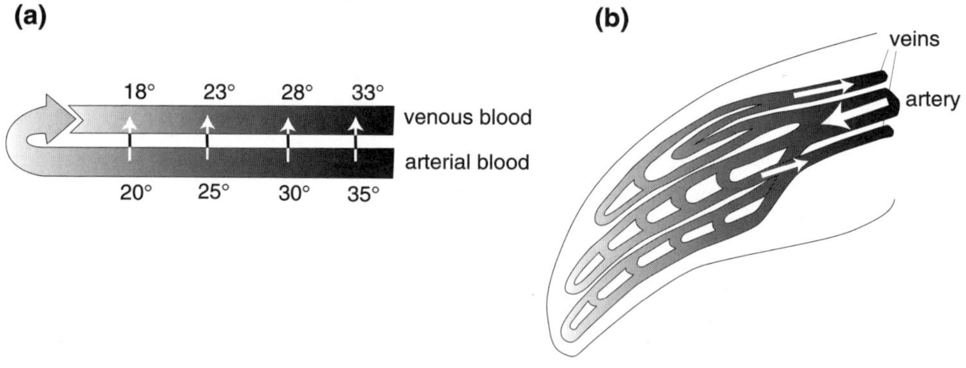

Figure 7.17. General pattern of heat exchange in a countercurrent system (a), and a simplified vascular exchange network (b).

In dolphins, spermatic arteries in the posterior abdomen are juxtaposed to veins returning cooled blood from the surfaces of the dorsal fin and tail flukes (Fig. 7.18). Immediately after vigorous swimming, temperatures at the CCHE decreased relative to resting and pre-swim values; post-swim temperatures at the CCHE were maximally 0.5° C cooler than pre-swim temperatures (Rommel *et al.,* 1992). These data suggest that the CCHE has an increased ability to cool the arterial blood supply to the testes when the dolphin is swimming. Subsequently, Rommel *et al.* (1994) reported deep body temperature measurements in male dolphins which supported this thermoregulatory hypothesis. Low temperatures were present in the region of the pelvic countercurrent heat exchanger in males. Female dolphins and phocid seals use a similar countercurrent exchange system with cool blood flowing directly to the fetus from the tail and fin in the case of dolphins or from the hindflipper for seals. This keeps the fetus (which has a metabolic rate about twice that of the mother's) from overheating and experiencing fetal distress, developmental disorders, or death (Rommel *et al.,* 1993, 1995).

It has been reported that baleen whales possess countercurrent heat exchangers in their mouths, enabling them to reduce heat loss when feeding in cold waters (Ford and Kraus, 1992; Heyning and Mead, 1997; Fig. 7.19). Another example of a countercurrent exchange system, the nasal structure of elephant seals which enables them to reduce their water loss, is discussed in Chapter 9.

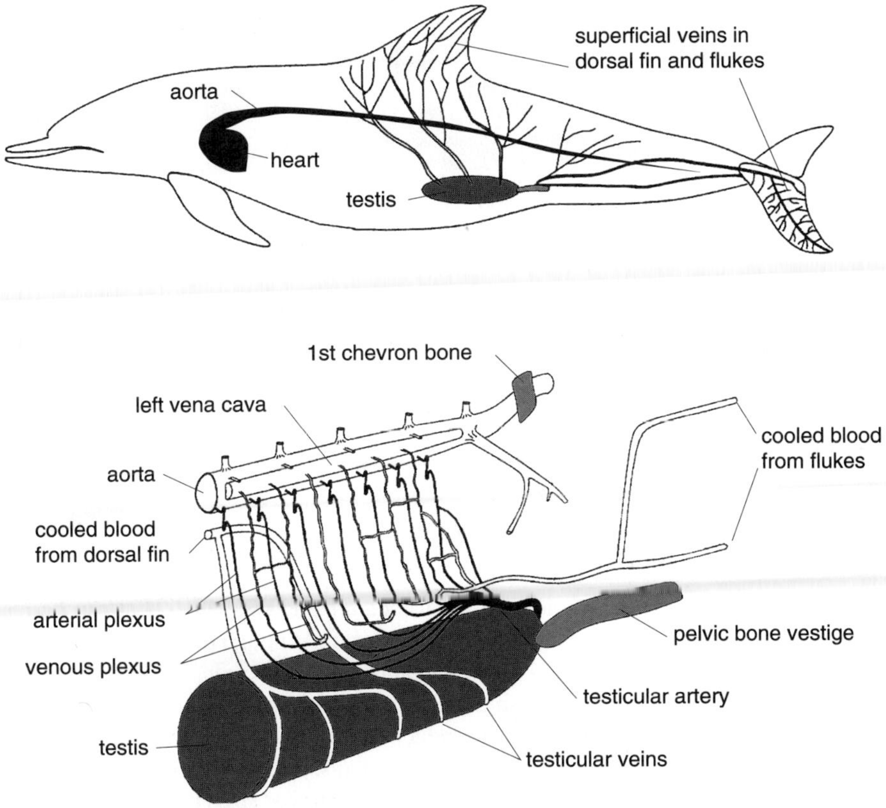

Figure 7.18. Dolphin testes as countercurrent exchange system (modified from Pabst *et al.,* 1995).

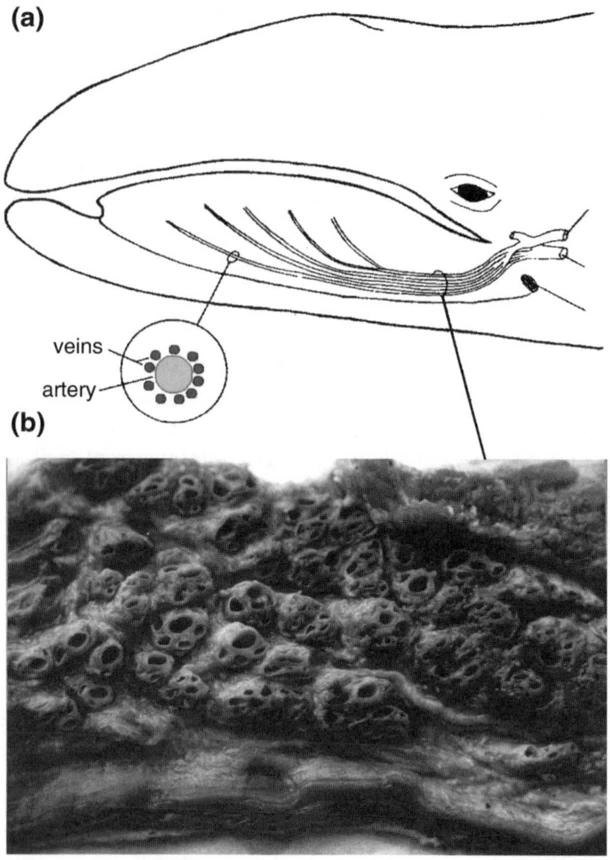

Figure 7.19. Countercurrent exchange system in gray whale mouth (a) schematic diagram and (b) cross section through lingual rete. From Heyning and Mead, 1997; courtesy of John Heyning.

The retia of sirenians are in the form of vascular bundles rather than networks and are scattered throughout the body, including the body walls, face and jaw, tail and, spinal cord (Husar, 1977), but they are best developed in the flippers (Caldwell and Caldwell, 1985).

7.2.2.3. Surface-to-Volume Ratio

Marine mammals may reduce the amount of surface area across which heat can be lost by modifying their shape toward an optimum spherical form. Although marine mammals are not spherical, they are torpedo shaped and projecting appendages are reduced. This shape confers the minimum surface area while still maintaining a shape that is within the parameters needed for efficient locomotion, foraging, and reproduction, among other activities. The surface areas of marine mammals (including pinnipeds, cetaceans, and the sea otter) are, on average, about 23% smaller than those of terrestrial mammals of similar size (Innes *et al.,* 1990).

Another way to reduce surface area is to take advantage of the surface-to-volume relationship. The surface area of a body increases as the square of its linear dimension while its volume increases as the cube. It follows that for bodies of the same general shape, the larger ones will have relatively low surface area: volume ratio (Fig. 7.20). Most marine mammals are large and they are thus capable of producing considerable heat with relatively little loss at the surface. The sea otter, although small in comparison to most marine mammals, is more than twice as large as the largest terrestrial mustelid, the European badger. In addition to reduced surface areas, marine mammals can reduce heat loss to the environment in a number of other ways (e.g. peripheral vasoconstriction and nasal mucosa, discussed in relation to ventilatory and circulatory adjustments during diving in Chapter 9).

It is important to remember that these same anatomical adaptations (i.e. an insulative layer of blubber or fur) out of the water function to inhibit heat dissipation rather than to conserve it. For those marine mammals living in warm environments, overheating may also pose a problem. When temperatures rise, fur seals, sea lions, and seals enter the water or rest in tidepools. Some pinnipeds, such as northern elephant seals, New Zealand sea lions, and Southern sea lions, cool off by flipping sand onto their backs. The characteristic "sand flipping" behavior during exposure to direct sunlight affords the animal a layer of damp sand that decreases heat gain and provides exposure to cool moist sand, enhancing conductive heat loss (references cited in Hansen *et al.,* 1995). The northern fur seal actually pants like a dog to dissipate heat (Gentry, 1981). The monk seal, the only phocid living in a tropical environment, cools off on warm days by resting near the water in damp sand, often digging holes to expose cooler layers (Riedman, 1990). When on land, Galapagos fur seal pups too young to cool off in the sea resort to seeking shelter in the shade of boulders and to curtailing their activities during the heat of the day (Linberger *et al.,* 1986).

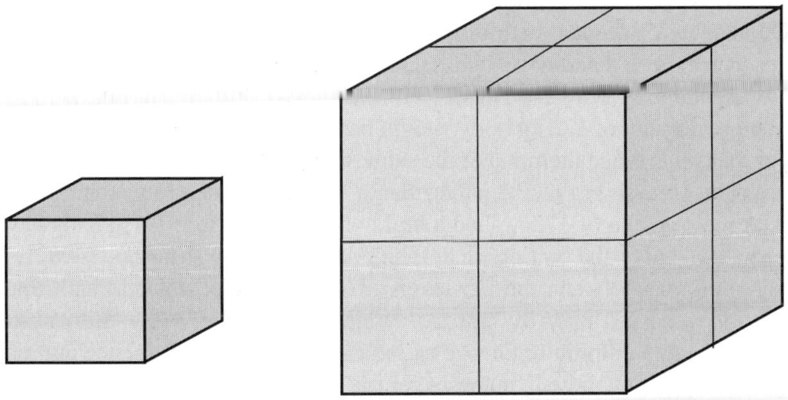

Surface area:	6	24
Volume:	1	8
Ratio:	6:1	3:1

Figure 7.20. Surface-to-volume relationship. As a body increases in size (left to right), its surface area and volume also increase; however, the ratio of its surface area to its volume decreases.

7.3. Nerves and Sense Organs

7.3.1. Nervous System

7.3.1.1. Brain

Descriptions of the anatomy of the pinniped brain are summarized in Harrison and Kooyman (1968), Harrison and Tomlinson (1963), and Flanigan (1972). Representative brain weights range from 320 g for the gray seal, 550 g for the Weddell seal, and 1020 g for the walrus (Table 7.1). The pinniped brain is more spherical than the brain of terrestrial carnivores and is more highly convoluted, especially in phocids. Compared with terrestrial carnivores, the olfactory area in pinnipeds is reduced (more so in phocids than in odobenids or otariids). The auditory area and the cerebellum are large (King, 1983). Comparisons among pinnipeds of the **encephalization quotient** (EQ, defined by Jerison, 1973), a ratio of brain size relative to body size, reveals similar values to those of terrestrial carnivores (Worthy and Hickie, 1986).

Comparative reviews of cetacean brain anatomy are found in Breathnach (1960), Kruger (1966), and Morgane and Jacobs (1972). Descriptions of the dolphin brain anatomy and its evolution are found in Morgane *et al.* (1986) and Ridgway (1986a,b, 1990). Fossil whales apparently did not have large brains. Study of relative brain sizes in archaeocetes reveals that they had smaller brains than expected for mammals of the same size living today (Gingerich, 1998). Among extant taxa, although EQ is high in cetaceans, there is considerable variation in cetacean brain size, ranging from 840 g in common dolphins to a reported high of 7820 g for the largest odontocete, the sperm whale. The brains of mysticetes such as the fin whale weigh 6930 g (Table 7.1). Some delphinids have brains as large as the human brain. While the brain weight, expressed as a percentage of body weight, is not widely different between cetaceans and pinnipeds (Bryden, 1972), the body weights of some cetaceans is considerably larger than those of pinnipeds (Table 7.1).

Odontocete cetaceans, with the exception of the sperm whale, have relative brain sizes larger than expected and have values similar to anthropoid primates (gorillas, chimpanzees, and orangutans; Worthy and Hickie, 1986; Ridgway, 1986a; Marino, 1998). An adult male bottlenose dolphin of 172 kg body weight had a brain of 1629 g and an EQ almost 4.5 times larger than an average mammal of the same size (cf. Jerison, 1973; Wood and Evans, 1980). The closest rival in brain size, other than a few related delphinids and humans, is the gorilla. A male gorilla of 172 kg had a brain of 570 g (Jerison, 1973; Ridgway, 1990) and an EQ equal to that of the bottlenose dolphin. Another study (Marino, 1998) reported an even closer similarity between the EQ levels of some odontocetes and anthropoid primates, a similarity surpassed only by humans. While some authors (e.g. Lilly, 1962, 1964) have viewed the large dolphin brain size as indicative of high intelligence and possibly even of language capability, these hypotheses remain largely untested and there is no general agreement as to what adaptations to aquatic life could be responsible for a large brain (Ridgway, 1990). Although EQ is high in cetaceans and moderate in pinnipeds, by comparison, sirenians, the only other mammal group totally adapted to an aquatic life, have relatively small brains. The EQs for sirenians are among the lowest known for mammals (O'Shea and Reep, 1990).

EQ and related measures of relative brain size also are positively correlated with a number of life history patterns in terrestrial mammals, such as dietary strategy, social group

Table 7.1 Brain and body weights of some marine mammals as compared to humans (Pinniped data from original sources listed in Bryden, 1972; Spector, 1956; Sacher and Staffeldt, 1974; Bryden and Erickson, 1976; Vaz-Ferreira, 1981; cetaceans from Bryden and Corkeron, 1988; sirenians from O'Shea and Reep, 1990)

Species	Brain weight (gms)	Body weight (kg)	(Brain Weight/ Body Weight) × 100
Pinnipeds			
Otariids			
No. fur seal	355	250 (male)	.142
California sea lion	363	101	.359
Southern sea lion	550	260	.211
Phocids			
Bearded seal	460	281	.163
Gray seal	320	163	.196
Weddell seal	550	400	.138
Leopard seal	542	222	.244
Walrus	1020	600	.170
Odontocetes			
Bottlenose dolphin	1600	154	1.038
Common dolphin	840	100	.840
Pilot whale	2670	3178	.074
Killer whale	5620	5448	.103
Sperm whale	7820	33596	.023
Mysticetes			
Fin whale	6930	81720	.008
Sirenian			
Florida manatee	360	756	.047
Human	1500	64	2.344

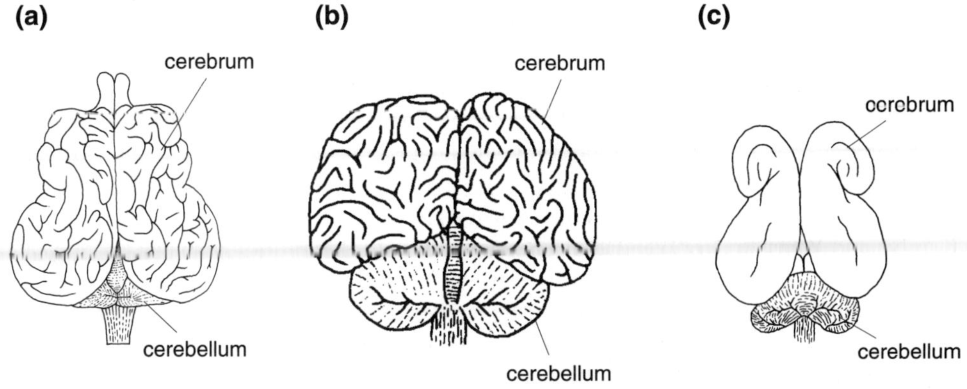

Figure 7.21. Comparison of pinniped, *Otaria byronia* (a), cetacean, *Tursiops truncatus* (b), and sirenian, *Dugong dugon* (c) brain in dorsal views, (Illustrated by P. Adam)

size, and weaning age (Marino, 1997, and references cited therein). The overall patterns of relationship between EQ and gestation, body mass, and encephalization within odontocetes differ from those found in most mammals. It is suggested that a correction factor, which takes into consideration nonallometric increases in body mass in cetaceans, will need to be defined in order to interpret the relationship between life history factors in cetaceans so that they may be compared to terrestrial mammals (Marino, 1997). In sirenians, low metabolic rate and prolonged postnatal growth have been factors implicated in the low EQs found in this group (O'Shea and Reep, 1990).

Although it has been suggested that dolphins' brains shrink as much as 30% when the animals are maintained in captivity (Pilleri, 1983), this hypothesis was questioned by Ridgway (1990). In a related study, he reported no significant difference in the body length to brain weight ratio between newly captured animals and those that died after having been in captivity for 5, 10, or more years.

Delphinids are born with brains at an advanced stage of development. From the very limited data available on animals of known age, Ridgway (1990) estimated that Atlantic coastal bottlenose dolphins reach full brain development in 9 or 10 years, about half the total growth period required for human brains but considerably longer than for brains of most "higher" mammals. A feature of the cetacean brain, similar to the human brain, is the large size of the cerebral hemispheres. The surface of the cetacean brain is highly convoluted, and for some odontocetes, it is even more convoluted than the human brain, although the cortex is thinner (Fig. 7.21). Hypertrophy of the auditory region may be the primary reason for the large brain in dolphins. Considerable experimental work has involved the use of evoked potentials to study dolphin hearing and auditory processing (Morgane *et al.*, 1986; see also Chapter 10). These studies illustrate the comparatively well-developed auditory region of the cetacean brain.

Dolphins also are competent performers of complex tasks when the only information provided about the task is auditory. In a series of experiments (summarized in Herman, 1991; Herman *et al.*, 1994), simple artificial computer-generated languages have been created that dolphins have learned to understand. Rule-based sentences of these languages are created from artificial "words" referring to objects in the animal's tank, words referring to actions to take on those objects, and modifier words to express place or relative time. With these words and the rules for linking them, dolphins can, for example, distinguish the auditory instruction "Put the ball in the ring" from the instruction "Take the ring to the ball." Probably no other non-primate mammal performs as competently on these types of tasks when the information about the task is solely auditory.

The absolute size of the cerebellum of the largest mysticetes is huge, approximately 1500 g. In these species, the cerebellum may be more than 20% of total brain weight. In the bottlenose dolphin, the cerebellum is more typically about 15% of total brain weight, compared with about 11% in humans.

The brain of sirenians is relatively small (250–282 g for dugongs) (Dexler, 1913; Kamiya and Yamsaki, 1979) and approximately 364 g for the Florida manatee (O'Shea and Reep, 1990) with few and shallow sulci (grooves in the cerebrum; Fig. 7.21). The hemispheres of the manatee brain are divided by a deep, wide, longitudinal fissure and there is a deep Sylvian fissure. A notable feature of sirenian brains is the general absence of convolutions on the surface of the cerebral cortex (Reep and O'Shea, 1990). The cerebellum in both the manatee and dugong is well developed.

Although manatees have a relatively small brain with few surface convolutions, volume estimates of the major brain regions indicate that the manatee cerebral cortex is comparable to those seen among a diversity of taxa having large relative brain size, including primates (Reep and O'Shea, 1990). As previously suggested, the low encephalization quotient of the manatee may be representative of other factors (i.e. large relative body size, low metabolic rate) rather than related to small relative brain size. This is further supported by the finding that the internal architecture of the manatee cerebrum is well defined, providing evidence that it is capable of extensive amount of information processing (e.g. control of tactile bristles of the upper lips; Reep *et al.,* 1989; Marshall and Reep, 1995).

The dugong brain is more elongate than that of the manatee and the cerebral hemispheres are even more widely separated by the median longitudinal fissure. A shallow Sylvian fissure is present (Fig. 7.21). A detailed description of the brain and spinal cord can be found in Dexler (1913).

Gittleman (1986b) reported brain sizes of sea otters that are not significantly different than those of other mustelids. In another study, Gittleman (1986a) showed that relative brain size for mustelids is somewhat smaller than that for carnivores overall.

7.3.1.2. Spinal Cord

The spinal cord of pinnipeds is short, terminating between the eighth and twelfth thoracic vertebrae (King, 1983). A functional relationship between neural canal size and locomotor type was found among marine carnivores (Giffin, 1992). This relationship was interpreted to be the result of differential innervation and areas of musculature involved in generating movement of the limbs. Among otariids, lumbosacral (lower back to pelvis) enlargement of the neural canal is less than brachial (arm) enlargements. This pattern is correlated to their forelimb-dominated pattern of locomotion. The phocid neural canal is unique among marine carnivores. The forelimb enlargement is similar to that in otters or otariids, but the lumbosacral enlargement is always higher than the forelimb peak. This is related to their mode of locomotion in which the hind limbs are principally employed. The walrus neural canal displays a hind limb enlargement, a pattern that is very similar to that of phocids. This is reflected in their locomotor pattern in which both the fore- and hind limb are used (see also Chapter 8).

The length of the cetacean spinal cord varies greatly depending on the body size of the species. The body length/spinal cord length ratio in the whale is 4.1, approximately the same as that found in humans (Jansen and Jansen, 1969). Among characteristic features of the cetacean spinal cord is its nearly cylindrical form throughout. Associated with development of the flippers is a prominent cervical enlargement of the spinal cord. A lumbar enlargement is much less prominent, due no doubt to the vestigial character of the hind limbs. There are 40–44 pairs of spinal nerves (Flanigan, 1966). Dorsal (sensory) structures appear relatively small in comparison to ventral (motor) structures. While this is not unique to cetaceans, the sensory component (dorsal roots and horns) is relatively more reduced in cetaceans than in other mammals. This disparity has been attributed to a relative lack of peripheral sensory innervation and, especially in the lumbosacral region, the innervation of the powerful tail musculature.

The spinal cord of the manatee ends at the last lumbar or first caudal vertebra (Quiring and Harlan, 1953). In sea otters, the neural canal cross section increases in size posteriorly in the thoracic and lumbar region suggesting extensive neural supply to the posterior torso and hind limb muscles. Polar bears differ in showing enlargements of the neural canal at both the forelimb and hind limb levels (Giffin, 1992).

7.3.1.3. Endocrine Glands

Pinnipeds differ from cetaceans in possessing a pituitary gland characterized by a thick pars intermedia in the anterior lobe of the gland (Harrison, 1969). Based on the presence of numerous somatotroph cells in the anterior lobe, it has been suggested that the pituitary gland may be actively secreting growth hormone during the rapid early postnatal growth of elephant seal pups (Bryden, 1994). The pituitary of the Amazon manatee is described as being divided into anterior and posterior lobes by a thick layer of dense connective tissue; no pars intermedia is present (Oldham *et al.,* 1938). The pituitary of the West Indian manatee, much like that of that of the dugong, is described as having well-developed anterior and posterior lobes but with reduced pars tuberalis and pars intermedius (Hill, 1945; Husar, 1977). For the dugong, there are histological descriptions of the pituitary and adrenal gland (Cave and Aumonier, 1967) and the thymus and thyroid glands (Fernand, 1957).

In addition to the pituitary gland, also located in the brain is the pineal gland. In elephant seals and Weddell seals the pineal gland is particularly large at birth. It has been suggested that the pineal, like the thyroid, is involved in thermoregulation early in postnatal life. A rhythmic activity of the pineal in adults also is suggested, having some correlation with the amount of light available and probably also with the reproductive cycle (King, 1983). In the southern elephant seal there is some evidence that the amount of daylight controls the breeding period of males through the pineal gland (Griffths and Bryden, 1981). The pineal gland is absent in odontocetes. There is a single report of a small pineal from a mysticete, the humpback whale (Gersch, 1938). The organ also is reported in embryonic stages of the blue whale (Pilleri, 1965).

The thyroid gland is two-lobed, with one lobe lying on each side of the larynx. The pinniped thyroid gland probably is very active within a few hours after birth, based on morphologic and physiologic evidence in those phocid seals that have been studied (i.e. common seal and harp seal by Dadydov and Makarova (1964) and elephant seal by Bryden (1994). It has been suggested that this increase in hormonal activity increases metabolic rate. Because the growth of fat increases markedly after the first week (Bryden, 1969), it is likely that the insulation provided reduces heat loss leading to a lowered metabolic rate and presumeably lowered thyroid activity. The relatively large size of the thyroid in cetaceans has been related to its important role in the regulation of metabolism. In baleen whales the average weight of the thyroid varies from between 0.06 and 0.6 g/kg body weight (Slijper, 1959). Quiring (1943) recorded a thyroid weight of 3450 g in a blue whale with a body weight just over 58,000 kg (0.06 g/kg) and of 3049 g for the humpback whale with average body weight of a little over 39,000 kg (about 0.08 g/kg). Bottlenose dolphins have large thyroid glands (Harrison, 1969) and a high level of circulating thyroid hormones (Ridgway and Patton, 1971). The thyroid gland of sirenians is exceptional in the relatively great abundance and density of its interfollicular connective tissue (Harrison, 1969). Colloid, a protein substance, is profuse, suggesting low thyroid activity. The pachyostotic bone, sluggish behavior, and relatively low rate of oxygen consumption all have been linked to the unusual structure of the thyroid gland (Harrison and King, 1965).

The adrenal gland in pinnipeds displays marked lobulation and folding. It differs from most other mammals in having more cortical than medullary tissue (Harrison, 1969). The adrenal glands have been described as smooth ovoid organs in delphinids but distinctly lobulated on the outside in mysticetes (Harrison, 1969). The histology of the adrenal gland of the West Indian manatee has been described as atypical because it apparently has no cortical zones (Husar, 1977).

7.3.2. Sense Organs

7.3.2.1. Visual System: Morphology of the Eye and Visual Acuity

The size and pattern of growth of the eye of marine mammals is discussed by Bryden (1972). The pattern of growth in the eyes of the southern elephant seal indicates that the most rapid period of growth occurs when the seal first goes out to sea, suggesting that good vision under water is important whereas acute vision in air is less important.

Most pinniped eyes are large relative to body size. Walruses are an exception and possess relatively small eyes by comparison. The exposed part of the eye is protected by a highly keratinized corneal epithelium and a thick sclera. The sclera prevents deformation of the eye as a result of the pressure variations to which it is subjected (Pilleri and Wandeler, 1964) and provides protection during swimming (Jamieson and Fisher, 1972). Additionally, the observation that the sclera is thinner in the equatorial region of pinniped eyes suggests that it may function to flatten the eye when exposed to air outside of the water, thereby reducing myopia (Pardue *et al.,* 1993). The thicker epithelial layer of the cornea in the bearded seal, in comparison to other phocids, may function in protecting the eye against debris and sand encountered when they feed on slow moving, sedentary or burrowing animals as is their habit (Pardue *et al,* 1993). The choroid, which lines much of the internal region of the sclera, is highly vascularized and contains a large cell layer, the **tapetum lucidum**, which makes the eye more light sensitive by acting as a mirror and reflecting the light so that it traverses the photoreceptive cells of retina twice. The tapetum reaches its greatest development in seals (Jamieson and Fisher, 1972) and it is apparently lacking in the manatee (Walls, 1942). The lens is nearly spherical, an adaptation that compensates for the loss of corneal refractive power when the eye is in water (Fig. 7.22; Sivak, 1980). The iris is very muscular and well-vascularized and the contracted pupil is a vertical slit, except in the bearded seal in which it is diagonal and the walrus in which it is a broad horizontal oval. In a study of the range of diameter of the pupil and lower limit of pupillary adjustment in the northern elephant seal, the harbor seal, and the California sea lion, the northern elephant seal exhibited the largest range of pupillary area (Levenson and Schusterman, 1997). Furthermore, the elephant seal's visual system was found to function in dimmer conditions and to respond to greater changes in light levels than that of the other pinnipeds. The Harderian glands located in the outer corners of the eye produce an oily mucus that protects the eye and prevents the cornea from drying out. Lacrimal glands, which produce tears, are small and there is no nasolacrimal duct (King, 1983).

When outside of the water, the combination of the cornea and the bulbous lens probably makes the eyes strongly myopic (nearsighted), with the image focused in front of the retina (Fig. 7.22). However, in most pinnipeds this is partly compensated for by a reduction in the size of the pupils. When the light level increases (the usual situation when going from the water into the air), the pupil of many pinnipeds becomes a narrow slit or pinhole. As such, pinnipeds probably have poor depth perception out of the water. The presence of a well-developed ciliary muscle in pinnipeds suggests accomodative movement of the lens by the ciliary muscle which would reduce myopia when the eye is exposed to air (West *et al.,* 1991). In this same study, the presence of circular muscle bundles indicated that the ciliary muscle is better developed in the elephant seal and California sea lion than in the walrus.

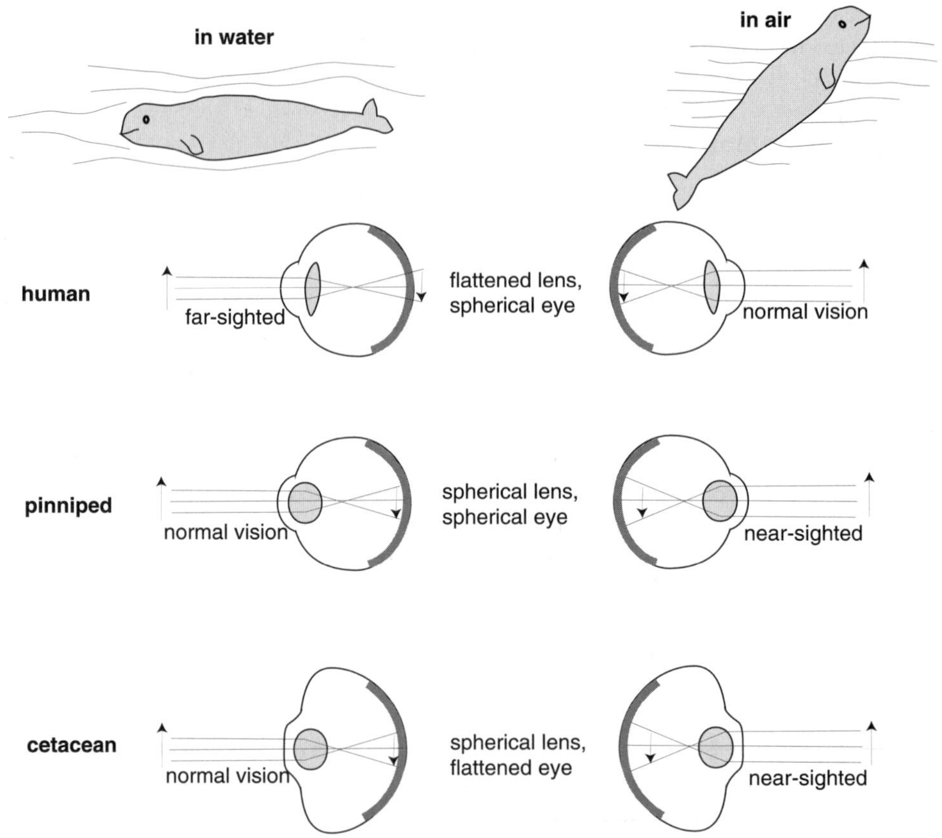

Figure 7.22. Comparison of the eye and lens shape of a human, pinniped, and cetacean and optics in air and water.

Pinnipeds, which make frequent transitions to land, require an accomodative mechanism. In contrast, in completely aquatic mammals, the ciliary muscle is rudimentary (narwhal and manatee) or lacking (beluga whale; West *et al.,* 1991).

The pinniped eye is well adapted for high visual acuity under water because of the almost circular lens, the increased light sensitivity due to the thick retina, and the well-developed tapetum lucidum. Vision is relatively clear because the image is focused on the retina. The retina is dominated by rods which give the animal increased sensitivity in dim light. Much of the interest in psychophysical research on pinniped visual acuity was initiated by Schusterman and his coworkers (e.g., for summaries, see Schusterman 1968, 1971). Visual acuity in the walrus is probably lower than in most other pinnipeds (most of which catch fast-moving prey) because the retina of the walrus eye is smaller than that of other pinnipeds and has relatively few rods per unit of surface area and many rods per optical nerve fiber (Kastelein *et al.,* 1993). Walrus eyes are placed laterally and provide limited binocular vision (Fay, 1985). Whether the optic nerves cross completely or partially in the walrus as is necessary for stereoscopic vision has not been investigated.

Demonstration of color discrimination by pinnipeds and cetaceans has been difficult. There is considerable evidence for the presence of both rods and cones in phocid and otariid retinas (Lavigne *et al.,* 1977). The walrus retina shows at least two different light receptors, one of which might have cone properties (Kastelein *et al.,* 1993). Despite the presence of two types of receptor cells in pinnipeds and the bottlenose dolphin, however, it is unclear whether this allows for color discrimination or whether instead it allows the animal to use multiple pigment systems to enhance their object detection capabilities (Watkins and Wartzok, 1985). A female spotted seal was trained to discriminate between two different targets that differed only in color (Wartzok and McCormick, 1978). Behavioral experiments with the California sea lion indicate that they possess dichromatic color vision. The sea lions were able to discriminate blue and green from a series of grays, but they could not discern red and blue-green from certain shades of gray (Griebel and Schmid, 1992). The elephant seal has been shown to possess a modified photopigment, resembling that of deep-sea fishes (Lythgoe and Dartnall, 1970), and it has been suggested that these seals use their modified photopigments to respond to the illumination of bioluminescent squid on which they feed.

In cetaceans, the eyes are located on the sides of the head but are directed forward. Rather than being spherical as in most mammals, the cetacean eye is markedly flattened anteriorly (Fig. 7.22). The susu, a river dolphin, has no lens and only a flat membrane (Purves and Pilleri, 1973; Dral and Beumer, 1974). A reflective tapetum lucidum also is present behind the retina. The sclera of whales is very thick and may serve to hold the inner globe of the eye in an elliptical shape (Pilleri and Wandeler, 1964). Although cetaceans have no tear glands, the Harderian glands and glands in the conjunctiva of the eyelids regularly bathe the cornea in a viscous solution, thus protecting it from the effects of sea water (Dawson *et al.,* 1972, 1987). Tarpley and Ridgway (1991) proposed that these special "tears" of the bottlenose dolphin, composed mainly of mucopolysaccharides, in addition to protecting the eye would help reduce frictional forces, especially when swimming at speeds where normal tears would be readily washed away.

Dolphins possess a "double pupil" (Herman *et al.,* 1975). A curtain-like extension of the upper iris margin, the operculum, comes down over the pupil proper in bright light leaving only two tiny openings in each of the two lower lateral quadrants of the eye. Several possible functions for the double pupils of dolphins have been suggested (Herman *et al.,* 1975; Norris *et al.,* 1994). These small pupils may help to avoid the problem of focusing very intense light on a single point on the retina. Instead, two points of lesser intensity can be used. Another possibility is that the pupils in spinner dolphins are on the lower quadrant of the eye, which, in a horizontally swimming dolphin, generally point slightly downward in the direction of the water beneath the animal rather than directly into the flickering glare of the surface. It also has been suggested and supported by experimental evidence (Herman *et al.,* 1975) that these two pupils working together in the same eye, by their minor overlap and by differential motion of a subject across the retina through the two pupils, may impart a measure of depth perception in the dolphin. A final benefit for the double slit pupil is that it allows dolphins to have sharp vision both above and below water during strong daylight (Herman *et al.,* 1975).

As is true for pinnipeds, the retina of some cetaceans (notably the bottlenose dolphin) is duplex, meaning that it is composed of two classes of light sensitive cells. Duplicity is a necessary but not sufficient requirement for color vision. Although rod-like and cone-like receptor cells are present in cetacean eyes, the inability of dolphins to discriminate colors is supported by several behavioral studies (Madsen and Herman, 1980). Large ganglion cells have been reported in dolphins and porpoises. Their specialized distribution in two high density areas has been used to suggest that one of these areas, the temporal, may function for frontal vision, with the rostral area functioning for side vision (Murayama *et al.,* 1995). The possibility of binocular vision has been suggested for some cetaceans based on behavioral observations (Caldwell and Caldwell, 1972). Similar kinds of evidence indicated that dolphins do not have binocular vision, although Ridgway (1990) suggested that bottlenose dolphins have small areas of overlap in the visual field.

The eye of the manatee is small compared with the size of the orbital cavity and the optic nerve is slender. There is a well-developed nictitating membrane which functions to close the conjunctival sac (Harrison and King, 1965). The shape of the lens is nearly spherical and the sclera appears thicker posteriorly than elsewhere (Griebel and Schmid, 1992). The dugong eye is small, round, and black with a well-developed nictitating membrane. As is true for cetaceans, secretions from glands under the eyelids create a copious flow of viscous tears (Kingdon, 1971). Absence of a well-developed ciliary muscle has been reported for both the dugong (Walls, 1942) and the manatee (West *et al.,* 1991) and is consistent with the poor visibility of their natural environment.

Behavioral observations of manatees in the wild indicate that they can see for considerable distances in clear water, but that they may be farsighted inasmuch as they tend to bump into objects within close range. Well-developed tapeta lucida indicate the likelihood of good vision under low light intensities. The presence of binocular vision was suggested by an additional behavioral observation, their tendency to encounter objects head-on (Hartman, 1979). The retina of the West Indian manatee has been shown to have rod-like and cone-like receptors (Cohen *et al.,* 1992). Behavioral experiments support this conclusion and provide evidence that the West Indian manatee possesses dichromatic color vision (Griebel and Schmid, 1996).

The sea otter eye is characterized by extensively developed ciliary musculature associated with a unique and well-developed accomodative mechanism that is able to change the refractive power of the lens; their accomodative range is at least three times greater than that reported for any terrestrial mammal (Sivak, 1980). In addition, the well-developed anterior epithelium may be an adaptation that helps the sea otter cope with salinity in its environment (Murphy *et al.,* 1990). Sea otters appear to have a well-developed tapetum lucidum (Riedman and Estes, 1990).

Visual acuity in the sea otter seems to be good both above and under water. Murphy *et al.* (1990) found that sea otters are able to focus clearly on targets both under water and in the air. Sea otters depend on accomodation of the eyeball to compensate for the loss of the eye's corneal refractive power when underwater. Gentry and Peterson (1967) examined underwater visual discrimination in the sea otter. Results were compared with those of a similar study of the California sea lion and they suggested that the sea lion was better at making visual size discriminations than the sea otter. However, subsequent research has indicated that the visual size discrimination task is contaminated as a test for acuity by the brightness differences caused by differently sized targets (Forbes and Smock, 1981; Schusterman, 1968).

7.3.2.2. Olfactory System

The olfactory lobes of pinnipeds are small. Pinnipeds have both peripheral (Kuzin and Sobolevsky, 1976) and central (Harrison and Kooyman, 1968) olfactory structures, and there is extensive behavioral evidence (e.g. nose to nose muzzlings) for an olfactory component in pinniped social interactions (e.g., Evans and Bastain, 1969; Ross, 1972; Miller, 1991).

Adult toothed whales typically do not possess olfactory bulbs or nerves. In the early development of the harbor porpoise, however, there is evidence for development of the olfactory bulb (Oelschläger and Buhl, 1985). The olfactory bulb and nerves are greatly reduced but not completely absent in baleen whales. The fact that mysticetes have retained some sense of smell is inferred primarily from the presence of small invaginations of the nasal cavity (ethmoturbinals of other mammals) that are covered with olfactory epithelium. In addition, their ethmoid bones, like those of most mammals, have a cribriform plate perforated with small holes, allowing the terminal branches of the olfactory nerve to pass through. Although poorly developed, the latter possesses a swelling at its extremity, the olfactory bulb (Slijper, 1936).

Manatees have a large olfactory organ and behaviorally they are often very selective in their food choice, but whether the selection is through smell, taste, or touch, or a combination of these, is not known.

Olfaction is virtually unstudied in the sea otter. They have well developed turbinates and acute olfactory sensitivity, typical of terrestrial carnivores. The social behavior of sea otters also suggests that scent production and acute olfactory sensitivity are important. Adult males may possibly locate and identify estrous females by olfactory cues (Riedman and Estes, 1990).

7.3.2.3. Taste

Although pinnipeds possess tastebuds (King, 1983) there are no known studies on the gustatory sense of pinnipeds (Watkins and Wartzok, 1985). Anatomical studies have revealed that cetaceans possess taste buds at the base of the tongue, and common and bottlenose dolphins and harbor porpoises have been shown in captivity to be able to distinguish different chemicals, even small concentrations of citric acid (Nachtigall, 1986).

In comparison to cetaceans, taste buds are more numerous in sirenians. In the dugong they are located in a row of pits along the lateral margins of the tongue. The West African manatee possesses a pair of swellings corresponding to the pits of the dugong tongue. Serous glands open into the pits and swellings and neighboring mucous glands open directly onto the surface of the tongue. The product of the glands may be used to rinse the taste buds, particularly in the case of the dugong, which feeds on sea grasses. It is also possible that some enzymes contained in the fluid convert the polysaccharides of sea grasses and algae into smaller molecules which in turn stimulate the taste buds. Another characteristic feature of the dugong tongue is the presence of patches, fungiform papillae, on the lateral surface, which may serve as tactile organs (Yamasaki *et al.,* 1980).

7.4. Urinary System

7.4.1. Kidneys

Although it has been reported that the kidneys of marine mammals are very large (Slijper, 1962), this is not true of all marine mammals. For example, the relative size of the kidneys of elephant seals differs little from that of terrestrial mammals (Bryden, 1971). Interestingly, in the elephant seal there is no change in the relative size or growth of the kidneys after the animal goes to sea, when presumably it begins ingesting sea water with its food (Bryden, 1971).

Pinnipeds, cetaceans, the polar bear, and the sea otter possess a **reniculate** kidney (Figure 7.23). In these animals each kidney is made up of small discrete lobes, the reniculi. Each reniculus is like a small single kidney with its own cortex, medulla, and calyx, and the duct from it joins with others to form the ureter.

The number of reniculi in cetaceans ranges from hundreds to thousands per kidney (Ommanney, 1932; Gihr and Kraus, 1970). One structure in the reniculus which appears unique to certain marine mammals (cetaceans and some pinnipeds, see Vardy and Bryden, 1981) is the sporta perimedullaris musculosa, an extension of muscle and cartilaginous tissue from the calyx, which penetrates the reniculus and surrounds the medullary pyramid. This feature together with other features of the cetacean reniculus, such as large reservoirs of glycogen and unique medullary blood vessels, are considered specialized adaptations in the kidney which may facilitate diving (Pfeiffer, 1997).

Dugong kidneys are elongate and quite unlike the lobulate kidneys of cetaceans and pinnipeds (Fig. 7.23). Batrawi (1953, 1957) considered the dugong kidney to combine features seen in other ungulates. Unlike manatees, the dugong appears to be physiologically independent of fresh water. Its salt metabolism is thus potentially very interesting and needs further investigation (Nishiwaki and Marsh, 1985). The kidneys of manatees are only superficially lobulate and lie on the surface of the diaphragm (Caldwell and Caldwell, 1985).

The kidneys of sea otters are large relative to body size and consist of oval clusters divided into reniculi. The lobulation of the kidneys allows the sea otter to produce large volumes of moderately concentrated urine (Kenyon, 1969; Costa, 1982; Riedman and Estes, 1990). The polar bear has the highest number of lobules (65) recorded for a carnivore (Raven, 1936).

7.4.2. Water Balance

Most marine mammals are **hypoosmotic**, that is their body fluids have a lower salt content then the surrounding environment and they are constantly in danger of losing water to the

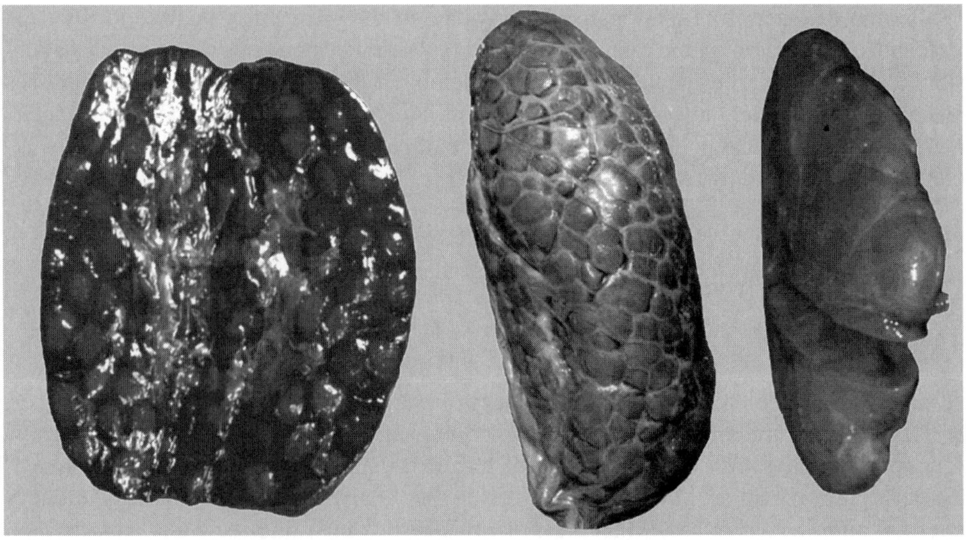

Figure 7.23. Comparison of pinniped (a), cetacean (b), and sirenian kidney (c) (courtesy of D. Odell).

more concentrated or salty ocean water in which they live. Among the ways that seals reduce their water loss is through countercurrent heat exchangers located in the nasal passages and through ventilatory patterns discussed in Chapter 9. It has been shown experimentally that seals can obtain all the water they need from the food they eat. If, however, sea water is given to seals, the stomach becomes upset and the excess salts have to be eliminated using body water.

Despite this, seals from warm climates have been seen drinking seawater (King, 1983), a practice called **mariposia**. It has been suggested that seals consume small amounts of seawater at intervals that would not be enough to cause digestive problems but would be sufficient for facilitating nitrogen excretion. Mariposia is especially common among adult male otariids including California sea lions, Steller sea lions (California population only), northern fur seals (California and St. George's Island), New Zealand fur seals (South Neptune Island only), South American fur seals, and South African fur seals (Riedman, 1990). Why do pinnipeds drink seawater? Gentry (1981) noted that most of the otariids observed ingesting sea water live in warmer climates and lose water by urination, panting, and sweating. He suggested that such water loss, along with prolonged fasting by territorial males, may be severe enough to promote the drinking of seawater. The behavior may play a role in nitrogen excretion by supplementing water produced oxidatively from fat reserves.

A study of renal function in the Baikal seal, an inhabitant of freshwater, and in the ringed seal, its marine counterpart, revealed no major differences in renal function. It was concluded that the Baikal seal, isolated from seawater and living in freshwater for 0.5 my, remarkably retained the renal function they possessed at the time of isolation (Hong *et al.,* 1982).

Experiments conducted by Hui (1981) indicated that although small odontocetes drink some seawater, it is not essential for survival. The high water turnover rate found in Hui's experiments indicates that water conservation is not a characteristic of dolphin physiology, unlike terrestrial animals forced to eat foods with relatively low moisture content in arid or semi-arid environments. The concentration range of urea produced by cetaceans is comparable to that of most terrestrial mammals (Ridgway, 1972).

The isotopic concentration of mammalian tooth phosphate reflects the type of water ingested (i.e. marine vs fresh water), and it is possible to determine when cetaceans adapted to the excess salt load associated with ingesting sea water. From studies of isotopic concentrations of fossil and living cetacean teeth (and bone) it was determined that the earliest whales (e.g. the pakicetids) were tied to terrestrial sources of freshwater and food. By the middle Eocene the first fully marine cetaceans (i.e. protocetids and remingtonocetids) appeared (Thewissen *et al.,* 1996; Roe *et al.,* 1998). The transition of cetaceans from terrestrial to marine life reflected by changes in osmoregulatory function and diet allowed them to leave the coast and rapidly disperse across the oceans. In a study of the isotopic concentrations of fossil and living cetacean teeth, it was determined that the oldest whales (e.g. the pakicetids) were not marine. By the middle Eocene the osmoregulatory organs of cetaceans (i.e. *Indocetus*) had adapted to increased salt loads, allowing them to leave the coast and disperse quickly across the oceans and ultimately to colonize the globe (Thewissen *et al.,* 1996).

Costa (1976, 1978) demonstrated that sea otters drink seawater. Because sea otters consume primarily invertebrates (which possess higher electrolyte concentrations than bony fish or mammals), they must process large amounts of electrolytes, nitrogen, and water. Ingestion of seawater promotes urea elimination by increasing the urinary osmotic space without increasing the electrolyte concentration in the urine (Costa, 1982; Riedman and Estes, 1990).

7.5. Summary and Conclusions

The integumentary system of marine mammals functions in protection, thermoregulation, and communication. The skin of cetaceans and sirenians is distinguished from other marine mammals by the absence of glands and pelage hair. The outer epidermal layer of skin in beluga whales is unique among cetaceans in undergoing an annual molt. The inner layer of skin (hypodermis, or blubber) is of variable thickness and lipid content and is subject to age- and sex-related, individual, and seasonal changes. Color patterns of the skin and pelage of marine mammals primarily function in either concealment or communication. Barnacles and whale lice attached to the skin of cetaceans are probably best considered mutualists or commensals rather than parasites. The hair of pinnipeds, the sea otter, and the polar bear consists of longer, thicker guard hairs underlain by shorter, finer underfur. Unlike phocids, fur seals and sea lions do not molt annually but instead renew their pelt gradually all year long. Vibrissae function in tactile receptivity and may be particularly important in prey detection. A layer of brown fat under the skin of newborn seals helps keep them warm by nonshivering thermogenesis until this fat is converted into insulative blubber. Because the thermal conductivity of blubber is partly a function of its thickness, temperate water porpoises have thicker blubber than tropical spotted dolphins. Research on the thermoregulation of seals indicates that ambient air temperatures play an important role in limiting their geographic distribution. Further work is necessary to test whether this is a more general phenomenon among pinnipeds. Countercurrent heat exchangers (CCHE) which regulate temperature occur in the flippers, fins, and flukes as well as the reproductive organs of marine mammals. Marine mammals also reduce heat loss to the environment by reducing their surface areas.

One of the most discussed aspects of the nervous system of marine mammals is the large relative brain size of some odontocete cetaceans and its purported relation to intelligence. Comparisons of the encephalization quotient among marine mammals indicate that dolphins have the highest brain size to body size ratio and this is likely related to life history patterns, including dietary strategy and social group size. The EQ of sirenians is among the lowest known for mammals and has been related to their low metabolic rate and long period of postnatal growth. The differing degree of development of brachial and lumbosacral regions of the spinal cord have been related to the locomotor specializations of various marine mammals. The functioning of various endocrine glands has been related to the sluggish behavior of sirenians (thyroid gland) and the breeding cycle of some seals (pineal gland).

Of the three sensory systems reviewed in this chapter (vision, olfaction, and taste), the best developed and most studied is the visual system. The eye of marine mammals is characterized by a well-developed tapetum lucidum which functions to make the eye more light sensitive, especially under low light conditions, and by Harderian glands which produce an oily mucus to protect the eye. The accomodative mechanism (i.e. the ciliary musculature) which changes the refractive power of the lens is especially well developed in pinnipeds and the sea otter in comparison to either cetaceans or sirenians. Demonstration of color discrimination in pinnipeds, cetaceans, and sirenians has been difficult, although behavioral experiments and the presence of both rods and cones in the retina have been documented for various species. Olfactory bulbs are small in pinnipeds and completely lacking in toothed whales. This is in contrast to both manatees and the sea otter which have relatively large olfactory organs and presumably more acute olfactory sensitivity.

Pinnipeds, cetaceans, the polar bear, and the sea otter possess a reniculate kidney which allows the production of large volumes of concentrated urine. The practice of drinking seawater, or mariposia, seen in seals in warmer climates, has been related to nitrogen excretion and may provide a supplement to water produced oxidatively from fat reserves. Study of the isotopic concentrations of fossil and living cetacean teeth indicates that the oldest whales were freshwater animals and that their adaptation to a marine environment occurred later.

7.6. Further Reading

For reviews of the anatomy and physiology of pinnipeds see Ridgway (1972), Harrison (1972–1977), and King (1983). For summaries of cetacean anatomy see Slijper (1962), Norris *et al.* (1966), and Yablokov *et al.* (1972). Accounts of sirenian anatomy can be found in Ridgway and Harrison (1985), Nishiwaki and Marsh (1985), and Caldwell and Caldwell (1985). The capabilities of various sensory systems of marine mammals have been reviewed (Popper, 1980; Dawson, 1980; Schusterman, 1981; Forbes and Smock, 1981) and their results highlighted by Watkins and Wartzok (1985), Thomas and Kastelein (1990), and Kastelein *et al.* (1995).

References

Ashwell-Erikson, S., F. H. Fay, R. Elsner, and D. Wartzok (1986). Metabolic and hormonal correlates of molting and regeneration of pelage in Alaskan harbour and spotted seal (*Phoca vitulina* and *Phoca largha*). *Can. J. Zool.* **64**: 1086–1094.

Batrawi, A. (1953). The external features of the dugong kidney. *Bull. Zool. Soc. Egypt* **11**: 12–13.

Batrawi, A. (1957). The structure of the dugong kidney. *Publ. Mar. Biol. Stn., Ghardaqa, Red Sea* **9**: 51–68.

Beck, G. G. and T. G. Smith (1995). Distribution of blubber in the northwest Atlantic harp seal, *Phoca groenlandica. Can. J. Zool.* **73**: 1991–1998.

Blix, A. S., L. K. Miller, M. C. Keyes, H. J. Grav, and R. Elsner (1979). Newborn mother fur seals (*Callorhinus*)—Do they suffer from cold? *Am. J. Physiol.* **236**: 322–327.

Blix, A. S., H. J. Grav, and K. Ronald (1973). Brown adipose tissue and the significance of the venous plexes in pinnipeds. *Acta Physiol. Scand.* **94**: 133–135.

Boily, P. (1995). Theoretical heat flux in water and habitat selection of phocid seals and beluga whales during the annual molt. *J. Theor. Biol.* **172**: 235–244.

Bonner, N. (1994). "Seals and Sea Lions of the World." Facts on File, New York.

Bowen, W. D. (1991). Behavioural ecology of pinniped neonates. *In* "Behavior of Pinnipeds" (D. Renouf, ed.), pp. 66–127. Chapman & Hall, London.

Boyd I. L., T. Arnbom, and M. Fedak (1993). Water flux, body composition and metabolic rate during molt in female elephant seals (*Mirounga leonina*) *Physiol. Zool.* **66**: 43–60.

Breathnach, A. S. (1960). The cetacean nervous system. *Biol. Rev. Cambridge Philos. Soc.* **35**: 187–230.

Bryden, M. M. (1964). Insulating capacity of the subcutaneous fat of the southern elephant seal. *Nature* **203**: 1299–1300.

Bryden, M. M. (1967). Testicular temperature in the southern elephant seal, *Mirounga leonina* (L.) *J. Reprod. Fertil.* **13**: 583–584.

Bryden, M. M. (1969). Relative growth of the major body components of the southern elephant seals, *Mirounga leonina* (L.). *Australian J. Zool.* **17**: 153–177.

Bryden, M. M. (1971). Anatomical and allometric adaptations in elephant seals, *Mirounga leonina. J. Anat.* **108**: 208.

Bryden, M. M. (1972). Growth in pinnipeds. *In* "Functional Anatomy of Marine Mammals" (R. J. Harrison, ed.), Vol. 1, pp. 2–79. Academic Press, London.

Bryden, M. M. (1994). Endocrine changes in newborn southern elephant seals. *In* "Elephant Seals: Population Ecology, Behavior, and Physiology" (B. J. Le Boeuf and R. M. Laws, eds.), pp. 387–397. University of California Press, Berkeley.

Bryden, M. M. and A. W. Erickson (1976). Body size and composition of Crabeater seals (*Lobodon carcinophagus*), with observations on tissue and organ size in Ross seals (*Ommatophoca rossi. J. Zool. Lond.* **179**: 235–247.

Bryden, M. M. and P. Corkeron (1988). Intelligence, pp. 160–167. *In* "Whales, Dolphins and Porpoises" (R. Harrison and M. M. Bryden, eds.), Facts on File, New York.

Caldwell, D. K., and M. C. Caldwell (1972). Senses and communication. *In* "Mammals of the Sea: Biology and Medicine" (S. H. Ridgway, ed.), pp. 419–465. Charles C Thomas, Springfield, IL.

Caldwell, D. K. and M. C. Caldwell (1985). Manatees—*Trichechus manatus, Trichechus sengalensis,* and *Trichechus inuguis.* pp. 33–36. Handbook of Marine Mammals, vol. 3, The Sirenians and Baleen Whales (S. H. Ridgway and R. J. Harrison, eds.) Academic Press, London.

Cave, A. J. E., and F. J. Aumonier (1967). Observations on dugong histology. *J. R. Microsc. Soc.* **87**: 113–121.

Cohen, J. L., G. S. Tucker and D. K. Odell (1982). The photoreceptors of the West Indian manatee. *J. Morphol.* **173**: 197–202.

Costa, D. P. (1978). The sea otter: Its interaction with man. *Oceanus* **21**: 24–30.

Costa, D. P. (1982). Energy, nitrogen, and sea-water drinking in the sea otter, *Enhydra lutris. Physiol. Zool.* **55**: 35–44.

Davydov, A. F. and A. R. Makarova (1964). Changes in heat regulation and circulation in newborn seals on transition to aquatic form of life. *Frizol. Zhur. SSSR* **50**: 894–897.

Dawson, W. W. (1980). The cetacean eye. *In* "Cetacean Behavior" (L. Herman, ed.), pp. 53–100. Wiley-Interscience, New York.

Dawson, W. W., L. A. Birndorf, and J. M. Perez (1972). Gross anatomy and optics of the dolphin eye. *Cetology* **11**: 1–11.

Dawson, W. W., J. P. Schroeder, and S. N. Sharpe (1987). Corneal surface properties of two marine mammal species. *Mar. Mamm. Sci.* **3**: 186–197.

Denhardt, G. (1994). Tactile size discrimination by a California sea lion (*Zalophus californianus*) using its mystacial vibrissac. *J. Comp. Physiol., A* **175**: 791–800.

Denhardt, G., and A. Kaminski (1995). Sensitivity of the mysticial vibrissae of harbour seals (*Phoca vitulina*) for size differences of actively touched objects. *J. Exp. Biol.* **198**: 2317–2323.

Dexler, H. (1913). Das hirn von Halicore dugong Erxl. *Morphol. Jahrb.* **45**: 95–195.

Domning, D. P., and de Buffrénil (1991). Hydrostasis in the Sirenia: Quantitative data and functional interpretations. *Mar. Mamm. Sci.* **7**(4): 331–368.

Dosch, F. (1915). "Structure and Development of the Integument of the Sirenia" (D. A. Sinclair, transl.), Tech. Trans. No. 1624. National Research Council of Canada.

Dral, A. D. G. and L. Beumer (1974). The anatomy of the eye of the Ganges River dolphin *Platanista gangetica* (Roxburgh, 1801). *Z. f. Saugetierk* **9**: 143–167.

Ebling, F. J. and P. A. Hale (1970). The control of the mammalian molt. *Mem. Soc. Endocrinol.* **18**: 215–235.

Elsner, R., D. D. Hammond, D. M. Dension, and R. Wyburn (1977). Temperature regulation in the newborn Weddell seal *Leptonychotes weddelli. In* "Adaptation within Antarctic ecosystems," (G. A. Llano, ed.), pp. 531–540. Proceedings of the third SCAR Symposium on Antarctic Biology, Aug. 26–30, 1974, Smithsonian Institution, Washington D.C.

Estes, J. (1980). *Enhydra lutris. Am. Soc. Mammal. Mamm. Species* **133**: 1–8.

Evans, W. E., and J. Bastain (1969). Marine mammal communication: Social and ecological factors. *In* "The Biology of Marine Mammals" (H. T. Andersen, ed.), pp. 425–476. Academic Press, New York.

Fay, F. (1982). Ecology and biology of the Pacific walrus, *Odobenus rosmarus divergens* Illiger. *North Am. Fauna Ser., U.S. Dep. Int., Fish Wildl. Serv.,* No. 74.

Fay, F. (1985). *Odobenus rosmarus. Mamm. Species* **238**: 1–7.

Fernand, V. S. V. (1951). The histology of the pituitary and the adrenal glands of the dugong (*Dugong dugong*), *Ceylon. J. Sci.* **8**: 57–62.

Flanigan, N. J. (1966). The anatomy of the spinal cord of the Pacific striped dolphin, *Lagenorhynchus obliquidens. In* "Whales, Dolphins and Porpoises" (K. S. Norris, ed.). pp. 207–231. University of California Press, Berkeley.

Flanigan, N. J. (1972). The central nervous system. *In* "Mammals of the Sea: Biology and Medicine" (S. Ridgway, ed.), pp. 215–246. Thomas, Springfield, IL.

Forbes, J. L. and C. C. Smock (1981). Sensory capabilities of marine mammals. *Psychol. Bull.* **89**: 288–307.

Ford, T. J. and S. D. Kraus (1992). A rete in the right whale. *Nature* **359**: 680.

Gentry, R. L. (1981). Sea water drinking in eared seals. *Comp. Biochem. Physiol.* **68A**: 81–86.
Gentry, R. L. and R. S. Peterson (1967). Underwater vision of the sea water. *Nature* **216**: 435–436.
Geraci, J. R., D. J. St. Aubin, and B. D. Hicks (1986). The epidermis of odontocetes: A view from within. *In* "Research on Dolphins" (M. M. Bryden and R. Harrison, eds.). pp. 3–31. Oxford Science Publ., Oxford.
Gersh, I. (1938). Note on the pineal gland of the humpback whale. *J. Mamm.* **19**: 477–480.
Giffin, E. (1992). Functional implications of neural canal anatomy in Recent and fossil marine carnivores. *J. Morphol.* **214**: 357–374.
Gihr, M., and C. Kraus (1970). Quantitative investigation on the cetacean kidney. *In* "Investigations on Cetacea" (G. Pilleri, ed.), Vol. 2, pp. 168–176. Berne, Switzerland.
Gingerich, P. D. (1998). Paleobiological perspectives on Mesonychia, Archaeoceti, and the origin of whales. *In* "The Emergence of Whales: Patterns in the Origin of Cetacea" (J. G. M. Thewissen, ed.), pp. 423–449. Plenum Press, New York.
Gittleman, J. L. (1986a). Carnivore brain size, behavioral ecology and phylogeny. *J. Mammal.* **67**: 23–36.
Gittleman, J. L. (1986b). Carnivore life history patterns: Allometric, ecological and phylogenetic associations. *Am. Nat.* **127**: 744–771.
Grav, H. H. and A. S. Blix (1975). Brown adipose tissue—A factor in the survival of harp seal pups. *Vitam impendere vero. In* "Depressed metabolism and cold thermogenesis" (L. Jansky, ed.), Academia, Rague.
Grav, H. H., A. S. Blix and A. Pasche (1974). How do seal pups survive birth in Arctic winter? *Actas Physiol. Scand.* **92**: 427–429.
Griebel, U., and A. Schmid (1992). Color vision in the California sea lion (*Zalophus californianus*). *Vision Res.* **32**(3): 477–482.
Griebel, U., and A. Schmid (1996). Color vision in the manatee (*Trichechus manatus*). *Vision Res.* **36**(17): 2747–2757.
Griffiths, D. J., and M. M. Bryden (1981). The annual cycle of the pineal gland of the elephant seal (*Mirounga leonina*). *In* "Pineal function" (C. Matthews and R. Seamark, eds.), pp. 57–66. Elsevier.
Hansen, S., and D. M. Lavigne (1997a). Ontogeny of the thermal limits in the harbor seal (*Phoca vitulina*). *Physiol. Zool.* **70**(1): 85–92.
Hansen, S., and D. M. Lavigne (1997b). Temperature effects on the breeding distribution of gray seals (*Halichoerus grypus*). *Physiol. Zool.* **70**(4): 436–443.
Hansen, S., D. M. Lavigne, and S. Innes (1995). Energy metabolism and thermoregulation in juvenile harbor seals (*Phoca vitulina*). *Physiol. Zool.* **68**: 290–315.
Harrison, R. J. (1969). Endocrine organs: Hypophysis, thyroid, and adrenal, *In* "The Biology of Marine Mammals" (H. T. Andersen, ed.), pp. 349–390. Academic Press, New York.
Harrison, R. J. (1972–1977). Functional Anatomy of Marine Mammals, vols. 1–3. Academic Press, London.
Harrison, R. J., and J. E. King (1965). "Marine Mammals." Hutchinson, London.
Harrison, R. J. and J. D. W. Tomlinson (1963). Anatomical and physiological adaptations in diving mammals, pp. 115–162. *In* "Viewpoints in Biology," Butterworth, London.
Harrison, R. J. and G. L. Kooyman (1968). General physiology of the Pinnipedia. *In* "The Behavior and Physiology of the Pinnipeds" (R. J. Harrison, R. C. Hubbard, R. S. Peterson, C. E. Rice, and R. J. Schusterman, eds.), pp. 211–296. Appleton-Century-Crofts, New York.
Harrison, R. J., and Thurley (1974). Structure of the epidermis in *Tursiops, Delphinus, Orcinus* and *Phocoena. In* "Functional Anatomy of Marine Mammals" (R. J. Harrison, ed.), Vol. 1, pp. 45–71. Academic Press, New York and London.
Hartman, D. S. (1979). Ecology and behavior of the manatee (*Trichechus manatus*) in Florida, *Am. Soc. Mammal. Spec. Publ.* **3**: 1–153.
Herman, L. M. (1991). What The Dolphin Knows, Or Might Know, In Its Natural World. *In* "Dolphin Societies," pp. 349–363. Pryor, K. K. S. Norris. University of California Press, Berkeley.
Herman, L. M., M. Peacock, M. Yunker, and C. Madsen (1975). Bottlenosed dolphin: double-slit pupil yields equivalent aerial and underwater diurnal acuity. *Science* **189**: 650–652.
Heyning, J., and J. Mead (1997). Thermoregulation in the mouths of feeding gray whales. *Science* **278**: 1138–1139.
Hill, W. C. O. (1945). Notes on the dissection of two dugongs. *J. Mammal.* **26**: 153–175.
Hong, S. K., R. Elsner, J. R. Claybaugh, and K. Ronald (1982). Renal functions of the Baikal Seal *Pusa sibirica* and Ringed Seal *Pusa hispida. Physiol. Zool.* **55**(3): 289–299.
Howell, A. B. (1930). Aquatic Mammals. Charles C Thomas, Springfield, Ill.
Hui, C. A. (1981). Seawater consumption and water flux in the common dolphin *Delphinus delphis. Physiol. Zool.* **54**: 43–440.
Husar, S. (1977). "The West Indian Manatee: *Trichechus manatus*," Wildl. Res. Rep. No. 7. U.S. Department of the Interior, Fish and Wildlife Service, Washington, DC.

Hyvvärinen, H. (1989). Diving in darkness: Whiskers as sense organs of the ringed seal (*Phoca hispida saimensis*). *J. Zool. Soc. London* **218**: 663–678.

Hyvvärinen, H. (1995). Structure and function of the vibrissae of the ringed seal (*Phoca hispida* L.). *In* "Sensory Systems of Aquatic Mammals" (R. A. Kastelein, J. A. Thomas, and P. E. Nachtigall, eds.), pp. 429–445. De Spil Publishers, Woerden, The Netherlands.

Innes, S., G. A. J. Worthy, D. M. Lavigne, and K. Ronald (1990). Surface area of phocid seals. *Can. J. Zool.* **68**: 2531–2538.

Iverson, S. J. (1998). Blubber of marine mammals: An ecological tool. *In* "Abstracts of World Marine Mammal Science Conference," p. 67. Monaco, January 20–24, 1998.

Jamieson, G. S., and H. D. Fisher (1972). The pinniped eye: A review. *In* "Functional Anatomy of Marine Mammals" (R. J. Harrison, ed.), Vol. 1. Academic Press, London.

Jansen, J. and J. K. S. Jansen (1969). The nervous system of Cetacea. *In* "The Biology of Marine Mammals" (H. T. Andersen, ed.), pp. 175–252. Academic Press, New York.

Jerison, H. J. (1973). "Evolution of the Brain and Intelligence." Academic Press, New York.

Kamiya, Y., and F. Yamsaki (1979). A morphological note on the sinus hair of the dugong. *In* "The Dugong, Proceedings of a Seminar/Workshop held at James Cook University of North Queensland" (H. Marsh, ed.), pp. 193–197.

Kastelein, R. A., and M. A. van Gaalen (1988). The sensitivity of a Pacific walrus (*Odobenus rosmarus divergens*). Part 1. *Aqua. Mamm.* **14**(3): 123–133.

Kastelein, R. A. S. Stevens, and P. Mosterd (1990). The tactile sensitivity of the mystacial vibrissae of a Pacific walrus (*Odobenus rosmarus divergens*). Part 2: Masking. *Aquat. Mamm.* **16**(2): 78–87.

Kastelein, R. A., R. C. V. J. Zweypfenning, H. Spekreijse, J. L. Dubbeldam, and E. W. Born (1993). The anatomy of the walrus head (*Odobenus rosmarus*). Part 3: The eyes ant their function in walrus ecology. *Aquat. Mamm.* **19**(2): 61–92.

Kastelein, R. A., J. A. Thomas, and P. E. Nachtigall (eds.) (1995). "Sensory Systems of Aquatic Mammals." De Spil Publishers, Woerden, The Netherlands.

Kenyon, K. W. (1969). The sea otter in the eastern Pacific Ocean. *North Am. Fauna Ser., U.S. Dep. Int., Fish Wildl. Serv.* No. 68.

Kenyon, K. W., and D. W. Rice (1959). Life history of the Hawaiian monk seal. *Pac. Discovery* **13**: 215–252.

Kim, K. C. (1971). The sucking lice (Anoplura: Echinopthiriidae) of the northern fur seal. Descriptions and morphological adaptation. *Ann. Entomol. Soc. Am.* **64**: 280–292.

Kim, K. C. (1975). Ecology and morphological adaptation of the sucking lice (Anoplura: Echinophthiriidae) on the northern fur seal. *Rapp. Reun. Cons. Int. Explor. Mer.* **169**: 504–515.

Kim, K. C., C. A. Repenning, and G. V. Morejohn (1975). Specific antiquity of the suckling lice and evolution of otariid seals. *Rapp. P-v. Reun Cons. Int. Explor. Mer.* **169**: 544–549.

King, J. E. (1983). "Seals of the World," 2nd ed. Cornell University Press, Ithaca, NY.

Koon, D. W. (1998). Is polar bear hair fiber optic? *Applied Optics* **37**(15): 3198–3200.

Kingdon, J. (1971). East African mammals, an atlas of evolution in Africa. Vol. 1, p. 446. Academic Press, London.

Kruger, L. (1966). Specialized features of the cetacean brain. *In* "Whales, Dolphins and Porpoises" (K. S. Norris, ed.), pp. 232–254. University of California Press, Berkeley.

Kuzin, A. Ye. and Ye. I. Sobololevsky (1976). Morphological and functional characteristics of the fur seal's respiratory system. Proc. of the 6th All-Union Conf. of Publ. Serv., Arlington.

Kvadsheim, P. V., A. R. L. Gotaas, L. P. Folkow, and A. S. Blix (1997). An experimental validation of heat loss models for marine mammals. *J. Theor. Biol.* **184**: 15–23.

Lavigne, D. M., and K. M. Kovacs. (1988). "Harps and Hoods." University of Waterloo Press, Ontario, Canada.

Lavigne, D. M., C. D. Bernholz, and F. Ronald (1977). Functional aspects of pinniped vision. *In* "Functional Anatomy of Marine Mammals" (R. J. Harrison, ed.), Vol. 3, pp. 135–173. Academic Press, London.

Leatherwood, S. and R. R. Reeves (1983). The Sierra Club Handbook of Whales and Dolphins, Sierra Club Book, San Francisco.

Leung, Y. M. (1967). An illustrated key to the species of whale lice. *Crustaceana* **12**: 279–291.

Levenson, D. H. and R. J. Schusterman (1997). Pupillometry in seals and sea lions: Ecological implications. *Can. J. Zool.* **75**: 2050–2057.

Lewin, R. A., and P. T. Robinson (1979). The greening of polar bears in zoos. *Nature* **278**: 445–447.

Lilly, J. C. (1964). Animals in aquatic environments: adaptation of mammals to the ocean. *In* "Handbook of physiology-environment." pp. 741–747. American Physiological Society, Washington, D. C.

Lilly, J. C. (1967). "The mind of the dolphin." Doubleday, Garden City, New York.

Linberger, D., F. Trillmich, H. Biebach, and R. D. Stevenson (1986). Temperature regulation and microhabitat choice by free-ranging Galapagos fur seals (*Arctocephalus galapagoensis*). *Oecologia* **69**: 53–59.

Ling, J. K. (1965). Functional significance of sweat glands and sebaceous glands in seals. *Nature* **208**: 560–562.

Ling, J. K. (1970). Pelage and molting in wild mammals with special reference to aquatic forms. *Q. Rev. Biol.* **45**: 16–54.

Ling, J. K. (1974). The integument of marine mammals. *In* "Functional Anatomy of Marine Mammals" (R. J. Harrison, ed.), Vol. 2, pp. 1–44. Academic Press, London.

Ling, J. K. (1977). Vibrissae of marine mammals. *In* "Functional Anatomy of Marine Mammals" (R. J. Harrison, ed.), Vol. 3, pp. 387–415. Academic Press, London.

Ling, J. K., and C. E. Button (1975). The skin and pelage of gray seal pups (*Halichoerus grypus* Fabricus): With a comparative study of foetal and neonatal moulting in the Pinnipedia. *Rapp. P.-V. Renun., Cons. Int. Explor. Mer* **169**: 112–132.

Ling, J. K. and C. D. B. Thomas (1967). The skin and hair of the southern elephant seal, *Mirounga leonina* (L.) 2. Pre-natal and early post-natal development and moulting. *Aust. J. Zool.* **15**: 349–365.

Lythgoe, J. N., and H. J. A. Dartnall (1970). A deep sea rhodopsin in a mammal. *Nature* **227**: 955–956.

MacDonald, D., ed. (1984). "Sea Mammals." Torstar Books, New York.

Madsen, C. J., and L. M. Herman (1980). Social and ecological correlates of cetacean vision and visual appearance. *In* "Cetacean Behavior" (L. Herman, ed.). Wiley-Interscience, New York.

Marino, L. (1997). The relationship between gestation length, encephalization, and body weight in odontocetes. *Mar. Mamm. Sci.* **13**(1): 133–138.

Marino, L. (1998). A comparison of encephalization between odontocete cetaceans and anthropoid primates. *Brain, Behavior and Evolution* **51**(4): 230–238.

Marshall, C. D., and R. L. Reep (1995). Manatee cerebral cortex: Cytoarchitecture of the caudal region in *Trichechus manatus latirostris*. *Brain, Behav. Evol.* **45**: 1–18.

Marshall, C. D., L. A. Clark, and R. L. Reep (1998). The muscular hydrostat of the Florida manatee (*Trichechus manatus latirostris*): functional morphological model of perioral bristle use. *Mar. Mamm. Sci.* **14**(2): 290–305.

McLaren, I. A. (1966). Taxonomy of harbor seals of the western North Pacific and the evolution of certain other hair seals. *J. Mammal.* **47**: 466–473.

Melnikov, V. V. (1997). The arterial system of the sperm whale (*Physeter macrocephalus*). *J. Morphol.* **234**: 37–50.

Mills, F., and D. Renouf (1986). Determination of the vibrational sensitivity of the harbour seal, *Phoca vitulina* vibrissae. *J. Exp. Mar. Biol. Ecol.* **100**: 3–9.

Mitchell, E. D. (1970). Pigmentation pattern evolution in delphinid coloration: An essay in adaptive coloration. *Can. J. Zool.* **48**: 717–740.

Morgane, P. J. and M. Jacobs (1972). Comparative anatomy of the cetacean nervous system. *In* "Functional Anatomy of Marine Mammals" (R. J. Harrison, ed.), pp. 117–244. Academic Press, London.

Morgane, P. J., M. S. Jacobs, and A. Galaburda (1986). Evolutionary morphology of the dolphin brain. *In* "Dolphin Cognition and Behavior: A Comparative Approach" (R. J. Schusterman, J. A. Thomas, and F. G. Wood, eds.), pp. 5–28. Hillsdale, NJ.

Murayama, T., H. Somiya, I. Aoki, and T. Ishii (1995). Retinal ganglion cell size and distribution predict visual capabilities of Dall's porpoise. *Mar. Mamm. Sci.* **11**(2): 136–149.

Murie, J. (1871). Researchers upon the anatomy of the Pinnipedia. Part I. On the walrus (*Trichechus rosmarus* Linn.) *Trans. Zool. Soc.* (London) **7**: 411–464.

Murphy, C. J., R. W. Bellhorn, R. W. Williams, T. Burns, M. S. Schaeffel, and H. C. Howland (1990). Refractive state, ocular anatomy, and accomodative range of the sea otter. *Vision Res.* **30**: 23–32.

Nachtigall, P. E. (1986). Vision, audition, and chemoreception in dolphins and other marine mammals. *In* "Dolphin Cognition and Behavior: A Comparative Approach" (R. J. Schusterman, J. A. Thomas, and F. G. Wood, eds.), pp. 79–113. Erlbaum, Hillsdale, NJ.

Nemoto, T. (1956). On the diatoms of the skin film of whales in the northern Pacific. *Sci. Rep. Whales Res. Inst. Tokyo* **11**: 99–132.

Nemoto, T., P. B. Best, K. Ishimaru, and H. Takano (1980). Diatom films on whales in South African waters. *Sci. Rep. Whales Res. Inst.* **32**: 97–103.

Nishiwaki, M., and H. Marsh (1985). *Dugong dugon* (Muller, 1776). *In* "Handbook of Marine Mammals" (S. H. Ridgway and R. Harrison, eds.), Vol. 3, pp. 1–31. Academic Press, New York.

Norris, K. S., ed. (1966). "Whales, Dolphins and Porpoises." Univ. California Press, Berkeley.

Norris, K. S., R. S. Wells, and C. M. Johnson (1994). The visual domain. *In* "The Hawaiian Spinner Dolphin" (K. S. Norris, B. Wursig, R. S. Wells, and M. Wursig, eds.), pp. 141–160. University of California Press, Berkeley.

O'Dea, J. D. (1990). The mammalian rete mirabile and oxygen availability. *Comp. Biochem. Physiol. A* **95A**(1): 23–25.

Oelschläger, H. A., and E. H. Buhl (1985). Development and rudimantation of the peripheral olfactory system in the harbor porpoise *Phocoena phocoena* (Mammalia: Cetacea). *J. Morphol.* **184**: 351–360.

Oftedal, O. T., W. D. Bowen, E. M. Widdowson, and D. J. Boness (1991). The prenatal molt and its ecological significance in hooded and harbor seals. *Can. J. Zool.* **69**: 2489–2493.

Oldham, F. K., D. P. McCleery and E. N. K. Geiling (1938). A note on the histology and pharmacology of the hypophysis of the manatee (*Trichechus inunguis*). *Anat. Rec.* **71**: 27–32.

Ommanney, F. C. (1932). The uro-genital system of the fin whale (*Balaenoptera physalus*). With appendix: The dimensions and growth of the kidney of blue and fin whales. *Discovery Rep.* **5**: 363–466.

Øritsland, N. A. (1971). Wavelength-dependent solar heating of harp seals (*Pagophilus groenlandicus*). *Comp. Biochem. Physiol.* **40A**: 359–361.

Øritsland, T. (1970). Energetic significance of absorption of solar radiation in polar homeotherms. *In* "Antarctic Ecology," Vol. 1 (M. W. Holgate, ed.), pp. 464–470. Academic Press, London.

O'Shea, T. J., and R. L. Reep (1990). Encephalization quotients and life-history traits in the Sirenia. *J. Mammal.* **71**(4): 534–543.

Pabst, D. A., S. A. Rommel, W. A. McLellan (1998). Evolution of the thermoregulatory function in the cetacean reproductive systems. *In* "The Emergence of Whales: Patterns in the Origin of Cetacea" (J. G. M. Thewissen, ed.), pp. 379–397. Plenum Press, New York.

Pabst, D. A., S. A. Rommel, W. A. McLellan, T. M. Williams, and T. K. Rowles (1995). Thermoregulation of the intra-abdominal testes of the bottlenose dolphin (*Tursiops truncatus*) during exercise. *J. Exp. Biol.* **198**: 221–226.

Pardue, M. T., J. G. Sivak, and K. M. Kovacs (1993). Corneal anatomy of marine mammals. *Can. J. Zool.* **71**: 2282–2290.

Parry, D. A. (1949). The structure of whale blubber, and a discussion of its thermal properties. *Q. J. Microsc. Sci.* **90**: 13–25.

Perrin, W. F. (1972). Color patterns of spinner porpoises (*Stenells* cf. *S. longisrostris*) of the eastern Pacific and Hawaii, with comments on delphinid pigmentation. *Fish. Bull.* **70**(3): 983–1003.

Pfeiffer, C. J. (1997). Renal cellular and tissue specializations in the bottlenose dolphin (*Tursiops truncatus*) and beluga whale (*Delphinapterus leucas*). *Aqua. Mamm.* **23**(2): 75–84.

Pilleri, G. (1965). Morphologie des Gehirnes des Blauwals, *Balaenoptera musculus* Linnaeus (Cetacea, Mysticeti, Balaenopteridae) *Jahrb. Naturhist. Museum Bern.* 187–203.

Pilleri, G. (1983). Cetaceans in capativity. *In* "Investigations on Cetacea" (G. Pilleri, ed.), pp. 221–249. Brain Anatomy Institute, Berne, Switzerland, 258 pp.

Pilleri, G., and A. Wandeler (1964). Ontogeny and functional morphology of the eye of the fin whale (*Balaenoptera physalus*). *Acta Anat., Suppl.* **50**(1): 179–245.

Popper, A. N. (1980). Sound emission and detection by delphinids. *In* "Cetacean Behavior" (L. M. Herman, ed.), pp. 1–52. Wiley-Interscience, New York.

Purves, P. E. and G. Pilleri (1973). Observations on the ear, nose, throat and eye of (*Platanista indi*). *Invest. Cetacea* **5**: 13–57.

Quiring, D. P. (1943). Weight data on five whales. *J. Mammal.* **24**: 39.

Quiring, D. P., and C. F. Harlan (1953). On the anatomy of the manatee. *J. Mammal.* **34**: 192–203.

Raven, H. C. (1936). Notes on the anatomy of the viscera of the giant panda (*Ailuropoda melanoleuca*). *Amer. Mus. Novit.* **877**: 1–23.

Reep, R. L., and T. J. O'Shea (1990). Regional brain morphometry and lissencephaly in the Sirenia. *Brain, Behav. Evol.* **35**: 185–194.

Reep, R. L., J. I. Johnson, R. C. Switzer, and W. J. Welker (1989). Manatee cerebral cortex: Cytoarchitecture of the frontal region in *Trichechus manatus latirostris. Brain, Behav. Evol.* **34**: 365–386.

Reep, R. L., C. D. Marshall, M. L. Stoll and D. M. Whitaker (1998). Distribution and innervation of facial bristles and hairs in the Florida manatee (*Trichechus manatus latirostris*). *Mar. Mamm. Sci.* **14**(2): 257–273.

Reeves, R. R., B. S. Stewart and S. Leatherwood (1992). "The Sierra Club Handbook of Seals and Sirenians." Sierra Club Books, San Francisco.

Renouf, D. (1979). Preliminary measurements of the sensitivity of the vibrissae of harbour seals (*Phoca vitulina*) to low frequency vibrations. *J. Zool. Soc. London* **188**: 443–450.

Renouf, D. (1980). Fishing in captive harbour seals (*Phoca vitulina concolor*): A possible role for vibrissae. *Neth. J. Zool.* **30**: 504–509.

Ridgway, S. H. (1972). Homeostasis in the aquatic environment. *In* "Mammals of the Sea: Biology and Medicine" (S. H. Ridgway, ed.), pp. 590–747. Charles C Thomas, Springfield, Illinois.

Ridgway, S. H. (1986a). Dolphin brain size. *In* "Research on Dolphins" (M. M. Bryden and R. Harrison, eds.), pp. 59–70. Oxford Science Publications, Oxford.

Ridgway, S. H. (1986b). Physiological observations on dolphin brains. *In* "Dolphin Cognition and Behavior: A Comparative Approach" (R. J. Schusterman, J. A. Thomas, and F. G. Wood, eds.), pp. 31–55. Erlbaum, Hillsdale, NJ.

Ridgway, S. H. (1990). The central nervous system of the bottlenose dolphin. *In* "The Bottlenose Dolphin" (S. Leatherwood and R. R. Reeves, eds), pp. 69–97. Academic Press, San Diego, CA.

Ridgway, S. H., and R. J. Harrison (eds.) (1985). "Handbook of Marine Mammals," Vol. 3. Academic Press, New York.

Ridgway, S. H. and G. S. Patton (1971). Dolphin thyroid: some anatomical and physiological findings. *Z. Verg. Physiol.* **71**: 129–141.

Riedman, M. L. (1990). "The Pinnipeds: Seals, Sea Lions and Walruses." University of California Press, Berkeley.

Riedman, M. L., and J. A. Estes (1990). The sea otter (*Enhydra lutris*): Behavior, ecology, and natural history. *U.S. Fish Wildl. Serv., Biol. Rep.* **90**(14).

Roe, L. J., J. G. M. Thewissen, J. Quade, J. R. O'Neill, S. Bajpal, A. Sahni, and S. T. Hussain (1998). Isotopic approaches to understanding the terrestrial-to-marine transition of the earliest cetaceans. *In* "The Emergence of Whales: Patterns in the Origin of Cetacea" (J. G. M. Thewissen, ed.), pp. 399–422. Plenum Press, New York.

Rommel, S. A., D. A. Pabst, W. A. McLellan, J. G. Mead, and C. W. Potter (1992). Anatomical evidence for a countercurrent heat exchanger associated with dolphin testes. *Anat. Rec.* **232**(1): 150–156.

Rommel, S. A., D. A. Pabst, W. A. McLellan, T. M. Williams, and W. A. Friedl (1994). Temperature regulation of the testes of the bottlenose dolphin (*Tursiops truncatus*): evidence from colonic temperatures. *J. Comp. Physiol. B* **164**: 130–134.

Rommel, S. A., D. A. Pabst, and W. A. McLellan (1993). Functional morphology of the vascular plexuses associated with the cetacean uterus. *Anat. Rec.* **237**: 538–546.

Rommel, S. A., G. A. Early, K. A. Matassa, D. A. Pabst, and W. A. McLellan (1995). Venous structures associated with thermoregulation of phocid seal reproductive organs *Anat. Rec.* **243**: 390–402.

Ross, G. J. B. (1972). Nuzzling behavior in captive Cape fur seals. *Int. Zool. Yearbook* **12**: 183–184.

Rowntree, V. J. (1983). Cyamids: the louse that moored. Whalewatcher. *J. Am. Cetacean Soc.* **17**: 14–17.

Rowntree, V. J. (1996). Feeding, distribution, and reproductive behavior of cyamids (Crustacea: Amphipoda) living on humpback and right whales. *Can. J. Zool.* **74**: 103–109.

Ryg, M., T. G. Smith, and N. A. Oritsland (1988). Thermal significance of the topographical distribution of blubber in ringed seals (*Phoca hispida*). *Can. J. Fish. Aquat. Sci.* **45**: 985–992.

Sacher, G. A. and E. F. Staffeldt (1974). Relation of gestation time to brain weight for placental mammals: Implications for the theory of vertebrate growth. *Am. Naturalist* **108**(963): 593–615.

Scheffer, V. (1964). Hair patterns in seals (Pinnipedia). *J. Morphol.* **115**: 291–304.

Schevill, W. E., W. A. Watkins, and G. C. Ray (1966). Analysis of underwater *Odobenus* calls with remarks on the development and function of the pharyngeal pouches. *Zoologica* **51**: 103–106.

Schusterman, R. J. (1968). Experimental laboratory studies of pinniped behavior. *In* "The Behavior and Physiology of Pinnipeds" (R. J. Harrison, R. C. Hubbard, R. S. Peterson, C. E. Rice, and R. J. Schusterman, eds.), pp. 87–171. Appleton-Century-Crofts, New York.

Schusterman, R. J. (1971). Aerial and underwater activity in the California sea lion, *Zalophus californianus,* as a function of luminance. *Ann. NY Acad. Sci.* **188**: 37–47.

Schusterman, R. J. (1981). Behavioral capabilities of seals and sea lions: a review of their hearing, visual, learning and diving skills. *Psychol. Rec.* **31**: 125–143.

Shoemaker, P. A., and S. H. Ridgway (1991). Cutaneous ridges in odontocetes. *Mar. Mamm. Sci.* **7**(1): 66–74.

Sivak, J. G. (1980). Accomodation in vertebrates: A contemporary survey. *Curr. Top. Eye Res.* **3**: 281–330.

Slijper, E. J. (1936). Die Cetaceen, vergleichend anatomisch und systematisch, Diss. Utrecht, *Capita Zoologica* **7**.

Slijper, E. J. (1958). Organ weights and symmetry problems in porpoises and seals. *Arch. Neerl, Zool.* **13**(suppl.) 1: 97.

Slijper, E. J. (1979). "Whales." 2nd ed. Hutchinson, Univ. Press, London.

Sokolov, V. E. (1982). "Mammal Skin." Univ. California Press, Berkeley.

Spector, W. S. (1956). "Handbook of Biological Data." Saunders, Philadelphia.

St. Aubin, D. J., T. G. Smith, and J. R. Geraci (1990). Seasonal epidermal molt in beluga whales, *Delphinapterus leucas. Can. J. Zool.* **68**: 359–367.

Stutz, S. S. (1967). Moult in the Pacific harbour seal, *Phoca vitulina richardsi. J. Fish. Res. Board Can.* **24**: 435–441.

Tarasoff, F. J. (1974). Anatomical adaptations in the river otter, sea otter and harp seal with reference to thermal regulation. *In* "Functional Anatomy of Marine Mammals" (R. J. Harrison, ed.), Vol. 2. pp. 111–142. Academic Press, London.

Tarpley, R. J., and S. A. Ridgway (1991). Orbital gland structure and secretions in the Atlantic bottlenose dolphin (*Tursiops truncatus*). *J. Morphol.* **207**: 173–184.

Thewissen, J. G. M., L. J. Roe, J. R. O'Neill, S. T. Hussain, A. Sahni, and S. Bajpal (1996). Evolution of cetacean osmoregulation. *Nature* **381**: 379–380.

Thomas, J. A. and R. A. Kastelein, eds. (1990). Sensory Abilities of Cetaceans: Laboratory and Field Evidence. Plenum Press, New York.

Vardy, P. H., and M. M. Bryden (1981). The kidney of *Leptonychotes weddelli* (Pinnipedia: Phocidae) with some observations on the kidneys of two other southern phocid seals. *J. Morphol.* **167**: 13–34.

Vaz-Ferreira, R. (1981). South American sea lion—*Otaria flavescens. In* "Handbook of Marine Mammals" (S. H. Ridgway and R. J. Harrison, eds.), pp. 39–66. Academic Press, London.

Walls, G. L. (1942). "The Vertebrate Eye and its Adaptive Radiation." Cranbrook Institute of Science, Bloomfield Hills, MI.

Wartzok, D., and M. G. McCormick (1978). Color discrimination by a Bering Sea spotted seal, *Phoca larga. Vision Res.* **18**: 781–784.

Wartzok, D., R. Elsner, H. Stone, B. P. Kelly, and R. W. Davis (1992). Under-ice movements and sensory basis of hole finding by ringed and Weddell Seals. *Can. J. Zool.* **70**: 1712–1722.

Watkins, W. A., and D. Wartzok (1985). Sensory biophysics of marine mammals. *Mar. Mamm. Sci.* **1**(3): 219–260.

West, J. A., J. G. Sivak, C. J. Murphy, and K. M. Kovacs (1991). A comparative study of the anatomy of the iris and ciliary body in aquatic mammals. *Can. J. Zool.* **69**: 2594–2607.

Williams, T. D., D. D. Allen, J. M. Groff, and R. L. Glass (1992). An analysis of California sea otter (*Enhydra lutris*) pelage and integument. *Mar. Mamm. Sci.* **8**(1): 1–18.

Williams, T. M., J. E. Haun, W. A. Friedl, and L. W. Bivens (1992). Assessing the thermal limits of bottlenose dolphins: A cooperative study between trainers, scientists, and animals. *IMATA Strandings* **4**: 16–17.

Wood, F. G., and W. E. Evans (1980). Adaptiveness and ecology of echolocation in toothed whales. *In* "Animal Sonar Systems" (R.-G. Busnel and J. F. Fish, eds.), pp. 381–425. Plenum Press, New York.

Worthy, G. A. J., and E. F. Edwards (1990). Morphometric and biochemical factors affecting heat loss in a small temperate cetacean (*Phocoena phocoena*) and a small tropical cetacean (*Stenella attenuata*). *Physiol. Zool.* **63**: 432–442.

Worthy, G. A., and J. P. Hickie (1986). Relative brain size in marine mammals. *Am. Nat.* **128**(4): 445–449.

Worthy, G. A., P. A. Morris, D. P. Costa, and B. J. Le Boeuf (1992). Moult energetics of the northern elephant seal (*Mirounga angustirostris*). *J. Zool.* **227**: 257–265.

Wyss, A. R. (1987). The walrus auditory region and the monophyly of pinnipeds. *Am. Mus. Novit.* **2871**: 1–31.

Wyss, A. R. (1988). On "retrogression" in the evolution of the Phocinae and phylogenetic affinities of the monk seals. *Am. Mus. Novit.* **2924**: 1–38.

Yablokov, A. V., Bel'kovich, V. M. and V. I. Borisov (1972). Whales and Dolphins, Israel Programs for Scientific Translations, Jerusalem.

Yamasaki, F., S. Komatsu, and T. Kamiya (1980). A comparative morphological study on the tongues of manatee and dugong (Sirenia). *Sci. Rep. Whales Res. Inst.* **32**: 127–144.

8

Musculoskeletal System and Locomotion

8.1. Introduction

Rather than providing detailed anatomical descriptions for individual marine mammal taxa, the focus of this chapter will be one of comparing and considering variation in the musculoskeletal anatomy of the major marine mammal groups, especially as it relates to locomotion. Propulsion for swimming by marine mammals is derived from paired flipper movements (pinnipeds and sea otters) or vertical movements of caudal flukes (cetaceans and sirenians). Paired flipper propulsion is more efficient at low speeds where maneuverability is critical. The evolution of locomotion in each of the major groups of marine mammals also is reviewed. Those anatomical specializations that specifically relate to sound production are covered in Chapter 10 and those related to feeding are further discussed in Chapter 11. The nomenclature and topographical and directional terms used are from the Nomina Anatomica Veterinaria (1983).

8.2. Pinnipeds

This discussion of pinniped musculoskeletal anatomy is based on Howell (1929) and King (1983).

8.2.1. Skull and Mandible

The pinniped skull is characterized by large eye orbits, a relatively short snout, a constricted interorbital region, and large orbital vacuities (unossified spaces in the ventromedial wall of the eye orbit; Figs. 3.3 and 8.1). The skull of otariids is readily distinguishable from those of phocids and the walrus in the development of large, shelf-like supraorbital processes of the frontal bones (Fig. 8.1). In addition, the relationship of the nasals to the

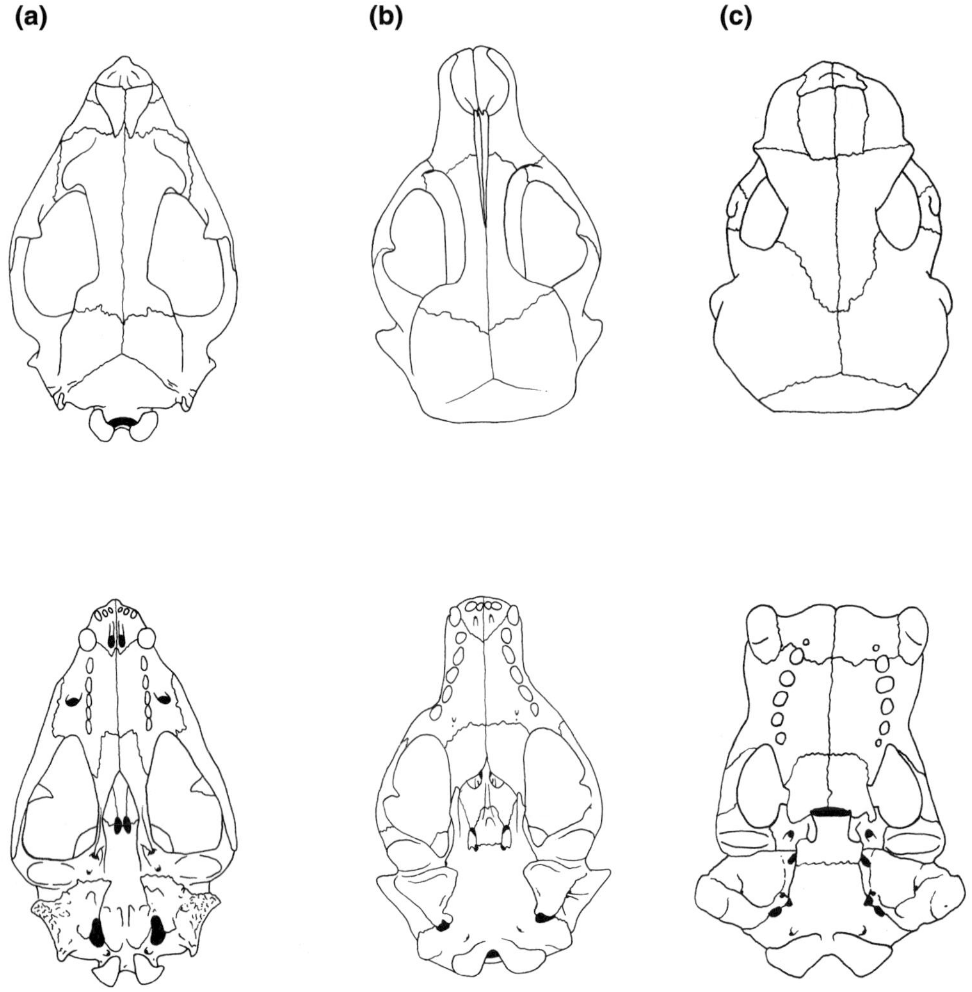

Figure 8.1. Dorsal and ventral views of skulls of representative pinnipeds. (a) otariid, *Callorhinus ursinus,* (b) phocid, *Phoca hispida* (modified from Howell, 1929), and (c) walrus, *Odobenus rosmarus.* Illustrated by P. Adam.

frontals is unique among otariids; the frontals extend anteriorly between the nasals forming a W-shape naso-frontal contact (Figs. 3.11 and 8.1).

The modern walrus skull is distinctive; the large maxilla accommodates the upper canine tusks. The entire skull is heavily ossified and shortened anteriorly (Fig. 8.1). The modern walrus lacks development of supraorbital processes. Prominent antorbital processes formed of the maxilla and frontal bones and enlarged infraorbital foramina are diagnostic features of the walrus. One of the principal eye muscles, the mm. orbicularis oculi, which closes the upper and lower eyelids, is attached to the antorbital process. The short supercilaris muscle, which functions to lift the upper eyelid, also is attached to this process. The modern walrus is characterized by a highly vaulted palate. This vaulting occurs in both the transverse and longitudinal planes, with the degree of vaulting greatest between the anterior teeth (incisors) and the end of the postcanine toothrow (Deméré, 1994). The external nares are elevated above the toothrow.

The phocid skull is characterized by the lack of supraorbital processes, an inflated tympanic bulla, and nasals that narrow greatly posteriorly and terminate far posterior of the frontal-maxillary contact in a V-shaped suture with the frontals (Figs. 3.11 and 8.1).

In otariids, the angular (pterygoid) process is well developed and positioned near the base of the ascending ramus of the mandible. This process is the point of attachment of the pterygoideus medialis muscle which elevates the mandible. In walruses and phocids this process is reduced and elevated above the base of the ascending ramus (Fig. 8.2). The phocid lower jaw is characterized by a thinning and ventral extension of the posterior end to form a thin bony flange (Fig. 8.2). The modern walrus is characterized by a solid joint between the anterior ends of the lower jaws, referred to as a fused mandibular symphysis.

8.2.2. Hyoid Apparatus

In pinnipeds, the hyoid bone, which serves for the attachment of tongue muscles, is composed of the same elements seen in other carnivores: the basihyal, thryohyal, epihyal, and ceratohyal. In two phocids, the Ross seal and the leopard seal, only the ceratohyal and epihyal are present. In addition, these taxa have proximal unossified ends of the epihyal which lie freely inside a fibrous tube (King, 1969).

The prehyoid (mylohyoid and stylohyoid) and pharyngeal and tongue musculature are well developed in the Ross seal (King, 1969; Bryden and Felts, 1974). This musculature may be involved in feeding by allowing grasping and swallowing of large cephalopods. This musculature, and particularly the pharyngeal musculature, also may be involved in sound production by the Ross seal because the throat is expanded considerably before sounds are produced. The muscles of the walrus tongue are involved in suction feeding and are discussed further in Chapter 11.

8.2.3. Vertebral Column and Axial Musculature

The typical pinniped vertebral formula is C7, T15, L5, S3, C10-12. The cervical (neck) vertebrae of otariids are large, with well-developed transverse processes and neural spines associated with muscles for movement of the neck and head (Fig. 8.3). Extensive movements of the head and neck in otariids occur during terrestrial locomotion and help maintain balance

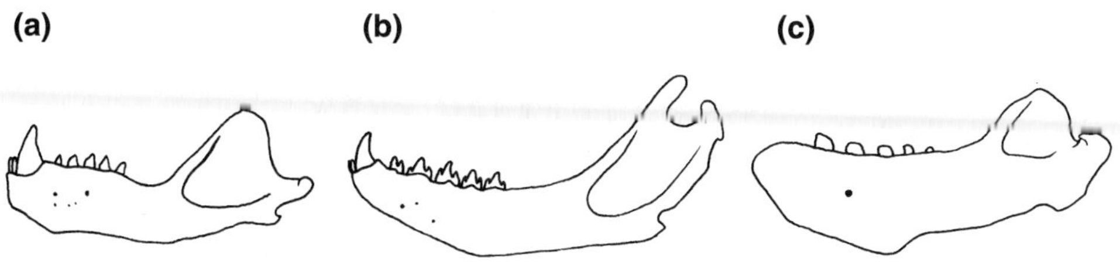

Figure 8.2. Lateral views of lower jaw of representative pinnipeds. (a) otariid, *Callorhinus ursinus,* (b) phocid, *Phoca hispida* (modified from Howell, 1929), and (c) walrus, *Odobenus rosmarus.* Illustrated by P. Adam.

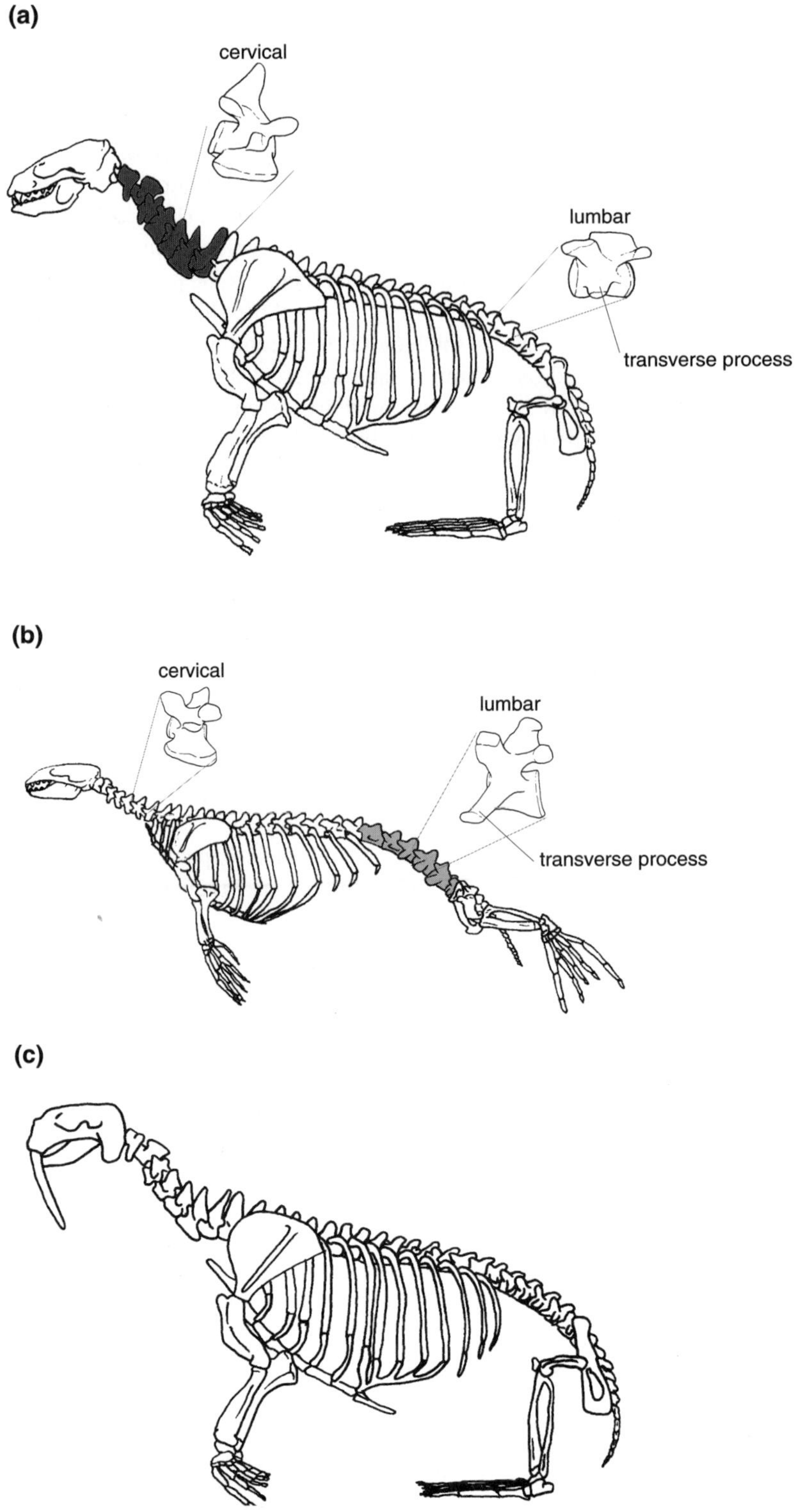

Figure 8.3. Lateral view of generalized skeleton of representative pinnipeds. (a) otariid (modified from Macdonald, 1984), (b) phocid (modified from Macdonald, 1984), and (c) walrus. Illustrated by P. Adam.

by lifting the forelimbs from the ground (English, 1976). The walrus and phocids have cervical vertebrae that are smaller than the thoracic and lumbar vertebrae with small transverse processes and neural spines (Fay, 1981). In contrast to the low neural spines of phocids and the walrus, the thoracic vertebrae of otariids possess large neural spines. Increased height of neural spines provides larger attachment points for epaxial (dorsal to the spine) musculature (mm. multifidus lumborum and longissimus thoracics).

The lumbar vertebrae of otariids have small transverse processes and closely set zygopophyses (one of the processes by which a vertebra articulates with another), whereas those of phocids have larger transverse processes and more loosely fitting zygopophyses (King, 1983). In the walrus and in phocids the transverse processes are two or three times as long as they are wide (Fay, 1981) whereas in otariids these processes are about as long as they are wide. In all pinnipeds except the walrus, the number of lumbar vertebrae is five. Walruses typically have six lumbar vertebrae (Fay, 1981). In phocids, the elongated transverse processes provide larger attachment points for the hypaxial (ventral to the spine) musculature (mm. quadratus lumborum, longissimus thoracics, and iliocaudalis), which is correlated with horizontal movements in the posterior end of the body (Fig. 8.3). Because the tail is not used in swimming, the caudal vertebrae are small, cylindrical, and without strong processes.

8.2.4. Sternum and Ribs

Pinnipeds are characterized by elongated manubria (one of the bones that makes up the sternum). In otariids, the length of the manubrium is increased by a bony anterior extension at the point of attachment of the first pair of ribs. In phocids and the walrus, the length of the manubrium is increased by cartilage (King, 1983). Ribs have a well-developed capitulum and head, and are firmly articulated to the thoracic vertebrae. There are typically eight true ribs, four false ribs, and three floating ribs.

8.2.5. Flippers and Locomotion

8.2.5.1. Pectoral Girdle and Forelimb

Front and hind limb bones are relatively short and lie within the body outline. The axilla (arm pit) in otariids and the walrus falls at about the middle of the forearm, and in phocids at the wrist. The hind flipper is free distal to the ankle.

The otariid scapula is unique among pinnipeds in possessing at least one ridge (called accessory spines) subdividing the supraspinous fossa (King, 1983; Figs. 3.11 and 8.4). A large supraspinous fossa is a consistent feature of otariids and the walrus. Enlargement of the supraspinous fossa and the development of a scapular ridge in otariids are correlated with strong development of the supraspinatus muscle which possesses pinnated heads divided by an aponeurosis (fibrous or membranous sheets). In relation to the size of the infraspinous fossa, the supraspinous fossa tends to be substantially reduced in phocids, particularly among phocines (Fig. 8.4; Wyss, 1988).

The humerus is short and robust. In pinnipeds the greater and lesser tuberosities are prominent relative to those in terrestrial carnivores. In otariids the greater tuberosity is elevated above the head; in phocids it is the lesser tuberosity that is elevated above the head. These enlarged humeral tuberosities serve not only as expanded areas of insertion for the

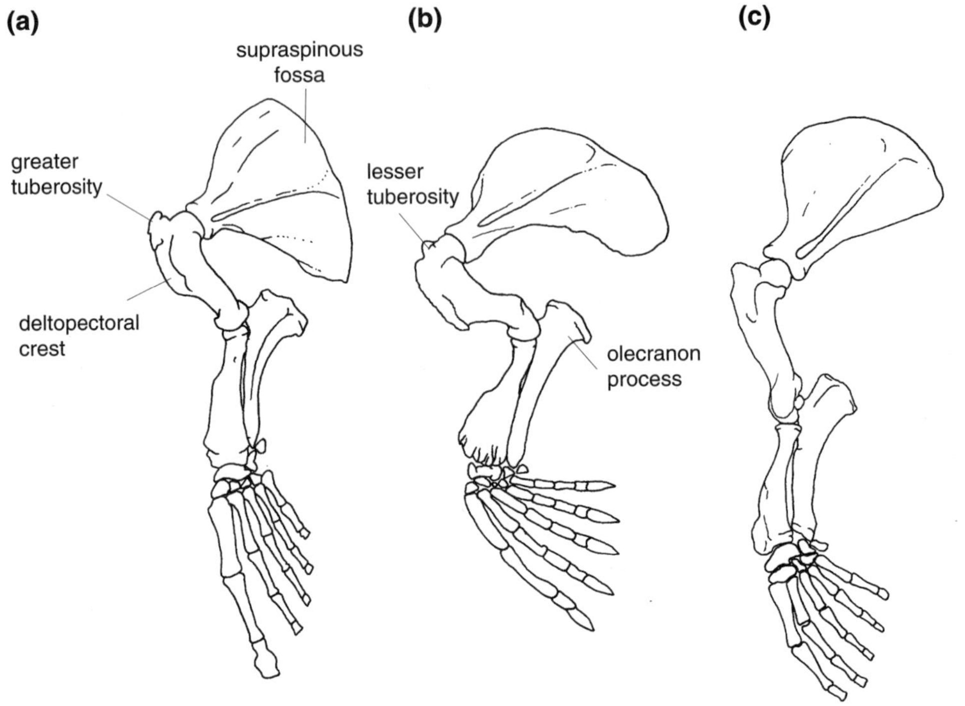

Figure 8.4. Forelimb of representative pinnipeds in anatomical position. (a) otariid, *Zalophus californianus* (modified from Howell, 1930), (b) phocid, *Phoca hispida* (modified from Howell, 1930a), and (c) walrus, *Odobenus rosmarus*. Illustrated by P. Adam.

large rotator cuff musculature (mm. deltoideus, infraspinatus, subscapularis, supraspinatus), but by lying above the proximal joint surface of the head, the moment arm of these muscles as protactors and humeral rotators is greater than in animals without enlarged humeral tuberosities (English, 1974). In "monachines," otariids, and odobenids the deltopectoral crest is elongated, extending two-thirds to three-quarters the length of the shaft where it ends abruptly, forming an acute angle with the shaft in lateral view. In phocines, the crest is shorter and terminates more abruptly (Wyss, 1988). The extraordinary development of the deltopectoral crest is associated with enlargement of the sites of attachment of the deltoid and pectoralis muscles and the pectoral portion of the latissimus dorsi muscle (English, 1977). A supracondylar (=entepicondylar) foramen is usually found in phocines but not in "monachines" (some fossil "monachines" are exceptions; Wyss, 1988).

There are several unique structural features of the elbow joint of otariid pinnipeds. One is the position of the annular ligament, which in terrestrial carnivores forms a ring around the neck of the radius, attaching to the sides of the articular surface of the ulna, and the semilunar notch, to help secure the proximal radioulnar articular surfaces. In fur seals and seal lions, the annular ligament is not continuous but terminates on the articular capsule and lateral epicondyle. This arrangement of the annular ligament inhibits or stops rotary forearm movements in otariids. A second major structural feature of the elbow joint of otariids is the shape of the articular surface of the ulna. In fur seals and sea lions, the lateral half of the semilunar notch is poorly developed, unlike the condition in terrestrial carnivores. A prominent coronoid process forms the medial border of an expanded trough for articulation with the radius (English, 1977, Fig. 15). This modification of joint structure may be advantageous in loading of the joint that occurs during locomotion.

The radius and ulna are short and flattened anteroposteriorly. The olecranon process of the ulna is laterally flattened and very enlarged in all pinnipeds (Fig. 8.4). The olecranon process of the ulna of otariids forms the sole source of origin of the mm. flexor and extensor carpi ulnaris, both of which display some humeral origin in terrestrial carnivores (English, 1977). The large flattened olecranon allows insertion on the ulna by muscles of the triceps complex, which extend the elbow.

Pinnipeds (except phocines) are characterized by having the first metacarpal in the hand greatly elongated and thicker in comparison to metacarpal II (King, 1966; Wyss, 1988). Strong reduction of the fifth intermediate phalanx of the hand occurs in all pinnipeds. Pinnipeds possess cartilaginous rods distal to each digit which support an extension of the flipper border. Long cartilaginous extensions occur on both the fore and hindflipper of otariids, short extensions occur in walruses, and shorter extensions occur in at least some phocids (see Fig. 7.14; King, 1969, 1983).

8.2.5.2. Pelvic Girdle and Hind Limb

The hip (or innominate bone) of pinnipeds has a short ilium and elongated ischium and pelvis. The connection of the hip bones anteriorly, at the pubic symphysis, is unfused but has a ligament binding adjoining bones. This differs from the condition in terrestrial carnivores in which the symphysis is bony and fused. Phocines, except the bearded seal, are characterized by lateral eversion of the ilium accompanied by a deep lateral excavation of the iliac wing (King, 1983). The great eversion of the phocid ilium means that the medial surface of the bone now faces almost anteriorly. This presumably gives a much greater attachment area to the strong iliocostalis lumborum muscle which is, to a large extent, responsible for much of the lateral body movements used in swimming (King, 1983). This flaring also results in an increased area of origin of the mm. gluteus medius, minimis, and pyriformis. These muscles attach to the greater trochanter of the femur and upon contraction cause the femur to be adducted and rotate. As noted by King (1983), a strongly developed dorsally directed ischiatic spine is present only in phocids, where the deep head of m. biceps femoris and the muscles attached to it helps in elevating the hind flippers to produce the characteristic phocid posture (Fig. 8.5).

The femur is short, broad, and flattened anteroposteriorly (Figs. 3.5 and 8.6). The position of the fovea capitis is barely visible on the head, and the round ligament between the head of the femur and the acetabulum does not occur in pinnipeds. This ligament fixes the femoral head within the acetabulum to provide a more secure joint when the weight of the animal is borne on the hind limb. As pinnipeds spend more time in water, the need of the round ligament has been lost (Tarasoff, 1972). The lesser trochanter (one of several bony processes at the proximal end of the femur) is present only as a small knob distal to the head in otariids and is reduced or absent in phocids. In the walrus, the lesser trochanter is marked by a slightly raised area (Fig. 3.5). In phocid seals (that do not bring their hind limbs forward), decrease in size or loss of the lesser trochanter represent a decrease in the area of insertion of muscles that rotate the femur posteriorly (mm. iliacus and psoas major). In phocid seals insertion is onto the iliac wing (m. psoas major) or distal to medial femur (m. iliacus). The new points of attachment for these muscles aid in increasing the strength of lateral undulation of the lumbosacral region of the spine and flexion of the leg.

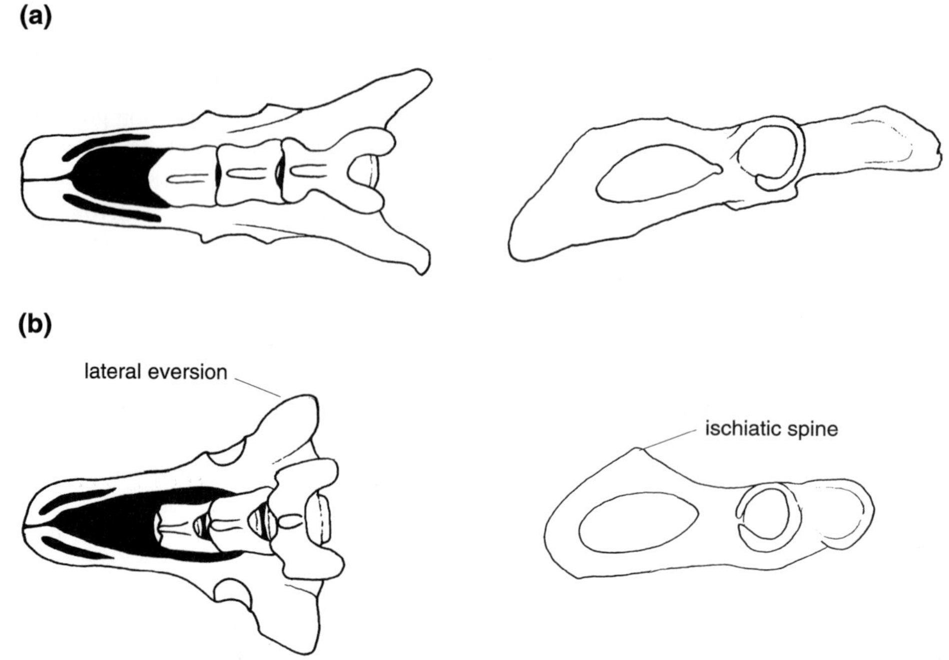

Figure 8.5. Pelvis of representative pinnipeds in dorsal and lateral views. (a) otariid, *Callorhinus ursinus,* (b) phocid, *Monachus schauinslandi*. Illustrated by P. Adam.

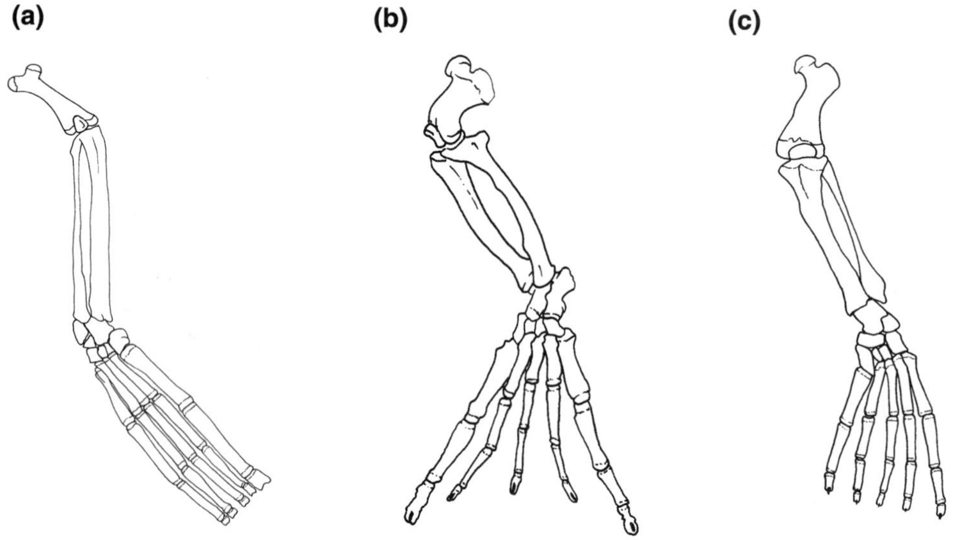

Figure 8.6. Hind limb of representative pinnipeds. (a) otariid, *Callorhinus ursinus,* (b) phocid, *Monachus tropicalis,* and (c) walrus, *Odobenus rosmarus.* Illustrated by P. Adam.

Correlated with morphology of the foreflipper is that of the foot. Pinnipeds (except phocines) are characterized by relatively long, flattened metatarsal shafts with flattened heads associated with smooth, hinge-like articulations (Wyss, 1988). They also are characterized by having elongated digits I and V (metatarsal I and proximal phalanx) in the foot (Fig. 8.6). In "monachines" and the hooded seal, the third metatarsal is considerably shorter than the others. The phocid ankle bone (astragalus) is characterized by a strong caudally directed process (calcaneal process) over which passes the tendon of the flexor hallucis longus (see Fig. 3.17). Tension on this tendon prevents the foot from being dorsiflexed in phocids such that the foot lies at right angles to the leg, as in an otariid. In walruses there is a slight posterior extension of this process; in otariids there is not. There are also differences between the heel bone (calcaneum) of phocids and otariids. Among the more obvious of these are the presence of a groove for the Achilles tendon on the tuberosity and the presence of a medially-directed process (the sustentaculum) in the otariid heel bone. Both of these characters are lacking in phocids (King, 1983).

8.2.5.3. Locomotion

The energetic cost of locomotion by mammals is expensive and therefore represents a major expenditure of their available resources. The cost of swimming is affected by water flow patterns around the swimmer as dictated by physical properties of the aquatic medium. Most important are density and viscosity. Water is over 800 times denser than air and at least 30 times more viscous. Thus the resistance to moving through water is considerably greater than in air. As a consequence, movement through water imposes severe limitations on speed and energetic performance for swimming mammals. There are, however, advantages to moving in water. Propulsive forces are easier to generate in water than in air. Because the density of mammalian bodies is similar to that of water, a swimmer is neutrally buoyant. Consequently, swimming mammals can maintain their vertical position in the water with little energy expenditure as they do not need to create lift during locomotion (as do terrestrial mammals and flyers; Rayner, 1986; Withers, 1992; Fish, 1993).

Among modern pinnipeds, terrestrial and aquatic locomotion are achieved differently. Three distinct patterns of swimming are recognized. One of these patterns, pectoral oscillation (forelimb swimming), is seen in otariids. This is where sea lions and fur seals use the forelimbs in a "flapping" manner to produce thrust in a manner similar to flapping birds in flight. Observations indicate that the hind limbs are essential in providing maneuverability and directional control but play little role in propulsion (Godfrey, 1985). The pectoral flippers move in unison, acting as oscillatory hydrofoils in a stroke that includes power, paddle, and recovery phases (Fig. 8.7; Feldcamp, 1987; English, 1976). The power stroke is generated by medial rotation and adduction and retraction of the forelimbs, in contrast to nearly pure limb retraction seen in walking terrestrial carnivores. The otariid terrestrial posture allows weight to be borne on all four limbs, with the hind flippers facing forward. On land, locomotion is limb based, although extensive movements of the head and neck rather than hind limb movements provide propulsion (Fig. 8.8). Beentjes (1990) documented walk and gallop gaits in the New Zealand sea lion and the New Zealand fur seal. He observed that these gaits are associated with ecological variables. Gaits in which the limbs are moved in sequence alternately and independently, as seen in the sea lion, are typical of otariids that live on relatively sandy substrates. The New Zealand fur seals, as well as other fur seals, move with a bounding gait that displaces their center of gravity vertically.

Figure 8.7. Oblique view of aquatic locomotion in the otariid, *Zalophus californianus*. Tracings of limb and body movements (from English, 1976).

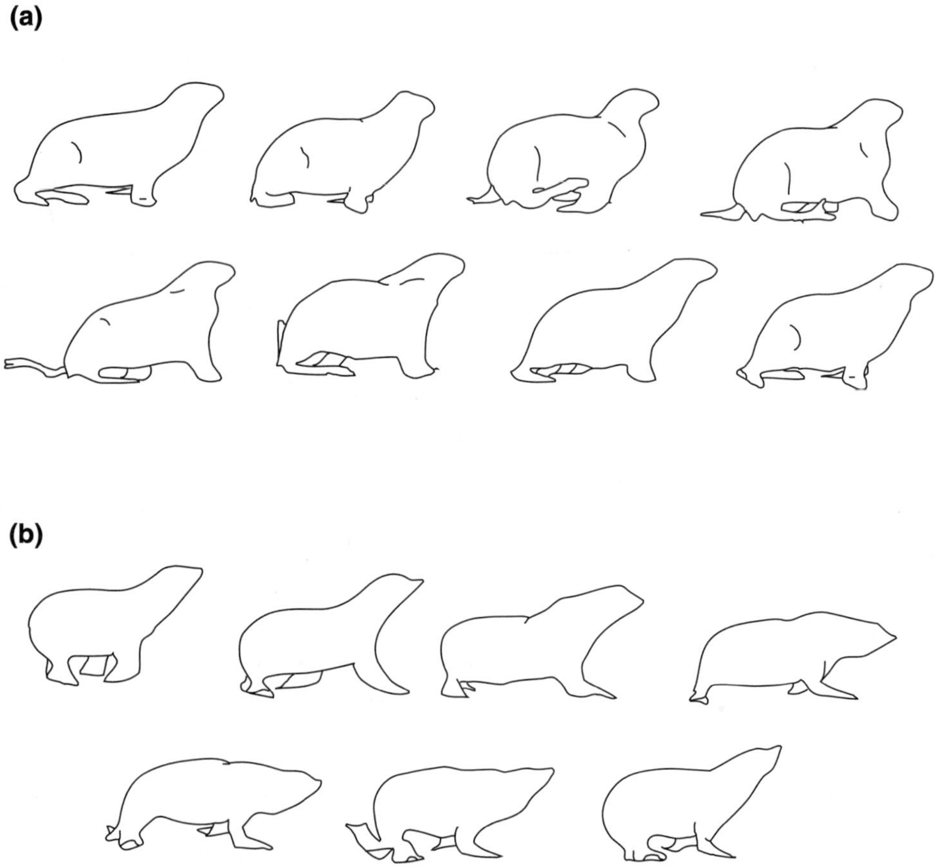

Figure 8.8. Terrestrial locomotion in otariids. Tracings of limb and body movements. (a) New Zealand sea lion, *Phocarctos hookeri,* and (b) New Zealand fur seal, *Arctocephalus forsteri* (from Beentjees, 1990).

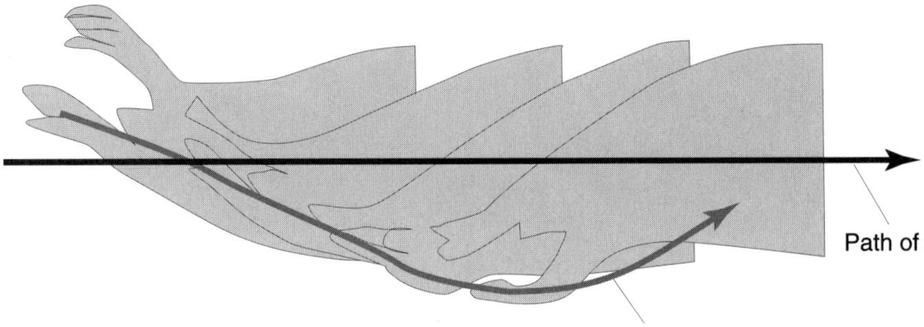

Figure 8.9. Aquatic locomotion in phocids, tracings in dorsal view of the hindflipper (adapted from Fish *et al.,* 1988).

This type of gait, in which the hind limbs are moved in unison, is more often used by otariids that live on rocky substrates.

A second method of aquatic locomotion in pinnipeds is the pelvic oscillation (hind limb swimming) of seals. Among phocids, the hind limbs are the major source of propulsion in the water and the forelimbs function principally for steering (Fig. 8.9). During swimming, seals also laterally undulate the lumbosacral region of their bodies. This enhances propulsive forces produced by the hind limbs, as well as produces other forces that give the animal a forward movement. Phocids are incapable of turning the hind limbs forward, and consequently the hind limbs are not used in terrestrial locomotion. Movement on land by phocids is accomplished generally by vertical undulations of the trunk. Arching of the lumbar region allows the pelvis to be brought forward while the weight of the body is carried by the sternum. This action is followed by extension of the anterior end of the body while the weight is carried by the pelvis (Fig. 8.10). The foreflippers may facilitate this movement by lifting and/or thrusting the anterior body off of the substrate; hind limbs are typically held up and do not contribute to this shuffling movement. The exceptional role of forelimbs in undulatory terrestrial locomotion of the gray seal was noted by Backhouse (1961). A second, apparently more rapid, mode of terrestrial locomotion has been noted in a few species. Crabeaters, ribbons, harps, and leopard seals have been observed moving in a sinuous fashion with lateral undulations of the body, particularly when on an icy substrate (O'Gorman, 1963; Burns, 1981; Kooyman, 1981). This pattern involves backward strokes by the foreflippers and lateral movement by the posterior torso with the hind flippers lifted well above the substrate. The unusually rapid aquatic and terrestrial locomotion of the leopard seal has been noted (O'Gorman, 1963).

A variant of pelvic oscillation, similar to that described for seals, is exhibited by the walrus (Fig. 8.11). The hind limbs of the walrus generate the dominant propulsive force; forelimbs are used either as rudders or as paddles at slower speeds. The forelimb stroke cycle is bilateral and contains both power and recovery strokes. The power stroke consists of adduction and retraction of the medially rotated limbs. The recovery stroke is accomplished by lateral rotation followed by abduction and protraction of the forelimb. The hind limb stroke is unilateral and consists also of a power and recovery stroke. The power stroke is a rearward translation of the flipper followed by a medial flexion of the flipper and lower leg. The recovery stroke returns the flipper to its protracted position but represents the power stroke of the opposing leg. In walruses, as in otariids, the hind limbs can be rotated forward

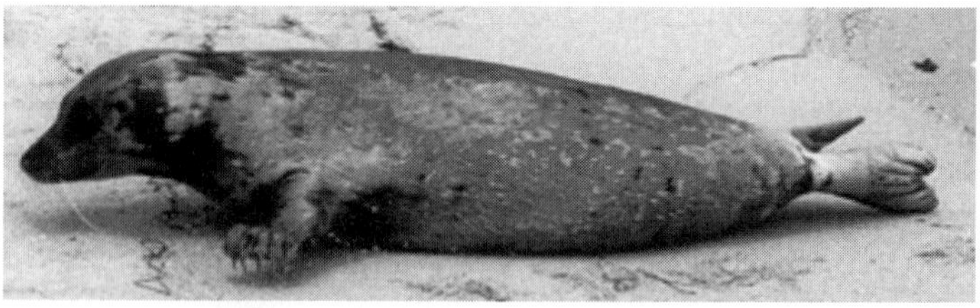

Figure 8.10. Terrestrial locomotion in the harbor seal, *Phoca vitulina* (courtesy of T. Berta).

in terrestrial locomotion. Terrestrial locomotion is unusual in that the body of the animal is supported in large part by the belly, not by the limbs (Fig. 8.12). The movement of the feet is a lateral sequence walk that alternates with a lunge that is responsible for forward progression. In the lunge, the chest is raised off the ground by the forelimbs while the lumbar and posterior thoracic regions of the torso are flexed. The hind limbs and torso then extend, pushing the body forward. Young (small) walruses are able to execute a walk similar to that of sea lions without the lunge (Gordon, 1981). Fay (1981) reported observing terrestrial locomotion of a walrus on ice using only the forelimbs, with the hindquarters and limbs being dragged passively.

Swimming speeds for a variety of pinnipeds have been determined in both controlled laboratory and unrestrained natural situations. California sea lions swimming in tanks exhibited velocities ranging from 2.7 to 3.5 m/s (Feldkamp, 1987; Godfrey, 1985), and Ponganis *et al.* (1990) reported swimming velocities between 0.6 and 1.9 m/s for surface swimming and between 0.9 and 1.9 m/s for diving in four species of otariids. Le Boeuf *et al.* (1992) obtained similar velocities (0.9–1.7 m/s) for an unrestrained adult female elephant seal foraging at sea.

8.2.5.3.1. Case Study: Integration of Phylogeny and Functional Morphology

The evolution of pinniped locomotor patterns was investigated by mapping skeletal characters associated with a particular locomotor mode (forelimb or hind limb) propulsion onto a phylogeny for pinnipeds (Fig. 8.13). The distribution of skeletal characters suggests the following transformations. Forelimb swimming appears to be primitive for the group, but was lost to hind limb swimming once within the Phocoidea (*Desmatophoca* and all later diverging phocids) and once within the Odobenidae (*Imagotaria* and all later diverging walruses). The basal phocoid *Allodesmus* retains several features consistent with forelimb propulsion, but also displays adaptations for hind limb swimming. Forelimb swimming was independently regained in the fossil walrus *Gomphotaria.* Although this case study focused on aquatic locomotion, researchers are incorporating terrestrial locomotion into a more general framework of locomotor evolution (Adam and Berta, 1997; Adam and Berta, 1998).

8.3. Cetaceans

The following discussion is based on the broad comparative treatments of cetacean anatomy found in Slijper (1936) and Yablokov *et al.* (1972).

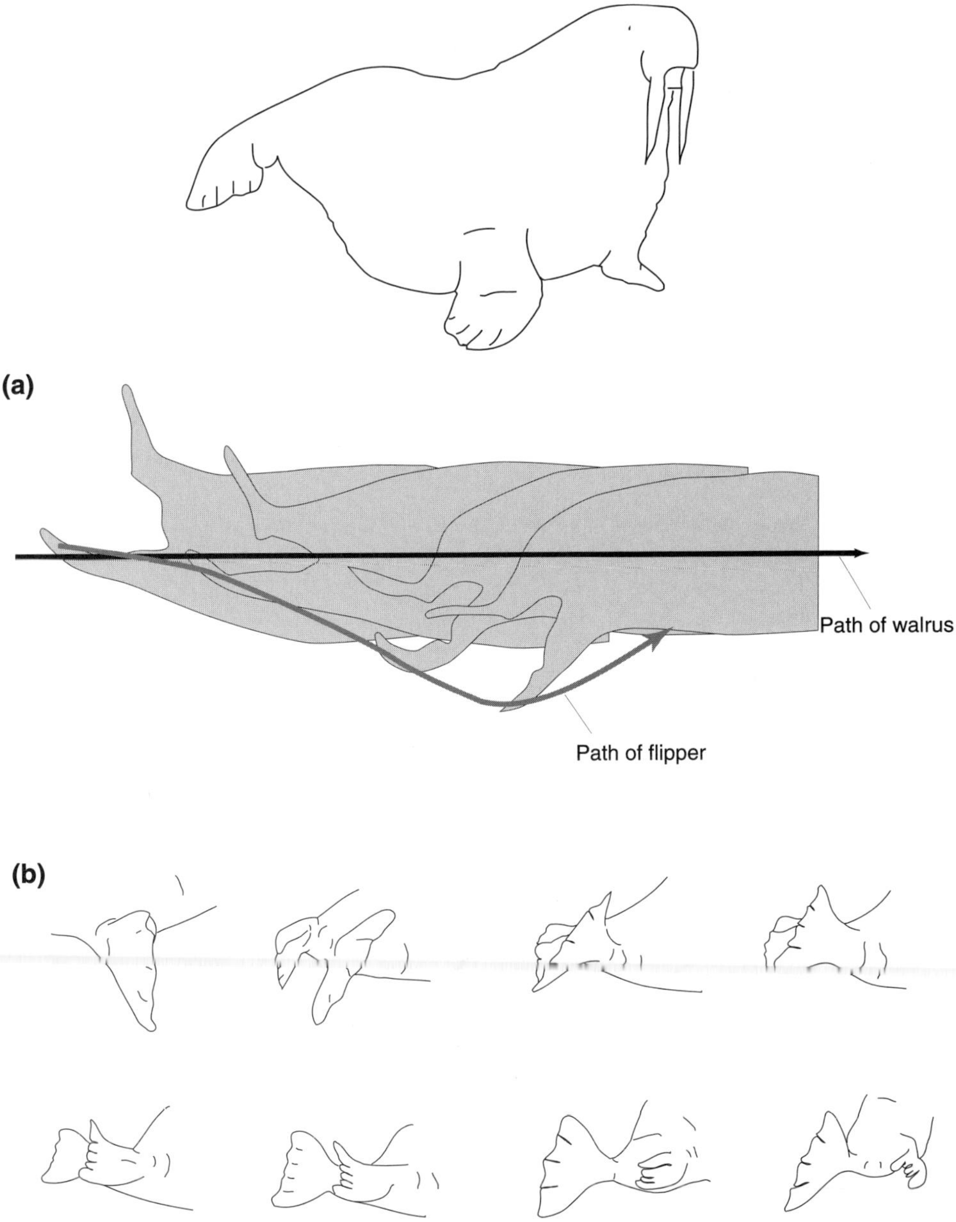

Figure 8.11. Aquatic locomotion in the walrus, *Odobenus rosmarus*. Tracings in dorsal view of the hind-flipper, (a) power stroke and (b) recovery stroke (modified from Gordon, 1981).

8.3.1. Skull

In comparison to the typical mammalian skull, the cetacean skull is telescoped (as described in Chapter 4); the braincase, or the portion of the skull behind the rostrum, has been shortened (Fig. 4.11). This telescoping has altered the size, shape, and relationship of many

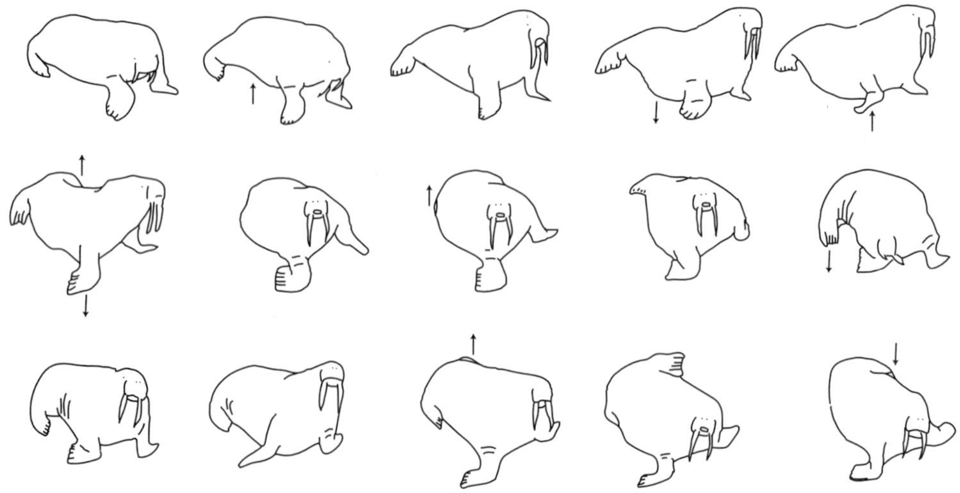

Figure 8.12. Terrestrial locomotion in the walrus, *Odobenus rosmarus*. Tracings of limb and body movements (modified from Gordon, 1981).

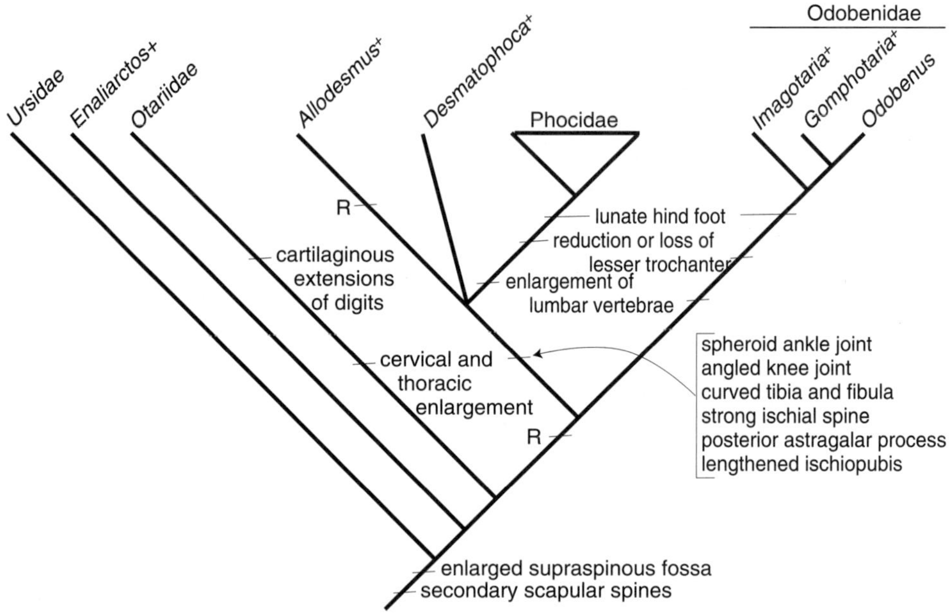

Figure 8.13. Evolution of aquatic locomotion in pinnipeds (phylogeny from Berta and Wyss, 1994; not all taxa are shown). R = reversals, *Allodesmus* reversals: curved fibia and fibula, posterior astragalar process, Phocomorpha (Phocidae + *Allodesmus* + *Desmatophoca* + Odobenidae reversals: enlarged supraspinous fossa and secondary scapular spines.

of the skull bones. For example, the external narial opening (blowhole(s)) has migrated posteriorly to a more dorsal position on the head, and the nasals have become small, tabular bones situated immediately behind it. Telescoping of the cranial bones in the mysticete skull involves the maxilla extending posteriorly underneath the frontal. In odontocetes, the premaxilla and maxilla extend posteriorly and laterally so as to override the frontals and crowd the parietals laterally.

Typically, the odontocete skull displays cranial and facial asymmetry in which those bones and soft anatomical structures on the right side are larger than those on the left side (Fig. 8.14; see also Chapter 4). It has been suggested that asymmetry is involved in sound production, perhaps with the right side being more specialized for producing sound and the left side primarily adapted for respiration (Norris, 1964; Wood, 1964; Mead, 1975).

The skulls of several odontocetes are variously ornamented. A cranial feature unique to phocoenids is the presence of small rounded protuberances on the premaxillae (Heyning, 1989; see Fig. 4.33). The facial region of the beluga is unique among odontocetes because the entire surface is slightly convex rather than concave. The spiracular plates of the premaxilla also differs from those in delphinids and ziphiids in that it is slightly rugose (Heyning, 1989). The susu has unique maxillary crests that overhang the facial region anteriorly (Heyning, 1989). The ventral surface of these crests is covered by a thin, flat, complicated

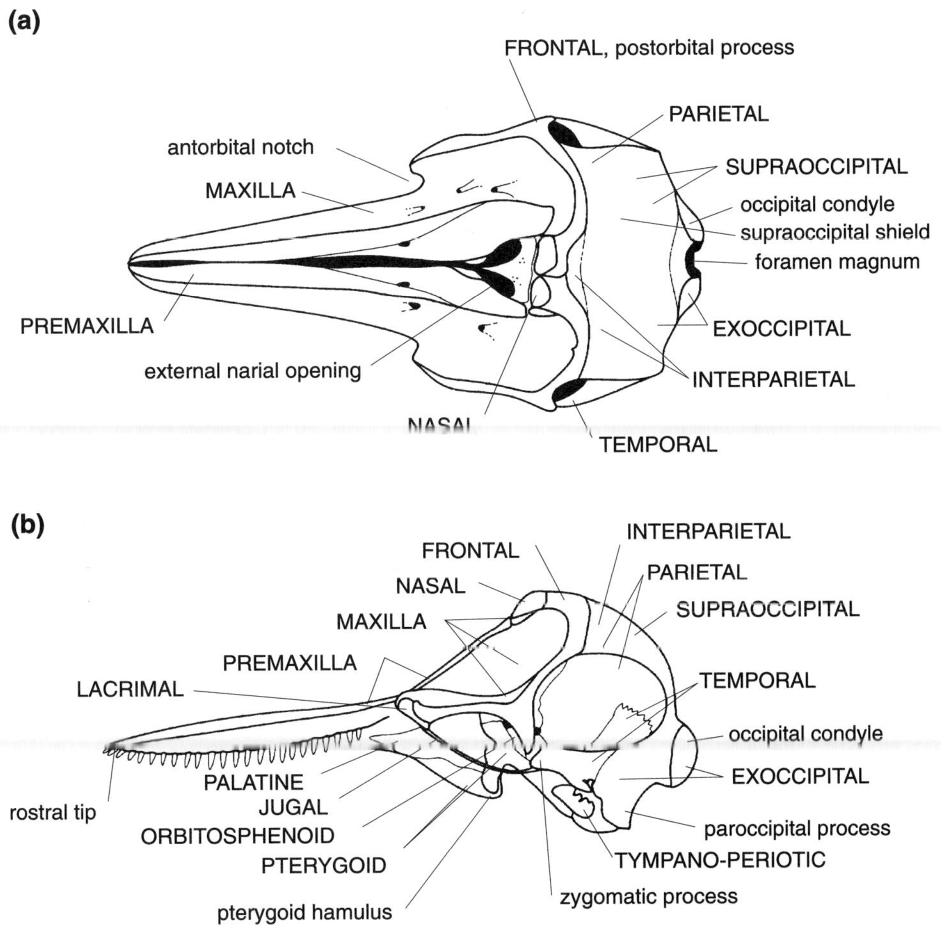

Figure 8.14. The skull of a representative odontocete, *Tursiops truncatus.* (a) Dorsal, and (b) Lateral views (modified from Rommel, 1990).

air sac derived from the pterygoid air sinus system (Fraser and Purves, 1960; Purves and Pilleri, 1973; see Fig. 4.26).

The rostra of many toothed whales differ from those of baleen whales in being made of dense bone. This is especially true of beaked whales, particularly Blainville's beaked whale (de Buffrénil and Casinos, 1995; Zioupos *et al.,* 1997). Several hypotheses have been proposed to explain the functional significance of a dense rostrum. Heyning (1984) suggested that the compaction of the rostrum in various beaked whales increases the strength of the rostrum and reduces the risk of fracture during intraspecific fights between adult males. De Buffrénil and Casinos (1995) and Zioupos *et al.* (1997) presented data demonstrating that the rostrum, in addition to being highly mineralized, was a stiff, brittle, and fragile structure. They suggested that similarity in composition and mechanical properties between the rostrum and the tympanic bulla indicated an acoustics-related function for the rostrum.

In the mysticete skull, the entire facial region is expanded and the rostrum is arched to accommodate the baleen plates that hang from the upper jaw (Fig. 8.15). The rostral arch varies; it is slightly arched in balaenopterids (less than 5% between the basicranium and the base of the rostrum), moderately arched in *Eschrichtius* and *Caperea* (10 and 17%, respectively), and greatly arched (over 20%) in the balaenids (Barnes and McLeod, 1984). The high rostral arch of balaenids accommodates the long baleen plates. In mysticetes, unlike odontocetes, there is strong development of several facial and skull bones (i.e. vomer, temporal, and palatine bones).

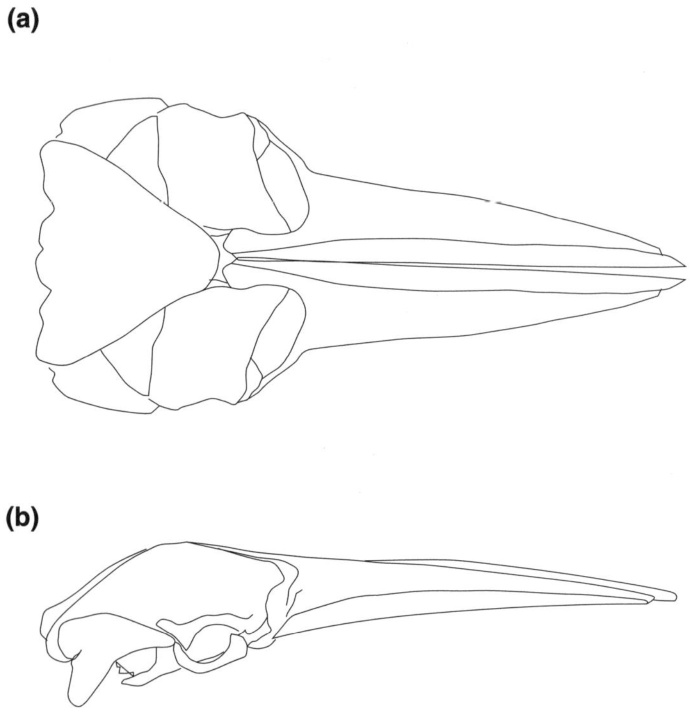

Figure 8.15. The skull of a representative mysticete, Sei whale, *Balaenoptera borealis.* (a) Dorsal and (b) Lateral views (after Kellogg, 1928).

All mysticetes have two nasal passages, or blowholes. In odontocetes (with the exception of physeterids), the single nasal passage (vestibule) extends vertically to the bony nares. A series of blind-ended sacs branch off the nasal passage. The nasal air spaces are variable, both within a single species and between species. Detailed descriptions of these nasal sacs are provided by Heyning (1989). The musculature associated with the nasal passages is extremely complex (see Lawrence and Schevill, 1956; Mead, 1975; Heyning, 1989). Sperm whales are unique among odontocetes in the retention of two nasal passages (Fig. 8.16). The left nasal passage extends posteroventrally in nearly a straight line to the enlarged left bony naris and lacks air sacs. The right nasal passage extends ventrally from the blowhole and expands into an air sac (vestibular air sac). On the posterior wall of this sac is a muscular ridge with a narrow slit-like orifice that opens to the right nasal passage. The gross appearance of this valve-like structure gives it the name **museau de singe**, or monkey's muzzle (Pouchet and Beauregard, 1892). Just superficial to the bony naris, there is another air sac off the right nasal passage.

The facial structure of odontocetes undoubtedly serves a number of functions. A primary function is respiration. Two main theories have been proposed regarding nonrespiratory functions of the facial region: 1) facial structures are responsible for sound production used in echolocation, and 2) this region, at least in sperm whales, plays some role in buoyancy control (see later discussion of the spermaceti organ). Most researchers favor the sound production theory discussed in greater detail in Chapter 10.

Occluding the bony nares of cetaceans are a pair of large fleshy masses of tissue, the **nasal plugs**, which consist of connective tissue, muscle, and fat. Relative to odontocetes, the nasal plugs of mysticetes contain less fatty tissue but are otherwise similar in general morphology. The nasal plugs are retracted by paired nasal plug muscles that originate from the premaxillae. Contraction of the nasal plug muscles pulls the nasal plugs anterolaterally. When the nasal plugs are retracted during inhalation and exhalation, the nasal passage remains fully open. In addition to this respiratory function, it also has been suggested that nasal plugs function in sound production (see Chapter 10).

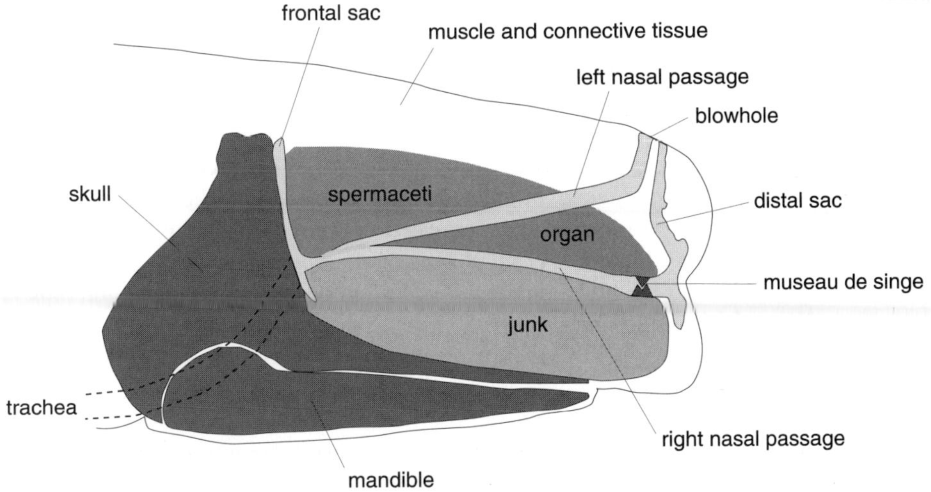

Figure 8.16. Diagram of skull of sperm whale, *Physeter macrocephalus* with nasal passages (modified from Evans, 1987).

Farther anterior on the facial region of odontocetes is a large ovoid melon. The melon typically is asymmetrically positioned, slightly off to the right side. It rests on a pad of dense connective tissue on top of the bony rostrum of the skull. The core region of fatty tissue has a higher lipid content and a different lipid composition than the surrounding outer melon and blubber (Litchfield *et al.*, 1975; Norris and Harvey, 1974) and is an important component of the echolocation system. Lipid composition of the melon also varies between major groups of odontocetes (Litchfield and Greenberg, 1974; Litchfield *et al.*, 1975).

As discussed in Chapter 4, a vestigial melon has been described in baleen whales by Heyning and Mead (1990). They suggest that the original function of the melon in cetaceans was to allow the free movement of the nasal plugs as they are drawn posteriorly over the premaxillae during contraction of the nasal plug muscles. Alternatively, Milinkovitch (1995) suggests that the presence of a melon in mysticetes indicates that the ancestor of all whales may have possessed a well-developed melon and correspondingly well-developed echolocation abilities.

In the forehead of sperm whales is a large structure, the **spermaceti organ**, that may occupy more than 30% of the whale's total length and 20% of its weight (Fig. 8.16). The fatty tissue in the facial region of physeterids is highly modified and very different in structure than the melon of all other odontocetes. Because it is situated posterodorsal to the nasal passages, the spermaceti organ is not thought to be homologous with the melon. In adults there is an elongate connective tissue sac, or case, that is filled with a viscous waxy fluid called **spermaceti**. This is the sperm whale oil that was most sought after by whalers for candlemaking and for burning in lanterns. The spermaceti organ is contained within a thick case of muscles and ligaments. Below the spermaceti organ is a region of connective tissue alternating with spaces filled with spermaceti oil. This region was called the **junk** by whalers because it has a lesser quantity of oil in it (Clarke, 1978; Fig. 8.16). The spermaceti "junk" is probably homologous with the melon of other odontocetes. It has been proposed that the function of the spermaceti organ is the control of buoyancy (Clarke, 1970, 1978, 1979). According to Clarke's hypothesis, as sperm whales dive into cooler, deeper water, the flow of water in the head passages lowers the temperature of the wax which solidifies, shrinks, and in doing so, increases the density of the head, so aiding the animal's descent. When the whale starts to ascend, the wax is warmed by increasing blood flow in the capillaries of the head; this increases buoyancy and allows the animal to rise with the minimum expenditure of effort. This hypothesis, however, has serious flaws (Ridgway, 1971; Schenkkan and Purves, 1973) and was proposed with little consideration of the detailed anatomy of the head. For example, because the head is not a closed circuit with respect to blood circulation, when sperm whales dive into cooler, deeper water the entire body temperature would be reduced, not just the head temperature. The small size and low density of blood vessels penetrating the spermaceti organ make his suggestion of "rapid warming" untenable. In addition, the small size of the spermaceti organ in the pygmy sperm whale would result in an insignificant decrease in density of the head and thus precludes its role as a hydrostatic organ.

8.3.2. Mandible

The lower jaws, or mandibles, appear straight when viewed dorsally in odontocetes. The posterior non-tooth bearing part of the jaw has thin walls that form the fat filled **pan bone** (Fig. 8.17). Norris (1964, 1968, 1969) proposed that this region is the primary site of sound reception in odontocetes (discussed in Chapter 10).

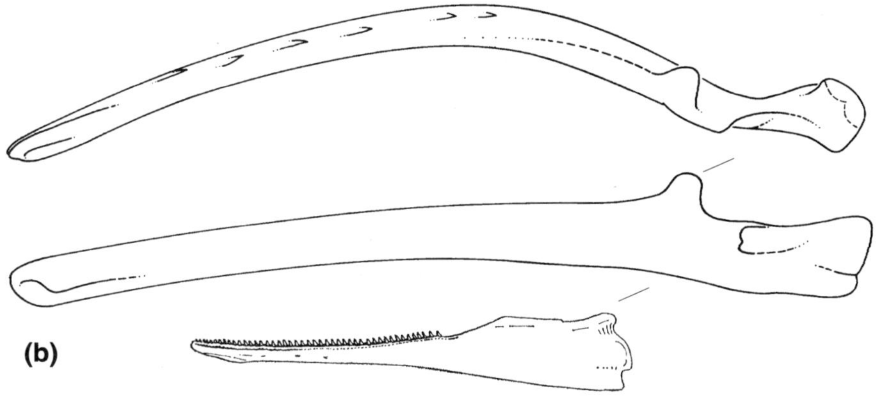

Figure 8.17. Lateral views of lower jaw of representative cetaceans. (a) Mysticete, Minke whale, *Balaenoptera acutorostrata* (from Deméré, 1986), and (b) Odontocete, spotted dolphin, *stenella* sp.

In mysticetes the mandible curves laterally and there is no pan bone. The mandibular symphysis, a fibrocartilage articulation, connects the tapered distal ends of the paired dentary bones. It is analogous in structure to the intervertebral joints; its center, filled with a gelatinous substance, is surrounded by a dense fibrocartilaginous capsule.

The coronoid process for attachment of the temporalis muscles is reduced in most odontocetes (an exception is the susu which retains a distinct process). Among mysticetes, it is of moderate size in balaenopterids and developed as a slightly upraised area in the gray whale, pygmy right whale, and the balaenids (Barnes and McLeod, 1984). The function of the coronoid process in mysticete feeding is discussed in Chapter 11.

8.3.3. Hyoid Apparatus

The hyoid bone is well developed in all cetaceans. In odontocetes the hyoid is divisible into a basal portion (basihyal, paired thyrohyals) and a suspensory portion (paired ceratohyals, epihyals, stylohyals, and tympanohyals; Reidenberg and Laitman, 1994). Muscles which retract the hyoid apparatus (e.g. sternohyoid) or control the tongue (e.g. styloglossus, hyoglossus) are enlarged and it is suggested that they may be important in suction feeding (see Chapter 11).

8.3.4. Vertebral Column and Axial Musculature

In cetaceans, the vertebral column does not contain a sacral region because the pelvic girdle is lacking. The boundaries between cervical, thoracic, and lumbar regions are established according to the presence of ribs, and the boundary between the lumbar and caudal segments is determined by the presence of **chevron bones** (Fig. 8.18). The typical cetacean vertebral formula is C7, T11-12, L usually 9-24 (range 2 to 30), C usually 15-45 (range 15 to 49) (Yablokov *et al.,* 1972).

All cetaceans have seven cervical vertebrae (Fig. 8.19). The centra of cervical vertebrae differ from those in other mammals in being extremely flat and occasionally consisting of

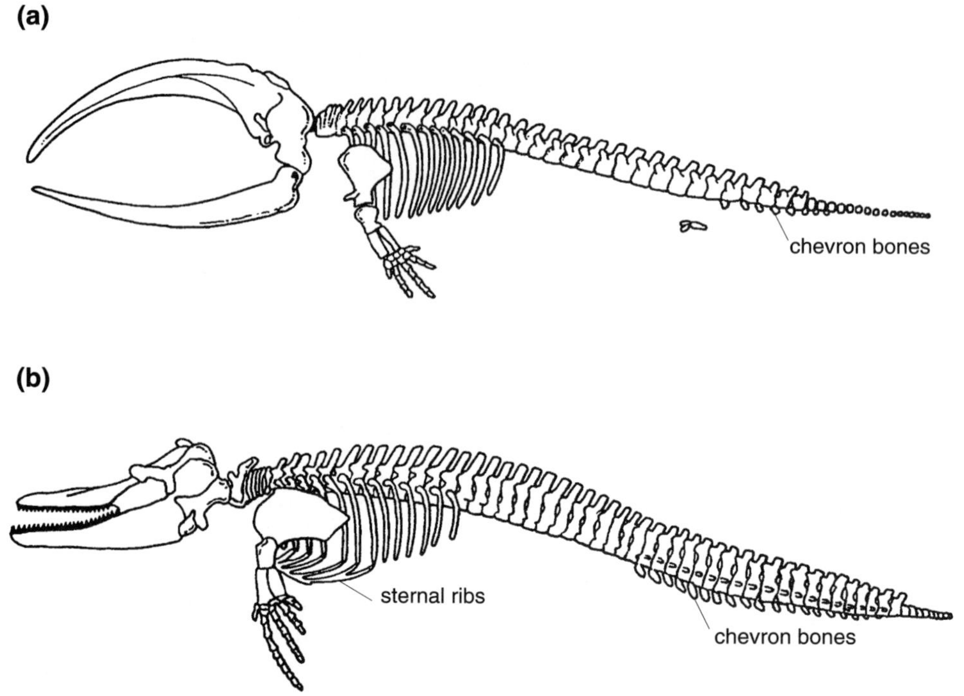

Figure 8.18. Vertebral columns of representative cetaceans, (a) mysticete, (b) odontocete. Chevron bones are indicated in both and sternal ribs in odontocetes (modified from Harrison and Bryden, 1988).

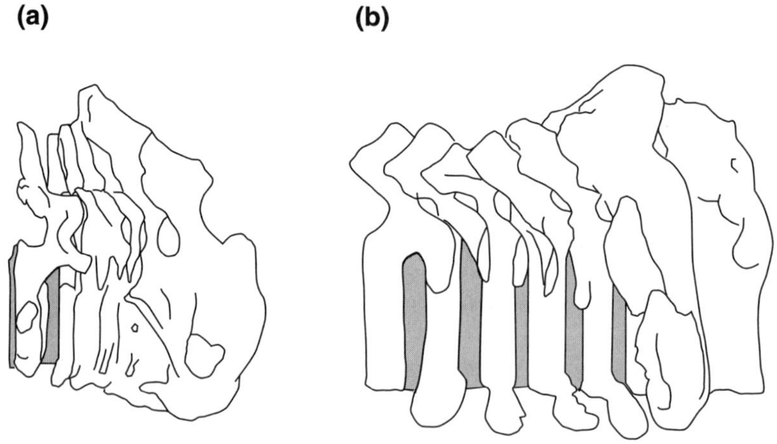

Figure 8.19. Lateral view of the cervical vertebrae of a Pilot whale, *Globicephala* sp. (a) and a Blue whale, *Balaenoptera musculus* (b). The first six vertebrae of the pilot whale are fused. The vertebrae of the blue whale are unfused and are separated by intervertebral disks (gray) (redrawn from Slijper, 1962).

only thin, osseous plates that have lost the main characteristics of vertebrae. Most cetaceans, including balaenids, neobalaenids, and odontocetes (e.g. bottlenose whale, pygmy sperm whale, bottlenose dolphin) have two or more of the cervicals fused (Rommel, 1990; Fig. 8.19a). In the sperm whale, the last six vertebrae are fused (DeSmet, 1977). The resulting short, rigid neck adds to the streamlining of the body by stabilizing the head and aids in propulsion (Slijper, 1962). The unfused condition (Fig. 8.19b) is seen in balaenopteriids, eschrictiids, platanistids, iniids, and pontoporiids (Barnes and McLeod, 1984) and in the beluga (Yablokov *et al.,* 1972). The existence of cervical ribs is not uncommon in cetaceans and in several species, such ribs are of general occurrence (for example in the sei whale). Often they are fused to the first true rib (see Slijper, 1936, pp. 280–285, for other examples).

The thoracic vertebrae are flanked by ribs. This definition presents several difficulties for cetaceans, not only because of the frequent occurrence of cervical ribs but also because the last ribs often are floating or are much smaller than the others and do not contact an articular facet on the corresponding vertebra. Typically, 11 or 12 pairs of thoracic vertebrae are present. The common feature of thoracic vertebrae is relatively poor development of the articular surfaces on the vertebral bodies; usually only thoracic vertebrae 1–4 or 5 have these articulations developed (Yablokov *et al.,* 1972). In mysticetes, the relative size of the vertebral body is considerably larger than the size in odontocetes; usually in the latter the vertebral body comprises more than 50% of vertebral height. Sternal ribs are absent in mysticetes but present in odontocetes (Fig. 8.18).

Posterior to the thoracic vertebrae, the vertebral series continues as far as the notch of the tail flukes. The first lumbar vertebra lacks a rib. The lumbar vertebrae possess the largest vertebral bodies and best-developed transverse and spinous processes. There is considerable variation in the number of lumbar vertebrae. The maximum number (29–30) is reported in Dall's porpoise; the fewest are reported from the pygmy sperm whale (2), the Platanistidae (3–5), and the Monodontidae (6; Yablokov *et al.,* 1972). There are 16–18 lumbar vertebrae in the bottlenose dolphin (Rommel, 1990).

There are no sacral vertebrae in cetaceans. Early whale evolution is characterized by reduction in the number of sacrals, loss of fusion between sacral vertebrae and the loss of articulation of sacral vertebrae with the pelvis (Buchholtz, 1998). The tail or caudal vertebrae of cetaceans are defined as the first vertebra with a chevron bone immediately posterior to its caudal epiphysis and all vertebrae posterior to this (Fig. 8.18). Chevron bones are paired ventral intervertebral ossifications found in the caudal region of many vertebrates. They articulate via paired vertebral facets of the vertebra in front of them and are held in position by ligaments. When seen from the front they have a Y or a V shape. Variation also exists in the number of caudal vertebrae, ranging from a minimum of 15–17 in the false killer whale to a maximum of 49 in the finless porpoise, the Cuvier's beaked whale, and the pygmy sperm whale (Yablokov *et al.,* 1972). There are 25–27 caudal vertebrae in the bottlenose dolphin (Rommel, 1990). The thoracic and lumbar vertebrae of cetaceans during normal swimming are restrained by a strong collagenous **subdermal connective tissue sheath** which gives rigidity to the thorax and provides an enlarged surface to anchor the flexor and extensor muscles of the tail (Pabst, 1993; Fig. 8.20).

Among the dorsal axial muscles, the position of the semispinalis muscle suggests that its action is to change the position of the skull relative to the vertebral column (providing extension and lateral flexion of the skull). The muscle also helps tense the anterior superficial and deep tendon fibers. The action of another major epaxial muscle group, the multifidus, is to stiffen its deep tendon of insertion, thereby forming a stable platform for the m. longissimus,

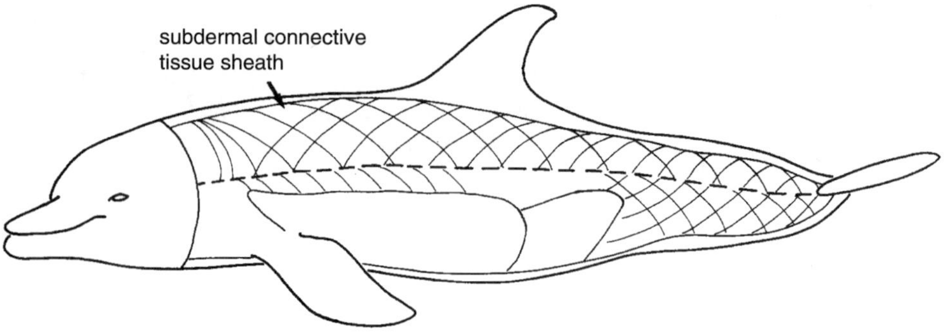

Figure 8.20. Subdermal connective tissue sheath (SDS) of the bottlenose dolphin, *Tursiops truncatus* (blubber and m. cutaneous trunci removed) (from Pabst, 1990).

another epaxial muscle. The longissimus muscle transmits the majority of its force to the caudal spine by way of a novel interaction between its insertional tendons and the subdermal connective tissue sheath (Pabst, 1993).

The vertebral column is the primary structure used by dolphins to generate the dorsoventral bending characteristic of cetacean swimming (discussed later in this chapter). In dorsoventral bending, the intervertebral joints of the saddleback dolphin are stiff near the middle of the body and become more flexible toward the head and tail (Long *et al.*, 1997). The pattern of intervertebral joint stiffness is consistent with the hypothesis that axial muscles anchored in the lumbar spine cause extension of the tail (Pabst, 1993). Results of a mechanical study of the bending dynamics of the saddleback dolphin suggest that the intervertebral joint at the base of the flukes acts as a "low resistance hinge, permitting subtle and continuous alterations of the angle of attack of the flukes" on the water (Long *et al.*, 1997, p. 75). These workers propose a novel structural mechanism that functions to stiffen the joint in both tail extension and flexion. This mechanism works by placing ligaments in tension during both of these movements. As the articular processes of a caudal vertebra shear past the neural spine of the cranial vertebrae, mediolaterally-oriented ligaments are lengthened (Fig. 8.21). Another conclusion from this study was that the dolphin vertebral column has the capacity to store elastic energy and to dampen oscillations as well as to control the pattern of body deformation observed during swimming.

8.3.5. Sternum and Ribs

The sternum of odontocetes differs from that of mysticetes in several features. In odontocetes, usually 5–7 pairs of ribs are attached to the sternum (sternal ribs) which consists of a long, flat bone, usually segmented and widened anteriorly, with recesses at the site of attachments for ribs (Fig. 8.18). In mysticetes, there is only one pair of ribs attached to the sternum and the sternum is shorter and broader than in odontocetes (Yablokov *et al.*, 1972).

Cetaceans are unique in having single-headed ribs (but see below) that attach only to the transverse processes instead of to the centra plus transverse processes, as in most mammals. There are 12–14 vertebral ribs in the bottlenose dolphin (Rommel, 1990). The anterior-most 4–5 vertebral ribs are double headed, with a proximal capitulum and distal tuberculum. In the sperm and beaked whales, true ribs, of which there are only 3–5 pairs, are cartilaginous. True ribs are lacking in mysticetes and only the first pair of ribs is attached by a lig-

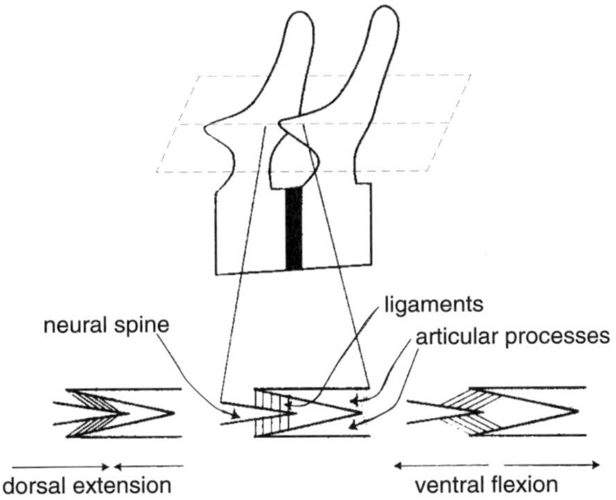

Figure 8.21. Articular process stiffening mechanism. Left lateral view of a vertebral pair; the dashed and obliquely oriented plane is the frontal section through the articular processes shown below (from Long *et al.*, 1997).

ament to the extremely small sternum. The first pair of ribs do not have a head in mysticetes (the gray whale is an exception; Yablokov *et al.*, 1972). Cetaceans have poorly-developed intercostal muscles and depend on the diaphragm for forceful inhalation.

8.3.6. Flippers and Locomotion

In cetaceans, the forelimb proportions are so altered from those of terrestrial mammals that the elbow is at approximately the body contour and the visible extremity consists almost entirely of the forearm and hand. Cetacean flippers are variable in size and shape. The flippers of sperm, killer, and beluga whales are almost round (in the beluga, the posterior edge may even be curved upward). The flippers are triangular in the La Plata, Amazonian, and Ganges river dolphins.

The humpback whale has the longest flipper of any cetacean, with its length varying from 25 to 33% of the total body length (Fish and Battle, 1995). The flipper shape is long, narrow, and thin. The humpback whale flipper also is unique because of the presence of large protuberances, or tubercles, located on the leading (anterior) edge which give the flippers a scalloped appearance (Fig. 8.22). Typically, barnacles are found on the upper leading edge of the tubercles. The flipper has a cross-sectional design typical of airplane wings, where airfoils are used for lift generation. The position and number of tubercles on the flipper suggest that they function as enhanced lift devices to control flow over the flipper and to maintain lift at high angles of attack. The morphology of the humpback whale flipper further suggests that it is adapted for high maneuverability associated with the whale's unique "bubble-cloud" feeding behavior (Fish and Battle, 1995; discussed in detail in Chapter 11).

The ratio of radius–ulna length to that of the humerus varies slightly among odontocetes; generally the forearm skeleton is longer, and in mysticetes, this is particularly true of the long and slender radius and ulna. The interphalangeal (finger) joints have nearly flat surfaces and, as in other joints distal to the shoulder, capsules and dorsal and ventral ligamentous arrangements provide almost complete immobilization between bones (Felts, 1966).

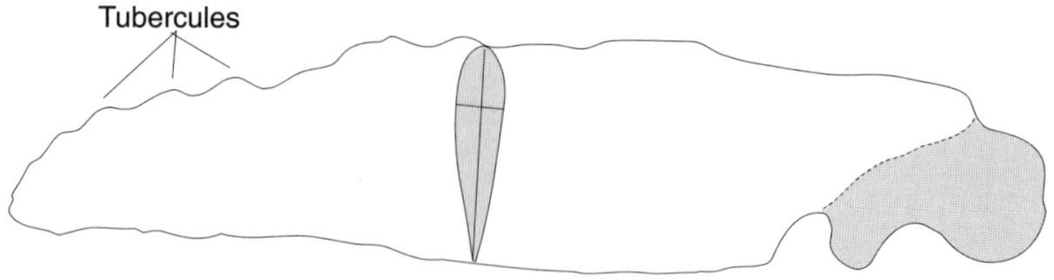

Figure 8.22. Flipper of humpback whale with tubercles marked and cross-section shown illustrating aerodynamic design (from Fish and Battle, 1995).

The reduced density of cetacean limb bones (de Buffrénil *et al.,* 1986) is accompanied by extensive development of a dense connective tissue matrix which may help to maintain flipper strength. A study of the allometric scaling relationships of the cetacean forelimb suggests that either large cetacean bones are underbuilt and less robust than expected or that limb bones of small cetaceans are more robust than expected. A possible explanation for this negative allometry is the greater relative swimming speed of small delphinids and phocoenids, as well as the greater stresses incurred by high speed swimming (Dawson, 1994).

8.3.6.1. Pectoral Girdle and Forelimb

The scapula is typically wide, flat, and fan-shaped (Fig. 8.23). In odontocetes, the coracoid and acromial processes are well developed. In some mysticetes (e.g. the humpback whale), the acromion is reduced (Howell, 1930a). The infraspinous fossa occupies practically the entire lateral aspect of the bone (although the muscle covers only 1/2 to 2/3 of the area), while the bony area of the supraspinous fossa is insignificant. The supraspinous muscle is therefore of lessened importance (Howell, 1930a). The scapula of the franciscana differs from those of described delphinoids (dolphins, porpoises, narwhal, beluga) and physeteroids (sperm and dwarf sperm whales) in the relatively large size of the supraspinous fossa (Strickler, 1978). Cetaceans lack the trapezius muscle. Among odontocetes, the serratus muscle occurs only in the franciscana, although it exists in rorquals among the mysticetes. The pectoralis abdominalis and three rhomboideus divisions are found in the franciscana and the pygmy sperm whale, but in relatively few dolphins. Strickler (1978) suggests that these characteristics are associated with a more generalized use of the forelimb in the franciscana.

The humerus, radius, and ulna are relatively short and flattened in cetaceans (Fig. 8.23). The radius and ulna exceed the humerus in length and have dorsoventrally compressed shafts. The elbow joint is immobile due to flattened articular facets. The lesser tuberosity of the humerus is medially positioned and reduced in size, indicated only by a pronounced rugosity. The lack of development of the lesser tuberosity indicates that either the subscapularis is unusually weak, which its extent belies, or else that it has a somewhat altered function (i.e. to effect rotation of the humerus when the arm is considerably flexed). The latter is regarded as more likely (Howell, 1930a). In mysticetes, the greater tuberosity is well developed and may be nearly as high as the head. Although this process appears homologous with the greater tuberosity it is hardly so, except in position, and is actually a deltoid process. In odontocetes, the proximal humerus differs. Instead of the head being located toward the rear of the shaft it is situated to the lateral side. Because of the shift of the head, the greater tuberosity is located so as to allow the subscapularis (which inserts on it) to act as an efficient adductor (Howell, 1930a). Some fossil archaeocete whales retained a moveable elbow joint, a long humerus, and a flipper that is not as streamlined as in extant cetaceans.

The cetacean hand, unique among mammals, exhibits **hyperphalangy** (they have more than the standard number of phalanges; Fig. 8.23). The development of hyperphalangy, which occurs in only one other vertebrate group, the extinct ichthyosaurs (reptiles), is described by Sedmera *et al.* (1997b). The maximum number of phalanges that may develop is found in the pilot whale (as many as 5, 15, and 11 in the first, second, and third digits, respectively). Balaenids have five digits, and all other mysticetes with the exception of the gray whale have four digits.

Watson (1994) reported a rare case of the congenital malformation **polydactyly**, or the presence of additional digits, in the bottlenose dolphin. In this case, one flipper had duplicated the fourth digit making the number of digits total six. The development of polydactylous limbs has been linked to altered activity of the homeobox genes during limb bud development caused by genetic, developmental, and environmental influences.

8.3.6.2. Pelvic Girdle and Hind Limb

Only a few altered and reduced pelvic bones remain in cetaceans. They have no direct connection to the vertebral column and are imbedded in the body musculature. In some cases the femur and/or tibia remains; in even rarer cases, elements of the foot exist (Yablokov *et al.*, 1972). Hind limb buds reported in the embryos of different cetacean species regress in early fetal life (for a review, see Sedmera *et al.*, 1997a). Various mechanisms are likely involved in the loss of the hind limb, including the nonexpression of certain homeobox genes.

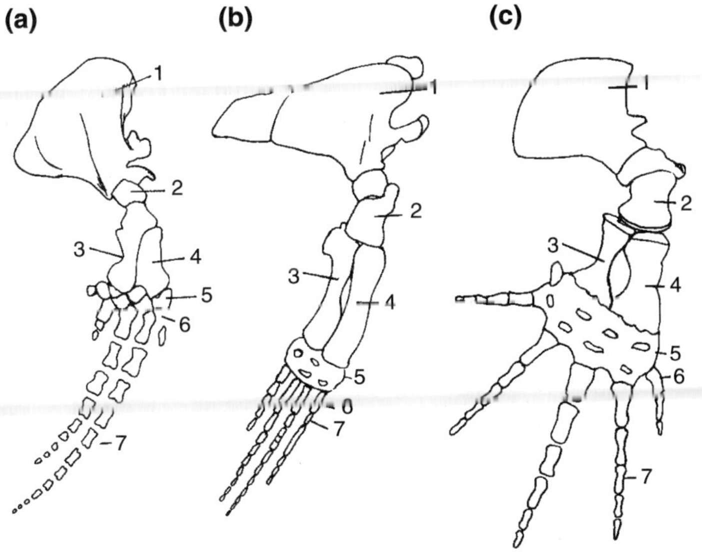

Figure 8.23. Forelimb of representative cetaceans, (a) pilot whale, *Globicephala* sp. (b) blue whale, *Balaenoptera musculus,* and (c) right whale, *Eubalaena* sp. Numbers: 1=scapula, 2=humerus, 3=ulna, 4=radius, 5=carpals, 6=metacarpals, 7=phalanges (from Evans, 1987).

Some (possibly all) archaeocete cetaceans had external hind limbs. The pelvic facets on sacral vertebrae of *Protocetus* suggest a well-developed pelvis, hind limbs have been discovered on *Prozeuglodon, Ambulocetus natans* has a large hindleg and foot, *Rodhocetus kasrani* has a large pelvis, and a protocetid from Georgia also has a pelvis (Hulbert and Petkewich, 1991; Hulbert, 1998). Archaeocetes may have been able to haul out on beaches as do pinnipeds. It has been suggested that the small functional hind limbs of *Basilosaurus isis* perhaps aided copulation (Gingerich *et al.,* 1990) or locomotion in shallow waters (Fordyce and Barnes, 1994; see also Chapter 4).

8.3.6.3. Tail (Fluke)

The tails, or **flukes**, of cetaceans have the following basic components: 1) a cutaneous layer not significantly different from that described for other regions of the body, 2) a blubber layer far thinner than that of the body, 3) a ligamentous layer extending from the caudal keels and sides of the tail, 4) a core of extremely tough, dense, fibrous tissue within the ligamentous envelope, forming the bulk of the fluke (Felts, 1966).

The flukes are an outgrowth of the lateral caudal region (similar to the development of limb buds from the lateral body wall). The shape of the flukes differs among cetaceans (Fig. 8.24) in response to varying hydrodynamic parameters (Fish, 1998). The trailing edges of most are slightly convex, but some are almost straight (sperm whale); while others are conspicuously curved (humpback), falcate (sickle-shaped; rorquals) or even biconvex (narwhal).

The evolution of cetacean flukes remains speculative although it seems likely that they evolved by the middle of the Eocene as judged from the vertebral characteristics of protocetids (i.e. *Rodhocetus;* Gingerich *et al.,* 1994; Buchholtz, 1998).

8.3.6.4. Dorsal Fin

There is generally a prominent dorsal fin on the back of cetaceans (Fig. 8.25). Some cetaceans lack a dorsal fin (balaenids, sperm whales, beluga, narwhal, and some porpoises such as *Phocoena*). In some it is poorly developed and too small to function as a mechanism preventing rolling during swimming. In most odontocetes it is quite large, culminating in the killer whales in which it may attain a length of almost two meters in adult males. The fin is supported not by bone but by tough fibrous tissue inside it. It has been suggested that it serves to assist in the maintenance of balance and for thermoregulation.

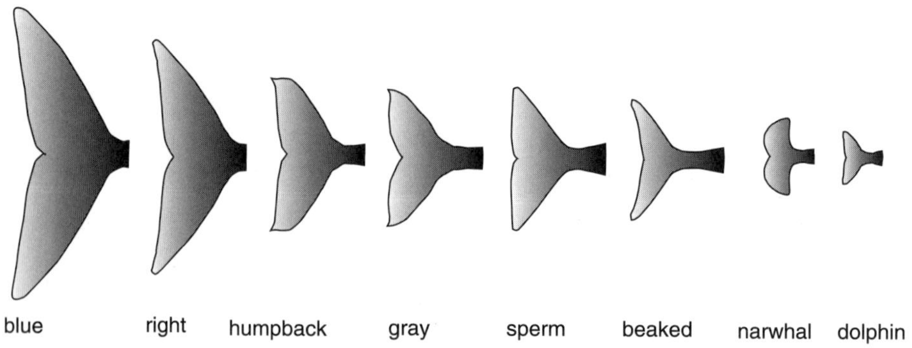

Figure 8.24. Different shaped flukes of various cetaceans (from Harrison and Bryden, 1988).

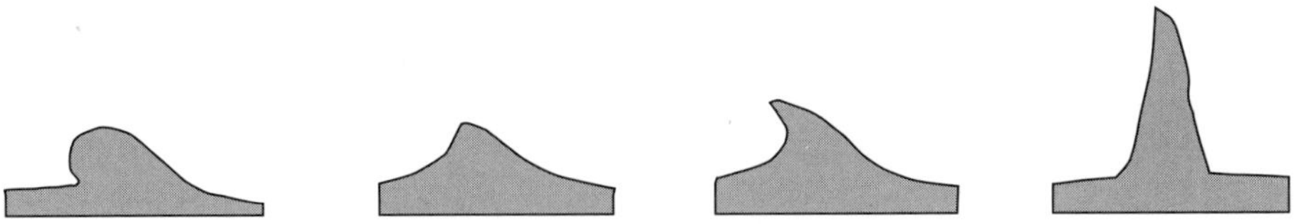

Figure 8.25. Representative dorsal fins of various cetaceans (from Harrison and Bryden, 1988).

8.3.6.5. Locomotion

Modern cetaceans swim by vertical movements of the tail (Fig. 8.26) via the alternate actions of the epaxial and hypaxial muscles. This derived mode of locomotion differs from that of all other marine mammals with the exception of sirenians. Caudal propulsion provides improved efficiency at sustained higher velocities. Differences between the sizes of the epaxial and hypaxial muscle masses led to the early contention that the up and down movements of the tail were not equivalent; the upstroke was considered to produce thrust while the downstroke was passive, functioning as a recovery stroke. Other data indicate thrust is produced during both phases, although the magnitude of thrust differs between the up- and downstroke with the upstroke being more powerful (Fish and Hui, 1991). The upstroke, which involves muscles that extend the tail, is powered primarily by two epaxial muscles: (1) the m. multifidus with its caudal extension (the m. extensor caudae medialis), and (2) the m. longissimus, with its caudal extension (the m. extensor caudae lateralis; Pabst, 1990, 1993). The caudal extension of the m. longissimus is the only epaxial muscle that acts to control the angle of attack of the flukes. The downstroke, which involves muscles that flex the tail and depress the flukes, is powered by the mm. flexor caudae lateralis and flexor caudae medialis; both are extensions of the m. hypaxalis lumborum. Another major tail flexor is the m. ischiocaudalis which also provides some lateral torque. Strong connective tissues in the flukes of cetaceans have been found to help in the transmission of force. For example, in dolphins, at the end of each stroke, kinetic energy is moved from the fluke and then returned. This energy is temporarily stored as elastic strain energy in the connective tissue (e.g. tendons) in the fluke, and then is recovered in an elastic recoil instead of dissipating and subsequently being replaced (at metabolic cost) by muscular work (Blickhan and Cheng, 1994).

A trained oceanic spinner dolphin has been clocked in a controlled test situation at better than 11 m/s (40 km/hr; Lang and Pryor, 1966), and peak velocities of killer whales are estimated to be 40 to 55 km/hr. At these velocities, fine maneuvering becomes difficult. However, most marine mammals seldom approach their peak swimming velocities because these velocities are energetically very expensive and they usually require a cost of reduced maneuverability.

The body shape of a fast swimming marine mammal, such as a dolphin, is a compromise between different hypothetical body forms, each of which reduces some component of the total drag and allows the animal to slip through the water with as little resistance as possible. **Frictional drag** results from the interaction of the animal's surface with the water surrounding its body and is reduced by reducing the animal's surface area relative to the animal's volume. However, an animal swimming through water also must overcome **pressure drag**, created by the need to displace an amount of water equal to the animal's largest

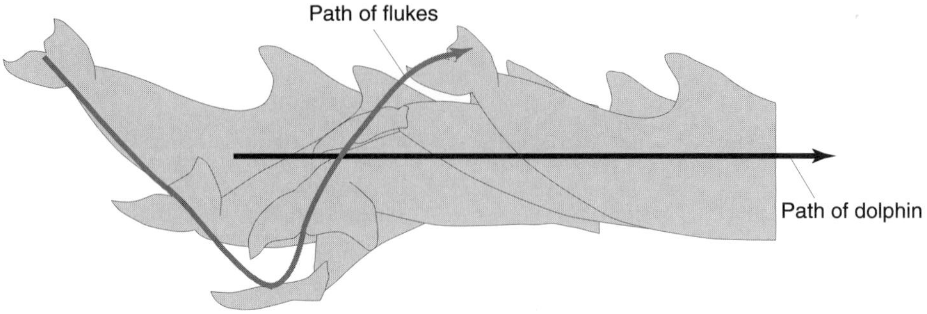

Figure 8.26. Cetacean propulsion, tracings of flukes of bottlenose dolphin (modified from Coffey, 1977).

cross-sectional area (from a head-on view). The ideal shape for the least overall, or total, drag of a fast swimmer is a streamline form that is roundly blunt at the front end, tapered to a point in the rear, and round in cross section. The fineness ratio (the ratio of maximum body length to maximum body diameter; Fig. 8.27) for efficient swimmers ranges from 3–7, with the ideal near 4.5. Most cetaceans exhibit fineness ratios near 6–7, with only killer whales and right whales having ratios of 4.0–4.5.

Three main forces act on bodies moving in fluids: inertial, viscous, and gravitational. For submerged swimming marine mammals, both inertial and viscous forces are important. Although the inertial forces dominate, the viscosity of the fluid is responsible for the formation of the boundary layer which is important in the creation of skin friction due to the shear forces near the surface of the animal. A widely used comparative indicator of the forces acting on such submerged bodies, the **Reynolds number** (R), provides an order of magnitude approximation of these forces (Webb, 1975).

$$R = (\text{body length} \times \text{swimming velocity})/(\text{water viscosity}/\text{water density})$$

Because the lower term of this equation changes little over typical ranges of sea water temperatures, calculated R values are influenced primarily by body lengths and swimming velocities. For submerged swimming animals with streamlined bodies and R values $<5\text{x}10^5$, water flow over the body remains laminar and stable, with low total drag characteristics. At R values $> 5\text{x}10^6$, the pattern of water flow becomes unstable and turbulent, resulting in greatly increased drag characteristics (when $5\text{x}10^5<R<5\text{x}10^6$, flow is transitional between laminar and turbulent conditions; Webb, 1975). Thus, low R values and patterns of laminar water flow are associated with small or slow-moving swimmers.

Models of hydrodynamic performance indicate that power requirements for submerged swimming by streamlined animals are proportional to the cube of the swimming velocity. Predicted power requirements (P) for streamlined swimmers can be generalized by the following equation (Webb, 1975):

$$P = 0.5\rho C_t S_w V_3$$

where ρ = water density
C_t = coefficient of total drag
S_w = wetted surface area of the swimmer
V = swimming velocity

The magnitude of C_t for rigid streamlined forms is estimated to be at least an order of magnitude greater for animals experiencing turbulent boundary conditions than it is for animals swimming with laminar flow characteristics. Empirical determinations of C_t are available

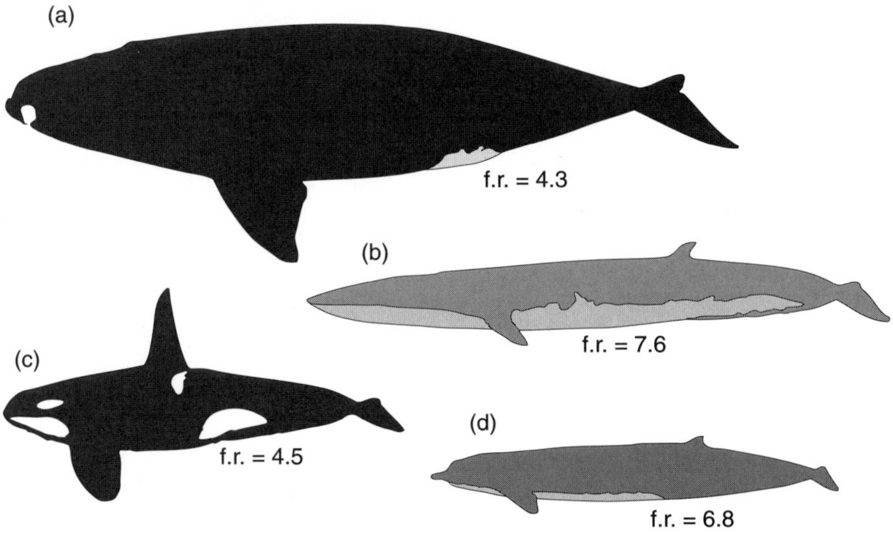

Figure 8.27. Fineness ratios (f.r.) of two mysticetes, (a) *Balaena* and (b) *Balaenoptera,* and two odontocetes, (c) *Orcinus* and (d) *Berardius.*

for only a few species of small odontocetes (C_t = 0.03–0.04; Lang, 1975) and one mysticete (C_t = 0.06; Sumich, 1983). The lower C_t value for the small odontocetes is attributed to laminar water flow characteristics over at least a substantial part of the body. Completely turbulent patterns characterize the water flow over the much larger bodies of mysticetes, and the resulting calculated value of C_t is correspondingly greater.

Swimming and diving represent major energetic expenditures in marine mammals. In wild bottlenose dolphins, locomotor activities can represent more than 82% of the animal's daytime activity budget (Hansen and Defran, 1993). The **cost of transport** (COT) is useful for comparing the locomotory efficiencies between different modes of locomotion or between different species employing the same mode of locomotion. COT for a swimming animal is defined as the power (P) required to move a given body mass (M) at some velocity (V). Thus, in appropriate units, COT = P/MV. Tucker (1975) summarized the known minimum COT for a variety of swimming, flying, and running animals spanning several orders of magnitude in body size (Fig. 8.28). The power:velocity curve for most swimming animals is U-shaped, with the power requirements reaching a minimum at some intermediate velocity. The COT at that velocity is the COT_{min}. This is analogous to determining the minimum amount of fuel necessary to drive an automobile between two cities.

It is apparent from Figure 8.28 that, within any one mode of locomotion (running, flying, or swimming), the COT_{min} decreases with increasing body size and is essentially independent of taxonomic affiliation. Of the three general modes of transport, swimming is the least costly because swimmers need not support their body weight against the constant pull of gravity. Conspicuously absent from Tucker's summary were estimates of the COT for cetaceans or other swimming endotherms. The general relationship between body size and COT_{min} suggests that large swimming animals should have exceedingly low COT_{min}, but experimental evidence to test that prediction was not available until the early 1990s. To measure power output rates, the metabolic rates of a subject animal must be measured, and that is difficult to do with a large, unrestrained, swimming animal. Williams *et al.* (1992) trained two Atlantic bottlenose dolphins to swim in open water beside a pace boat and to

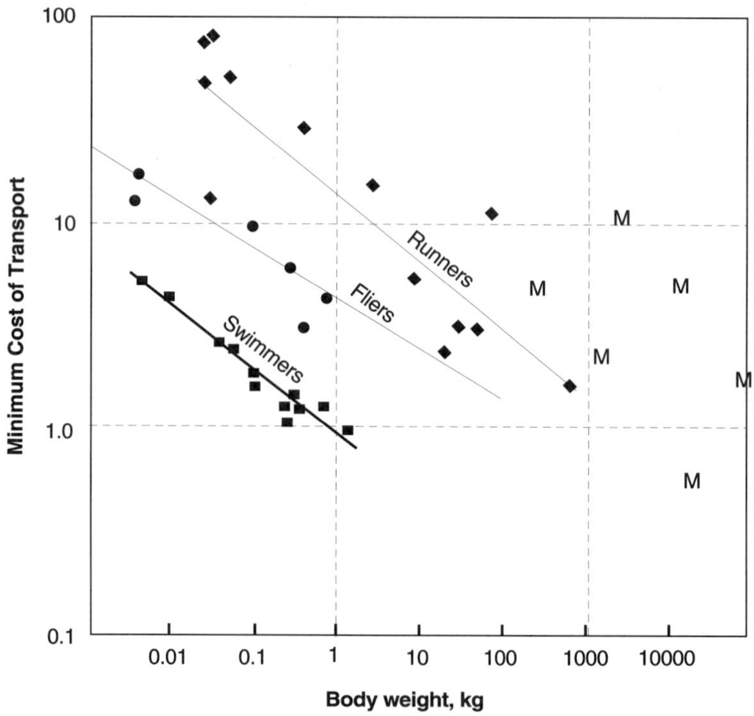

Figure 8.28. Relationships between COT_{min} and body weight for swimmers, fliers, and runners, regardless of taxonomic affiliation. M=machines. (Adapted from Tucker, 1975).

match its speed. Heart and respiratory rates, previously calibrated to oxygen consumption rates, were monitored and recorded continuously during each 20–25 minute test session to estimate metabolic rate. Blood samples for lactate analysis (a product of anaerobic respiration) were collected immediately after each session.

The results of this study indicate that the COT is minimum for these swimmers at speeds of 2.1 m/s and that COT_{min} is doubled at 2.9 m/s. These results, at least for COT_{min}, have since been confirmed for dolphin swimming speed measurements made in the wild using a multidirectional video sonar (Ridoux *et al.,* 1997). However, when speeds were increased above approximately 3 m/s, the dolphins in the Williams *et al.* (1992) study invariably switched to **wave riding**, a behavior that is best described as surfing the stern wake of the pace boat. When wave riding at 3.8 m/s, the COT was only 13% higher than the minimum at 2.1 m/s. The large energetic saving that accompanies wave riding at higher speed explains the common practice of dolphins riding the bow or stern waves of ships and even other large whales, apparently with little effort.

How does the COT of dolphins compare to the COT of other swimmers? Williams *et al.* (1992) demonstrated that dolphins are efficient swimmers, with COT_{min} about an order of magnitude lower than that of humans or other surface swimmers (Fig. 8.29). However, the dolphin COT_{min} is still several times higher than that of a hypothetical fish of comparable size. The additional costs incurred by dolphins are presumably associated with the mammalian requirement of thermoregulation. In essence, this is the overhead cost of keeping the motor warmed up and running. The COT_{min} of dolphins is substantially lower than that of pinnipeds and is comparable (when body mass differences are accommodated) to the es-

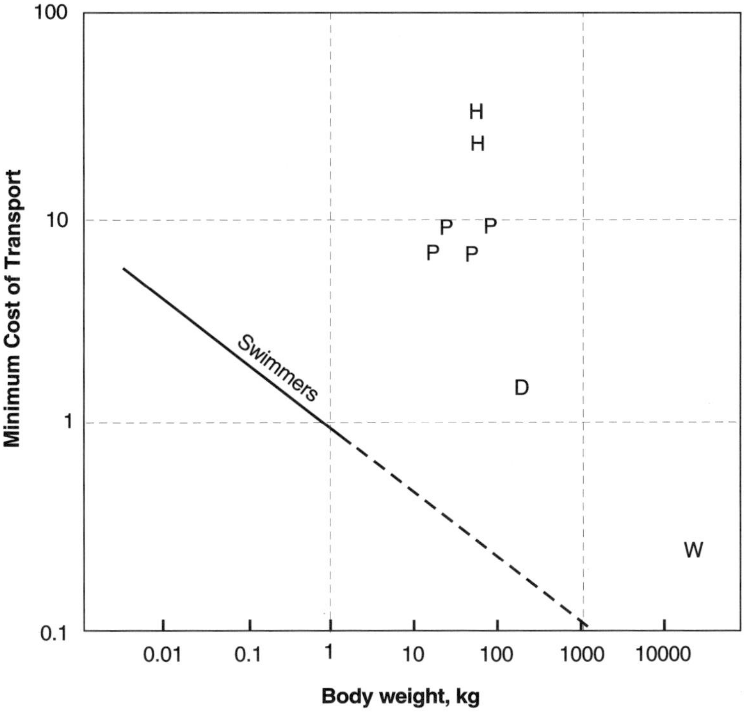

Figure 8.29. Measured COT_{min} as a function of body weight for humans (H), pinnipeds (P), a bottlenose dolphin (D), and a gray whale (W). The regression line for poikilothermic swimmers from Fig. 8.28 is extrapolated to larger body weights (data from Williams *et al.*, 1992).

timated COT_{min} of migrating adult gray whales (Sumich, 1983). Interestingly, the swimming velocity at which COT was minimum is identical, 2 m/s, for both dolphins and gray whales, and is within 10% of the mean migrating speeds of southbound gray whales. The energetic implications of swimming at speeds which minimize their COT and maximize their range, as gray whales do, are likely critical factors in successfully covering the exceedingly long migratory distances that they travel. Observations of Ridoux *et al.* (1997) on the swimming speed and activities of wild dolphins indicate that they continue their foraging activities during rising tides and that the additional cost of such a foraging strategy must be balanced by an increased prey density, availability, or catchability during rising tides.

When submerged swimming mammals approach the sea surface to breathe, they encounter additional drag due to gravitational forces associated with creating waves at the air-sea interface. At depths below three times an animal's greatest body diameter, these gravitational forces are negligible, but as a swimming mammal ascends, its total drag increases to a maximum of five-fold at the sea surface due to energy lost in the formation of surface waves. This pattern of increasing drag nearer the sea surface is shown in Figure 8.30. Any mammal can reduce its COT by swimming at depths below 2.5 body diameters for a period approaching the duration of its aerobic breathhold capacity (defined in Chapter 9), then surfacing to breathe only as frequently as O_2 demands dictate. This is reflected in the breathing patterns of many swimming mammals (Fig. 8.30), featuring extended submerged breathhold swims punctuated by surface bouts of several closely-spaced ventilatory

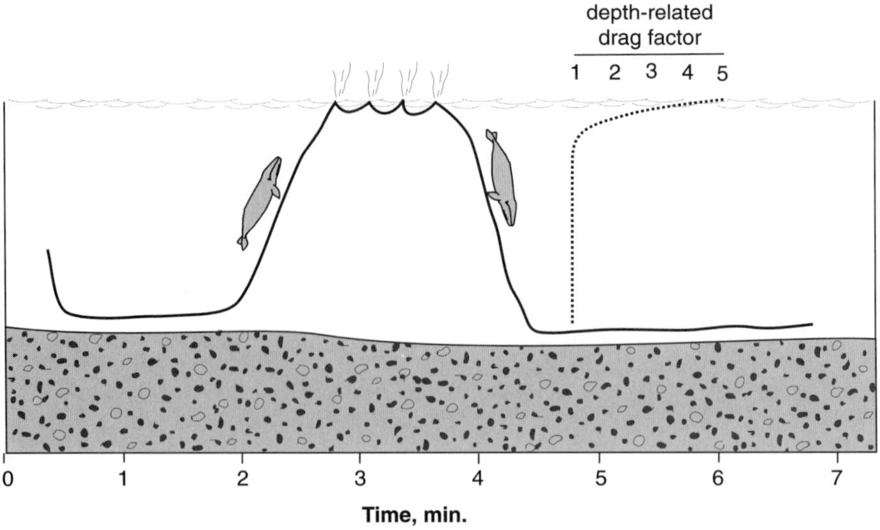

Figure 8.30. Apneustic breathing pattern of a migrating gray whale. Graph at right illustrates the relative increase in drag as the whale approaches the surface.

cycles. Thus, short breath holds apparently serve to achieve efficient rates of oxygen utilization, whereas long breath holds permit more efficient transport over extended or even migratory distances.

Smaller marine mammals must necessarily surface to breathe more frequently at higher swimming velocities. At high speeds, the high drag associated with surfacing can be partly avoided by leaping above the water–air interface and gliding airborne for a few body lengths. The aerial phase of this type of **porpoising** or leaping locomotion removes the animal from the high drag environment of the water surface (Norris and Johnson, 1994) while simultaneously providing an opportunity to breathe. The velocity at which it becomes more efficient to leap rather than to remain submerged is known as the crossover speed (Fish and Hui, 1991). The crossover speed is estimated to be about 5 m/s for spotted dolphins and increases with increasing body size until leaping becomes a prohibitively expensive mode of locomotion in cetaceans longer than about 10 m in length. Diving dolphins also may use burst-and-glide swimming to reduce locomotor costs. In an experiment in which dolphins were trained to dive in a straight line path to submerged targets at different depths, Williams *et al.* (1996) reported that rather than swim at constant speeds, the dolphins descended slower and ascended faster than predicted for transit swimming. Subsequent video sequences of the dives showed that the dolphins switched from the energetically expensive constant propulsion to an intermittent mode of swimming, thus incurring less cost during the ascent from longer dives. In another study which linked the cost of locomotion to the cost of thermoregulation, the COT_{min} and the optimal swim speed were found to be both a function of water temperature and to vary between marine mammals (Hind and Gurney, 1997).

8.3.6.5.1. Evolution of Cetacean Locomotor Patterns

According to Fish's (1996) model, modified by Thewissen and Fish (1997), the cetacean mode of swimming, caudal oscillation, evolved in stages from a mesonychian condylarth ancestor that swam by quadrupedal paddling. This ancestor went through a pelvic paddling phase (*Ambulocetus*), a caudal undulation phase (*Rodhocetus*), and finally adopted caudal oscillation as its swimming mode (all modern cetaceans) (Fig. 8.31).

Fossil discoveries in Eocene rocks of Pakistan have revealed several of the critical evolutionary steps involved in the transition from land to the sea (Thewissen *et al.,* 1996; Thewissen and Fish, 1997). *Ambulocetus natans,* the "walking whale," walked on land but could also swim using a combination of pelvic paddling provided by the hind limbs and dorsoventral undulations of the tail. Its locomotion in the water has been compared to that of the modern otter *Lutra.* The hand of *Ambulocetus* was small relative to the foot and probably did not provide any propulsion. The thumb was mobile at the wrist but the arm was rigid. Forelimb motions were limited and the shoulder and thumb were the primary means of modifying the position of the forelimb during swimming. Joints of the remaining digits were mobile and were likely used for locomotion on land. The large feet with elongated, flattened phalanges, similar to those of pinnipeds, suggest that *Ambulocetus* may have had webbed feet.

A slightly later diverging archaic whale, *Rodhocetus kasrani* from Pakistan, spent most of its time in the water but could walk a little on land. The femur was relatively short and it is likely its small rear legs did not help in swimming. The presence of four unfused sacral vertebrae and strong dorsal spines indicates that flexion and extension of the lumbar and caudal vertebral column were well developed. All modern whales swim by dorsoventral oscillations of their tail flukes, referred to as caudal oscillation.

Another stage in the evolution of locomotion in cetaceans is represented by recent discoveries of two still later diverging archaic whales from the southeastern U.S. (Hulbert *et al.,* 1998; Uhen, 1999). One new genus and species of protocetid whale, *Georgiacetus vogtlensis,* has been described as having a pelvis that did not articulate with the hind limb, suggesting a loss of any significant locomotor function of the hind limb in terrestrial locomotion. Aquatic locomotion in *Georgiacetus* is inferred to have been primarily caudal oscillation with a secondary contribution from the hind limb (Hulbert *et al.,* 1998).

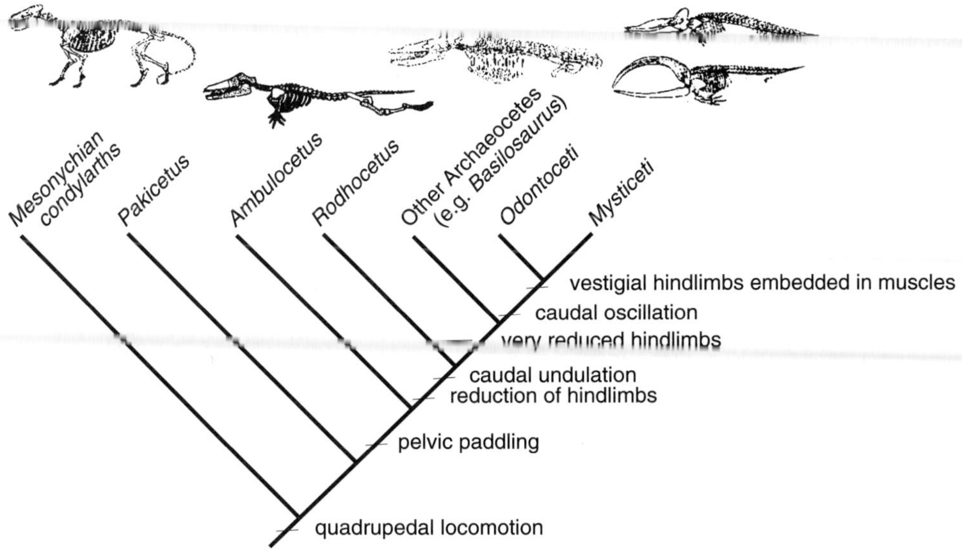

Figure 8.31. Evolution of locomotion in cetaceans (based on Thewissen and Fish, 1997).

8.4. Sirenians

8.4.1. Skull and Mandible

The dugong skull has remarkably enlarged downturned premaxillae (Fig. 8.32). Nasal bones are absent. Several features of the skull show sexual dimorphism, the most obvious of which is a difference in thickness of the premaxillae; they are more robust in the male, presumably because of the difference in tusk eruption (Nishiwaki and Marsh, 1985).

The manatee skull is broad with a relatively short snout and an expanded nasal basin. The premaxillae are only slightly downturned, relatively small, and lack tusks (Figure 8.32b). The vomer is short, extending anteriorly only to the level of the middle of the orbit, in the West African manatee, whereas in the West Indian manatee the vomer extends to the posterior edge of the incisive foramina or beyond. The lower jaw is massive. Manatees possess a specialized, lipid-filled structure (the zygomatic process of the squamosal) that has been suggested to function in sound reception in a similar manner to the fatty-filled mandibular canal of odontocetes; both are further discussed in Chapter 10.

Domning (1978), in his description of the musculature of the Amazonian manatee, made comparisons with other manatees and the dugong. Several notable differences exist. In the Amazonian manatee, the rectus capitis muscle has been modified from its function of bending the head laterally and strengthened to serve also as an extensor of the atlantooccipital joint in conjunction with the semispinalis muscle.

8.4.2. Vertebral Column and Axial Musculature

Sirenians have experienced a lengthening of the thorax which has resulted in a shortening of the lumbar region. There are 57–60 vertebrae in the dugong (C7, T17-19, L4, S3, C28-29). Vertebrae number 43–54 in manatees (C6, T15-19, and LSC23 to 29; Husar, 1977). In sirenians, the articulations of the vertebrae in the lumbocaudal region are reduced, more markedly in the manatee (Howell, 1930a). The presence of six rather than seven cervical vertebrae in manatees (also seen in two sloth lineages) is most likely the result of developmental reorganization of segmentation pattern that appears to have evolved independently in mammals at least three times (Giffin and Gillett, 1996).

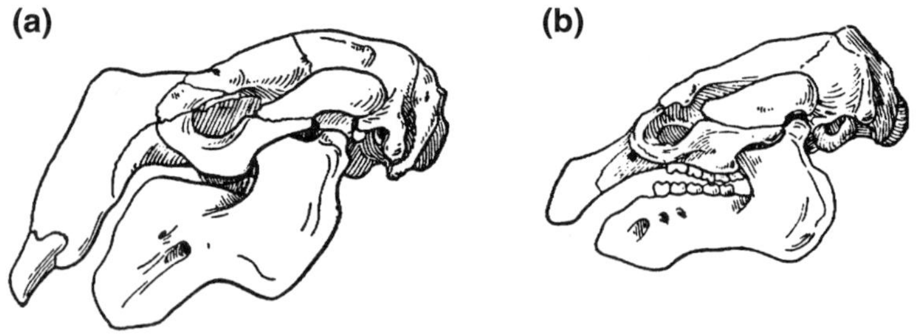

Figure 8.32. Lateral views of (a) dugong and (b) manatee skulls (from Gregory, 1951).

8.4.3. Sternum and Ribs

The sternum in both the dugong and manatee is a broad, flat, single bone (the manubrium), with no indication of additional separate or fused sternal elements as is the normal mammalian condition. The manubrium of the West Indian manatee has a deep median notch in the anterior border, whereas that of the West African manatee lacks a deep notch (Husar, 1977, 1978). Only the first three pairs of ribs join the sternum; the others are free of distal articulation.

8.4.4. Flippers and Locomotion

8.4.4.1. Pectoral Girdle and Forelimb

The axilla in sirenians is situated just proximal to the elbow. Since sea cows, like all other marine mammals, lack a clavicle, the shoulder girdle is composed only of the scapula. The scapula of the dugong has a short acromion and a well-developed coracoid. The acromion is better developed in manatees. The humerus has prominent tuberosities (Fig. 8.33). The humeral head in both the manatee and dugong is situated fairly posterior to the main shaft axis. This suggests that the chief direction of movement is in the sagittal plane. This is

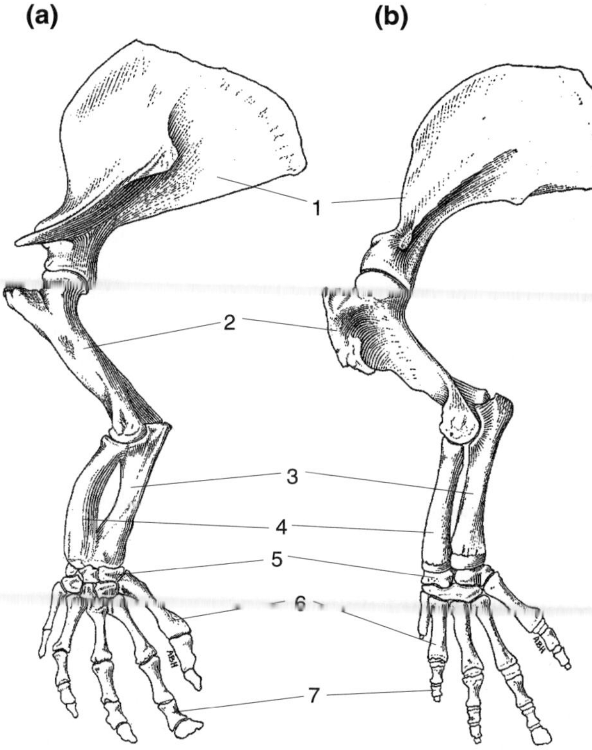

Figure 8.33. Forelimb of manatee (a) and dugong (b). Numbers: 1=scapula, 2=humerus, 3=ulna, 4=radius, 5=carpals, 6=metacarpals, 7=phalanges (from Howell, 1930a).

also supported by the fact that the lesser tuberosity is not medially positioned. Instead it is continuous with the greater tuberosity and the two are conjoined to form a broad, transverse ridge anterior to the head. There is no teres minor muscle in the dugong so the scapular muscles inserting upon this ridge, are the subscapularis upon the medial part, the infraspinatus on the lateral portion, and the supraspinatus between them. In the manatee, the deltoid is inserted not upon a ridge but on a rugosity on the middle of the shaft (Howell, 1930a). In the dugong, the humeral head is also posterior to the shaft axis, indicating that flexion and extension are the chief movements. The greater tuberosity is higher than the lesser, the former is located cranial of the head as usual, and both are distinct instead of continuous as in manatees. In addition, there is a heavy and high deltoid crest continuous distally with the greater tuberosity (Howell, 1930a).

The humerus, radius, and ulna are well developed in the dugong. This is especially true with regard to the proximal portion of the humerus, with its much stouter processes. The radius and ulna of both the manatee and the dugong are proximally fused and the dugong also exhibits fusion distally (Fig. 8.33). The olecranon process of the ulna is also much better developed in the dugong. The elbow joint is movable in both (Kaiser, 1974). The trochlea spiral of the humeroulnar joint of sirenians is in the opposite direction from that of terrestrial mammals (i.e. it is expanded posteriorly and medially and anteriorly and laterally). Domning (1978) suggests that this may be because the principal propulsive force is transmitted from the shoulder muscles through the humerus and elbow to the forearm, with negligible force exerted in the opposite direction; that is, the forearm flexors play little role in propulsion.

The forelimbs of the Steller's sea cow are described as short, blunt, and hook-like and therefore would have been of little use in paddling. This animal probably remained in shallow water and employed the forelimbs to pull the body forward along the bottom.

The wrist joint of sirenians is moveable. The pisiform (one of the wrist bones) is absent. The carpals of the dugong show a tendency for fusion (Harrison and King, 1965). The fifth digit is poorly developed with a single phalanx present (Kaiser, 1974). In the dugong, the carpal elements are reduced to three but in manatees there are six carpals (five carpals according to Quiring and Harlan, 1953, with fusion of the radiale and intermedium). The metacarpals and phalanges are flattened, especially in manatees. Two phalanges occur in four of the five digits; the first digit has one phalanx (Quiring and Harlan, 1953). The ungual phalanges (equivalent to finger tips) are of irregular shape and are particularly flat, and the thumb is reduced. The fourth digit is the longest and represents the tip of the flipper (Howell, 1930).

The shoulder musculature in the dugong and manatees differs and Domning (1978) suggested that this may reflect the requirements of maneuvering in different habitats; the marine habitat of the dugong is more open than that of the manatee (Nishiwaki and Marsh, 1985).

8.4.4.2. Pelvic Girdle and Hind Limb

The pelvic girdle is vestigial; pubic bones are absent and the ischium and ilium, which are both rod-like, are fused in adults into an innominate bone. Sexual dimorphism in the innominate bone of dugongs was observed by Domning (1991). The pelvic girdle is absent in the West African manatee; innominate bones are reduced in both the West Indian manatee and West African manatee (Husar, 1977). Distal elements of the hind limbs are absent.

8.4.4.3. Hydrostatic Adaptations

The skeleton of sirenians is both pachyostotic and osteosclerotic. Pachyostosis and osteosclerosis, the patterns of growth in weight of the skeleton, the positions of gravity and buoyancy centers, and the lung morphology all are involved in hydrostatic regulation which may free locomotory efforts from the additional requirement of providing lift (Domning and de Buffrénil, 1991).

8.4.4.4. Locomotion

Sirenians, like cetaceans, use caudal oscillation to effect propulsion. Nearly all of our information comes from Hartman's (1979) work on the West Indian manatee. Compared to cetaceans, manatees are poor swimmers and are unable to reach or sustain high speeds. According to Hartman (1979: Fig. 16) movement is initiated from a stationary position by an upswing of the tail followed by a downswing, repeated until undulatory movement is established. Each stroke of the tail displaces the body vertically, the degree of pitching increasing with the power stroke (Fig. 8.34). The tail also serves as a rudder. Cruising animals can bank, steer, and roll by means of the tail alone. The use of the flippers in locomotion differs somewhat from cetaceans. While cruising, the flippers of adult manatees are held motionless at the sides. Juvenile manatees have been reported to swim exclusively with their flippers (Moore, 1956, 1957). Flippers (either independently or simultaneously) normally are used only for precise maneuvering and for corrective movements to stabilize and orient the animal while it is feeding. The primary use of flippers is to turn an animal to the right or left. This is in contrast to dugongs which may employ the flippers when cruising; dugongs also employ the flippers to turn and maintain balance. Cetaceans often use the flippers as planing surfaces to assist diving and surfacing.

Dugongs and manatees are considered to swim in a leisurely manner (0.6–0.8 m/s; Hartman, 1979; Nishiwaki and Marsh, 1985). As herbivores, sirenians do not require speed and rapid acceleration to catch prey. Low speed swimming allows for precise maneuverability. Swimming velocities of manatees vary greatly depending on activity; idling speed is 2–3 km/h and cruising speed is 3–7 km/h (Hartman, 1979). During flight sprint speeds of over 6 m/s (22km/h; Hartman, 1979; Nishiwaki and Marsh, 1985) aid in escape from predators such as sharks and crocodiles (Reynolds and Odell, 1991).

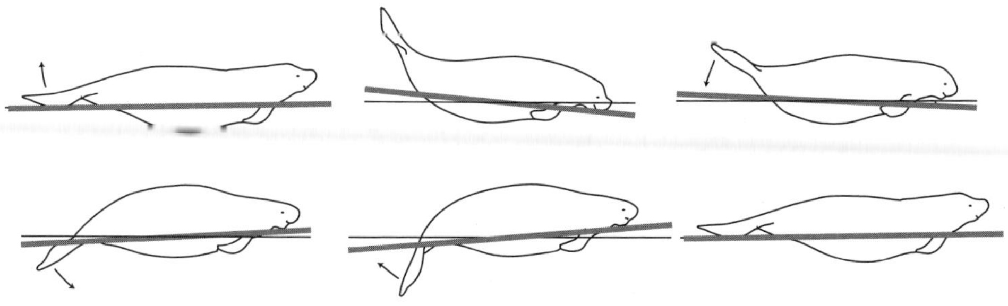

Figure 8.34. Lateral view of manatee swimming, tracings of body, limb and tail movements. Arrows indicate direction of movement. (From Hartman, 1979).

8.4.4.4.1. Evolution of Sirenian Locomotor Patterns

According to Domning (1996; Fig. 8.35), sirenians passed through the following stages in their return to the water: 1) as mostly terrestrial quadrupeds, swimming by alternate thrusts of the limbs, followed by 2) amphibious quadrupeds swimming by dorsoventral spinal undulation and bilateral thrusts of the hind limbs, and 3) completely aquatic animals swimming with the tail only. The earliest stage in the evolution of sirenian locomotor patterns is represented by prorastomids from the early and middle Eocene of Jamaica (Fig. 8.35). Prorastomids have well developed pelvic and hind limb bones. The development of large and expanded neural processes of the posterior vertebrae suggests unusual development of longissimus dorsi muscles for spinal extension. Because the caudal vertebrae lack transverse processes, it is likely that the hind limbs rather than the tail were the major propulsive organs. Also apparent at this early stage of locomotor evolution were pachyostotic and osteosclerotic bones suggesting the need for heavy ballast when swimming. The next stage is represented by *Protosiren* from the middle Eocene of Egypt. Although this animal retained a complete hind limb, the pelvis is modified and the sacrum is only weakly connected to the pelvis. The caudal vertebrae have broad transverse processes typical of later sirenians, suggesting that the tail had become the major propulsive organ, although the hind limbs probably played some role in swimming. Shortening of the neck occurred simultaneously with a reduction of the hind limbs and is apparent in *Protosiren.* Archaic dugongids living contemporaneously with some species of *Protosiren* represent a more advanced stage of evolution. The pubis was very reduced and it is clear that these animals could no longer support their weight on the hind limbs. Late Eocene and Oligocene dugongids show considerable variation in the pelvic and hind limb bones. The Recent *Dugong* and *Hydrodamalis* lack femora and elements of the pelvis (including the acetabulum) entirely. Trichechids have completely lost the pelvis and with it, connection to the vertebral column.

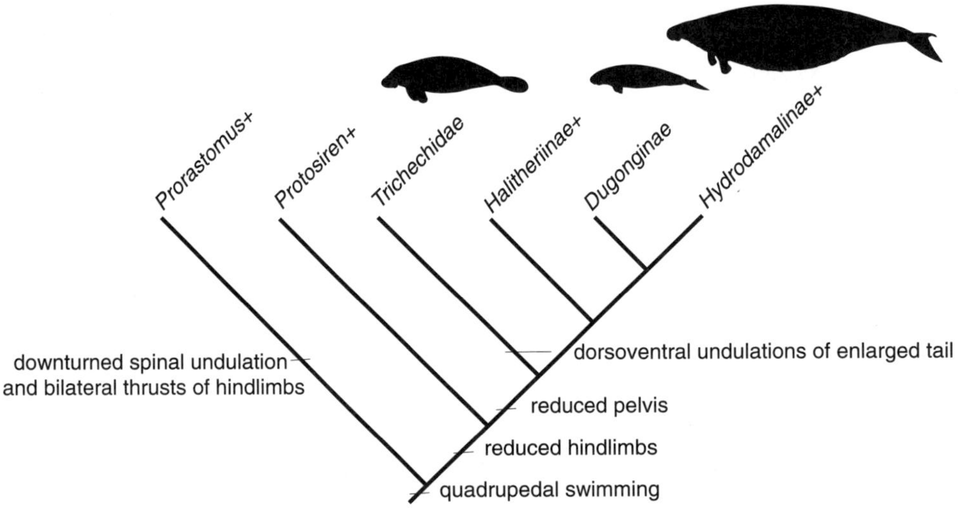

Figure 8.35. Evolution of sirenian locomotion, +=extinct taxa (based on Domning, 1996).

8.5. Sea Otter

8.5.1. Skull and Mandible

The sea otter skull is short and robust and is characterized by a blunt rostrum, prominent zygomatic arches, and well-developed sagittal and occipital crests. Auditory bullae are large and inflated. The lower jaw exhibits a large coronoid process and weakly developed angular process (see Fig. 5.15). Skull length data indicate significant sexual dimorphism (Estes, 1989).

Asymmetry has been reported in the sea otter skull (Barabash-Nikiforov *et al.,* 1947, 1968) in which the left side of the cranium tends to be larger in most individuals. More detailed study of this phenomenon indicates that the asymmetry varies both between individuals and between populations (Roest, 1993).

8.5.2. Vertebral Column and Axial Musculature

Sea otters possess 50–51 vertebrae with a typical vertebral formula, C7, T14, L6, S3, C20-21. The vertebrae of the sea otter differ from those of the river otter in having larger intervertebral foraminae, especially posteriorly, and very reduced vertebral processes. The neck of the sea otter is shorter relative to the length of the trunk in comparison to the river otter (Taylor, 1914). This shortness of the neck is associated with streamlining of the body and the development of the thoracolumbar and caudal regions used for propulsion.

During rapid aquatic locomotion in the sea otter (as well as in the river otter), the lumbosacral region is moved vertically, paralleling the activity of the tail and hindfoot movements. As one would expect, there is an increased development of these regions displayed by increased muscle mass of the epaxial musculature (mm. multifidis lumborum and longissimus thoracis (Gambarajan and Karapetjan, 1961) and an increased height of the neural spines and transverse processes which provide attachment points for those muscles.

8.5.3. Sternum and Ribs

Sea otters possess 14 pairs of ribs. The first 10 pairs of ribs articulate loosely with the sternum and contribute to the mobility of the thoracic region.

8.5.4. Pectoral Girdle and Forelimb

The sea otter scapula is relatively smaller than in the river otter, and not so long anteroposteriorly. This has been related to the lack of dependence on forelimbs for support (Taylor, 1914). There is no clavicle, allowing extreme mobility of the pectoral girdle. The forelimbs are proportionally smaller than in the river otter. The forelimb in general and the wrist in particular are highly mobile. The forefeet are small as evidenced by reduced metacarpals and phalanges (Fig. 8.36).

8.5.5. Pelvic Girdle and Hind Limb

The sea otter pelvis is elevated, lying more nearly parallel to the vertebral column than is found in the river otter. The ilia are markedly turned outward anteriorly. The femur, tibia, and fibula are relatively short. There is no round ligament in the sea otter, which confers

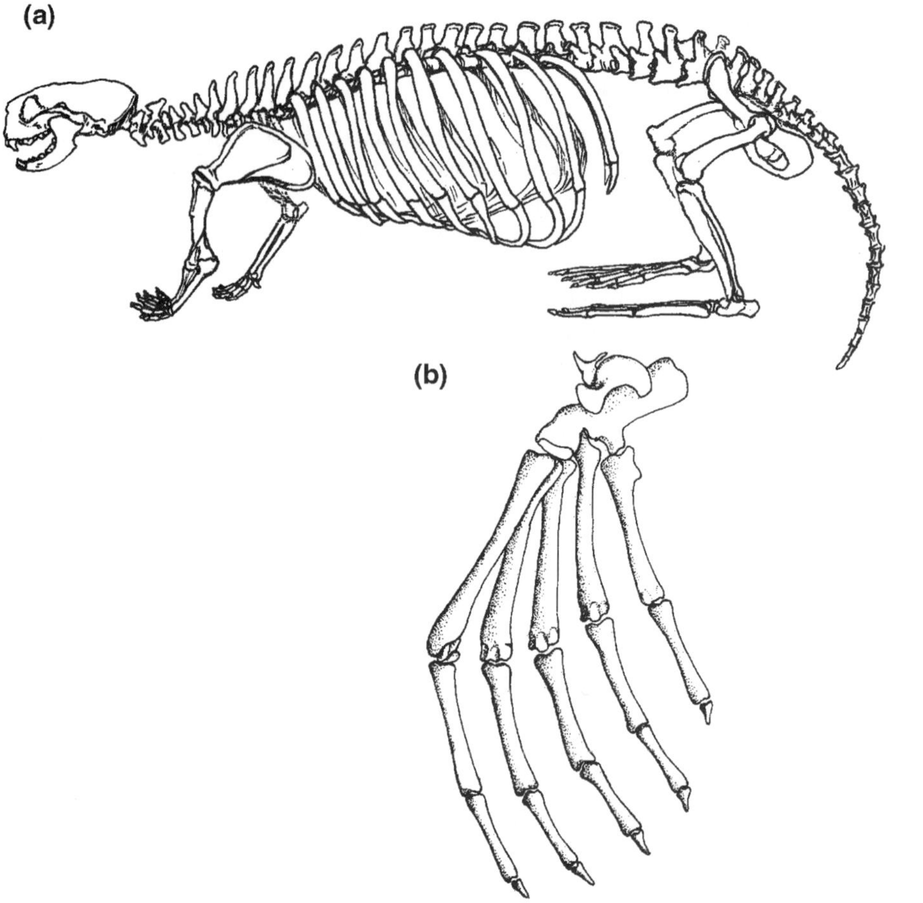

Figure 8.36. Sea otter, *Enhydra lutris* (a) Skeleton (from Chanin, 1985), (b) hindfoot (from Taylor, 1989).

greater mobility to the femur (Fig. 8.36). Both the metatarsals and phalanges are elongated (Fig. 8.36b) and a large web of skin exists between the digits of the hindfeet, so that the foot becomes twice as wide when the digits are spread out (Taylor, 1989). The fourth and fifth digits are closely bound to give rigidity to the hindflipper for propulsion. In the sea otter, the proportion of the hind limb protruding from the body contours is reduced.

8.5.6. Locomotion

The hind limbs of sea otters are so much larger than the forelimbs that terrestrial locomotion is clumsy and slow (Tarasoff and Whitt, 1972; Kenyon, 1981; Fig. 8.36). The sea otter on land exhibits two patterns of locomotion: walking and bounding. Unlike the river otter, there are no running movements. Instead, for rapid forward locomotion, bounding occurs. For walking, the general pattern of movement is one of forward movement of alternate limbs.

Aquatic locomotion in modern sea otters is achieved by pelvic paddling involving hind limb propulsion and pelvic undulation provided by the vertebral column (Fig. 8.37). This is in contrast to a forelimb-specialized swimming that has been suggested for the extinct giant otter *En-*

Figure 8.37. Aquatic locomotion in the sea otter, tracings of body, limb, and tail movements (from Tarasoff *et al.*, 1972).

hydritherium (Lambert, 1997; further discussed in Chapter 5; Thewissen and Fish, 1997). Specializations for pelvic paddling in modern sea otters include a robust femur and elongated distal hind limb elements (Tarasoff and Whitt, 1972). Three primary modes of swimming were observed by Williams (1989): 1) ventral up swimming, 2) ventral down swimming, and 3) alternate ventral up and down swimming. Ventral up swimming was used during periods of food manipulation and ingestion, and in the initial stages of an escape response from a disturbance. In this position, the animal's body is partially submerged with the head and chest held above the water surface. The forefeet are folded close to the chest above the water line while the hind feet provided propulsion. Both alternate and simultaneous strokes of the hind feet were observed. Occasionally otters maneuver slowly by making lateral undulations of the tail while the hind feet are raised above the water surface. During ventral down swimming, the head and scapular region of the back remain above the water surface. Propulsion is provided by either alternate or simultaneous strokes of the hind feet (Fig. 8.37). The forepaws are held against the submerged chest. Neither the forefoot nor the tail appear to play a role in propulsion. This position often is used during intermediate speed travel between areas and prior to a dive and high speed submerged swimming. An intermediate form of surface swimming also is observed that is associated with grooming behavior. Rather than maintain a fixed position, the animals alternatively swam with their ventral surface up or down. Such rolling along the long axis of the body is superimposed on the forward progression. As with the other forms of surface swimming, the hind paws provided the propulsion.

In the same study, sea otters were found to have two distinct speed ranges that varied with swimming mode (Williams, 1989). Sustained surface swimming, including ventral surface up, ventral surface down, and rolling body positions, occurred at speeds less than 0.8 m/s. Generally, ventral up swimming was used at the lower range of preferred speeds (0.1 to 0.5 m/s). With increases in surface swimming speed, this position was replaced by ventral surface down and rolling positions. Often ventral down swimming preceded submerged swimming; consequently, submerged swimming occurred over a higher range of speeds. Steady swimming by submerged sea otters ranged from 0.6 to 1.4 m/s. Based on these results, crossover speeds between surface and submerged swimming ranged from 0.6 to 0.8 m/s.

8.6. Polar Bear

In comparison to other marine mammals, considerably less information is available on the anatomy of the polar bear. Modern polar bears are the largest bear species, although they are smaller than their Pleistocene ancestors. Males are larger than females and this is reflected in skull as well as body measurements.

Polar bears (Fig. 8.38) possess 39–45 vertebrae distributed to the formula C7, T14-15, L5-6, S4-6, and C9-11. The neck muscles of the polar bear are especially well developed (Uspenskii, 1977).

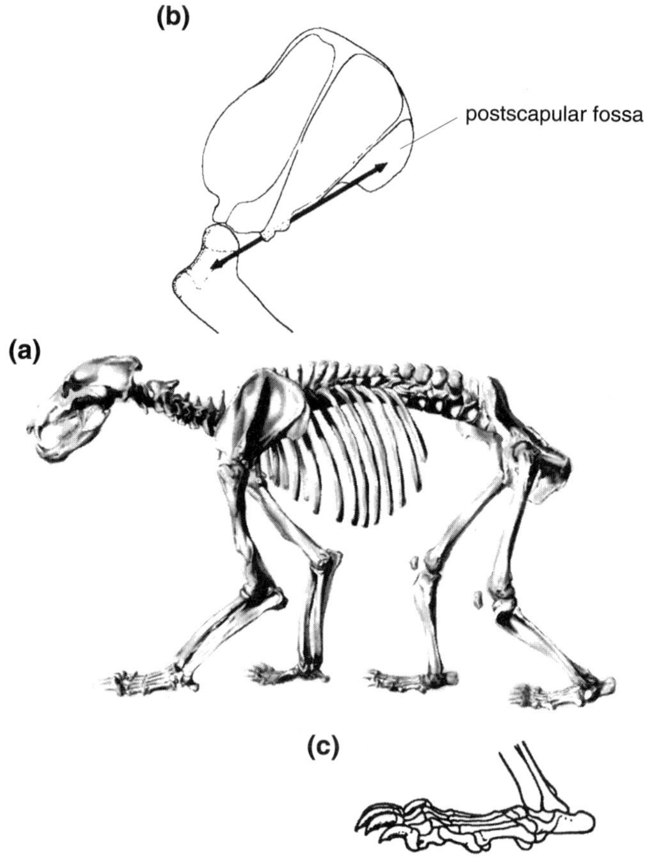

Figure 8.38. Polar bear, *Ursus maritimus* (a) Skeleton, (b) Scapula with arrow showing line of action of subscapularis muscle, and (c) Plantigrade foot (from Ewer, 1973).

Polar bears have large **plantigrade** feet which aid in propulsion during swimming. The polar bear swims with a stroke like a crawl, pulling itself through the water with its forelimbs while its hind legs trail behind (Flyger and Townsend, 1968). This is reflected in the development of a wide flange on the posterior margin of the scapula called the postscapular fossa (Davis, 1949; Fig. 8.38). The subscapularis muscle arises in part from this fossa and the unusual position of this muscle in bears is correlated with their method of climbing, or in the case of polar bears, with swimming, which involves pulling up the heavy body by the forelimbs.

When traveling on land, huge paws help distribute their body weight while their foot pads, covered with small soft papillae, increase friction between the feet and the ice (Stirling, 1988). The polar bear uses a terrestrial walk (Dagg, 1979) similar to that of other large carnivores; lateral legs are used to a large extent, whereas diagonal legs are seldom used (Taylor, 1989). Terrestrial locomotion in polar bears has been measured at various speeds and they can run up to 25 mph (Hurst *et al.,* 1982).

8.7. Summary and Conclusions

The pinniped skull is characterized by large orbits, a relatively short snout, a constricted interorbital region, and large orbital vacuities. The modern walrus skull is easily distinguished from that of other pinnipeds by being foreshortened and having large maxillae for accommodation of the upper canine tusks. The axial skeleton is differently developed among otariids, phocids, and the walrus. The neck vertebrae of otariids are large with well-developed processes associated with muscles for movements of the head and neck. In the walrus and in phocids the enlarged processes of the lumbar vertebrae provide attachment surfaces for hypaxial muscles associated with horizontal movements of the posterior end of the body. The bones of the pinniped fore and hind limb are short, flattened, and modified as flippers. Propulsion for swimming by marine mammals is derived from paired flipper movements (pinnipeds and the sea otter) or vertical movements of caudal flukes (cetaceans and sirenians). Among modern pinnipeds, aquatic and terrestrial locomotion are achieved differently. Otariids use pectoral oscillation and phocids and the walrus use pelvic oscillation for propulsion in water. Terrestrial locomotion is likewise achieved differently: ambulatory in walruses and otariids, sagittal undulation in phocids.

The cetacean skull differs from the typical mammalian skull because it is telescoped, the result of migration of the external narial opening to a dorsal position on the skull. In cetaceans, the vertebral column does not contain a sacral region because the pelvic girdle is lacking. The subdermal connective tissue sheath provides an enlarged surface to anchor flexor and extensor muscles of the tail. The elbow joint of modern cetaceans is uniquely immobile. The cetacean foreflipper is used primarily for steering rather than for propulsion. The cetacean flipper is unique among mammals in exhibiting hyperphalangy. The cost of transport (COT) is a useful comparison of the locomotor efficiencies between different or similar locomotor mode(s). Wave riding and porpoising behaviors of dolphins reduces their COT. The fossil record has revealed several critical steps in the transition of whales from land to sea. Archaic whales possessed a well-developed pelvis and hind limbs and walked on land. Later diverging whales reduced the hind limbs and developed large processes on the sacral vertebra indicating that caudal undulation of the body was well developed, like in modern whales.

The sirenian skull is distinguished from other marine mammals by its down-turned premaxilla. It is more sharply inclined in the dugong than in manatees. The skeleton of sirenians is pachyostotic and osteosclerotic, features involved in hydrostatic regulation. As in cetaceans, the forelimb flipper is primarily used for steering. The pelvic girdle is vestigial.

The sea otter skull is short and robust and is characterized by a blunt rostrum, prominent cheeks, and well-developed bony crests for the attachment of powerful jaw-closing muscles. Because the hind limbs are larger than the forelimbs, locomotion on land is slow and clumsy. Swimming involves undulations of the vertebral column, tail, and hindfoot. Correlated with this is an increased development of vertebral processes in the lumbosacral region for attachment of the epaxial musculature involved in swimming. Polar bears, the largest bears, use their huge plantigrade forefeet to generate propulsion in swimming. Terrestrial locomotion involves walking and running with their large paws serving for weight distribution.

8.8. Further Reading

The classic comparative treatment of the functional anatomy of pinnipeds, cetaceans, sirenians, and the sea otter is found in Howell (1930a); a summary focused on the energetics of aquatic locomotion is provided by Fish (1992). A good general introduction to pinniped musculoskeletal anatomy is King (1983). The osteology and myology of fossil and extant phocids is described by de Muizon (1981). The most thorough comparative survey of the morphology of skulls of southern fur seals is provided by Repenning *et al.* (1971). Descriptions of pinniped osteology and musculature in varying degrees of detail are given for the bearded seal (Mikker, 1888), Ross seal (King, 1969; Pierard and Bisaillon, 1979), Weddell seal (Howell, 1929; Pierard, 1971), hooded seal, Antarctic fur seal (Miller, 1888), California sea lion (Howell, 1929; Mori, 1958), Steller sea lion (Murie, 1872, 1874), Pacific walrus (Murie, 1871; Bisaillon and Pierard, 1981; Kastelein *et al.,* 1991), harbor seal (Miller, 1888), baikal seal (Koster *et al.,* 1990), ringed seal (Miller, 1888; Howell, 1929), and the southern elephant seal (Bryden, 1971).

Accounts of the cetacean skeleton are provided for the right whale (Eschricht and Reinhardt, 1866), minke whale (Omura, 1975), pygmy blue whale (Omura *et al.,* 1970), Cuvier's beaked whale (Omura, 1972), and the bottlenose dolphin (Rommel, 1990). Detailed descriptions of cetacean musculature are given for the pygmy sperm whale (Schulte and Smith, 1918), sperm whale (Berzin, 1972), porpoises (Boenninghaus, 1902; Schulte, 1916; Howell, 1927; Moris, 1969; Sokolov and Rodinov, 1974; Mead, 1975; Smith *et al.,* 1976; Kastelein *et al.,* 1997), Sei whale (Carte and McAlister, 1868; Schulte, 1916), Risso's dolphin (Murie, 1871), pilot whale (Murie, 1874), narwhal (Hein, 1914; Howell, 1930b), bottlenose dolphin (Huber, 1934), and susu (Pilleri *et al.,* 1976). Principal references for descriptions of the facial anatomy of odontocetes include Lawrence and Schevill (1956), Mead (1975), Purves and Pilleri (1973), Schenkkan (1973), Heyning (1989), Curry (1992), and Cranford *et al.* (1996).

An atlas of the osteology of sirenians is provided by Kaiser (1974). Detailed description of the myology of the dugong is given by Domning (1977) and for the Amazonian manatee see Domning (1978). The osteology of the West Indian manatee is described by Quiring and Harlan (1953). Brief reviews of the musculoskeletal anatomy and locomotion in the manatee are in Caldwell and Caldwell (1985); for the dugong see Nishiwaki and Marsh (1985) and Reynolds and Odell (1991).

Principal contributors to the osteology and myology of the sea otter include Taylor (1914), Gambarajan and Karapetjan (1961), and Howard (1973, 1975). For an account of the limb anatomy of the sea otter with reference to locomotion see Tarasoff and Whitt (1972).

References

Adam, P. J. and A. Berta. (1998). Using a phylogenetic paradigm to test hypotheses of the evolution of locomotor styles in the Pinnipedimorpha (Mammalia). Paleobios, 1998 Conference Abstracts Supplement, 1A.

Adam, P. J. and A. Berta (1997). Osteo indicators of locomotor type and their utility in determining evolutionary pattern in the Pinnipedimorpha. *Abst. 57th Ann. Meet. Soc. Vert. Paleo.* Chicago, p. 28A.

Backhouse, K. M. (1961). Locomotion of seals with particular reference to the forelimb. *Symp. Zool. Soc. London* **5**: 59–75.

Barabash-Nikiforov, I. I. (1947). "Kalan" (The sea otter). Soviet Ministrov RSFSR. (Translated from Russian, Israel Program for Scientific Translations, Jerusalem, 1962).

Barabash-Nikifrov, I. I., S. V. Marakov, and A. M. Nikolaev (1968). Otters (sea otters). Izd-vo Nauka, Leningrad, 184 pp. [in Russian].

Barnes, L. G., and S. A. McLeod (1984). The fossil record and phyletic relationships of gray whales. *In* "The Gray Whale" (M. L. Jones and S. L. Swartz, eds.), pp. 3–28. Academic Press, New York.

Beentjes, M. P. (1990). Comparative terrestrial locomotion of the Hooker's sea lion (*Phocarctos hookeri*) and the New Zealand fur seal (*Arctocephalus forsteri*): Evolutionary and ecological implications. *Zool. J. Linn. Soc.* **98**: 307–325.

Berta, A., and C. E. Ray (1990). Skeletal morphology and locomotor capabilities of the archaic pinniped *Enaliarctos mealsi. J. Vertebr. Paleontol.* **10**(2): 141–157.

Berzin, A. A. (1972). "The Sperm Whale" (A. V. Yablokov, ed.). (Translated from Russian, Israel Program for Scientific Translations, Jerusalem).

Bisaillon, A., and J. Pierard (1981). Oseologie du Morse de l'Atlantique (*Odobenus rosmarus,* L., 1758) Ceintures et membres. *Zentralbl. Veterinaer med., Reihe C.* **10**: 310–327.

Blickhan, R., and J.-Y. Cheng (1994). Energy storage by elastic mechanisms in the tail of large swimmers—a re-revaluation. *J. Theor. Biol.* **168**: 315–321.

Boenninghaus, G. (1902). Der Rachen von *Phocaena communis. Zool. Jahrb.* **17**(1-2): 1–98.

Buchholtz, E. A. (1998). Implications of vertebral morphology for locomotor evolution in early Cetacea. *In* "The Emergence of Whales: Patterns in the Origin of Cetacea" (J. G. M. Thewissen, ed.), pp. 325–351. Plenum Press, New York.

Bryden, M. M. (1971). Myology of the southern elephant seal *Mirounga leonina* (L.). *Antarc. Res. Ser.* **18**: 109–140.

Bryden, M. M. and W. J. L. Felts (1974). Quantitative anatomical observations on the skeletal and muscular system of four species of Antarctic seals. *J. Anat.* **118**(3): 589–600.

Burns, J. J. (1981). Ribbon Seal-*Phoca fasciata* Zimmerman, 1783 pp. 89–109, *In* "Handbook of Marine Mammals" (S. H. Ridgway and R. J. Harrison, eds.), Academic Press, London.

Caldwell, D. K., and M. C. Caldwell (1985). Manatees. *In* "Handbook of Marine Mammals" (S. H. Ridgway and R. Harrison, eds.), pp. 33–66. Academic Press, New York.

Carte, A. and A. McAlister (1868). On the anatomy of *Balaenoptera rostrata. Phil. Trans. Royal Soc. London* **158**.

Chanin, P. (1985). The Natural History of Otters. Croom Helm, London,

Clarke, M. R. (1970). Function of the spermaceti organ of the sperm whale. *Nature (London)* **228**: 873–974.

Clarke, M. R. (1978). Buoyancy control as a function of the spermaceti organ in the sperm whale. *J. Mar. Biol. Assoc. U.K.* **58**: 27–51.

Clarke, M. R. (1979). The head of the sperm whale. *Sci. Am.* **240**(1): 106–117.

Coffey, D. L. (1977). "Dolphins, Whales and Porpoises." MacMillan Press, New York.

Cranford, T. W., M. Amundin, and K. S. Norris (1996). Functional morphology and homology in the odontocete nasal complex: Implications for sound generation. *J. Morphol.* **228**: 223–285.

Curry, B. E. (1992). Facial anatomy and potential function of facial structures for sound production in the harbor porpoise (*Phocoena phocoena*) and Dall's porpoise (*Phocoenoides dalli*). *Can. J. Zool.* **70**: 2103–2114.

Dagg, A. I. (1979). The walk of the large quadrupedal mammals. *Can. J. Zool.* **57**: 1157–1163.

Davis, D. D. (1949). The shoulder architecture of bears and other carnivores. *Fieldiana, Zool.* **31**: 285–305.

Dawson, S. D. (1994). Allometry of cetacean forelimb bones. *J. Morphol.* **222**: 215–221.

de Buffrénil, V., J. Y. Sire, and D. Schoevaert (1986). Comparaison de la structure et du volume squelettique entre un delphinidé (*Delphinus delphis* L.) et un mammifere terrestre. (*Panthera leo* L.) *Can. J. Zool.* **64**: 1750–1756.

de Buffrénil, V. and Casinos, A. (1995). Observations histologiques sur le rostre de *Mesoplodon densirostris* (Mammalia, Cetacea, Ziphiidae): Le tissu osseux le plus dense connu. *Ann. Sci. Nat., Zool. Biol. Anim.* [14] **16**: 21–32.

Deméré, T. A. (1986). The fossil whale *Balaenoptera davidsonii* (Cope, 1872), with a review of other Neogene species of *Balaenoptera* (Cetacea: Mysticeti). *Mar. Mamm. Sci.* **2**(4): 277–298.

Deméré, T. A. (1994). The Family Odobenidae: A phylogenetic analysis of fossil and living taxa. *Proc. San Diego Soc. Nat. Hist.* **29**: 99–123.

DeSmet, W. M. A. (1977). The regions of the cetacean vertebral column. *In* "Functional Anatomy of Marine Mammals" (R. J. Harrison, ed.), Vol. 3, pp. 59–79. Academic Press, London.

Domning, D. P. (1977). Observations on the myology of *Dugong dugong* (Muller). *Smithson. Contrib. Zool.* **226**: 1–56.

Domning, D. P. (1978). The myology of the Amazonian manatee, *Trichechus inunguis* (Natterer) (Mammalia: Sirenia). *Acta Amazonica,* **8**(2): Suppl. 1.

Domning, D. P. (1991). Sexual and ontogenetic variation in the pelvic bones of *Dugong dugon* (Sirenia). *Mar. Mamm. Sci.* **7**(3): 311–316.

Domning, D. P. (1996). The readaptation of Eocene sirenians to life in the water. *In* "Abstracts of the Conference on Secondary Adaptation to Life in the Water" (J.-M. Mazin, P. Vignaud, and V. de Buffrénil, eds.), p. 5. Poitiers, France.

Domning, D. P., and V. de Buffrénil (1991). Hydrostasis in the Sirenia: Quantitative data and functional interpretations. *Mar. Mamm. Sci.* **7**(4): 331–368.

English, A. W. (1974). Functional anatomy of the forelimb in pinnipeds. Unpublished PhD thesis, University of Illinois at the Medical Center, Chicago.

English, A. W. (1976). Limb movements and locomotor function in the California sea lion (*Zalophus californianus*). *J. Zool. Soc. London* **178**: 341–364.

English, A. W. (1977). Structural correlates of forelimb function in fur seals and sea lions. *J. Morphol.* **151**: 325–352.

Eschricht, D. F. and J. Reinhardt (1866). I. On the Greenland right-whale (*Balaena mysticetus*). *In* "Recent Memoirs on the Cetacea" (W. H. Flower, ed.), pp. 1–45. Ray Society, London.

Estes, J. (1989). Adaptations for aquatic living by carnivores. *In* "Carnivore Behavior, Ecology and Evolution" (J. L. Gittleman, ed.), pp. 242–282. Cornell University Press, Ithaca, NY.

Evans, P. G. H. (1987). "The Natural History of Whales and Dolphins." Facts on File, New York.

Ewer, R. F. (1973). "The Carnivores," Cornell University Press, Ithaca, NY.

Fay, F. H. (1981). Walrus-*Odobenus rosmarus*. pp. 1–23. *In* "Handbook of Marine Mammals, I" (Ridgway, S. H. and R. J. Harrison, eds.), Academic Press, London.

Feldkamp, S. D. (1987). Forelimb propulsion in the California sea lion *Zalophus californianus*. *J. Zool. Soc. London* **212**: 4333–4357.

Felts, W. J. L. (1966). Some functional and structural characteristics of cetacean flippers and flukes. *In* "Whales, Dolphins and Porpoises" (K. S. Norris, ed.), pp. 255–276. University of California Press, Berkeley.

Fish, F. E. (1992). Aquatic locomotion. *In* "Mammalian Energetics: Interdisciplinary Views of Metabolism and Reproduction" (T. E. Tomasci and T. H. Horton, eds.), pp. 34–63. Cornell University Press, Ithaca, NY.

Fish, F. E. (1993). Influence of hydrodynamic design and propulsive mode on mammalian swimming energetics. *Aust. J. Zool.* **42**: 79–101.

Fish, F. E. (1996). Transition from drag-based to lift-based propulsion in mammalian swimming. *Am. Zool.* **36**: 628–641.

Fish, F. (1998). Biomechanical perspective on the origin of cetacean flukes. *In* "The Emergence of Whales: Patterns in the Origin of Cetacea" (J. G. M. Thewissen, ed.), pp. 303–324. Plenum Press, New York.

Fish, F. E., and J. M. Battle (1995). Hydrodynamic design of the humpback whale flipper. *J. Morphol.* **225**: 51–60.

Fish, F. E., and C. A. Hui (1991). Dolphin swimming—a review. *Mamm. Rev.* **21**(4): 181–195.

Fish, F. E., S. Innes, and K. Ronald (1988). Kinematics and estimated thrust production of swimming harp and ringed seals. *J. Exp. Biol.* **137**: 157–173.

Flyger, V., and M. R. Townsend (1968). The migration of polar bears. *Sci. Am.* **218**: 108–116.

Fordyce, E., and L. G. Barnes (1994). The evolutionary history of whales and dolphins. *Ann. Rev. Earth Planet. Sci.* **22**: 419–455.

Fraser, F. C., and P. E. Purves (1960). Hearing in cetaceans. *Bull. Br. Mus. (Nat. Hist.), Zool.* **7**(1).

Gambarajan, P. P., and W. S. Karpetjan (1961). Besonderheiten im Bau des Seelöwen (*Eumetopias californianus*), der Baikalrobbe (*Phoca sibirica*) und des Seotters (*Enhydra lutris*) in anpassung an die Fortbewegung im Wasser. *Zool. Jahrb. Anat.* **79**: 123–148.

Giffin, E. B. and M. Gillett (1996). Neurological and osteological definition of cervical vertebrae in mammals. *Brain Behav. Evol.* **47**: 214–218.

Gingerich, P. D., S. M. Raza, M. Arif, M. Anwar, and X. Zhou (1994). New whale from the Eocene of Pakistan and the origin of cetacean swimming. *Science* **368**: 844–847.

Gingerich, P. D., B. H. Smith, and E. L. Simons (1990). Hind limbs of *Basilosaurus:* Evidence of feet in whales. *Science* **249**: 403–406.

Godfrey, S. J. (1985). Additional observations of subaqueous locomotion in the California Sea Lion (*Zalophus californianus*). *Aquat. Mamm.* **11**(2): 53–57.

Gordon, K. (1981). Locomotor behaviour of the walrus (*Odobenus*). *J. Zool. Soc. London* **195**: 349–367.

Gregory, W. K. (1951). Evolution Emerging, vol. 2. Maximillan, New York.

Hansen, M. T., and R. H. Defran (1993). The behavior and feeding ecology of the Pacific coast bottlenose dolphin, *Tursiops truncatus*. *Aquat. Mamm.* **19**: 127–142.

Harrison, R. H., and M. M. Bryden (1988). "Whales, Dolphins and Porpoises." Facts on File, New York.

Harrison, R. H., and J. E. King (1965). Marine Mammals, 2nd ed., Hutchinson, London.

Hartman, D. S. (1979). Ecology and behavior of the manatee (*Trichechus manatus*) in Florida. *Am. Soc. Mammal. Spec. Publ.*, No. 5.

Hein, S. A. A. (1914). The larynx and its surrounding in *Monodon*. *Verhand. Kor. Adkad. Wetensch.* **2-18**(3): 4–54.

Heyning, J. E. (1984). Functional morphology involved in intraspecific fighting of the beaked whale *Mesoplodon carlhubbsi*. *Can. J. Zool.* **62**: 1645–1654.

Heyning, J. E. (1989). Comparative facial anatomy of beaked whales (Ziphiidae) and a systematic revision among the families of extant Odontoceti. *Nat. Hist. Mus. Los Angeles Cty.* **405**: 1–64.

Heyning, J. E., and J. G. Mead (1990). Function of the nasal anatomy of cetaceans. *In* "Sensory Abilities of Cetaceans" (J. Thomas and R. Kastelein, eds.), pp. 67–79. Plenum, New York.

Hind, A. T., and W. S. C. Gurney (1997). The metabolic cost of swimming in marine homeotherms. *J. Exp. Biol.* **200**: 531–542.

Howard, L. D. (1973). Muscular anatomy of the forelimb of the sea otter (*Enhydra lutris*). *Proc. Calif. Acad. Sci.* **39**(20): 411–500.

Howard, L. D. (1975). Muscular anatomy of the hind limb of the sea otter (*Enhydra lutris*). *Proc. Calif. Acad. Sci.* **40**(12): 335–416.

Howell, A. B. (1927). Contribution to the anatomy of the Chinese finless porpoise, *Neomeris phocaenoides. Proc. U.S. Natl. Mus.* **70**(Artic. 13): 1–43.

Howell, A. B. (1929). Contribution to the comparative anatomy of the eared and earless seals (Genera *Zalophus* and *Phoca*). *Proc. U.S. Natl. Mus.* **73**(Artic. 15): 1–142.

Howell, A. B. (1930a). "Aquatic Mammals." Thomas, Springfield, IL.

Howell, A. B. (1930b). Myology of the narwhal (*Monodon*). *Am. J. Sci.* **46**(2): 187–215.

Huber, E. (1934). Anatomical notes on Pinnipedia and Cetacea. *Carnegie Inst. Washington Publ.* **447**: 105–136.

Hulbert, R. C. and R. Petkewich (1991). Innominate of a middle Eocene (Lutetian) protocetid whale from Georgia. *Abst. 51st Ann. Meet. Soc. Vert. Paleo.,* San Diego, CA.

Hulbert, R. C. Jr., R. M. Petkewich, G. A. Bishop, D. Bukry and D. P. Aleshire (1998). A new middle Eocene protocetid whale (Mammalia: Cetacea: Archaeoceti) and associated biota from Georgia. *Journal of Paleontology* **72**: 907–927.

Hurst, R. J., M. L. Leonard, P. Beckerton, and N. A. Øritsland (1982). Polar bear locomotion: Body temperature and energetic cost. *Can. J. Zool.* **60**: 222–228.

Husar, S. (1977). The West Indian manatee (*Trichechus manatus*). *Res. Rep.—U.S. Fish Wildl. Serv.* **7**: 1–22.

Husar, S. (1978). *Trichechus sengalensis. Mamm. Species* **89**: 1–3.

Kaiser, H. E. (1974). "Morphology of the Sirenia: A Macroscopic and X-ray Atlas of the Osteology of Recent Species." Karger, Basel.

Kastelein, R. A. N. M. Gerrits, and J. L. Dubbledam (1991). The anatomy of the walrus head (*Odobenus rosmarus*). Part 2: Description of the muscles and of their role in feeding and haul-out behavior. *Aquat. Mamm.* **17**(3): 156–180.

Kastelein, R. A., J. L. Dubbledam, J. Luksenburg, C. Staal, and A. A. H. van Immerseel (1997). Anatomical atlas of an adult female harbour porpoise (*Phocoena phocoena*). *In* "The Biology of the Harbour Porpoise" (A. J. Read, P. R. Wiepkema, and P. E. Nachtigall, eds.), pp. 87–178. De Spil Publishers, Woerden, The Netherlands.

Kellogg, R. (1928). The history of whales—their adaptation to life in the water. *Quart. Rev. Biol.* **3**(1): 29–76.

Kenyon, K. (1981). Sea Otter-*Enhydra lutris. In* "Handbook of Marine Mammals" (S. H. Ridgway and R. J. Harrison, eds.), pp. 209–223, Academic Press, New York.

King, J. E. (1966). Relationships of the hooded and elephant seals (genera *Cystophora* and *Mirounga*). *J. Zool. Soc. London* **148**: 385–398.

King, J. E. (1969). Some aspects of the anatomy of the Ross Seal, *Ommatophoca rossi* (Pinnipedia: Phocidae). *Br. Antarct. Surv. Sci. Rep.* **63**:1–54.

King, J. E. (1983). "Seals of the World." Oxford Univ. Press, London.

Kooyman, G. (1981). Leopard seal, *Hydrurga leptonyx,* pp. 261–274. *In* "Handbook of Marine Mammals, vol. 2, Seals" (S. H. Ridgway and R. J. Harrison, eds.), Academic Press, London.

Koster, M. D., K. Ronald, and P. Van Bree (1990). Thoracic anatomy of the Baikal seal compared with some phocid seals. *Can. J. Zool.* **68**: 168–182.

Lambert, W. D. (1997). The osteology and paleoecology of the giant otter *Enhydritherium terranovae. J. Vertebr. Paleontol.* **17**(4): 738–749.

Lang, T. G. (1975). Speed, power, and drag measurements of dolphins and porpoises, pp. 553–571. *In* "Swimming and Flying in Nature" (T. Y. Wu, C. J. Brokaw, and C. Brennen, eds.), Plenum, New York.

Lang, T. G. and K. Pryor (1966). Hydrodynamic performance of porpoises (*Stenella attenuata*). *Science* **152**: 531–533.

Lawrence, B., and W. E. Schevill (1956). The functional anatomy of the delphinid nose. *Bull. Mus. Comp. Zool.* **114**: 103–151.

Le Boeuf, B. J., Y. Naito, T. Asaga, D. Crocker, and D. P. Costa (1992). Swim speeds in a female northern elephant seal: metabolic and foraging implications. *Can. J. Zool.* **70**: 786–795.

Litchfield, C., and A. J. Greenberg (1974). Comparative lipid patterns in the melon fats of dolphins, porpoises and toothed whales. *Comp. Biochem. Physiol.* **47**: 401–407.

Litchfield, C., A. J. Greenberg, D. K. Caldwell, M. C. Caldwell, J. C. Sipos, and R. G. Ackman (1975). Comparative lipid patterns in acoustical and nonacoustical fatty tissues of dolphins, porpoises and toothed whales. *Comp. Biochem. Physiol. B* **50B**: 591–597.

Long, J. H., D. A. Pabst, W. R. Shepard, and W. A. McLellan (1997). Locomotor design of dolphin vertebral columns: Bending mechanics and morphology of *Delphinus delphis. J. Exp. Biol.* **200**: 65–81.

Macdonald, D. (ed.) (1984). "All the World's Animals Sea Mammals." Torstar, New York.

Mead, J. (1975). Anatomy of the external nasal passages and facial complex in the Delphinidae (Mammalia: Cetacea). *Smithson. Contrib. Zool.* **207**: 1–72.

Milinkovitch, M. (1995). Molecular phylogeny of cetaceans prompts revision of morphological transformations. *Trends Ecol. Evol.* **10**(8): 328–334.

Miller, W. C. G. (1888). The myology of the Pinnipedia. *In* "Report on the Scientific Results of the Voyage of the H.M.S. Challenger," Vol. 26, No. 2, pp. 139–240. Challenger Office, 1880–1895, Edinburgh.

Moore, J. C. (1956). Observations of manatees in aggregations. *Am. Mus. Novit.* **1811**: 1–24.

Moore, J. C. (1957). Newborn young of a captive manatee. *J. Mamm.* **38**: 137–138.

Mori, M. (1958). The skeleton and musculature of *Zalophus. Okajimas Folia Anat. Jpn.* **31**: 203–284.

Moris, F. (1969). Étude anatomique de la région cephalique du marouin, *Phocoena phocoena* L. (cétacé odontocete). *Mammalia* **33**(4): 666–726.

Muizon, C. de (1981). "Les Vertébrés Fossiles de la Formation Piscou (Pérou) Part 1. Recherches sur les Grandes Civilisations," Mem. No. 6. Institut Français d'Etudes Andines, Paris.

Murie, J. (1870). Researches upon the anatomy of the Pinnipedia. Part I. On the walrus (*Trichechus rosmarus,* Linn.). *Trans. Zool. Soc. London* **7**: 411–464.

Murie, J. (1871). On Risso's *Grampus. J. Anat. Physiol. Norm. Pathol. Homme Anim.* **5**: 118.

Murie, J. (1872). Researches upon the anatomy of the Pinnipedia. Part 2. Descriptive anatomy of the sea lion (*Otaria jubata*). *Trans. Zool. Soc. London* **7**: 527–596.

Murie, J. (1874). Researches upon the anatomy of the Pinnipedia. Part 3. Descriptive anatomy of the sea lion (*Otaria jubata*). *Trans. Zool. Soc. London* **8**: 501–582.

Nishiwaki, M. and H. Marsh (1985). Dugong *Dugong dugon* (Muller, 1776). "Handbook of Marine Mammals." vol. 33, pp. 1–31. The Sirenians and Baleen Whales. Academic Press, New York.

Nomina Anatomica Veterinaria (1983). 5th ed. Williams and Wilkens, Baltimore, Maryland.

Norris, K. S. (1964). Some problems of echolocation in cetaceans. *In* "Marine Bio-acoustics" (W. N. Tavolga, ed.), pp. 317–336. Pergamon, Oxford.

Norris, K. S. (1968). The evolution of acoustic mechanisms in odontocete cetaceans. *In* "Evolution and Environment" (E. T. Drake, ed.), pp. 297–324. Yale Univ. Press, New Haven.

Norris, K. S. (1969). The echolocation of marine mammals. *In* "The Biology of Marine Mammals" (H. T. Anderson, ed.), pp. 391–423. Academic Press, New York.

Norris, K. S., and G. W. Harvey (1974). Sound transmission in the porpoise head. *J. Acoust. Soc. Am.* **56**: 659–664.

Norris, K. S., and C. M. Johnson (1994). Locomotion. *In* "The Hawaiian Spinner Dolphin" (K. S. Norris, B. Wursig, R. S. Wells, and M. Wursig, eds.), pp. 201–205. University of California Press, Berkeley.

O'Gorman, F. (1963). Observations on terrestrial locomotion in Antarctic seals. *Proc. Zool. Soc. London* **141**: 837–850.

Omura, H. (1972). An osteological study of the Cuvier's beaked whale *Ziphius cavirostris,* in the northwest Pacific. *Sci. Rep. Whales Res. Inst.* **24**: 1–34.

Omura, H. (1975). Osteological study of the minke whale from the Antarctic. *Sci. Rep. Whales Res. Inst.* **27**: 1–36.

Omura, H., T. Ichihara, and T. Kasuya (1970). Osteology of pygmy blue whale with additional information on external and other characteristics. *Sci. Rep. Whales Res. Inst.* **22**: 1–27.

Pabst, D. A. (1990). Axial muscles and connective tissues of the bottlenose dolphin. *In* "The Bottlenose Dolphin" (S. Leatherwood and R. R. Reeves, eds.), pp. 51–67. Academic Press, San Diego, CA.

Pabst, D. A. (1993). Intramuscular morphology and tendon geometry of the epaxial swimming muscles of dolphins. *J. Zool. Soc. London* **230**: 159–176.

Pierard, J. (1971). Osteology and myology of the Weddell Seal *Leptonychotes weddelli* (Lesson, 1826). *Antarct. Res. Ser.* **18**: 53–108.

Pierard, J., and A. Bisaillon (1979). Osteology of the Ross Seal, *Ommatophoca rossi* Gray, 1844. *Antarct. Res. Ser.* **31**: 1–24.

Ponganis, P. J., E. P. Ponganis, K. V. Ponganis, G. L. Kooyman, G. L. Gentry, and F. Trillmich (1990). Swimming velocities in otariids. *Can. J. Zool.* **68**: 2105–2112.

Pouchet, M. G. and H. Beauregard (1892). Sur "l'organe des spermaceti." *Comptes Rendus de Societe Biologique* **11**: 343–344.

Purves, P. E., and G. Pilleri (1973). Observations on the ear, nose, throat and eye of *Platanista indi. Invest. Cetacea* **5**: 13–57.

Quiring, D. P., and C. F. Harlan (1953). On the anatomy of the manatee. *J. Mammal.* **34**(2): 192–203.

Rayner, J. M. V. (1986). Pleuston: animal which moves in water and air. *Endeavour* **10**: 58–64.

Reidenberg, J. S., and J. T. Laitman (1994). Anatomy of the hyoid apparatus in Odontoceti (Toothed whales): specializations of their skeleton and musculature compared with those of terrestrial mammals. *Anat. Rec.* **240**: 598–624.

Repenning, C. E., R. S. Peterson, and C. L. Hubbs (1971). Contributions to the systematics of the southern fur seals, with particular reference to the Juan Fernandez and Guadalupe species. *In* "Antarctic Pinnipedia" (W. H. Burt, ed.), pp. 1–34. *Antarct. Res. Ser.* **18**, American Geophysical Union, Washington, D.C.

Reynolds, J., and D. Odell (1991). "Manatees and Dugongs." Facts on File, New York.

Ridgway, S. (1971). Buoyancy regulation in deep diving whales. *Nature* **232**: 133–134.

Ridoux, V., C. Guinent, C. Liret, P. Creton, R. Steenstrup, and G. Beauplet (1997). A video sonar as a new tool to study marine mammals in the wild: Measurements of dolphin swimming speed. *Mar. Mamm. Sci.* **13**(2): 196–206.

Roest, A. I. (1993). Asymmetry in the skulls of California sea otters (*Enhydra lutris nereis*). *Mar. Mamm. Sci.* **9**(2): 190–194.

Rommel, S. (1990). Osteology of the bottlenose dolphin. *In* "The Bottlenose Dolphin" (S. Leatherwood and R. R. Reeves, eds.), pp. 29–49. Academic Press, San Diego, CA.

Schenkkan, E. J. (1973). On the comparative anatomy and function of the nasal tract in odontocetes (Mammalia, Cetacea). *Bijdra. Dierkd.* **43**: 127–159.

Schenkkan, E. J., and P. E. Purves (1973). The comparative anatomy of the nasal tract and the function of the spermaceti organ in the Physeteridae (Mammalia, Odontoceti). *Bijdr. Dierkd.* **43**: 93–112.

Schulte, H. von W. (1916). Anatomy of a fetus of *Balaenoptera borealis. Mem. Am. Mus. Nat. Hist.* **1**(6): 389–502.

Schulte, H. von W., and M. De F. Smith (1918). The external characters, skeletal muscles and peripheral nerves of *Kogia breviceps. Bulle. Am. Mus. Nat. Hist.* **38**(7).

Sedmera, D., I. Misek, and M. Klima (1997a). On the development of cetacean extremities: I. Hind limb rudimentation in the spotted dolphin (*Stenella attenuata*). *Eur. J. Morphol.* **35**(1): 25–30.

Sedmera, D., I. Misek, and M. Klima (1997b). On the development of cetacean extremities: II. Morphogenesis and histogenesis of the flippers in the spotted dolphin (*Stenella attenuata*). *Eur. J. Morphol.* **35**(2): 117–123.

Slijper, E. J. (1936). Die Cetaceen, vergleichendantomisch und systematisch. *Capita Zool.* **6/7**: 1–600.

Slijper, E. J. (1962). "Whales." Hutchinson, London.

Smith, G. J. D., K. W. Browne, and D. E. Gaskin (1976). Functional myology of the harbour porpoise, *Phocoena phocoena* (L.). *Can. J. Zool.* **54**: 716–729.

Stirling, I. (1988). "Polar Bears." University of Michigan Press, Ann Arbor.

Strickler, T. L. (1978). Myology of the shoulder of *Pontoporia blainvillei,* including a review of the literature on shoulder morphology in the Cetacea. *Am. J. Anat.* **152**(3): 419–432.

Sumich, J. (1983). Swimming velocities, breathing patterns, and estimated costs of locomotion in migrating gray whales, *Eschrichtius robustus. Can. J. Zool.* **61**: 647–652.

Tarasoff, F. J. (1972). Comparative aspects of the hind limbs of the river otter, sea otter and seals. *In* "Functional Anatomy of Marine Mammals" (R. J. Harrison, ed.), Vol. 1, pp. 333–359. Academic Press, London.

Tarasoff, F. J., A. Bisaillon, J. Pierard, and A. P. Whitt (1972). Locomotory patterns and external morphology of the river otter, sea otter, and harp seal (Mammalia). *Can. J. Zool.* **50**: 915–929.

Taylor, M. E. (1989). Locomotor adaptations by carnivores. *In* "Carnivore Behavior, Ecology and Evolution" (J. L. Gittleman, ed.), pp. 382–409. Cornell University Press, Ithaca, NY.

Taylor, W. P. (1914). The problem of aquatic adaptation in the Carnivora, as illustrated in the osteology and evolution of the sea-otter. *Univ. Calif., Berkeley, Publ. Dep. Geol.* **7**(25): 465–495.

Thewissen, J. G. M., and Fish, F. E. (1997). Locomotor evolution in the earliest cetaceans: Functional model, modern analogues, and paleontologic evidence. *Paleobiology* **23**(4): 482–490.

Thewissen, J. G. M., S. I. Madar, and S. T. Hussain (1996). *Ambulocetus natans,* an Eocene cetacean (Mammalia) from Pakistan. *CFS, Cour. Forschungsinst. Senckenberg* **191**: 1–86.

True, F. W. (1904). The whale bone whales of the western North Atlantic. Smithsonian Contributions to Knowledge, **33**: 192–210.

Tucker, V. A. (1975). The energetic cost of moving about. *Am. Sci.* **63**: 413–419.

Uhen, M. D. (1999). New species of protocetid archaeocete whale, *Eocetus wardii* (Mammalia: Cetacea), from the middle Eocene of North Carolina. *Journal of Paleontology* **73**: 512–528.

Uspenskii, S. M. (1977). Belyi Medved (The Polar Bear) Moscow: Navka. Unedited translation by Government of Canada Translation Bureau, No. 1541321, June, 1978.

Watson, A. (1994). Polydactyly in a bottlenose dolphin, *Tursiops truncatus. Mar. Mamm. Sci.* **10**(1): 93–100.

Webb, P. W. (1975). Hydrodynamics and energetics of fish propulsion. *Bull. Fish. Res. Board Can.* **190**: 1–158.

Williams, T. M. (1989). Swimming by sea otters: Adaptations for low energetic cost locomotion. *J. Comp. Physiol., A* **164**: 815–824.

Williams, T. M., W. A. Friedl, M. L. Fong, R. M. Yamada, P. Sedivy, and J. E. Haun (1992). Travel at low energetic cost by swimming and wave-riding bottlenose dolphins. *Nature* **355**: 821–823.

Williams, T. M., S. F. Shippee, and M. J. Rothe (1996). Strategies for reducing foraging costs in dolphins. *In* "Aquatic Predators and their Prey" (S. P. R. Greenstreet and M. L. Tasker, eds.), pp. 4–9. Fishing News (Blackwell Science, Ltd.), London.

Withers, P. C. (1992). "Comparative Animal Physiology." Saunders, Fort Worth, TX.

Wood, F. G. (1964). General Discussion. *In* "Marine Bio-Acoustics, vol 1." (W. N. Tavolga, ed.), pp. 395–398. Pergamon, New York.

Wyss, A. R. (1988). On "retrogression" in the evolution of the Phocinae and phylogenetic affinities of the monk seals. *Am. Mus. Novit.* **2924**: 1–38.

Yablokov, A. V., Bel'kovich, V. M., and V. I. Borisov (1972). Whales and Dolphins, Israel Programs for Scientific Translations, Jerusalem.

Zioupos, P., J. D. Currey, A. Casinos, and V. de Buffrénil (1997). Mechanical properties of the rostrum of the whale *Mesoplodon densirostris,* a remarkably dense bony tissue. *J. Zool.* **241**: 725–737.

9

Respiration, Diving, and Breath-Hold Physiology

9.1. Introduction

A prominent feature of the normal behavior of marine mammals is their frequent and often prolonged breath-hold diving. The details of diving behavior often are difficult to observe and interpret, for they usually occur well below the sea surface. Whether making extended dives below the surface to forage for food, to increase swimming efficiency by diving below the high drag conditions found at the surface, or to avoid predators, many marine mammals are well adapted to dive to great depths, or to stay below the surface for extended periods of time, or both.

Measured either as maximal depth of dive or maximal duration of breath hold, the diving capabilities of marine mammals vary immensely. Some are little better than the Ama pearl divers of Japan who, without the aid of supplementary air supplies, repeatedly dive to depths of 25 m and remain underwater for 30 to 90 seconds (Karmiol, 1978). The maximal free-diving depth for humans is greater than 70 m; breath holds lasting as long as six minutes have been independently achieved, although not while diving (Arnold, 1985). However, even the best efforts of humans pale in comparison to the dives of some whales and pinnipeds (Table 9.1). With dive times sometimes exceeding one hour, these exceptional divers are no longer closely tied to the surface by their need for air. Instead, they have increased freedom to explore and exploit the deeper portions of their environment, surfacing only occasionally for air.

9.2. Problems of Deep and Prolonged Dives for Breath-Holders

Aristotle recognized over 20 centuries ago that dolphins are air-breathing mammals. However, it was not until the middle of the twentieth century that the physiological basis for the deep and prolonged breath-holding dives by marine mammals was explored. Unlike human SCUBA divers who carry air for breathing under water, marine mammals must cease breathing during

Table 9.1. Maximum dive depths and breath-holding capabilities of marine mammals.

Species	Maximal depth (m)	Maximal duration of breath hold (min.)	Source
Pinnipeds			
Phocids			
Northern elephant seal			
male	1530	77	Schreer and Kovacs (1997)*
female	1273	62	Schreer and Kovacs (1997)*
Southern elephant seal			
female	1430	120	Slip *et al.* (1994)
male	1282	88.5	Slip *et al.* (1994)
Weddell seal	626	82	Castellini *et al.* (1992)
Crabeater seal	528	10.8	Schreer and Kovacs (1997)*
Harbor seal	508	?	Schreer and Kovacs (1997)*
Harp seal	370	16	Schreer and Kovacs (1997)*
Gray seal	268	32	Schreer and Kovacs (1997)*
Hawaiian monk seal		12	Hochachka and Mottishaw (1998)
Ross seal		9.8	Hochachka and Mottishaw (1998)*
Otariids			
California sea lion	482	15	Schreer and Kovacs (1997)*
Hooker's sea lion	474	12	Schreer and Kovacs (1997)*
Steller sea lion	424	16	Schreer and Kovacs (1997)*
New Zealand fur seal	238	11	Schreer and Kovacs (1997)*
Northern fur seal	207	8	Schreer and Kovacs (1997)*
South African fur seal	204	8	Schreer and Kovacs (1997)*
Antarctic fur seal	181	10	Schreer and Kovacs (1997)*
South American fur seal	170	7	Schreer and Kovacs (1997)*
Galapagos fur seal	115	8	Schreer and Kovacs (1997)*
Southern sea lion	112	6	Schreer and Kovacs (1997)*
Australian sea lion	92	6	Schreer and Kovacs (1997)*
Guadalupe fur seal	82	18	Schreer and Kovacs (1997)*
Walrus	100	12.7	Schreer and Kovacs (1997)*
Cetaceans			
Odontocetes			
Sperm whale	3000	138	Schreer and Kovacs (1997)*
Narwhal	1000	20	Schreer and Kovacs (1997)*
Bottlenose whale	1000	120	Schreer and Kovacs (1997)*
Beluga	647	20	Schreer and Kovacs (1997)*
Pilot whale	610	20	Schreer and Kovacs (1997)*
Bottlenose dolphin	535	12	Schreer and Kovacs (1997)*
Killer whale	260	15	Schreer and Kovacs (1997)*
Pacific white sided dolphin	214	6	Schreer and Kovacs (1997)*
Dall's porpoise	180	?	Schreer and Kovacs (1997)*

continues

continued

Mysticetes			
Fin whale	500	30	Schreer and Kovacs (1997)*
Bowhead whale	300	80	Schreer and Kovacs (1997)*
Right whale	184	50	Schreer and Kovacs (1997)*
Gray whale	170	26	Schreer and Kovacs (1997)*
Humpback	148	21	Schreer and Kovacs (1997)*
Bluewhale	100	50	Schreer and Kovacs (1997)*
Sirenians			
West Indian manatee	600	6	Schreer and Kovacs (1997)*
Dugong	400	8	Schreer and Kovacs (1997)*
Sea Otter	23	2.3	Kvitek *et al.* (1993)

Note: depths and duration do not necessary correspond to same dive.
*See for original sources.

dives, and that leads to several worsening, or at least conflicting, physiological conditions during those **anaerobic** conditions (Castellini, 1985). First, oxygen stores begin to deplete when the intensity of activity is increasing and the demand for oxygen is highest. Second, without ventilation, CO_2 and **lactate** (a metabolic end product produced in vertebrates when oxygen stores are depleted) increase in both blood and muscle tissues, making the blood serum and cell fluid more acidic. During these periods of **hypoxia**, continued muscle activity is maintained anaerobically, accumulating even more lactate. Some organs, such as the brain and heart, are limited in their ability to survive prolonged periods of hypoxia, whereas kidney and liver tissue can experience dramatically reduced enzyme activity during anaerobic conditions but still maintain cell and tissue integrity (Castellini, 1985).

As mammals dive below the sea surface, they must tolerate an increase in water pressure of 1 atmosphere (atm) for each 10 m of water depth (300 atm for a sperm whale at 3000 m, Table 9.1). Increasing water pressure on the outside of an animal can squeeze air filled tissue spaces inside the animal, causing the spaces to distort or collapse as the air they contain is compressed. Absorbing gases from air at these high pressures poses some potentially serious problems for diving mammals, for oxygen can be toxic at high concentrations, nitrogen can have a narcotic (sleeping) effect on the central nervous system, and both can form damaging bubbles in tissues and blood vessels during and immediately following ascent (Moon *et al.,* 1995).

9.3. Pulmonary and Circulatory Adaptations to Diving

9.3.1. Anatomy and Physiology of the Cardiovascular System

9.3.1.1. Heart and Blood Vessels

Marine mammals undergo important circulatory changes during diving. In general, the structure of the heart of cetaceans and pinnipeds closely resembles that of other mammals (Fig. 9.1). At the ultrastructural level, several distinctive differences are observed in the hearts of ringed and harp seals, such as enlarged stores of glycogen, which may represent a

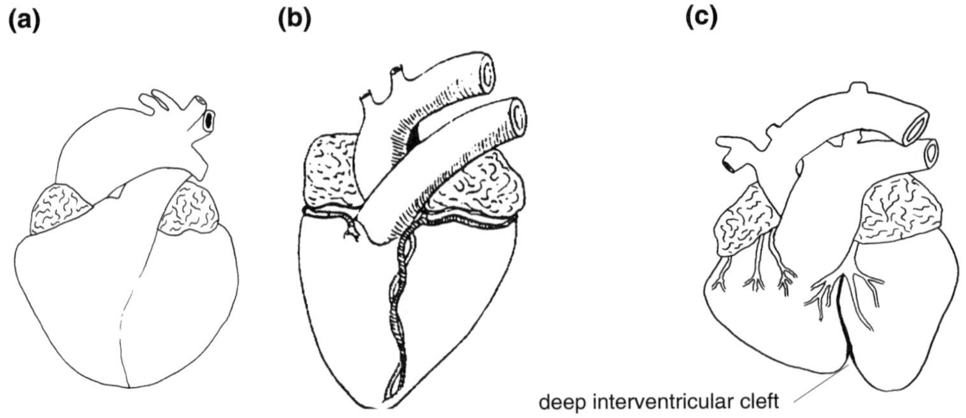

Figure 9.1. Ventral view of heart of (a) pinniped (Weddell seal) (modified from Drabek, 1977), (b) cetacean (porpoise) (modified from Slijper, 1979), and (c) sirenian (dugong) (modified from Rowlatt and Marsh, 1985).

diving adaptation (Pfeiffer and Viers, 1995). The presence of enhanced glycogen storage also occurs in the bowhead whale heart (Pfeiffer, 1990). A change in allometry of the heart with a change in physiological activity was suggested as a behavioral response to diving by Bryden and Lim (1969) who showed that the relative size of the heart of the southern elephant seal increases when diving activity begins. Ridgway and Johnston (1966) related the relatively larger heart size of the Dall's porpoise, when compared to the inshore less active Atlantic bottlenose dolphin, to its pelagic deep-diving habit.

The ascending aorta in pinnipeds increases in diameter by 30–40% immediately outside the heart to form an expanded elastic aortic bulb (aortic arch). After all the great vessels (i.e., brachiocephalic, left common carotid and left subclavian arteries) have branched from the aorta, at about the level of the ductus arteriosus, there is a sudden decrease in the diameter of the aorta by about 50%, and it then continues posteriorly as a relatively slender abdominal aorta. Although the enlarged aortic bulb is characteristic of all pinnipeds (Drabek, 1975, 1977; King, 1977), there is some correlation between the size of the bulb and the diving habits of the species. The shallow water leopard seals, for example, have a smaller bulb than the deep-diving Weddell seal. The aortic bulb and smaller arteries at the base of the brain serve to dampen blood pressure pulses at each heart beat.

A similar bulbous expansion of the aortic arch has been described in fin whales (Shadwick and Gosline, 1994; Gosline and Shadwick, 1996) and sperm whales (Melnikov, 1997). Further examination of the structural properties of the aorta and associated vessels in the fin whale (Gosline and Shadwick, 1996) indicates that most of the arterial compliance in the whale's circulation results from huge volumetric expansion in the aortic arch and differences in the mechanical properties of its walls such as the thickness and organization of elastic tissues.

In addition to having a heart with a deep interventricular cleft (double ventricular apex) extending almost the full length of the ventricles, sirenians are distinguished from other marine mammals in having a dorsally located left atrium (Fig. 9.1). In most respects the manatee heart is very similar to the dugong heart. Among the differences are the quadrate shape of the manatee left ventricle, as opposed to its conical shape in the dugong, and the bulbous swelling of the aortic arch in the manatee, similar to that seen in pinnipeds (Drabek, 1977) and fin whales (Shadwick and Gosline, 1994). It seems unlikely that expansion of the aortic arch in manatees can be attributed to differences in diving performance because all sirenians are modest divers in comparison to many other marine mammals (Rowlatt and Marsh, 1985, and see Table 9.1).

The circulatory system of marine mammals is characterized by groups of blood vessels (retia mirabilia) arranged for heat conservation (discussed in Chapter 7) in addition to serving as blood reservoirs to increase oxygen stores for use during diving (e.g. Pfeiffer and Kinkead, 1990). The main changes in the venous system of pinnipeds are the enlargement and increased complexity of veins to enhance their capacity. Most of our knowledge of these adaptations comes from work done on the venous system of phocid seals (Harrison and Kooyman, 1968; Ronald *et al.,* 1977; Fig. 9.2). In phocids, the posterior vena cava frequently is developed as paired vessels each capable of considerable distension of their thin, elastic walls. Each branch drains extensive plexi of veins in the flippers, pelvis, and lateral abdominal wall. Each branch also receives several tributaries of varying sizes from the stellate plexus which encloses the kidneys (Fig. 9.2). Just posterior to the diaphragm and covered by the lobes of the liver, lies the hepatic sinus, formed from enlarged hepatic veins and also receiving blood from the posterior vena cava and conveying it to the heart. Immediately anterior to the diaphragm, the vena cava has a muscular caval sphincter surrounding it (Fig. 9.2). Anterior to the sphincter the veins from the pericardial plexus enter the vena cava. This convoluted mass of interconnected veins (encased in brown adipose tissue) forms a ring around the base of the pericardium and sends out leaf-like projections into the pleural cavities containing the lungs. The vein walls in this region are relatively thick and contain coiled collagenous elastic, and smooth muscle fibers, all of which suggest considerable capacity for expansion.

In phocids, the greatest number of these venous modifications are combined, including the pericardial plexus, renal stellate plexus, large extradural vein receiving the main cranial drainage, hepatic sinus, and caval sphincter (King, 1983; Munkasci and Newstead, 1985). Walruses resemble phocids in having a large hepatic sinus and a well-developed caval sphincter, but resemble otariids in having a single azygous vein, no well developed pericardial plexus, and no prominent stellate plexus (Fay, 1981).

Relative to body size, the veins of cetaceans are not as enlarged as those of pinnipeds, although the posterior vena cava is enlarged in the hepatic region in some species. The posterior

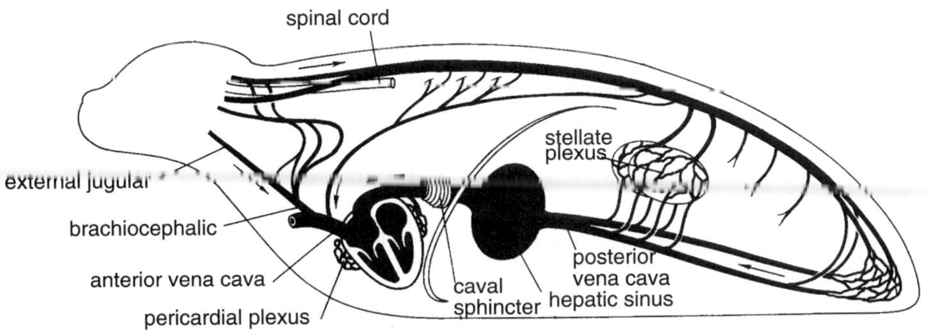

Figure 9.2. Diagram of the venous circulation in a phocid with the major vessels labeled (from King, 1983).

vena cava shows marked variation in its anatomy not only in different species but even within a species (Harrison and Tomlinson, 1956). As in pinnipeds, the posterior vena cava frequently forms paired vessels. A vascular distinction of most cetaceans is the development of a pair of large veins ventral to the spinal cord which have been related to their diving ability (Slijper, 1979). There is no real caval sphincter nor hepatic sinus in cetaceans (Harrison and King, 1980).

9.3.1.2. Spleen

It has been noted that the spleen of seals and sea lions is large (4.5% of body weight). The elephant seal has the largest spleen, its relative weight being more than three times that of terrestrial mammals. The spleen acts as a storage tank for oxygenated red blood cells in much the same way as a SCUBA tank. Diving capacity in phocids (but not in otariids) is strongly correlated with spleen size (Hochachka and Mottishaw, 1998).

The spleen of cetaceans is very small (0.02% of body weight) in comparison with most terrestrial mammals (0.3% of body weight; Bryden, 1972). No correlation has yet been described between diving ability and spleen size in cetaceans.

9.3.1.3. Other Oxygen Stores

In addition to the spleen, large stores of oxygen are maintained in chemical combination with **hemoglobin** of the blood or with **myoglobin**, the oxygen binding molecule found in muscle cells that gives them a dark red appearance. Red blood cells (which contain hemoglobin) are about the same size in diving and nondiving mammals; however, diving mammals have higher relative blood volumes, more red blood cells, and each cell tends to be somewhat inflated by its extra load of hemoglobin. These last two features together effectively increase the **hematocrit**, or packed red blood cell volume, and consequently the hemoglobin volume of the blood. Hematocrit values range from 40–45% in gray whales and 48% in California sea lions to about 50–60% in elephant seals (Table 9.2). Hedrick and Duffield (1991) have suggested that those species of marine mammals with the greatest adaptation for increased oxygen storage (with higher hematocrit levels) actually experience a decreased capacity for oxygen transport and limited ability to sustain fast swimming speeds.

Table 9.2 Blood Values that Relate to Oxygen Capacity in Selected Marine Mammals

Species	Blood vol. (ml/kg)	Hematocrit (%)	Source
Pinnipeds			
Phocids			
N. elephant seal	100–175	50–62	Thorson and Le Boeuf (1994)
Otariids			
California sea lion	?	48	Ridgway (1972)
Cetaceans			
Odontocetes			
Sperm whale	204	52	Sleet *et al.* (1981)
Bottlenose dolphin	71–95	42–52	Ridgway and Johnston (1966)
Mysticetes			
Gray whale	61–81	40–45	Gilmartin *et al.* (1974)

Much of the total store of oxygen available for use during a dive is bound to the myoglobin of the skeletal muscles (Fig. 9.3). These muscles are very tolerant of the hypoxic conditions occurring during dives; when the muscles deplete their myoglobin-oxygen store, they and other peripheral organs (such as the kidneys and digestive organs) may be deprived of the circulating hemoglobin-bound oxygen stored in the blood.

The total blood volume (relative to body mass) of diving mammals is two to three times greater than in nondiving mammals. Much of the additional blood volume is accommodated in numerous retia mirabilia (Figure 7.16) or in enlarged blood vessels (Fig. 9.2). Comparison of the total oxygen stores of various marine mammals (Figure 9.3) reveals that phocid seals maintain total oxygen reserves that are 21–79% higher than those calculated for dolphins (Kooyman, 1989). The total oxygen reserve of Atlantic coastal bottlenose dolphins resembles levels reported for otariids rather than those of phocids (Williams *et al.*, 1991; see Ridgway and Johnson, 1966).

9.3.2. Anatomy and Physiology of the Respiratory System

In this section we deal with the ventilatory adaptations necessary to achieve prolonged dives in species such as those listed in Table 9.1. The respiratory tract of marine mammals begins with the external nares of pinnipeds and sirenians and blowhole(s) of cetaceans and ends with the lungs.

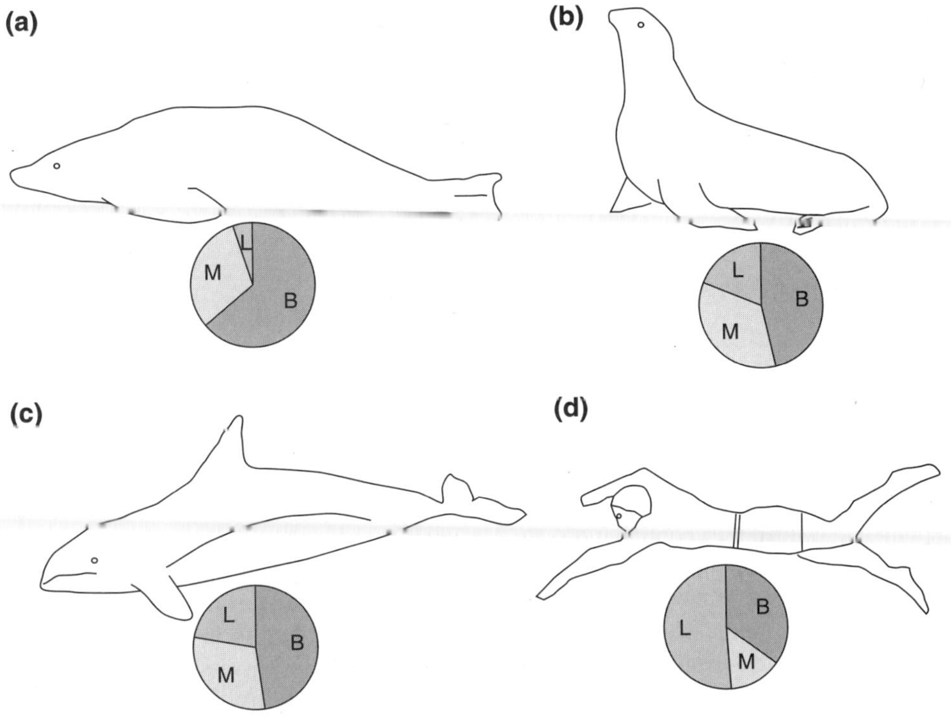

Figure 9.3. Generalized comparison of relative blood (B), muscle (M), and lung (L) oxygen stores for (a) phocids, (b) otariids, (c) odontocetes, and (d) humans (after Kooyman, 1985).

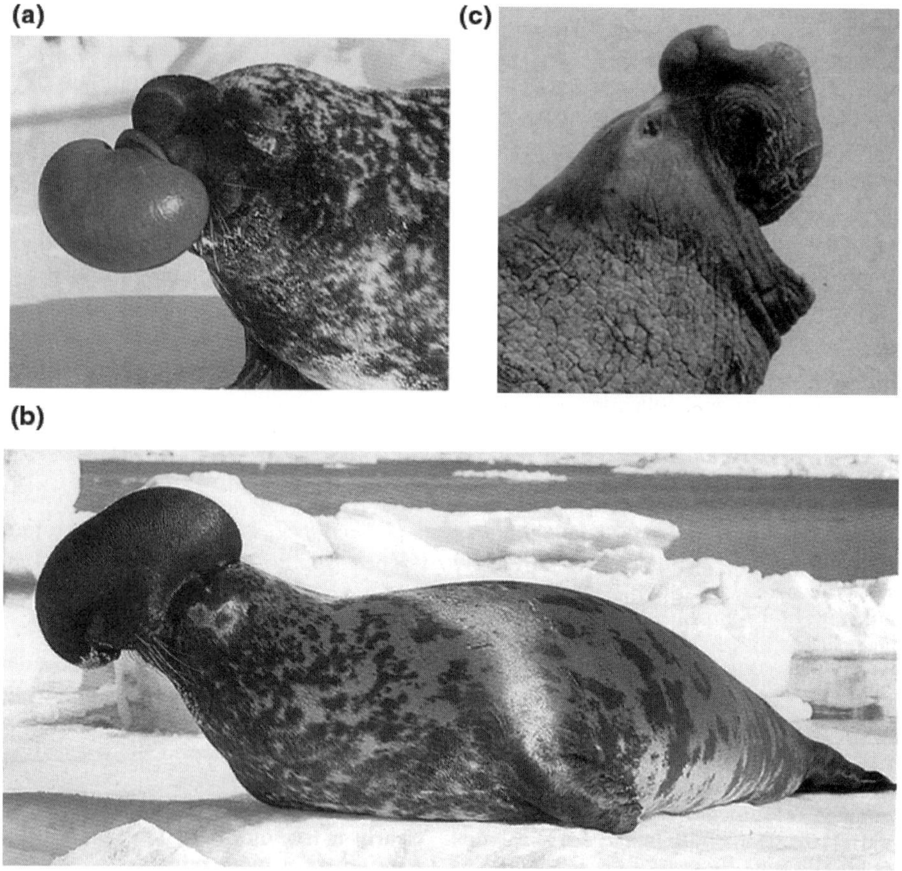

Figure 9.4. Balloon blown from (a) left nostril and (b) inflatable hood of hooded seal (from Macdonald, 1984) and (c) proboscis of mature male northern elephant seal (from the Le Boeuf and Laws, 1994).

9.3.2.1. The Hood of Hooded Seals

An enlargement of the nasal cavity forms an inflatable hood on top of the head in adult male hooded seals (Fig. 9.4). It reaches its maximum size in sexually mature bulls which use it for courtship display (Reeves and Ling, 1978). The hood starts developing at about four years of age and increases in size with age and increasing body size. By age 13, males possess large hoods. The hood may be inflated with air when the animal is disturbed or during the pupping and mating season, and at other times. The hood is divided by the nasal septum and is lined by a continuation of the mucous membrane of the nose. The skin of the hood is very elastic, and the hairs that are present are shorter and grow less thickly than those on other parts of the body. No blubber is found in the hood as it is replaced by elastic tissue. There are muscle fibers around the nostrils where they form annular constrictor muscles that trap exhalant within the hood. Hooded seals also possess the ability to blow (from the left nostril only) a red balloon-shaped structure formed from the extensible membranous part of the internasal septum (Fig. 9.4). The seal produces this balloon by closing the left nostril and blowing air into the hood. Only the side of the hood with the closed nostril will start to inflate, and if the hood is kept uninflated by muscular action, the air pressure causes the elastic internasal septum to bulge and eventually to appear as a balloon through the open nostril of the other side (King, 1983).

9.3.2.2. The Elephant Seal Nose

The inflatable proboscis is arguably the most conspicuous feature of the adult male elephant seal (Fig. 9.4). In females there is no enlargement. Although flattened and less obvious in the non-breeding season, it is used in male dominance displays during the breeding season. The development of the proboscis begins at about two years of age and its full size is attained by about eight years of age. As in the hooded seal, the protuberance is an enlargement of the nasal cavity internally divided by the nasal septum. Inflation, however, is attained through muscular action and blood pressure with minor assistance from the respiratory system. When inflated it forms a high, bolster-shaped cushion on top of the snout with its open tip hanging down in front of the open mouth. The snorts and other vocalizations are thus directed downwards into the open mouth and pharynx, which act as a resonating chamber (King, 1983).

9.3.2.3. Respiratory Tract of Other Marine Mammals

Cetaceans breathe through the blowholes (external nares) which have migrated to a position high on the top of the head. The sperm whale, in which the blowhole is on the anterior top end of the head, slightly left of center, is the exception. Mysticetes possess two blowholes in contrast to the single blowhole of odontocetes. Opening of the nares is accomplished by contraction of skeletal muscle, whereas closure is a passive process by dense fibrous connective tissue rich with adipose tissue. The active opening of the blowhole is an adaptation to spending life in an aquatic medium. If muscle contraction were needed to maintain closed blowholes, much energy would be required to keep water out of the respiratory tract.

Manatees breathe through two-valved nostrils situated at the tip of the rostrum. The nostrils of the dugong lie close together and are situated anterodorsally, thereby allowing the dugong to breathe with most of its body submerged. The nostrils are closed during diving by anteriorly hinged valves (Nishiwaki and Marsh, 1985).

No valve is present in the external nares of pinnipeds. Instead, the flat medial surfaces of two throat (arytenoid) cartilages lie in close approximation, which also abut the posterior surface of the epiglottis, providing a tight seal against the entry of water into the trachea. The powerful muscles of the larynx also help to keep this entrance closed (King, 1983).

The cetacean larynx is composed of a cartilaginous framework held together by a series of muscles. To keep inhaled air separate from food the larynx of odontocetes (but not mysticetes) has two elongate cartilages (Fig. 9.5; Slijper, 1979; Lawrence and Schevill, 1965; Reidenberg and Laitman, 1987). This provides a more direct connection between the nose and trachea than is found in mysticetes.

The trachea in most pinnipeds is supported by cartilaginous rings that either form complete circles or are incomplete and overlap dorsally. The cartilaginous rings are reduced to ventral bars in Ross, Weddell, and leopard seals (King, 1983). In the ribbon seal, a longitudinal slit occurs between the ends of the incomplete cartilage rings on the dorsal surface of the trachea just before it bifurcates to form the bronchi. A membranous sac of unknown function extends both anteriorly and posteriorly from the trachea on the right side of the

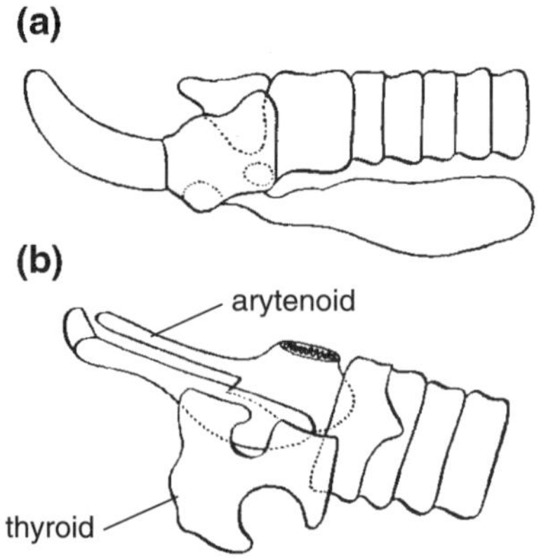

Figure 9.5. Lateral view of cetacean larynx in (a) mysticete (fin whale) and (b) odontocete (narwhal). Note the elongated arytenoid and thyroid cartilages in the odontocete (from Slijper, 1979).

body. Male ribbon seals possess this sac, and it increases in size with age. The tracheal slit is present in females, but the sac is small or absent (King, 1983). In phocids and the walrus, the trachea divides into two primary bronchi immediately outside the substance of the lung. In otariids this bifurcation is located more anteriorly, at approximately the level of the first rib, and the two elongated bronchi run parallel until they diverge to enter the lungs dorsal to the heart (see Fig. 3.11).

In cetaceans the trachea is short and broad and consists of several cartilaginous rings (varying from five to seven rings in the beluga and sperm whale to 13–15 in the fin whale) that are interconnected with each other. Unlike baleen whales, the tracheal rings of toothed whales are closed and form a noncollapsing tube (Yablokov *et al.,* 1972).

The dugong trachea is short (only four cartilage rings) and it is deeply divided by a medial septum (Hill, 1945; Harrison and King, 1980). The manatee trachea is longer, supported by 8–12 tracheal rings (Harrison and King, 1980).

9.3.2.4. Lungs

Some important differences exist between the lungs of marine mammals and those of terrestrial mammals. The left and right lungs of pinnipeds are approximately equal in size and are lobulated as in terrestrial carnivores; both lungs have three main lobes, but the right lung has an additional small intermediate lobe. There appears to be a tendency to reduce lobulation, and the lungs of the walrus, ribbon, harp, and spotted seals have been reported as having little or no lobulation (King, 1983). The bronchi subdivide within the lungs to form bronchioles and eventually end in alveoli, but the details of this transition vary among the three families (Fig. 9.6; see King, 1983).

The lungs of cetaceans are distinct from those of all other mammals in their overall sacculate shape and lack of lobes (Fig. 9.7). Only occasionally is the apical part of the right lung somewhat prominent, resembling the apical lobe of the lungs of other mammals. There is some difference between the shape of the right and left lungs; the right lung is usually larger, longer, and heavier. Such asymmetry of lung size, which is related in whales as in other mammals to the somewhat asymmetric position of the heart in the chest cavity, is seen in virtually all studied cetaceans: rorquals, various dolphins, sperm, and beluga whales.

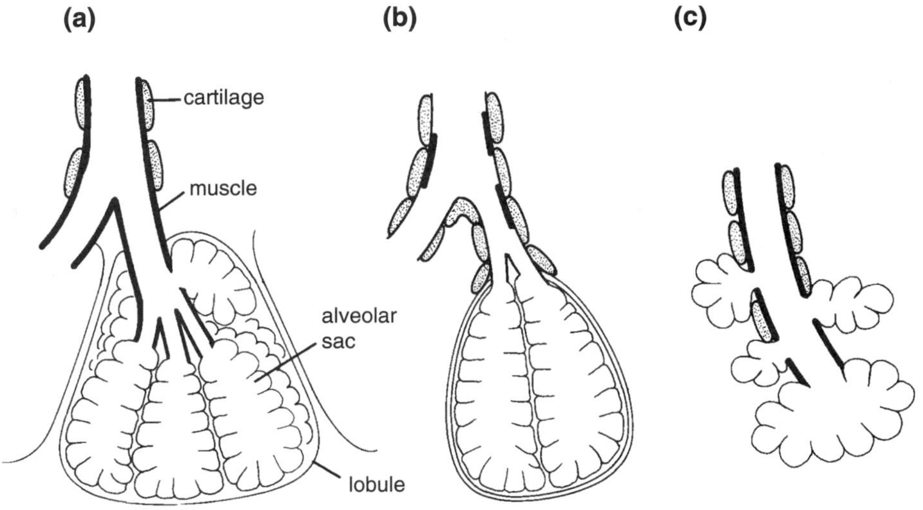

Figure 9.6. Diagram of the structure of alveoli and associated cartilage and muscle in pinnipeds (a) phocid, (b) otariid, and (c) odobenid (from King, 1983).

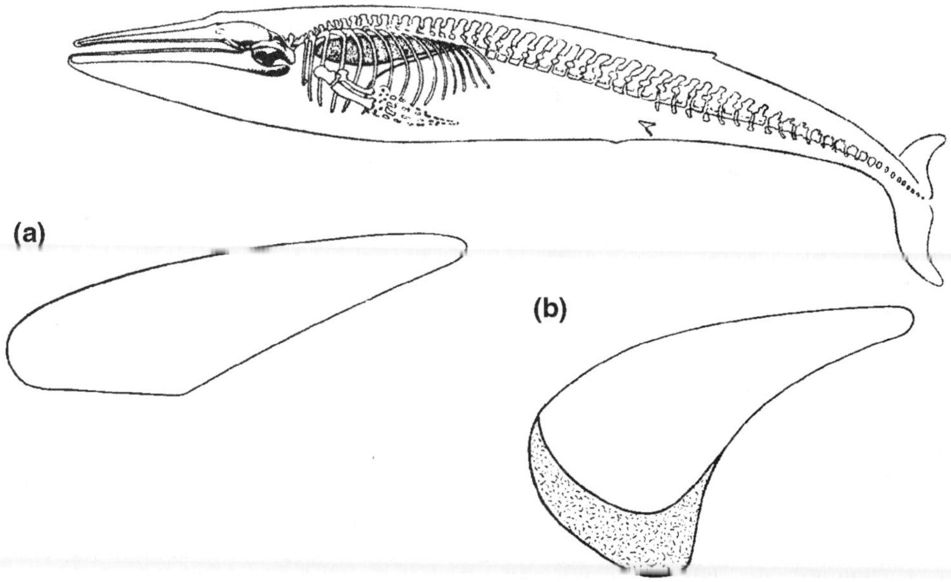

Figure 9.7. Diagram showing position of the cetacean lung and comparison of (a) mysticete (fin whale) and (b) odontocete (bottlenose dolphin) lung on right. Stippled area indicates particularly thin section of lung (from Slijper, 1979).

Comparative lung volume is lower for cetaceans than terrestrial mammals. A number of studies have confirmed that the quantity of air in the lungs is not as important to the capacity for deep diving as is the total volume of stored and hemoglobin-bound oxygen (e.g., Kolchinskaya *et al.,* 1980; Ridgway *et al.,* 1969). Another possible explanation for the relatively small lung volume of deep diving species is that with less air in the lungs when the animal is at considerable depth, fewer gases will pass to the blood, which reduces the danger of an **embolism** when surfacing rapidly (Kooyman and Anderson, 1969; Yablokov *et al.,* 1972).

The lungs of cetaceans, compared to those of terrestrial mammals, show greater rigidity and elasticity because of increased cartilaginous support. In baleen, sperm, and bottlenose whales the septa projecting into the proximal portion of the air sacs contain heavy myoelastic bundles. In the smaller toothed whales these bundles are atrophied, but there are a series of myoelastic sphincters in the smallest bronchioles. In both the bundles and the sphincters, the muscular part may act to close the air sacs whereas the elastic part may facilitate rapid expiration. Airway closure should delay alveolar collapse during dives and allow additional pulmonary gas exchange to occur for those odontocete families known to possess myoelastic terminal airway sphincters (Drabek and Kooyman, 1983).

The lungs of sirenians are long and extend posteriorly almost as far as the kidneys. They are separated from the abdominal viscera by a large obliquely sloped diaphragm, bronchial tree, and respiratory tissue (Engel, 1959a,b, 1962). The primary bronchi run almost the length of the lungs with only a few smaller side branches or secondary bronchi. The secondary bronchi pass into smaller tubes, which in turn give rise to minute tubules supplying the respiratory vesicles. Another unique sirenian feature is that these vesicles arise laterally along the length of the bronchioles rather than from their ends, as is the typical mammalian condition (Engel, 1959a). The bronchioles are very muscular and may function to close off respiratory vesicles when desired. For example, the dugong may use this technique to compress the volume and density of air in the lungs, thus enabling it to surface or sink without the use of flippers or tail and without expelling air (Engel, 1962). Cartilage occurs throughout the length of the air passages (Nishiwaki and Marsh, 1985).

The thoracic cavity of the sea otter is large and the diaphragm is positioned obliquely (Barabash-Nikiforov, 1947). The right lung has four lobes and the left has two lobes (Tarasoff and Kooyman, 1973a,b). The lungs are large in relation to body size, nearly 2.5 times that found in mammals of similar size. Large lungs serve more to regulate buoyancy than to store oxygen (Lenfant *et al.,* 1970; Kooyman, 1973; Leith, 1976; Costa and Kooyman, 1982).

9.3.2.5. Breathing

Elephant seals possess anatomical and physiological features associated with respiration that allow them to prolong the time that they can stay out of water (Huntley *et al.,* 1984). Their nasal structure is similar to that of desert rodents for which water conservation is of great importance. Countercurrent blood flow in the nose sets up temperature gradients which allow recycling and retention of moisture in the nasal passages. This moisture would normally be lost with exhalation, but because of the temperature gradient and the increased surface area of the nasal passages, much of the moisture in the exhaled air condenses on the epithelium of the nasal passage. This moisture is used during inhalation to humidify the air on its way to the lungs. Gray seals conserve their water in a similar manner (Folkow and Blix, 1987).

The flow of air escaping from the lungs of cetaceans at the time of expiration blows upward the drops of water that are around the blowhole. A particularly large amount of water may be spouted in baleen whales, whose blowholes are located in rather deep folds. The water which is sprayed constitutes the spouting, or **blow**, that is typical for large whales (Fig. 9.8). Vapor formed by contact between air heated in the lungs and the cold external air also is involved in formation of the blow; it also contains an emulsion of fine oil droplets from cells lining the air sinuses, mucus from the tracheal glands, and **surfactants** from the

Figure 9.8. Surface "blow" of three gray whales.

lungs. Surfactants are a mixture of lipoproteins which reduce surface tension in pulmonary fluids and facilitate easy inflation of the whale's lungs upon surfacing. The blow leaves a greasy film on the water after a whale has surfaced (sometimes referred to as a "footprint"). The size, shape, and direction of the blow can help to identify some species of whales from a distance (Fig. 9.8).

During inhalation, extensive elastic tissue in the lungs and diaphragm (Fig. 9.9) is stretched by muscular activity in the diaphragm and intercostal musculature. These fibers recoil during exhalation to rapidly and nearly completely empty the lungs. Oxygen uptake within the alveoli of the lungs may be enhanced as lung air is moved into contact with the walls of the alveoli by the kneading action of small muscle fibers scattered throughout the lungs. In some species, the alveoli are highly vascularized to promote rapid uptake of oxygen. Bottlenose dolphins, for example, can remove nearly 90% of the oxygen contained in each breath (Ridgway *et al.,* 1969). In comparison, humans and most other terrestrial mammals use only about 20% of the inspired oxygen.

It has been proposed that foreign particulate matter in inspired air or sea water may result in the formation of biomineral concretions, or calculi, recently discovered in the nasal sacs of some delphinids (Curry *et al.,* 1994).

Breathing patterns of marine mammals vary. Cetaceans exhale and inhale singly but very rapidly upon surfacing, whereas pinnipeds breathe vigorously and frequently during the recovery phase after diving. Manatees exhale after surfacing and like cetaceans can renew about 90% of the air in the lungs in a single breath. By comparison, humans at rest renew about 10% of the air in the lungs in a single breath (Reynolds and Odell, 1991).

9.3.2.6. Diving

Cetaceans typically dive with full lungs whereas pinnipeds often exhale prior to diving. These differences suggest that the volume of lung air at the beginning of a dive is of little

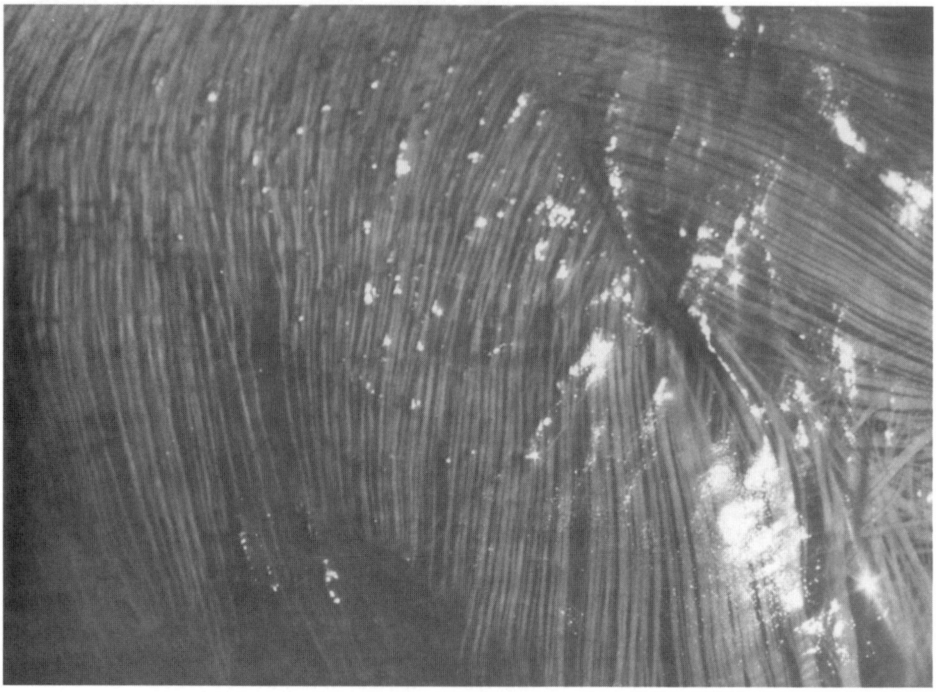

Figure 9.9. Extensive elastic fibers of diaphragm tissue of dolphin *Stenella.*

importance in supplying oxygen during a dive, but it may be adjusted to achieve neutral buoyancy during the dive. Moreover, the lungs and their protective rib cage are modified to allow the lungs to collapse as the water pressure increases with depth (Fig. 9.10). Complete lung collapse occurs at depths of 25–50 m for Weddell seals (Falke *et al.,* 1985), 70 m for the bottlenose dolphin (Ridgway and Howard, 1979), and probably occurs in the first 50–100 m for most marine mammals. Any air remaining in the lungs below that depth is squeezed out of the alveoli and into the bronchi and trachea of the lungs. Even the cartilage rings of the trachea of toothed whales are flexible and undergo partial collapse during deep dives. The smooth collapse and reinflation of the lungs are facilitated by the position of the diaphragm, which is set at an acute angle to the long axis of the body.

By tolerating complete lung collapse, these animals sidestep the need for respiratory structures capable of resisting the extreme water pressure experienced during deep dives. They also receive an additional bonus. As the air is forced out of the collapsing alveoli during a dive, the compressed air still within the larger air passages is blocked from contact with the thin, gas-exchanging walls of the alveoli. Consequently, little of this compressed gas is absorbed by the blood during dives and marine mammals avoid the potentially serious diving problems of decompression sickness (also called the **bends**) and **nitrogen narcosis** that sometimes plague human divers breathing compressed air (Moon *et al.,* 1995).

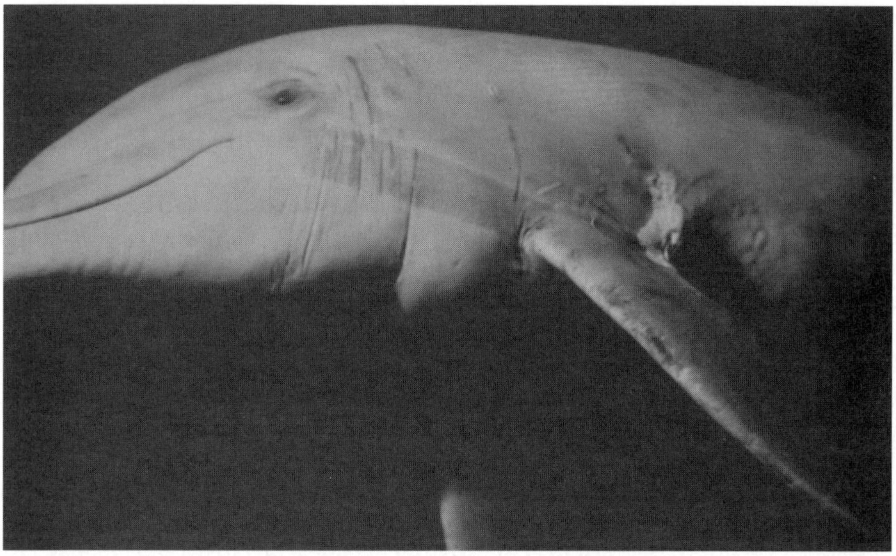

Figure 9.10. Bottlenose dolphin at a depth of 300 m, experiencing obvious thoracic collapse visible behind the left flipper (courtesy S. Ridgway and used by permission).

9.4. Diving Biochemistry and Metabolism

Marine mammal tissues have characteristics which allow them to survive repeated bouts of hypoxia and/or **ischema**. Early workers analyzed tissues from various marine mammals and suggested that hypoxia tolerance was related to the activity level of glycolytic enzymes, such as pyruvate kinase (PK) and lactate dehydrogenase (LDH) (e.g., Hochachka and Storey, 1975). Later work revealed that glycolytic enzyme activity was not directly related to diving ability but was probably more related to tissue activity level (e.g., Murphy *et al.* 1980). For example, the muscle enzyme PK, which was suggested to be directly proportional to dive durations in seals, was found to be even higher in rabbit, porpoise, and penguin muscle (Castellini *et al.,* 1981). Enzyme activity levels varied by tissue and species. Tissues of marine mammals do not have unusually high capacities for anaerobic glycolysis, supporting other evidence demonstrating that marine mammals power most of their natural dives using aerobic metabolic pathways (Castellini and Somero, 1981). No study has described any extreme alteration in glycolytic enzyme activity that would give a marine mammal tissue an enhanced ability to survive hypoxia (Castellini, 1991).

In an extensive comparison of diving and nondiving mammals, the most significant differences in tissue biochemistry were found in the levels of myoglobin and muscle buffering capacity (Castellini *et al.,* 1981). Buffering capacity is the ability to hold tissue pH constant in the face of an increasing amount of acidic end products created by anaerobic metabolism. Marine mammals have a greater buffering ability than terrestrial mammals, and phocids have higher noncarbonate plasma buffering capacities than either otariids or most cetaceans (Boutilier *et al.,* 1993). This probably reflects their general patterns of breath-hold diving and relative potentials for tolerating low oxygen and metabolic acidosis. Most current work on marine mammal tissue biochemistry is focused on cell membrane defenses against hypoxia and ischemia (e.g., Hochachka, 1988, 1992; Hochachka and Guppy, 1987; Hochachka and Foreman, 1993; Castellini, 1991).

9.5. Do Marine Mammals Have High Metabolic Rates?

Attempts to estimate metabolic rates of marine mammals often are complicated by the animals' large size, their habit of staying in an environment that is not thermally neutral, and by the lack of agreement on how allometric relationships developed from studies of small cetaceans and other captive mammals might serve as appropriate metabolic models for much larger animals (Lavigne *et al.,* 1986; McNab, 1988).

The issue of whether marine mammals have higher metabolic rates than terrestrial mammals continues to be debated. Several studies of pinniped metabolism (as measured by oxygen consumption) have shown that the resting metabolic rates of pinnipeds are about 1.5–3 times greater than those of terrestrial mammals of similar size (e.g., Kooyman, 1981). Similarly it has been argued that cetaceans have a higher metabolic rate than average terrestrial mammals of similar size (Irving *et al.,* 1941; Pierce, 1970; Ridgway and Patton, 1971; Hampton *et al.,* 1971; Kasting *et al.,* 1989). Lavigne *et al.* (1986) and Huntley (1987) have argued that metabolic rates of pinnipeds are not significantly different from those of terrestrial mammals and suggest that previous studies did not always make comparisons under standardized conditions. When resting metabolism was measured by oxygen consumption rates in captive harp, gray, and ringed seals (Innes and Ronald, 1985) and in captive hooded seals (Rea, 1987), their metabolic rates were found to be only slightly higher (1.1–1.2 times) than those typical of a terrestrial mammal of similar size (Riedman, 1990). Opposing evidence has also been presented for cetaceans (Karandeeva *et al.,* 1973; Lavigne *et al.,* 1986; and Innes and Lavigne, 1991) using similar data to reject claims of higher metabolic rates.

Metabolic rates of West Indian manatees are one-fifth of the values predicted on the basis of body size in a general mammalian regression (Irvine, 1983), while metabolic rates of Amazon manatees are one-third of predicted values (Gallivan and Best, 1980). Dugongs also are presumed to have low metabolic rates (Marsh *et al.,* 1978). It has been suggested that the low metabolic rates reported for the West Indian manatee and the Amazon manatee are a result of their relatively poor quality diet, as discussed further in Chapter 11. A lifestyle based on foraging aquatic plants does not demand complex foraging strategies or elaborate sensory systems. Additionally, as suggested by O'Shea and Reep (1990), it is likely that the low metabolic rate of sirenians placed constraints on potential selection for larger relative brain size. Thus, sirenians evolved larger body size which was advantageous in food processing, mobility, and energy conservation, but not larger relative brain size (see also Chapter 7).

9.6. Metabolism and Physiological Responses to Breath Holding in Seals

Investigators in the late 1930s noted that despite the increased oxygen storage capacity of marine mammals there was insufficient oxygen to support the maximum observed dive times if the metabolic rate of the animal remained at resting levels. Thus, it was suggested that during longer dives when the animal exceeded its aerobic metabolic limits, a recovery time at the surface would be necessary to replenish oxygen stores and to readjust pH and process lactates and other metabolites resulting from anaerobic metabolism.

It was the lack of agreement between predicted **aerobic dive limits** (based on measured oxygen-storage capacity) and actual observed dive times that led Scholander and Irving to propose in a series of articles (i.e. Scholander, 1940; Scholander and Irving, 1941; Scholander *et al.,* 1942; Irving *et al.,* 1935) a widely accepted explanation for long breath holds in essentially all diving air-breathing vertebrates. During observed dives of a variety of marine mammals in controlled laboratory conditions, the arteries leading to skeletal muscles and organs constrict, shunting most of the circulating blood (and its oxygen store) to a few vital organs, primarily the heart and brain. Simultaneously, the heartbeat rate slows dramatically to accommodate pressure changes in a much-reduced circulatory system comprised principally of the heart, brain, and connecting blood vessels.

These two responses, **peripheral vasoconstriction** and **bradycardia** (the marked slowing of the heartbeat rate that accompanies a dive), probably occur in all diving air-breathing vertebrates, including birds, reptiles, and mammals. The intensity of bradycardia varies widely between marine mammal groups. During experimental dives under laboratory conditions, heartbeat rates of restrained cetaceans are reduced to 20 to 50% of their predive rates. Many seals in controlled experimental dives drop their resting heartbeat rates of 100 to 150 beats/min to 10 beats/min when diving. The combination of bradycardia, peripheral vasoconstriction, and other circulatory adjustments to diving has been commonly referred to as "the mammalian dive response" (Elsner and Gooden, 1983). The major components of this response are summarized in Table 9.3 and illustrated in Figure 9.11.

In spite of variable and even conflicting data for some cetaceans and semivoluntary diving pinnipeds, this set of characteristics was widely applied to explain long-duration breath holds by marine mammals. Subsequent studies of free-diving Weddell seals in Antarctic waters (Fig. 9.12) by Kooyman and other researchers support a substantially different picture of diving responses in unrestrained divers in their natural habitat (Kooyman, 1966, 1985; Kooyman and Campbell, 1972; Kooyman *et al.,* 1981). These researchers attached instrument packages to numerous free-diving seals to monitor and record dive time, depth, heartbeat rate, core body temperature, and blood chemistry. Weddell seals were ideal subjects for this type of study because they breathe by surfacing at holes maintained in the fast sea ice. Each seal returning to its own hole to breathe after a dive offered convenient opportunities to attach and retrieve recording instrument packs.

Kooyman and others found that Weddell seals perform breath-holding dives up to about 20 minutes in length without employing "the mammalian dive response" presented in Table 9.3. These results suggest that Weddell seals have sufficient stored oxygen at the beginning of a dive to last about 20 minutes. Only during dives lasting longer than about 20 minutes

Table 9.3. A Summary of "The Mammalian Dive Response"

1. Cessation of breathing
2. Extreme bradycardia regardless of dive duration
3. Strong peripheral and some central vasoconstriction
4. Reduced aerobic metabolism in most organs
5. Rapid depletion of muscle O_2
6. Lactic acid accumulation in muscles (see Fig. 9.13)
7. Variety of blood chemistry changes during and immediately following dive

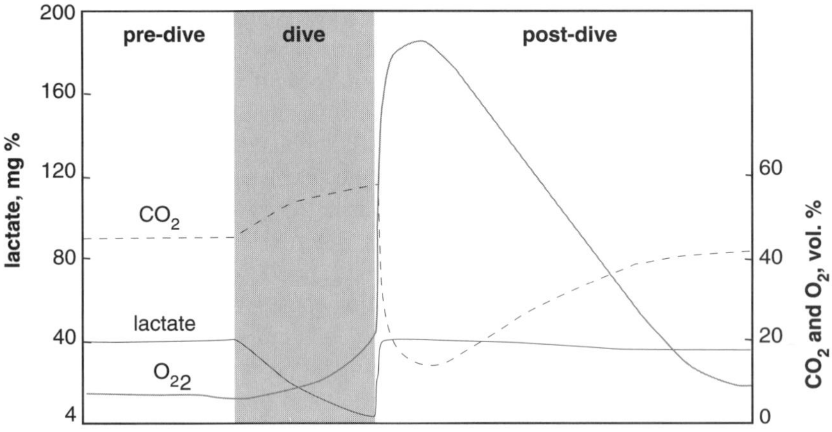

Figure 9.11. Monitored changes in arterial blood lactate, O_2 and CO_2 before, during, and immediately following an 18 min. forced immersion by a 42 kg gray seal (redrawn from Scholander, 1940).

(a)

(b)

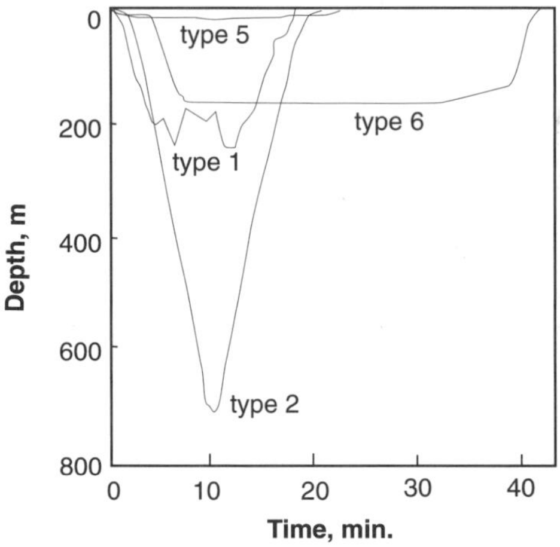

Figure 9.12. (a) Weddell seal in breathing hole (courtesy of G. Kooyman) and (b) Profiles of four different dive types of Weddell seals as characterized by Schreer and Testa, 1996.

(their apparent **aerobic dive limit**, or **ADL**; Fig. 9.13) are circulatory responses observed that resemble the expected dive response described in Table 9.3. An animal's ADL as defined by Kooyman (1985) is the longest dive that does not lead to an increase in blood lactate concentration during the dive. Therefore, if an animal dives within its ADL, there is no lactate accumulated to metabolize after the dive, and a subsequent dive can be made as soon as the depleted blood oxygen is replenished. The ADL can be calculated by measur-

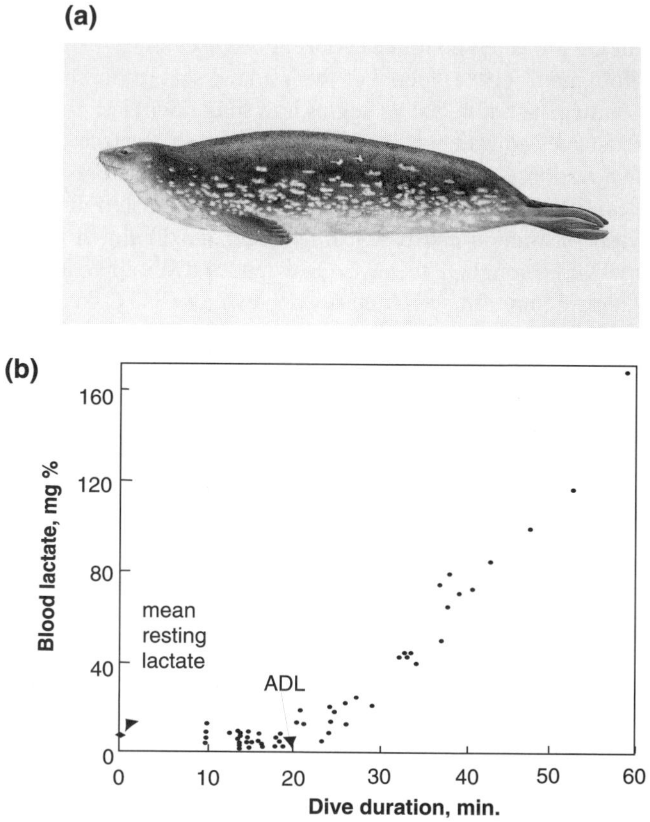

Figure 9.13. (a) Weddell seal (illustrated by P. Folkens), (b) Peak arterial lactate concentrations obtained following dives of varying durations for three Weddell seals. Commencement of post-dive increases in arterial lactate define ADL (redrawn from Kooyman *et al.,* 1981).

ing available oxygen stores and dividing by either a measured or an estimated metabolic rate (measured as oxygen consumption), and is therefore dependent on the animal's level of activity. Only the Weddell seal has had its ADL verified by the measurement of blood lactic acid concentrations, and in no species has this been verified under wholly free-ranging conditions (Kooyman *et al.,* 1983). However, studies have shown that many species appear to exceed their theoretical aerobic dive time (TADT) during a substantial portion of their dives (Boyd, 1997).

For dives longer than the ADL, the magnitude of physiological responses is generally related to the length of the dive, yet the picture is not a simple one. Peripheral vasoconstriction and bradycardia do occur, with the magnitude of those responses generally proportional to the duration of the part of the dive that exceeded the animal's ADL. During dives exceeding the ADL, the glomerular filtration rate of the kidneys, for example, is reduced, yet hepatic blood flow to kidney tissue is maintained. The length of the ADL is related to the size of the animal, but the more the dive exceeds the ADL, the greater the accumulation of lactate and the longer it takes for the level of lactate to return to resting levels. After very long dives (1 h or more), Weddell seals are exhausted and sleep for several hours (Kooyman *et al.,* 1980; Castellini *et al.,* 1988). Although Weddell seals are capable of remaining submerged for more than an hour, they seldom do. Approximately 85% of the dives observed by Kooyman and Campbell (1972) were within the projected 20 minute ADL of this species.

According to Kooyman's (1985) model of the Weddell seal response to diving, it appears that these animals anticipate before a dive begins how long it will last, then consciously make the appropriate circulatory adjustments prior to leaving the sea surface. This is why it should not be called a dive response, but rather an integrated set of related responses. During short dives (<20 minutes), no adjustments are necessary. For anticipated dives of long duration, both peripheral vasoconstriction and bradycardia occur maximally at the beginning of the dive and remain that way throughout the dive. On extended dives approaching one hour in duration, core body temperature can be voluntarily depressed to 35° C, kept depressed between dives, then rapidly elevated after the last dive of a dive series. Together, these responses (summarized in Table 9.4) allow Weddell seals to accomplish some of the longest breath holds known for mammals. They also indicate that, at least in this species, peripheral vasoconstriction, heartbeat rate, and core body temperature are under conscious control, and argue strongly against the earlier concept of a reflexive "dive response" for marine mammals.

Can these results be generalized to other species of marine mammals? The question is difficult to answer for more than a few species, because it is apparent that Kooyman's work with unrestrained Weddell seals, whose dive duration was under their own control, was a key to elucidating this species' physiological response to breath-hold diving. Opportunities to attach instrument packages to monitor physiological responses of a free-diving mammal, release the subject animal for a series of unrestrained dives, then recapture the subject animal for instrument package recovery and blood sampling have been limited in the past. However, such opportunities are becoming more frequent as improvements in electronic monitoring and radio telemetry techniques expand our studies of animals diving without restraint (e.g., Nowicki *et al.*, 1997).

The exceptional breath-holding abilities of several other species of seals, for example, have become known because of these techniques. Experimental monitoring of diving behaviors of northern and southern elephant seals has been accomplished by fitting adults with long-duration dive profile recorders, then recovering the recorders later when the animals return to their island rookery after several weeks at sea. Elephant seal adults, for example, have a postreproductive feeding excursion in the open sea of more than two months, after which they return to their breeding rookery. They spend their time at sea foraging for squid and fish at depths between 300 and 1500 m (see Table 9.1). The foraging dives of northern elephant seals are typically 20 to 25 minutes long, with females usually going to

Table 9.4. A Summary of Dive Response in Weddell Seals

1. Cessation of breathing
2. Variable bradycardia depending on dive duration
3. Variable peripheral and central vasoconstriction depending on dive duration
4. Reduced aerobic metabolism in most organs
5. Rapid depletion of muscle O_2
6. Lactic acid accumulation in muscles beginning after 20 minutes
7. Variety of blood chemistry changes during and immediately following dive, depending on dive duration
8. Voluntary reduction of core body temperature during very long dives

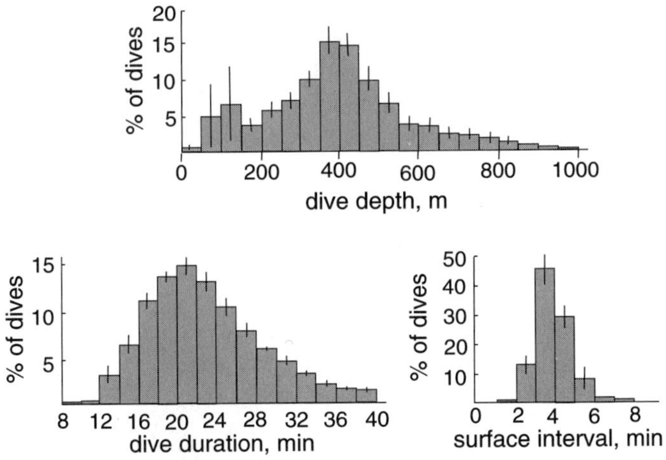

Figure 9.14. Summaries of depths, durations, and post-dive intervals of over 36,000 dives made by six adult male northern elephant seals (error bars = ±1 s.e.) (redrawn from DeLong and Stewart, 1991; Fig. 1).

depths of about 400 m (Le Boeuf *et al.,* 1989) and males to depths of 750 to 800 m (DeLong and Stewart, 1991; see also Chapter 11). Both sexes dive night and day for days at a time without prolonged rest periods at the sea surface. After each dive, they typically spend only a few minutes at the surface before the next dive (Fig. 9.14). The short duration of these surface bouts suggests that the 20–25 min dives are not unusual but are within the ADL of this species. These seals probably adjust their swimming speeds and metabolic rates to sustain almost all dives aerobically, so that little surface recovery time is required before commencing the next dive. Diving patterns of juvenile northern elephant seals exhibit a pattern like that of adults, diving deep, long, and continuously while at sea. The level of performance increased with age and experience up to two years of age, when diving performance became comparable to that of adults (Le Boeuf *et al.,* 1996).

Andrews *et al.* (1997) monitored heart rates of northern elephant seals diving at sea and resting on the beach. Their results suggest that elephant seals do not anticipate dive duration but instead adjust their heart rate response throughout a dive. As the seal descends deeper, its heart rate falls to a lower level, so that deeper, longer dives elicit correspondingly lower heart rates. This pattern of a gradual and continual adjustment of the heart rate response does not support Kooyman's threshold model for the Weddell seal. Such a gradual reduction in heart rate also may represent a gradual reduction in metabolic rate with increasing dive duration. Furthermore, if metabolic rate, like heart rate, is continuously being adjusted then there can be no single time limit for aerobic dives, as has been estimated for many species (Andrews *et al.,* 1997). Instead, the ADL would be lengthened by changes in metabolic rate, a difficult pattern to predict.

Studies of the diving behavior of adult southern elephant seals (e.g., Hindell *et al.,* 1992) showed that 44% of all dives made by postmolt females exceeded the calculated ADL, compared to 7% for postbreeding females and less than 1% for adult males. Most of these extended dives were thought to be foraging dives, and they often occurred in bouts. The longest bout consisted of 63 consecutive dives over a 2-day period, with apparently little extended post-dive recovery time required between dives. Similarly, for free-ranging gray seals, recovery from unusually long dives did not require a longer period at the surface (Thompson and Fedak, 1993). These authors suggest that there is a reduction in overall metabolic rate, rather than a switch to anaerobic metabolism.

Data from Antarctic fur seals indicate that although less than 6% of individual dives exceed the estimated ADL (Boyd and Croxall, 1996), some dive bouts are of significantly longer duration and are followed by longer surface intervals. Although these seals exceeded their ADL, this did not appear to have any effect on their subsequent diving behavior. Deep foraging dives (>75 m) are common for northern fur seals (Fig. 9.15) and in one study 92% of dives exceeded the calculated ADL, whereas only 8% of shallow foraging dives (<40 m) exceeded the ADL (Ponganis *et al.,* 1992). Results of this study confirm previous suggestions that for longer dives exceeding the estimated ADL a different metabolic strategy may be involved instead of a switch to anaerobic metabolism. This metabolic strategy likely involves how divers manage heat and oxygen at varying body sizes, an area requiring further research (Boyd and Croxall, 1996; Boyd, 1997).

In summary, both physiological and behavioral evidence from a number of marine mammals indicates that the majority of dives they perform are aerobic. On occasions, excessively long dives are performed and in some species, such as the Weddell seal, accumulation of high levels of lactate during such dives may be related to subsequently long periods at the surface, when these animals appear to be exhausted. For elephant seals and gray seals, however, recovering from long dives does not require a longer period at the surface. It is suggested that during extended dives in these species, there is a reduction in overall metabolic rate, rather than a switch to anaerobic metabolism. It is clear that any attempt to understand the biology of diving must consider the complex interplay of behavioral, physiological, and biochemical components.

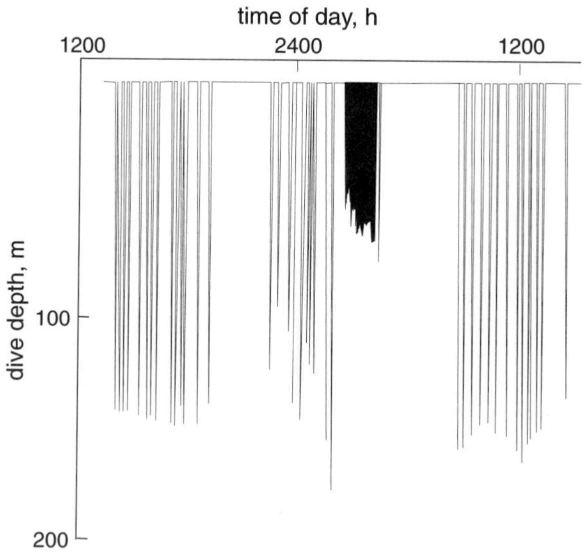

Figure 9.15. Deep dive bouts during foraging by an adult female northern fur seal (redrawn from Gentry and Kooyman, 1986).

9.7. Functions of Diving Behavior

The deep diving patterns exhibited by many pinnipeds function, in part, for energy conservation. Laboratory studies have confirmed that the metabolic rates of elephant seals are lower during periods of diving than when the seals are simply resting at the surface (Thorson and Le Boeuf, 1994). Based on these results it has been hypothesized that elephant seals may dive continuously while traveling and foraging because, by lowering their metabolic rate, they expend less energy by diving than by resting or swimming at the surface (Le Boeuf, 1994).

There is evidence that sleeping can effectively reduce metabolic rate by 20–50% in fasting northern elephant seals, harp seal pups, and gray seal pups (Hansen and Lavigne, 1997, and references cited therein). Furthermore, seals periodically experience **apnea** (cessation of breathing) during sleep as well as when diving. Due to the difficulty of studying animals at sea, the study of sleep apnea while the animal is on land is easier. This phenomenon has been studied extensively in the northern elephant seal (Huntley *et al.*, 1984; Andrews *et al.*, 1997).

In addition to their function in energy conservation and foraging, the diving patterns of pinnipeds also may play a role in the avoidance of predators. Le Boeuf and Crocker (1996) proposed that northern elephant seals exhibit a diving pattern consistent with this hypothesis: diving deeply with no swimming at the surface, short surface intervals, and long duration dives may help elephant seals to minimize encounters with white sharks. They may also avoid these predators along the routes to and from the rookery over the continental shelf by swimming faster in waters over the shelf than off it, surfacing for shorter intervals, and swimming near the bottom. Newly weaned pups learn to swim and dive at night, remaining close to shore in shallow water. Breeding age males spend more time in the "high risk zones" near islands, than do females and juveniles and are more frequently injured by sharks. Southern elephant seals exhibit similar diving behaviors (e.g. females exhibit higher diving rates and shorter durations on the continental shelf than off it), suggesting avoidance of their major predator, the killer whale. It is unknown whether other phocids exhibit a diving pattern that may have functions other than feeding. Otariids do not exhibit the diving behavior associated with avoidance of near-surface predators and, in fact, typically swim at the surface during transit.

9.8. Phylogenetic Implications of Diving Patterns in Pinnipeds

Different evolutionary strategies for diving in phocids and otariids have been proposed based on a comparative study of physiological characters of diving responses in pinnipeds (Mottishaw *et al.*, 1999). The phocid diving strategy, described as "energy conserving," enables phocids to dive longer than otariids. Otariids do not spend as much time diving and average dive durations are on the order of a few minutes. The otariid strategy is energy dissipative (Table 9.5).

For the greater diving capacity in phocids, all of the above characteristics are incorporated. A large body weight maximizes the amount of oxygen that can be carried while minimizing mass-specific energy demands during diving by allometric effects. A slow swimming speed

Table 9.5. Comparison of phocid and otariid diving strategies (based on Mottishaw *et al.*, 1999)

Otariid characteristics	Phocid characteristics
1. apnea, initiated on inhalation and a gas exchange system that does not completely collapse	1. apnea, with exhalation upon initiation of diving
2. bradycardia	2. bradycardia in 1:1 proportion with changes in cardiac output
3. peripheral vasoconstriction, with propulsive muscle microvasculature presumably more relaxed than in phocids	3. peripheral vasoconstriction and hypoperfusion (to conserve O_2 for central nervous system and the heart)
4. hypometabolism of ischemic tissues	4. hypometabolism of (vasoconstricted) ischemic tissues
5. O_2 carrying capacity intermediate between large phocids and terrestrial mammals	5. enhanced O_2 carrying capacity (enlarged blood volume, expanded red blood cell mass within the blood volume—i.e. higher hematocrit, higher hemoglobin concentration, possibly higher myoglobin concentration in muscles and heart)
6. spleen not much larger as a percentage of body weight than in terrestrial mammals	6. enlarged spleen (for regulating the hematocrit so that very high RBCs need not be circulated under all physiological conditions)

while at sea minimizes the cost of locomotion while maximizing submergence, hence foraging, time. In contrast, otariids have a relatively small and hydrodynamically sleek body consistent with a high speed predator lifestyle. The tradeoff seems to require sacrificing extended foraging time for energy needed for higher speed swimming (Costa, 1991). There are, however, exceptions to these generalizations of phocid and otariid dive patterns. For example, the New Zealand sea lion has the highest blood volume yet reported for an otariid, one which falls within the range of phocids (Costa *et al.,* 1998). This high blood volume determination which enables increased oxygen storage capability supports the deep, prolonged diving pattern exhibited by this species. Future work is needed to determine whether this species shows other adaptations that would increase its diving capability (e.g., higher myoglobin, larger spleen). Although walruses are among the largest pinnipeds they are one of the shortest duration and shallowest divers (Table 9.1). It has been suggested that walruses may be able to dive to greater depths than the maximum recorded but have little reason to do so because of the abundance of their benthic prey in shallower waters (Fay and Burns, 1988).

9.9. Diving and Breath-Holding Patterns in Whales

On the basis of body size it would be expected that cetaceans should be able to dive longer and deeper than other marine mammals because they can store more oxygen and have lower mass-specific metabolic rates. This, however, is not the case and cetaceans (with the exception of the sperm whale) are surpassed in average diving capacity by considerably smaller phocids (Schreer and Kovacs, 1997). There are several likely reasons for this. First, cetacean diving behavior is extremely difficult to measure and much of the data are based on single observations or inferences from feeding ecology. Secondly, the feeding ecology of most cetaceans involves exploitation of resources located at shallower depths than other groups and therefore they may not need to dive as deep or for as long (Schreer and Kovacs, 1997).

Generally, cetaceans (like pinnipeds) exhale and inhale lung air rapidly, then retain that air in their lungs for prolonged periods of apnea before exhaling again, even when resting at the sea surface. Small dolphins, for instance, exhale and inhale in about 0.1 s, then hold their breath for 20 to 30 s before taking a breath. Even adult blue whales can empty their lungs of 1500 liters of air and refill them in as little as 2 seconds. In the larger species of whales, dives of several minutes duration, whether for feeding or during migration, typically are followed by a series of several blows 20 to 30 seconds apart before another prolonged dive is initiated (Fig. 9.16 and see Fig. 8.30).

These short breath-hold ventilatory patterns of whales optimize oxygen uptake relative to their time spent at the sea surface. Most extraction of oxygen by gray whale calves, for example, is accomplished with rapid uptake of oxygen during the first 20–25 s of each breath hold, followed by diminishing oxygen gains at longer breath holds (Fig. 9.17). This reflects a breathing pattern marked by a well-defined breath-hold duration at about 20 s for gray whales of all ages, including migrating adults, foraging calves, and adults outside winter lagoons (Sumich, 1983, 1986).

The ventilatory rhythms of animals involved in activities which require submergence have evolved in ways which maximize the net gain of oxygen with each surfacing, or optimize oxygen uptake relative to their time spent at the sea surface (Kramer, 1988). Apneustic ventilatory rhythms permit diving mammals to maintain aerobic diving schedules by staying within their ADL between breaths. By avoiding long periods of hypoxia which require longer surface recovery times, they have more time available for submerged activity such as foraging (Kramer, 1988; Sumich, 1994).

This pattern also is expressed in the ventilatory and diving behavior of foraging humpback whales studied in Alaska (Dolphin, 1987). Dive durations, surface times, and the numbers of blows per surfacing all were correlated with the depths of foraging dives. Dives tended to be short (most were less than 3 min) and shallow (84.6% were to depths of less than 60 m). Dolphin postulated that dives to depths of 41–60 m (1–6 min in duration) approximate the aerobic dive limit of humpback whales because the percentage of time spent at the surface tended to increase with increasing depth of dive and exhibited a marked increase at depths greater than 60 m.

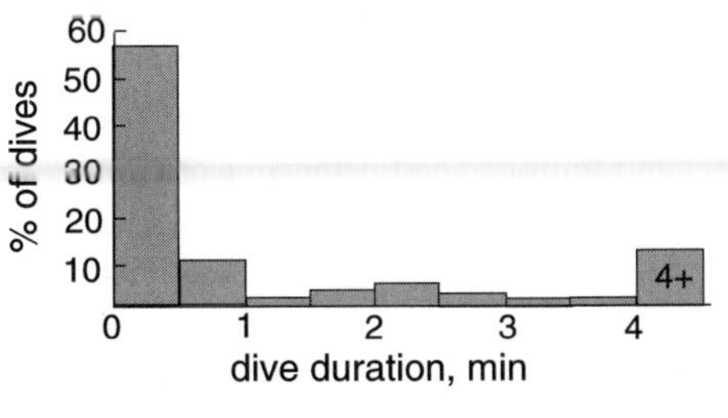

Figure 9.16. Thirty second increment frequency distribution of dive durations of migrating gray whales (n = 349; modified from Sumich, 1983).

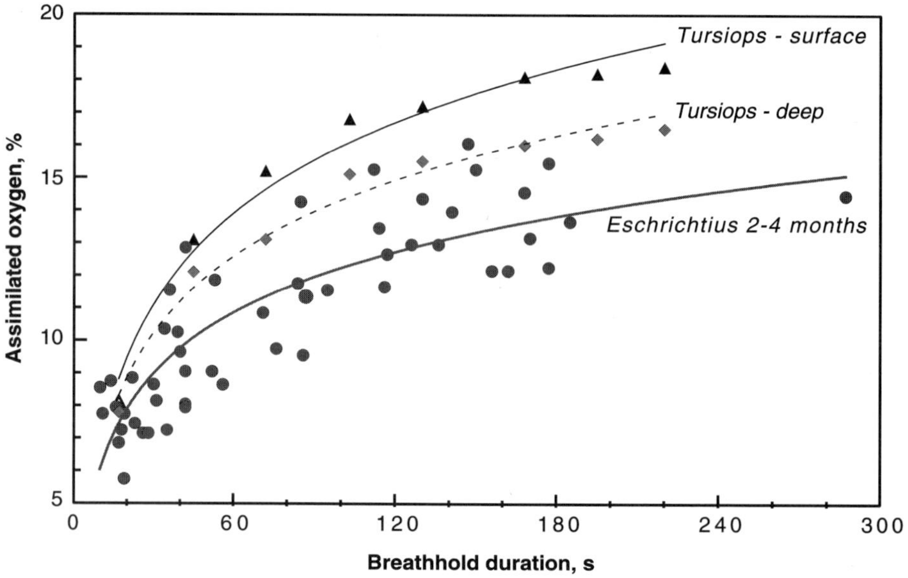

Figure 9.17. Influence of breathhold duration on % oxygen uptake for a bottlenose dolphin at the surface and 30 m deep, and for a young captive gray whale (from Ridgway, 1972 and Sumich, unpublished data).

Sperm whales exhibit yet another pattern of diving. Small social groups of these whales spend hours together at the surface each day, then initiate a series of long and deep foraging dives. Adult Caribbean sperm whales tracked with acoustic transponders exhibited dive profiles like those in Fig. 9.18, with extended periods of resting and socializing at the surface, especially during afternoon hours (Watkins *et al.,* 1993). Diving was most common at night and during early morning hours. Dives typically lasted more than 30 min to depths usually below 400 m. Like the dives of foraging elephant seals and migrating gray whales, little surface recovery time was apparent between dives. Sperm whales, like the other species of marine mammals discussed in this chapter, presumably dive within their ADL or are compensating by other mechanisms.

9.10. Summary and Conclusions

The effects of pressure on the diving animal involve circulatory and respiratory adaptations. Among circulatory changes in pinnipeds and cetaceans are enlargement and increased complexity of blood vessels, including the development of retia mirabilia throughout the body which serve as oxygen reservoirs during deep dives. The muscles, blood, and spleen are important for oxygen stores in marine mammals. Respiratory adjustments that occur during diving involve modifications in the structure of the lungs, especially the bronchioles.

Most of the evidence supports the view that marine mammals do not have significantly higher metabolic rates than terrestrial mammals of similar size. Bradycardia, peripheral

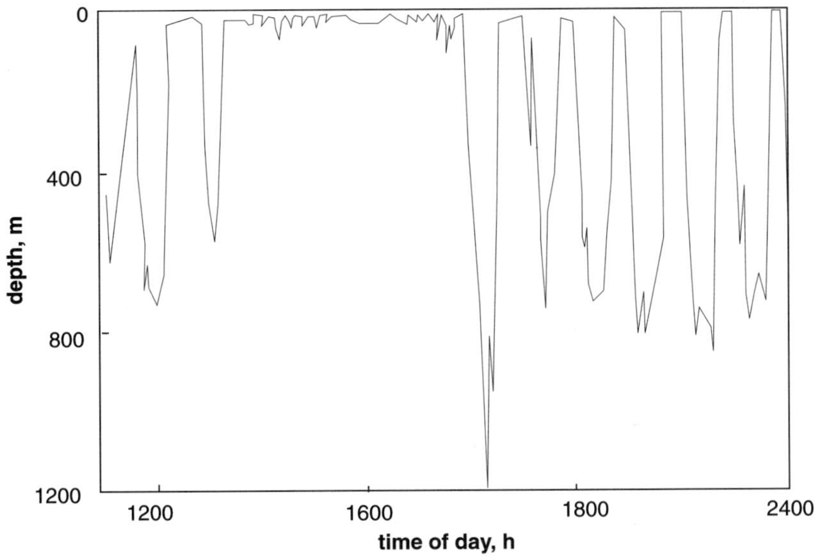

Figure 9.18. Continuous dive profile of a single sperm whale, generated by connecting depth points recorded by a digital depth monitor tag (redrawn from Watkins *et al.*, 1993).

vasoconstriction, and other circulatory adjustments are important components of an integrated set of diving responses. Research on the Weddell seal and other pinnipeds revealed that the majority of dives are aerobic and that only dives exceeding an animal's aerobic dive limit (ADL) elicited one or more of the diving responses. The phylogenetic implications of the diving patterns indicate two strategies among pinnipeds, an otariid "energy dissipative" strategy and a phocid "energy conserving" strategy. It is suggested that the walrus is capable of deep dives but has little reason to do so because of the availability of their prey in shallow water. In addition to their function in energy conservation and foraging, the diving patterns of pinnipeds may also play a role in the avoidance of predators. The diving and breath-hold capacities of most whales (with the exception of the sperm whale) are exceeded by considerably smaller phocid seals. Possible explanations for this include less accurate measurements of cetacean diving behavior and their exploitation of prey located at shallower depths.

9.11. Further Reading

For a general introduction to diving physiology and behavior in marine mammals see Kooyman (1989); a popular account of diving in the Weddell seal can be found in Kooyman (1981). A comprehensive account of elephant seal diving behavior is summarized in an edited volume of their biology (Le Boeuf and Laws, 1994) and see Gentry and Kooyman (1986) for diving behaviors of various fur seals. Summary accounts of cetacean diving include Ridgway (1986) and Ridgway and Harrison (1986).

References

Andrews, R. D., D. R. Jones, J. D. Williams, P. H. Thorson, G. W. Oliver, D. P. Costa, and B. J. Le Boeuf (1997). Heart rates of Northern elephant seals diving at sea and resting on the beach. *J. Exp. Biol.* **200**: 2083–2095.

Arnold, R. W. (1985). Extremes in human breath hold, facial immersion bradycardia. *Undersea Biomed. Res.* **12**: 183–190.

Barabash-Nikiforov, I. I. (1947). "Kalan" (The sea otter). Soviet Ministrov RSFSR. (Translated from Russian, Israel Program for Scientific Translations, Jerusalem, 1962).

Boutilier, R. G., M. Nikinmaa, and B. L. Tufts (1993). Relationship between blood buffering properties, erythrocyte pH and water content, in gray seals *(Halichoerus grypus). Acta. Physiol. Scand.* **147**: 241–247.

Boyd, I. L., and J. P. Croxall (1996). Dive durations in pinnipeds and seabirds. *Can. J. Zool.* **74**: 1696–1705.

Boyd, I. L. (1997). The behavioural and physiological ecology of diving. *Trends in Ecology and Evolution* **12**(6): 213–217.

Bryden, M. M. (1972). Growth and development of marine mammals. *In* "Functional Anatomy of Marine Mammals" (R. J. Harrison, ed.), Vol. 1, pp. 1–79. Academic Press, New York.

Bryden, M. M., and G. H. K. Lim (1969). Blood parameters of the southern elephant seal *(Mirounga leonina)* in relation to diving. *Comp. Biochem. Physiol.* **28**: 139–148.

Castellini, M. A. (1985). Metabolic depression in tissues and organs of marine mammals during diving: Living with less oxygen. *Mol. Physiol.* **8**: 427–437.

Castellini, M. A. (1991). The biology of diving mammals: Behavioral, physiological, and biochemical limits. *Adv. Comp. Physiol.* **8**: 105–134.

Castellini, M. A., and G. N. Somero (1981). Buffering capacity of vertebrate muscle: Correlations with potentials for anaerobic function. *J. Comp. Physiol.* **143**: 191–198.

Castellini, M. A., G. N. Somero, and G. L. Kooyman (1981). Glycolytic enzyme activities in tissues of marine and terrestrial mammals. *Physiol. Zool.* **54**: 242–252.

Castellini, M. A., Davis, R. W., and G. L. Kooyman (1988). Blood chemistry regulation during repetitive diving in Weddell seals. *Physiol. Zool.* **61**: 379–386.

Castellini, M. A., D. P. Costa, and M. Castellini (1992). Blood glucose distribution, brain size and diving in small odontocetes. *Mar. Mamm. Sci.* **8**: 294–298.

Costa, D. P. (1991). Reproductive and foraging energetics of pinnipeds: Implications for life history patterns. *In* "The Behavior of Pinnipeds" (D. Renouf, ed.), pp. 300–344. Chapman & Hall, London.

Costa, D. P., and G. L. Kooyman (1982). Oxygen consumption, thermoregulation, and the effect of fur oiling and washing on the sea otter, *Enhydra lutris. Can. J. Zool.* **60**: 2761–2767.

Costa, D. P., N. J. Gales, and D. E. Crocker (1998). Blood volume and diving ability of the New Zealand sea lion, *Phocarctos hookeri. Physiol. Zool.* **71**(2): 208–213.

Curry, B. E., J. Mead, and A. P. Purgue (1994). The occurrence of calculi in the nasal diverticula of porpoises (Phocoenidae). *Mar. Mamm. Sci.* **10**(1): 81–86.

DeLong, R. L., and B. S. Stewart (1991). Diving patterns of northern elephant seal bulls. *Mar. Mamm. Sci.* **7**: 369–384.

Dolphin, W. F. (1987). Dive behavior and estimated energy expenditure of foraging humpback whales in southeast Alaska. *Can. J. Zool.* **65**: 354–362.

Drabek, C. M. (1975). Some anatomical aspects of the cardiovascular system of Antarctic seals and their possible functional significance in diving. *J. Morph.* **145**(1): 85–106.

Drabek, C. M. (1977). Some anatomical and functional aspects of seal hearts and aortae. *In* "Functional Anatomy of Marine Mammals" (R. J. Harrison, ed.), Vol. 3, pp. 217–234. Academic Press, London.

Drabek, C. M., and G. L. Kooyman (1983). Terminal airway embryology of the delphinid porpoises, *Stenella attenuata* and *S. longirostris. J. Morphol.* **175**: 65–72.

Elsner, R., and B. Gooden (1983). "Diving and Asphyxia: A Comparative Study of Animals and Men." Cambridge University Press, New York.

Engel, S. (1959a). The respiratory tissue of dugong *(Halicore dugong). Anat. Anz.* **106**: 90–100.

Engel, S. (1959b). Rudimentary mammalian lungs. *Gegenbaurs Morphol. Jahrb.* **106**: 95–114.

Engel, S. (1962). The air passages of the dugong lung. *Acta Anat.* **48**: 95–107.

Falke, K. J., R. D. Hill, J. Qvist, R. C. Schneider, M. Guppy, G. C. Liggins, P. W. Hochachka, R. E. Elliott, and W. M. Zapol (1985). Seal lungs collapse during free diving: Evidence from arterial nitrogen tensions. *Science* **229**: 556–557.

Fay, F. (1981). Walrus—*Odobenus rosmarus*. *In* "Handbook of Marine Mammals" (S. H. Ridgway and R. J. Harrison, eds.), pp. 1–23. Academic Press, London.

Fay, F. H., and J. J. Burns (1988). Maximum feeding depth of walruses. *Arctic* **41**: 239–240.

Folkow, L. P., and A. S. Blix (1987). Nasal heat and water exchange in gray seals. *Am. J. Physiol.* **253**: R883–R889.

Gallivan, G. H., and R. C. Best (1980). Metabolism and respiration of the Amazonian manatee. (*Trichechus inunguis*). *Physiol. Zool.* **53**(3): 245–253.

Gentry, R. L., and G. L. Kooyman (1986). "Fur Seals: Maternal Strategies on Land and at Sea." Princeton Univ. Press, New Jersey.

Gentry, R. L., G. L. Kooyman and M. E. Goebel (1986). Feeding and diving behavior of northern fur seals. *In* "Fur Seals: Maternal Strategies on Land and at Sea," pp. 61–78. Princeton Univ. Press, New Jersey.

Gilmartin, W. G., R. W. Pierce, and G. A. Antonelis (1974). Some physiological parameters of the blood of the California gray whale. *Marine Fisheries Rev.* **36**: 28–31.

Gosline, J. M., and R. E. Shadwick (1996). The mechanical properties of fin whale arteries are explained by novel connective tissue designs. *J. Exp. Biol.* **199**: 985–997.

Hampton, I. F. G., G. C. Whitlow, J. Szekercezes, and S. Rutherford (1971). Heat transfer and body temperature in the Atlantic bottlenosed dolphin, *Tursiops truncatus*. *Int. J. Biometeorol.* **15**: 247–253.

Hansen, S., and D. M. Lavigne (1997). Ontogeny of the thermal limits in the harbor seal (*Phoca vitulina*). *Physiol. Zool.* **70**(1): 85–92.

Harrison, R. J. and J. E. King (1980). Marine Mammals, 2nd ed. Hutchinson, London.

Harrison, R. J., and G. L. Kooyman (1968). General physiology of the pinnipedia. *In* "The Behavior and Physiology of the Pinnipeds" (R. J. Harrison, R. C. Hubbard, R. S. Peterson, R. E. Rice, and R. J. Schusterman, eds.), pp. 211–296. Appleton-Century-Crofts, New York.

Harrison, R. J. and J. D. W. Tomlinson (1956). Observations on the venous system in certain Pinnipedia and Cetacea. *Trans. Zool. Soc. London* **126** (part 2): 205–233.

Hedrick, M. S., and D. A. Duffield (1991). Haematological and rheological characteristics of blood in seven marine mammal species: Physiological implications for diving behaviour. *J. Zool.* **225**: 273–283.

Hill, W. C. O. (1945). Notes on the dissection of two dugongs. *J. Mammal.* **26**: 153–175.

Hindell, M. A., D. J. Slip, H. R. Burton, and M. M. Bryden (1992). Physiological implications of continuous, prolonged, and deep dives of the southern elephant seal (*Mirounga leonina*). *Can. J. Zool.* **70**(2): 370–379.

Hochachka, P. W. (1988). Metabolic suppression and oxygen availability (marine mammals). *Can. J. Zool.* **66**: 152–158.

Hochachka, P. W. (1992). Metabolic biochemistry and the making of a mesopelagic mammal. *Experentia* **48**: 570–575.

Hochachka, P. W., and R. A. Foreman, III (1993). Phocid and cetacean blueprints of muscle metabolism. *Can. J. Zool.* **71**: 2089–2098.

Hochachka, P. W., and M. Guppy (1987). "Metabolic Arrest and the Control of Biological Time." Harvard University Press, Cambridge, MA.

Hochachka, P. W., and P. D. Mottishaw (1998). Evolution and adaptation of the diving response: Phocids and otariids. *In* "Cold Ocean Symposia" (H. O. Portwer and R. C. Playle, eds.), pp. 391–431. Cambridge Univ. Press, Cambridge, Massachusetts.

Hochachka, P. W., and K. B. Storey (1975). Metabolic consequences of diving in mammals and man. *Science* **187**: 613–621.

Hong, S. K. (1988). Man as a breath-hold diver. *Can. J. Zool.* **66**: 70–74.

Huntley, A. C. (1987). Determination of basal metabolic rate by extrapolation in mammals that breathe periodically. *In* "Marine Mammal Energetics" (A. C. Huntley *et al.*, eds.), Spec. Publ. No. 1, pp. 97–107. *Soc. Mar. Mammal.*

Huntley, A. C., D. P. Costa, and R. D. Rubin (1984). The contribution of nasal countercurrent heat exchange to water balance in the northern elephant seal, *Mirounga angustirostris*. *J. Exp. Biol.* **113**: 447–454.

Husar, S. (1977). A review of the literature of the dugong (*Dugong dugon*). *Res. Rep.—U.S. Fish Wildl. Serv.* **4**: 1–25.

Innes, S., and D. M. Lavigne (1991). Do cetaceans really have elevated metabolic rates? *Physiol. Zool.* **64**(4): 1130–1134.

Innes, H. S., and K. Ronald (1985). Daily energy expenditure, heat increment of feeding, and postabsorptive, resting metabolic rates of ringed, harp and gray seals. *In* "Proceedings of the Sixth Biennial Conference on the Biology of Marine Mammals." Nov 22–26, Vancouver, British Columbia.

Irvine, A. B. (1983). Manatee metabolism and its influence on distribution in Florida. *Biol. Conserv.* **25**: 315–334.

Irving, L., O. M. Solandt, D. Y. Solandt, and K. C. Fisher (1935). Respiratory characteristics of the blood of the seal. *J. Cell. Comp. Physiol.* **6**: 393–403.

Irving, L., P. F. Scholander, and S. W. Grinnell (1941). The respiration of the porpoises, *Tursiops truncatus*. *J. Cell. Comp. Physiol.* **17**: 145.

Karadeeva, O. G., S. K. Matisheva, and V. M. Shapunov (1973). Features of external respiration in the delphinidae. *In* "Morphology and Ecology of Marine Mammals. Seals, Dolphins, Porpoises" (K. K. Chapskii and V. E. Soklov, eds.), pp. 196–206. Wiley, New York.

Karmiol, E. (1978). Ama: The diving women of Japan. *Oceans* **11**: 38–41.

Kasting, N. W., S. A. L. Adderley, T. Safford, and K. Hewlett (1989). Thermoregulation in beluga (*Delphinapterus leucas*) and killer (*Orcinus orca*) whales. *Physiol. Zool.* **62**: 687–701.

King, J. E. (1977). Comparative anatomy of the blood vessels of the sea lions *Neophoca* and *Phocarctos;* with comments on the differences between the otariid and phocid vascular systems. *J. Zool.* **181**: 69–94.

King, J. E. (1983). "Seals of the World," 2nd ed. Comstock, Ithaca, NY.

Kolchinskaya, A. Z., I. N. Man'koyskaya, and A. G. Misura (1980). "Respiration and Oxygen Regimes of the Dolphin." Naukova Dumka Publishing House, Kiev, USSR.

Kooyman, G. L. (1966). Maximum diving capacities of the Weddell seal (*Leptonychotes weddelli*). *Science* **151**: 1553–1554.

Kooyman, G. L. (1973). Respiratory adaptations in marine mammals. *Am. Zool.* **13**: 457–468.

Kooyman, G. L. (1981). "Weddell seal: Consummate diver." Cambridge Univ. Press, Cambridge.

Kooyman, G. L. (1985). Physiology without restraint in diving mammals. *Mar. Mamm. Sci.* **1**: 166–178.

Kooyman, G. L. (1989). "Diverse Divers: Physiology and Behavior." Springer-Verlag, New York.

Kooyman, G. L., and H. T. Anderson (1969). Deep diving. *In* "Biology of Marine Mammals" (H. T. Anderson, ed.), pp. 65–94. Academic Press. New York.

Kooyman, G. L., and W. B. Campbell (1972). Heart rates in freely diving Weddell seals, *Leptonychotes weddellii*. *Comp. Biochem. Physiol. A* **43A**: 31–36.

Kooyman, G. L., E. A. Wahrenbrock, M. A. Castellini, R. W. Davis, and E. E. Sinnett (1980). Aerobic and anaerobic metabolism during voluntary diving in Weddell seals: Evidence of preferred pathways from blood chemistry and behavior. *J. Comp. Physiol.* **138**: 335–346.

Kooyman, G. L., M. A. Castellini, and R. W. Davis (1981). Physiology of diving in marine mammals. *Annu. Rev. Physiol.* **43**: 343–356.

Kooyman, G. L., M. A. Castellini, R. W. Davis, and R. A. Mauae. (1983). Aerobic diving limits of immature Weddell seals. *J. Comp. Physiol., B* **151**: 171–174.

Kramer, D. L. (1988). The behavioral ecology of air breathing by aquatic animals. *Can. J. Zool.* **66**: 89–94.

Kvitek, R. G., C. E. Bowley, and M. Staedler (1993). Diet and foraging behavior of sea otters in southeast Alaska. *Mar. Mamm. Sci.* **9**(2): 168–181.

Lavigne, D. M., S. Innes, G. A. Worthy, K. M. Kovacs, O. J. Schmitz, and J. P. Hickie (1986). Metabolic rates of seals and whales. *Can. J. Zool.* **64**: 279–284.

Lawrence, B., and W. E. Schevill (1965). Gular musculature in delphinids. *Bull. Mus. Comp. Zool.* **133**: 1–65.

Le Boeuf, B. J. (1994). Variation in the diving pattern of Northern elephant seals with age, mass, sex and reproductive condition. *In* "Elephant Seals" (B. J. Le Boeuf and R. M. Laws, eds.), University of California Press, Berkeley.

Le Boeuf, B. J., and D. E. Crocker (1996). Diving behavior of elephant seals: Implications for predator avoidance. *In* "Great White Sharks, The Biology of *Carcharodon carchias*" (A. P. Klimley and D. G. Ainley, eds.), pp. 193–206. Academic Press, San Diego, CA.

Le Boeuf, B. J., and R. M. Laws, eds. (1994). "Elephant Seals." Univ. Calif. Press, Berkeley.

Le Boeuf, B. J., Y. Naito, A. C. Huntley, and T. Asaga (1989). Prolonged, continuous, deep diving by northern elephant seals. *Can. J. Zool.* **67**: 2514–2519.

Le Boeuf, B. J., P. A. Morris, S. B. Blackwell, D. E. Crocker, and D. P. Costa (1996). Diving behavior of juvenile northern elephant seals. *Can. J. Zool.* **74**: 1632–1644.

Leith, D. (1976). Physiological properties of blood of marine mammals. *In* "The Biology of Marine Mammals" (H. T. Anderson, ed.), pp. 95–116. Academic Press, New York.

Lenfant, C., K. Johansen, and J. D. Torrance (1970). Gas transport and oxygen storage capacity in some pinnipeds and the sea otter. *Respir. Physiol.* **9**: 227–286.

MacDonald, A. A., I. L. Boyd, and C. Dixon (1995). Comparative anatomy of the cardiac foramen ovale in the Pinnipedia. *Can. J. Zool.* **73**: 850–857.

Marsh, H. D., A. V. Spain, and G. Heinsohn (1978). Minireview: Physiology of the dugong. *Comp. Biochem. Physiol.* Part A, **61**(2): 159–168.

McNab, B. K. (1988). Complications inherent in scaling the basal rate of metabolism in mammals. *Q. Rev. Biol.* **63**: 25–54.

Melnikov, V. V. (1997). The arterial system of the sperm whale (*Physeter macrocephalus*). *J. Morphol.* **234**: 37–50.

Moon, R. E., R. D. Vann, and P. B. Bennett (1995). The physiology of decompression illness. *Sci. Am.* **273**: 70–77.

Mottishaw, P. D., S. J. Thornton, and P. W. Hochachka (1999). The diving response mechanism and its surprising evolutionary path in seals and sea lions. *Amer. Zool.* **39**: 434–450.
Munkacsi, I. M., and J. D. Newstead (1985). The intrarenal and pericapsular venous systems of kidneys of the ringed seal, *Phoca hispida. J. Morphol.* **184**: 361–373.
Murphy, B., W. M. Zapol, and P. W. Hochachka (1980). Metabolic activities of heart, lung, and brain during diving and recovery in the Weddell seal. *J. Appl. Physiol.* **48**: 596–605.
Nishiwaki, M., and H. Marsh (1985). Dugong *Dugong dugon* (Muller, 1776). "Handbook of Marine Mammals," vol. 3, pp. 1–31. The Sirenians and Baleen Whales. Academic Press, New York.
Nowicki, S. N., I. Stirling, and B. Sjare (1997). Duration of stereotyped underwater vocal displays by male Atlantic walruses in relation to aerobic dive limit. *Mar. Mamm. Sci.* **13**(4): 566–575.
O'Shea, T. J., and R. L. Reep (1990). Encephalization quotients and life history traits in the Sirenia. *J. Mammal.* **71**(4): 334–342.
Pfeiffer, C. J. (1990). Observations on the ultrastructural morphology of the bowhead whale (*Balaena mysticetus*) heart. *J. Zool. Wild. Med.* **21**: 48–55.
Pfeiffer, C. J., and T. P. Kinkead (1990). Microanatomy of retia mirabilia of bowhead whale foramen magnum and mandibular foramen. *Acta Anat.* **139**: 141–150.
Pfeiffer, C. J., and V. S. Viers (1995). Cardiac ultrastructure in the ringed seal, *Phoca hispida* and harp seal, *Phoca groenlandica. Aquat. Mamm.* **21**(2): 109–119.
Pierce, R. W. (1970). Design and operation of a metabolic chamber for marine mammals. Ph.D. dissertation, University of California, Berkeley.
Ponganis, P. J., R. L. Gentry, E. P. Ponganis, and K. V. Ponganis (1992). Analysis of swim velocities during deep and shallow dives of two northern fur seals, *Callorhinus ursinus. Mar. Mamm. Sci.* **8**: 69–75.
Rea, L. D. (1987). Post-absorptive metabolism of hooded seals, *Cystophora cristata. In* "Proceedings of the Seventh Biennial Conference on the Biology of Marine Mammals," December 3–9, Miami, Fla.
Reeves, R. R., and J. K. Ling (1978). Hooded Seal-*Cystophora cristata. In* "Handbook of Marine Mammals," vol. 2, pp. 171–194. Academic Press, London.
Reidenberg, J. S., and J. T. Laitman (1987). Position of the larynx in Odontoceti. *Anat. Rec.* **218**: 98–106.
Reynolds, J., and D. Odell (1991). "Manatees and Dugongs." Facts on File, New York.
Ridgway, S. H. (1972). Homeostasis in the aquatic environment. *In* "Mammals of the Sea" (S. H. Ridgway, ed.), pp. 590–747. Thomas, Springfield, Ill.
Ridgway, S. H. (1986). Diving by cetaceans. *In* "Diving in Animals and Man" (A. O. Brubakk, J. W. Kanwisher, and G. Sundness, eds.), pp. 33–62. The Royal Norwegian Society of Science and Letters, Trinheim, Norway.
Ridgway, S. H., and R. J. Harrison (1986). Diving dolphins. *In* "Research on Dolphins" (M. M. Bryden and R. H. Harrison, eds.), pp. 33–58. Oxford Univ. Press, Oxford.
Ridgway, S. H. (1990). The central nervous system of the bottlenose dolphin. *In* "The Bottlenose Dolphin" (S. Leatherwood and R. R. Reeves, eds.), pp. 69–97. Academic Press, San Diego, CA.
Ridgway, S. H., and R. Howard (1979). Dolphin lung collapse and intramuscular circulation during free diving: Evidence from nitrogen washout. *Science* **206**: 1182–1183.
Ridgway, S. H., and D. G. Johnston (1966). Blood oxygen and ecology of porpoises of three genera. *Science* **151**: 456–458.
Ridgway, S. H. and G. S. Patton (1971). Dolphin thyroid: Some anatomical and physiological findings. *Z. Vergl. Physiol.* **71**: 129–141.
Ridgway, S. H., B. L. Scronce, and J. Kaniwisher (1969). Respiration and deep diving in the bottlenose porpoise. *Science* **166**: 1651–1653.
Riedman, M. (1990). "The Pinnipeds: Seals, Sea Lions, and Walruses." University of California Press, Berkeley.
Ronald, K., R. McCarter, and L. J. Selley (1977). Venous circulation in the harp seal (*Pagophilus groenlandicus*). *In* "Functional Anatomy of Marine Mammals" (R. J. Harrison, ed.), Vol. 3, pp. 235–270. Academic Press, New York.
Rowlatt, U., and H. Marsh (1985). The heart of the dugong (*Dugong dugon*) and the West Indian Manatee (*Trichechus manatus*) Sirenia. *J. Morphol.* **186**: 95–105.
Scholander, P. F. (1940). Experimental investigations on the respiratory function in diving mammals and birds. *Hvalradets Skr.* **22**: 1–131.
Scholander, P. F., and L. Irving (1941). Experimental investigations on the respiration and diving of the Florida manatee. *J. Cell. Comp. Physiol.* **17**: 169–191.
Scholander, P. F., L. Irving, and S. W. Grinell (1942). Aerobic and anaerobic changes in seal muscles during diving. *J. Biol. Chem.* **142**: 431–440.
Schreer, J. F., and K. M. Kovacs (1997). Allometry of diving capacity in air-breathing vertebrates. *Can. J. Zool.* **75**: 339–358.

Schreer, J. F., and J. W. Testa (1996). Classification of Weddell seal diving behavior. *Mar. Mamm. Sci.* **12**: 227–250.

Shadwick, R. E., and J. M. Gosline (1994). Arterial mechanics in the fin whale suggest a unique hemodynamic design. *Am. J. Physiol.* **267**: R805–R818.

Sleet, R. B., J. L. Sumich, and L. J. Weber (1981). Estimates of total blood volume and total body weight of a sperm whale (*Physeter catadon*). *Can. J. Zool.* **59**: 567–570.

Slijper, E. J. (1936). Die Cetaceen Vergleichend-Anatomisch und Systematisch. *Capita Zool.* **7**: 1–589.

Slijper, E. J. (1979). "Whales." 2nd ed. Hutchinson, London.

Slip, D. J., M. A. Hindell, and H. R. Burton (1994). Diving behavior of southern elephant seals from Macquarie Island. *In* "Elephant Seals" (B. J. Le Boeuf, and R. M. Laws, eds.), pp. 253–270. University of California Press, Berkeley.

Sumich, J. L. (1983). Swimming velocities, breathing patterns, and estimated costs of locomotion in migrating gray whales, *Eschrichtius robustus. Can. J. Zool.* **61**: 647–652.

Sumich, J. L. (1986). Latitudinal distribution, calf growth and metabolism, and reproductive energetics of gray whales, *Eschrichtius robustus.* Ph.D. Dissertation, Oregon State University, Corvallis.

Sumich, J. L. (1994). Oxygen extraction in free-swimming gray whale calves. *Mar. Mamm. Sci.* **10**: 226–230.

Tarasoff, F. J., and G. L. Kooyman (1973a). Observations on the anatomy of the respiratory system of the river otter, sea otter, and harp seal I. The topography, weight, and measurements of the lungs. *Can. J. Zool.* **51**(2): 163–170.

Tarasoff, F. J., and G. L. Kooyman (1973b). Observations on the anatomy of the respiratory system of the river otter, sea otter, and harp seal II. The trachea and bronchial tree. *Can. J. Zool.* **51**(2): 171–177.

Tarpley, R. J., D. J. Hillmann, W. G. Henk, and J. C. George (1997). Observations on the external morphology and vasculature of a fetal heart of the bowhead whale, *Balaena mysticetus. Anat. Rec.* **247**: 556–581.

Thompson, D,. and M. A. Fedak (1993). Cardiac responses of gray seals during diving at sea. *J. Exp. Biol.* **174**: 139–164.

Thorson, P. H., and B. J. Le Boeuf (1994). Developmental aspects of diving in northern elephant seal pups. *In* "Elephant Seals" (B. J. Le Boeuf and R. M. Laws, eds.), pp. 271–289. University of California Press, Berkeley.

Watkins, W. A., M. A. Daher, K. M. Fristrup, T. J. Howard, and G. N. Sciara (1993). Sperm whales tagged with transponders and tracked under water by sonar. *Mar. Mamm. Sci.* **9**: 55–67.

Williams, T. M., G. L. Kooyman, and D. A. Croll (1991). The effect of submergence on heart rate and oxygen consumption of swimming seals and sea lions. *J. Comp. Physiol.* **160B**: 637–644.

Yablokov, A. V., V. M. Bel'kovich, and V. I. Borisov (1972). Whales and Dolphins, Israel Programs for Scientific Translations, Jerusalem.

10

Sound Production for Communication, Echolocation, and Prey Capture

10.1. Introduction

This chapter deals with the production, transmission, and reception of sounds produced by vocalizing marine mammals in air and underwater. The manner in which vocalizations are produced and received differs between marine mammal taxa and also between air-borne and water-borne sounds. The purpose of these vocalizations ranges from communicating with the same species to locating unseen targets with echolocation.

10.1.1. Air-Borne Sounds

10.1.1.1. Pinnipeds

Air-borne sounds of pinnipeds usually are within the range of human hearing and often are described as grunts, snorts, or barks, or are identified with their presumed social function, such as "threat calls" of breeding males or "pup-attraction calls" of mothers. With the exception of the reduction in size (in otariids) or complete absence (in phocids and walruses) of the pinnae, the system for sound reception in pinnipeds is not markedly different from the typical mammalian ear. Most pinniped vocalizations are produced in the larynx, although male walruses also make clacking noises with their teeth and produce distinctive gong-like sounds in air and underwater by striking inflated pharyngeal (throat) pouches with their front flippers. These pouches are only present on males, and the gong-like sounds are produced almost exclusively by adult males during the breeding season as part of a courting display (Fig. 10.1). The hood and nasal septum of hooded seals (described in

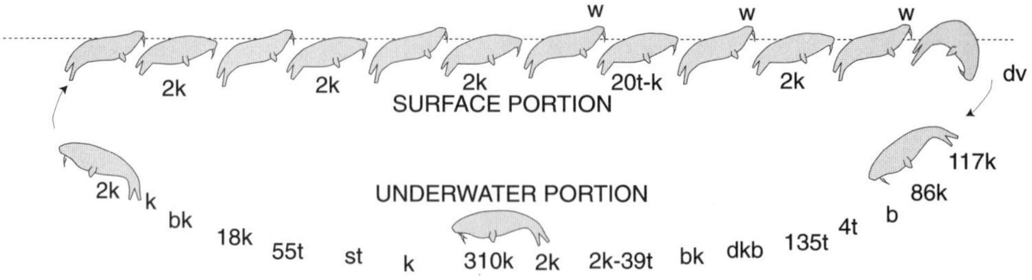

Figure 10.1. Spatial and vocal structure of a single courting display of a male walrus, with eight discrete phonations: b=bell phonation; bk=bell knock phonation; dk=double knock phonation; dkb=double knock bell phonation; dv=diving phonation; k=knock phonation; st=strum phonation; t=tap phonation; w=whistle; numerals=number of repetitions. (Redrawn from Stirling *et al.*, 1987.)

Chapter 9) produce sounds both underwater and in air. In air, these sounds are primarily emitted by adult males and may be used either in a competitive or social context depending on the sex of neighboring seals (Terhune and Ronald, 1973; Ballard and Kovacs, 1995).

In air vocalizations of pinnipeds can be grouped by species, age, and sex class, and whether individuals are in breeding or nonbreeding groups. Female harbor seals, for example, rarely vocalize on land unless they are attending pups. At the other extreme is the almost incessant barking of California and northern sea lions. Male California sea lions produce a loud directional bark that advertises dominance as well as threatens other males. Fur seal males exhibit a more complex repertoire of vocalizations, including a nondirectional "trumpeted roar" threat call that is sufficiently distinctive to allow males occupying neighboring breeding territories to recognize one another and respond less often to vocalizations of immediate neighbors than to those of strange males encroaching upon their territory (Antonelis and York, 1985; Roux and Jouventin, 1987).

Dominant male elephant seals also produce loud and repetitive vocalizations in their crowded breeding rookeries, presumably to communicate their relative breeding status to other nearby males over the cacophony of background rookery noises. These threat vocalizations differ sufficiently from one rookery to another to be considered distinctive regional **dialects** (Le Boeuf and Petrinovich, 1975). Such geographic variation of a species' vocal calls also has been found in high-latitude Weddell and bearded seals and is discussed later in this chapter.

Walruses utter sounds in most social interactions on land or on ice. Among the air-borne sound classes produced by walruses are roars, grunts, and guttural sounds used in threat displays, sometimes in combination with tusk presentation. They also produce barks, distinctive loud calls with a variety of functions that range from a submissive bark given only by adults to the bark of young calves when they are distressed (Miller, 1985). Walruses also produce what is considered a rutting whistle (Verboom and Kastelein, 1995a).

A final class of above-water pinniped vocalizations includes mother–pup calls. Mothers and pups of most species of pinnipeds have specific vocalizations to assist mother–pup pairs in recognizing and locating each other. For pinnipeds such as elephant seals, whose mothers and pups remain together throughout the nursing period, these calls help a pair to maintain contact in crowded breeding rookeries. Sea lion and fur seal mothers produce distinctive calls to attract their pups when returning from foraging at sea. Even though several pups may respond to the call of a single female, her own pup is capable of recognizing her mother's vocalizations, and individual pups are identified by their mothers by a combination of its vocalizations and probably visual and olfactory cues (Roux and Jouventin, 1987; Hanggi, 1992; Reiman and Terhune, 1993). Harp seals differ from other pinniped species in having very complex pup vocalizations. This seems anomalous because the mother–pup bond is very brief. It has been suggested that these vocalizations may instead represent a developmental step toward the complex system of adult underwater communication (Miller and Murray, 1995).

10.1.1.2. Other Marine Mammals

The vocal repertoire of sea otters consists of above-water, low frequency, low intensity signals that are similar in complexity to those of certain pinnipeds, notably the California sea lion and the northern elephant seal (McShane *et al.,* 1995). One known moderately long distance (<1 km) signal is likely important for mother–pup recognition. Of particular interest is the presence of graded signals (i.e. those that vary over a continuum of frequencies rather than forming discrete units) that are most appropriate for short range communication between familiar individuals (McShane *et al.,* 1995).

Field observations suggest that polar bears lack most of the distinctive vocalizations that characterize other carnivores (Stirling and Derocher, 1990). Females may produce mother–cub recognition calls and males snort and chuff. The latter is a low intensity repetitive call during interactions with one another (Wemmer *et al.,* 1976).

Cetaceans also produce some sounds above the sea surface and the sounds made by slapping the sea surface with flukes, flippers, or body flanks are thought to have a signal function for many odontocetes (Norris and Prescott, 1961; Norris *et al.,* 1994).

10.1.2. Sound Propagation in Water

Soon after the first microphones were lowered into the sea in the early part of the twentieth century, it became apparent that the ocean is a very noisy environment. Nonbiological sounds from waves and surf as well as sounds from biological sources contribute to the symphony of underwater sounds. Fish and crustaceans, as well as whales and pinnipeds, generate a tremendous repertoire of underwater sounds. While the emphasis of this chapter is on the active uses of phonation, many animals with acute hearing may be able to obtain substantial information about their immediate acoustic environment without giving away similar information about themselves just by quietly, intensively listening to the sounds made by others.

Several distinct functions of intentionally produced sounds have been demonstrated or suggested. Dolphins produce a large variety of whistle-like sounds (Popper, 1980), and captive individuals have been shown to understand complex linguistic subtleties (Herman, 1991). Many of the moans, squeals, and wails are evidently for communication. Several species of whales produce unique signature sounds for individual identification, including whistles of dolphins, click **codas** of sperm whales, and very low frequency tones of blue and fin whales. Other sounds, especially those of the humpback whale (*Megaptera*), have a fascinating musical quality and are thought to be produced primarily by adult males during courtship. Loud impulse sounds, so far recorded from *Tursiops, Orcinus,* and *Physeter,* have been suggested, although not yet confirmed, as possible acoustic mechanisms to overload the sensory systems in other individuals, either for debilitation of prey, self-defense, or intimidating conspecifics (Norris and Møhl, 1983). Finally, the most studied function of underwater vocalization is **echolocation**, the active detection and ranging of acoustic targets. It is this function that will receive most of the emphasis in the remainder of this chapter.

Sound energy propagates well in water and some marine mammals have co-opted this property to compensate partially for diminished light transmission and consequent poor vision in water. The velocity of sound in water is almost always between 1450 and 1550 m/s at depths less than 2000 m (Sverdrup *et al.,* 1970). The frequency and wavelength of sound are related to velocity by the following equation:

$$\text{Frequency (vibrations/s = Hz)} \times \text{wavelength (m)} = \text{Velocity (m/s)}$$

With the velocity of sound in water nearly constant, the wavelength of any underwater sound varies with its frequency. Low frequency sounds attenuate more slowly and, if used for echolocation, their ability to resolve target size cannot be finer than the wavelength of the sound (about 15 m at 100 Hz and 1.5 cm at 100 kHz). Higher frequency sounds attenuate more quickly, yet they have the potential to provide more information on target resolution because of their shorter wavelengths.

The important characteristics of any acoustic signal, its frequency, duration, and energy level, are conventionally portrayed graphically as a **sonogram** (frequency with time; Fig. 10.2a) or a **frequency (power) spectrum** (sound pressure levels with frequency; Fig. 10.2b). Both representations will be used in this chapter to assist in visualizing the sound characteristics being discussed. The time scales of sonograms are represented in appropriate units (varying from milliseconds to minutes), frequency is measured in Hz or kHz, and sound pressure level is measured in a logarithmic decibel scale (Au, 1993).

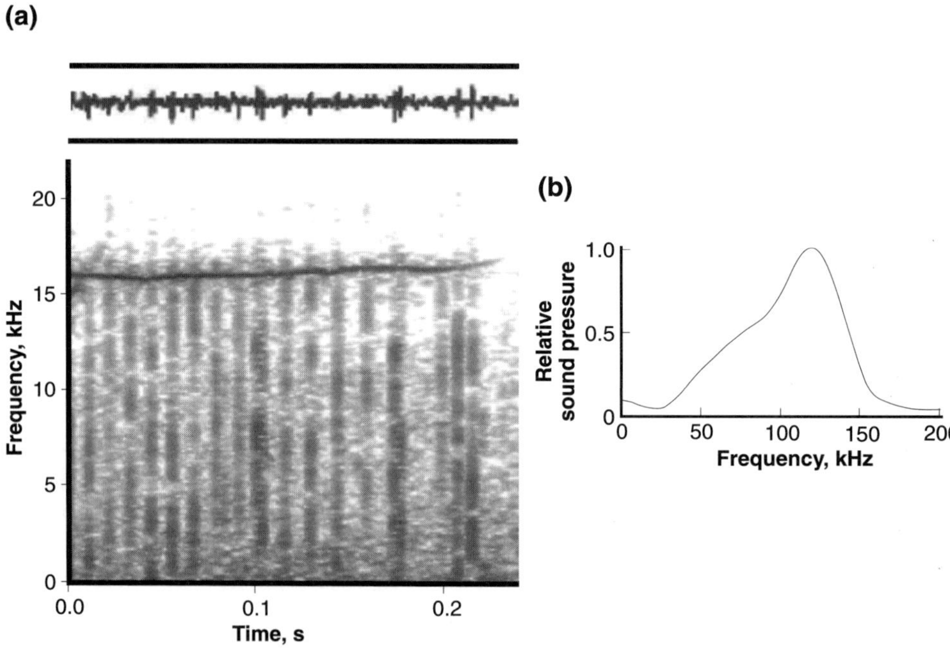

Figure 10.2. Examples of typical graphical displays of a sonogram plotting frequency and time (a), and a power spectrum plotting relative amplitude and frequency (b). The sonogram of a bottlenose dolphin echolocation click series (vertical bands) and a whistle at 16kHz. The power spectrum is of a single click of the series. Many sonograms, including this one, indicate relative amplitude with intensity of shading (or color) and with a waveform (top of sonogram). (Sonogram courtesy Hubbs/Sea World Research Institute; power spectrum adapted from Au, 1993.)

The conventional measure of propagated sound energy in water is sound pressure rather than intensity (volume). It is defined in terms of sound pressure level (SPL) in units of decibels:

$$\text{SPL in decibels} = 20 \log (p/p_o),$$

where p_o is a standardized reference pressure (typically 1 μ Pascal of pressure underwater). Decibels are used in underwater acoustics as a convenient measure of the ratio of the measured sound pressure relative to the reference sound pressure. These units provide a convenient logarithmic scale by which to compare vastly different sound pressure levels.

10.2. Anatomy and Physiology of Sound Reception

The mammalian ear evolved for the detection of sound vibrations in air. The typical mammalian ear includes an outer ear or pinna which collects sound waves and funnels them into an auditory canal (Fig. 10.3a) to the tympanic membrane, or eardrum, which separates the outer and middle ear (Fig. 10.3b). The middle ear is an air-filled chamber containing a chain of three small bony elements, or ossicles (the malleus, incus, and stapes; Fig. 10.3b). These bones form a continuous bony bridge to conduct sound vibrations from the inside of the tympanic membrane to the oval window of the inner ear, amplifying them considerably along the chain. The organ of sound reception is the cochlea, located in the inner ear. The ossicles and cochlea are enclosed in the earbone, or auditory bulla. The cochlea is a coiled organ that is divided lengthwise into three parallel tubular canals which become progressively narrower toward the apex (Fig. 10.3c). The base of the vestibular canal is formed by the oval window contacting the stapes. The tympanic canal is continuous with the vestibular canal and is closed by the round window. Between these two parallel canals lies the cochlear duct containing the actual sensory structure, the organ of Corti (Fig. 10.3c). Within the organ of Corti are rows of thousands of sensory hair cells, each connected with neurons of the auditory nerve. These hair cells are supported on the basilar membrane with the tectorial membrane directly over them. The entire organ of Corti is bathed in the endolymph of the cochlear duct. The mammalian inner ear houses two organs of equilibrium, the vestibule and the semicircular canals. As an animal's head changes position, moving fluid in the semicircular canals and vestibule puts shearing force on hair cells. Changes in shearing forces are transmitted into neuronal impulses.

The energy of air-borne sound waves striking the tympanic membrane is conducted and amplified through the bones of the middle ear to the oval window, where its oscillations are transmitted to the fluids of the vestibular and tympanic canals. These oscillating fluids simultaneously cause the basilar membrane supporting the hair cells to vibrate. Different portions of the basilar membrane respond to different frequencies, or pitches, of sound depending on the membrane's width and stiffness. The amplitude of sound, or loudness, is determined by the number of hair cells stimulated, and its timbre, or pitch, depends on the distribution pattern of stimulated hair cells.

The human ear is an extremely sensitive instrument for analyzing, characterizing, and comparing air-borne auditory signals of other animals. The range of frequencies detectable by most people lies between about 18 vibrations/s, or hertz (Hz), and 15,000 Hz (or 15 kHz). Marine mammal vocalizations often extend both above and below the range of human hearing; those with frequencies lower than 18 Hz are labeled as **infrasonic** and those higher than 20 kHz as **ultrasonic**.

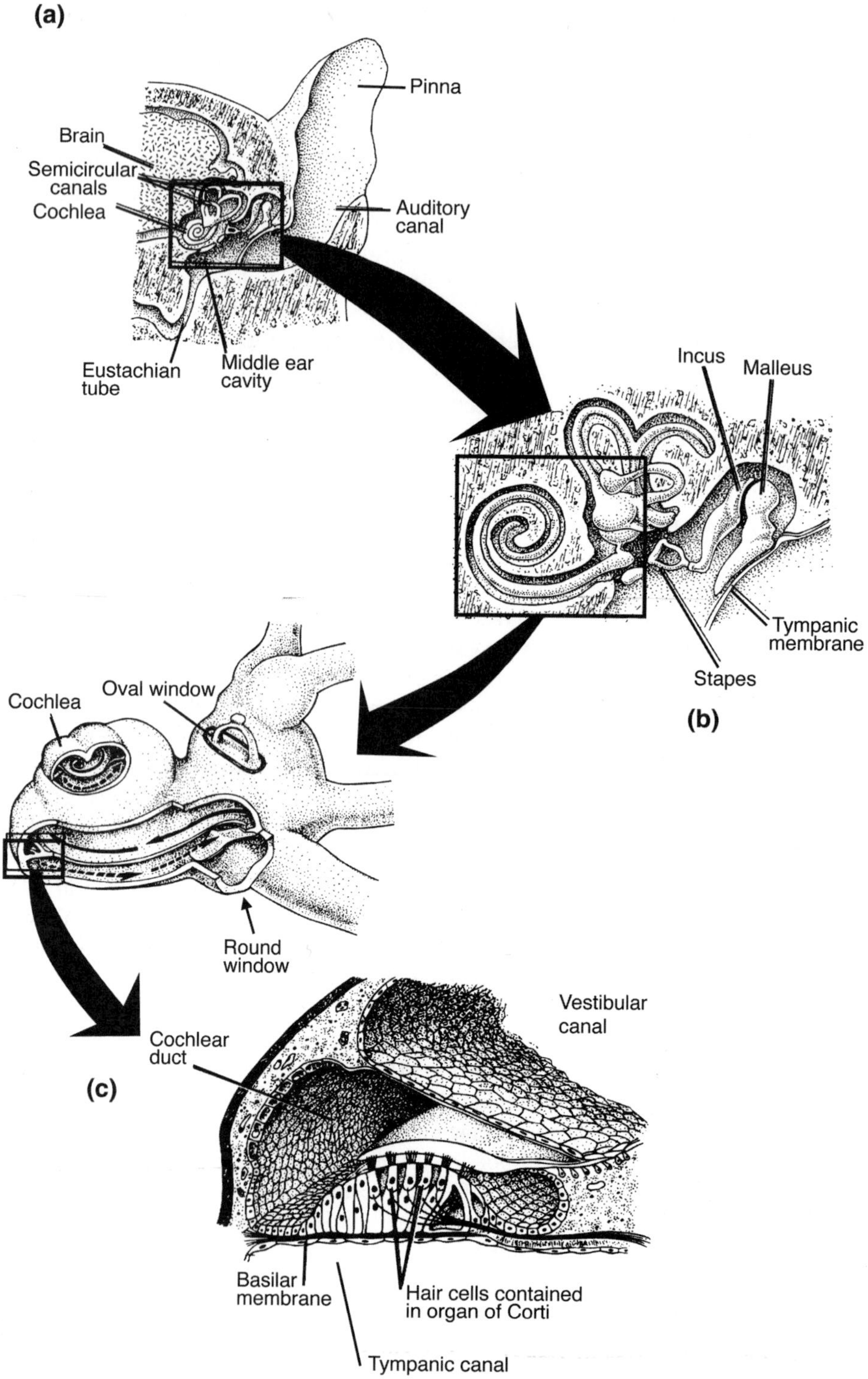

Figure 10.3. Typical mammalian ear. (a) Cross section through a typical mammalian skull, (b) Internal structure of the cochlea, (c) Section through the organ of Corti. (From Kardong, 1995.)

10.3. Functions of Sound for Marine Mammals

10.3.1. Echolocation in Toothed Whales

About 20% of all mammalian species (mostly bats) have overcome the problem of orienting themselves and locating objects in the dark or where vision is otherwise limited by producing short-duration sounds and listening for reflected echoes as the sounds bounce off objects. Essentially, echolocation is a specialized type of acoustic communication in which an animal sends information to itself. Echolocation has arisen independently at least five times in mammalian history. Microchiropteran bats are well-known echolocators, and so too are some shrews, golden hamsters, flying lemurs, and some marine mammals, notably odontocete cetaceans. By 1938, the echolocating abilities of bats were clearly demonstrated (Pierce and Griffin, 1938); yet another twenty-five years passed before echolocation in dolphins was reported. Kellogg *et al.* (1953) reported that captive dolphins could hear sounds up to 80 kHz, and McBride (1956) presented some of the first evidence that bottlenose dolphins could use echolocation to detect underwater objects. For a more detailed account of the early dolphin echolocation studies, see Au (1993).

Since those first reports, the echolocating abilities of odontocetes (especially captive dolphins) have been the subject of intense research. As echolocation can only be confirmed for captive animals that are deprived of access to their other senses, six species of small odontocetes are the only marine mammals unequivocally known to echolocate. However, all species of odontocetes known to produce pulse-like sounds in the wild are assumed to possess echolocation capabilities, and echolocation is suspected in some other groups of marine mammals. Several new investigative techniques, such as CAT and NMR scanning of the structures involved in the production and reception of these complex sounds, can only be used on captive animals.

Behavioral studies of the echolocation sensitivities of captive animals typically have involved a training regime to establish stimulus control of the behavior of an animal (Au, 1993). Thus, when any stimulus is changed, such as the size or shape of a target object presented to a dolphin wearing opaque eyecups, a resulting change in behavioral performance can be measured. From such behavioral evidence, captive odontocetes have uniformly performed well on target discrimination tests and sound frequency and intensity tests. They also can localize sound sources to within a couple of degrees, comparable to humans, and resolve time down to tens of millionths of a second, an order of magnitude finer than humans.

To accomplish these discrimination tasks, odontocetes must have an extremely sensitive sound reception information processing system to be effective, and, with the exception of passive listeners, they also require a sophisticated sound production system. These capabilities are the result of the evolution of unique sound generation and propagation organs (the melon and nasal passages), pathways for sound reception that are specifically adapted to water-borne sounds (the lower jaw and possibly the melon), and the integrative activity of the auditory areas of the central nervous system (although data is almost completely lacking in this area).

10.3.1.1. Characteristics of Echolocation Clicks

Bottlenose dolphins have been the principal subjects of captive echolocation studies. To produce the types of echolocation sounds actually recorded, the sound production system

Figure 10.4. Pattern of click train production and echo return for an echolocating dolphin. Outgoing clicks occur between returning echos to reduce interference.

of *Tursiops* generates trains or pulses of broad-frequency **clicks** of very short duration. As each click strikes a target, a portion of its sound energy is reflected back to the source (Fig. 10.4). *Tursiops* uses clicks that are composed of a wide range of frequencies often exceeding 150 kHz, with most of the acoustic energy between 30 and 150 kHz (Fig. 10.5). Each click lasts from 10 to 100 ms and may be repeated as many as 600 times each second.

While these trains of rapidly repeated clicks are being produced, their rate of repetition is adjusted to allow the click echo to return to the animal during the time between outgoing clicks. The time required for a click to travel from its producer to the reflecting target and back again is a measure of the distance to the target. As that distance varies, so will the time necessary for the echo to return. Continued evaluation of returning echoes from a moving target can indicate the target's speed and direction of travel.

To make this acoustic picture more complicated, at the same time a dolphin is producing a train of click pulses, it can simultaneously produce frequency-modulated tonal whistle signals that vary in pitch from 2–30 kHz and direct those emitted sound signals forward

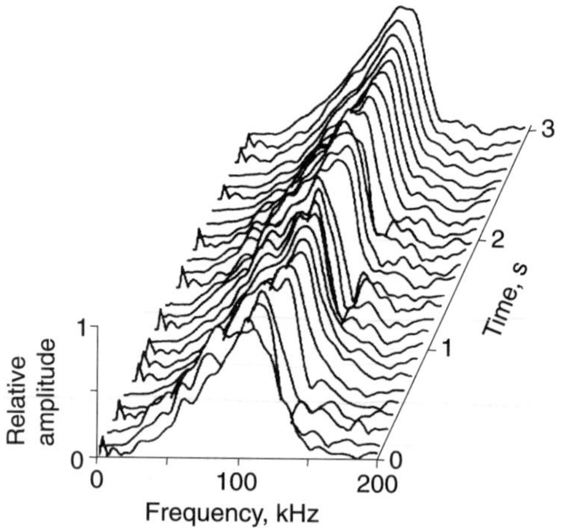

Figure 10.5. Power spectra of a single sequence of dolphin echolocation clicks. (Redrawn from Au, 1993.)

from the melon in different beam patterns. It can do this while continually varying the spectral content of the clicks to adjust to the changing background noise or to the acoustic characteristics of the target.

The echolocation sounds produced by sperm whales consist of reverberant pulses that are repeated more slowly and at lower frequencies than those of *Tursiops*. Each click pulse lasts about 24 ms and consists of a series of up to nine individual rapidly reverberating clicks (Fig. 10.6). The repetition rate of the pulses is adjusted so that the echo of one click pulse returns from the target before the next pulse is emitted. The click pulses of sperm whales are intense and may travel for several kilometers in the sea. Figure 10.7 is a sonogram of a portion of a sequence of click pulses emitted by a sperm whale at sea. The boat from which the recording hydrophone was suspended was apparently the target of the whale's echolocation efforts. As the whale swam toward the boat to investigate, the time required for successive pulses to travel from the whale to the boat and back to the whale decreased and the whale compensated by increasing the repetition rate of click pulses (middle of Fig. 10.7).

Acoustic signals produced by harbor porpoises cover a very broad frequency range, from 40 Hz to at least 150 kHz (Verboom and Kastelein, 1995b, 1997). Individual signals consist of low frequency (80–10 kHz), mid-frequency (10 kHz), and high frequency (100–160 kHz) components. The low frequency components of high amplitude sounds probably are used for detection. The mid-frequency components have such a low energy level that they may not be of much practical function. The high frequency components are used for bearing detection and classification of objects such as prey items. Commerson's dolphins produce a narrow band frequency with nearly all of the energy above 100 kHz and in a narrow region around 4 kHz (Evans and Awbrey, 1988; Fig. 10.8).

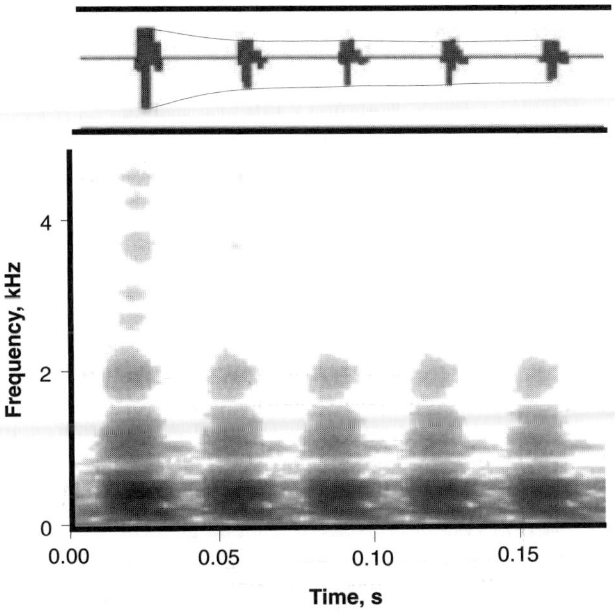

Figure 10.6. Single click pulse of sperm whale. Note the decreasing amplitude (top) of successive clicks within the pulse. (Courtesy J. Fish and Hubbs/Sea World Research Institute.)

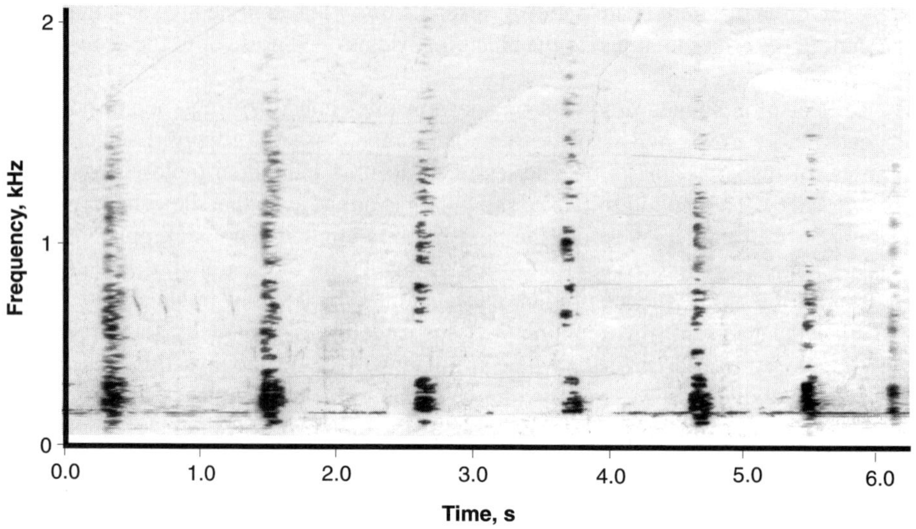

Figure 10.7. Pulse train of an echolocating sperm whale. The structure of a single pulse in this series is shown in Fig. 10.6. (Courtesy J. Fish.)

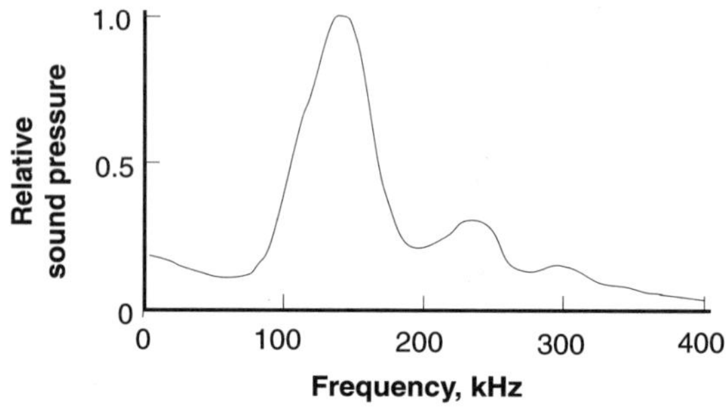

Figure 10.8. Frequency (power) spectrum of Commerson's dolphin. (Redrawn from Evans and Awbrey, 1988.)

10.3.1.2. Echolocation Sound Production and Reception

After decades of study, there is little debate about the anatomical source of echolocation sound production in odontocetes. The tubed extension of the larynx as the source of echolocation sounds has been favored by Purves, Pilleri, and their associates (e.g., Purves and Pilleri, 1983), partly because most mammals produce vocalizations with their larynx. The results of other studies, however, conclusively support the region of the nasal sac system just inside the blowhole as the click-generating structures in odontocetes (Fig. 10.9).

The basic sound-production system consists of a sound generator, the structural complex associated with the upper nasal passages termed the **"monkey lips"/dorsal bursa (MLDB complex)**. All odontocetes except sperm whales possess two bilaterally placed MLDB complexes. Each MLDB complex is located just below the ventral floor of the vestibular air sac and is composed of a pair of fatty-filled anterior and posterior dorsal bursae embedded in a

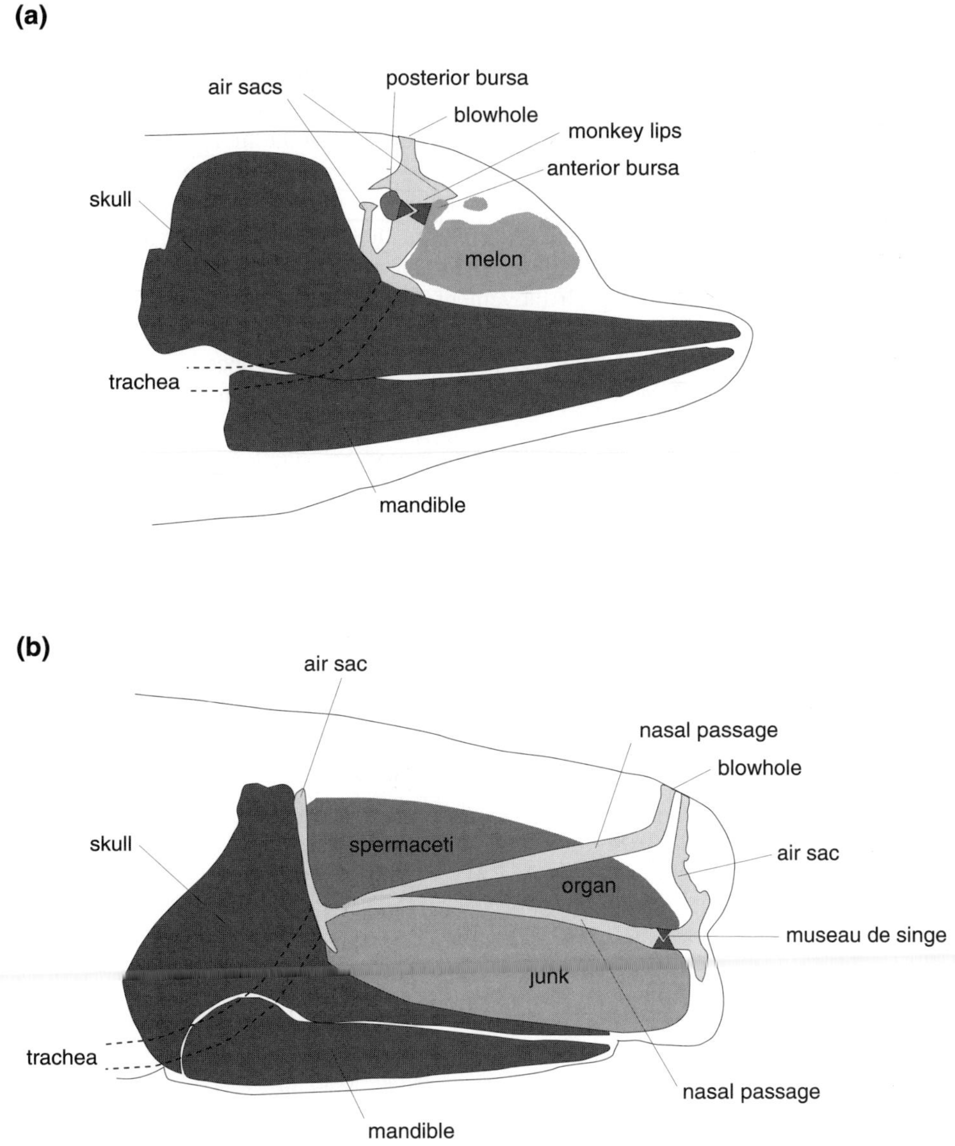

Figure 10.9. Schematic diagram of homologous structures in the foreheads of dolphin (a) and sperm whale (b). Similarly shaded structures are hypothesized to be homologous. Solid black interlocking triangles, monkey lips; light gray, anterior bursae/melon/junk; medium gray, posterior bursae, spermaceti organ; dark gray, skull (modified from Cranford, 1996).

pair of "monkey lips" (a slit-like opening; Fig. 10.9), a resilient cartilaginous blade (bursal cartilages), and a stout blowhole ligament, all suspended within a complex array of muscles and air spaces (Cranford *et al.,* 1996). Cranford (1988, 1992, 1996) has proposed that, in spite of the obvious structural differences between the heads of a dolphin and a sperm whale, the mechanism for click production is homologous between sperm whales (physeterids) and other odontocetes. For example, he suggests that the junk of the sperm whales is homologous to the melon in other odontocetes, and that the spermaceti organ of sperm whales is homologous to the right posterior bursa.

Comparison of these homologous structures suggests that all odontocetes may be making their pulsed echolocation signals by a similar mechanism. Cranford *et al.* (1996) hypothesized that sounds are generated as air is forced between the monkey lips, setting the MLDB complex into vibration. The periodic opening and closing of the monkey lips breaks up the air flow and determines the click repetition rate of the train. When the monkey lips slap together during click production, vibrations in the bursae are likely produced. The nasal plugs and their nodes along with the blowhole ligament and other membranes are most likely involved in regulating air movement in the passages dorsal to the nares, and perhaps are used in whistle production. Direct observations by T. W. Cranford (personal communication) of vocalizing bottlenose dolphins using a high-speed video endoscope have confirmed the MLDB as the only structure responsible for echolocation and signal generation.

The sound generation system is coupled to the sound-propagation structure, the melon. The core of the melon consists of low density lipids which serve as an acoustic lens to create focused directional beams in front of the melon (Fig. 10.10).

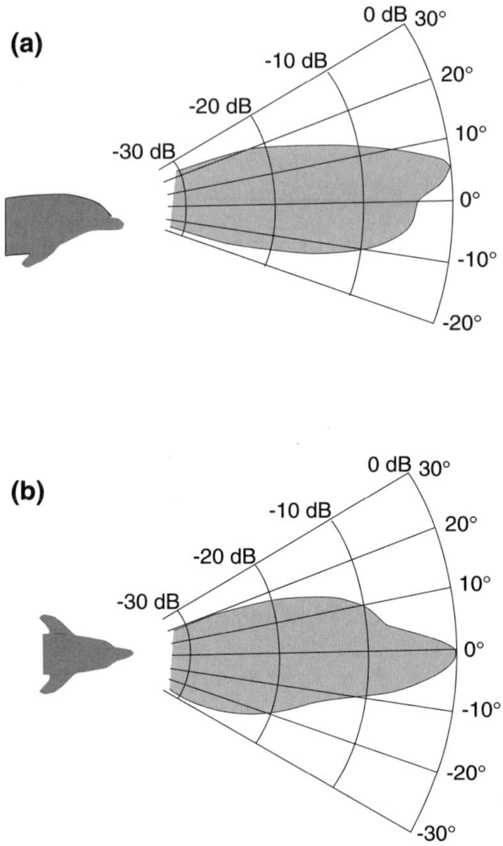

Figure 10.10. Focused transmission beam patterns of three different bottlenose dolphins in the vertical (a) and horizontal (b) planes. (Redrawn from Au, 1993.)

No anatomical studies have shown equivalent structural specializations for sound generation or transmission in mysticetes. Mysticetes have a larynx but lack vocal cords. The cranial sinuses of mysticetes are thought to be involved in phonation although no precise or general mechanism has so far been demonstrated.

Behavioral studies of both wild and captive subjects suggest that all species of marine mammals have good hearing. Experimental evidence, however, is again largely restricted to studies of captive small toothed whales (Fig. 10.11). Their sound-detection systems must be attuned to very weak echoes of their own clicks but must simultaneously withstand the powerful blast of outgoing clicks generated in adjacent regions of the head.

The external auditory canal is the typical mammalian sound-conducting channel connecting the external and middle ears. The external auditory meatus of cetaceans has an extremely narrow or plugged opening and there is debate regarding whether it is functional (Fig. 10.12). In mysticetes, an extension of the eardrum pushes into the ear canal. This **glove finger** ends in a horn like plug (composed of dead cells from the canal lining) that may be a meter long. Mapping of acoustically sensitive areas of dolphins' heads has shown the external auditory canal to be about six times less sensitive to sound than the lower jaw. Additionally, in experimental discrimination tests, the echolocating performance of a dolphin was significantly reduced when a sound-attenuating rubber hood was worn over the lower jaw (Brill *et al.,* 1988). These results support the hypothesis first proposed by Norris (1964) of a unique sound reception pathway in odontocetes. The bones of the lower jaw are flared toward the rear, known as the pan bone, and often are thin enough to be translucent

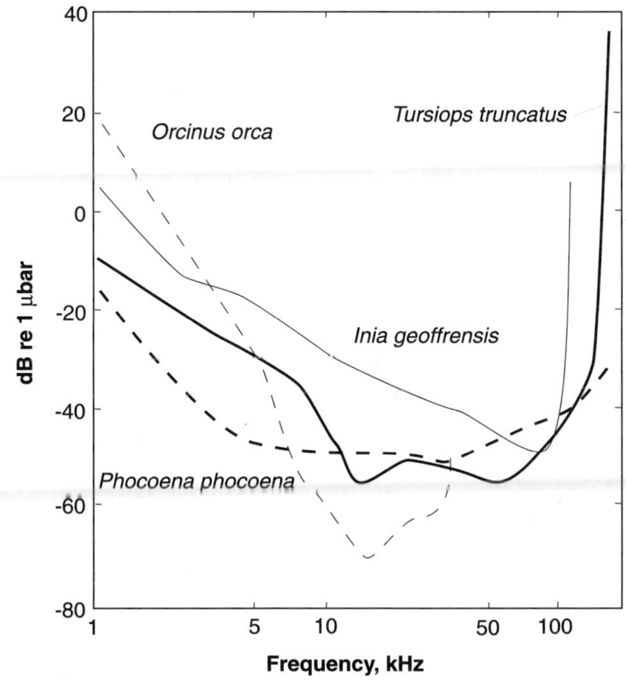

Figure 10.11. Auditory sensitivity curves (audiograms) for several species of odontocetes. (Redrawn from Au, 1993.)

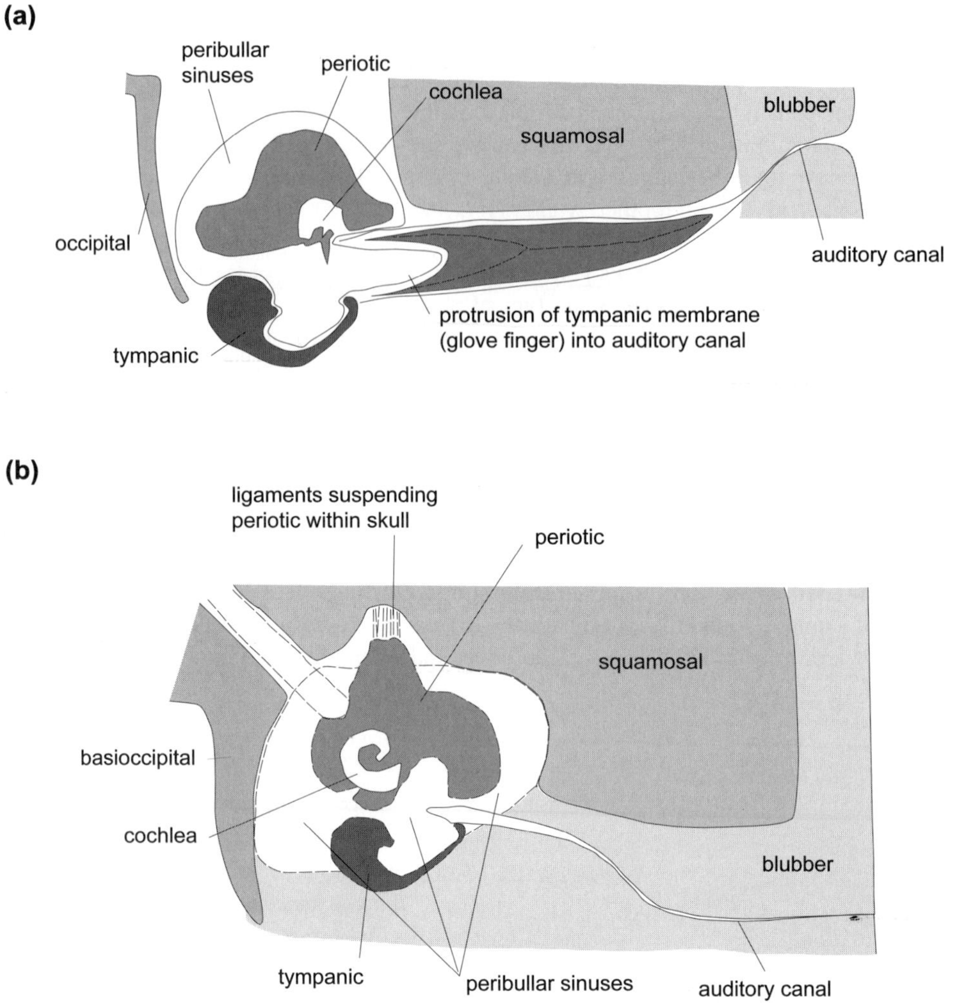

Figure 10.12. Simplified cross-sections of the ear region of a mysticete (a) and an odontocete (b). (Adapted from Reysenbach de Haan, 1956.)

(Fig. 10.13). Within each half of the lower jaw is a fat body (liquid oil at body temperature) that directly connects with the wall of the bulla of the middle ear. These fat or oil bodies, like the fat of a dolphin's melon or the oil of the sperm whale's spermaceti organ, act as low density sound channels to conduct sounds from the flared portions of the lower jaw directly to the middle ear. An area on either side of the forehead is nearly as sensitive as the lower jaw, suggesting that dolphins may possess two other very sensitive hearing channels for sound reception. It is likely that mysticetes differ in their sound reception mechanism and receive sound from the ear canal rather than from the jaw, although this has not yet been demonstrated.

The auditory bulla has two distinct components, the tympanic and the periotic bones (**tympano-periotic complex**), both of which are constructed from very dense or pachyostotic bone (see Oelschläger, 1986a,b, for discussion of the evolution of this region in toothed whales). The sound-processing structures of the middle ear are enclosed in the

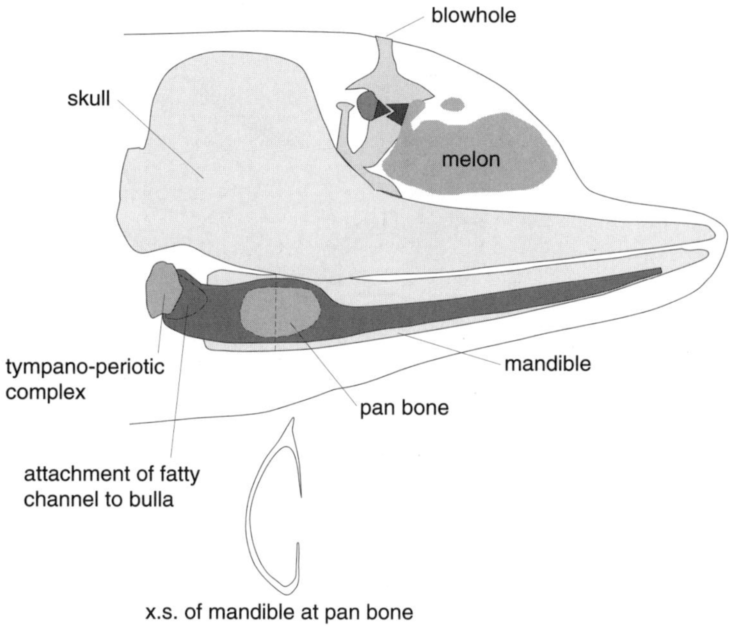

Figure 10.13. Sound reception structures of the head of a dolphin, including the fatty channel (gray) of the pan bone. (Redrawn from Norris, 1968.)

bulla. Cetacean bullae differ from those of other mammals in appearance, construction, and cranial associations. Mysticete and odontocete bullae differ in size, shape, and in the relative volumes of the tympanic and periotic. Bullar dimensions are strongly correlated with animal size; mysticete bullae are two to three times larger than those of most odontocetes. In toothed whales, the bulla is separated from adjacent bones of the skull by peri-tympanic sinuses filled with an insulating emulsion of mucus, oil, and air. The bulla is suspended in this emulsion by a sparse network of connective tissue (Fig. 10.14). Thus, each middle ear functions as an sound receiver isolated from the skull to better localize sound sources.

Some disagreement exists about the actual mechanism of sound transmission within the middle ear, for in odontocetes the tympanic membrane is reduced to a calcified ligament that is not coupled to the large and dense bones of the middle ear (i.e. malleus, incus, stapes; Fig. 10.15). The bones in odontocetes are stiffened with ligaments, presumably to enhance high frequency sensitivity. Mysticete ossicles are equally massive but have none of the high frequency specializations of odontocetes. In the inner ear of dolphins, the cochlea is similar to that of humans, with about the same number of hair cells, but the ganglion cell:hair cell ratio (2:1 in humans) is 5:1 in *Tursiops*. In addition, the basilar membrane is thicker and stiffer, again presumably to enhance higher frequency sensitivity. Other cochlear differences seen in odontocetes are the number of cochlear turns and the distribution of membrane support structures (see Ketten, 1992c, for further discussion).

Cetaceans are exceptional in having semicircular canals that are significantly smaller than the cochlear canal. If the semicircular canals are vestigial, these animals may not have any rotational or three-dimensional positioning sense, which may permit the flying turns of spinner dolphins without the side effects of motion sickness (Ketten, 1992a).

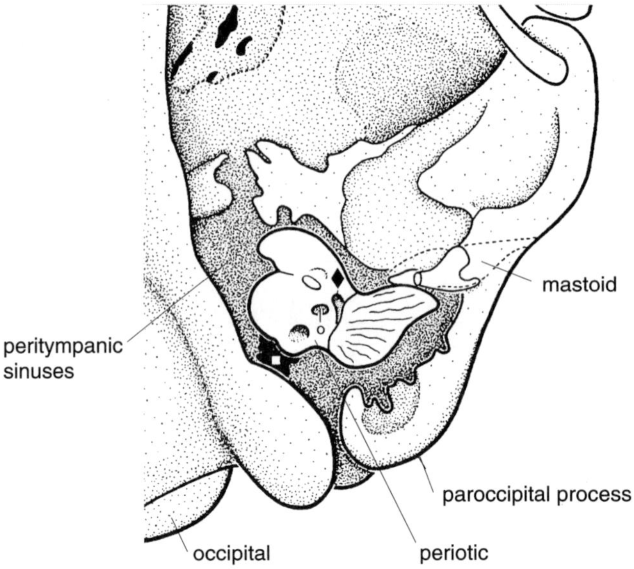

Figure 10.14. Schematic drawing of odontocete ear region in ventral view (without tympanic bone) illustrating periotic, peribullar sinuses, mastoid, occipital, and paroccipital process. (From Oelschläger, 1986a.)

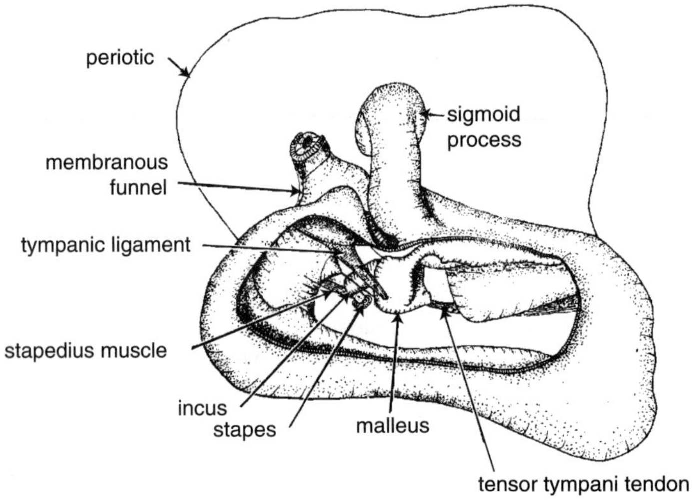

Figure 10.15. Right auditory bulla of bottlenose dolphin, *Tursiops truncatus* opened to show middle ear. Tympanic bone is shown in detail with the periotic shown only in outline. (From McCormick *et al.*, 1970.)

10.3.1.3. Resulting Echolocation Capability

The echolocation clicks of most odontocetes consist of broadband frequency spectra and short duration pulses, with the actual frequency used being continually adjusted to avoid competing background noises and to maximize the return of information about the target. These clicks are of high intensity, with repetition rates adjusted to changing animal–target distance. The echolocation abilities of blindfolded captive dolphins are sufficiently refined to discriminate target diameter ratios as small as 1:1.25 for different metal targets of the same size and shape, and for different thicknesses of the same metals. By extension, it is presumed that these discriminatory abilities are sufficient to acoustically identify preferred prey and other similar items in the dolphin's natural habitat. The maximum range exhibited in target discrimination tests by *Tursiops* is about 100 m (Au and Snyder, 1980), and it is presumably much greater for sperm whales.

There is some evidence to suggest that the same type of clicks used by sperm whales for echolocation also serve as a means of communication. Rhythmic patterns of clicks, known as **codas**, last up to 1–2 s and consist of 3–30 click pulses (Fig. 10.16). By localizing and recording sperm whale sound sources with arrays of hydrophones, Watkins and Schevill (1977) found that individual whales repeatedly produce unique codas, and they suggest that these codas may serve as recognition codes for individual whales. These identity codas may allow pod members to keep track of each other when they disperse over several km^2 during foraging dives (see Chapter 11). Other sperm whale codas are shared by several whales in local groups, suggesting that some communication function other than individual identity is served (Moore *et al.*, 1993; Weilgart and Whitehead, 1993). Coda repertoires distinctive to groups seem to persist over several years and show significant, but weaker, geographical differences (Weilgart and Whitehead, 1997). The group-specific coda repertoires in sperm whales have, in fact, been likened to group dialects in killer whales (discussed later in this chapter).

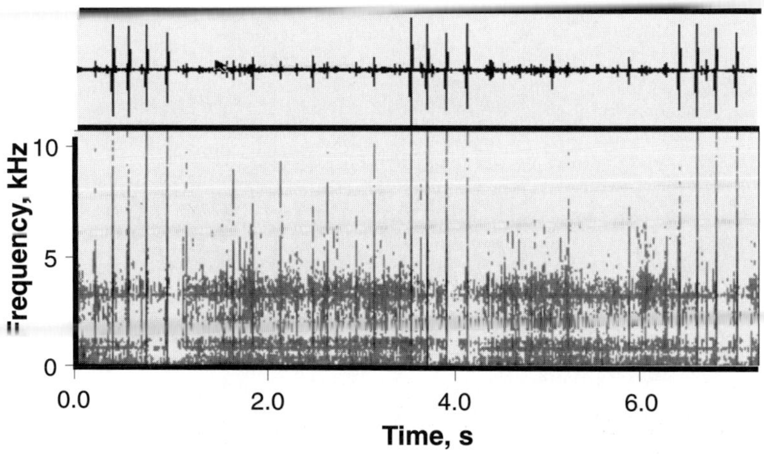

Figure 10.16. Sonogram (bottom) and power spectrum (top) of a series of three regular 4-click codas recorded in the presence of a female/young unit of sperm whales near the Azores. (Recording courtesy P. Colla.)

In a study comparing whistle structure among various odontocetes, the observed differences were correlated with taxonomic relationships, habitats, and body lengths (Ding *et al.*, 1995a). For example, whistles of the freshwater river dolphin *Inia geoffrensis* were very different from whistles of oceanic delphinid species and the differences were related to habitat differences. The low and narrow frequency signals of *Inia* have better refractive capabilities, important to species whose habitats are rivers, which have higher noise levels than pelagic environments and carry more suspended material (Evans and Awbrey, 1988). Finally, a limitation of sound production capability related to body length is suggested because, in general, the longer the body the lower the maximum whistle frequency range that can be produced.

10.3.1.4. Evidence for Echolocation in Mysticetes and Pinnipeds

How common is echolocation in marine mammals? Presently, it is uncertain because it is difficult to establish whether wild populations are indeed using echolocation-like clicks for the purposes of orientation and location. If judgments can be made from the types of sounds produced, then echolocation probably occurs in all toothed whales. Underwater clicks have also been recorded from several phocids, including harbor, ringed, harp, gray, and hooded seals (Ballard and Kovacs, 1995, and references cited therein). Renouf and Davis (1982) have speculated that these clicks are used for echolocation, although this theory is still controversial. Broad-spectrum trains of clicks or short pulses have been recorded in the presence of gray whales in the North Pacific (Fig. 10.17) and blue and minke whales in the North Atlantic. The fact that the majority of sounds produced by gray whales along their migration route are at frequencies below 200 Hz and that they have a pattern of repetition with long periods of silence in between, suggest their use is in communication rather than echolocation (Crane and Lashkari, 1996).

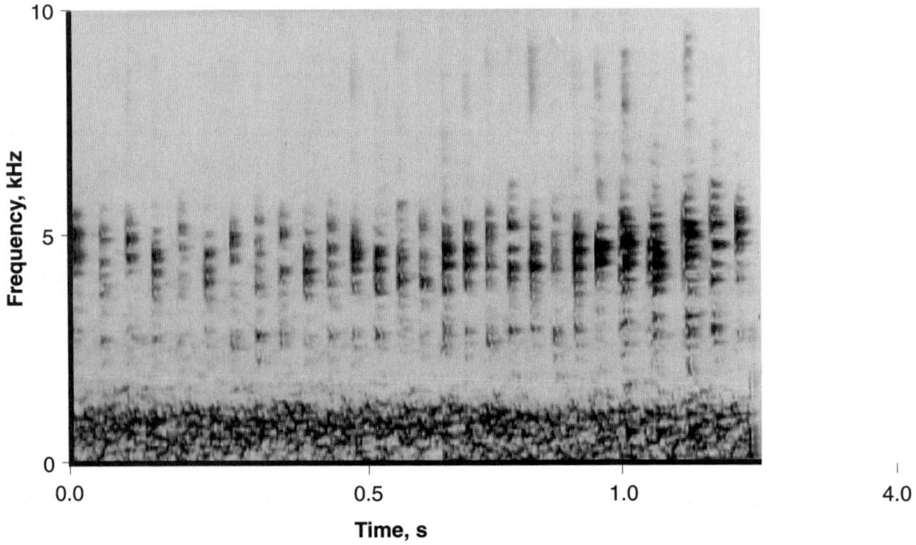

Figure 10.17. Sonogram of click series from a feeding gray whale. (From Fish *et al.*, 1974.)

In 1992, the U.S. Navy initiated a test program to make available to marine mammal scientists the North Atlantic Ocean undersea listening capabilities of the Integrated Undersea Surveillance System (IUSS). IUSS is part of the U.S. submarine defense system developed over three decades ago to acoustically detect and track Soviet submarines. The system consists of networks of hydrophone arrays, some towed by ships and others affixed to the sea bottom; it is sufficiently sensitive to locate and track individual whales over hundreds of km for weeks.

Prior to 1992, the Navy made no systematic effort to record and archive any of the whale sounds detected. The IUSS study has resulted in a wealth of acoustical data on large baleen whales, especially blue, fin, and minke whales. The vocalizations of these whales are typically very loud, low frequency pulses of varying spectral complexity (Fig. 10.18). The pulses of blue whales are between 15–20 Hz, mostly below the range of human hearing, while those of fin whales are only slightly higher at 20–30 Hz (Fig. 10.18). Their function is not known, but two plausible explanations have been put forward. It is reasonable to conclude that if we can detect these sounds at long distances, other whales should be able to as well. They may therefore function in long-distance communication. These loud, low-frequency, patterned sequences of tones propagate through water with much less attenuation than do the higher frequency whistles or echolocation clicks of small toothed whales.

In addition to signature or identity calls, it has been proposed that these low-frequency, short duration tone pulses may serve an echolocation function, although a different one than that described for small toothed whales. A typical blue whale call like that shown in Fig. 10.18 lasts for 20 s and, in water, is approximately 30 km in length. The low frequency of blue and fin whale tones have very long wavelengths, from 50 m at 30 Hz to 100 m at 15 Hz, and, if used for echolocation, cannot resolve target features finer than those wavelengths. Clark (1994) has speculated that these tone pulses are used by large mysticetes to detect very large scale oceanic features, such as continental shelves, islands, and possibly sharp differences in water density associated with upwelling of cold water. Currently, however, the experimental evidence needed to support the sound reception capability needed for echolocation in mysticetes is completely lacking.

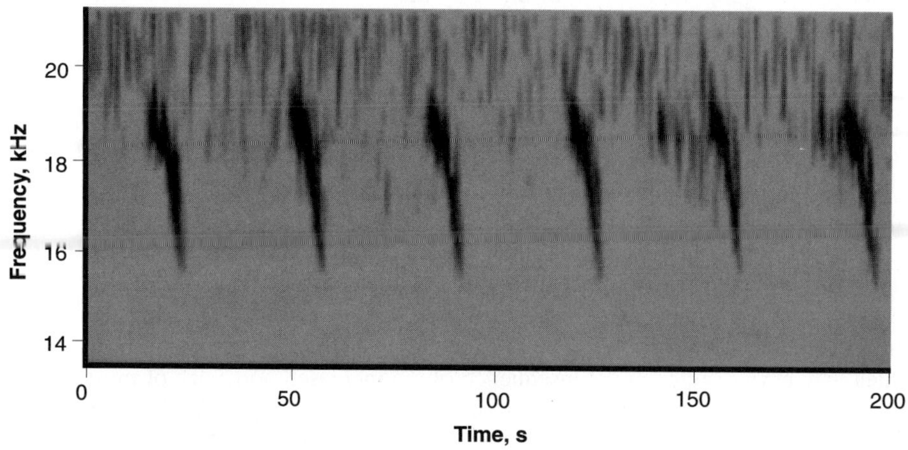

Figure 10.18. Sonogram of a series of calls from a blue whale. (From Clark, 1994.)

10.3.1.5. The Evolution of Echolocation

Fossil evidence suggests that the ability to use high frequencies may have originated early in cetacean history. The recent discovery of the ability of clupeid fish (herring and shad) to detect ultrasound pulses from odontocetes indicates that echolocation may have evolved prior to the appearance of odontocetes (Mann *et al.,* 1997). We are not able to link specific auditory structures with entry into the water. In the absence of any evidence for a melon in early archaeocetes it is unlikely that they were aquatic echolocators. In fact, the morphology of a middle ear bone (incus) and the jaw as well as the bony connections between the ear and the skull suggest that with respect to hearing, *Pakicetus* may more closely resemble certain pinnipeds (e.g. phocid seals and the walrus; Thewissen and Hussain, 1993).

Among early cetaceans, *Ambulocetus* achieved the greatest degree of acoustic isolation, created by development of peritympanic sinuses. The unique odontocete pathway of sound through the lower jaw can be seen in the morphology and size of the mandibular canal and foramen and in the position of the fat pad. An enlarged mandibular foramen is seen in *Ambulocetus,* intermediate in size between that of *Pakicetus* and later cetaceans. Among the hypotheses proposed to explain the origin of the new cetacean sound pathway to the middle ear is one which suggests that *Ambulocetus,* while resting on land, may have kept its lower jaw in contact with the ground and thus used the jaw as a low frequency sound receiver, as do some modern mammals such as the mole rat. The fat pad of modern cetaceans has been considered an exaptation, as mentioned in Chapter 2. Accordingly, it arose for a different function (transmission of low frequency substrate-borne sounds) than the function it took on later (transmission of high frequency water-borne sounds; Thewissen *et al.,* 1996).

Basilosaurids have bullar modifications similar to those of modern cetaceans, although the tympano-periotic complex remains attached to the braincase. The dorudontine ear had enlarged sinuses, massive ossicles, and a periotic decoupled from the mastoid, all of which are features of a functional aquatic ear (Ketten, 1992b).

The presence of related osteological changes (telescoping of the skull, concave mandible, separate bullae, and enlarged peribullar spaces) in the earliest odontocetes, the agorophids, indicates the development of echolocation because in modern odontocetes, these features are associated with soft tissue developments principally related to high frequency sound reception. The presence of high frequency hearing structures (i.e. numerous foramina for the ganglion cells of the auditory nerve) and the highly specialized vestibule and semicircular canals in squalodontoids (including agorophids) suggests that high frequency hearing and other specializations of the inner ear among cetaceans occurred before the early Oligocene (Luo and Eastman, 1995).

Since the earliest cetaceans, common ancestors of odontocetes and mysticetes, probably used high, but not ultrasonic, frequencies, and it is likely that the low frequency hearing of mysticetes evolved subsequently. Why did low frequency hearing evolve? The appearance of mysticetes coincides with the opening of new oceanic regions in the southern hemisphere. In addition to an increase in primary productivity (see Chapters 6 and 11) there was a substantial reduction in surface temperatures at higher latitudes. In colder regions, an increase in body size would offer a substantial metabolic advantage. As cochlea measurements scale isometrically to body size, Ketten (1992a) proposes that a lower frequency cochlea may have resulted as a consequence of the increased body size of mysticetes. She further suggests that with less pressure to use echolocation as a foraging strategy in more productive waters, a decrease in the reception of higher frequency sounds may not have been a significant disadvantage. Therefore, as larger mysticetes evolved, increased size of cochlear structures may have constrained the resonance characteristics of the ear to progressively lower frequencies.

10.3.2. Social Sounds

10.3.2.1. Signature Whistles of Dolphins

In addition to echolocation clicks and loud impulse sounds, dolphins also produce another type of vocalization, a narrow band frequency modulated (FM) sound often with a harmonic structure, usually described as a whistle or squeal. Typically, the frequency of these pure-tone emissions rises and falls between about 7 and 15 kHz and averages less than one second in duration (but some may continue for 2–3 s; Fig. 10.19).

Since 1965, the Caldwells (see Caldwell *et al.,* 1990 for a detailed review) have studied the acoustic characteristics of over one hundred captive *Tursiops* of all ages and both sexes. They observed that each individual dolphin in a group produces an individual whistle contour so distinct that each animal can be identified from the whistle contour on a sonogram. These sounds came to be called **signature whistles**. The Caldwells hypothesized that the distinctiveness of an individual's whistle served to broadcast the identity of the animal producing the whistle, and possibly to communicate other information, such as their state of arousal or fear, to group mates.

In addition to individual identification, a broader social function of signature whistles is suggested by a growing body of evidence. Dolphins often whistle when separated from other group members or in response to the whistles of group members. Captive dolphins

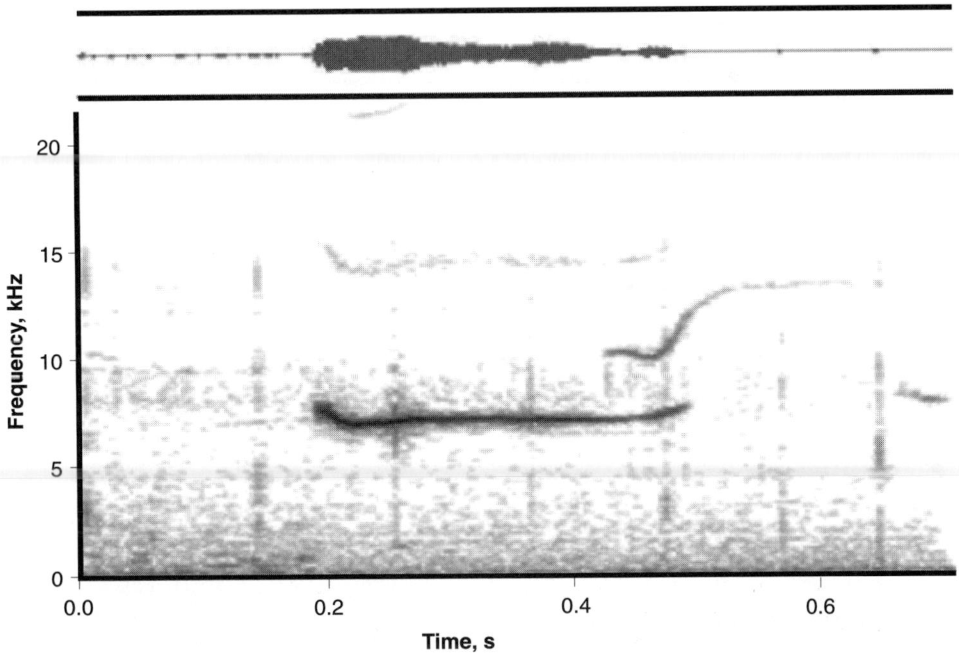

Figure 10.19. Sonogram of a bottlenose dolphin whistle call. (Courtesy Hubbs/Sea World Research Institute.)

have been trained to mimic electronically generated dolphin-like whistles and may imitate each other's signature whistle up to 20% of the time (Tyack, 1991). Tyack proposed that a dolphin in a large group will mimic the signature whistle of another group member to initiate a social interaction. Dolphin species that are more social also are known to whistle more. There are, however, suggestions that the signature whistle hypothesis needs to be reevaluated. The results of McCowan and Reiss (1995) indicate that captive bottlenose dolphins share several different whistle types and that signature whistles may play a less predominant role than previously suspected. Other studies have investigated the whistle repertoires of wild dolphins. Comparisons of the whistles of several bottlenose dolphin populations suggest that although there may be differences between whistles from different or the same individuals within the same population, there are still some characteristics which are unique for each population (Ding *et al.,* 1995b). In another study, the fact that common dolphin whistle repertoires were not individual-specific nor context-specific led Moore and Ridgway (1995) to suggest that they may represent a portion of a regional dialect, similar to the pod-specific dialects proposed for killer whales (see below). Future work analyzing dolphin whistle repertoires with respect to behavioral contexts and social relationships is needed.

10.3.2.2. Dialects of Killer Whales

Killer whales have been found to produce repetitious calls that are now considered to be group dialects (Ford, 1991). Repertoires consisting of a small number of discrete calls (averaging about 10, such as those shown in Fig. 10.20) are shared by individuals within a pod and appear to persist unchanged for several decades. These pod-specific repertoires seem to serve as vocal indicators of pod affiliation and help to make vocal communication within

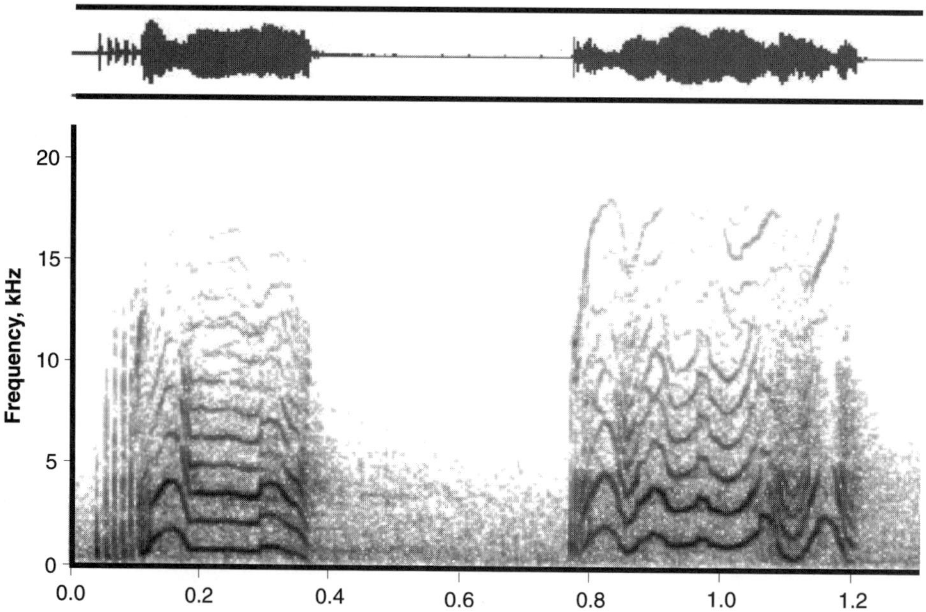

Figure 10.20. Sonogram of a killer whale vocal call. (Courtesy Hubbs/Sea World Research Institute.)

a pod more efficient. Sixteen pods of resident killer whales studied by Ford in British Columbia coastal waters formed four distinct acoustic associations, or clans. All the pods within a clan shared several but not all calls, no sharing of calls occurred between different clans. This hierarchy of call associations, with individuals within a pod sharing a repertoire of pod calls, pods within a clan sharing some of those calls, and different clans sharing no calls, led Ford (1991) to propose that each group's vocal tradition had evolved over generations, with related pods in a clan having descended from a common ancestral group through growth and division of the group along matrilineal lines (Fig. 10.21). Paralleling these group divergences were divergences of the group's vocal traditions as innovations of new calls and loss of old calls accumulated over time. These results have been confirmed by other studies of call repertoires in killer whale pods (Strager, 1995).

10.3.2.3. Humpback Whale Sounds

Humpback whales are the most sonorous of the mysticetes. While on their winter breeding grounds, they sing long and acoustically complex songs which are shared by all singing whales occupying the same breeding ground (Payne and McVay, 1971). Consequently, the songs of North Atlantic humpback whales are identifiably different from those in the North Pacific Ocean. Each song, although often repeated for hours, lasts 10–15 minutes and is composed of repeated themes, phrases, and subphrases (Fig. 10.22). Individual units that make up subphrases are typically a few seconds in duration with frequencies generally below 1.5 kHz (Payne *et al.,* 1983). In general terms, the songs of southern hemisphere humpback whales resemble those published for northern hemisphere humpback whales (Jenkins *et al.,* 1995).

The structure of humpback whale songs changes progressively over time. Most of the changes occur during winter months on breeding grounds and typically include changes in the frequency and duration of individual units as well as deletion of old and insertion of new phrases or themes (Payne *et al.,* 1983). The composition and sequence of themes within a song also change with time so that the song structure at the beginning of a winter

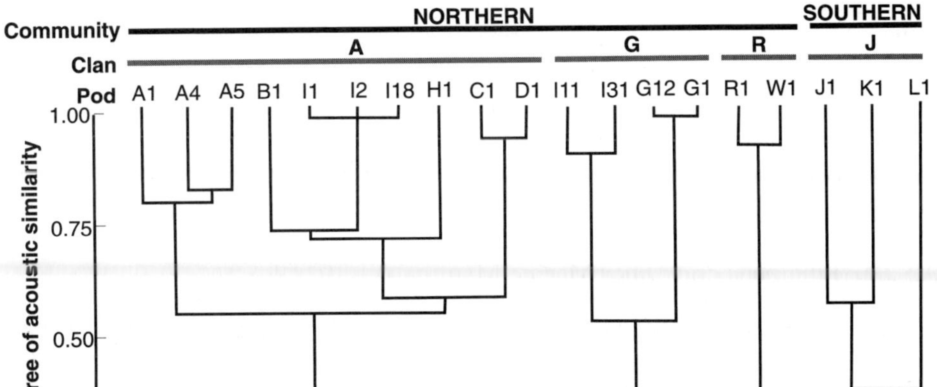

Figure 10.21. Clan association diagram, showing the likely genealogies for the resident pods of killer whales in the Puget Sound/Vancouver Island region. (Redrawn from Ford, 1991.)

Figure 10.22. Hierarchical structure of humpback whale songs, each illustrated with spectogram tracings. (From Payne, 1983.)

breeding season is modified substantially by the end of that season a few months later, although all whales sing the same song at any point in time. Individual whales express the same changes at the same rate as the rest of the group of singing whales (Guinee *et al.,* 1983). Thus, singing whales seem to actively learn songs from each other; forgetfulness or changing membership in a singing population does not seem to account for the changes in song structure over time.

Underwater observations of singing humpbacks in the clear tropical waters of the Hawaiian breeding grounds (Chapter 12) have established that only adult males sing. The identification of the sex of the singers has also been confirmed by DNA analysis of humpbacks from the breeding grounds of the Mexican Pacific Ocean (Medrano *et al.,* 1994). These observations support the notion that humpback songs play a reproductive role similar to that of bird songs, communicating a singer's species, sex, location, readiness to mate with females, and readiness to engage in competitive behavior with other whales (Tyack, 1981). Additionally, the simultaneous singing by many males may serve as a communal display to synchronize the ovulation of females (Mobley and Herman, 1985). These songs also are thought to function as acoustic signals to mark underwater territories of adult males (Tyack, 1981; Darling *et al.,* 1983). Occasionally, humpback whales have been heard singing in pelagic waters during the spring migration well away from known breeding areas (Barlow, personal communication), as well as in summer feeding grounds in southeast Alaska (McSweeney *et al.,* 1989). These songs were essentially an abbreviated composite of the breeding ground songs recorded in Hawaii in the previous and following winters. The gender of the Alaska singers was not determined, and the function of singing during migration or feeding is not known.

10.3.2.4. Pinnipeds and Other Marine Mammals

Pinnipeds produce a variety of underwater sounds that appear most often related to breeding activities and social interactions. Whistles, chirps, trills, and low pitched buzzes characterize Weddell seals and are used in territorial defense (Thomas and Kuechle, 1982; Fig. 10.23). Trills similar to those of Weddell seals have been recorded for hooded seals (Ballard and Kovacs, 1995) and bearded seals (e.g., Cleator *et al.,* 1989) and it has been suggested that they may be used in establishing and maintaining aquatic territories. Harp seal calls described as trills, warbles, cooing, and squeaks are produced underwater only during

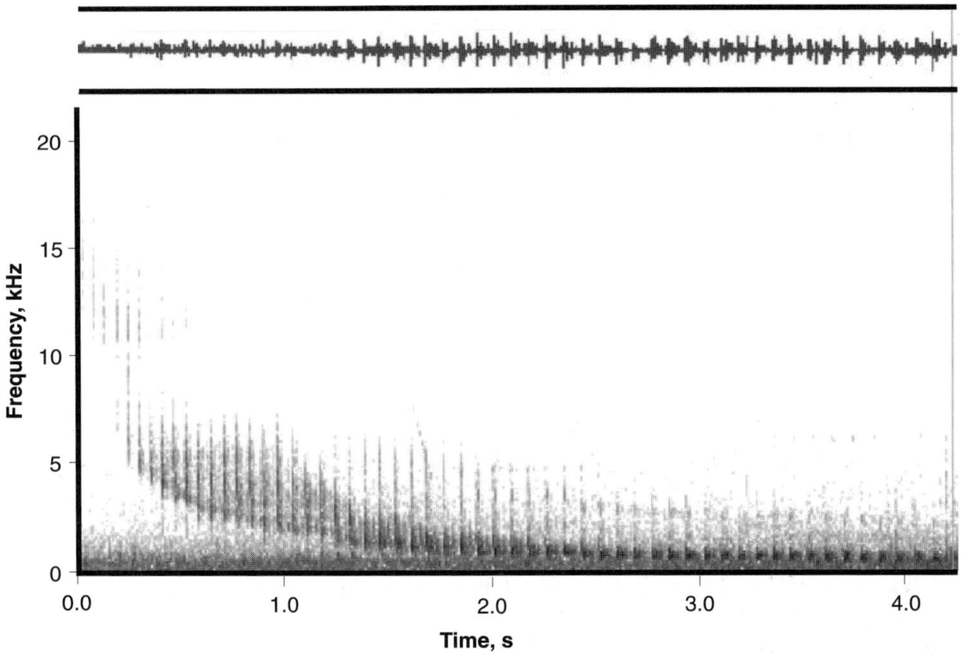

Figure 10.23. Sonogram of a descending trill of a Weddell seal. (Courtesy Hubbs/Sea World Research Institute.)

the breeding season (Møhl *et al.,* 1975). Complex musical underwater songs, consisting of oscillating warbles that change frequencies and are punctuated by brief unmodulated low frequency moans, are produced by bearded seal males and possibly also by females (Ray *et al.,* 1969). Leopard seal vocalizations are described as soft, lyrical calls rather than the aggressive sounding grunts, barks, and groans found in most other phocids and may be related to their solitary social system which does not require calls for territorial defense or interanimal disputes (Rogers *et al.,* 1995; Thomas and Golladay, 1995). The variation in the call repertoires of leopard seals on opposite sides of the Antarctic suggests that there is geographic variation between repertoires (Thomas and Golladay, 1995). Similar research has suggested that this is also true for populations of Weddell seals around Antarctica (Pahl *et al.,* 1997, and references cited therein). Study of the behavioral context of leopard seal vocalizations revealed that vocalizations are used by mature males to advertise their sexual receptivity and possibly by mature males in search of mates (Rogers *et al.,* 1996). Similarly, evidence that male harbor seals are vocal underwater during the breeding season was reported by Hangii and Schusterman (1994). Results of this study suggested that these vocalizations are used in male–male competition and/or advertisement displays to attract females.

Among the most distinctive underwater pinniped sounds are those made by male walruses during and outside the breeding season. Males produce a series of knocking sounds (including bells, bell-knocks, double knocks, and double-knock bell phonations) often described as "ringing bells" that are produced both in air and underwater (Schevill *et al.,* 1966; Fay *et al.,* 1984; Miller, 1985; Stirling *et al.,* 1987). Underwater knocking sounds also have been recorded from hooded seals (Ballard and Kovacs, 1995), Weddell seals (Thomas and Kuechle, 1982) and gray seals (Asselin *et al.,* 1993).

The pinniped ear shows several modifications for hearing underwater. These modifications amplify sound reception and allow directionality. Several of the bones associated with the middle ear (squamosal, tympanic bulla) have flattened surfaces to receive and direct sound waves. The tympanic bulla, isolated from most bones of the skull, would otherwise amplify and limit source detection of sounds. The outer and middle ear contain cavernous tissue capable of being engorged with blood when the animal is submerged. In addition to helping in pressure equalization when diving, these cavernous tissues may enhance the transmission of sound to the inner ear (Fig. 10.24), in particular making the ear more sensitive to high frequencies (Repenning, 1972; Kastelein *et al.,* 1996). Phocid middle ear bones show a number of modifications (e.g. extreme expansion of the incus to form a head, and in some, extra articulations on the malleus) not seen in otariids, the walrus, or other carnivores. The middle ear bones are enlarged in both the walrus and phocids and they also share specializations of the malleus (Wyss, 1987).

Sounds described as chirp-squeaks, identified as short, frequency modulated signals, have been reported for both manatees and dugongs (2.5–8 kHz range for manatees, Evans and Herald, 1970; 3–18 kHz range for dugongs, Anderson and Barclay, 1995; Fig. 10.25). Hartman (1979) described chirp-squeaks, squeals, and screams for the West Indian manatee. Additional categories of sound were reported for this same species and further distinguished by gender and age (Steel, 1982). Observations in the field indicate that manatee vocalizations play a key role in keeping mothers and calves together. In addition to chirp-squeaks, other vocalizations of dugongs have been described as barks and trills (Anderson and Barclay, 1995). According to Anderson and Barclay, low pitched whistles previously attributed to dugongs are more likely, given their production during breathing, to reflect an abnormality in the respiratory system rather than a means of communication. On the basis of behavioral observations, it appears that the chirp-squeaks and other sounds, of the dugong, originate in the frontal region of the head, suggesting a mechanism similar to that in whales, rather than in the larynx as previously suggested. Chirp-squeaks are emitted as male dugongs feed at the bottom or patrol territories. Barks have physical characteristics

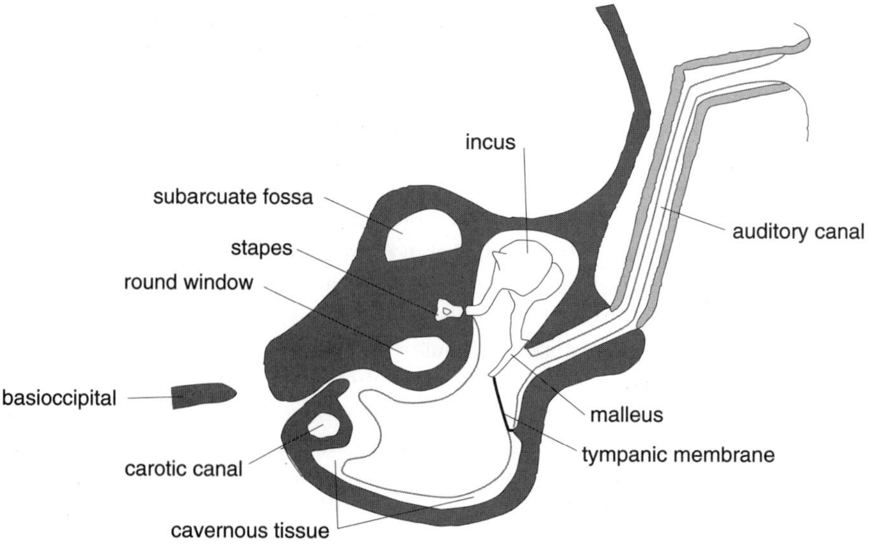

Figure 10.24. Simplified cross section of a pinniped (phocid) ear. (From Møhl, 1968.)

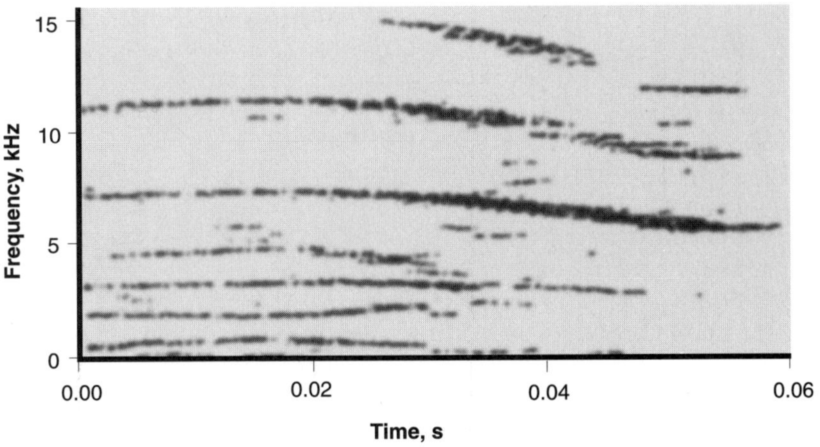

Figure 10.25. Sonogram of dugong. (From Anderson and Barclay, 1995.)

appropriate for aggressive behavior and have been recorded in situations suggesting a role in territorial defense. Trills have characteristics more appropriate in advertisement of a territory or readiness for mating (Anderson and Barclay, 1995). The vocal cords of sirenians are absent and are replaced by fleshy, prominent cushions (Harrison and King, 1980).

As in cetaceans, the external pinnae of manatees are absent and the external meatus is reduced to a tiny opening which leads to a narrow external auditory canal. The bullae are composed of a large bilobed periotic and a smaller tympanic. The tympano-periotic complex is composed of exceptionally dense bone, similar to that of cetaceans. Unlike the cetacean tympano-periotic complexes, which are external to the skull, manatee tympano-periotics are attached to the inner wall of the cranium and are attached to bone (Fig. 10.26). The intracranial position of the periotic and its fusion with the squamosal has important implications for hearing. The squamosal connects via a bony bridge to an enlarged zygomatic process of the jugal. The zygomatic process is an inflated, oil-filled, bony sponge that is analogous to the fatty filling of the mandibular canal of odontocetes and may have a significant role in manatee sound reception as a low frequency sound channel. Their inner ear structures imply that manatee ears lack sensitivity and directionality compared to most mammals. There is no indication that any species of manatee has ultrasonic hearing. The low frequency reception of the manatee ear may explain the large number of manatee deaths that occur each year from boat collisions.

The tympano-periotic complexes of extinct sirenians are very similar to those of the modern Florida manatee and are consistent with fully aquatic animals. They imply that few functional changes have occurred in the sirenian auditory system since the appearance of the group 50 Ma. Thus, manatees appear to represent an exception to the convention that hearing is the most significant and developed of marine mammal senses.

10.3.3. Prey Capture Sounds

It has been discovered that one of the major prey of odontocetes, clupeid fish, can detect ultrasound clicks up to 180 kHz (Mann *et al.,* 1997). The ability of clupeids to detect ultrasound may be an example of convergent evolution such as that seen in moths and other

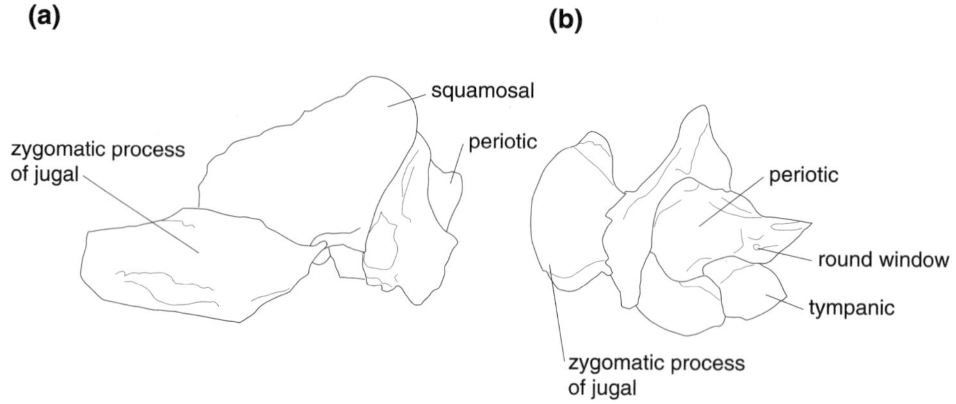

Figure 10.26. Diagram of manatee tympano-periotic complex in (a) lateral and (b) posterior views. (From Ketten, 1992.)

insects capable of detecting ultrasounds of their predators. Shad readily detect echolocating pulses of dolphins, and like moths, their response to detection is escape behavior. Since fossil clupeids are known from the early Cretaceous (130 Ma), long before the first odontocetes in the Oligocene (25–38 Ma), it is likely that the ultrasound detection capability of clupeids was present before there were echolocating predators.

To counter the possibility of acoustic detection and avoidance by prey species, some species of toothed whales may debilitate or temporarily disorient small prey with loud blasts of sound called "bangs." Presumably the same sound production system employed for echolocation is used to produce these bangs. The concept of stunning prey with acoustic energy was first proposed for sperm whales by Bel'kovich and Yablokov (1963), and was supported by the work of Berzin (1971). The concept has been evaluated in the context of other odontocete species by Norris and co-workers (i.e. Norris and Møhl, 1983; Marten *et al.,* 1988). In addition, it has been suggested (Johnson and Norris, 1994) that jaw claps, loud long-duration multipulsed sounds associated with rapid jaw closure in odontocetes, may be similar to sounds implicated in debilitation of prey. The general arguments used to support the concept of prey debilitation are based on anatomical, behavioral, and acoustic evidence as well as anecdotal information. Among the anatomical arguments used to support the concept is the serious mismatch between successful prey capture (based on examinations of stomach contents) and the feeding structures exhibited by several predaceous odontocete species. This mismatch is especially noticeable in the absence of functional teeth in most beaked whales, the narwhal, and in sexually immature sperm whales. That these whales successfully capture fast, slippery prey without functional teeth suggests that they must be able to approach very closely before engulfing their prey with a piston-like action of the tongue (see also Chapter 11).

Acoustic evidence for prey debilitation is difficult to collect, for sound bursts of sufficient pressure to damage or disorient small fish (estimated at 240–250 dB by Zagaeski, 1987) are very difficult to record in natural conditions, and captive animals are unlikely to emit such loud sounds in reverberant concrete tanks. Norris and Møhl (1983) calculated that sperm whales may emit click pulses at 265 dB. However, recording such an emission in a natural setting usually saturates the electronics of standard recording systems, and, unless the orientation angle and precise location of the whale are known, evaluating the SPL of bangs is difficult.

Some recordings in natural settings have been made that are suggestive of prey debilitation (Fig. 10.27). Similar loud, low-frequency stunning sounds have been recorded from wild bottlenose dolphins feeding in coastal Australia and California waters, from killer whales in the North Atlantic and Northeast Pacific Oceans, and from sperm whales in the Indian Ocean (Marten *et al.,* 1988). Although the SPL of these sounds could not be measured, they were typically much higher than the SPL of the presumed echolocation clicks immediately preceding the bang.

In summary, despite more than a decade of discussion and research, it remains unclear whether odontocetes actually use these sounds to debilitate prey and, if they do, which species produce these sounds and at what frequencies.

10.4. ATOC and Related Programs

In 1991, oceanographers from the U.S. and other countries conducted an experiment to determine if measuring the transmission time of low-frequency sounds across ocean basins

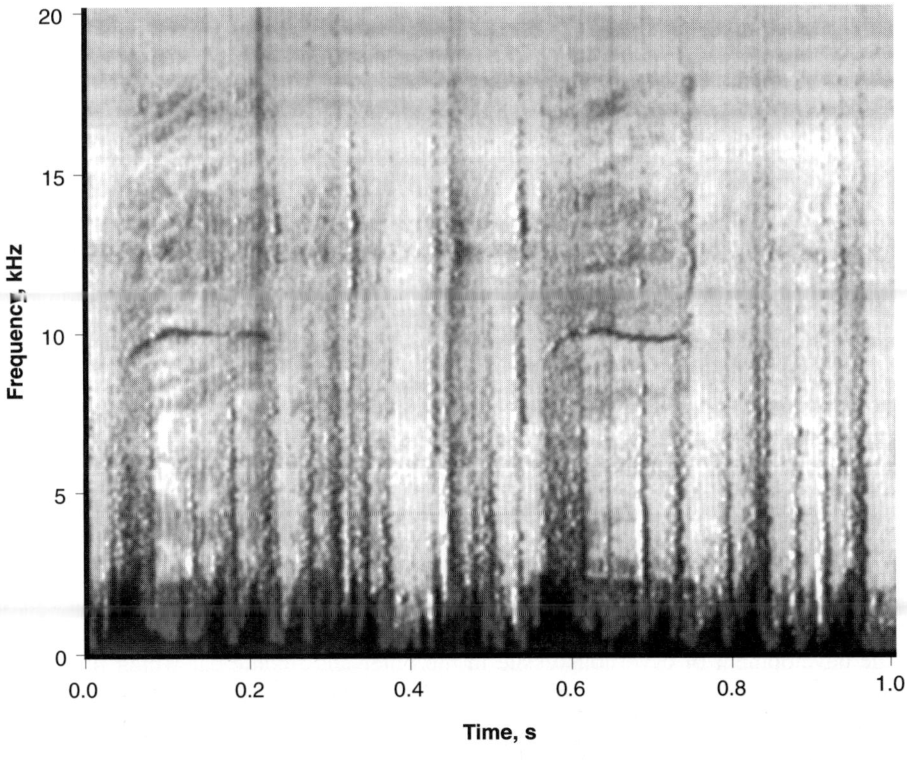

Figure 10.27. Sonogram of a series of popping sonations (vertical bands) produced by bottlenose dolphin(s), with higher amplitude, longer durations, and lower frequencies than typical echolocation clicks shown in Fig. 10.2. (Courtesy V. Dudley.)

could be used to detect changes in ocean temperature to monitor global warming. This experiment, referred to as the Heard Island Feasibility Test, was successful and a follow-up study was authorized. This study, the **Acoustic Thermometry of Ocean Climate (ATOC)** Program, called for installing 260-watt, low-frequency sound generators in deep water off the coast of Hawaii and central California. A research program was later included to ensure that the sounds produced by ATOC would not have a negative impact on marine mammals and other ocean animals. The location of the planned California sound source was moved further north to a location off the San Francisco coast and testing was begun late in 1995. Although not yet complete, analysis of the data collected indicates that the ATOC transmissions have had few detectable effects on marine mammals (Marine Mammal Commission, 1998).

10.5. Summary and Conclusions

Air-borne and water-borne sounds are produced by marine mammals for echolocation, communication, and prey capture. The majority of air-borne sounds of pinnipeds are produced in the larynx. Other air-borne pinniped vocalizations include those of the walrus, produced by the teeth and throat pouches, and those produced by the harp seal by inflating the hood and nasal septum. Sea otter vocalizations are low intensity, low-frequency signals similar to those of pinnipeds. Sound energy propagates well in water and the frequency and wavelength of sound are related to velocity. The frequency, duration, and energy level of sound are portrayed as a sonogram or a frequency spectrum.

Echolocation involves the production of short duration sounds (clicks) and listening for reflected echos as sounds bounce off objects. The echolocation abilities of toothed whales have been the subject of intense research. The source of production of echolocation sounds has been determined to be a structural complex associated with the upper nasal passages ("monkey lips"/dorsal bursae, or MLDB complex). The periodic opening and closing of the monkey lips break up the air flow between the lips and determines the click repetition rate. This sound generation system is coupled to a sound propagation structure, the melon, which serves as an acoustic lens to focus sound. The sound reception system of odontocetes involves a number of anatomical specializations of the ear (e.g. development of air sinuses, increase in number of receptors for hearing (hair cells), and lower jaw (e.g. fat pad that acts as sound channel to conduct sound to middle ear)). Experimental evidence to support the claim that some mysticetes and pinnipeds echolocate is lacking. Echolocation evolved among early cetaceans as judged by the transformation of the ear and jaw.

Social sounds produced by marine mammals for communication include the signature whistles of dolphins, dialects of killer whales, and the songs of humpback whales. Underwater sounds of pinnipeds range from the soft lyrical sounds of the leopard seal to the aggressive sounding grunts, barks, and groans of most other phocids. Modifications of the pinniped ear for underwater hearing include isolation of the auditory bulla, as in cetaceans, and the development of cavernous tissue in the outer and middle ear which functions to equalize pressure when diving as well as to enhance the transmission of high frequency sound to the inner ear. Sirenian vocalizations described as chirp-squeaks, short-frequency modulated signals, have been identified. It has been suggested that these sounds originate in the frontal region of the head, indicating a mechanism similar to whales. Sound reception may occur via a low-frequency sound channel in an oil filled bony sponge in the cheek region of the skull. Finally considered are loud blasts of sound, "bangs," produced by toothed whales that may debilitate or temporarily disorient small prey. Various experiments conducted to determine if the transmission of low-frequency sounds could be used to detect changes in ocean temperature, and by extension global warming, were found to have negligible effects on marine mammals.

10.6. Further Reading

A general review of echolocation in dolphins can be found in Au (1983) and see Cranford *et al.* (1996) for recent developments in the mechanics of sound production in dolphins and other odontocetes. Summaries of the function of acoustic communication in marine mammals can be found in a number of edited volumes (Busnel and Fish, 1980; Nachtigall and Moore, 1988; Thomas and Kastelein, 1990; Renouf, 1991; Thomas *et al.*, 1992; Webster *et al.*, 1992; Kastelein *et al.*, 1995). More information about ATOC and its effect on marine mammals can be found at the following internet address: http://atoc.ucsd.edu; and see the Acoustical Society of America (http://asa.aip.org), a professional organization with an animal bioacoustics group interested in cetacean sonar and vocalizations among other topics.

References

Anderson, P. K., and R. M. R. Barclay (1995). Acoustic signals of solitary dugongs: Physical characteristics and behavioral correlates. *J. Mammal.* **76**(4): 1226–1237.

Antonelis, G. A., and A. E. York (1985). Identification of individual male northern fur seals, *Callorhinus ursinus,* from their vocalizations. Proceedings of the 6th Biennial Conference on the Biology of Marine Mammals, Vancouver, British Columbia.

Asselin, S., M. O. Hammill, and C. Barette (1993). Underwater vocalisations of icebreeding gray seals. *Can. J. Zool.* **71**(11): 2211–2219.

Au, W. W. L. (1993). "The Sonar of Dolphins." Springer-Verlag, New York.

Au, W. W. L., and K. J. Snyder (1980). Long-range target detection in open waters by an echolocating Atlantic Bottlenose Dolphin (*Tursiops truncatus*). *J. Acoust. Soc. Am.* **68**: 1077–1084.

Ballard, K. A., and K. M. Kovacs (1995). The acoustic repertoire of hooded seals (*Cystophora cristata*). *Can. J. Zool.* **73**: 1362–1374.

Bel'kovich, V. M., and A. V. Yablokov (1963). Marine mammals 'share experience' with designers. *Nauka—Zhizn.* **30**: 61–64.

Berzin, A. A. (1971). The sperm whale. *Pac. Sci. Res. Inst. Fish. Oceanogr.,* pp. 1–394.

Brill, R. L., M. S. Sevenich, T. J. Sullivan, J. D. Sustman, and R. E. Witt (1988). Behavioural evidence for hearing through the lower jaw by an echolocating dolphin (*Tursiops truncatus*). *Mar. Mamm. Sci.* **4**: 223–230.

Bushel, R. G., and J. F. Fish (eds.). 1980. "Animal Sonar Systems." Plenum Press, New York.

Caldwell, M. C., D. K. Caldwell, and P. L. Tyack (1990). Review of the signature-whistle hypothesis for the Atlantic Bottlenose Dolphin. *In* "The Bottlenose Dolphin" (S. R. Leatherwood and R. Reeves, eds.), pp. 199–234. Academic Press, San Diego, CA.

Clark, C. W. (1994). Blue deep voices: Insights from the Navy's whales '93 program. *Whalewatcher* **28**: 6–11.

Cleator, H. J., I. Stirling, and T. G. Smith (1989). Underwater vocalizations of the bearded seal (*Erignathus barbatus*). *Can. J. Zool.* **67**: 1900–1910.

Crane, N. L., and K. Lashkari (1996). Sound production of gray whales, *Eschrichtius robustus,* along their migration route: A new approach to signal analysis. *J. Acoust. Soc. Am.* **100**(3): 1878–1886.

Cranford, T. W. (1988). The anatomy of acoustic structures in the spinner dolphin forehead as shown by X-ray computed tomography and computer graphics. *In* "Animal Sonar: Processes and Performance" (P. E. Nachtigall and P. W. Moore, eds.), pp. 67–77. Plenum, New York.

Cranford, T. W. (1992). Functional morphology of the odontocete forehead: Implications for sound generation. Ph.D. Dissertation, Univ. of Calif., Santa Cruz.

Cranford, T. W., M. Amundin, and K. S. Norris (1996). Functional morphology and homology in the odontocete nasal complex: Implications for sound generation. *Jour. Morphology* **228**: 223–285.

Darling, J. D., K. M. Gibson, and G. K. Silber (1983). Observations on the abundance and behavior of humpback whales (*Megaptera novaeangliae*) off West Maui, Hawaii, 1977–1979. *In* "Communication and Behavior of Whales" (R. Payne, ed.), pp. 201–222. Westview Press, Boulder, CO.

Ding, W., B. Wursig, and W. Evans (1995a). Comparisons of whistles among seven odontocete species. *In* "Sensory Systems of Aquatic Mammals" (R. A. Kastelein, J. A. Thomas, and P. E. Nachtigall, eds.), pp. 299–323. De Spil Publishers, Woerden, The Netherlands.

Ding, W., B. Wursig, and W. Evans (1995b). Whistles of bottlenose dolphins: Comparisons among populations. *Aquat. Mamm.* **21**(1): 65–77.

Evans, W. E., and F. Awbrey (1988). High frequency pulses produced by free-ranging Commerson's dolphin (*Cephalorhynchus commersonii*) compared to those of phocoenids. *IWC Spec. Iss.* **9**: 173–181.

Evans, W. E., and E. S. Herald (1970). Underwater calls of a captive Amazon manatee, *Trichechus inunguis. J. Mammal.* **51**: 820–823.

Fay, F. H., G. C. Ray, and A. A. Kibal'chich (1984). Time and location of mating and associated behavior of the Pacific walrus, *Odobenus rosmarus divergens* Illiger. *In* "Soviet-American Cooperative Research on Marine Mammals: vol. 1. Pinnipeds." NOAA Tech. Rep. NMFS 12.

Fish, J. F., J. L. Sumich, and G. L. Lingle (1974). Sounds produced by the gray whale *Eschrichtius robustus. Mar. Fish. Rev.* **36**: 38–49.

Ford, J. B. (1991). Vocal traditions among resident killer whales (*Orcinus orca*) in coastal waters of British Columbia. *Can. J. Zool.* **69**: 1454–1483.

Guinee, L. N., K. Chu, and E. M. Dorsey (1983). Changes over time in the songs of known individual Humpback whales (*Megaptera novaeangliae*). *In* "Communication and Behavior of Whales" (R. Payne, ed.), pp. 59–80. Westview Press, Boulder, CO.

Hanggi, E. (1992). Importance of vocal cues in other-pup recognition in a California sea lion. *Mar. Mamm. Sci.* **8**(4): 430–432.

Hanggi, E., and R. J. Schusterman (1994). Underwater acoustic displays and individual variation in male harbor seals, *Phoca vitulina. Anim. Behav.* **48**: 1275–1283.

Harrison, R. H., and J. E. King (1980). "Marine Mammals," 2nd. ed., Hutchinson, London.

Hartman, D. S. (1979). Ecology and behavior of the manatee (*Trichechus manatus*) in Florida. *Am. Soc. Mamm. Spec. Publ.* **5**: 1–153.

Herman, L. M. (1991). What the dolphin knows, or might know, in its natural world. *In* "Dolphin Societies" (K. Pryor and K. S. Norris, eds.), pp. 349–363. University of California Press, Berkeley.

Jenkins, P. F., D. A. Helweg, and D. H. Cato (1995). Humpback whale song in Tonga: Initial findings. *In* "Sensory Systems of Aquatic Mammals" (R. A. Kastelein, J. A. Thomas, and P. E. Nachtigall, eds.), pp. 335–348. De Spil Publishers, Woerden, The Netherlands.

Johnson, C. H., and K. S. Norris (1994). Social behavior. *In* "The Hawaiian Spinner Dolphin" (K. S. Norris, B. Wursig, R. S. Wells, M. Wursig, eds.), pp. 243–286. Univ. California Press, Berkeley.

Kardong, K. V. (1995). "Vertebrates." William C. Brown, Dubuque, Iowa.

Kastelein, R. A., J. L. Dubbledam, M. A. G. de Bakker, and N. M. Gerrits (1996). The anatomy of the walrus head (*Odobenus rosmarus*). Part 4: The ears and their function in aerial and underwater hearing. *Aquat. Mamm.* **22**(2): 95–125.

Kellogg, W. N., R. Kohler, and H. N. Morris (1953). Porpoise sounds as sonar signals. *Science* **117**: 239–243.

Ketten, D. M. (1992a). The marine mammal ear: Specializations for aquatic audition and echolocation. *In* "The Evolutionary Biology of Hearing" (D. B. Webster, R. R. Fay, and A. N. Popper, eds.), pp. 717–750. Springer-Verlag, New York.

Ketten, D. M. (1992b). The cetacean ear: Form, frequency, and evolution. *In* "Marine Mammals Sensory Systems" (J. Thomas, R. A. Kastelein, and A. Ya. Supin, eds.), pp. 53–75. Plenum, New York.

Ketten, D. M. (1992c). Structure, function, and adaptation of the manatee ear. *In* "Marine Mammals Sensory Systems" (J. Thomas, R. A. Kastelein, and A. Ya. Supin, eds.), pp. 77–95. Plenum, New York.

Le Boeuf, B. J., and L. F. Petrinovich (1975). Elephant seal dialects: Are they reliable? *Cons. Int. Explor. Mer.* **169**: 213–218.

Luo, Z., and E. R. Eastman (1995). Petrosal and inner ear of a squalodontoid whale: Implications for evolution of hearing in odontocetes. *Journal of Vertebrate Paleontology* **15**(2): 431–442.

Luo, L., and K. Marsh (1996). Petrosal (periotics) and inner ear of a Pliocene kogiine whale (Kogiinae: Odontoceti): Implications on relationship and hearing evolution of tooth whales. *J. Vertebr. Paleontol.* **16**(2): 328–348.

Mann, D. A., Z. Lee, and A. N. Popper (1997). A clupeid fish can detect ultrasound. *Nature* **389**: 341.

Marine Mammal Commission (1998). Annual Report to Congress 1997. Washington, D.C.

Marten, K., K. S. Norris, P. W. B. Moore, and K. Englund (1988). Loud impulse sounds in odontocete predation and social behavior. *In* "Animal Sonar: Processes and Performance" (P. E. Nachtigall and P. W. B. Moore, eds.), pp. 281–285. Plenum, New York.

McBride, A. F. (1956). Evidence for echolocation by cetaceans. *Deep-Sea Res.* **3**: 153–154.

McCormick, J. G., E. G. Wever, G. Palin, and S. H. Ridgway (1970). Sound conduction in the dolphin ear. *J. Acoustic Soc. America* **48**: 1418–1428.

McCowan, B., and D. Reiss (1995). Quantitative comparison of whistle repertoires from captive adult bottlenose dolphins (Delphinidae, *Tursiops truncatus*): A re-evaluation of the signature whistle hypothesis. *Ethology* **100**: 194–209.

McShane, L. J., J. A. Estes, M. L. Riedman, and M. M. Staedler (1995). Repertoire, structure, and individual variation of vocalizations of the sea otter. *J. Mammal.* **76**(2): 414–427.

McSweeney, D. J., K. C. Chu, W. F. Dolphin, and L. N. Guinee (1989). North Pacific humpback whale songs: A comparison of Southeast Alaskan feeding ground songs with Hawaiian wintering ground songs. *Mar. Mamm. Sci.* **5**: 139–148.

Medrano, L., M. Salinas, I. Salas, P. Ladronde Guevara, and A. Aguayo (1994). Sex identification of humpback whales, *Megaptera novaeangliae,* on the wintering grounds of the Mexican Pacific Ocean. *Can. J. Zool.* **72**: 1771–1774.

Miller, E. H. (1985). Airborne acoustic communication in the walrus *Odobenus rosmarus. Nat. Geogr. Res.* **1**: 124–145.

Miller, E. H., and A. V. Murray (1995). Structure, complexity, and organization of vocalizations in harp seal (*Phoca groenlandica*) pups. *In* "Sensory Systems of Aquatic Mammals" (R. A. Kastelein, J. A. Thomas, and P. E. Nachtigall, eds.), pp. 237–264. De Spil Publishers, Woerden, The Netherlands.

Mobley, J. R. J., and L. M. Herman (1985). Transcience of social affiliations among humpback whales (*Megaptera novaeangliae*) on the Hawaiian wintering grounds. *Can. J. Zool.* **63**: 762–772.

Møhl, B. (1968). Hearing in seals. *In* "The Behavior and Physiology of Pinnipeds" (R. J. Harrison, R. C. Hubbard, R. S. Peterson, C. E. Rice, and R. J. Schusterman, eds.), pp. 172–195. Appleton-Century-Crofts, New York.

Møhl, B., J. M. Terhune, and K. Ronald. (1975). Underwater calls of the harp seal, *Phoca groenlandica. Rapp. P.-V. Reun. Cons. Int. Exp. Mer* **169**: 533–543.

Moore, K. E., W. A. Watkins, and P. L. Tyack (1993). Pattern similarity in shared codas from sperm whales (*Physeter catodon*). *Mar. Mamm. Sci.* **9**: 1–9.

Moore, S. E., and S. H. Ridgway (1995). Whistles produced by common dolphins from the southern California bight. *Aquat. Mamm.* **21**(1): 55–63.

Nachtigall, P. E., and P. W. B. Moore (eds.) (1988). "Animal Sonar: Processes and Performance." Plenum Press, New York.

Norris, K. (1964). Some problems of echolocation in cetaceans, pp. 317–336. *In* Marine Bio-Acoustics (ed. W. N. Tavolga), Pergamon Press, New York.

Norris, K. S. (1968). The evolution of acoustic mechanisms in odontocete cetaceans. *In* "Evolution and Environment" (E. T. Drake, ed.), pp. 297–324. Yale Univ. Press, New Haven.

Norris, K. S., and B. Møhl (1983). Can odontocetes debilitate prey with sound? *Am. Nat.* **122**: 85–104.

Norris, K. S., and J. H. Prescott (1961). Observations on Pacific cetaceans of Californian and Mexican waters. *Univ. Calif. Publ. Zool.* **63**: 291–402.

Norris, K. S., B. Wursig, and R. S. Wells (1994). Aerial behavior. *In* "The Hawaiian Spinner Dolphin" (K. S. Norris, B. Wursig, R. S. Wells, and M. Wursig, eds.), pp. 103–121. University of California Press, Berkeley.

Oelschläger, H. A. (1986a). Comparative morphology and evolution of the otic region in toothed whales (Cetacea, Mammalia). *Am. J. Anat.* **177**: 353–368.

Oelschläger, H. A. (1986b). Tympanohyal bone in toothed whales and the formation of the tympano-periotic complex (Mammalia: Cetacea). *J. Morphol.* **188**: 157–165.

Pahl, B. C., J. M. Terhune, and H. R. Burton (1997). Repertoire and geographic variation in underwater vocalisations of Weddell seals (*Leptonychotes weddellii,* Pinnipedia: Phocidae) at the Vestfold Hill, Antarctica. *Aust. J. Zool.*, 171–187.

Payne, K., P. Tyack, and R. Payne (1983). Progressive changes in the songs of Humpback whales (*Megaptera novaeangliae*): A detailed analysis of two seasons in Hawaii. *In* "Communication and Behavior of Whales" (R. Payne, ed.), pp. 9–57. Westview Press, Boulder, CO.

Payne, R. (ed.) (1983). "Communication and Behavior of Whales," pp. 59–80. Westview Press, Boulder, CO.

Payne, R., and S. McVay (1971). Songs of the humpback whales. *Science* **173**: 587–597.

Pierce, G. W., and D. R. Griffin (1938). Experimental determination of supersonic notes emitted by bats. *J. Mammal.* **19**: 454–455.

Popper, A. N. (1980). Sound emission and detection by delphinids. *In* "Cetacean Behavior: Mechanisms and Functions" (L. M. Herman, ed.), pp. 1–49. Wiley, New York.

Purves, P. E., and G. E. Pilleri (1983). "Echolocation in Whales and Dolphins." Academic Press, London.

Ray, C., W. A. Watkins, and J. Burns (1969). The underwater song of *Erignathus barbatus* (bearded seal). *Zoologica (N.Y.)* **54**: 79–83.

Reiman, A. J., and J. M. Terhune (1993). The maximum range of vocal communication in air between a harbor seal (*Phoca vitulina*) pup and its mother. *Mar. Mamm. Sci.* **9**(2): 182–189.

Renouf, D., and M. B. Davis (1982). Evidence that seals may use echolocation. *Nature* **300**: 635–637.

Repenning, C. A. (1972). Adaptive evolution of sea lions and walruses. *Systematic Zoology* **25**: 375–390.

Reysenbach de Haan, F. W. (1956). Hearing in whales. *Acta Otolaryngol Suppl.* **134**: 1–114.

Riedman, M. (1990). "The Pinnipeds: Seals, Sea Lions, and Walruses." University of California Press, Berkeley.

Rogers, T., D. Cato, and M. M. Bryden (1995). Underwater vocal repertoire of the leopard seal (*Hydrurga leptonyx*) in Prydz Bay, Antarctica. *In* "Sensory Systems of Aquatic Mammals" (R. A. Kastelein, J. A. Thomas, and P. E. Nachtigall, eds.), pp. 223–236. De Spil Publishers, Woerden, The Netherlands.

Rogers, T., D. Cato, and M. Bryden (1996). Behavioral significance of underwater vocalizations of captive leopard seals, *Hydrurga leptonyx. Mar. Mamm. Sci.* **12**(3): 414–427.

Roux, J. P., and P. Jouventin (1987). Behavioral cues to individual recognition in the subantarctic fur seal, *Arctocephalus tropicalis. In* "Status, Biology and Ecology of Fur Seals" (J. R. Croxall and R. L. Gentry, eds.), NOAA Tech Rep., pp. 95–102. Natl. Oceanic Atmos. Admin., Washington, DC.

Schevill, W. E., W. A. Watkins, and G. C. Ray (1966). Analysis of underwater *Odobenus* calls with remarks on the development and function of the pharyngeal pouches. *Zoologica* **51**: 103–106.

Steel, C. (1982). Vocalization patterns and corresponding behavior of the West Indian manatee (*Trichechus manatus*). Ph.D. dissertation, Florida Institute of Technology, Melbourne, 188 pp.

Stirling, I., and A. E. Derocher (1990). Factors affecting the evolution and behavioral ecology of the modern bears. *Int. Cont. Bear Res. Manag.* vol. 8, pp. 189–204.

Stirling, I., W. Calvert, and C. Spencer (1987). Evidence of stereotyped underwater vocalizations of male Atlantic walruses (*Odobenus rosmarus rosmarus*). *Can. J. Zool.* **65**: 2311–2321.

Strager, H. (1995). Pod specific call repertoires and compound calls of killer whales, *Orcinus orca* Linnaeus, 1758 in the waters of northern Norway. *Can. J. Zool.* **73**(6): 1037–1047.

Sverdup, H. U., M. W. Johnson, and R. H. Fleming (1970). "The Oceans: Their Physics, Chemistry, and Biology." Prentice-Hall, Englewood Cliffs, NJ.

Terhune, J. M., and K. Ronald (1973). Some hooded seal (*Cystophora cristata*) sounds in March. *Can. J. Zool.* **51**: 319–321.

Thewissen, J. G. M., and S. T. Hussain (1993). Origin of underwater hearing in whales. *Nature* **361**: 444–445.

Thewissen, J. G. M., S. I. Madar, and S. T. Hussain (1996). *Ambulocetus natans,* an Eocene cetacean (Mammalia) from Pakistan. *CFS, Cour. Forschungsinst. Senckenberg* **191**: 1–86.

Thomas, J. A., and R. A. Kastelein (eds.) (1990). Sensory Abilities of Cetaceans: Laboratory and Field Evidence, Plenum Press, New York.

Thomas, J. A., and C. L. Golladay (1995). Geographic variation in leopard seal (*Hydrurga leptonyx*) underwater vocalizations. *In* "Sensory Systems of Aquatic Mammals" (R. A. Kastelein, J. A. Thomas, and P. E. Nachtigall, eds.), pp. 201–221. De Spil Publishers, Woerden, The Netherlands.

Thomas, J. A., and V. B. Kuechle (1982). Quantitative analysis of the Weddell seal (*Leptonychotes weddellii*) underwater vocalizations at McMurdo Sound, *Antarct. J. Acoust. Soc. Am.* **72**: 1730–1738.

Tyack, P. (1981). Interactions between singing Hawaiian Humpback whales and conspecifics nearby. *Behav. Ecol. Sociobiol.* **8**: 105–116.

Tyack, P. (1991). Use of a telemetry device to identify which dolphin produces a sound. *In* "Dolphin Societies" (K. Pryor and K. S. Norris, eds.), pp. 319–344. University of California Press, Berkeley.

Verboom, W. C., and R. A. Kastelein (1995a). Rutting whistles of a male Pacific walrus (*Odobenus rosmarus divergens*). *In* "Sensory Systems of Aquatic Mammals" (R. A. Kastelein, J. A. Thomas, and P. E. Nachtigall, eds.), pp. 287–298. De Spil Publishers, Woerden, The Netherlands.

Verboom, W. C., and R. A. Kastelein (1995b). Acoustic signals by harbour porpoises (*Phocoena phocoena*). *In* "Harbour Porpoises, Laboratory Studies to Reduce Bycatch" (P. E. Nachtigall, J. Lien, W. W. Au, and A. J. Read, eds.), pp. 1–40. De Spil Publishers, Woerden, The Netherlands.

Verboom, W. C. and R. A. Kastelein (1997). Structure of harbour porpoises (*Phocoena phocoena*) click train signals. *In* "The Biology of the Harbour Porpoise" (A. J. Read, P. R. Wiepkema, and P. E. Nachtigall, eds.), pp. 343–363. De Spil Publishers, Woerden, The Netherlands.

Watkins, W. A., and W. E. Schevill (1977). Spatial distribution of *Physeter catodon* (sperm whales) underwater. *Deep-Sea Res.* **24**: 693–699.

Webster, D. B., R. R. Fay, and A. N. Popper (eds.) (1992). "The Evolutionary Biology of Hearing." Springer-Verlag, New York.

Weilgart, L., and H. Whitehead (1993). Coda communication by sperm whales (*Physeter macrocephalus*) off the Galapagos Islands. *Can. J. Zool.* **71**: 744–752.

Weilgart, L., and H. Whitehead (1997). Group-specific dialects and geographical variation in coda repertoire in South Pacific sperm whales. *Behav. Ecol. Sociobiol.* **40**: 277–285.

Wemmer, C., M. von Ebers, and K. Scaw (1976). An analysis of the chuffing vocalization of the polar bear. *J. Zool. Soc. London* **180**: 425–439.

Wyss, A. R. (1987). The walrus auditory region and the monophyly of pinnipeds. *Am. Mus. Novit.* **2871**: 1–31.

Zagaeski, M. (1987). Some observations on the prey stunning hypothesis. *Mar. Mamm. Sci.* **3**: 275–279.

11

Diet, Foraging Structures, and Strategies

11.1. Introduction

Marine mammals occupy the "large" end of the range of body sizes displayed by animals that live in the sea. One consequence of this large size is that the great majority of marine food items, phytoplankton and small zooplankton, are unavailable to marine mammals simply because the size disparity between predator and prey is too great. Mysticetes and pinnipeds (i.e. crabeater and leopard seals) have anatomical specializations that permit exploitation of these smaller (one to several cm long) prey existing at lower trophic levels; no marine mammals, however, can harvest phytoplankton or the smallest zooplankton. Most pinnipeds and odontocetes prey on relatively large (and less abundant) animals several trophic levels removed from the primary producers. Only the sirenians graze directly on the plants of the primary trophic level, and these animals are restricted to shallow coastal waters where larger rooted vegetation occurs. In this chapter, the diet of marine mammals is examined as are several of the more obvious structural and behavioral specializations employed by marine mammals to capture their prey. We also compare the foraging energetics and the anatomy and physiology of digestion.

Research on the foraging activities of marine mammals is difficult, for feeding typically occurs below the sea surface. Standard approaches to analyzing foraging behavior, in addition to direct observations of predators pursuing and capturing prey, include stomach content analysis of dead, stranded, or net-entangled animals, stomach lavage of healthy restrainable animals, studies of fecal remains and diet-derived patterns of stable isotope deposits in teeth (Hobson and Sease, 1998). Molecular genetic techniques also contribute to diet analyses. Mitochondrial and nuclear DNA markers have been used to assign individual, sex, and species identities of prey to fecal samples from pinnipeds and have enabled assessments of dietary preferences (Reed et al., 1997). A relatively new tool for studying the foraging behavior of marine mammals is an animal-borne video system and data recorder (Davis *et al.*, 1999).

11.2. Seasonal and Geographical Patterns of Prey Abundance

Marine mammal diets and foraging behaviors are direct consequences of both the spatial and temporal patterns of marine primary productivity (see Chapter 6). In general terms, marine primary productivity is highest over continental shelves and other shallow banks, in regions of upwelling, and in areas that cool appreciably in winter months. Most tropical and subtropical areas of the open sea are characterized by very low rates of primary production with little seasonal variability. Only extremely small phytoplankton cell sizes occur at the primary trophic level, and several trophic levels exist between these phytoplankton and the sparse populations of animals sufficiently large enough to be preyed upon by pinnipeds or odontocetes (see Fig. 6.2).

At higher latitudes, phytoplankton cells are individually much larger and more abundant in spring and summer months, but essentially disappear during the cold months of the year. These higher latitude primary producers, although seasonal in occurrence, form the bases of shorter food chains supporting abundant, but much more seasonally variable, aggregations of larger animals (see Fig. 6.2). Consequently, marine mammal predators in these high latitude waters must make adjustments to cope with the seasonal variability in their food supplies, including extended wintertime fasting periods and migratory excursions to lower latitude waters.

11.3. General Diet, Mechanisms, and Strategies for Prey Capture

Like all other animals, marine mammals must, on average, acquire more energy in their foraging activities than they expend. For most pinnipeds and odontocetes, large and relatively sparse prey items are located and taken one at a time. For mysticetes, smaller and more abundant shoaling or schooling prey are taken in large numbers during each feeding bout. Because marine mammals are incapable of feeding directly on phytoplankton, they typically focus their foraging activities where higher trophic level prey species congregate. Most of the animal species commonly preyed upon by marine mammals tend to concentrate near their own food supplies in the near surface photic zone: at sharp density interfaces, such as the sea surface, the sea floor, and the thermocline near the bottom of the photic zone, or at open-ocean eddies and fronts between differing water masses or along ocean current boundaries.

The feeding ecology of marine mammals is complex and requires knowledge of prey species as well as their nutritive values. Differences in prey type reflect differences in energy content. For example, in calculating energy budgets of whales (the energy content) of plankton (such as euphausids) and many pelagic fish is around 4–10 kJoules (0.96–2.39 kcal) per g body weight. The corresponding values for squid are lower at about 3–3.5 kJ (0.72–0.84 kcal) per g of body weight. This implies that more energy per unit body weight could be obtained by feeding on fish or plankton than on squid (Evans, 1987, see especially Table 6.3). However, the digestibility of the food item by the marine mammal in this equation also needs to be considered. For example, fish protein has a high digestibility (i.e. most of the available energy can be absorbed) whereas the chitin present in euphausids makes them relatively undigestible. Further, some fish have higher caloric content due to differences in the relative amount of fat they contain. The total energy consumed in a day by a marine mammal will depend not only on the caloric content of its prey but also on the number and size of individuals eaten. An important reason to understand the nutritive values of prey species is also well illustrated by studies of the Hawaiian monk seal and Steller sea lion, for whom lack of prey abundance and quality have been suggested as contributing to recent population declines in these species. One of the problems of calculating energy budgets is to distinguish between theoretical estimates and those that actually occur in the wild. Considerable information exists on the energetic benefits of selective prey consumption in whales (Gaskin, 1982; Lockyer, 1981a,b), pinnipeds (e.g. Gentry et al., 1986; Costa, 1993), and sea otters (Riedman and Estes, 1990). A less well-studied area is the energetic cost of foraging discussed later in this chapter.

11.4. Feeding Specializations of Pinnipeds

11.4.1. Teeth

Pinniped teeth, following the typical mammalian convention, are named according to their type and position in the toothrow. Premolar and molar teeth are typically similar in size and shape, and are often collectively called postcanines. Abbreviations used for each tooth type are as follows: I=incisors, C=canines, P=premolars, M=molars, PC=postcanines. Numbers affixed to these letters refer to specific teeth of each type; superscript numbers refer to teeth in the upper jaw (e.g. I^3=upper third incisor), while subscript numbers refer to teeth in the lower jaw (e.g. PC_2=lower second postcanine). Small letters indicate milk dentition. The number of teeth of each type (i.e. incisors, canines, premolars, and molars) is referred to as the **dental formula**. It is written as the number of each type of tooth in one side of the upper jaw over the corresponding number occurring in one side of the lower jaw. For humans, the dental formula is written as incisors 2/2, canines 1/1, premolars 3/3, and molars 2/2. Because the tooth types are always presented in the same order, this formula may be abbreviated as I2/2, C1/1, P3/3, M2/2 $\times$ 2 = 32(total). There is a reduction in the number of teeth in pinnipeds compared to most carnivores. In all pinnipeds, a double rooted condition of the cheek teeth (teeth posterior to the canines) is the ancestral condition, apart from the first premolar which is single rooted. There is a trend in all lineages toward evolution of single rooted teeth (King, 1983).

In pinnipeds the deciduous, or milk, teeth are very small and simple in shape. The permanent incisors and canines have deciduous precursors, as is the typical mammalian condition, but of the postcanines only P2-4 are preceded by milk teeth. The first permanent teeth to erupt are the upper and lower incisors, In phocids the milk teeth are usually resorbed before birth or shed shortly after birth. They are also relatively smaller compared to those of otariids (King, 1983).

The deciduous dentition of the walrus consists of three incisors, a canine, and three postcanines in each side of both upper and lower jaws, the first permanent postcanine not being preceded by a milk tooth. The formula for the deciduous dention is therefore i3/3, c1/1, p3/3, m0/0$\times$2=28. The milk teeth are shed shortly after birth but not all of them are replaced. Apart from the canines, the four teeth usually found in one-half of the upper jaw of an adult walrus are the third incisor and three postcanines. In the lower jaw there are no permanent incisors and the four teeth are the molariform canine and three postcanines. A small tooth sometimes erupts behind the third milk postcanine. This usually belongs to the permanent dentition (a vestigial p4/4) and is usually shed quite early, although it may persist into adult life. Because the teeth that erupt after the milk teeth do not all remain into adult life, the functional dentition, I1/10, C1/1, P3/3×2=18, although considerable variation may be observed (King, 1983).

The most noticeable aspect of the walrus dentition is a pair of long tusks, present in both sexes but more slender in females. The tusks are modified upper canines, and their large size has resulted in changes to the shape of the anterior end of the skull. The permanent upper canines erupt at about four months of age. They have persistently open pulp cavities and continue to grow throughout the life of the animal, although the tips are abraded constantly during feeding (Fig. 11.1). The granular nature of the tooth material filling the pulp cavity (globular dentine) is structurally unique and characteristic of walrus ivory. The tusks of males are larger, thicker, spaced farther apart at the base, and more divergent at the tips than those of females, and a single tusk may reach one meter in length (35 cm is average) and weigh as much as 5.4 kg (King, 1983; Fay, 1982, 1985). Male walruses use their tusks mainly in dominance displays and females use them to defend themselves and their young, and they are occasionally used by both sexes to pull themselves onto ice floes. Tusks are not usually used in feeding, although rarely they are used to stab seal prey. The abrasion to the tips, noted above, is the result of the tusks being scratched by sediment as an animal is searching for molluscs, its primary prey.

Otariids have more teeth (34–38) than phocids (22–36), and both have more than the walrus (18–24). The permanent teeth of otariids are less diverse in morphology than are those of phocids. The typical otariid dental formula is I3/2, C1/1, PC 5-6/5 with some interspecific differences and individual variation. Without the need for slicing or chewing while processing food (prey are swallowed whole), the cheek teeth of pinnipeds are typically homodont with a single pointed cusp (Fig. 11.2) for gripping slippery prey. Posterior cusps also may be present and are more frequent on the posterior cheek teeth. The cheek teeth of crabeater seals and, to a lesser extent, of leopard seals, are highly modified with complex elongated cusps to trap and strain krill (Fig. 11.2). Both crabeater and leopard seals are thought to suck krill into their open mouths by retracting their tongues, then forcing excess water out through the sieving cheek teeth (Bonner, 1982). Leopard seals also possess well-developed canines for preying on penguins and other sea birds and occasionally on fur seal pups.

Among phocids, the phocines have incisors 3/2 (except for the hooded seal which has 2/1) and the monachines have incisors 2/2 (except for the elephant seal which has 2/1). In all other phocids the rest of the dental formula is C1/1, PC5/5. There is considerable variation in tooth shape and degree of cusping (Fig. 11.2).

11.4.2. Diet and Feeding Strategies

Like most cetaceans, pinnipeds typically prey on animals small enough to be swallowed whole, although some bring larger prey to the surface to be consumed in bite-sized pieces. Fish and squid are common in the diets of pinnipeds. Other common food items taken include other invertebrates, especially crustaceans and bivalve molluscs, zooplankton (mostly krill), and warm-blooded birds and other pinnipeds (Riedman, 1990, see especially Table 7 and 8). Leopard seals are perhaps the best known, but other pinnipeds known to prey on sea birds include the New Zealand, Antarctic, sub-Antarctic, and South African fur seals, as well as New Zealand, Australian, and southern sea lions and the walrus. The northern fur seal

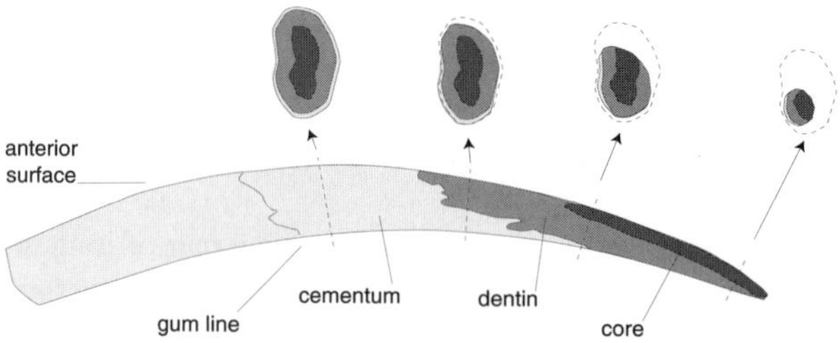

Figure 11.1. Lateral view of a mature walrus tusk with several cross-sections indicating the extent of tusk abrasion. Dashed line = original tusk surface. (Redrawn from Fay, 1982).

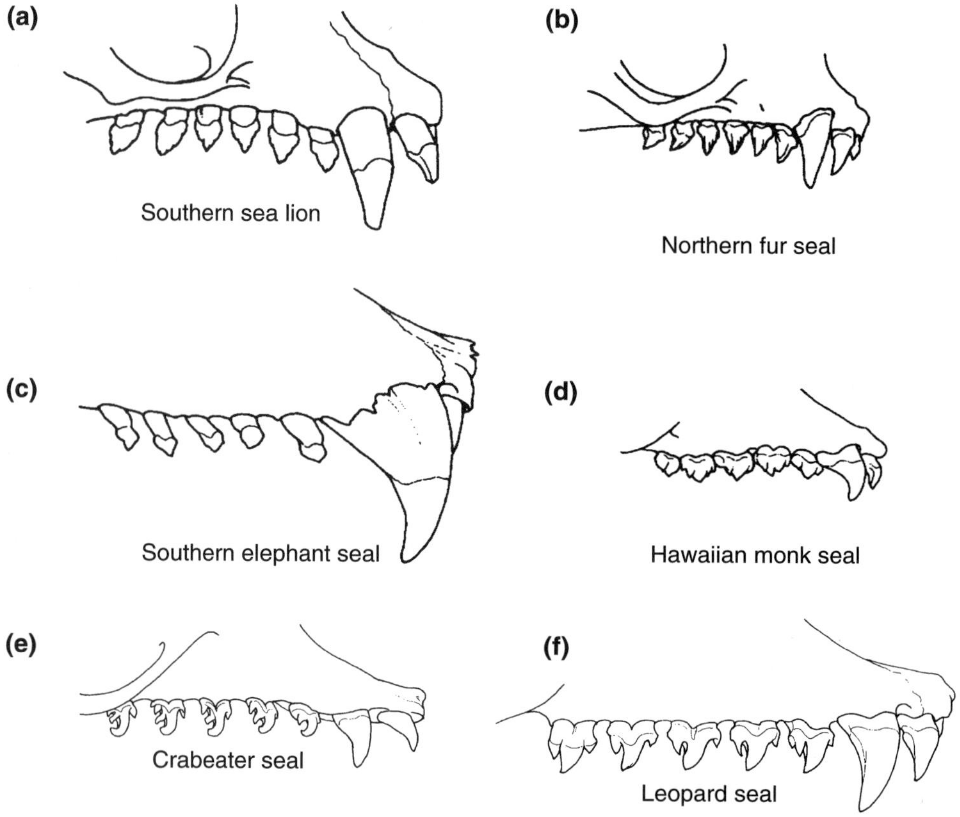

Figure 11.2. Representative otariid (a, b) and phocid (c, d, e, f) upper dentitions. (From King, 1983.)

also sometimes eats birds, although they represent an insignificant part of the diet. A number of pinnipeds, including leopard seals, New Zealand sea lions, southern sea lions, Steller sea lions, and walruses prey on other species of pinniped (Riedman, 1990, and references cited therein).

There are both geographic and seasonal variations in the diet of many pinnipeds. This is especially true for otariids living in temperate and tropical areas where there is considerable inter-annual variability related to ENSO events (discussed in Chapter 6). Diet also varies with age, with juvenile diets differing from those of adult animals. For example, adult harp seals typically feed on fish and some crustaceans whereas pups eat mainly zooplankton. Riedman (1990) suggested that one reason for this difference may be that juveniles require prey that are easier to capture. A difference in foraging strategies by young and adult female Steller sea lions has been implicated as a factor in the recent decline in their Alaskan populations (Merrick and Loughlin, 1997). It was suggested that because the young have a more limited diving ability they are more affected by changes in prey distribution.

Pinnipeds forage both individually and cooperatively in groups. Those resources most efficiently captured by an individual animal include nonschooling fish, slow moving or sessile invertebrates, or relatively small warm-blooded prey. Many phocids, including elephant and harbor seals, are solitary foragers (Riedman, 1990). Cooperative foraging occurs most frequently among pinnipeds that exploit large, patchily distributed schools of fish or squid. Many fur seal and sea lions cooperate and forage in groups. Foraging strategies exhibit considerable plasticity depending on the type and distribution of the food resource. For example, Steller sea lions forage together in large groups when feeding on schooling fish or squid, but feed singly or in small groups otherwise (Fiscus and Baines, 1966). The foraging strategies of pinnipeds in relation to maternal care strategies are discussed in Chapter 13 and diving patterns are reviewed in Chapter 9.

Walruses forage for clams, their typical prey, by swimming along the sea bottom in a head-down position, stirring up sediments with their snout and sensitive vibrissae (Fig. 11.3). When a clam is located, it is either sucked into the mouth directly or is first excavated with jets of water squirted from the mouth. The soft tissue of large clams is sucked out of the shell by the tongue, which acts as a piston creating very low pressure in the mouth cavity. Pressure changes are caused by retraction of the tongue by the large styloglossus muscle and its depression by the large genioglossus muscles (see illustrations in Kastelein *et al.,* 1991). Fay (1982) reported that the walrus tongue can create a vacuum with a pressure of –76 cm Hg in the mouth cavity. The tip of the walrus tongue has a well-developed tactile sense as evidenced by the presence of a large number of mechanoreceptors (i.e. lamellated corpuscles). Compared to many terrestrial mammals, the walrus has relatively few, but large, taste buds (Kastelein *et al.,* 1997a).

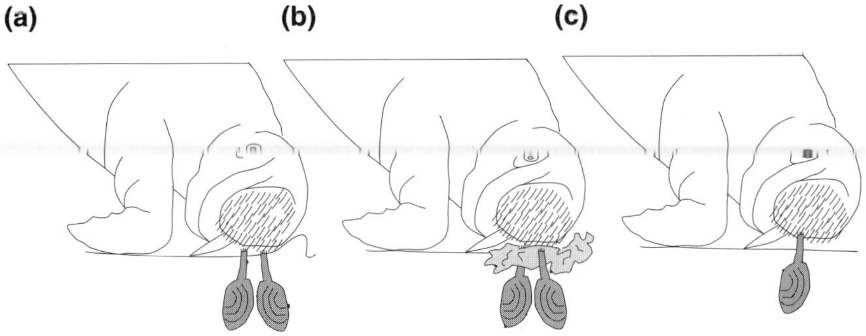

Figure 11.3. Walrus excavation techniques for benthic mollusks. (Redrawn from Kastelein and Mosterd, 1989.) Courtesy R. Kastelein.

Because the walrus consumes a large quantity of clams per day (up to 6000 individual prey per meal as reported by Fay, 1985) the feeding activities described above have to be performed very fast and very often. Oliver *et al.* (1983) recorded a feeding rate of six clams per minute, for the walrus. This would require 16–17 hours foraging time in order to capture enough prey for a full meal. In their foraging activities, walruses produce long furrows and pits on the sea bottom and can be important agents of disturbance in shallow soft-bottom Arctic benthic communities. Some walruses occasionally eat ringed and bearded seals and birds using the tongue vacuum pump to suck away the skin, blubber, and intestines (Fay, 1982).

11.4.3. Seasonal Migrations of Elephant Seals

One of the best studied foraging patterns among pinnipeds is that of the elephant seal. Adults of both species of elephant seals stay at sea for 8–9 months each year to forage. During this time they make two round-trip migrations between nearshore island breeding rookeries and offshore foraging regions. With the development of microprocessor-based **geographic location dive time and depth recorders (GLTDRs)**, details of the foraging behavior of these deep-diving seals have been documented. By attaching GLTDRs to adults as they leave their island rookeries, dive behaviors of individual animals can be recorded continuously for several months until they return to their rookeries where their GLTDRs and their recorded data can be recovered (Le Boeuf *et al.,* 1989; DeLong and Stewart, 1991; Stewart and DeLong, 1993, 1994, 1995). As GLTDRs have been used more extensively with northern elephant seals, the following discussion will focus on this species, although some generalizations apply to both species. For a summary of the movements of southern elephant seals monitored by satellite telemetry, see McConnell and Fedak (1996).

Although many vertebrates migrate long distances between breeding seasons, elephant seals are the first reported to make a double migration each year. Their individual annual movements of 18,000–21,000 km rival the gray whale in terms of the greatest distance travelled. When ashore for breeding or for molting, adult elephant seals fast (see Chapter 12), and each fasting period is followed by prolonged periods of foraging in offshore waters of the North Pacific Ocean. The first migration begins in February or early March, when seals return to sea after spending 1–3 months ashore fasting and breeding. The postbreeding migration averages 2.5 months for females and 4 months for males (Stewart and DeLong, 1993). After returning to their breeding rookery for a short molting period of 3–4 weeks, they again migrate north and west into deeper water. During this postmolt migration, females forage for about 7 months, whereas males again feed at sea for about 4 months (Fig. 11.4). Both males and females then return again to their rookeries for breeding. Individuals return to the same area during postbreeding and postmolt migrations.

While at sea, both males and females dive almost continuously, remaining submerged for about 90% of the total time. Dives for both sexes average 23 min, with males having slightly longer maximum dive durations. These dive durations probably are near the aerobic dive limit for this species (see Chapter 9; Stewart and DeLong, 1991). Elephant seals of both sexes spend about 35% of their dive time near maximum depth, between 200 and 800 m. In general, daytime dives are 100–200 m deeper than nighttime dives.

Antonelis *et al.* (1994) used stomach lavage and identification of hard parts of prey to show that the principal prey of elephant seals are mesopelagic squid and fish that spend daylight hours below 400 m and ascend nearer the surface at night. This upward nighttime movement reflects the general daily behavior of many common deep scattering layer

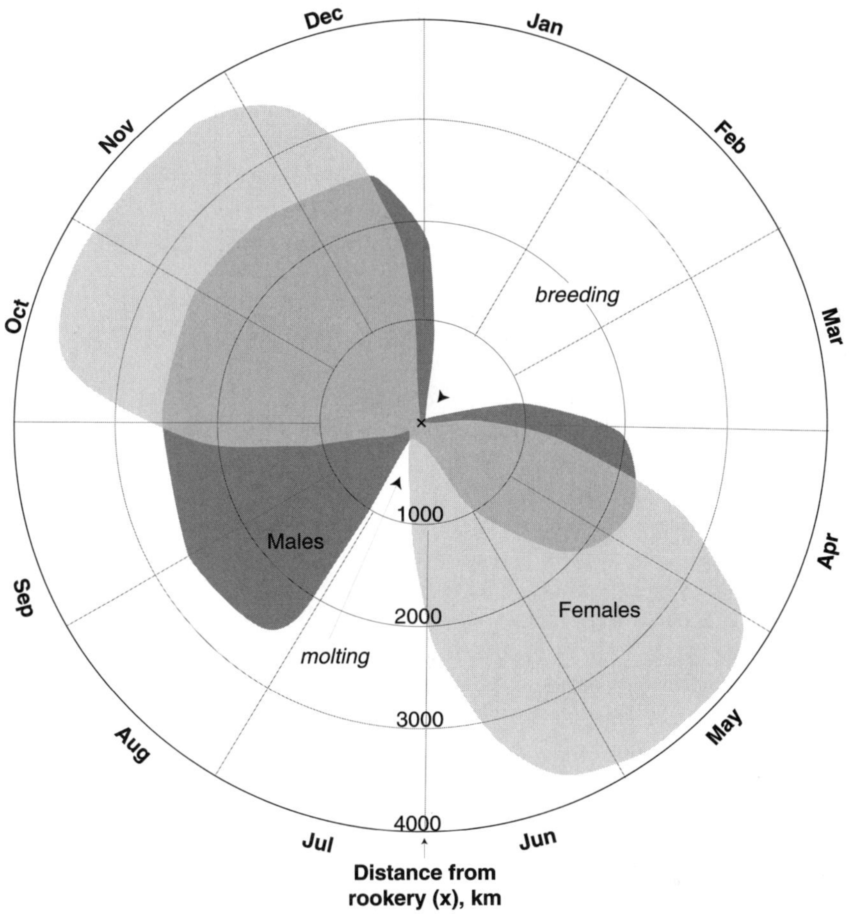

Figure 11.4. Seasonal patterns of foraging distances from breeding/molting rookeries for male and female northern elephant seals. (From Stewart and DeLong, 1993.)

species and is likely the basis for the marked difference in maximum depths between day and night dives of elephant seals. The preferred squid prey of elephant seals are slow-swimming, neutrally buoyant animals of relatively low nutritional quality. Stewart and DeLong (1993) suggest that, in selecting neutrally buoyant squid of lower nutritional quality over more muscular, faster-swimming, and more nutritious squid, elephant seals are trading nutritional content of their prey for ease of capture and shortened pursuit times.

Foraging elephant seals are widely dispersed over the northeast Pacific Ocean and exhibit strong gender differences for preferred foraging locations. Females tend to remain south of 50° N. latitude, particularly in the subarctic Frontal Zone (Fig. 11.5). Adult males transit farther north, through the feeding areas of females, to subarctic waters of the Gulf of Alaska and the offshore boundary of the Alaska Current flowing along the south side of the Aleutian Islands (Fig. 11.5). These areas of aggregation are regions of high primary productivity and contain abundant fish and squid communities.

The geographical segregation of foraging areas by male and female northern elephant seals may reflect the preferences of males for larger and more oil-rich species of squid

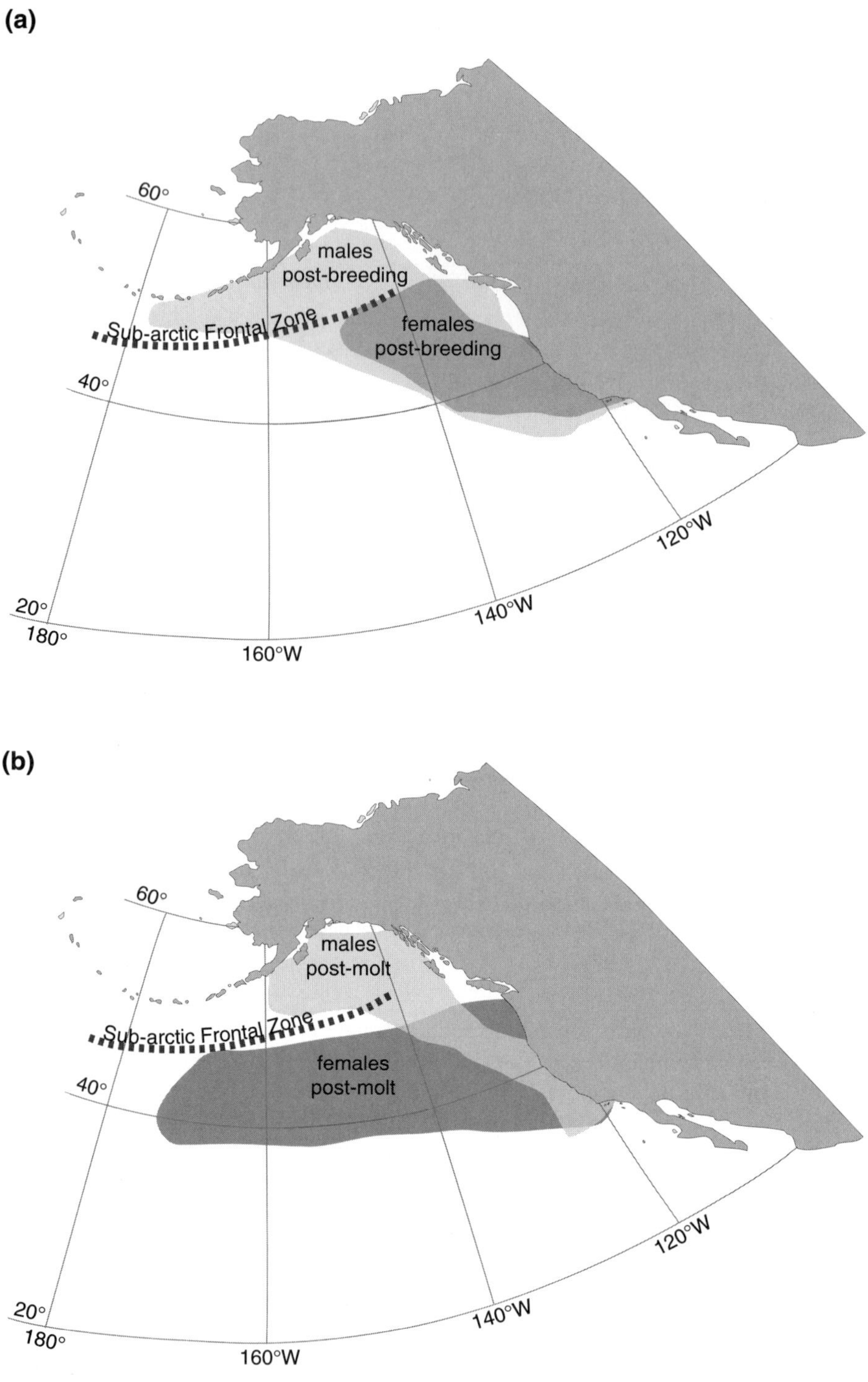

Figure 11.5. Geographical distribution of male and female northern elephant seals during post-breeding (a) and post-molt (b) foraging migrations. (From Stewart and DeLong, 1993.)

found in higher latitude subarctic waters, even though they must travel farther through the foraging areas of the females to get to these high latitude foraging grounds (Stewart and DeLong, 1993). The smaller females of this species also may have different energetic requirements that encourage them to undertake shorter migratory distances at the expense of access to energy-rich prey at higher latitudes. Strikingly similar patterns of latitudinal segregation by gender in North Pacific foraging areas are exhibited by sperm whales. Their prey are also primarily mesopelagic squid, and their seasonal migrations and diving patterns may also reflect the geographic and vertical distribution of their preferred squid prey. (Jaquet and Whitehead, 1999).

In a study further investigating the cause of differential migrations of northern elephant seals, Stewart (1997) reported that it appears to develop during puberty, when growth rates of males are substantially greater than those of females. These patterns are well established by the time males are 4.5–5 years old. His results suggest that the development of sexual segregation results from different metabolic needs of males during the period of sexual maturation and accelerated growth rather than to sexual differences in the energy requirements of adults. Segregation apparently confers survival benefits to pubescent males which more than compensate for the higher mortality generally associated with rapid growth during puberty.

11.4.4. Evolution of Feeding Strategies in Pinnipeds

The feeding behaviors of modern pinnipeds can be characterized in the following way. Most otariids and phocids employ a generalist or biting strategy and feed on a variety of fish and squid. In contrast, walruses employ a specialized suction feeding strategy using their powerful tongues to suck meat out of the shells of invertebrates. Preliminary study (DeLuis and Adam, 1998) of the structure of the palate, jaws, and teeth of pinnipeds indicates a number of features that can be used to distinguish generalist from specialist feeding strategies (e.g. palate shape and length, tooth reduction). In an effort to understand the evolution of these feeding patterns in pinnipeds, morphologic evidence for feeding pattern was mapped onto the phylogenetic framework for pinnipeds (Fig. 11.6). A generalist (biting) strategy, presumably an adaptation for a piscivorous diet, appears to be the ancestral feeding condition in archaic pinnipeds, otariids, phocids, and archaic walruses (i.e. *Neotherium* and *Imagotaria*). The specialist (suction) feeding strategy evolved secondarily in both dusignathine and odobenine walruses. This shift in feeding strategy among walruses occurred at least 11 mya.

11.4.5. Anatomy and Physiology of Digestion

Pinniped salivary glands are relatively small. They produce mucus to help in swallowing, but as the food is usually swallowed whole with no mastication, the saliva has no digestive enzymes (e.g. salivary amylase). The salivary glands are slightly better developed in otariids and the walrus than in phocids. The largest salivary gland is usually the submandibular. The sublingual gland is variably present and the parotid gland is very small or may be absent. Palatine tonsils have been reported in embryonic Weddell seal and harbor seals but have not been observed in adult Weddell seals. In the nasopharynx a pharnygeal tonsil is present in Weddell seals (Eastman and Coalson, 1974).

The esophagus frequently has deep longitudinal folds and is well supplied with mucous glands. The esophagus appears particularly muscular and dilatable in the Ross

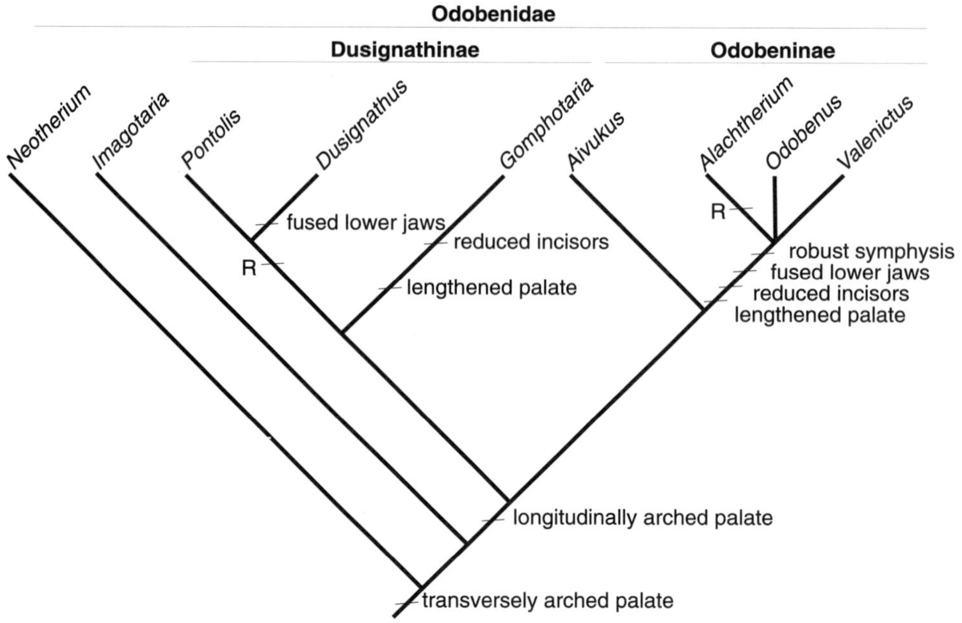

Figure 11.6. Evolution of suction feeding in walruses (phylogeny from Deméré, 1994). R = reversals, *Pontolis* and *Dusignathus* reversals: loss of transversely arched palate and longitudinally arched palate, *Alachtherium* reversals: loss of lengthened palate, reduced incisors and fused lower jaws.

seal (Bryden and Erikson, 1976). In adult Weddell seals, the large size and extensive distribution of the esophageal glands indicates that they probably augment salivary gland secretions to facilitate the passage of food through the esophagus to the stomach (Eastman and Coalson, 1974).

The stomach is simple and similar in structure to terrestrial carnivores. A characteristic feature is that the pyloric region is sharply bent back on the body of the stomach. The inner mucosal layer is arranged with well-developed rugae. Gastric glands are the most widely distributed gland in the pinniped stomach.

In most species of marine mammals there is no cecum (first part of the large intestine) and no clear division between small and large intestines. The first segment of the small intestine, the duodenum, is only indistinctly recognizable from the much longer segments of the small intestine, the jejuneum and ileum. The small intestine of pinnipeds is between eight (California sea lion) and 25 times (elephant seal) their body length (Helm, 1983). It has been suggested that intestine length is related to diet and prey digestibility. Those animals (e.g. southern elephant seal) that have a diet composed of large quantities of hard to digest squid have relatively long intestines, whereas those animals (e.g. leopard seal) that eat readily digested warm-blooded prey or fish have much shorter intestines (Bryden, 1972). It also has been suggested that the great length of the pinniped small intestine may provide a greater area for food absorption, which is related to a possibly higher metabolic rate (Eastman and Coalson, 1974). A strictly dietary explanation for the long intestine of pinnipeds now seems unlikely because other squid-eating pinnipeds such as the Ross seal do not have a long intestine. A more likely explanation, according to Krockenberger and Bryden (1994), is that it is an adaptation to frequent, deep, and long-term diving. The long intestine increases the volume of the digestive tract which serves as an extended storage compartment when the animal is submerged. Most absorption occurs during brief times when the animal is at the surface and the gut is perfused with blood. In another study, the different dietary habits of two Antarctic seals (crabeater and Weddell seals) revealed subtle rather than major morphological differences (Schumacher *et al.,* 1995; see also Martenssen *et al.*, 1998).

The large intestine is relatively short and only slightly larger in diameter than the small intestine. It has been suggested that the shorter large intestine of the elephant seal in comparison to that of the California sea lion and harbor seal may be related to their highly efficient water conservation ability. This renders the resorptive function of the large intestine of minor importance (Helm, 1983). Pinnipeds also lack an appendix.

The liver is relatively larger in pinnipeds than it is in terrestrial carnivores. It is deeply divided into five to eight long, and weakly pointed, lobes which surround the hepatic sinus. A gall bladder is present in pinnipeds and serves to store and concentrate bile, which is involved in emulsifying fats during digestion. The pancreas is an elongated organ extending transversely across the dorsal abdominal wall from the duodenum to the spleen and posteriorly to the stomach. The relative size and growth of the pancreas is probably related to diet to some extent. For example, in the southern elephant seal the relative growth of the pancreas changes during different growth phases associated with changes in diet (Bryden, 1971).

11.5. Diet, Mechanisms, and Strategies for Prey Capture in Whales

11.5.1. Mysticetes

Mysticetes feed primarily on planktonic or micronectonic crustaceans (e.g. krill) and/or small pelagic fish (Gaskin, 1982) found at relatively shallow depths, usually between 100 and 500 m. Mysticetes are characterized by a complete absence of teeth (although teeth may be found in fetal whales). Instead, a row of **baleen** (also called **whalebone**) plates projects ventrally from the outer edges of the roof of the mouth. The base of each plate is deeply embedded into the epidermal pad of the palate. The plates grow continuously out from the base but are also continually worn down by movements of the tongue. The baleen plates grow out of a foundation layer of cells that sends small projections (papillae) into the underlying layer. The papillae are covered by sheaths of keratin-filled cells (the same material that makes up hair, claws and fingernails), which form a single fringe on the border of the baleen plate. An intermediate layer of tissue produces a sheet of keratin on each side of the row of fringes, binding them into plates (Fig. 11.7). The sheets thicken into a solid mass, anchoring the adjacent plates to the soft tissue of the palate. As the outer fringes are gradually worn away through use, the inner fringes become frayed and tangled. Collectively these tangled fiberous strands overlap each other to form an extended filtering surface on the inner side of each row of baleen plates. The density of the resulting baleen fringe (# of baleen fibers/cm^2) varies at least ten-fold among species. The number and length of individual baleen plates on each side of the mouth ranges from about 100 (each less than 1 m long) in gray whales (Fig. 11.8) to more than 350 in right whales (some exceeding 3 m in length). The flexible and light yet strong characteristics of baleen plates of most mysticete species made them commercially valuable in the nineteenth century, serving many of the roles that plastics do today.

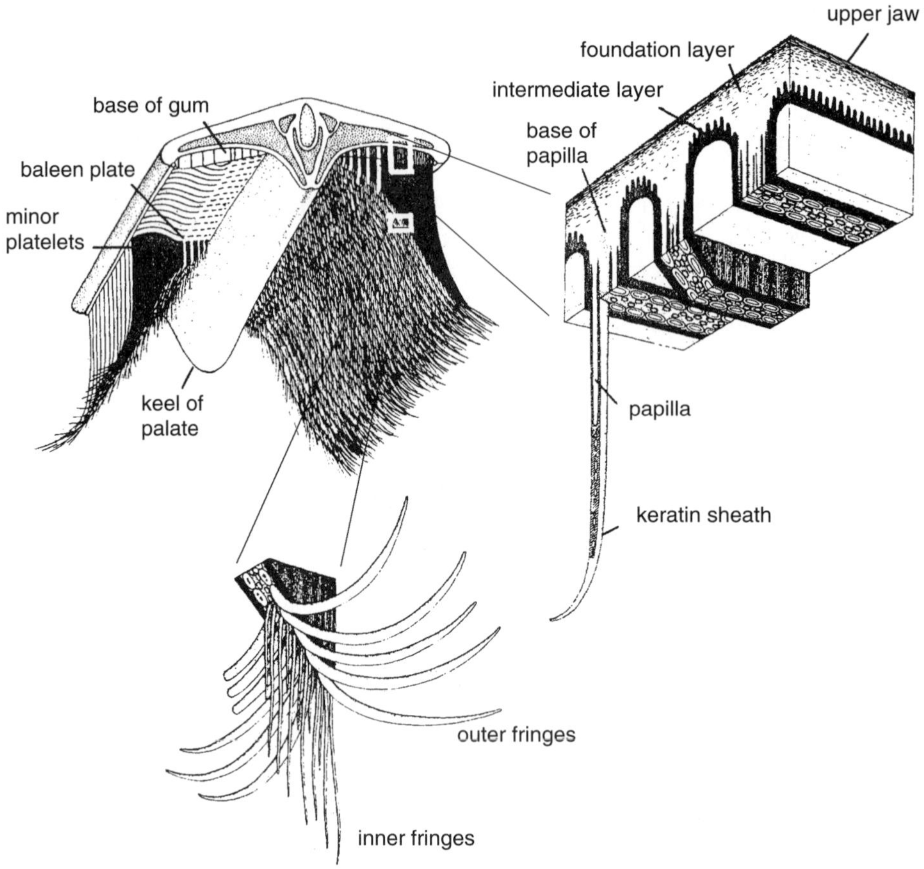

Figure 11.7. Generalized structure of baleen. (Redrawn from Pivorunas, 1979.)

Figure 11.8. Baleen of a gray whale. (Courtesy R. Botten.)

11.5.1.1. Strategies of Prey Capture

Mysticetes have evolved three different strategies for efficiently feeding on small prey: 1) skimming, 2) engulfment, and 3) mud scooping. These strategies are reflected in characters of the baleen (see Kawamura, 1980), mouth, tongue, and the method by which the mouth is expanded (Heyning and Mead, 1996). Right and bowhead whales (Balaenidae) are slow swimmers, with a highly arched rostrum and very long and finely textured baleen housed within a tall and blunt mouth. These whales feed by skimming the surface of the water collecting prey on the baleen, as water is expelled by the tongue (Fig. 11.9).

In contrast to right whales, rorquals (Balaenopteridae) are fast, streamlined swimmers with shorter and coarser baleen. The mouths of all rorqual species are enormous, extending posteriorly nearly half the total length of the body (Fig. 11.10). All members of this family have 70–80 external grooves (furrows) in the ventral wall of the mouth and throat, collectively referred to as **throat grooves** (Fig. 11.10). During feeding in blue and fin whales, this grooved mouth floor can open like pleats to lengths of up to four times its circumferential resting length as it inflates with a volume of water equivalent to 70% of the animal's body weight. It has been estimated that a mature blue whale may engulf as much as 70 tons of water at one time (Pivorunas, 1979). Alternating longitudinal strips of muscle and blubber, both with large amounts of the protein elastin, facilitate this extension (Pivorunas, 1979; Orton and Brodie, 1987). During extension, capillary networks within the tissue give the throat a reddish color. This feature has conferred the name "rorqual" or red throat to the balaenopterids.

Water and the small prey it contains enters the open mouth by negative pressure produced by the backward and downward movement of the tongue and by the forward swimming motion of the feeding animal. This method of prey capture, in which large volumes of water and prey are taken in, is referred to as engulfment feeding (Fig. 11.10). After engulfing entire shoals of euphausiids, sand lances, capelin and other prey in this manner, the lower jaw is slowly closed around the mass of water and prey. Then the muscular tongue acts in concert with contraction of the ventral wall muscles of the mouth (and sometimes with vertical surfacing behavior) to force the water out through the baleen and to assist in swallowing trapped prey (Kawamura, 1980). During feeding the tongue is capable of invaginating to form a hollow, sac-like structure called the **cavum ventrale** which lines the ventral pouch of the body. In this way the everted, elastic tongue acts to enlarge the capacity of the mouth (Lambersten, 1983). Examination of the morphology of the grooved ventral pouch reveals that in addition to fat tissue, thick layers of elastic connective tissue and

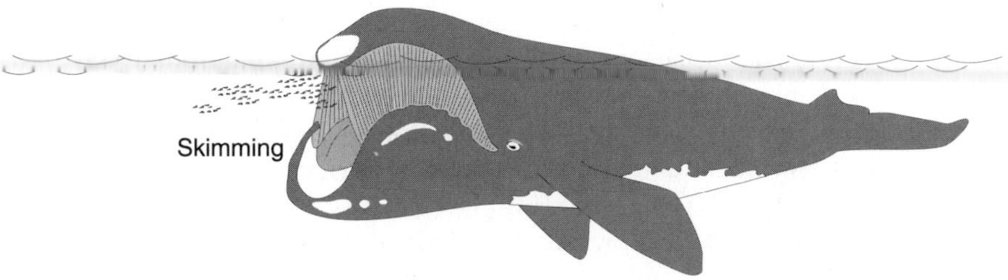

Figure 11.9. Skimming feeding style of a right whale. (Redrawn from Pivorunas, 1979.)

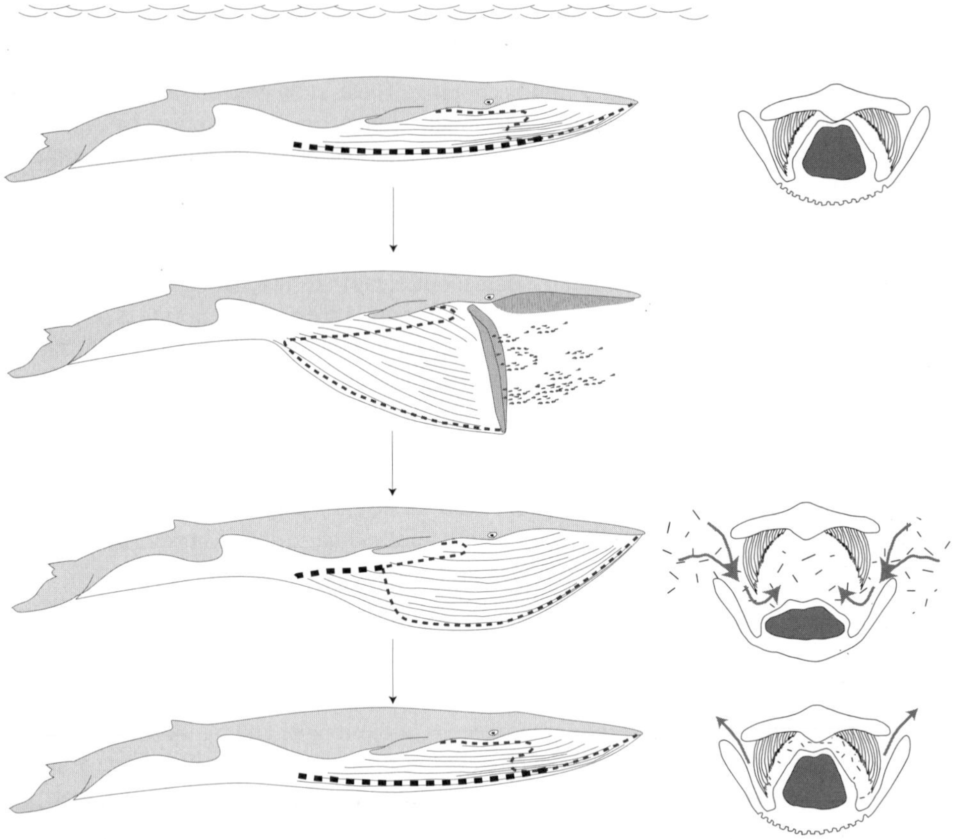

Figure 11.10. Lateral and cross-sectional views of engulfment feeding of a fin whale, illustrating the action of the tongue (dark gray) within the baleen basket. Dashed line defines the cavum ventrale. (Redrawn from Pivorunas, 1979, and Bonner, 1989.)

muscle with layered corpuscles are found closely associated with the grooves. It has been suggested that these corpuscles may have a sensory function in the timing of mouth closure during feeding (Bakker *et al.,* 1996).

A functionally important component of the rorqual engulfment feeding mechanism is the well-developed coronoid process of the lower jaw. It serves principally as the site of insertion of the large temporalis muscle. By comparison, balaenid, neobalaenid, and eschrichtiid species, which are not specialized for engulfment feeding, lack a distinctive coronoid process. A tendinous part of the temporalis muscle, the **frontomandibular stay**, provides a continuous, mechanical linkage between the skull and lower jaw and serves to optimize the gape (angle of mouth opening) during engulfment feeding. In addition, the frontomandibular stay may act to amplify the mechanical advantage of the temporalis during mouth closure (Lambertsen *et al.,* 1995) (Fig. 11.11).

It also has been proposed for fin whales that during the brief period of full gape during feeding, prey might be startled and retained within the ventral pouch by noise generated by the rapid opening of the jaw (Brodie, 1993). The sounds produced at full gape and their resonance along the mandibles might effect an escape reaction in prey contained within the

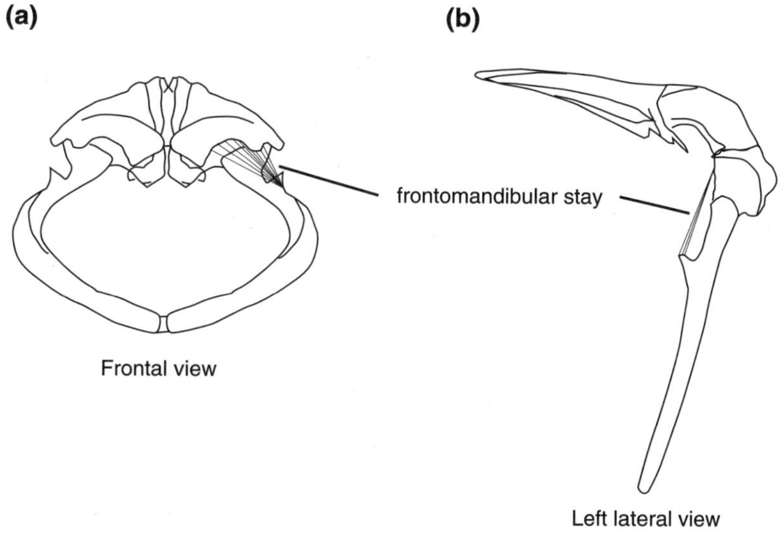

Figure 11.11. Frontomandibular stay of balaenopterids. (From Lambertsen *et al.,* 1995.) Courtesy R. Lambertsen.

mouth cavity. This may direct the movement of prey away from the jaws, resulting in their concentration and retention within the mouth.

Humpback whales display a wide variety of engulfment feeding strategies. Bottom feeding has been observed in recent years at several locations off the North American Atlantic coast (Swingle *et al.,* 1993; Hain *et al.,* 1995). Freshly abraded areas on the right side of the rostrum and tips of the flukes also suggest bottom feeding in some individuals.

When feeding on herring, humpback whales often produce a large (about 10 m diameter) cloud of ascending grapefruit-sized bubbles of expired air, referred to as **bubble-cloud feeding** (Fig. 11.12). This net of bubbles is produced by one member of a group of several co-operating whales that form long term foraging associations. These bubble clouds seem to confuse prey or cause them to clump into tight food balls for more efficient feeding by the whales (Weinrich *et al.,* 1992). As one whale produces the bubble curtain, other members of the group dive below the target herring school and force it into the curtain, then lunge through the confused school from below (Fig. 11.12). Low-frequency calls are sometimes produced as the whales lunge through the school of prey and may aid in orienting whales during this complex maneuver (A. Sharpe and L. M. Dill, personal communication, 1995). Observations of humpbacks feeding in New England waters shows that bubble-cloud feeding was followed by a tail slap, or lobtail, referred to as **lobtail feeding** (Weinrich *et al.,* 1992). It is hypothesized that this behavior is initiated as the whales switched from feeding on herring to the smaller sand lance, which may react to a lobtail by clumping more densely, making the bubble cloud more effective. The release of bubbles during foraging activities has also been reported for spotted dolphins, and killer, gray, fin, and Bryde's whales (Sharpe and Dill, 1997, and references cited therein). A series of laboratory experiments conducted to determine the effects of bubbles on schooling prey concluded that herring have a strong aversion to bubbles and can readily be manipulated or contained within bubble nets by predators. Some further experimental evidence suggests that herring may be responding to the acoustic and visual aspects of the bubbles (Sharpe and Dill, 1997).

Figure 11.12. Surface view of bubble curtain produced by humpback whales foraging on herring in southeastern Alaska waters. Courtesy F. Sharpe.

Differences in rorqual feeding patterns are best observed in the northern hemisphere, where competition has encouraged partitioning of available food resources (Nemoto, 1959). In contrast, in the southern Hemisphere, large baleen whale species exploit a single but abundant species, krill of the Antarctic upwelling region. In both hemispheres, extreme seasonal variations in the abundance of high-latitude prey forces large mysticetes to meet their total annual food requirements in 4–6 months, then abandon their feeding areas during the dark and cold months of winter when prey are rare. These annual migrations are discussed later in this chapter.

Gray whales (Eschrichtiidae) have shorter and coarser baleen than do rorquals, and lack numerous throat grooves and mouth distensibility. Gray whales exhibit the most unusual feeding behavior of all mysticetes, foraging principally on bottom invertebrates, especially small amphipod crustaceans, in their shallow summer feeding grounds of the Bering and Arctic seas (Nerini, 1984). Gray whales possess from three to five throat grooves that may function in allowing the floor of the mouth to expand during feeding. Direct observations on the feeding behavior of gray whales demonstrate that these animals roll to one side and suck their prey into the side of the mouth and expel water out the other side (Fig. 11.13) in a mud scooping strategy. Gray whales leave a record of their feeding activities, mouth-sized depressions in bottom sediments. Similar feeding behaviors are employed by some gray whales which do not make the complete northward migration; rather, they forage on a wide variety of benthic invertebrates and shoaling mysid crustaceans in shallow coastal waters throughout the gray whale's migratory range south of the Aleutian Islands (Darling, 1984; Darling *et al.,* 1995, 1998; Nerini, 1984).

(a)

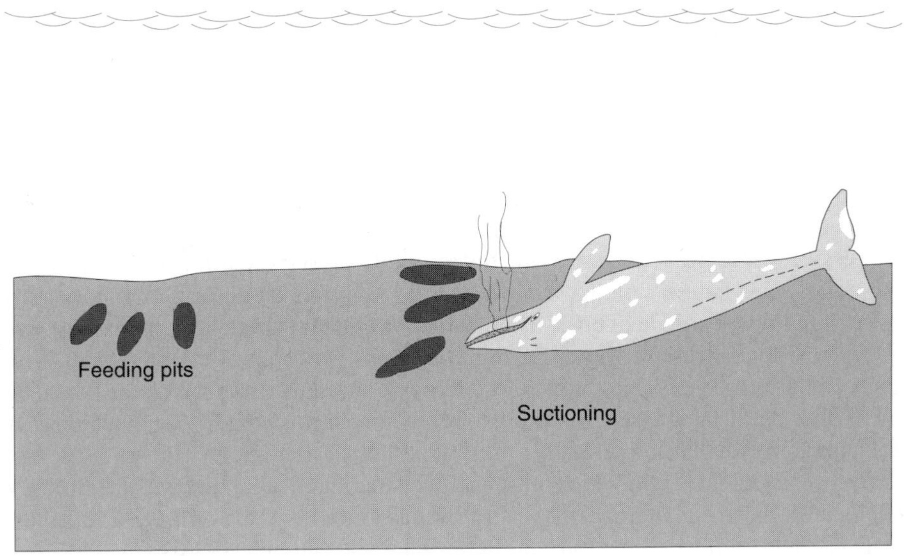

(b)

Figure 11.13. Bottom feeding by a gray whale (a) and flushing mud from baleen basket at the surface after a bottom feeding bout (b). [(a) Redrawn from Nerini, 1984.]

11.5.1.2. Seasonal Latitudinal Migrations for Feeding

Intensive high latitude summer feeding followed by long distance migrations to low latitudes in winter months is typical of large mysticetes of both hemispheres (Fig. 11.14). When away from high latitude feeding grounds, these whales reduce their intake of food or completely cease feeding. The seasonal variations of feeding intensity impose annual cycles of fattening and fasting on these animals that can be as extreme as those of small hibernating terrestrial mammals. Although neither the migratory routes nor the patterns of energy apportionment for these migrations are known in detail for most mysticete species, a few generalizations can be made.

Successful winter migrations to low latitudes while fasting require that sufficient energy be stored as lipids before summer feeding ceases. Additionally, fasting migrators must be large enough to have sufficient body volume to accommodate these lipid stores. The threshold body size for successful winter fasting migrations is unclear. Certainly small juvenile animals of all mysticete species tend to feed throughout the year. So too do the adults of the smallest species of mysticetes, the minke and pygmy right whales (Sekiguchi and Best, 1992), although only the former makes annual latitudinal migrations. Hinga (1978) has argued that the much larger fin whale must also feed, although at a reduced rate, during winter months. However, adult gray whales fast for most or all of the 5–6 months that they are away from their summer feeding grounds (Nerini, 1984; Sumich, 1986).

Gray whales accomplish one of the longest annual migrations of any mammal, covering 15,000–20,000 km. This migration spans as much as 50° of latitude and links summer feeding areas in the Bering, Chukchi, and Okhotsk Seas with warmer breeding, calving, and assembling grounds along subtropical Pacific coastlines in winter (Fig. 11.15). Almost all of this migration occurs within 10 km of shore, and the details of this migration have been intensively studied (Gilmore, 1960; Pike, 1962; Rice and Wolman, 1971; Reilly, 1981; Herzing and Mate, 1984; Poole, 1984; Perryman *et al.*, 1999). As with other mysticete species, the highest energy costs during migration are incurred by the pregnant or lactating

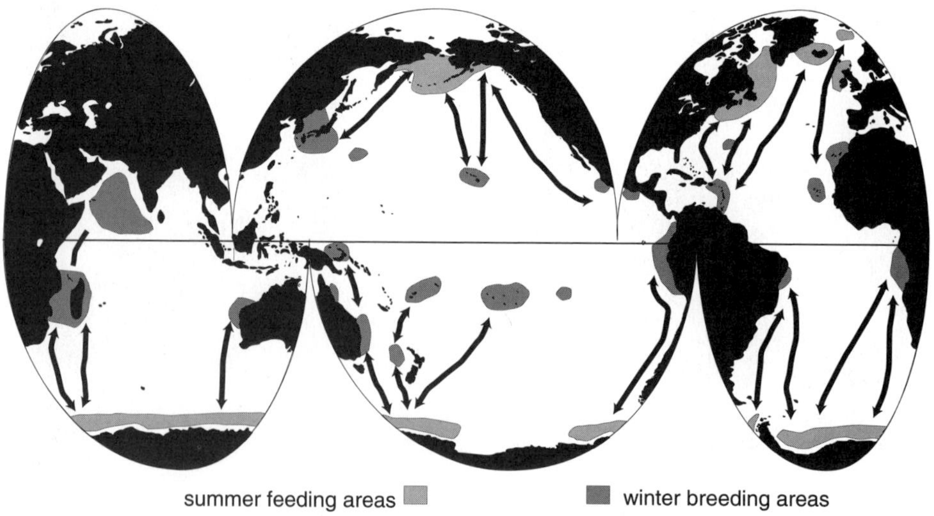

Figure 11.14. Distribution of principal humpback whale feeding and breeding areas and the migration routes linking them. (Redrawn from Slijper, 1979.)

females. Small lactating female gray whales require about 3.2 metric tons of lipids, out of an estimated reserve of 4.4 metric tons, for feeding their young and for their own maintenance costs through the end of the winter lagoon season. Small adults must resume feeding during their northbound migration, whereas whales unburdened with the costs of lactation, as well as older, larger pregnant females, have the necessary lipid reserves to complete the north migration without feeding.

During the Last Glacial Maximum (LGM, 18,000 years before present) the sea level was about 150 m below its present stand (Imbrie *et al.,* 1983). With the shift of polar and subpolar waters southward, all of the shallow sea floor areas presently used by and accessible to gray whales were inaccessible during the LGM. The shallow portions of the Bering, Chukchi, and Okhotsk Seas now used intensively for summer foraging were either drained of water during the last glacial maximum or they were completely icebound. Thus, the extensive prey assemblages presently exploited by gray whales either did not exist or were unavailable in these areas to gray whales during the LGM. Most of the present continental shelves in both the North Pacific and North Atlantic Oceans were also exposed above sea level, leaving much narrower continental shelves than exist at present.

The strong contrast between present and LGM oceanographic conditions in both the North Pacific and North Atlantic Oceans leads to the conjecture that gray whales may be thriving now because a particularly fortuitious set of environmental circumstances exists in polar seas during this (and possibly earlier) interglacial period, but which disappears during glacial maxima. The present foraging flexibility expressed by gray whales feeding in their migratory corridor suggests that they always have been food generalists, but have specialized temporarily into a narrow ecological niche to capitalize on benthic amphipods which are presently abundantly available. During glacial advances and consequent sea level lowering and polar sea exclusion by ice, this food resource disappears or at least becomes unavailable to gray whales.

Gray whales exhibit evolutionarily conservative feeding structures, especially the relatively small head with few extensible throat pleats, in addition to short, coarse baleen, which seem to make them poor competitors with other mysticete whales for pelagic food

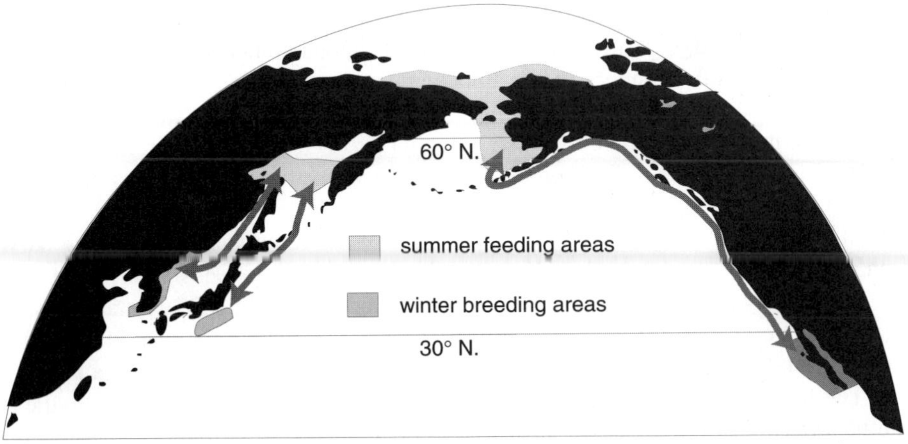

Figure 11.15. Distribution of principal gray whale feeding and breeding areas and the migration routes linking them.

resources in high latitudes. The present abundance of shallow water benthic prey which are not exploited by any other whale species, permits gray whales to avoid such competition.

11.5.2. Odontocetes

Fish, squid, large crustaceans, birds, and, more rarely, other marine mammals are the principal prey of modern odontocetes. The shape of the mouth and jaw, and the number, size, and shape of teeth vary considerably between odontocete families, yet most exhibit strong differences in tooth numbers and shapes from typical placental mammals.

Most often the teeth of odontocetes are simple and peg-shaped with single, open roots. There is no milk or deciduous dentition. In odontocetes most of the tooth consists of dentin covered by a thin layer of cementum (on root) and a very thin layer of enamel (on crown). In many toothed whales there is wide individual variation in tooth number. For example, in the sperm whale, pilot whale, and common dolphin the total number of teeth may exhibit a 1.5 to 4.5-fold difference among individuals. Other odontocetes (e.g. beaked whales) possess a relatively constant number of teeth. Teeth are loosely socketed in irregularly shaped alveoli.

In many marine mammals, because of the nearly homodont or peg-like condition of the teeth (Fig. 11.16), it is impossible to make distinctions between tooth types (premolars vs molars, for example). As such the total tooth number for each side of the jaw is simply combined as a single number, without indication of tooth type (e.g. 15/18 indicates 15 teeth per side in the upper jaw and 18 per side in the mandible). In some odontocetes (i.e. beaked whales, pygmy and true sperm whales, Dall's porpoise, etc.) there is reduction in the number of teeth in the jaws (Fig. 11.16); for some there are few or no teeth in the upper jaw but numerous teeth in the lower jaw (e.g. 0/25 for the sperm whale and 0/8–16 for the pygmy sperm whale).

Among beaked whales, the strap-toothed whale with its very reduced dentition (only 1 tooth is present in the lower jaw) and small mouth has raised questions about how adult males feed. This is because their erupted mandibular teeth curve medially above the rostrum, thereby limiting the extent to which they can open their mouths. It has been suggested that the erupted teeth may function to guide prey in the mouth (Leatherwood *et al.*, 1983), but because females and immature males lack these teeth, Heyning (1984) suggested that it was more likely they function in intraspecific fighting.

Finally, there is a large group of cetaceans with an equal number of teeth in the upper and lower jaws (e.g. tooth numbers in the Phocoenidae vary from 15/15 to 30/30). Among members of the Delphinidae the number varies from 0/2 in the short-snouted Risso's dolphin to 65/58 in the long-snouted spotted dolphin (Fig. 11.16). Tooth morphology also differs between these groups. Phocoenids have spatulate teeth and delphinids have conical teeth.

Much attention has been given to the presence of the remarkable tusk in the narwhal which may exceed a length of 3 m (Tomilin, 1957). The tusk extends anteriorly from the head, and is likely responsible for the myth of the unicorn (see Fig. 4.35). As a general rule, the left canine erupts as a tusk only in males. The outer surface of the tusk is marked by a series of prominent spiral ridges which may number five or six 360° turns on a large specimen. The spiral of the tusk is always sinistral (or left-handed) when viewed from the root. Male narwhals occasionally develop two tusks or may lack an erupted tusk, and females may develop a left tusk or both tusks. When present, the tusks of females are shorter and less robust than those of males.

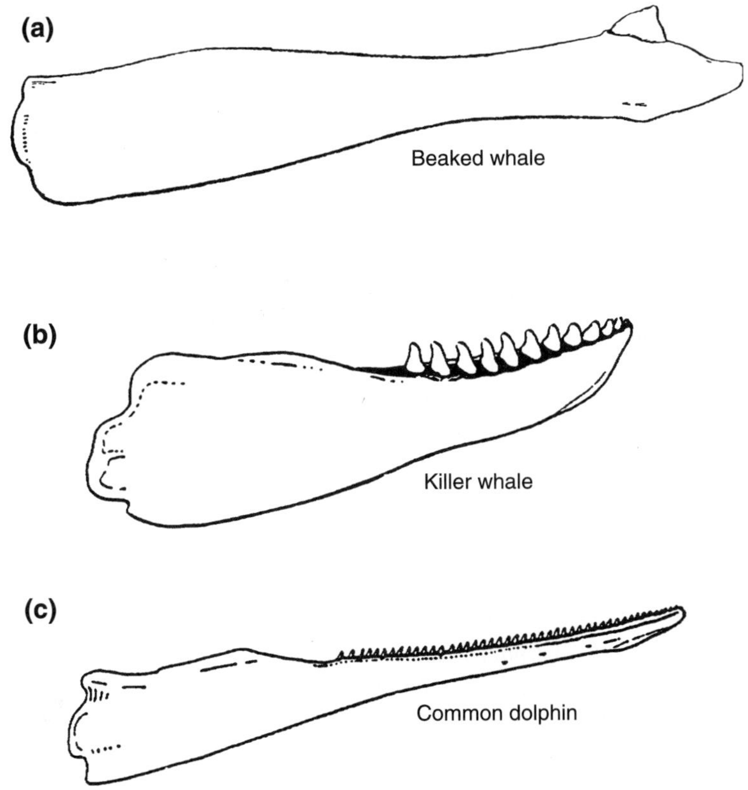

Figure 11.16. Representative lower dentitions of odontocetes: (a) beaked whale, (b) killer whale, and (c) common dolphin. (Redrawn from Slijper, 1979.)

There have been many suggestions regarding the function of the narwhal tusk ranging from its possible use in feeding to one of defense against predators. The large disparity in size between male and female narwhals and the later attainment of sexual maturity in the male strongly suggest that the tusks are used in sexual display between males. It has been suggested that the tusk is used for nonviolent assessment of hierarchical status on the basis of relative tusk size during frontal encounters (Best, 1981), but evidence from head scarring and broken tusks indicates that adult males may indulge in aggressive displays that involve violent fighting. Ford and Ford (1986) describe the only known instance of a narwhal being speared in the abdomen by the tusk of another whale. The injured animal subsequently died, almost certainly as a result of this massive injury. The attacked animal was not a male, as one might expect, but a female that had recently given birth (Hay and Mansfield, 1989).

11.5.2.1. Prey Capture Strategies

Odontocetes differ from mysticetes in feeding principally on fish and/or squid which live at greater depths than mysticete prey. The diet of odontocetes is reflected in the morphology of the jaw, type and number of teeth, and depends on aspects of the distribution and ecology of their prey. For a summary of the diet of various odontocete species see Evans (1987, Table 6.2). Among species that subsist largely or entirely on squid are the sperm and beaked whales. Those species that feed on squid exhibit a number of adaptations for employing the tongue as a piston and sucking squid into the mouth. This suction feeding strategy is characterized by a reduced number of teeth and a small gape to allow unobstructed entry of small prey, a ribbed palate to help to hold slippery-bodied squid, and throat grooves to allow for expansion of the throat region (Heyning and Mead, 1996). The suction feeding mechanism in beaked whales as described by Heyning and Mead (1996) involves distension of the floor of the mouth provided by the throat grooves and retraction of the tongue by the styloglossus and hyoglossus muscles (Fig. 11.17). The extensive sliding movement of the tongue is facilitated by smooth connective tissue between the tongue and the genioglossus muscles, similar to the cavum ventrale of rorquals; in the latter, however, there is significant lateral movement of the throat floor as the tongue inverts during feeding. After distension it is hypothesized that the throat region returns to its resting position primarily as the result of elastic recoil of surrounding tissues, again acting in a similar manner to the cavum ventrale in rorquals (Fig. 11.17).

It has been suggested that other odontocetes use suction to obtain prey and an analysis of suction feeding in delphinid cetaceans is in progress (Werth, 1989, 1991, 1993). Pelagic dolphins, for example *Stenella* and *Delphinus,* are wide-ranging in the subtropical and tropical regions of the world and are opportunistic feeders. Their diets can vary seasonally and from one year to the next. The pincer-like action of the jaws of these long-snouted forms allows fish to be trapped by the interlocking tips of the teeth when the jaw closes and water is forced out (Norris and Møhl, 1983). The suggestion that the short-snouted forms which capture prey by suction feeding, such as beaked whales, the narwhal, and immature sperm whales, may be more effective if the prey were first debilitated by high intensity sounds before engulfment (discussed in Chapter 10). As described by Kastelein *et al.* (1997b), the harbor porpoise also employs a suction feeding strategy in which the tongue tip creates a watertight seal around a fish, while the base of the tongue moves down to create suction toward the throat.

Perhaps the most intriguing foraging specialization is that suggested for a small number of female bottlenose dolphins in Shark Bay, Australia. These animals have been observed consistently over a number of years carrying sponges (Smolker *et al.,* 1997). Suggestions for how the sponges might be used range from their employment as "tools" to disturb bottom sediments and flush out prey species, to protection for the dolphin's face from the spines and stingers of stingrays, stone fish, and scorpionfish. Future work is needed to address such questions as how the behavior is acquired and the cost and benefits of sponge carrying as a foraging specialization (Smolker *et al.,* 1997).

The broad ecological and latitudinal range of killer whales corresponds to a wide variety of known prey species, including fish, cetaceans, pinnipeds, birds, cephalopods, sea turtles and sea otters (Hoyt, 1984; Estes *et al.*, 1998; Pyle *et al.*, 1999). Although killer whales have been described as feeding opportunists or generalists, Felleman *et al.* (1991) suggest that they have opportunistic foraging abilities but also can behave as feeding specialists, with the necessary flexibility to respond to variations in the type and abundance of their preferred prey.

In Icelandic coastal waters, some pods of killer whales sometimes feed on marine mammals, then switch to fish prey at other times of the year. In both Antarctic and Pacific Northwest waters, prey specialization between killer whale populations occurs. In Washington and British Columbia coastal waters, a resident population feeds almost exclusively

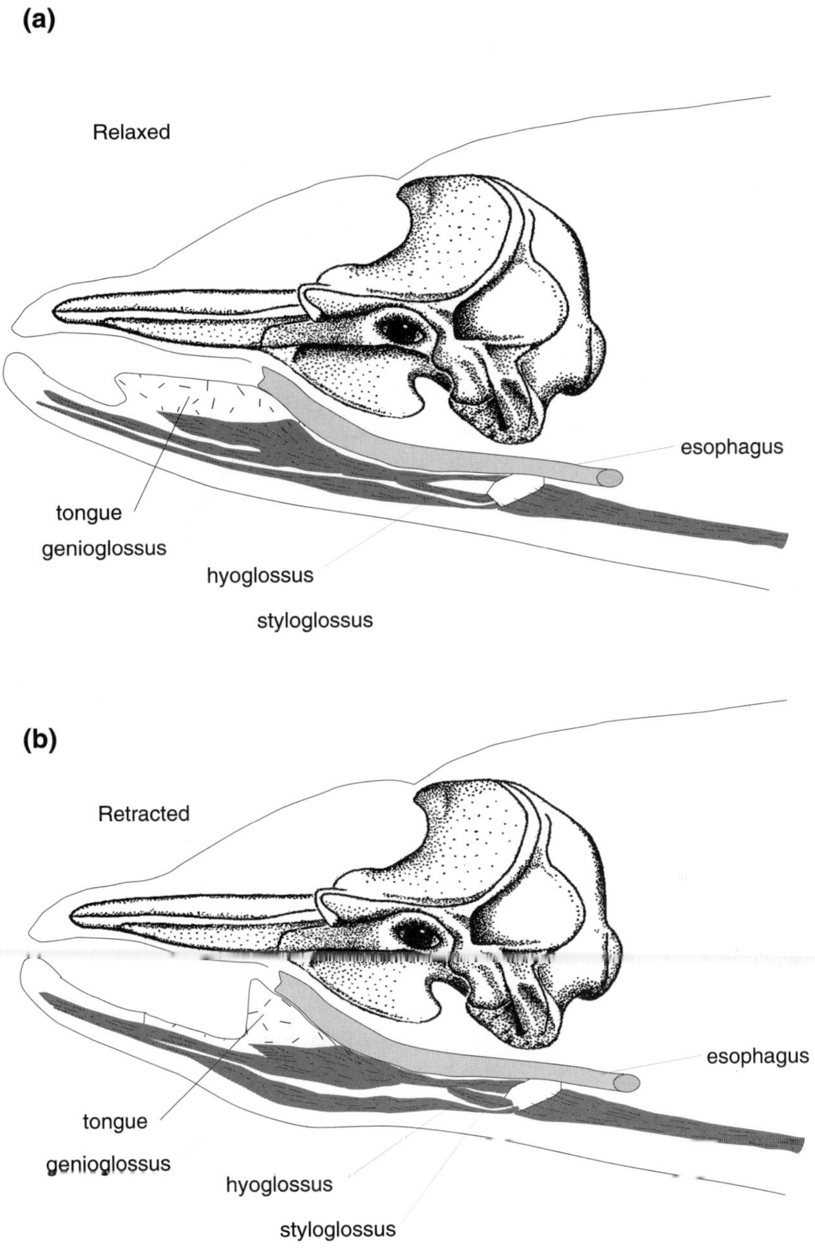

Figure 11.17. Mechanics of suction feeding in beaked whales with the tongue in the relaxed (a) and retracted (b) positions. (After Heyning and Mead, 1996.)

on fishes, whereas a nonresident or transient population preys principally on marine mammals, especially harbor seals and sea lions (Bigg *et al.,* 1987; Ford *et al.*, 1998). Sightings of foraging resident pods correlate strongly with seasonal variations in their most common prey, salmon and steelhead. During months when salmon are unavailable, residents switch prey to herring or bottom fish (Felleman *et al.,* 1991) and may disperse northward several hundred kilometers. In contrast the prey of transient groups is available year-round, and in spite of their label, these whales tend to remain in a small area for extended periods of time. Table 11.1 summarizes some important differences between these two populations.

Different populations use different foraging strategies, even when in close proximity to each other. These strategies reflect different prey types and possibly different pod traditions. Resident whales typically swim in a flank formation, possibly to maximize prey detection, although individual hunting is sometimes seen at the periphery of the main pod group. Resident pods appear to prefer foraging at slack tidal periods when salmon tend to aggregate. Echolocation and other vocalizations are common when resident pods feed on fish. These vocalizations are less frequent in transient groups preying on other marine mammals. The latter are more likely to exhibit avoidance responses. Relative to residents, transients use short and irregular echolocation trains composed of clicks that appear structurally variable and low in intensity, more closely resembling random noise (Barrett-Lennard *et al.,* 1996). Yablokov (1966) has suggested that the contrasting black and white coloration patterns of killer whales facilitate visual coordination and communication within feeding groups of transients. Transient groups commonly encircle their prey, taking turns hitting it with their flippers and flukes (Felleman *et al.,* 1991). This extended handling of prey may continue for 10–20 minutes before the prey is killed and consumed. When hunting alone, transient whales often employ repeated percussive tail-slaps or ramming actions to kill their prey before consuming it (Fig. 11.18). Foraging by transient groups occurs at high tides when more of their pinniped prey are in the water and vulnerable to predation.

An interesting consequence of this prey specialization is the pattern of indirect trophic interactions that have evolved between these two populations of orcas. Resident whales compete directly for fish that are also the prey of pinniped species consumed by transient killer whales. Any increase in the carrying capacity of residents will have the effect of decreasing the carrying capacity of transients, since residents compete with the pinniped prey of transients for available fish resources. However, an increase in the carrying capacity of transients will have the opposite effect on residents by reducing competitive pressures from pinnipeds on fish resources (Baird *et al.,* 1992). These indirect trophic interactions and resulting trophic level efficiencies suggest that residents should be more numerous than transients, and present estimates of the sizes of the two populations support this (Bigg *et al.,* 1987).

In Antarctic killer whales, a similar dichotomy exists, with an offshore population consisting of groups of 10–15 animals each preying mostly (nearly 90%, based on content

Table 11.1. A Comparison of Foraging-Related Differences between Transient and Resident Killer Whales of the Pacific Northwest (Modified from Baird *et al.,* 1992).

Character	Residents	Transients
Group size	Large (3–80)	Small (1–15)
Dive pattern	Short and consistent	Long and variable
Temporal occurrence	With salmon runs	Unpredictable
Foraging areas	Deep water	Shallow water
Vocalize when hunting?	Frequently	Less frequently
Prey type	Salmon & other fish	Mammals
Relative prey size	Small	Large
Prey sharing	Usually no	Usually yes

Figure 11.18. Transient killer whale attacking a Dall's porpoise in Chatham Strait, Alaska. Courtesy R. Baird.

analyses of 785 stomachs) on other species of marine mammals. Inshore Antarctic populations occur in groups ten times as large and feed almost exclusively on fishes (Berzin and Vladimirov, 1983).

Differences in the foraging behaviors of the two overlapping populations in the Pacific Northwest persist through time, with each group expressing different vocalizations (see Chapter 10) and different social group sizes as well as different prey preferences and foraging behaviors. A similar discreteness likely exists between inshore and offshore Antarctic killer whale populations, where differences in the distribution, foraging behavior, group size, and even average body size prompted Soviet researchers to propose separate species status for the two populations (Berzin and Vladimirov, 1983). Baird *et al.* (1992) suggest that the two populations in the Pacific Northwest are in the process of speciation. However, this picture may become more complicated as more is learned about a third group of killer whales occupying offshore waters from California to Alaska (Hoelzel *et al.,* 1995).

Killer whales are cooperative foragers, and take advantage of an ability, probably unique among marine mammals, to capture prey larger than themselves. The degree of foraging cooperation is variable, depending on the type of prey; it can involve cooperative prey encirclement and capture, division of labor during an attack (Tarpy, 1979; Frost *et al.,* 1992), and sharing of prey after capture (Lopez and Lopez, 1985). In the study by Lopez and Lopez, individual killer whales repeatedly swam up sloping beaches in Patagonia (South America) at high tide to capture hauled-out southern elephant seals and sea lions. This hunting strategy, termed intentional stranding, also is observed among juvenile female killer whales in the capture of elephant seal pups (Guinet and Bouvier, 1995). These studies suggest that adults teach this behavior to juveniles and that apprenticeship likely plays an important part in the transfer of hunting techniques from one generation to the next.

Although diets and prey capture strategies have been described for whales, less attention has been given the various energetic costs associated with foraging. Energy is expended through movement during prey searching and capture. Small cetaceans display a variety of foraging methods that vary in energetic costs and deplete their oxygen reserves in accordance with metabolic demands. For example, consider swimming at high speed. Although an energetically costly strategy when searching for prey, high speed swimming may be advantageous in capturing prey that is patchy in distribution and ephemeral in time has been identified (Williams *et al.*, 1996). In addition to the costs of foraging, there are other related energy losses including thermoregulation, locomotion, reproduction, and lactation. These are discussed in other chapters (Chapters 7, 8, and 13, respectively).

11.5.3. Evolution of Prey Capture Mechanisms and Strategies Among Whales

Archaic whales (i.e. protocetids) have simple heterodont teeth. *Pakicetus* could probably shear and grind its prey as well as snap the jaw shut during capture (Gingerich and Russell, 1990). The feeding morphology of *Ambulocetus* has been compared to that of crocodilians. Both have long snouts, pointed teeth, strong jaw adductors (especially the temporalis muscle), and they do not masticate their food. It has been suggested that *Ambulocetus* was an ambush predator that caught large struggling fish and aquatic reptiles that were trapped in shallow water with its jaws (Thewissen *et al.,* 1996). Basilosaurids show a greater range of tooth and jaw form as well as body size (in comparison to protocetids) and may have exploited offshore or deeper water prey (Fordyce *et al.,* 1995).

The tooth and rostrum structure in the earliest toothed mysticetes (i.e. aetiocetids) is consistent with filter feeding. It has been suggested that filter feeding in mysticetes evolved in response to the availability of new food and in turn to new oceanic circulation patterns associated with the creation of the Southern Ocean and the final breakup of Gondwana. Migration perhaps evolved at the same time, allowing seasonal high latitude feeding alternating with breeding in thermally less stressful temperate-tropical latitudes. Baleen-bearing mysticetes evolved by the late Oligocene, 4–5 Ma after toothed mysticetes appeared in the fossil record. Balaenopterids appeared by the late Miocene and differed from cetotheres in having abruptly depressed frontal bones which suggests a marked functional shift in the origin and action of the temporalis muscle and perhaps the origin of engulfment feeding. Early Miocene balaenids with their narrow arched rostra indicate that the skim feeding method of modern balaenids had already evolved by this time. The origin of the mud scooping feeding method of gray whales is not known because there is no record of this group before the Pleistocene.

The earliest known odontocetes probably used echolocation to hunt single prey items. Fordyce (1980) suggests that, as for mysticete feeding, echolocation evolved in response to changing food resources, ocean circulation, and continental positions. Tooth number and form vary widely among odontocetes. A reduced role for teeth in processing food is shown by convergent tooth loss in diverse groups including some sperm, beaked, pygmy sperm, pilot whales, and narwhals.

The most bizarre feeding adaptation so far recorded among cetaceans is that of the extinct taxon *Odobenocetops peruvianus* (Muizon, 1993a,b). This strange toothed whale lived during the early Pliocene along coastal Peru. Only a skull is known, and this has large, downturned, asymmetrical tusks and a blunt snout. Strong muscle scars on the anterior edge of the premaxillae suggest the presence of a powerful upper lip. This feature together with the deeply vaulted palate and absence of teeth suggests a convergent feeding adaptation with the walrus for eating benthic mollusks using suction (Fig. 11.19).

11.5.4. Anatomy and Physiology of Digestion

The striking feature of both cetacean and pinniped digestive systems is the extreme length of the alimentary canal. This may be related to the increased metabolic demands of a larger body size and not directly related to dietary demands. The esophagus of cetaceans consists of a long, thick-walled tube. Its length depends on the size of the animal, constituting approximately one quarter of the total body length in toothed whales (Yablokov *et al.,* 1972).

All cetaceans are characterized by a complex stomach with multiple divisions which resemble those of ruminants (e.g. cattle, goats, and sheep). The four main compartments are 1) a **forestomach** devoid of glands and lined by squamous epithelium, 2) a **fundic chamber or main stomach** with a folded mucosa and gastric glands, 3) a **connecting stomach**, between the main stomach and pyloric stomach, and 4) a relatively smooth **pyloric stomach** which may be bent on itself or show several dilations and which has some glands in its walls (Fig. 11.20). The organization of the cetacean stomach differs from that of ruminants. In whales, only the initial chamber is nonglandular (vs. the first three chambers of the ruminant stomach) and the multichambered arrangement primarily involves compartmentalization of the glandular stomach (Olsen *et al.,* 1994). The cetacean forestomach is homologous with the rumen, reticulum, and omasum of ruminants, and is where digestion is initiated. The forestomach of baleen whales is lined with keratinized, stratified squamous epithelium (Olsen *et al.,* 1994). It often contains stones and pebbles of various sizes which, with the powerful contractions of the muscular walls, help to grind up fish bones and crustaceans. Additionally, high concentrations of volatile fatty acids and anaerobic bacteria have been observed in the forestomach of baleen as well as small toothed whales, indicating that microbial fermentation occurs here as it does in the rumen (Olsen *et al.,* 1994). The forestomach is usually larger in odontocetes but it is lacking in beaked whales and the franciscana (see references cited in Langer, 1996). The forestomach of dolphins, reported to hold up to several liters of water, has a muscular sphincter between the esophagus and the forestomach (Harrison *et al.,* 1970). These researchers also observed dolphins ejecting water from the mouth in such volume as to suggest that some of it came from the forestomach. As hypothesized by Heyning and Mead (1996), one function of the dolphin forestomach may be to hold swallowed water while they secure prey against the palate and then release the water past the secured prey. The fundic chamber is equivalent to the fundic portion of the simple mammalian stomach or to the abomasum of ruminants. Its gastric glands contain parietal and chief cells which produce a gastric juice containing pepsin, hydrochloric acid, and some lipase. The forestomach and main stomach of a large blue whale can hold up to 1000 kg of krill. The connecting stomach acts as a third chamber, separated from the main and pyloric chanber by sphincters. It is lined with a glandular mucus-secreting mucosa that is thought to protect the epithelium from mechanical damage and to facilitate transport of digested food through the channel. The pyloric chamber is equivalent to the pyloric region of the abomasum of ruminants. It is lined by columnar mucous cells. Gastric digestion continues in this chamber and much of the solid food is broken down before passing

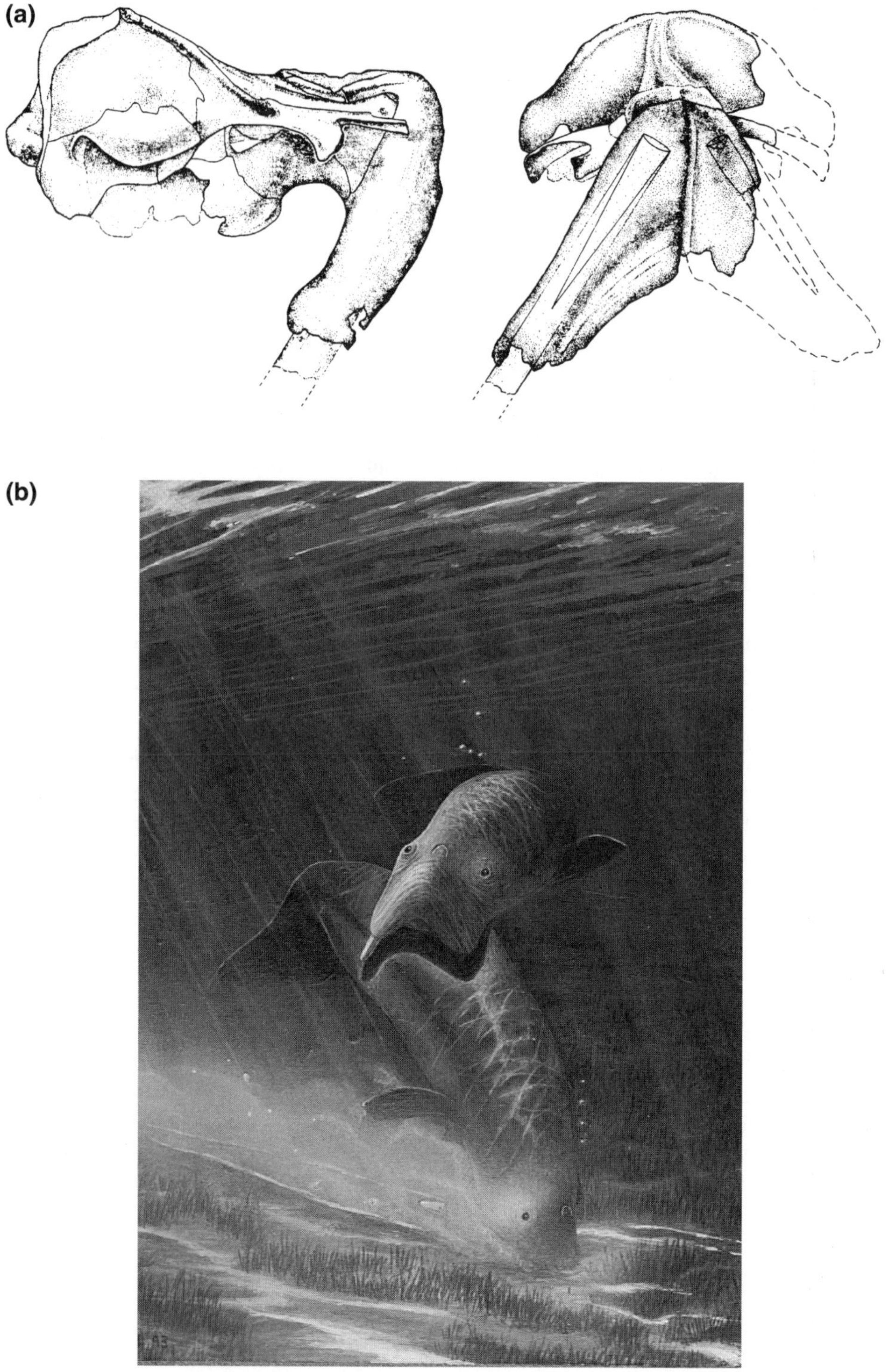

Figure 11.19. *Odobenocetops peruvianus,* skull (a) and life reconstruction (b). (From Muizon, 1993a,b. Life reconstruction courtesy M. Parrish.)

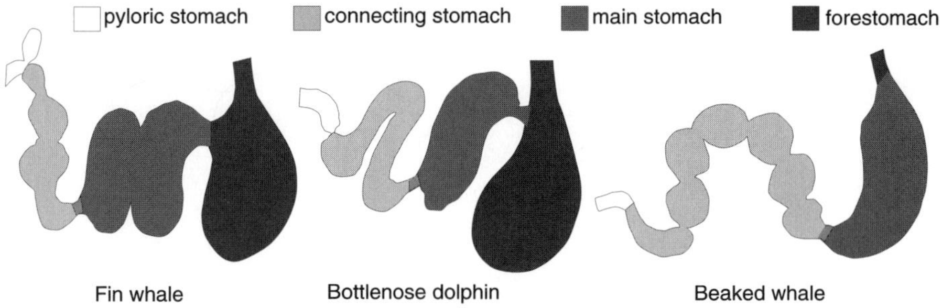

Figure 11.20. Representative cetacean stomachs. (Redrawn from Slijper, 1979.)

through the connecting channel. It leads by a narrow pylorus into the duodenum, the first part of which is sometimes markedly dilated and called the duodenal ampulla. This allows further digestion of food before it reaches the duodenum proper, indicating that enzymatic digestion may have a greater significance in cetaceans compared to ruminants (Olsen *et al.,* 1994). It has been suggested that differences in the stomachs of odontocetes (i.e. number of forechambers, number of main chambers, shape of connecting channel, and number and shape of pyloric chambers) may be phylogenetically informative (Rice and Wolman, 1990; Langer, 1996).

The basic difference between the intestine of baleen and toothed whales is that there is a cecum in baleen whales and none (with the exception of the Ganges River dolphin) in toothed whales (Yablokov *et al.,* 1972; Takahashi and Yamasaki, 1972). High concentrations of volatile fatty acids and anaerobic bacteria in the colon of fin and minke whales indicate the occurrence of bacterial fermentation in the colon of these animals (Herwing and Staley, 1986). Because they possess relatively shorter small intestines relative to those of pinnipeds with a similar diet, the multichambered stomach of minke whales is essential for optimal utilization of prey (Olsen *et al.,* 1994). According to Cowan and Smith (1995), cetaceans lack an appendix. A complex of lymphoepithelial organs called "anal tonsils," is a consistent structure of the anal canal of the bottlenose dolphin, and is likely to occur in most, if not all, cetaceans. It is possible that the anal tonsil fulfills some of the functions of the appendix.

The whale liver is usually bilobed, but a third lobe is sometimes present (Harrison and King, 1980). Whales do not have a gall bladder.

The pancreas is firm, elongated, and connected to the intestine through a special duct. It is larger in adult females than in males. Data (Kamiya, 1962; Bryden, 1966) indicate that there are two main ducts leading from the pancreas to the common bile duct, whereas in the toothed whales examined, there is only a single main duct (Yablokov *et al.,* 1972).

11.6. Feeding Specializations of Sirenians

11.6.1. Teeth

In the manatee there are usually five to seven functional teeth in each upper and lower jaw and it has been estimated that from 20 to 30 teeth per jaw are possible within the life span of a given individual (Fig. 11.21). The cheek teeth are **brachyodont**, or short-crowned, and

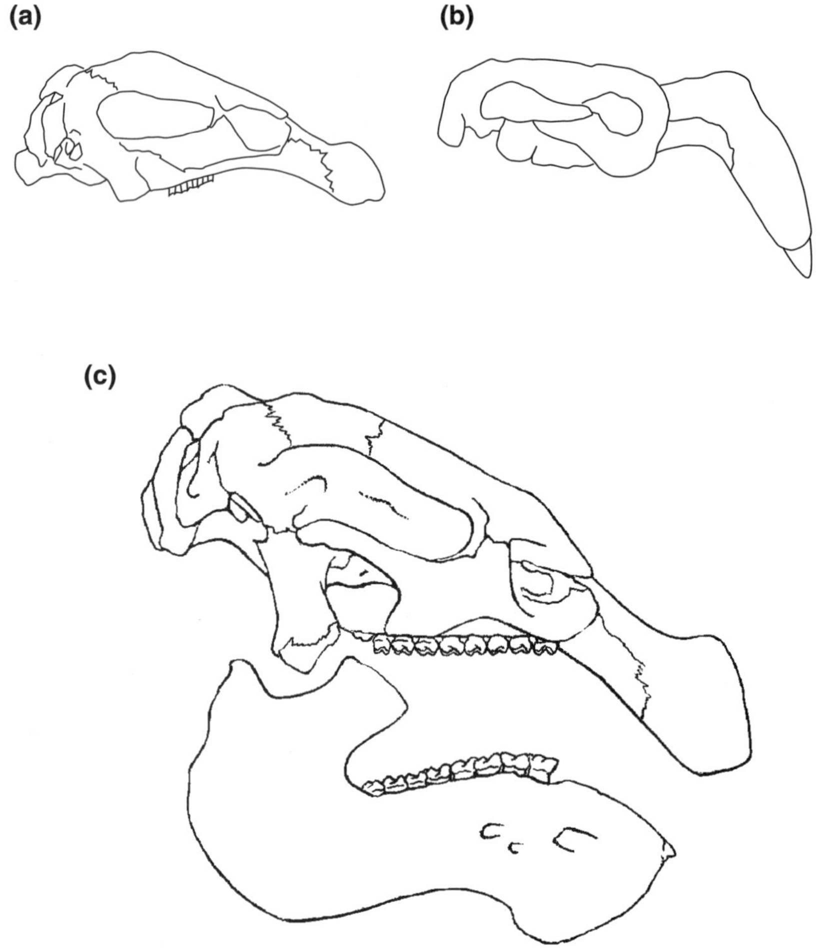

Figure 11.21. Lateral views of skull of a manatee (a,c) and dugong (b) illustrating difference in snout deflection. (Adapted from Hall and Kelson, 1959.)

are enameled but lack cementum. There are two vestigial incisors in each jaw at birth, but these are later resorbed (Harrison and King, 1980).

It was thought that tooth replacement in the manatee occurs throughout the life of the individual but there is evidence that this may not be the case (Husar, 1977). The teeth are replaced from the rear and, as the anterior teeth wear from excessive amounts of sand and grit in the manatee's normally vegetable diet, they fall out. Domning and Magnor (1977) confirmed observations that the increase in solid food intake after weaning, and hence more chewing, acts as a mechanical stimulus for the initiation and continuation of toothrow movement. Although often and misleadingly compared to tooth replacement in elephants, this combination of horizontal movement with an apparent limitless supply of supernumary (extra) molars is found in no other mammal, including the dugong. The elephant has a fixed number of teeth which are replaced by a similar mechanism, but once an elephant has completely worn its teeth it can no longer crush its food.

Dugongs, in contrast to manatees, have a fixed dental formula of I1/0, C0/0, P0/0, M2-3/2-3, with vertical replacement as in most other mammals. Two milk incisors are present in juveniles. The deciduous incisors are small and do not erupt, but are instead resorbed. In males, the deciduous incisors are lost around the time of tusk eruption and their tooth sockets disappear as the tusks expand. In females, small partially resorbed incisors may persist until the animal is about 30 years old (Nishiwaki and Marsh, 1985). The permanent incisors (tusks) develop in both sexes but only erupt in males and some old, probably postreproductive females. In some old females the tusks erupt and wear, presumably because they have reached the bases of the premaxillae and cannot grow posteriorly any further. Male tusks erupt when the animal is 12–15 years old. Adult male tusks may be up to 15 cm long but because they protrude from the mouth only a couple of centimeters, they do not seem to be formidable weapons. Up to three pairs of vestigial incisors and one pair of canines may occur. However, apart from the erupted tusks, only the cheek teeth are functional.

In situ replacement of the milk dentition does not occur in dugongs. During the life of the animal there are a total of four to six cheek teeth on each side of the upper and lower jaws but these are never simultaneously all erupted and in use (Nishiwaki and Marsh, 1985). Three premolars are erupted at birth, but all the roots of the anterior teeth are resorbed, causing them to fall out. Their sockets then become occluded with bone without eruption of permanent premolars. The molars progressively erupt during growth, the entire process continuing until usually only molars 2 and 3 (and occasionally molar 1) are present in each quadrant of old animals. Molars 2 and 3 have persistent pulp cavities and continue to grow throughout life so that the total occlusal area of the cheek teeth is maintained and increased even after the anterior cheek teeth have been lost. The pattern of cheek tooth replacement can be used to age dugongs; however, more precise age estimates can be obtained by counting dentinal growth layers (Nishiwaki and Marsh, 1985).

11.6.2. Feeding Strategies

Even though sea grass meadows are very productive, sirenians and sea turtles are the only large herbivores to commonly graze on them. A wide variety of tropical and subtropical sea grasses are consumed, including *Enhalus, Halophila, Halodule, Cymodocea, Thalassia, Thalasodendron, Syringodium,* and *Zostera.* Algae also are eaten but only in very small amounts if sea grasses are abundant (Nishiwaki and Marsh, 1985). A study presents evidence that dugongs in subtropical Moreton Bay, Australia selectively consume sessile benthic invertebrates including ascidians (sea squirts) and polychaetes (worms). Nutritional stress, particularly the lack of dietary nitrogen, caused by seasonality in the abundance of sea grasses may explain the omnivory of the Moreton Bay animals, which live at the southern edge of the dugongs' range (Preen, 1995). Manatees graze on a large variety of coastal and freshwater vegetation, including several species of submerged sea grasses, floating freshwater plants (*Hydrilla* and water hyacinths), and even the leaves and shoots of emergent mangroves.

The degree of snout deflection in manatees and dugongs appears to be correlated with the degree of specialization for bottom feeding (Fig. 11.21). The strongly downturned snout of the dugong causes its mouth to open almost straight downward, and it is virtually an obligate bottom feeder subsisting on sea grasses less than 20 cm high. Manatees, in contrast, have only relatively slight deflection, and are generalists feeding at any level in the water column from bottom to surface and are able to easily take floating vegetation (Domning, 1977).

Sirenians appear to be the only marine mammals that use the snout in a prehensile manner. In a study of facial musculature of the Florida manatee, it was determined that the short, muscular snout (especially the upper lip of the **rostral or oral disc**) is covered with modified vibrissae that achieve a prehensile function to bring vegetation to the mouth (Marshall *et al.,* 1998a,b; Fig. 11.22).

Similarly, the rostral disc of the dugong is also used in feeding. During feeding, dugongs gouge tracks into the bottom sediments (Anderson and Birtels, 1978). It is apparent that the tracks represent the action of the snout while grubbing sea grasses from the bottom (Fig. 11.23). Each track follows a serpentine course and appears to represent the continuous feeding effort of a single dive. The feeding trails suggest that the disc may be forced against the substrate while muscular contractions of its surface move the heavy bristles in a raking action which extracts sea grasses from the bottom and gathers them toward the mouth. Although male dugongs have erupted tusks, they do not appear to be used in feeding. The cheek teeth of both of these obligate herbivores are, like terrestrial mammalian herbivores, adapted for grinding cellulose-rich vegetation.

11.6.3. Evolution of Sirenian Feeding

Domning (1982) suggested that the "conveyor belt" tooth replacement pattern of manatees is an adaptation to an abrasive diet and increased tooth wear that results from their exploitation of a new high silica-containing resource, true grass, during the late Miocene. In the Indo-Pacific, dugongids responded slightly differently by evolving ever-growing teeth

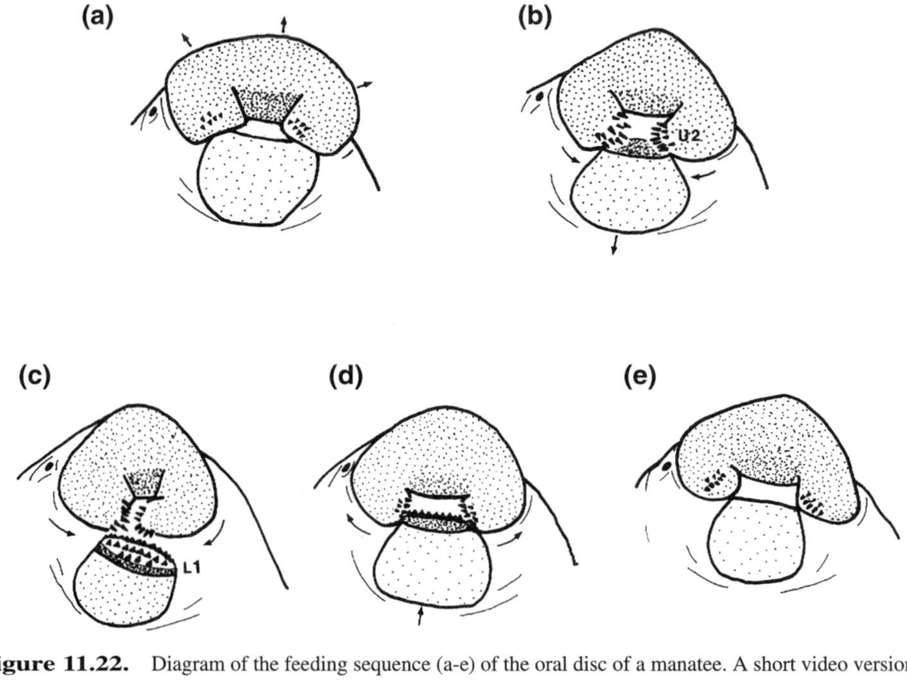

Figure 11.22. Diagram of the feeding sequence (a-e) of the oral disc of a manatee. A short video version of this action is available at http://www.vetmed.ufl.edu/ufmrg/manatee. (From Marshall *et al.,* 1998a.)

Figure 11.23. Photo of dugong feeding tracks. (From Anderson and Birtels, 1978. Courtesy P. Anderson.)

as an adaptation to increased tooth wear. Among sirenians, Steller's sea cow shows a number of unique cold water adaptations, including reaching a body length double that of other sea cows, an extraordinarily thick epidermis, inability to dive, and loss of teeth and phalanges. Domning (1977) suggests that these adaptations reflect a change in diet away from bottom feeding to feeding on plants growing at the surface (and mainly on algae growing in exposed rocky shallows). He correlates the loss of phalanges as a specialization for surface and rough-water feeding and suggests that stout claw-like forelimbs are adapted to grasp or fend against rocks and pull the animal forward while grazing in the shallows during bottom feeding. The relative ease of chewing algae compared to stringier sea grasses probably led to loss of the teeth. Although "overkill" by humans is usually blamed for the ultimate demise of Steller's sea cow, an intriguing explanation for their small, restricted populations was proposed by Anderson (1995) involving a competitive interaction between Steller's sea cow and the kelp-sea urchin-sea otter relationship. According to this relationship, described in more detail later in this chapter, shallow-water kelp communities are prolific only where sea otters are sufficiently abundant to limit sea urchin populations. Anderson (1995, p. 392) proposed that if the sea cow food supply was otter dependent, then the niche into which Steller's sea cow evolved was "precariously balanced" on sea otter carnivory. The aboriginal hunting of sea otters, urchin grazing, and replacement of shallow-water kelps by deep-water species could have destroyed sea cow foraging areas, thereby limiting their populations prior to their discovery in the early 1700s.

11.6.4. Anatomy and Physiology of Digestion

Large parotid glands are the only salivary glands in the dugong. Submaxillary salivary glands are prominent in the West Indian manatee (Quiring and Harlan, 1953) but sublingual glands are small (Murie, 1872). The most characteristic feature of the sirenian tongue is the form of the taste buds; in the dugong they are contained in pits and in the manatee they occur in swellings (Yamasaki *et al.,* 1980). Tonsils are absent (Hill, 1945).

The digestive tracts of both the dugong and the manatee are extremely long (Lomolino and Ewel, 1984). Detailed descriptions of the manatee stomach can be found in Langer (1988) and Reynolds and Rommel (1996). In both the manatee and dugong the stomach is a simple sac, differing from the typical mammalian simple stomach by the presence of a discrete cardiac gland which opens into the main sac via a single, small aperture (Marsh *et al.,* 1977; Reynolds and Rommel, 1996). The cardiac region of the Florida manatee stomach contains parietal, chief, and neck cells and secretes acid, mucus, and pepsin; its cellular composition corresponds to that of other mammals. The West African manatee lacks chief and parietal cells, except in the cardiac gland (Reynolds and Rommel, 1996, and references cited therein). The cardiac gland in the dugong contains all the chief cells and most of the parietal cells associated with the stomach (Marsh *et al.,* 1977). Reynolds and Rommel (1996) have shown that the Florida manatee has certain morphological adaptations, for production of copious mucus, and stratified lining of the pyloric stomach, such as submucosal mucous glands in the greater curvature of the stomach. Other sirenians apparently lack these adaptations.

The duodenum of the manatee and dugong possesses large duodenal ampullae and paired duodenal diverticula (Fig. 11.24). Marsh *et al.* (1977) suggested that the size of the

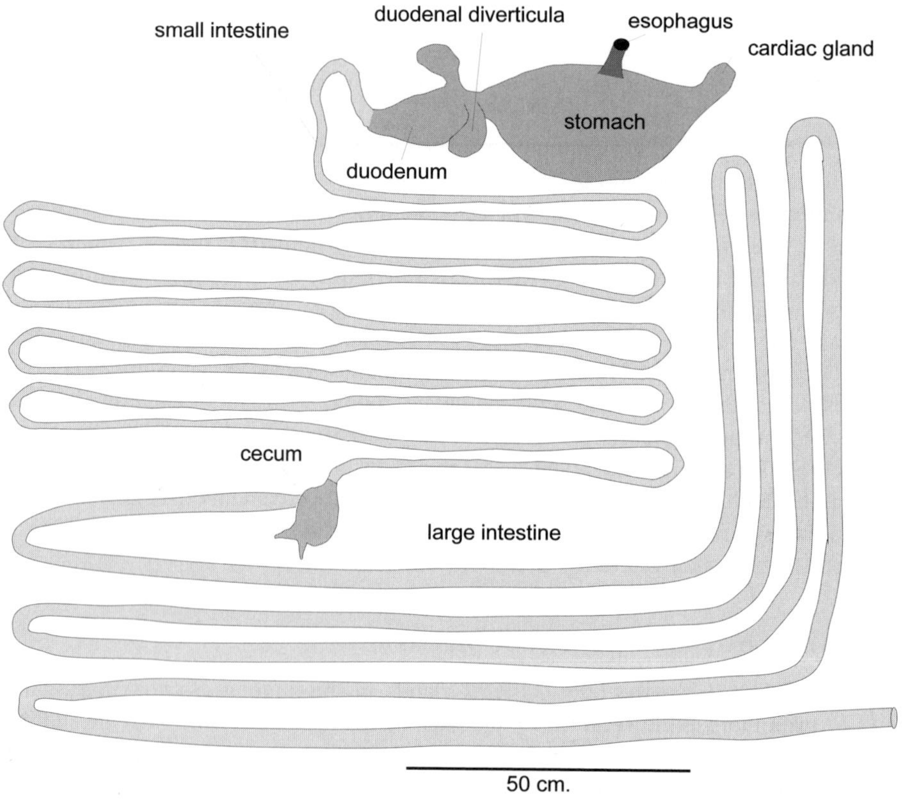

Figure 11.24. Diagram of a manatee digestive tract, drawn to scale. (Adapted from Reynolds and Rommel, 1996.)

ampullae and diverticulae allow the passage of large volumes of digesta from the stomach. The cecum and large intestine, the contents of which may weigh twice that of the stomach contents, have been shown to be the principal areas of absorption of the fiber portion of the diet (Murray *et al.,* 1977). In the adult dugong, the large intestine is up to 30 m long, about twice as long as the small intestine. This compares with the manatee's large intestine that has been measured at between 18 and 20 m or longer (references cited in Lanyon and Marsh, 1995). In comparison with other hindgut fermenting herbivores (e.g. the elephant has a 10 m hindgut), sirenians have longer hindguts (Lanyon and Marsh, 1995). Both the stomach shape and intestine size of the dugong and manatee provide evidence that they are nonruminant herbivores with a greatly enlarged hindgut and a rich microflora which enables them to digest cellulose and other fibrous carbohydrates (Nishiwaki and Marsh, 1985; Lanyon and Marsh, 1995). Both groups employ a digestive strategy atypical of hindgut fermenters; low-fiber material is retained for extended periods within the long hindgut and it is almost completely digested (Lanyon and Marsh, 1995). Similarities in the gross anatomy of the gastrointestinal tracts exist between sirenians and their close relatives, elephants, especially regarding the specialized cardiac stomach (cardiac gland in sirenians) and the cecum (Reynolds and Rommel, 1996).

The liver of the dugong has three main lobes and is positioned against the almost horizontal diaphragm. A long common bile duct and a small gall bladder occur in the dugong (Harrison and King, 1980). By contrast, a relatively large gall bladder is present in the manatee. The dugong pancreas is small, compact, and lobulated (Husar, 1975).

11.7. Feeding Specializations of Other Marine Mammals

11.7.1. Sea Otters

Unlike their fish-eating relatives of freshwater lakes and streams, sea otters preferentially forage on benthic invertebrates, particularly sea urchins, gastropod and bivalve mollusks, and crustaceans. The dental formula of sea otters is I3/2, C1/1, P3/3, M1/2, differing from that of most other carnivores in having a reduced number of lower incisors. In addition, the carnassials and molars are modified from their slicing role (terrestrial carnivores) to blunt crushing teeth suitable for breaking up exoskeletons and shells of invertebrate prey (Fig. 11.25). Captured prey are manipulated with the forepaws or are held temporarily in loose skin pouches in the armpits. For larger, heavier-shelled prey, otters will sometimes carry rocks to the surface to crack open their hard shells as they float on their backs (Fig. 11.26). Otters have exceptionally high metabolic and food consumption rates: typical adult otters in Alaskan waters daily consume prey equal to 23–37% of their body weight (Costa, 1978; Kvitek *et al.,* 1993).

Sea otters are completely restricted to shallow (generally < 35 m depth) coastal waters of the North Pacific Ocean, where substantial populations of invertebrates inhabit rocky or sandy substrates. Sea otters are most commonly affiliated with nearshore canopy-forming kelps (principally the brown algae *Macrocystis* or *Nereocystis*), although large numbers of otters have been observed as much as 30 km offshore (Kenyon, 1969). In portions of the sea otter range, where their numbers have recovered or where they have been reintroduced (see Chapter 15), sea otters are considered a keystone predator, playing a pivotal role in kelp bed communities by keeping populations of herbivorous invertebrates, mostly grazing sea urchins, low in number and allowing kelp plants to reestablish themselves and thrive

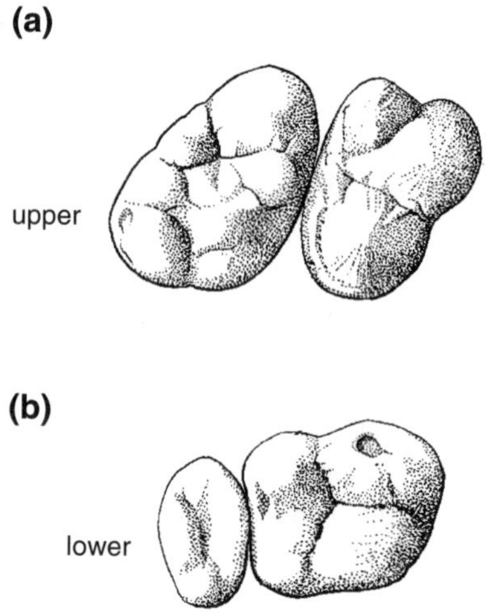

Figure 11.25. Occlusal surfaces of the upper (fourth premolar and first molar) and lower (first and second molars) teeth of a sea otter, with rounded cusps and a complete lack of shearing ability characteristic of most other carnivorans. (Adapted from Vaughn, 1986.)

(Duggins, 1980). In the southern part of their historical California and northern Baja California range, however, healthy kelp forests persist even though sea otters have been absent for more than a century. There, water temperature variations, storm surges, or other disturbances also may play important roles in the dynamics of these otter-free nearshore kelp communities.

In a novel study of the influences of sea otters on marine plant-herbivore interactions, Steinberg *et al.* (1995) examined contrasting biotic assemblages between the northern and southern hemispheres. The northeast Pacific Ocean assemblage has been influenced by the effect of sea otter predation on herbivorous invertebrates, and probably has been since the late Miocene. The temperate Australasia assemblage, in contrast, while containing similar guilds of plants and animals, lacks a comparable predator to the sea otter. Steinberg *et al.* (1995) suggested that in the northern hemisphere kelp forests evolved in a three-tiered food web, with sea otters and their recent ancestors at the top, herbivores in the middle, and macroalgae as the autotrophs. In such a food web herbivores are limited by predation, thus protecting the autotrophs from intense disturbance via herbivory. In contrast, in the southern hemisphere where kelp is not limited by herbivory, these autotrophs are left unprotected. These patterns led Steinberg *et al.* (1995) to predict that autotrophs defend against their herbivores in Australasia but not in the North Pacific. This prediction has been substantiated by the discovery of higher concentrations of secondary metabolites (defenses against herbivory) in brown algae in the southern hemisphere compared to the northern hemisphere. In addition, there is evidence that herbivores in the southern regions have evolved differing abilities to cope with chemical defenses (Estes, 1996, and references cited therein). Results of this study suggest that sea otter predation of sea urchins, by freeing North Pacific autotrophs from the need to defend themselves, has been a key factor in the evolution of a marine flora that is vulnerable to herbivory.

Sea otter foraging patterns, based on visual observations of unidentified individuals, were reviewed by Riedman and Estes (1990). Ralls *et al.* (1995) monitored instrumented individuals in California and summarized their results which indicate extensive variation in the pattern of individual otters with respect to dive duration and success rate, surface inter-

Figure 11.26. Sea otter at sea surface with cracking rock. (Courtesy P. Colla.)

val length, size and species of prey consumed, foraging bout length, and the degree of difference between diurnal and nocturnal foraging patterns. Differences between the foraging patterns of juvenile males and juvenile females were particularly striking. Juvenile males often forage further offshore over deeper water than otters in other age and sex classes and they also tended to make longer dives. It is possible that they were consuming larger prey but this was not confirmed since they could not be observed from shore. In contrast, juvenile females foraged closer to shore and made shorter dives. Juvenile females also tended to have longer foraging bouts with short surface intervals suggesting to Ralls *et al.* (1995) that they were perhaps capturing small prey of lower caloric value; this was confirmed by observations that they often fed on kelp crabs, turban snails, and mussels.

11.7.2. Polar Bears

Polar bears have 38–42 teeth and a dental formula of I3/3, C1/1, P2-4/2-4, M2/3. The molars are broad, flat and multicusped with an emphasis on grinding and crushing rather than slicing. Ice seals (ringed, bearded, and ribbon), and sometimes harbor and harp seals, are the major prey of polar bears, with walruses, beluga whales, and even birds occasionally taken (Amstrup and DeMaster, 1988). Bear predation of ice seals occurs primarily in unstable ice conditions where the bears can stalk seals resting out of water. Seal pups are especially vulnerable to bear predation. In the Canadian Arctic, ring seals give birth to pups in snow caves above breathing holes in the ice. At weaning, these pups are 50% fat, and it is from these pups that bears secure most of their annual energy supply during the short period just after the ring seal pups are weaned (I. Stirling, personal communication, 1995).

The extent of bear predation on walruses varies in different areas of the Arctic, with higher rates of predation in the Canadian Arctic than in the Bering Sea. Bears frequently fail to make a kill by stalking hauled-out walrus herds, yet manage to frighten herds into the water. In the ensuing stampede, walrus pups are sometimes injured or isolated, making them easy prey for the bears (Riedman, 1990). It is not known whether bears commonly prey on seals underwater.

As reviewed by Atkinson *et al.* (1996) one of the most interesting aspects of the foraging ecology of polar bears, indeed of bears in general, is their prolonged seasonal fasting as a result of declines in food availability or when reproductive activities prevent foraging. In polar bears the ability to endure prolonged fasts may not be restricted to the denning period over winter. For example, polar bears in western Hudson Bay are forced to stay onshore in summer as the ice melts. During this ice-free period, they have little or no access to food and are forced to fast for up to 4 months until late autumn when most individuals return to the newly formed ice to feed. Although most polar bears (except pregnant females) do not occupy dens regularly, there are data (i.e. urea:creatinine ratio as an indicator of protein loss through catabolism of body fat) suggesting that individuals are able to adopt an otherwise efficient state of protein conservation similar to that of denning bears during the winter. Such a fasting response also has been suggested to function at other times of the year, for example during the mating season in spring when adult males may forgo feeding to compete for access to females. Results of a study of fasting in polar bears suggests that among ursids in general, the ability to minimize protein loss during fasts may be largely dependent on the relative fatness of the animal at the start of a fast, which is in turn dependent on the extraordinary magnitude of fat stores that some individuals can accumulate in seasons where food is abundant (Atkinson *et al.,* 1996).

11.8. Summary and Conclusions

Marine mammal diets and foraging strategies are direct consequences of patterns of primary productivity, although the majority prey on relatively large animals several trophic levels removed from the primary producers. The cheek teeth of pinnipeds and odontocetes are typically homodont with single pointed cusps adapted for feeding on fish and squid. Walruses employ a suction feeding strategy using the tongue as a piston to suck clams out of their shells. Tusks are used in social display rather than for feeding. The seasonal migration of the elephant seal, one of the best-studied feeding patterns among pinnipeds, involves an annual double migration with prolonged periods of offshore feeding.

Mysticetes employ rows of baleen plates to filter feed plankton and small fish from the water. They employ three different feeding strategies: skimming (balaenids), engulfment (rorquals), and mud scooping (gray whale). In engulfment feeding the mouth is enlarged by expansion of the throat grooves and invagination of the tongue to create a large ventral cavity. Large mysticetes (e.g. gray whales) typically feed at high latitudes during the summer and migrate long distance to low latitudes in winter months. Odontocete foraging strategies are varied. Some odontocetes, characterized by reduced numbers of teeth (e.g. beaked and sperm whales), employ a suction feeding strategy in which throat grooves and muscles of the tongue function in retraction and distension of the floor of the mouth. Sponge carrying has been proposed as a foraging specialization in some dolphins. Transient and resident killer whales not only employ different foraging strategies but also feed on different prey. The evolution of prey capture mechanisms and strategies in whales has been related to the availability of new food resources and oceanic circulation patterns for mysticetes and to echolocation for odontocetes. Cetaceans are characterized by multi-chambered stomachs similar to ruminant artiodactyls, their close living relatives.

As the only herbivorous marine mammals, sirenians have modified short, broad-crowned teeth. Tooth replacement in manatees is unique among mammals. Teeth follow a "conveyor belt" replacement and they are replaced throughout life. The degree of snout deflection in manatees and dugongs is correlated with the degree of specialization for bottom feeding on sea grasses and/or floating vegetation. The dugong, with its strongly downturned snout, is a bottom feeder, in contrast to manatees which have relatively slight snout deflection and feed at all levels of the water column. Dugongs employ a rostral disc as a grazing mechanism; it gouges tracks into bottom sediments during feeding. The evolution of the "conveyor belt" replacement in manatees is related to the abrasive diet and increased tooth wear that resulted from exploitation of a new resource, sea grasses, approximately 10 Ma. The relatively long large intestine of sirenians may be related to the high fiber content of their diets.

Sea otters possess blunt teeth for crushing the shells of their invertebrate prey. They are considered keystone predators and play a pivotal role in kelp bed communities by keeping populations of grazing sea urchins low. Study of the influences of sea otters on marine plant–herbivore interactions reveal that in the North Pacific sea otter predation may have been a key factor in the evolution of a marine flora that is vulnerable to herbivory. The feeding ecology of polar bears differs from other marine mammals and is characterized by prolonged seasonal fasts that occur in part as a result of the decline of their food availability.

11.9. Further Reading

A general introduction to pinniped diet and foraging strategies is summarized by Riedman (1990); for cetaceans, see Evans (1987) and Gaskin (1982); for dugongs consult Anderson and Birtels (1978) and see Hartman (1979) for manatees. The anatomy and physiology of digestion for pinnipeds is summarized in King (1983); for cetaceans consult Slijper (1979) and for sirenians see Reynolds and Odell (1991). The evolution of feeding strategies in cetaceans is summarized by Fordyce *et al.* (1995); see also Thewissen *et al.* (1996) for archaic whales and for sirenians see Domning (1982).

References

Amstrup, S. C. and D. P. De Master (1988). Polar bear, *Ursus maritimus*. *In* "Selected marine mammals of Alaska" (J. W. Lentfer, ed.), pp. 39–56. Washington, DC.

Anderson, P. K. (1995). Competition, predation, and the evolution and extinction of Steller's sea cow, *Hydrodamalis gigas*. *Mar. Mamm. Sci.* **11**(3): 391–394.

Anderson, P. K., and A. Birtels (1978). Behavior and ecology of the dugong, *Dugong dugon* (Sirenia): Observations in Shoalwater and Cleveland Bays. *Queensl. Aust. Wildl. Res.* **5**: 1–23.

Antonelis, G. A., M. S. Lowry, C. H. Fiscus, B. S. Stewart, and R. L. DeLong (1994). Diet of the Northern Elephant Seal. In "Elephant Seals" (B. J. Le Boeuf and R. M. Laws, eds.), pp. 211–223. University of California Press, Berkeley.

Atkinson, S. N., R. A. Nelson, and M. A. Ramsay (1996). Changes in the body composition of fasting polar bears (*Ursus maritimus*): The effect of relative fatness on protein conservation. *Physiol. Zool.* **69**(2): 304–316.

Baird, R. W., P. A. Abrams, and L. M. Dill (1992). Possible indirect interactions between transient and resident killer whales: Implications for the evolution of foraging specializations in the genus *Orcinus*. *Oecologia* **89**: 125–132.

Bakker, M. A. G., R. A. Kastelein, and J. L. Dubbledam (1996). Histology of the grooved ventral pouch of the minke whale, *Balaenoptera acutorostrata,* with special reference to the occurrence of lamellated corpuscles. *Can. J. Zool.* **75**: 563–567.

Barrett-Lennard, L. G., J. K. B. Ford, and K. A. Heise (1996). The mixed blessing of echolocation: Differences in sonar use by fish-eating and mammal-eating killer whales. *Anim. Behav.* **51**: 553–565.

Berzin, A. A., and V. L. Vladimirov (1983). A new species of killer whale (Cetacea, Delphinidae) from the antarctic waters. *Zool. Zh.* **62**: 287–295.

Best, R. C. (1981). The tusk of narwhal (*Monodon monoceros* L.): Interpretation of its function (Mammalia: Cetacea). *Can. J. Zool.* **59**: 2386–2393.

Bigg, M. A., G. M. Ellis, J. K. B. Ford, and K. C. Balcomb (1987). "Killer Whales: A Study of Their Identification, Genealogy and Natural History in British Columbia and Washington State," pp. 1–79. Phantom Press & Publishers, Nanaimo, BC, Can.

Bonner, W. N. (1982). "Seals and Man. A Study of Interactions." University of Washington Press, Seattle.

Bonner, W. N. (1989). "Whales of the World." Facts on File, New York.

Brodie, P. (1993). Noise generated by the jaw actions of feeding fin whales. Can. J. Zool. **71**: 2546–2550.

Bryden, M. M. (1966). Twin foetuses in the southern elephant seal, *Mirounga leonina* (Linn.). *R. Soc. Tasmania, Pap and Proc.* **100**: 89–90.

Bryden, M. M. (1971). Anatomical and allometric adaptations in elephant seals, *Mirounga leonina. J. Anat.* **108**: 208.

Bryden, M. M. (1972). Growth and development of marine mammals. *In* "Functional Anatomy of Marine Mammals" (R. J. Harrison, ed.), Vol. 1, pp. 1–79. Academic Press, New York.

Bryden, M. M. and A. W. Erickson (1976). Body size and composition of crabeater seals (*Lobodon carcinophagus*), with observations on tissue and organ size in Ross seals (*Ommatophoca rossi*). *J. Zool.* **179**: 235–247.

Costa, D. P. (1978). The sea otter. Its interaction with man. *Oceanus* **21**(2): 24–30.

Costa, D. P. (1993). The relationship between reproductive and foraging energetics and the evolution of the Pinnipedia. *Symp. Zool. Soc. London* **66**: 293–314.

Cowan, D. F., and T. L. Smith (1995). Morphology of the complex lymphoepithelial organs of the anal canal ("Anal Tonsil") in the Bottlenose Dolphin, *Tursiops truncatus. J. Morphol.* **223**: 263–268.

Darling, J. D. (1984). Gray whales off Vancouver Island, British Columbia. *In* "The Gray Whale, *Eschrichtius robustus* (Lilljeborg, 1861)" (M. L. Jones, S. L. Swartz, and S. Leatherwood, eds.), pp. 267–288. Academic Press, New York.

Darling, J. D., K. E. Keogh, and T. Steeves (1995). Gray whale (*Eschrichtius robustus*) habitat utilization and prey species off Vancouver Island, B.C. *Abstr. 11th Bienn. Conf. Biol. Mar. Mamm.*, Orlando, FL, p. 28.

Darling, J. D., K. E. Koegh, and T. E. Steeves (1998). Gray Whale (*Eschrichtius Robustus*) Habitat Utilization And Prey Species Off Vancouver Island, B.C. *Mar. Mamm. Sci.* **14**: 692–720.

Davis, R. W., L. A. Fuiman, T. M. Williams, S. O. Collier, W. P. Hagey, S. B. Kanatous, S. Kohin, and M. Horning (1999). Hunting behavior of a marine mammal beneath the Antarctic fast ice. *Science* **283**: 993–996.

DeLong, R. L., and B. S. Stewart (1991). Diving patterns of northern elephant seal bulls. *Mar. Mamm. Sci.* **7**: 369–384.

DeLuis, M. and P. J. Adam (1998). Evolution of feeding types in the Pinnipedimorpha using functional morphology and phylogenetic methods. Abstracts California Paleontology Conference, Los Angeles, CA, *Paleo Bios* **18**(Suppl. 3): 2–3.

Domning, D. P. (1977). An ecological model for late Tertiary sirenian evolution in the North Pacific Ocean. *Syst. Zool.* **25**: 352–362.

Domning, D. P. (1982). Evolution of manatees: A speculative history. *Journal of Paleontology* **56**(3): 599–619.

Domning, D. P., and D. Magnor (1977). Taxa se substitiucao horizontal de dentes no peixe-boi. *Acta Amazonica* **7**(3): 435–438.

Duggins, D. O. (1980). Kelp beds and sea otters: An experimental approach. *Ecology* **61**: 447–453.

Eastman, J. T., and R. E. Coalson (1974). The digestive system of the Weddell seal, *Leptonychotes weddelli*—a review. *In* "Functional Anatomy of Marine Mammals" (R. J. Harrison, ed.), 2nd ed., pp. 253–320. Academic Press, London.

Estes, J. A. (1996). The influence of large, mobile predators in aquatic food webs: Examples from sea otters and kelp forests. *In* "Aquatic Predators and their Prey" (S. P. R. Greenstreet and M. L. Tasker, eds.), pp. 65–72. Fishing News (Blackwell Science, Ltd.), London.

Estes, J. A., M. T. Tinker, T. M. Williams, and D. F. Doak (1998). Killer whale predation on sea otters linking oceanic and nearshore ecosystems. *Science* **282**: 473–476.

Evans, G. H. P. (1987). "The Natural History of Whales and Dolphins." Facts On File. New York.

Fay, F. H. (1982). Ecology and biology of the Pacific walrus, *Odobenus rosmarus divergens* Illiger. *North Am. Fauna* Ser., U.S. Dep. Int., Fish Wildl. Serv., No. 74.

Fay, F. H. (1985). *Odobenus rosmarus. Mamm. Species.* **238**: 1–7.

Felleman, F. L., J. R. Heimlich-Boran, and R. W. Osborne (1991). The feeding ecology of killer whales (*Orcinus orca*) in the Pacific Northwest. *In* "Dolphin Societies" (K. Pryor and K. S. Norris, eds.), pp. 113–147. University of California Press, Berkeley.

Fiscus, C. H., and G. A. Baines (1966). Food and feeding behavior of Steller and California sea lions. *J. Mammal.* **47**: 195–200.

Ford, J., and D. Ford (1986). Narwhal: Unicorn of the Arctic seas. *National Geographic* **169**: 354–363.

Ford, J. K. B, G. M. Ellis, L. G. Barrett-Lennard, A. B. Morton, R. S. Palm, and K. C. Balcomb III (1998). Dietary specialization in two sympatric populations of killer whales (*Orcinus orca*) in coastal British Columbia and adjacent waters. *Can. J. Zool.* **76**: 1456–1471.

Fordyce, R. E. (1980). Whale evolution and Oligocene Southern Ocean environments. *Palaeogeogr., Palaeoclimatol., Palaeoecol.* **31**: 319–336.

Fordyce, R. E., L. G. Barnes, and N. Miyazaki (1995). General aspects of the evolutionary history of whales and dolphins. *Island Arc* **3**: 373–391.

Frost, K. J., R. B. Russell, and L. F. Lowry (1992). Killer whales, *Orcinus orca,* in the southeastern Bering Sea: Recent sightings and predation on other marine mammals. *Mar. Mamm. Sci.* **8**: 110–119.

Gaskin, D. E. (1982). "The Ecology of Whales and Dolphins." Heinemann, London.

Gentry, R. L., G. L. Kooyman, and M. E. Goebel (1986). Feeding and diving behavior of northern fur seals. *In* "Fur Seals: Maternal Strategies on Land and at Sea" (R. L. Gentry and G. L. Kooyman, eds.), pp. 61–78. Princeton University Press, Princeton, NJ.

Gilmore, R. M. (1960). A census of the California gray whale. *U.S. Fish Wildl. Serv., Spec. Sci. Rep.—Fish.* **342**: 1–30.

Gingerich, P. D., and D. E. Russell (1990). Dentition of early Eocene *Pakicetus* (Mammalia, Cetacea). *Contrib. Mus. Paleontol. Univ. Mich.* **28**(1): 1–20.

Guinet, C., and J. Bouvier (1995). Development of intentional stranding hunting techniques in killer whale (*Orcinus orca*) calves at Croizet Archipelago. *Can. J. Zool.* **73**: 27–33.

Hain, J. H. W., S. L. Ellis, R. D. Kenney, P. J. Clapham, B. K. Gray, M. T. Weinrich, and I. G. Babb (1995). Apparent bottom feeding by humpback whales on Stellwagen Bank. *Mar. Mamm. Sci.* **11**(4): 464–479.

Hall, E. R., and K. R. Kelson (1959). "The Mammals of North America." Ronald Press, New York, 2 vols.

Harrison, R. J., and J. E. King (1980). "Marine Mammals, 2nd ed." Hutchinson and Co., Ltd., London.

Harrison, R. J., F. R. Johnson, and B. A. Young (1970). The oesophagus and stomach of dolphins (*Tursiops, Delphinus, Stenella*). *J. Zool.* **160**: 377–390.

Hartman, D. S. (1979). Ecology and behavior of the manatee (*Trichechus manatus*) in Florida. American Society of Mammalogists, Special Publication no. 5, 153 pp.

Hay, K. A., and A. W. Mansfield (1989). Narwhal-*Monodon monoceros* Linnaeus, 1758. *In* "Handbook of Marine Mammals, vol. 4" (S. H. Ridgway and R. Harrison, eds.), pp. 145–176. Academic Press, London.

Helm, R. C. (1983). Intestinal length of three California pinniped species. *J. Zool.* **199**: 297–304.

Herwing, R. P., and J. T. Staley (1986). Anaerobic bacteria from the digestive tract of North Atlantic fin whales (*Balaenoptera physalus*). *FEMS Microbiol. Ecol.* **38**: 361–371.

Herzing, D. L., and B. R. Mate (1984). Gray whale migrations along the Oregon coast. *In* "The Gray Whale, *Eschrichtius robustus* (Lilljeborg, 1861)" (M. L. Jones, S. L. Swartz, and S. Leatherwood, eds.), pp. 289–308. Academic Press, New York.

Heyning, J. E. (1984). Functional morphology involved in intraspecific fighting of the beaked whale, *Mesoplodon carlhubbsi. Can. J. Zool.* **62**: 1645–1654.

Heyning, J. E., and J. G. Mead (1996). Suction feeding in beaked whales: Morphological and observational evidence. *Contrib. Sci. Los Angeles Mus. Nat. Hist.* **464**: 1–12.

Hill, W. C. O. (1945). Notes on the dissection of two dugongs. *J. Mammal.* **26**: 153–175.

Hinga, K. R. (1978). The food requirements of whales in the southern hemisphere. *Deep-Sea Res.* **25**: 569–577.

Hobson, K. A., and J. L. Sease (1998). Stable isotope analyses of tooth annuli reveal temporal dietary records: an example using Steller sea lions. *Mar. Mamm. Sci.* **14**: 116–129.

Hoelzel, A. R., C. Potter, and M. Dalheim (1995). Foraging specializations and the evolution of population genetic differentiation in delphinid cetaceans. *Abstr. 11th Bienn. Conf. Biol. Mar. Mamm.*, Orlando, FL, p. 55.

Hoyt, E. (1984). "The whale called killer." E. P. Dutton. N.Y.

Husar, S. (1975). A review of the literature of the dugong (*Dugong dugon*). *Res. Rep. U.S. Fish Wildl. Serv.* **4**: 1–30.

Husar, S. (1977). *Trichechus inunguis. Mamm. Species* **72**: 1–4.
Imbrie, J., A. McIntyre, and T. C. Moore, Jr. (1983). The ocean around North America at the last glacial maximum. *In* "Late Quaternary Environments of the United States" (S. C. Porter, ed.), pp. 230–236. University of Minnesota Press, Minneapolis.
Jaquet, N., and H. Whitehead (1999). Movements, distribution and feeding success of sperm whales in the Pacific Ocean, over scales of days and tens of kilometers. *Aquat. Mamm.* **25**(1): 1–13.
Kamiya, T. (1962). On the intramural cystic gland of the cetacean. *Acta Anat. Nipponica* **37**(5): 339–350.
Kastelein, R. A., and P. Mosterd (1989). The excavation technique for molluscs of Pacific walruses (*Odobenus rosmarus divergens*) under controlled conditions. *Aquat. Mamm.* **15**(1): 3–5.
Kastelein, R. A., N. M. Gerrits, and J. L. Dubbledam (1991). The anatomy of the walrus head (*Odobenus rosmarus*). Part 2: Description of the muscles and of their role in feeding and haul-out behavior. *Aquat. Mamm.* **17**(3): 156–180.
Kastelein, R. A., J. L. Dubbledam, and M. A. G. de Bakker (1997a). The anatomy of the walrus head (*Odobenus rosmarus*). Part 5: The tongue and its function in walrus ecology. *Aquat. Mamm.* **23**(1): 29–47.
Kastelein, R. A., C. Staal, A. Terlouw, and M. Muller (1997b). Pressure changes in the mouth of a feeding harbour porpoise (*Phocoena phocoena*). In "The Biology of the Harbour Porpoise" (A. J. Read, P. R. Wiepkema, and P. E. Nachtigall, eds.), pp. 279–291. De Spil Publishers, Woerden, The Netherlands.
Kawamura, A. (1980). A review of food of balaenopterid whales. *Sci. Rep. Whales Res. Inst.* **32**: 155–197.
Kenyon, K. W. (1969). "The Sea Otter in the North Pacific Ocean," North Am. Fauna, No. 68. U.S. Dept. of Interior, Bureau of Sport Fisheries and Wildlife, Washington DC.
King, J. E. (1983). "Seals of the World," 2nd ed. Cornell University Press, Ithaca, NY.
Krockenberger, M. B., and M. M. Bryden (1994). Rate of passage of digesta through the alimentary tract of southern elephant seals (*Mirounga leonina*) (Carnivora: Phocidae). *J. Zool.* **234**: 229–237.
Kvitek, R. G., C. E. Bowlby, and M. Staedler (1993). Diet and foraging behavior of sea otters in Southeast Alaska. *Mar. Mamm. Sci.* **9**: 168–181.
Lambertsen, R. H. (1983). Internal mechanism of rorqual feeding. *J. Mammal.* **64**(1): 76–88.
Lambertsen, R. H., N. Ulrich, and J. Straley (1995). Frontomandibular stay of Balaenopteridae: A mechanism for momentum recapture during feeding. *J. Mammal.* **76**(3): 877–899.
Langer, P. (1988). Sirenia. *In* "The Mammalian Herbivore Stomach," pp. 210–245. Fischer, New York.
Langer, P. (1996). Comparative anatomy of the stomach of the Cetacea. Ontogenetic changes involving gastric proportions-mesenteries-arteries. *Z. Säugetierkd.* **61**: 140–154.
Lanyon, J. M., and H. Marsh (1995). Digesta passage time in the dugong. *Aust. J. Zool.* **43**: 119–127.
Leatherwood, S., and R. R. Reeves (1983). "The Sierra Club Handbook of Whales and Dolphins." Sierra Club Books, San Francisco.
Lockyer, C. (1981a). Growth and energy budgets of large baleen whales from the southern hemisphere. *FAO Fish. Ser. (5)* [Mammals in the Sea] **3**: 379–487.
Lockyer, C. (1981b). Estimates of growth and energy budgets for the sperm whale, *Physter catadon. FAO Fish. Ser. (5)* [Mammals in the Sea] **3**: 489–504.
Le Boeuf, B. J., Y. Naito, A. C. Huntley, and T. Asage (1989). Prolonged, continuous, deep diving by northern elephant seals. *Can. J. Zool.* **67**: 2514–2519.
Lomolino, M. W., and K. C. Ewel (1984). Digestive efficiencies of the West Indian manatee (*Trichechus manatus*). *Florida Scientist* **47**: 176–179.
Lopez, J. C., and D. Lopez (1985). Killer whales (*Orcinus orca*) of Patagonia, and their behavior of intentional stranding while hunting nearshore. *J. Mammal.* **66**: 181–183.
Marsh, H., G. E. Heinsohn, and A. Spain (1977). The stomach and duodenal diverticula of the Dugong (*Dugong dugon*). In "Functional Anatomy of Marine Mammals" (R. J. Harrison, ed.), pp. 271–295. Academic Press, London.
Marshall, C. D., G. D. Huth, V. M. Edmonds, D. L. Halin, and R. L. Reep (1998a). Prehensile use of perioral bristles during feeding and associated behaviors of the Florida manatee (*Trichechus manatus latirostris*). *Mar. Mamm. Sci.* **14**(2): 274–289.
Marshall, C. D., L. A. Clark, and R. L. Reep (1998b). The muscular hydrostat of the Florida manatee (*Trichechus manatus latirostris*): A functional morphologic model of perioral bristle use. *Mar. Mamm. Sci.* **14**(2): 290–303.
Martensson, P.-E., E. S. Nordoy, E. B. Messelt, and A. S. Blix (1998). Gut length, food transit time and diving habit in phocid seals. *Pol. Biol.* **20**: 213–217.
McConnell, B. J., and M. A. Fedak (1996). Movements of southern elephant seals. *Can. J. Zool.* **74**: 1485–1496.
Merrick, R. L., and T. R. Loughlin (1997). Foraging behavior of adult female and young-of-the-year Steller sea lions in Alaskan waters. *Can. J. Zool.* **75**: 776–786.

Muizon, C. de (1993a). Walrus-like feeding adaptation in a new cetacean from the Pliocene of Peru. *Nature* **365**: 745–748.

Muizon, C de (1993b). *Odobenocetops peruvianus:* Una remarcable convergencia de adaptación alimentaria entre morosa y delfin. *Bull. Inst. fr. études andines* **22**(3): 671–683.

Murie, J. (1872). On the form and structure of the manatee. *Trans. Zool. Soc. London* **8**(3): 127–202.

Murray, R., H. Marsh, G. E. Heinsohn, and A. V. Spain (1977). The role of the midgut cecum and large intestine in the digestion of sea grasses by the dugong (Mammalia: Sirenia). *Comp. Biochem. Physiol.* **56A**: 7–10.

Nemoto, T. (1959). Food of baleen whales with reference to whale movements. *Sci. Rep., Whales Res. Instit.*, Tokyo **14**: 149–290.

Nerini, M. (1984). A review of gray whale feeding ecology. *In* "The Gray Whale, *Eschrichtius robustus* (Lilljeborg, 1861)" (M. L. Jones, S. L. Swartz, and S. Leatherwood, eds.), pp. 423–450. Academic Press, New York.

Nishiwaki, M., and H. Marsh (1985). Dugong. *In* "Handbook of Marine Mammals" (S. H. Ridgway and R. Harrison, eds.), pp. 1–32. Academic Press, New York.

Norris, K. S., and B. Mohl (1983). Can odontocetes debilitate prey with sound? *Am. Nat.* **122**: 85–104.

Oliver, J. S., P. N. Slattery, E. F. O'Connor, and L. F. Lowry (1983). Walrus, *Odobenus rosmarus,* feeding in the Bering Sea: A benthic perspective. *Fish. Bull.* **81**: 501–512.

Olsen, M. A., E. S. Nordøy, A. S. Blix and S. D. Mathiesen (1994). Functional anatomy of the gastrointestinal system of the northeastern Atlantic minke whale (*Balaenoptera acutorostrata*). *J. Zool.* **234**: 55–74.

Orton, L. S., and P. F. Brodie (1987). Engulfing mechanics of fin whales. *Can. J. Zool.* **65**: 2898–2907.

Perryman, W. L., M. A. Donahue, J. L. Laake, and T. E. Martin (1999). Diel variation in migration rates of eastern Pacific gray whales measured with thermal imaging sensors. *Mar. Mamm. Sci.* **15**: 426–445.

Pike, G. C. (1962). Migration and feeding of the gray whale (*Eschrichitus gibbosus*). *J. Fish. Res. Board Can.* **19**: 815–838.

Pivorunas, A. (1979). The feeding mechanisms of baleen whales. *Am. Sci.* **67**: 432–440.

Poole, M. M. (1984). Migration corridors of gray whales along the central California coast, 1980–1982. *In* "The Gray Whale, *Eschrichtius robustus* (Lilljeborg, 1861)" (M. L. Jones, S. L. Swartz, and S. Leatherwood, eds.), pp. 389–408. Academic Press, New York.

Preen, A. (1995). Diet of dugongs: Are they omnivores? *J. Mammal.* **76**(1): 163–171.

Pyle, P., M. J. Schramm, C. Keiper, and S. D. Anderson (1999). Predation on a white shark (*Carcharodon carcharias*) by a killer whale (*Orcinus orca*) and a possible case of competitive displacement. *Mar. Mamm. Sci.* **15**: 563–568.

Quiring, D. P. and C. F. Harlan (1953). On the anatomy of the manatee. *J. Mamm.* **34**: 192–203.

Ralls, K., B. B. Hatfield, and D. B. Siniff (1995). Foraging patterns of California sea otters as indicated by telemetry. *Can. J. Zool.* **73**: 523–531.

Rausch, R. L. (1953). On the status of some arctic mammals. *Arctic* **6**: 91–148.

Reed, J. Z., D. J. Tollit, P. M. Thompson, and W. Amos (1997). Molecular scatology: The use of molecular genetic analysis to assign species, sex and individual identity to seal faeces. *Mol. Ecol.* **6**: 225–234.

Reilly, S. B. (1981). Population assessment and population dynamics of the California gray whale, *Eschrichtius robustus*. Ph.D. dissertation. Univ. Wash. Seattle.

Reynolds, J. E., III, and D. E. Odell (1991). "Manatees and Dugongs." Facts on File, New York.

Reynolds, J. E., III, and S. A. Rommel (1996). Structure and function of the gastrointestinal tract of the Florida manatee, *Trichechus manatus latirostris*. *Anat. Rec.* **245**: 539–558.

Rice, D. W., and A. A. Wolman (1971). "The Life History and Ecology of the Gray Whale (*Eschrichtius robustus*)." *Am. Soc. Mammal., Spec. Publ.* **3**: 1–42.

Rice, D. W., and A. A. Wolman (1990). The stomach of *Kogia breviceps*. *J. Mammal.* **71**(2): 237–242.

Riedman, M. (1990). "The Pinnipeds: Seals, Sea Lions, and Walruses." University of California Press, Berkeley.

Riedman, M., and J. Estes (1990). The sea otter (*Enhydra lutris*): Behavior, ecology and natural history. *U.S., Fish Wildl. Serv., Biol. Rep.* No. 90.

Schumacher, U., P. Klein, J. Plotz, and U. Welsch (1995). Histological, histochemical, and ultrastructural investigations on the gastrointestinal system of Antarctic seals: Weddell Seal (*Leptonychotes weddellii*) and Crabeater seal (*Lobodon carcinophagus*). *J. Morphol.* **225**: 229–249.

Sekiguchi, K., and P. B. Best (1992). New information on the feeding habits and baleen morphology of the pygmy right whale *Caperea marginata. Mar. Mamm. Sci.* **8**: 288–293.

Sharpe, F. A., and L. M. Dill (1995). The bubble helix: Sonar structure of feeding humpback whales, *Abstr. 11th Bienn. Conf. Biol. Mar. Mam.*, Orlando, FL, p. 104.

Sharpe, F. A., and L. M. Dill (1997). The behavior of Pacific herring schools in response to artificial humpback whale bubbles. *Can. J. Zool.* **75**: 725–730.

Slijper, E. J. (1979). "Whales." Hutchison, London.

Smolker, R., A. Richards, R. Conner, J. Mann, and P. Berggren (1997). Sponge carrying by dolphins (Delphinidae, *Tursiops* sp.): A foraging specialization involving tool use? *Ethology* **103**: 454–465.

Steinberg, P. D., J. A. Estes, and F. C. Winter (1995). Evolutionary consequences of food chain length in kelp forest communities. *Proc. Natl. Acad. Sci. U.S.A.* **92**: 8145–8148.

Stewart, B. S. (1997). Ontogeny of differential migration and sexual segregation in northern elephant seals. *J. Mammal.* **78**(4): 1101–1116.

Stewart, B. S., and R. L. DeLong (1993). Seasonal dispersion and habitat use of foraging northern elephant seals. *Symp. Zool. Soc. London* **66**: 179–194.

Stewart, B. S., and R. L. DeLong (1994). Postbreeding foraging migrations of northern elephant seals. *In* "Elephant Seals" (B. J. Le Boeuf and R. M. Laws, eds.), pp. 290–309. University of California Press, Berkeley.

Stewart, B. S., and R. L. DeLong (1995). Double migrations of the Northern Elephant Seal, *Mirounga angustirostris. J. Mammal.* **76**(1): 196–205.

Stirling, I. (1995). Relationships between polar bears, ringed seals, and ecological variability. *Abstr. 11th Bienn. Conf. Biol. Mar. Mamm.,* Orlando, FL, p. 111.

Sumich, J. L. (1986). Latitudinal distribution, calf growth and metabolism, and reproductive energetics of gray whales, *Eschrichtius robustus.* Ph.D. Dissertation, Oregon State University, Corvallis.

Swingle, W. M., S. G. Barco, T. D. Pitvhford, W. A. McLellan, and D. A. Pabst (1993). Appearance of juvenile humpback whales feeding in the nearshore waters of Virginia. *Mar. Mamm. Sci.* **9**(3): 309–315.

Takahashi, K., and F. Yamasaki (1972). Digestive tract of Ganges dolphin, *Platanista gangetica.* II. Small and large intestines. *Okajimas Folia Anat. Jpn.* **48**: 427–452.

Tarpy, C. (1979). Killer whale attack! *National Geographic* **155**: 542–545.

Thewissen, J. G. M., S. I. Madar, and S. T. Hussain (1996). *Ambulocetus natans,* an Eocene cetacean (Mammalia) from Pakistan. *CFS, Cour. Forschungsinst. Senckenberg* **191**: 1–86.

Tomilin, A. G. (1957). "Animals of the USSR and neighboring countries, vol. 9." Cetaceans. Izd-vo AN SSSR, Moscow.

Vaughn, T. A. (1986). "Mammalogy, 3rd ed." W. B. Saunders, Philadelphia.

Weinrich, M. T., M. R. Schilling, and C. R. Belt (1992). Evidence for acquisition of a novel feeding behaviour: Lobtail feeding in humpback whales, *Megaptera novaeangliae. Anim. Behav.* **44**: 1059–1072.

Werth, A. (1989). Suction feeding in odontocetes: Water flow and head shape. *Am. Zool.* **29**(40): 92A.

Werth, A. (1991). Suction feeding in pilot whales: Kinematic and anatomical evidence. *Am. Zool.* **31**(5): 17A.

Werth, A. (1993). Functional morphology of balaenid whale tongues. *Abstr. 10th Bienn. Conf. Biol. Mar. Mamm.* Galveston, TX, 1993.

Williams, T. M., S. F. Shippe, and M. J. Rothe (1996). Strategies for reducing foraging costs in dolphins. *In* "Aquatic Predators and Their Prey" (ed. S. P. R. Greenstreet and M. L. Tasker), pp. 4–9. Fishing News Books (Blackwell Science Ltd.).

Yablokov, A. V. (1966). "Variability of mammals." NSF/Smithsonian Inst., Springfield, VA. NTIS. 350 pp.

Yablokov, A. V., V. M. Bel'kovich, and V. I. Botisov (1972). "Whales and dolphins." Nauka, Moscow.

Yamasaki, F., S. Komatsu, and T. Kamiya (1980). A comparative study on the tongues of manatee and dugong (Sirenia). *Sci. Rep. Whales Res. Inst.* **32**: 127–144.

12

Mating, Breeding, and Social Organization

12.1. Introduction

Marine mammals exhibit mating systems as varied as those of other groups of placental mammals, including monogamy, polygyny, and promiscuity. For example, some pinnipeds (e.g. hooded seals) are **monogamous**, with adult males mating with only one female. Many pinnipeds (e.g. elephant seals) are extremely **polygynous**, with successful males mating with dozens of females during a single breeding season. Some baleen whales (e.g. humpbacks), sea otters, and polar bears are also polygynous breeders. Mammals are predisposed for polygyny because of the disparity between genders in the number of gametes produced and the relatively minor role males usually play in the successful rearing of offspring. Males can mate with many females during a breeding season, but females, although able to mate numerous times, can only achieve one pregnancy (i.e. offspring can be sired by only one male) during each breeding season. Consequently, sexual selection pressures for males usually are fundamentally different from those for females because reproductive success is defined differently: male mating strategies may pay off well with numerous offspring sired in a single reproductive season, but the risk of being excluded from producing any offspring also is high. In contrast, female mating strategies result in low risks of reproductive exclusion, but the payoffs also are low, typically only one offspring is produced per reproductive cycle. In several species, this conflict between the reproductive best interests of males and females of the same species is associated with **sexual dimorphism**, an obvious and often dramatic difference in the size, appearance, and behavior of adult males and females. Odontocete cetaceans and sirenians have **promiscuous** mating systems, in which several adult males are associated with a group of females for a variable period of time. In some cases, adult males compete for access to females.

In this chapter, we will examine some of these differences for a variety of marine mammals. The term "breeding" includes two different components of the reproductive process: **mating** (mate selection and copulation) and **parturition** (calving in whales and sirenians;

pupping in pinnipeds and sea otters). Obviously, females are involved in both, males only in mating. For many species, these reproductive activities anchor one end of extended annual migrations (described in Chapter 13). Consequently, for mysticete cetaceans and some pinnipeds, mating and parturition typically occur in the same locality at nearly the same time of the year. For other marine mammals, such as sea otters (Jameson and Johnson, 1993) and many odontocetes (Barlow, 1984), the timing of breeding is spread broadly throughout the year with some seasonality. These species often remain in limited home ranges for both mating and parturition.

12.2. Pinniped Mating Systems

Pinniped mating systems cover the entire range from strict monogamy to extreme polygyny. Essentially all species of otariids and many species of phocids are polygynous, with only a few males mating with most of the females while simultaneously denying other males opportunities to mate (Boness, 1991; Le Boeuf, 1991). Le Boeuf (1991) defines slight polygyny as a male mating with 2–5 females (e.g. hooded seals), moderate polygyny as a male mating with 6–15 females (e.g. gray seals), and extreme polygyny as a male mating with 16–100 or more females during a breeding season (e.g. elephant seals). Polygyny is associated with moderate to extreme sexual dimorphism in adults, densely aggregated breeding groups when ashore, estrus and mating soon after pupping, and delayed implantation of the resulting **blastocyst** with a corresponding extension of gestation (discussed in Chapter 13).

12.2.1. Breeding on Land vs in the Water

Two thirds of all pinniped species breed and pup on land while the remainder mate and give birth on fast ice or pack ice. Almost all pinniped species that breed on land, including gray seals (Watkins, 1990), northern and southern elephant seals (Cassini and Vila, 1990; Le Boeuf, 1991), and all otariids (Boness, 1991), are extremely polygynous and strongly sexually dimorphic with males showing obvious secondary sex characteristics. Breeding male northern elephant seals are 5–6 times larger than adult females, and the largest southern elephant seal males may weigh ten times as much as the females with whom they copulate (Le Boeuf and Laws, 1994). In addition to their larger size, male elephant seals have an elongated proboscis, enlarged canine teeth, and thick cornified skin on the neck as secondary sexual characteristics. (Fig. 12.1). Species that pup on land prefer that their pupping and mating rookeries occur on islands free of large terrestrial predators or on isolated mainland beaches and sandbars not easily accessible to such predators. Consequently, available rookery space may become limiting, and females become densely aggregated in large breeding colonies. These dense aggregations establish conditions favorable to a polygynous mating system. As their rookery sites are geographically fixed and are used by the same adults in successive years, males can anticipate the return of females each year and can compete for breeding territories (in otariids) or establish dominance hierarchies (in elephant seals) prior to the return of the females. Females also can depend on the predictable presence of adequate pupping sites and on the presence of breeding males.

Species that breed in large colonies, such as northern and southern elephant seals, Weddell seals, and Hawaiian monk seals, also sometimes exhibit **alloparenting** or fostering behavior (also seen in sperm whales and discussed later in this chapter); this is the atten-

Figure 12.1. Male and female northern elephant seal, showing extreme sexual dimorphism.

dance, care, and nurturing of a young offspring by animals other than its parent(s). Because mother–pup separations may take place frequently on a crowded rookery, there are many opportunities for adoptive behavior (Riedman, 1990).

The remaining phocids that mate in the water or on ice include the Weddell, harp, ringed, ribbon, bearded, hooded, Baikal, Caspian, larga, crabeater, leopard, harbor, and monk seals (Le Boeuf, 1991). They typically show a reduced level of polygyny that is explained, in part, by the difficulty of gaining access to females in physically unstable environments such as tide-washed beaches or pack ice (Sjare and Stirling, 1996). Several Arctic phocid species use temporary or seasonal pack ice for breeding (Fig. 12.2). The extensive distribution of pack ice promotes dispersal of breeding females while providing protection from most predators and easy access to water and food. Yet the temporary and unpredictable nature of the location, extent, and break-up time of typical pack ice restricts pupping to a short time period when the ice is most stable. As females of ice-pupping species cannot reliably return to the same "place" for pupping year after year, males are forced to search for widely dispersed females. In-water mating is common in these species, providing males with even less opportunity to control the mating choices of females (Kovacs, 1990). Males can, however, increase their confidence of paternity by **mate guarding**, a mating strategy suggested for hooded seals that is well documented in birds (McRae and Kovacs, 1994). Behavioral observations summarized in this study revealed that this strategy involves male hooded seals displacing one another while attending nursing females. Supporting evidence for this strategy comes from the existence of intense competition for females, a brief nursing period, and estrus that occurs soon after weaning. This same breeding strategy also has been suggested for the crabeater seal. The main difference between the two is that a male crabeater seal guards a female on the ice for one or two weeks after her pup is weaned preventing her from returning to the water. This implies that some guarding after mating occurs (McRae and Kovacs, 1994, and references cited therein).

Figure 12.2. Ringed seal hauled on ice nursing her pup. (Photo by Kit and Christian, A.R.C.)

The vast extent of polar fast ice available to ice-breeding seals (Fig. 12.3) also allows breeding females to disperse widely, although access to cracks and holes in the ice may promote some clumping of individuals. Male Weddell seals of the Antarctic maintain under-ice breeding territories near breathing holes to exclude other males and are limited to mating with the females grouped around that ice hole. Weddell seals mate underwater, but it unclear which gender makes mate choice or how much polygyny occurs. In the Arctic,

Figure 12.3. An adult Weddell seal hauled on ice. (Courtesy C. Kooyman.)

ringed seal females pup in isolated and hidden snow caves above breathing holes in the fast ice to avoid polar bears. Because females are isolated and dispersed, individual male ringed seals typically have access to only one female and are considered monogamous.

Mating in water is especially difficult for human observers to study. However, even mating studies of land breeding species must be interpreted with caution. Using DNA fingerprint probes (see Chapter 14), Harris *et al.* (1991) demonstrated that behavioral observations during courtship and mating of a captive group of harbor seals were not reliable predictors of eventual paternity. In addition, gray seals observed on Rona Island by Amos *et al.* (1995) give the outward appearance of moderate polygyny, with relatively few large males monopolizing the observed matings ashore. However, the social structure of breeding gray seals has layers of complexity still not well-understood, for genetic paternity testing has established that the large males sire significantly fewer pups than expected from their observed mating opportunities. Additionally, the study by Amos *et al.* (1995) showed that females tended to produce several pups sired by the same male (often not the large attendant male), suggesting that mating seals must be capable of recognizing each other in successive years, and that mating during the females' estrus occurs away from the "breeding" beaches.

12.2.1.1. Mating Strategies

In monogamous seals, males can succeed reproductively by locating an estrus female and mating with her. With population gender ratios approximating 1:1, there will be approximately as many females available as there are males competing for them. These males apparently are limited to monogamy simply because the nonaggregated distribution of females does not allow them to access more than one female at a time or to exclude other males from access to females other than the one he is attending. The larger size and other sexually dimorphic characteristics seen in polygynous males confer no selective advantage, and monomorphism or even slight reverse sexual dimorphism becomes the norm for monogamous species. In Weddell seals, the smaller size of the male in comparison to the female has been suggested as making the male a more agile swimmer and therefore more attractive as a potential mate (Le Boeuf, 1991). In addition, ice breeding seals have developed complex vocalizations underwater to advertise attractiveness and mating receptivity (see Chapter 10).

Polygynous males, in contrast, must compete for reproductive control of females by excluding numerous other males from breeding activities. In otariids, this competition revolves around the establishment and defense of breeding territories. This type of mating system is referred to as **resource defense polygyny**. Several characteristics are common to those species that exhibit resource defense polygyny: 1) territorial males arrive before females, 2) females become receptive in close geographical proximity to where they give birth, 3) the rookery substrate is unstable and discontinuous, facilitating its defense, and 4) there may be a relatively low level of aggressive interaction among males (i.e. those males that are not large enough to maintain or capture a territory are seen infrequently and are usually peripheral to the main breeding activity (Boness, 1991)). The breeding behavior of northern fur seals is typical of this type of mating system. The results of a long-term study of northern fur seal populations at study sites on the Probilof Islands by Gentry (1998) are summarized below. Adult male northern fur seals usually maintain an established, very specific territory for life (Fig. 12.4). These territories are defended using aggressive behavior. Territorial defense most frequently is a two-male display using vocalizations and threat

Figure 12.4. Northern fur seal harem with territorial male in the right foreground. (Courtesy J. Harvey.)

displays rather than engaging in true fights. Males copulate more if they have larger body sizes, larger territories in good locations, fasts of longer duration, longer tenure in a territory, few interactions with females, and a higher frequency of territorial defense. Male reproductive success is highly variable. Males average only 2.5 copulations per year and only 3.6 per lifetime (range 0–116 copulations per lifetime). True values are undoubtedly higher, however, since the majority of copulations occur at night and were not observed.

By contrast, male Steller sea lions typically start out in poor territories with associated poor reproductive success and usually require about three years before achieving high reproductive success (Gisiner, 1985). Once a male Steller sea lion succeeds in acquiring and holding a territory, he seems to be able to remember relationships established with his territorial neighbors year after year (Higgins *et al.*, 1988). These memory and cognitive skills may be as important as physical attributes in enhancing a male's reproductive success over several years.

In those otariids that exhibit resource defense polygny, females are relatively sedentary between the time of parturition and estrus (Boness, 1991). This situation differs in the Juan Fernandez fur seal. Females are not sedentary and high temperatures contribute to male and female movements to the water. Males acquire access to females by controlling parturition sites. Males hold exclusively aquatic territories in areas when females predictably congregate. Other males hold either land-locked or shoreline territories where females give birth and nurse their young (Francis and Boness, 1991).

Polygynous elephant seals and gray seals do not defend breeding territories as do otariids; rather, they establish dominance hierarchies (Fig. 12.5) among groups of associating males within aggregations, or harems, of females. This type of mating system often is referred to as **female (or harem) defense polygyny**. Like otariid males, elephant seals fast for the duration of the breeding season (a period of over three months for northern elephant seals), and the increased lipid stores associated with large male body mass confer clear advantages in successfully withstanding these extended periods without food. The most dominant (or alpha) male in a dominance hierarchy defends nearby females against incursions by subordinate males. At Año Nuevo Island on the central California coast, northern elephant seal breeding behavior has been studied intensively for almost three decades (Le Boeuf and Laws, 1994). In areas crowded with females, an alpha male can dominate the breeding of about fifty females. As more females require even larger areas of the rookery, it becomes more difficult for an alpha male to exclude competing males from access to at least some females. Even so, fewer than 10% of a study group of males managed to mate at all during their lifetimes and the most successful male of that group mated with 121 females (Le Boeuf and Reiter, 1988). In male northern elephant seals, copulatory success is positively correlated with male size (Haley *et al.*, 1994), although this was not the case when controlling for age (Clinton and Le Boeuf, 1993). It is likely that other factors such

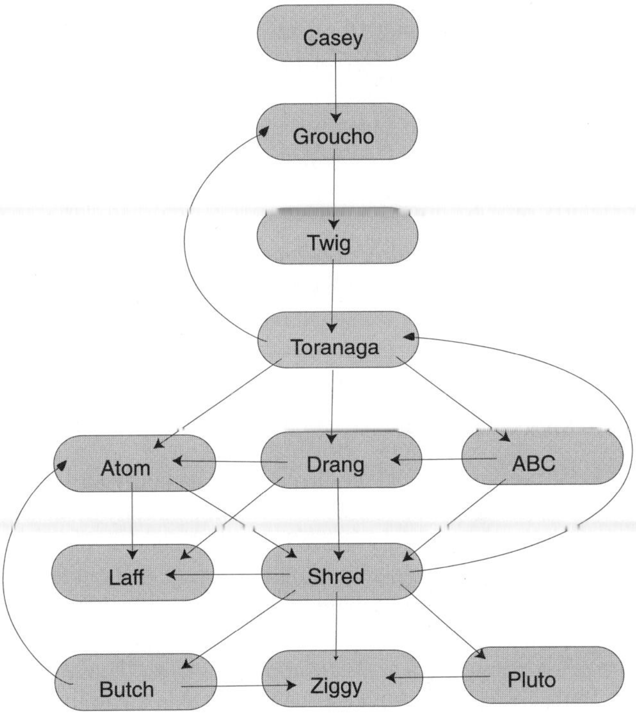

Figure 12.5. Dominance hierarchy patterns of northern elephant seal males during one season at Año Nuevo Island. Arrows point down the hierarchy. (Adapted from Riedman, 1990).

as fighting experience might influence copulatory success (Modig, 1996). Large aggregations of females are difficult to defend, and in addition to the alpha male, aggregations usually contain one or several lower ranking males (McCann, 1981). In a study of mating success in the southern elephant seal, among the factors correlated with large size in males and important for mating success are a central position in a harem (to which larger males gain access by having a higher dominance rank and therefore the ability to chase off other males) and maintenance of the central position in the harem for a long time [which also is the result of having energy reserves large enough to defend the central position against intruding males (Modig, 1996)].

Subdominant (usually younger) males utilize other strategies to gain access to at least a few females. Some male elephant seals occupy less preferred breeding beaches which attract fewer males with whom they must compete. However, these beaches also attract few females. In more crowded rookeries, subdominant males may accomplish occasional matings by sneaking into large harems in which alpha males are more likely to be distracted, or by mobbing a female as she departs from the rookery at the end of the breeding season (Riedman, 1990). However, these departing females almost definitely have been previously inseminated by a dominant male, so these late copulations by subdominant males are unlikely to lead to paternity. Another example of mobbing behavior are attacks by overly aggressive Hawaiian monk seal males attempting to mate with females (Alcorn, 1984). Some young adult female and juvenile seals have been injured as a result of this mobbing behavior (Johanos *et al.*, 1990) and a male-biased sex ratio is believed to increase the probability of these behaviors (Le Boeuf and Mesnick, 1990).

Several otariids have been described as exhibiting female defense polygny. Male southern and Australian sea lions without breeding territories of their own gain access to females by making large coordinated group raids into established territories of breeding males, and a few raiders attempt to mate with females or to abduct them in the temporary confusion (Campagna *et al.*, 1988; Cassini and Vila, 1990). How often these raiding behaviors actually result in successful fertilization is unknown.

Mating strategies of female pinnipeds have been less studied than those of males. This is in part due to the crowded rookery conditions of highly polygynous species. It is sometimes difficult to distinguish a female's behavior directed at defending her pup from strictly mating-related behavior. In land-breeding polygynous seals, females may move away from or vocally protest mounting attempts by subdominant males, thus attracting the notice of higher ranking males (Boness *et al.*, 1982). A female's position within a group, especially a large group, also may influence with whom she will mate. Older or more dominant females near the center of a harem will be more likely to mate with the dominant male, leaving females pushed to the edge of the harem more exposed to mating forays by subdominant males.

Mating in water is employed by most ice-breeding seals and walruses and may give females a selective advantage that does not occur on land: directly selecting the male with whom they will copulate. Pacific walruses have been described as having a **lek** or lek-like mating system. During the breeding season, female walruses and calves haul-out on ice or rest in the water while one or more adult males station themselves in the water alongside a herd and perform complex underwater visual displays (see Fig. 10.1) and produce a series of amazingly bell-like or gong-like sounds to attract females. These ritual courtship displays are similar to the well known lekking behavior of North American sage grouse and some African antelopes. In all lekking species, including the Pacific walrus, males only aggregate and display; females make the choice of their mating partners. The elaborate display behaviors of males allow females an opportunity to make the best genetic deal possible by getting males to show what they have before selecting a mate. In addition to the Pacific walrus, both the California sea lion and Hooker's sea lion have been reported to exhibit lek-like behavior and dispersion patterns (Heath and Francis, 1983, 1987).

A different mating system, female-defense polygyny rather than a lek-like system, was suggested for Atlantic walruses studied at the Dundas Island **polynya** (area of open water surrounded by stable fast ice) in the Canadian high Arctic (Sjare and Stirling, 1996). A large mature male had exclusive access to a herd of walruses containing several females for 1–5 days at a time. One or two males spent significantly more time with the herd and it was not evident that female preference was important in determining which male became the attending male (Fig. 12.6). When attending a herd, a male continuously repeated a complex, stereotyped underwater song. Other sexually mature males in the area behaved as silent herd members, vocal satellite males, or in some cases both (Sjare and Stirling, 1996). The herd attendance profile of males suggests that males maximize their reproductive success by roving between groups of females, a breeding strategy that also is characteristic of male sperm whales (Whitehead, 1993). Variability of the sea ice habitat is probably one of the factors contributing to the differences in the mating system and breeding behavior of Pacific and Atlantic walruses.

12.2.1.2. Rookery Utilization by Elephant Seals

Individuals of several pinniped species, including elephant seals, return year after year to the same breeding beach on which they were born. Consequently, repeated associations with the same individuals may recur several years in succession, alternating with periods of no association between individuals during the time away from the breeding site. Northern elephant seals provide a clear example of the shifting patterns of associations on a breeding site through time (Le Boeuf and Laws, 1994), and the dynamics of those associations

Figure 12.6. Herd of female and young walruses hauled along the edge of an Arctic polynya. An attending male is stationed in the water near the polynya edge and is singing. (Courtesy I. Stirling/B. Sjare.)

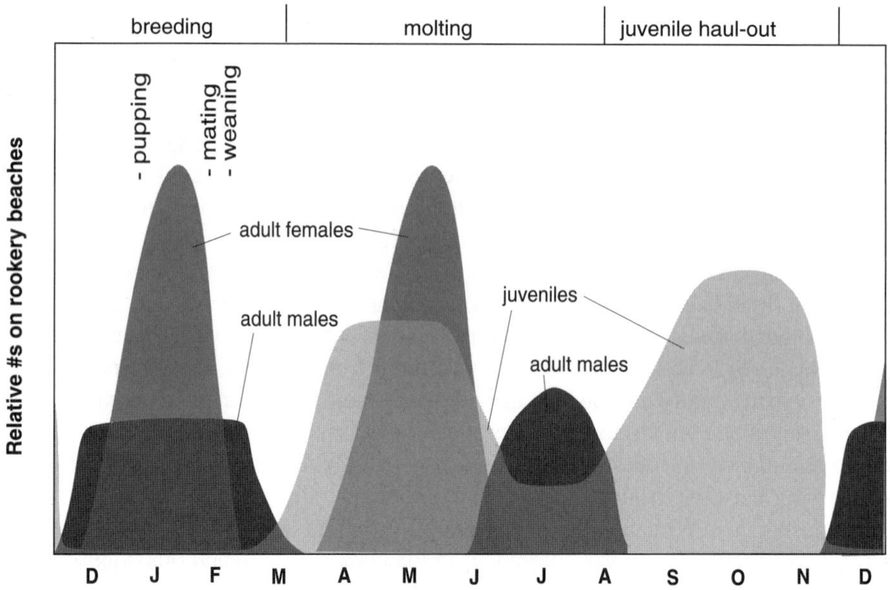

Figure 12.7. Seasonal sequence of rookery use by different gender and age groups of northern elephant seals. (Adapted from Le Boeuf and Laws, 1994).

for Año Nuevo Island are outlined in Figure 12.7. Juveniles utilize the beaches as haul-out sites through much of the nonbreeding season. Adult males arrive at rookery sites in early December, and successful breeders remain while fasting until late February or early March. The arrival of these males displaces the juveniles. Pregnant females arrive in late December and aggregate in preferred rookery sites occupied by dominant males. Pups are born and lactation commences about one week after females arrive. These lactating females enter estrus and mate about two weeks after pupping. Lactation continues for a total of about four weeks, after which females abruptly wean their offspring and depart for a two-month feeding migration at sea. Pups enter a 1–4 month postweaning period ashore, its duration dependent on the magnitude of their stored fat supplies (see Chapter 13). Adult males begin to depart in late February or early March. Adult females and juveniles return to the rookery for a one-month molting fast between mid-March and mid-May. Adult males return to the rookery in June and July for their molt. Then the juvenile animals return to use the beach as a haul-out site until the beginning of the next breeding season.

12.2.2. Evolution of Pinniped Mating Systems

Emlen and Oring (1977) proposed a model for the evolution of mammalian mating systems which emphasized the importance of environmental resources that allowed the simultaneous control by males of multiple mates or sequential access to single mates. A major factor in the evolution of pinniped mating systems, in addition to the fundamental conflict between gender roles referred to above, is the habitat available for pupping (i.e. land, pack ice, or fast ice); Stirling *et al.*, 1983; Le Boeuf, 1986). Pupping habitat controls the distribution of adult females which, in turn, influences male distribution and breeding behavior. Parturition in all pinnipeds occurs out of water. Although **precocious** at birth, most species of pinnipeds are not immediately capable of swimming. This, combined with their reduced mobility out of water, make pups especially vulnerable to terrestrial predators. As a result, pinnipeds exhibit a strong preference for pupping on ice or on oceanic islands.

Bartholomew (1970) proposed that the evolution and maintenance of polygyny and sexual dimorphism in pinnipeds are consequence of the interplay between conditions imposed by their mammalian heritage (sperm is cheaper and more abundant than eggs, and the costs of pregnancy and lactation are borne only be females) and their amphibious lifestyles (terrestrial pupping is isolated in time and space from offshore feeding). In the water, these pinnipeds are quite mobile and tend to disperse some distance from the rookery in search of food (see Chapter 11). Offshore feeding removes the competition for food from the rookery area and promotes the fullest use of the few isolated sites that are appropriate as pupping and breeding rookeries. In congested breeding rookeries, males, even with their limited mobility on land, can hypothetically contact and mate with several females while preventing other males from gaining access to those same females. The most successful males are the ones that most aggressively exclude other males from access to females.

Bartholomew's model does not explain all forms of pinniped polygyny. For example, walruses form dense aggregations on pack ice, are sexually dimorphic, but are only moderately polygynous (Stirling *et al.*, 1983; Le Boeuf, 1986). Their clumping may be a response to locally abundant but patchy food resources rather than due to a temporal and spatial isolation from those resources (Fay, 1982). Unlike elephant seals, walruses copulate in the water, in areas of drifting pack ice or polynyas.

Another exception to the Bartholomew model of polygyny occurs in sea lions. In California sea lions, mate choice is also done by females. Females copulate in areas away from the pupping sites where they spend most of their time, and the number of copulations a male accomplishes is unrelated to the number of females in his territory (Heath and Francis, 1987). Further, Bartholomew (1970) suggests that aquatic copulations seen in the California sea lion and pinnipeds in general are associated with reduced polygyny. This is based on the assumption that aquatic territories are more difficult to defend and more matings are performed by nonterritorial or marginal males. However, Francis and Boness (1991) reported that aquatic territories of the Juan Fernandez fur seal were defensible and all aquatic matings were performed by territorial males.

Harbor seals and gray seals are widespread in the northern hemisphere. Both species are monogamous when breeding on ice but tend toward polygyny and increased dimorphism when breeding on land (Bigg, 1981; Hoover, 1983). Thus, the type of habitat, or at least its extent, also is a strong influence on the development of polygyny in some pinniped species.

The evolution of ice breeding among phocid seals has been hypothesized to result from phocids having descended from an ice-breeding ancestor (Stirling, 1975; Stirling *et al.*, 1983). Reexamination of this and a related hypothesis (i.e. multiple origins for ice breeding; Bonner, 1984, 1990) in the context of a phylogenetic framework (Costa, 1993; Perry *et al.*, 1995; Berta and Deméré, 1993) has suggested alternative hypotheses. When the distribution of a breeding habit is mapped onto pinniped phylogeny, the data indicate that the ancestral breeding habit is land based (Fig. 12.8). Two derived states can be identified: 1) breeding on fast ice (seen in the Weddell seal) and 2) breeding on pack ice (seen in the walrus and most phocids). The data indicate that the previous hypothesis for multiple origins of ice breeding is incorrect. Ice breeding evolved only once in phocids, among lobodontine and phocine seals. The earliest diverging lineages of phocids, monk and elephant seals, retain the ancestral pattern for pinnipeds, that of breeding on land. The consequences of ice breeding in terms of the evolution of life history patterns is further considered in the next chapter.

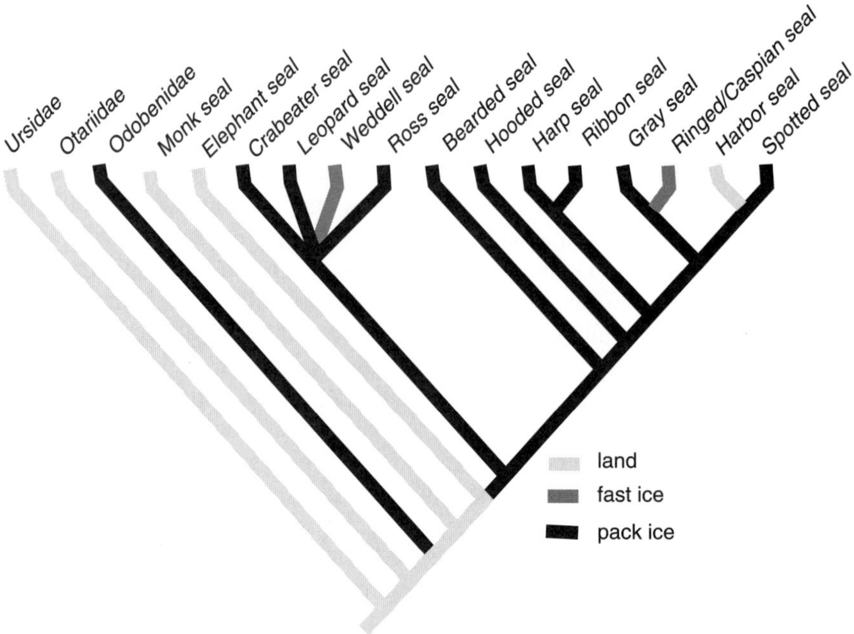

Figure 12.8. Breeding habit of pinnipeds mapped onto phylogeny.

12.2.3. Pinniped Social Organization

Social interactions of pinnipeds have only been studied for the time spent out of water and they vary with species, time of year, and location. Little is known of association patterns between individuals outside of breeding activities. In addition to breeding, pinnipeds haul-out of the water together to rest, avoid predators, molt, or warm themselves. Predator avoidance may be enhanced with the increased vigilance that occurs with larger group sizes. Renouf and Lawson (1986) suggest that, for harbor seals, scanning behavior by adult males is used to detect potential mating opportunities rather than predators, as other observers have proposed. The structure and composition of some walrus groups persist throughout the year, both in the water and on haul-out sites. This grouping may be a female strategy for pup defense against polar bear predation by providing a circle of adults to protect the more vulnerable calves (Fay, 1982). In addition, huddling by large numbers of walruses when out of the water may be important in reducing rates of body heat loss, especially in the smaller calves.

12.3. Cetacean Mating Systems

Unlike pinnipeds, all cetaceans mate and give birth in water. Consequently, our understanding of these events in most cetacean species is spotty. Only the general outlines of reproduction are documented for small odontocetes which can be observed in captivity, for species which have been exploited commercially (and for whom large numbers of carcasses have been available for examination), and for coastal tropical and subtropical species where direct underwater observations of courting, mating, and calving behaviors are facilitated by clear waters. With the advent of molecular techniques such as DNA fingerprinting (see Chapter 14), it has been possible to verify these behaviors and to determine paternity and kinship.

With few exceptions, notably cooperative feeding by humpback whales (see Fig. 11.13), mysticetes do not group closely together, school, or form pods. This probably reflects the need to feed more or less individually because restricted areas cannot sustain the daily food requirements of a large group. Unlike mysticetes, odontocetes exist in social groups (e.g. schools, units, and pods) of varying sizes whose structures persist longer than any individual member's lifespan. Most mysticetes show little evidence of persistent social behavior beyond mother–calf bonds which disappear at weaning. The presence or absence of persistent social bonds between individuals can, in turn, influence the evolution of mating behavior.

12.3.1. Social Odontocetes

Many odontocete species tend to group together in structured social groups, or **schools**, characterized by long-term association among individuals. The size of the school varies with species and location. Observational studies of spinner dolphins in the clear waters of Hawaii by Norris and his colleagues (1994) and the Bahamas by Herzing (1997) indicate that spinners aggregate in schools of up to one hundred individuals. Within each school are subgroups of up to a dozen individuals whose members maintain close association with each other by remaining close and synchronizing their movements. Most commonly the animals occur in a staggered arrangement, or **echelon formation** (Fig. 12.9), similar to that seen in flying formations of birds (Norris and Johnson, 1994). It has been suggested that this spatial arrangement might be part of a signaling system that allows organization and transmission of information throughout the school. Spinner dolphin societies are characterized by minimal sexual dimorphism and a high degree of cooperation among individuals. Both sexes are involved in birth, nurturing, instruction, and cooperative defense of the

Figure 12.9. Dorsal view of spinner dolphins swimming in echelon formation, with pectoral tips 1–2 body diameters apart. (Redrawn from a photograph in Norris and Johnson, 1994.)

young (Norris, 1994). Mating is seasonal and apparently promiscuous, with more than one male achieving intromission with the same female in rapid succession (Johnson and Norris, 1994).

Bottlenose dolphins inhabit nearshore waters of many temperate and warm coastlines, making many populations relatively easy to observe. One of the longest term studies of free ranging bottlenose dolphins is that of the Sarasota Bay community on the west coast of Florida initiated, in 1970 (Irvine and Wells, 1972; Wells *et al.*, 1987; Scott *et al.*, 1989). The community contains about 100 dolphins and is composed of smaller schools of socially interacting individuals. The groups are organized on the basis of age, sex, familial relationship, and reproductive condition. Although the composition of schools may fluctuate over the course of a day, many associations are relatively long term. The mother–calf bond is close and may persist for many years. Membership of the female bands is also relatively stable, and subadult and adult males may form lasting associations among themselves as well. Like spinner dolphins, bottlenose dolphins are probably promiscuous in their mating. In early adolescence, males form coalitions with one or two other adult males that last for years and may be life long (Connor *et al.*, 1992, 1999). These male coalitions exist as subgroups within larger schools and forage and swim together. Similar male coalitions have been described for spinner dolphins (Johnson and Norris, 1994). Coalitions of male bottlenose dolphins also aggressively attend adult females, and sometimes abduct females from other male coalitions. The extended period of calf dependence on their mothers means that females ovulate infrequently, and it may be in the males' reproductive best interest to abduct females and keep them in close proximity until estrus occurs. In the Sarasota Bay dolphin community, males typically sire offspring from their late twenties and continue to fertilize females for about a decade. Over that time span, individual males produce offspring with several females, and the calves of any one female are fathered by different males.

Social dominance and sex differences in competitive behavior, features of societies based on long-term relationship among individuals, have been described among captive odontocetes (reviewed in Samuels and Gifford, 1997). A zoo-based quantitative study of dominance relationships among bottlenose dolphins reveals that dominance was influenced by the gender of the participants. The study confirmed earlier work which reported male dolphins were dominant to females. Dominance relationships observed among female dolphins, however, differed from the prevalent view that female dominance relations are indistinct. The study indicated that a female's dominance status varied according to her mating partner and in some cases led to aggressiveness toward other females (Samuels and Gifford, 1997).

Although observations of births in wild dolphins are rare, reports of captive spinner and bottlenose dolphin births suggest that alloparenting or fostering behavior is probably common in many dolphin species. Both male and female dolphins may alloparent, although their behaviors observed in captivity differ (Johnson and Norris, 1994), especially in the level of apparent agonistic behavior directed toward the mother. "Babysitting" by older juveniles of both sexes has been described by Herzing (1995) for wild spinner dolphins, who suggested that the responsibility of this role is an important method for juvenile animals to practice adult behaviors that they will eventually need.

In all resident populations of killer whales so far studied, individuals exist in small stable social units knows as **pods**. Pods are characterized by their specific dialects (see Chapter 10) and foraging strategies (see Chapter 11) as well as by their individual members. Killer whale pods are **matrilineal** social groups, each typically consisting of an older mature female, her male and female offspring, and the offspring of the second generation's mature females. Mature males remain with the pod into which they were born, and movement or exchange of individuals among pods has not been documented (Bigg *et al.*, 1990). Mating behavior has rarely been observed, yet genetic studies support the notion that male killer whales do not mate with their closely related pod members. Instead it is thought that inter-pod matings occur when pods encounter each other in shared foraging or resting areas (Ford *et al.*, 1994).

Sperm whales occur in associations of varying sizes in all oceans. Gregarious adult females and immature whales occur throughout tropical and subtropical latitudes year-round (Fig. 12.10). These female/immature whale groups, or **units** (terminology of Whitehead *et al.*, 1991), are structurally equivalent to pods of killer whales and, like killer whales, appear to be matrilineal in structure (Whitehead *et al.*, 1991). Sperm whale social units average about a dozen whales and include closely related adult females and their offspring of both sexes (Whitehead and Waters, 1990). Unlike killer whales, however, male sperm whales leave these female groups at 4–5 years of age and gradually drift into higher latitudes as they grow, so adult males are not permanent members of the female units. It is those large, solitary, physically mature males that participate in most matings as they move from one female unit to another seeking estrus females (Whitehead, 1993). Sperm whales are characterized by adult males that can be about twice the length of females; they exhibit one of the greatest sexual size differences of any mammalian species.

Current evidence indicates that the social function of female sperm whale units is to provide a cooperative system of care for calves that are too young to accompany their mothers during deep foraging dives (described in Chapter 11). Shared communal care of

Figure 12.10. Sperm whale group.

vulnerable calves by other adult females, also referred to as "babysitting" (Whitehead, 1996, and references cited therein), provides protection from predators as well as the possibility of communal nursing while the mother is foraging (Whitehead *et al.*, 1991). Whitehead (1996) reports that babysitting sperm whales seem to show alloparental care, reducing periods during which calves are unaccompanied at the surface, and thus likely increasing protection for the calf while permitting greater foraging freedom to the mother. Such communal care behavior is likely to be selected for only if individuals within a sperm whale unit are closely related and remain together for extended time periods, perhaps even entire lifetimes. The benefits of this behavior may have been instrumental in the evolution of sociality in female sperm whales (Whitehead, 1996). Among female and immature sperm whales, two other levels of social organization, "groups" of associated units and even larger "aggregations" of associated, but unrelated groups, have been recognized (Whitehead and Kahn, 1992). Unlike units, however, temporal and geographic differences are observed in the sizes of groups and aggregations, probably caused by variations in the distribution and abundance of their food, although response to recent human exploitation may also be a factor.

Results of comparative study of the social systems of odontocetes are beginning to emerge. For example, sperm whales have been described as having a social system similar to elephants and bottlenose dolphin societies have been compared with those of chimpanzees (Connor *et al.*, 1998 and references cited therein). Future work based on long-term studies of identified individuals will allow us to extend these comparisons to a wider range of species.

12.3.2. Mysticetes

Baleen whales generally are observed in loose aggregations, with the basic stable unit being a cow and a calf. Usually animals occur singly or in groups of 2–6 whales, although larger groups of more than 20 have been observed both on and outside feeding grounds (Lockyer, 1984, and references cited therein). Mating in most baleen whale species that have been studied appears to be promiscuous. The mating behavior of baleen whales is intimately tied to a reproductive life cycle of breeding, migration, and feeding (described in greater detail in Chapter 11. All mysticetes show reverse sexual size dimorphism in which females are the larger of the two sexes. This may allow the larger females to offset the energetic costs associated with rapid fetal growth and lactation, especially because much of their time is spent in metabolically expensive cold water (Clapham, 1996).

The majority of gray whales mate during the southern portion of their migration in coastal or lagoon waters of limited underwater visibility. A persistent, yet unsubstantiated, myth describes the gray whale as typically mating in trios consisting of a receptive female and two males. Although courting trios are sometimes observed, the sexes of participants are usually unknown to the observer. Based on above-surface observations of courting activities, mating appears to be promiscuous, although actual paternity is impossible to establish from direct observations of their very active and vigorous courting encounters (Fig. 12.11). Courting/mating groups including as many as 17 individuals have been reported (Jones and Swartz, 1984), however the intensity of the physical interactions during these courting bouts precludes determining such basic features as gender and inter-whale contact patterns or even accurate determinations of group sizes.

In the absence of direct underwater observations of gray whale mating behavior, arguments for promiscuous mating must be based on other evidence. In comparison to most

Figure 12.11. A group of gray whales courting in a coastal lagoon in Baja California.

other baleen whales, gray, bowhead, and right whale males have substantially larger testes weight/body weight ratios (Fig. 12.12) and relatively larger penises. Larger testes are presumed to produce greater quantities of sperm. This has been interpreted as evidence of **sperm competition** (proposed for several species of birds and mammals, including some mysticetes; Brownell and Ralls, 1986), with copulating males competing with previous copulators by attempting to displace or dilute their sperm within a female's reproductive tract, thus increasing the probability of being the male to fertilize the female's single ovum.

Humpback whales form small, unstable groups on both summer feeding and winter breeding grounds (see Clapham, 1996, for a review). A unique feature of the mating behavior of this species is the performance by males of songs of extended duration (described

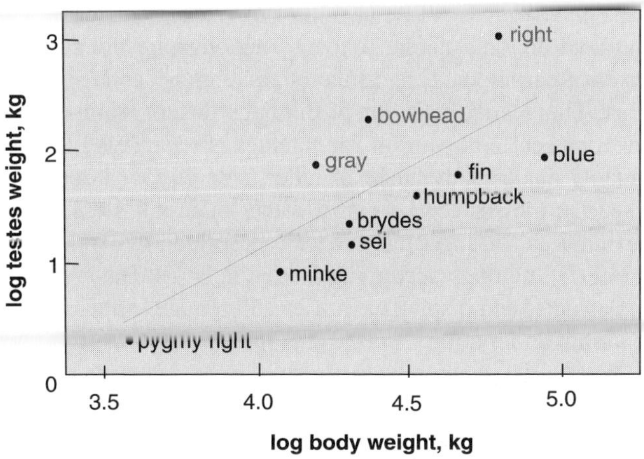

Figure 12.12. General relationship between body size and testis size of ten species of mysticetes. The three species with relatively larger testes (positioned above the diagonal line) are assumed to produce proportionally larger quantities of sperm with which to compete with the sperm of other males. (Redrawn from Brownell and Ralls, 1986)

in Chapter 10). This primarily occurs on the winter breeding grounds but also occasionally on the summer feeding grounds. During the winter breeding season, the social organization of humpback whales has been described in the context of competitive groups (Tyak and Whitehead, 1982; Clapham *et al.*, 1992). These typically contain a female humpback (even those with new calves) attended by another adult, termed the "principal **escort**." In the cases where gender had been determined, "principal escorts" have been male (Glockner-Ferrari and Ferrari, 1984; Medrano *et al.*, 1994). Other males, termed "secondary escorts," are sometimes present but do not play an active role in the group. Those males identified as "principal escorts" also have been observed alone and acting as singers. "Principal escorts" appear to be consorting with females to mate and will vigorously rebuff approaches by intruding males, termed "challengers" (Mobley and Herman, 1985), by ramming or thrashing of the flukes (Fig 12.13), by using trumpet blows, and by blowing bubble curtains or streams (see references cited in Weinrich, 1995, and Pack *et al.*, 1998). Baker and Herman (1984) have found that the incidence of these agonistic behaviors increases with increasing density of whales in the breeding areas. This mating system, in which males display (sing) or directly compete for access to females, has been further described by Clapham (1996) as being similar to both leks and male dominance polygyny. Because the mating system of humpbacks lacks the rigid spatial structure of leks, he referred to their unique mating system as a "floating lek."

12.4. Sirenian Mating Systems

Manatees and dugongs are solitary animals for most of the year. The few social interactions (apart from mother/calf pairs) observed appear to center on reproduction (O'Shea, 1994). Mating and calving occur throughout the year, although some seasonality in the occurrence of newborn calves has been reported for West Indian manatees and for the more tropical dugongs (Reynolds and Odell, 1991). A manatee cow attracts as many as 17 males that compete for copulation rights by vigorously pushing and shoving each other (Fig. 12.14; see also Bentgson, 1981; Rathbun and O'Shea, 1984). Mating may be promiscuous and Rathbun *et al.* (1995) reported that participatory roles and minimum ages of competing males were without pattern.

Less is known about dugong mating. Because dugongs are not conspicuously sexually dimorphic, the sexes of participants are difficult to distinguish and usually are inferred from behavioral patterns. The sexual behavior of dugongs differs from manatees primarily in their more intense physical competition for females (Preen, 1989). "Fighting" dugongs, with scars presumably made by the tusks of other male dugongs during courtship battles, frequently were seen at the surface lunging at other dugongs. Less male harassment and different mating behaviors for dugongs have been described by Anderson (1997). According to Anderson (1997), dugongs occupying a cove in Shark Bay, Australia exhibit a lek-strategy where males defended display territories and females appeared in the cove only in the context of courtship and mating.

12.5. Other Marine Mammals

Sea otters are polygynous breeders, and copulation occurs exclusively in the water. When not breeding, they are segregated by gender, with adult males occupying annual home

Figure 12.13. Above surface (a) and subsurface (b) views of humpback males competing. (Courtesy P. Colla.)

Figure 12.14. Courting/mating group of Florida manatees with focal female in lead. Courtesy T. O'Shea, Sirenia Project, U.S. Geological Survey.

ranges at the extremes of the females' home ranges. During the spring breeding season, adult males leave these "male areas" and establish breeding territories (usually about one km long, each running parallel to shore) within "female areas" (Jameson, 1989). As is typical of polygynous mammals, juvenile male sea otters in both California and Alaska tend to disperse farther than females. Juvenile males ultimately move to "female areas," while juvenile females remain within "female areas" (Ralls *et al.*, 1996). Territorial boundaries and preferred resting sites within territories are related to patterns of kelp canopy cover, with some males expressing strong fidelity for the same territory over several successive years. It is not known if nonterritorial males are occasionally successful at inseminating females.

Polar bears are also polygynous. Sexual dimorphism is not highly developed, although males are noticeably larger than females at birth. Possibly in relation to the dispersed nature of their seal prey, aggregations of receptive female bears do not occur, and, much like their prey (e.g. ringed seals), male bears can only attend one female at a time (Wiig *et al.*, 1992). Females typically do not mate when accompanied by cubs of the year. Therefore, only about one-third of the adult females mate in any one year. Mating occurs in the spring and mature male polar bears travel extensively during this time on sea ice in search of receptive females. The breeding condition of females may be advertised by **pheromones** deposited on the ice via urine or from footpad secretions (Stirling, 1988). Whatever the mechanism, males recognize the scent and follow the tracks of a receptive female (sometimes over distances up to one hundred km) until she is located. Physical competition among males for available females is evidenced by scarring on the head and neck and by the increased frequency of broken teeth in older males (Stirling, 1988), although direct observations of such interactions are sparse. A successful male will remain with the female for several days, repeatedly testing her receptivity for mating. Repeated matings over several days probably occur. Mated females continue to hunt and increase their fat stores through the summer, then enter maternity dens dug in snow in November. Only pregnant polar bears enter dens; mothers with older offspring and all other bears remain active throughout the year (Ramsay and Stirling, 1988). These dens occur both on land and in multi-year pack ice. It is unclear whether pack ice denning is a result of increased human disturbance in traditional denning areas ashore.

12.6. Summary and Conclusions

The mating systems of marine mammals include monogamy, polygyny, and promiscuity. Among pinnipeds, all otariids and many species of phocids are polygynous. Almost all pinniped species which breed on land are extremely polygynous and strongly sexually dimorphic. Because polygynous males must compete for reproductive control of females, this competition revolves around either the establishment and defense of breeding territories (resource defense polygyny) or the establishment of dominance hierarchies (female or harem defense polygyny). Those pinnipeds that mate in water or on ice (walrus and ice seals) typically show a reduced level of polygyny that is explained, in part, by the difficulty of defending a resource or access to a female in an unstable environment. In such an environment (unlike on land) females may have the selective advantage of choosing the male with whom she will mate. Lek or lek-like mating strategies have been suggested for the Pacific walrus, California sea lion, and Hooker's sea lion. The traditional model for the evolution of pinniped phylogeny does not explain all forms of polygyny. Multiple origins for the evolution of ice breeding among phocids have been hypothesized. However, when the distribution of breeding habits of pinnipeds is examined in the context of a phylogenetic framework, an alternate hypothesis is suggested for the number of times that ice breeding evolved in seals.

Mating in cetaceans and sirenians is typically promiscuous. Odontocetes exist in social groups (e.g. schools, units, and pods). Spinner dolphins and bottlenose dolphin schools are among the best studied. Killer whales live in pods which are matrilineal social groups, characterized by their specific dialects, foraging strategies, and individual members. Sperm whales occur in associations of female and immature groups, or units. The basic social unit in mysticetes is a cow and a calf. The larger testes of gray, bowhead, and right whales have been interpreted as evidence of sperm competition. The sexual behavior of dugongs differs from that of manatees primarily in the intensity of violent competition between males for females, although some data suggest less harassment by males and a lek strategy. Sea otters and polar bears are polygynous breeders.

12.7. Further Reading

Pinniped mating systems are summarized by Boness (1991) and Le Boeuf (1991). A general introduction to cetacean mating systems can be found in Evans (1987). Manatee and dugong mating behaviors are discussed in Rathbun *et al.* (1995) and Anderson (1997). The classic paper on the evolution of pinniped mating systems is Bartholomew (1970) and for a more recent discussion see Costa (1993).

References

Alcorn, D. J. (1984). The Hawaiian monk seal on Laysan Island, 1982. *NOAA Tech. Mem.NMFS-SNFC* NMFS-SWFC-42.

Amos, B., S. Twiss, P. P. Pomeroy, and S. Anderson (1995). Evidence for mate fidelity in the gray seal. *Science* **268**: 1897–1899.

Anderson, P. K. (1997). Shark Bay dugongs in summer. 1. Lekking. *Behaviour* **134**: 433–462.

Baker, C. S., and L. M. Herman (1984). Aggressive behavior between humpback whales (*Megaptera novaeangliae*) on the Hawaiian wintering grounds. *Can. J. Zool.* **62**: 1922–1937.

Barlow, J. (1984). Reproductive seasonality in pelagic dolphins (*Stenella* spp.): Implications for measuring rates. *Rep. Int. Whal. Comm., Spec. Issue* **6.**

Bartholomew, G. A. (1970). A model for the evolution of pinniped polygyny. *Evolution* **24**: 546–559.

Bengtson, J. L. (1981). Ecology of manatees (*Trichechus manatus*) in the St. Johns River, Florida. Ph.D. thesis, Univ. Minnesota, Minneapolis.

Bengtson, J. L., and D. B. Siniff (1981). Reproductive aspects of female crabeater seals, *Lobodon carcinophagus,* along the Antarctic Peninsula. *Can J. Zool.* **59**: 92–102.

Berta, A., and T. A. Deméré (1993). The evolution of pinniped aquatic locomotor patterns. *Abstr. 10th Bienn. Conf. Biol. Mar. Mamm.*, Galveston, TX.

Bigg, M. A. (1981). Harbour seal- *Phoca vitulina* and *P. largha. In* "Handbook of Marine Mammals" (S. H. Ridgway and R. J. Harrison, eds.), Vol. 2, pp. 1–27. Academic Press, London.

Bigg, M. A., P. F. Olesiuk, G. M. Ellis, J. K. B. Ford, and K. C. Balcomb (1990). Social organization and genealogy of resident killer whales (*Orcinus orca*) in the coastal waters of British Columbia and Washington State. *Rep. Int. Whal. Comm., Spec. Issue* **12**: 383–406.

Boness, D. J. (1991). Determinants of mating systems in the Otariidae (Pinnipedia). *In* "The Behaviour of Pinnipeds" (D. Renouf, ed.), pp. 1–44.

Boness, D. J., S. S. Anderson, and C. R. Cox (1982). Functions of female aggression during the pupping and mating season of gray seals, *Halichoerus grypus* (Fabricius). *Can. J. Zool.* **60**: 2270–2278.

Bonner, W. N. (1984). Lactation strategies in pinnipeds: Problems for a marine mammalian group. *In* "Physiological Strategies in Lactation" (M. Peaker, R. G. Vernon, and C. H. Knight, eds., 253–272). Academic Press, London.

Bonner, W. N. (1990). "The Natural History of Seals." Fact on File, New York.

Brownell, R. L. J., and K. Ralls (1986). Potential for sperm competition in baleen whales. *Rep. Int. Whal. Comm.*, Spec. Issue **8**: 97–112.

Campagna, C., B. J. Le Boeuf, and H. L. Cappozzo (1988). Group raids: A mating strategy of male southern sea lions. *Behavior* **105**: 224–246.

Cassini, M. H., and B. L. Vila (1990). Male mating behavior of the southern sea lion. *Bull. Mar. Sci.* **46**: 555–559.

Clapham, P. J. (1996). The social and reproductive biology of Humpback Whales: An ecological perspective. *Mamm. Rev.* **26**(1): 27–49.

Clapham, P. J., P. J. Palsboll, D. K. Mattila, and O. Vasquez (1992). Composition and the dynamics of humpback whales, *Megaptera novaeangliae,* in the southern Gulf of Maine. *Can. J. Zool.* **71**: 440–443.

Clinton, W. L. and B. J. Le Boeuf. (1993). Sexual selection's effects on male life history and the pattern of male mortality. *Ecology* **74**(6): 1884–1892.

Connor, R. C., M. R. Heithaus, and L. Barre (1999). Superalliance of bottlenose dolphins, *Nature* **397**: 571–572.

Connor, R. C., R. A. Smolker, and A. F. Richards (1992). Two levels of alliance formation among male bottlenose dolphins (*Tursiops* sp.). *Proc. Natl. Acad. Sci., USA* **89**: 987–990.

Connor, R. C., J. Mann, P. L. Tyak, and H. Whitehead (1998). Social evolution in toothed whales. *Trends in Ecology and Evolution* **13**: 228–232.

Costa, D. P. (1993). The relationship between reproductive and foraging energetics and the evolution of the Pinnipedia. *Symp. Zool. Soc. London* **66**: 293–312.

Emlen, S. T., and L. W. Oring (1977). Ecology, sexual selection, and the evolution of mating systems. *Science* **197**: 215–223.

Evans, P. G. H. (1987). "The Natural History of Whales and Dolphins" Facts on File, New York.

Fay, F. H. (1982). "Ecology and Biology of the Pacific Walrus, *Odobenus rosmarus divergens* Illiger, "North Am. Fauna, Ser. U.S. Dep. Int. Fish Wildl. Serv., No. 74.

Ford, J. K. B., G. M. Ellis, and K. C. Balcomb (1994). "Killer Whales: The Natural History and Genealogy of *Orcinus orca* in British Columbia and Washington State." University of Washington Press, Seattle.

Francis, J. M., and D. J. Boness (1991). The effect of thermoregulatory behavior on the mating system of the Juan Fernandez fur seal, *Arctocephalus philippii. Behaviour* **119**(1–2): 104–126.

Gentry, R. L. (1998). "Behavior and Ecology of the Northern Fur Seal." Princeton Univ. Press, New Jersey.

Gisiner, R. C. (1985). Male territoriality and reproductive behavior in the Steller sea lion, *Eumetopias jubatus.* Ph.D. dissertation, Univ. California, Santa Cruz.

Glockner-Ferrari, D. A., and M. J. Ferrari (1984). Reproduction in humpback whales, *Megaptera novaeangliae,* occurring in Hawaiian waters. *Rep. Int. Whal. Comm., Spec. Issue* **6**: 237–242.

Haley, M. P., C. J., Deutsch, and B. J. Le Boeuf (1994). Size, dominance and copulatory success in male northern elephant seals, *Mirounga angustirostris. Anim. Behav.* **48:** 1249–1260.

Harris, A. S., J. S. F. Young, and J. M. Wright (1991). DNA fingerprinting of harbour seals *(Phoca vitulina concolor)*: Male mating behaviour may not be a reliable indicator of reproductive success. *Can J. Zool.* **69**: 1862–1866.

Heath, C. B., and J. M. Francis (1983). Breeding behavior in the California sea lion, Mugu Lagoon and San Nicholas Island. *Ecol. Res. Symp.* **3**: 145–150.

Heath, C. B., and J. M. Francis (1987). Mechanisms and consequences of mate choice in the California sea lion. *Abstr. 7th Bienn. Conf. Biol. Mar. Mamm.*, Miami, FL.

Herzing, D. L. (1997). The life history of free-ranging Atlantic spotted dolphins *(Stenella frontalis)*: Age classes, color phases and female reproduction. *Mar. Mamm. Sci.* **13**: 576–595.

Higgins, L. V., D. P. Costa, A. C. Huntley, and B. J. Le Boeuf (1988). Behavior and physiological measurements of the maternal investment in the Steller sea lion, *Eumetopias jubatus. Mar. Mamm. Sci.* **4**: 44058.

Hoover, A. (1983). Behavior and ecology of harbor seals *(Phoca vitulina richardsi)* inhabiting glacial ice in Aialik Bay, Alaska. M.S. Thesis, University of Alaska, Anchorage.

Irvine, B., and R. S. Wells (1972). Results of attempts to tag Atlantic bottlenosed dolphins *(Tursiops truncatus). Cetology* **13**: 1–5.

Jameson, R. J. (1989). Movements, home range, and territories of male sea otters off central California. *Mar. Mamm. Sci.* **5**: 159–172.

Johanos, T. C., B. L. Becker, M. A. Brown, B. K. Choy, L. M. Hiruki, R. E. Brainard, and R. L. Westlake (1990). The Hawaiian monk seal on Laysan Island: 1988. *NOAA (Natl. Oceanic Atmos. Adm.) Tech. Mem. NMFS-SWMFS-151.*

Johnson, C. M., and K. S. Norris (1994). Social behavior. *In* "The Hawaiian Spinner Dolphin" (K. S. Norris, B. Würsig, R. S. Wells, and M. Würsig, eds.), pp. 243–286. University of California Press, Berkeley.

Jones, M. L., and S. L. Swartz (1984). Demography and phenology of gray whales *(Eschrichtius robustus)* in Laguna San Ignacio, Baja California Sur, Mexico. *In* "The Gray Whale, *Eschrichtius robustus* (Lilljeborg, 1861)" M. L. Jones, S. L. Swartz, and S. Leatherwood, eds.), pp. 309–374. Academic Press, New York.

Kovacs, K. M. (1990). Mating strategies in male hooded seals *(Cystophora cristata)? Can. J. Zool.* **68**: 2499–2502.

Le Boeuf, B. J. (1986). Sexual strategies of seals and walruses. *New Sci.* **1491**: 36–39.

Le Boeuf, B. J. (1991). Pinniped mating systems on land, ice, and in water: Emphasis on the Phocidae. *In* "The Behaviour of Pinnipeds" (D. Renouf, ed.), pp. 45–65. Chapman & Hall, London.

Le Boeuf, B. J., and R. M. Laws (1994). Elephant Seals: An introduction to the genus. *In* "Elephant Seals" (B. J. Le Boeuf and R. M. Laws, eds.), pp. 1–26. University of California Press, Berkeley.

Le Boeuf, B. J., and S. Mesnick (1990). Sexual behavior of male northern elephant seals. I. Lethal injuries to adult females. *Behaviour* **16**: 143–162.

Le Boeuf, B. J., and J. Reiter (1988). Lifetime reproductive success in northern elephant seals. *In* "Reproductive Success" (T. H. Clutton-Brock, ed.), pp. 344–362. University of Chicago Press, Chicago.

Lockyer, C. (1984). Review of baleen whale (Mysticeti) reproduction and implications for management. *Rep. Int. Whal. Comm., Spec. Issue* **6**: 27–50.

McCann, T. S. (1981). Aggression and sexual activity of male southern elephant seals, *Mirounga leonina* (L.). *Biol. J. Linn. Soc.* **14**: 133–150.

McRae, S. B., and K. M. Kovacs (1994). Paternity exclusion by DNA fingerprinting, and mate guarding in the hooded seal, *Cystophora cristata. Mol. Ecol.* **3**: 101–107.

Medrano, L. M. Salinas, I. Salas, P. Ladronde Guevara, and A. Aguayo (1994). Sex identification of humpback whales, *Megaptera novaeangliae,* on the wintering grounds of the Mexican Pacific Ocean. *Can. J. Zool.* **72**: 1771–1774.

Mobley, J. R. J., and L. M. Herman (1985). Transience of social affiliations among humpback whales *(Megaptera novaeangliae)* on the Hawaiian wintering grounds. *Can J. Zool.* **63**: 762–772.

Modig, A. O. (1996). Effect of body size on male reproductive behavior in the southern elephant seal. *Anim. Behav.* **51**: 1295–1306.

Norris, K. S. (Ed.) (1994). "The Hawaiian Spinner Dolphin." Univ. California Press, Berkeley. 408pp.

Norris, K. S., and C. M. Johnson (1994). Locomotion. *In* "The Hawaiian Spinner Dolphin" (K. S. Norris, B. Würsig, R. S. Wells, and M. Würsig, eds.), pp. 201–205. University of California Press, Berkeley.

O'Shea, T. J. (1994). Manatees. *Sci. Am.* **273**: 66–72.

Pack, A. A., D. R. Salden, M. J. Ferrari, D. A. Glockner-Ferrari, L. M. Herman, H. A. Stubbs, and J. M. Straley (1998). Male humpback whale dies in competitive group. *Mar. Mamm. Sci.* **14**: 861–873.

Perry, E. A., S. M. Carr, S. E. Bartlett, and W. S. Davidson (1995). A phylogenetic perspective on the evolution of reproduction behavior in pagophilic seals of the Northwest Atlantic as indicated by mitochondrial DNA sequences. *J. Mammal.* **76**: 22–31.

Preen, A. (1989). Observations of mating behavior in dugongs. *Mar. Mamm. Sci.* **5**: 382–386.

Ralls, K., T. C. Eagle, and D. B. Siniff (1996). Movement and spatial use patterns of California sea otters. *Can. J. Zool.* **74**: 1841–1849.

Ramsay, M. A. and I. Stirling (1988). Reproductive biology of female polar bears *(Ursus maritimus). J. Zool.* **214**: 601–634.

Rathbun, G. B., and T. J. O'Shea (1984). The manatee's simple social life. *In* "The Encyclopedia of Mammals" (D. Macdonald, ed.), pp. 300–301. Facts on File, New York.

Rathbun, G. B., J. P. Reid, R. K. Bonde, T. J. O'Shea, and J. A. Powell (1995). Reproduction in free-ranging Florida manatees. *In* "Population Biology of the Florida Manatee" (T. J. O'Shea, B. B. Ackerman, and H. F. Percival, eds.). U. S. Dept. of the Interior, Washington, DC.

Renouf, D., and J. W. Lawson (1986). Harbour seal vigilance: Watching for predators or mates. *Biol. Behav.* **11**: 44–49.

Reynolds, J. E., III, and D. E. Odell (1991). "Manatees and Dugongs." Facts on File, New York.

Riedman, M. (1990). "The Pinnipeds: Seals, Sea Lions, and Walruses." University of California Press, Berkeley.

Samuels, A., and T. Gifford (1997). A quantitative assessment of dominance relationships of dominance relationships among bottlenose dolphins. *Mar. Mamm. Sci.* **13**(1): 70–99.

Scott, M. D., R. S. Wells, and A. B. Irvine (1989). A long-term study of bottlenose dolphins on the west coast of Florida. *In* "The Bottlenose Dolphin" (S. Leatherwood and R. R. Reeves, eds.), pp. 235–244. Academic Press, Orlando, FL.

Sjare, B., and I. Stirling (1996). The breeding behavior of Atlantic walruses, *Odobenus rosmarus rosmarus,* in the Canadian high Arctic. *Can. J. Zool.* **74**: 897–911.

Stirling, I. (1975). Factors affecting the evolution of social behavior in the pinnipedia. *Rapp. P-V. Reun., cons. Int. Explor. Mer.* **169**: 205–212.

Stirling, I. (1988). "Polar Bears." University of Michigan Press, Ann Arbor.

Stirling, I., W. Calvert, and H. Cleator (1983). Underwater vocalizations as a tool for studying the distribution and relative abundance of wintering pinnipeds in the high arctic. *Arctic* **36**: 262–274.

Tyak, P., and H. Whitehead (1982). Male competition in large groups of wintering humpback whales. *Behaviour* **83**: 1–23.

Watkins, J. F. (1990). Observations of an aquatic gray seal (*Halichoerus grypus*) mating. *J. Zool.* **222**: 677–680.

Weinrich, M. (1995). Humpback whale competitive groups observed on a high-latitude feeding ground. *Mar. Mamm. Sci.* **11**(2): 251–254.

Wells, R. S., M. D. Scott, and A. B. Irvine (1987). The social structure of free-ranging bottlenose dolphins on the west coast of Florida. *In* "Current Mammalogy" (H. H. Genoways, ed.), Vol. 1, pp. 235–244. Plenum, New York.

Whitehead, H. (1993). The behaviour of mature male sperm whales on the Galapagos Islands breeding grounds. *Can J. Zool.* **71**: 689–699.

Whitehead, H. (1996). Babysitting, dive synchrony, and indications of alloparental care. *Behav. Evol. Sociobiol.* **38**: 237–244.

Whitehead, H., and B. Kahn (1992). Temporal and geographic variation in the social structure of female sperm whales. *Can. J. Zool.* **70**: 2145—2149.

Whitehead, H., and H. Waters (1990). Social organization and population structure of sperm whales off the Galapagos Islands, Ecuador (1985 and 1987). *Rep. Int. Whal. Comm., Spec. Issue* **12**: 1–440.

Whitehead, H., S. Waters, and T. Lyrholm (1991). Social organization of female sperm whales and their offspring: Constant companions and casual acquaintances. *Behav. Ecol. Sociobiol.* **29**: 385–389.

Wiig, O., I. Gjertz, R. Hansson, and J. Thomassen (1992). Breeding behaviour of polar bears in Hornsund, Svalbard. *Polar Rec.* **28**: 157–159.

13

Reproductive Structures, Patterns, and Strategies

13.1. Introduction

Successful reproduction, the transmission of genetic information from parents to offspring, can be defined in terms of genetic or reproductive fitness. Individuals with high genetic fitness survive longer, reproduce more, and through natural selection, transfer more copies of their genes to subsequent generations. Like other mammals, the exaggerated difference in the costs of gamete production between male and female marine mammals (sperm is abundant and cheap; eggs are rare and expensive) has set the stage for the evolution of very different roles in the reproductive process for males and females of the same species. Females, in addition to producing relatively expensive eggs, bear all the costs of pregnancy, lactation following birth, and most if not all other costs associated with postnatal care and teaching of offspring. Consequently, males are free to invest their energies in activities associated with controlling access of other males to females, or competing with other males in other ways (e.g. sperm competition), or mating with as many females as possible.

All groups of marine mammals share several features of reproduction which stem from their placental mammalian heritage. These basic conditions of reproduction are reflected in the strategies for care and nourishment of the young, and in the resulting life histories of these animals (discussed in this chapter and the following chapters). Sex determination is based on male **heterogamy** (males have XY sex chromosomes and female **homogamy** (females have XX sex chromosomes), resulting in male:female ratios very close to 1:1 (see Fredga, 1988, for mammalian exceptions). In contrast to the variety of sex determination mechanisms employed by some other vertebrates groups, male heterogamy of mammals has constrained the mechanics of mammalian sex determination into an evolutionary dead-end. Sex ratios are almost always very close to 1:1, even though other sex ratios might be adaptive in some reproductive conditions, such as moderate to intense polygyny (see Bull and Charnov, 1985, for a review of this topic). Males that are completely excluded from reproduction by the actions of other polygynous males have zero reproductive fitness, and male heterogamy disallows the possibility of gender transformation (as is possible in some other vertebrate groups) to achieve higher fitness as females.

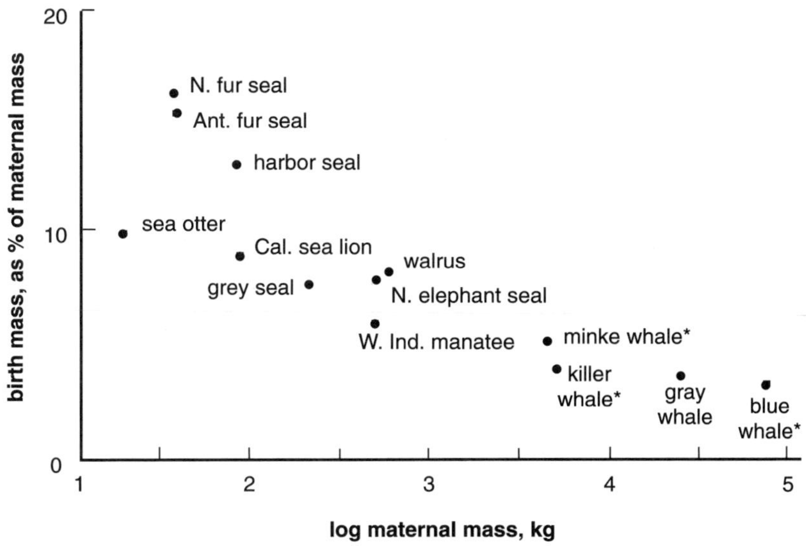

Figure 13.1. Birth mass, as percentage of maternal mass for 13 species of marine mammals, spanning several orders of magnitude in body mass. Sources listed in Tables 13.1 and 13.5* weights estimated from length and girth measurements

In all placental mammals, embryonic and fetal development occurs within the mother's uterus during extended **gestation** periods. Pregnancy is maintained by the production of chorionic gonadotropin, a placental hormone that acts as an ovulation blocker until birth (parturition) occurs. At birth, most young marine mammals are precocious, capable of swimming or moving on ice or land. For a time after birth, ranging from four days in hooded seals (Bowen *et al.*, 1985) to several years in some otariids, walruses, polar bears, odontocetes, and sirenians, mothers produce fat-rich milk as the sole source of nutrition for their developing and nutritionally dependent offspring. Neonates, being necessarily smaller than their mothers, have high surface to volume ratios with thinner fat or blubber layers and the resulting heat loss rate is higher than that that of adults (see Chapter 7). Therefore, species at the smaller end of the range of observed sizes of marine mammals tend to produce large offspring (relative to their mother's sizes; Fig. 13.1) that grow rapidly after birth.

The reproductive organs and associated structures are typically mammalian, with some specialization to accommodate body streamlining and, in pinnipeds, to protect testes and nipples during terrestrial locomotion. These specializations are described in the following section.

13.2. Anatomy and Physiology of the Reproductive System

13.2.1. Reproductive Structures

Male—In phocid seals, and the walrus, the testes are inguinal and lie lateral to the penis (Fig. 13.2). In otariids, as in other carnivores, the testes lie outside the inguinal ring termed scrotal. Pinnipeds possess a **baculum**, or penis bone, which is the ossified anterior end of

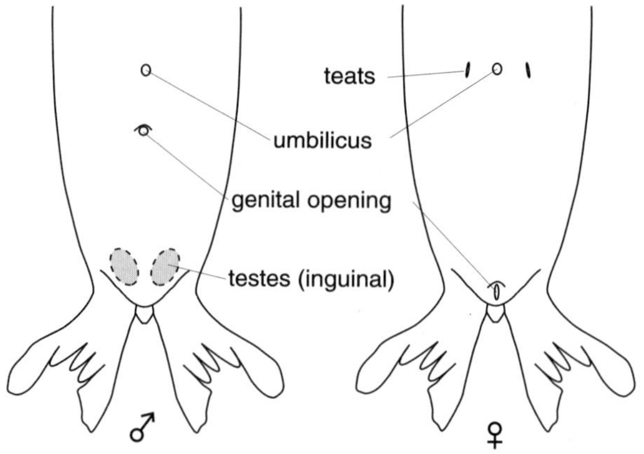

Figure 13.2. External sexual differences of pinnipeds. (Redrawn from Laws and Sinha, 1993.)

the corpus cavernosum (Fig. 13.3). The baculum of the walrus and phocid seals is large relative to that of otariids (King, 1983), but otariids have a more complex shape relative to phocids or the walrus (Morejohn, 1975). The testes are ovoid, circular in cross section, and twice as long as they are broad. The weight of each testis increases with age, with a rapid increase associated with the onset of sexual maturity.

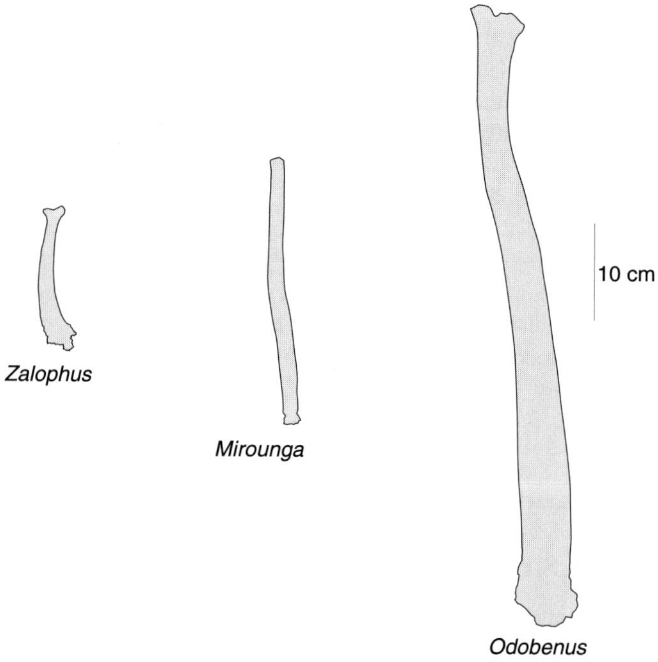

Figure 13.3. Bacula of adult males of three pinnipeds.

Sperm are produced in the testes, then pass into the epididymis, which as in all mammals are long, coiled tubes that lie alongside each testis. The sperm mature as they pass along this tube and are stored near its end, the tail of the epididymis. The ductus deferens, which arises from the epididymis, passes, together with the testicular ligament and blood vessels, through an opening into the abdominal cavity. The sperm pass from the short ductus deferens to the urethra and then out of the penis during ejaculation. The prostate gland, which contributes fluid that nourishes the sperm, surrounds the neck of the bladder (Laws and Sinha, 1993).

The only conspicuous external difference between the sexes in cetaceans is the distance between the anus and the genital slit, in which males is approximately 10% of the body length, but in females the genital slit appears to be continuous with the anal opening and has a mammary slit situated on either side (Fig. 13.4). In all cetaceans, the testes are located in the abdominal cavity, slightly behind and to the side of the kidneys. They are elongated, cylindrical and oval or round in cross section. The testicle weight to body weight ratio of cetaceans (see Fig. 12.12) can sometimes be very high, among the greatest recorded for mammals. According to data presented by Slijper (1966), for the largest cetacean, the blue whale, the testes may be 45 cm long and increase to 45 kg each during breeding seasons. The typical mammalian accessory glands are represented only by the prostate, which surrounds the urogenital canal.

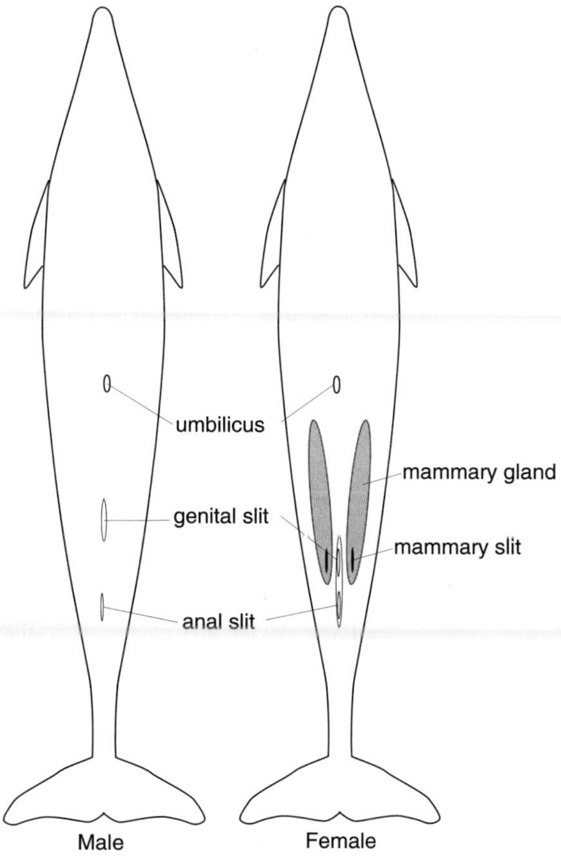

Figure 13.4. External sexual differences of cetaceans.

Neither cetaceans or sirenians possess a baculum. The penis is totally concealed in the body when in the retracted state (Fig. 13.5). The fibroelastic penis of large baleen whales reaches 2.5–3 m in length and up to 30 cm in diameter (Slijper, 1966). In all cetaceans, the penis is erected by muscle fibers and not by vasodilation. Both the firbroelastic penis and associated penis retractor muscle appear to be synapomorphies shared by artiodactyls and cetaceans (Pabst *et al.*, 1998). Based on anatomical constraints, copulation is assumed to occur belly-to-belly in all cetaceans, although it is rarely observed.

The testes in manatees and dugongs are abdominal and the seminal vesicles are large (Fig. 13.6). The nonglandular prostate of manatees is composed of erectile muscular tissue (Caldwell and Caldwell, 1985) and is absent in the dugong. Bulbourethral-type glandular tissue is dispersed among the muscles close to the base of the penis in dugongs (Nishiwaki and Marsh, 1985).

Female—The ovaries in pinnipeds lie close to the posterolateral wall of the abdominal cavity near the kidneys and are enclosed in large peritoneal bursae (Fig. 13.7). The size and shape of the ovaries depends on the age and reproductive status of the female. During pregnancy the follicle undergoes major physiological changes and develops into a **corpus luteum** which produces hormones that maintain the placenta for the duration of gestation. After birth, the corpus luteum degenerates into a small, hard structure termed a **corpus albicans** which, in cetaceans, persists for the life of the female. In other marine mammals the duration of a recognizable corpus albicans varies between species and individuals, and remnants of the corpus albicans may persist for several years in some species (Laws and Sinha, 1993). The uterus is bicornate (two horned) as in most mammals, but posteriorly the horns join to form a short uterus. The vagina is long and separated from the vestibule by a fleshy hymenal fold. Both the anus and vestibule open into a common furrow which is surrounded by muscular tissue that act as a sphincter. An os clitoridis (bone) is present in pinnipeds, but its appearance even within a single species is irregular (King, 1983).

In cetaceans, the two ovaries lie in the abdominal cavity (Fig. 13.8); in toothed whales the ovaries are held within well-developed deep ovarian pouches, but in baleen whales they are more exposed. Ovaries of baleen whales are oval, elongated, and convoluted and in toothed whales the ovaries are spherical and usually smooth. Ovaries of mature whales resemble a bunch of grapes in which the "grapes" are protruding follicles of different stages

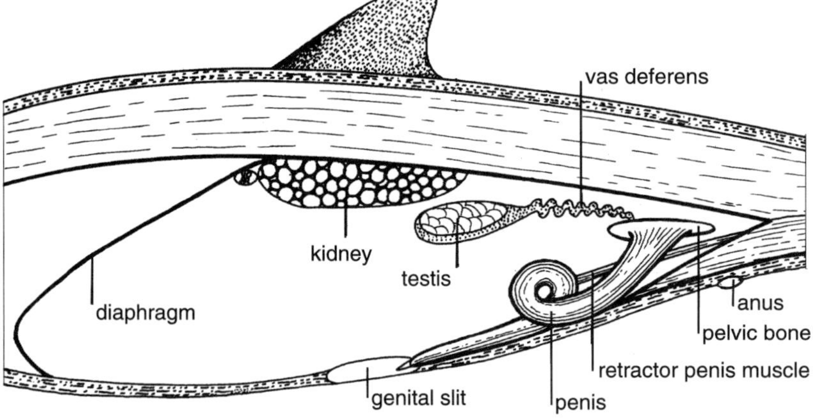

Figure 13.5. Cetacean male reproductive system. (Adapted from Slijper, 1966.)

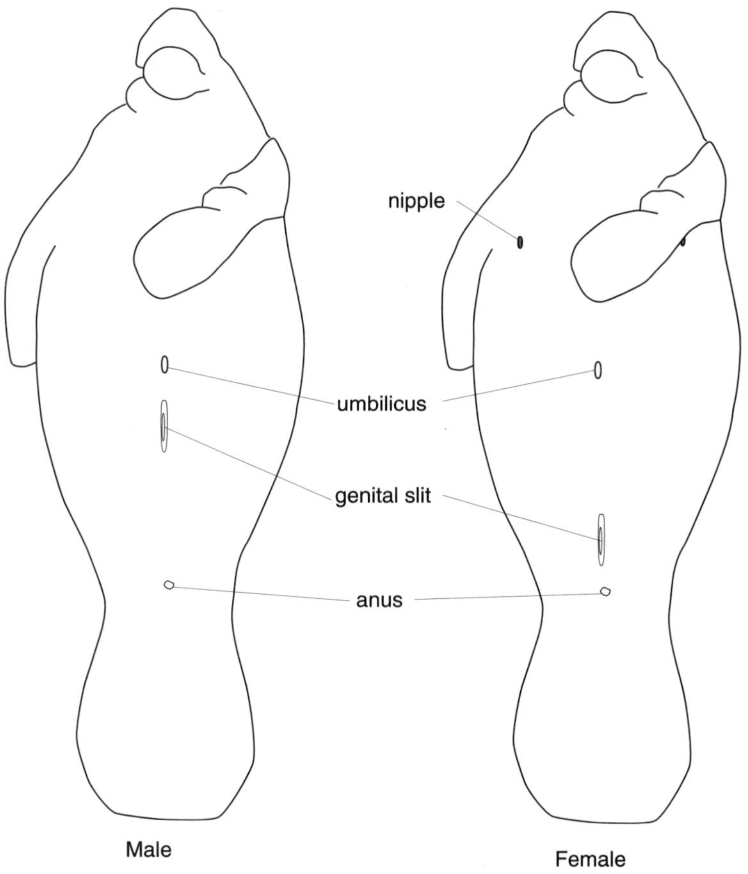

Figure 13.6. External sexual differences of sirenians (Adapted from Reynolds and Odell, 1991.)

of development (Fig. 13.9). For details of the morphology and histology of mysticete ovaries see Perrin and Donovan (1984). Follicular development is described in Laws (1962), Slijper (1966), and Harrison (1969) for fin whales, and in Rice and Wolman (1971) for gray whales.

A peculiarity of whales is that the corpora albicans remain for the entirety of an animal's life, providing a record of past ovulations. This makes it possible to examine the reproductive history and estimate ages of individual whales; each corpus albicans represents one ovulation (although not necessarily a pregnancy; see also Chapter 14). In mysticetes (unlike several odontocetes such as phocoenids, where the left ovary usually predominates and is more active at least initially), both ovaries are fully functional and able to ovulate from the onset of sexual maturity. The uterus of cetaceans is bicornate as in pinnipeds. The vagina is covered with longitudinal and transverse folds termed "pseudocervices" which are shared by artiodactyls and cetaceans (Pabst *et al.*, 1998). Distinctive vaginal plugs have been described for several toothed whales (Yablokov *et al.*, 1972).

Dugong ovaries are very large (up to 15 cm long), flattened, and ellipsoidal. Each lies in a peritoneal pouch hidden in the dorsal abdominal wall posterior to the kidney and lateral

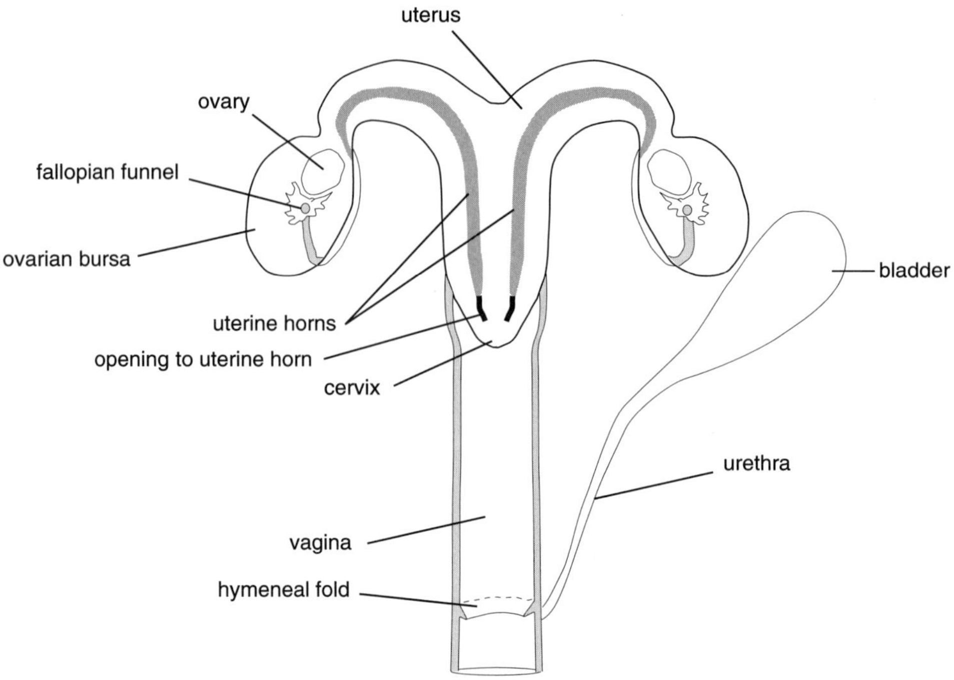

Figure 13.7. Pinniped female reproductive system. (Adapted from King, 1983.)

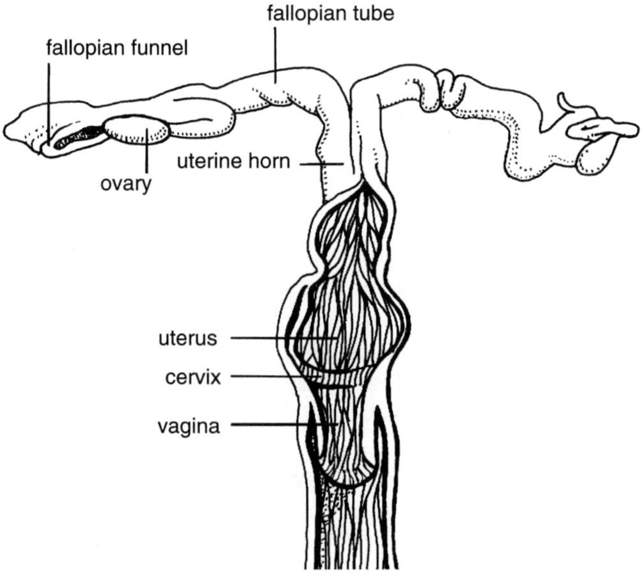

Figure 13.8. Cetacean female reproductive system.

to the ureter (Nishiwaki and Marsh, 1985). The ovaries of manatees consist of large masses of bead-like spherules and lack a heavy capsular coat (Caldwell and Caldwell, 1985). The uterus of sirenians is bicornate. The dugong vagina is a long straight tube with a very capacious lumen which possesses a raised shield-like region of keratinized material in its vault into which the cervix projects. The clitoris possesses a large conical glans (Nishiwaki and Marsh, 1985).

The ovary of the sea otter is a roughly lens-shaped, compressed oval with simple or complexly branched surface fissures (Estes, 1980). Changes in ovary form and in the gross anatomy and histology of the bicornate uterus through various stages of estrus and through pregnancy are described by Sinha *et al.* (1966).

The size and shape of the mammary glands differ between phocids and otariids. Otariids and the walrus possess four mammary teats, located on the ventral abdominal wall anterior and posterior to the umbilicus. The bearded seal and the monk seals also have four teats, whereas all other phocids have only two abdominal teats adjacent to or posterior to the umbilicus (Fig. 13.2; King, 1983). The nipples of all pinnipeds are retractile.

The mammae of cetaceans consist of long, flat glands located along the belly on either side of the urogenital fold (Fig. 13.4). Their ducts open to a single nipple on each side (retained within mammary slits), and both are retracted in a skin pouch at rest (Yablokov *et al.*, 1972). The thickness (depth) of the glands depends on the sexual status of the female. The immature gland in blue and fin whales is thin (about 2.5 cm thick) and thickens with the onset of sexual maturity. The depth and color of the glands are important criteria in assessing the sexual status of an individual female (Lockyer, 1984).

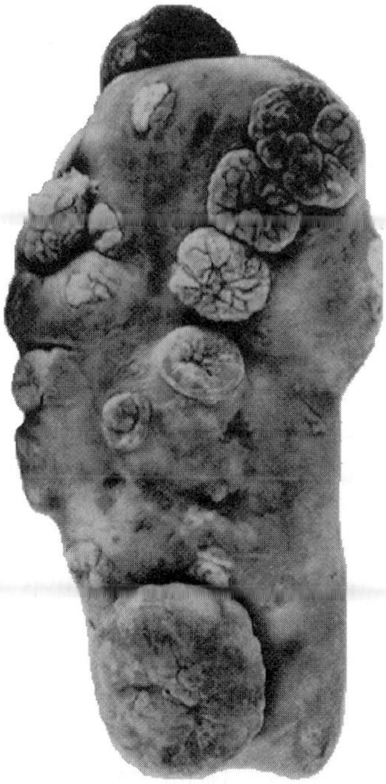

Figure 13.9. Left ovary of a Pacific white-sided dolphin showing corpora albicantia. (From Harrison and Bryden, 1988.)

The mammary glands of sirenians consist of a single teat on each side located in the axilla (armpit) almost at the posterior border of the flipper (Fig. 13.6; Harrison and King, 1980).

Sea otters and polar bears have four mammae. In comparison to their closest relative, the brown bear, and the black bear, which have 6 mammae, reduction of the number of mammae in polar bears may be a function of the smaller average litter size of polar bears (further discussed in Chapter 14; Derocher, 1990).

13.2.2. Ovulation and Estrus

Reproduction in marine mammals is characterized by a cycle of events regulated by both the nervous and endocrine systems, and especially by a reciprocal feedback regulation between reproductive hormones and the organs that secrete them. For many species this cycle is superimposed upon or entrained into annual patterns of migration to and from areas used for reproduction (described later in this chapter and in Chapter 11).

The ovulation cycle of marine mammals includes a period of follicle growth and release of an ovum (usually only one) from an ovarian follicle and the subsequent development of a corpus luteum at the site of the ruptured follicle. Both the follicle and the corpus luteum contribute hormones necessary to prepare the uterus for implantation of the egg if fertilization does occur. The term **estrus** defines both the time period of maximum reproductive receptivity of female mammals as well as the associated receptive behavior. Estrus occurs simultaneously with and immediately following ovulation, but the timing varies among marine mammal groups. Phocids and otariids have a **postpartum estrus** in which estrus follows immediately after parturition, when there is a rapid regression of the corpus luteum from the previous pregnancy in one ovary, accompanied by rapid growth of follicles in the opposite ovary; one of those follicles ovulates to initiate the next cycle. Most otariids mate between one and two weeks after parturition. The time delay between parturition and estrus and mating in phocids is more variable, but estrus is always near the end of lactation or soon after weaning has occurred (Riedman, 1990). Walruses are **polyestrous**: females enter one estrus period about four months postpartum when males are not producing sperm, then again about six months later when males are actively producing sperm and fertilization can occur. Phocids and otariids are often thought to be **monestrous**, with only one estrus cycle each year (Riedman, 1990). However, this has been challenged. Captive harbor and Hawaiian monk seals are definitely polyestrous and some evidence exists to suggest that this is also true for gray seals (Pomeroy, pers. comm.)

Estrus and mating is more difficult to document in cetaceans than in pinnipeds, and so less is known of the timing of these reproductive events for most species. Gestation periods usually last between 11 and 18 months, and almost all cetaceans exhibit multi-year reproductive cycles (Table 13.1), with mating and parturition usually separated by at least one, and sometimes two or more years. High latitude odontocetes, such as beluga whales, and all migratory mysticetes have well-defined seasonal periods of estrus and mating (Evans, 1987), although mating behaviors can be observed in many of these species throughout the year.

In mysticetes, some uncertainty exists concerning the timing of ovulation (and subsequent conception) for many species. For example, in a historical examination of gray whale ovaries, Rice and Wolman (1971) found that all (n=28) mature southbound female gray

Table 13.1. Birth Weights, Total Gestation Periods, and Reproductive Intervals in Some Marine Mammals.

Species	Approximate birth mass(kg)	Total gestation(mo)	Reproductive interval(yrs)	Source
Pinnipeds				
Phocids				
Harbor seal	11	9.5–12.5	1	Bowen (1991)*
Gray seal	16	11	1	Bowen (1991)*
N. elephant seal	40	11	1	Bowen (1991)*
Otariids				
N. fur seal	6	12	1	Bowen (1991)*
CA. sea lion	8	11	1	Bowen (1991)*
Antarctic fur seal	6	12	1	Bowen (1991)*
Walrus	50	14–16	2–4	Sease and Chapman (1988)
Cetaceans				
Odontocetes				
Dall's porpoise	na	7–11.4	na	Gaskin *et al.* (1984)*
Harbor porpoise	na	8–11	na	Gaskin *et al.* (1984)*
Bottlenose dolphin	na	12	na	Perrin and Reilly (1984)*
Spinner dolphin	na	9.5–10.7	na	
Killer whale	200	16–17	5	Ford *et al.* (1994)
Sperm whale	1050	14.5–16.5	3	Lockyer (1981)
Mysticetes				
Minke whale	230	10	1–2	Mitchell (1986)
Gray whale	920	11–13	2	Sumich (1986a,b)
Blue whale	2500	11–12	2–3	Rice (1986)
Sirenians				
Manatee	30	12–13	2–5	Reynolds and Odell (1991)
Dugong	na	13.9	3–7	Marsh (1995)
Other Marine Mammals				
Sea otter	2	6–7	1	Jameson and Johnson (1993)
Polar bear	0.7	8	2–4	Stirling (1988); Derocher and Stirling (1995)

Symbols: na=not available
*see for original sources.

whales not carrying near-term fetuses had recently ovulated and were presumably in very early stages of pregnancy. These animals were collected off central California, so the timing of ovulation and conception was assumed by Rice and Wolman (1971) to have occurred during earlier, more northerly portions of the southern migration. Vigorous and extensive courting and mating behaviors of adults, presumably with the goal of fertilization, are observed easily during the latter portion of their southern migration and especially for the month or so spent in winter "breeding" lagoons at the southern terminus of this migration.

If female gray whales have already ovulated and are indeed pregnant well before entering winter lagoons, our estimate of the timing of conception derived from direct histological examination is at odds with evidence based on field observations of copulatory behavior.

Manatees and dugongs are **polyovular**, producing numerous corpora lutea per pregnancy (Figure 13.10). Such large numbers of corpora may be necessary to produce sufficient progesterone to maintain pregnancy (Marmontel, 1995).

In sea otters mating may take place with or without the formation of pair bonds, which typically last from 1–4 days. Sexual receptivity of females ends soon after pair-bond dissolution suggesting that estrus averages 3–4 days (Riedman and Estes, 1990).

Field observations and observations of captive indicate that polar bears are **induced ovulators**, with ovulation occurring only when the female is stimulated by the presence and activity of a male. Mating occurs in the spring but implantation of the blastocyst is delayed until autumn. At the time of implantation females stop feeding and enter dens in which they spend the winter without food and water (Ramsay and Stirling, 1988). Polar bears have reproductive rates that are among the lowest for terrestrial mammals. The average reproductive interval for females is 2–3 or sometimes even 4 years. Low reproductive output is due to late maturation, small litters, and long birth intervals, all of which are influenced by fluctuation in marine productivity and the availability of seal prey (Derocher and Stirling, 1995).

13.2.3. Pregnancy and Birth

The duration of gestation in placental mammals ranges from 18 days in jumping mice to about 18 months in rhinoceroses to 22–24 months in elephants (Vaughan, 1986). In terres-

Figure 13.10. Multiple corpora (arrows) on the ovary of a mature Florida manatee. (From Marmontel, 1995.)

trial species, gestation duration is roughly related to the size of the fetus; larger fetuses require longer gestation periods to develop. For many marine mammals, both parturition and fertilization occur in the same geographic location and at the same time of year, but in successive years, and gestation periods are between one and three years in duration regardless of body size (Table 13.1). Consequently, large cetaceans must accelerate fetal development to complete gestation within one or more years whereas sea otters, polar bears, and most pinnipeds must stretch it out to prolong gestation for a year.

As all species of pinnipeds give birth out of water, and most also copulate onshore or on ice, gestation periods can be determined by observing known or identified individuals at least intermittently from the date of copulation to subsequent birth. For cetaceans and sirenians however, both copulation and birth occur in water, usually in conditions out of human sight. Observations of cetacean births in the wild are few (for descriptions of gray whale births, see Balcomb, 1974; Mills and Mills, 1979; for right whales, see Best, 1981). Furthermore, our attempts to visually determine when fertilization actually occurs are complicated by copulatory behaviors of some cetaceans that serve nonreproductive social purposes rather than insemination (Johnson and Norris, 1994).

The postpartum estrus characterizing most species of pinnipeds establishes a time frame of nearly one year between copulation and birth is, even when an entire year is not required to complete fetal development. Adjustments to fit gestation periods of less than one year into an annual time frame are accomplished by a reproductive phenomenon known as **seasonal delayed implantation** (see Sandell, 1990, for a review of this topic). In seasonal delayed implantation, the zygote undergoes several cell divisions to form a hollow ball of a few hundred cells, the blastocyst, which then lies undifferentiated in the female's uterus for periods of a few weeks to several months, depending on the species (Table 13.2). Following this delay, the blastocyst becomes implanted into the inner wall of the uterus, a

Table 13.2. Durations of Developmental Gestations and Delayed Implantations of Some Marine Mammals which, Together, Equal the Total Gestation Durations Listed in Table 13.1

Species	Developmental gestation(mo)	Delayed implantation(mo)	Source
Pinnipeds			
Phocids			
Harbor seal	8–9.5	1.5–3	Riedman (1990)*
Gray seal	7.8	3.4	Riedman (1990)*
N. elephant seal	7	4	Riedman (1990)*
Otariids			
N. fur seal	8	4	Riedman (1990)*
CA. sea lion	8	3	Riedman (1990)*
Antarctic fur seal	8	4	Riedman (1990)*
Walrus	10–11	4–5	Riedman (1990)*
Other Marine Mammals			
Sea otter	4	2–3	Jameson and Johnson (1993)
Polar bear	4	4	Stirling (1988)

*see for original sources.

placental connection develops between the embryo and the uterine wall, and normal embryonic growth and development resume through the remainder of the gestation period (Fig. 13.11). In effect, delayed implantation substantially extends the normal developmental gestation period to allow mating when adults are aggregated in rookeries rather than when dispersed at sea. By providing flexibility in the length of gestation, this reproductive strategy places parturition and mating into a relatively brief period of time and allows the young to be born when conditions are optimal for their survival. The physiological and hormonal mechanisms controlling delayed implantation are not well understood. Also, as most marine mammals are at sea and inaccessible when blastocyst implantation occurs, even the duration of the delay in some species has not been established with certainty (Riedman, 1990). However, delayed implantation is known or thought to occur in all species of pinnipeds, sea otters, and polar bears as well as in several species of terrestrial mammals, but not in sirenians or cetaceans. The reproductive strategy of delayed implantation requires precise timing of implantation in order to achieve the above noted benefits. As reviewed by Temte (1994) year-to-year precision in the mean date of birth for colonies of many pinnipeds has been documented and significant latitudinal variation in the timing of birth has been shown for several species. Research also has documented that the precision and latitudinal variation of birth timing in the harbor seal are both due to a response to photoperiod that occurs immediately prior to blastocyst implantation. Genetic regulation of reproductive timing was proposed as a mechanism for adjusting timing to different photoperiods (Temte, 1994).

Single-offspring births typify all species of marine mammals except polar bears. Confirmed multiple births are rare for pinnipeds or cetaceans in the wild, and only a few cases of captive-born "twins" and two verified cases of "triplets" (both by the same gray seal) have been reported (Spotte, 1982). The eventual success of the multiple in the wild is not

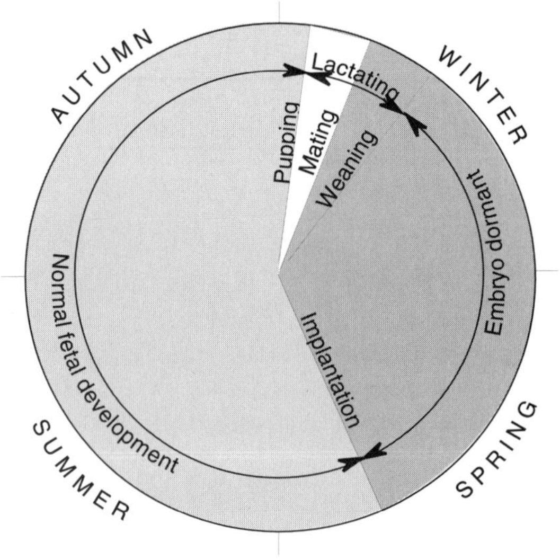

Figure 13.11. Generalized pinniped annual reproductive cycle, including durations of delayed implantation (dark gray) and developmental gestation (light gray). (Adapted from Sumich, 1996.)

known but the large energy costs of lactation likely select against pups survival of multiple offspring.

The gestation period of mysticetes ranges between 10 and 13 months (Table 13.1, Fig. 13.12). Long-distance fasting migrations to low latitudes in winter months is typical of large mysticetes in both hemispheres, with both mating and calving occurring in warm and often protected waters. A general picture of the relationship between these migrations and reproductive timing and behavior is well-illustrated by gray whales.

The migratory timing of gray whales was clarified by Rice and Wolman (1971) in their study of 317 gray whales taken off central California during their migration and by the more narrowly focused studies of Reilly *et al.* (1983), Rugh (1984), Herzing and Mate (1984), Poole (1984), Jones and Swartz (1984), Perryman *et al.* (1999), and Sumich and Show (1998). Collectively, these studies demonstrate that the annual migration of gray whales exists as two superimposed patterns related to the reproductive states of adult females (Fig. 13.13). Each year one-third to one-half of the adult females are pregnant. These near-term pregnant females depart the Bering Sea at the start of the southbound migration two weeks before other gray whales (Rice and Wolman, 1971; dotted line, Figure 13.13). Nonpregnant adult females start south later in company with adult males (although both groups overlap somewhat the earlier departure of pregnant females). These late-arriving whales are also the first to leave the lagoon (after approximately 30 days). While in the lagoons and adjacent coastal areas, most lactating cows with new calves maintain a spatial separation from other age and sex groups by occupying the inner, more protected reaches of the lagoons until the other animals depart (Norris *et al,* 1983; Jones and Swartz, 1984). The earlier arriving females, accompanied by their calves, are the last to leave Mexican calving lagoons the following spring (after 80 days; Jones and Swartz, 1984).

Odontocetes differ from baleen whales in not having such extensive latitudinal migrations. Gestation periods for odontocetes range from about 7 to 17 months (Table 13.1).

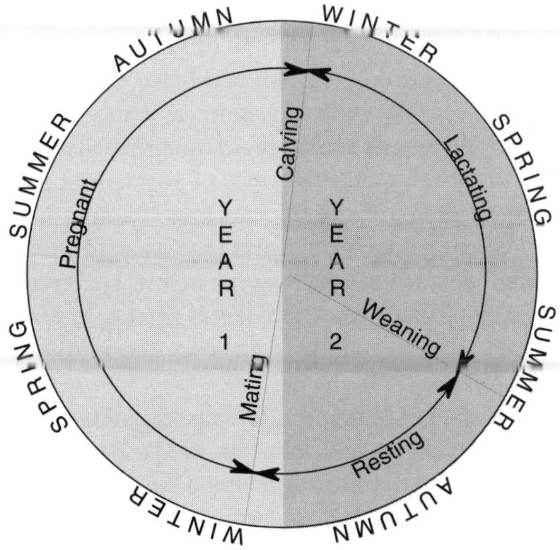

Figure 13.12. Two-year reproductive cycle of fin and gray whales. (Adapted from Mackintosh, 1966.)

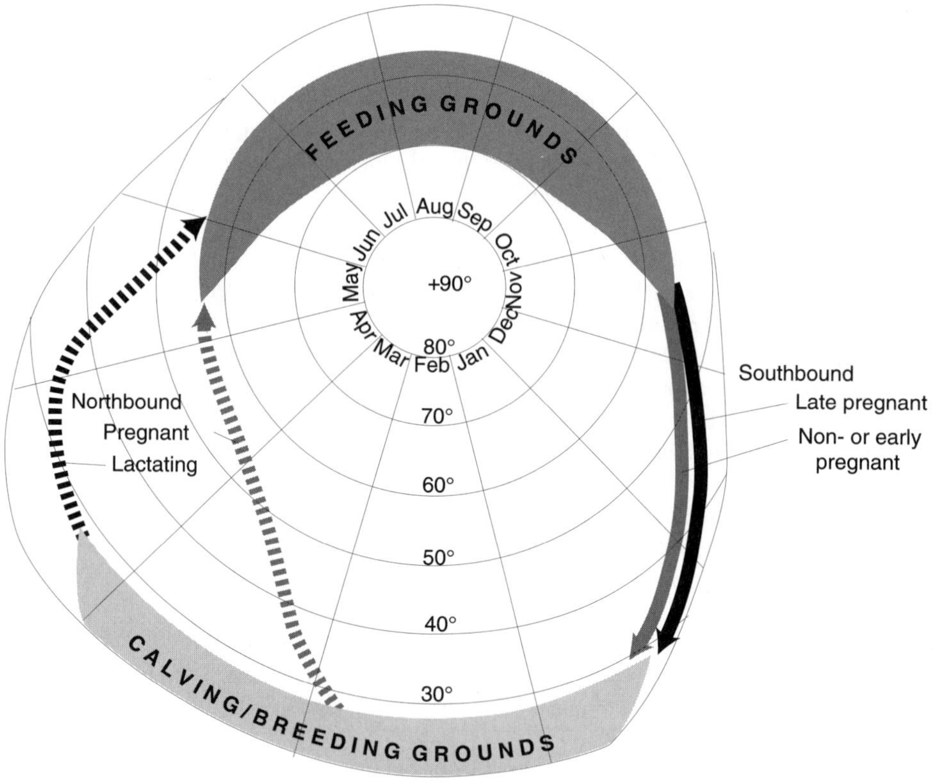

Figure 13.13. Latitudinal shifts of gray whales during their annual migratory cycle as a function of reproductive status. (Adapted from Sumich, 1986b.)

There seems to be a relationship between the length of gestation, fetal growth rate, and calf size at birth, such that larger delphinids (e.g. killer whales and pilot whales) have longer gestation periods than do smaller taxa such as spinner or white-sided dolphins (Perrin and Reilly, 1984). Odontocetes typically produce single offspring that are physically well developed but socially undeveloped. Extended periods of postnatal social learning are crucial elements of the normal development of odontocetes (see Herzing, 1997).

Gestation in manatees lasts about one year. Calves are weaned about one year after birth, but may remain with their mothers for another year before becoming independent (Marmontel, 1995). Thus, the calving interval of females is usually at least three years. Gestation in dugongs is estimated at 13.9 months with long interbirth intervals ranging from about 3 to 7 years (Marsh, 1995).

After a gestation period of about six months, female sea otters give birth to a single pup in late winter or early spring (Jameson and Johnson, 1993). Birth may occur on land or in the water. It appears that the seasonal timing of pupping has evolved so as to occur with the period of maximum food supply and thus maximize pup growth. Similarly gestation in polar bears is relatively short in comparison to other marine mammals, averaging about 8 months.

13.3. Reproductive Patterns

13.3.1. Maternal Care and Lactation Strategies

In placental mammals, provisioning offspring until they are nutritionally independent is the most energetically expensive event of reproduction. With very few exceptions, care and feeding of marine mammal offspring is the sole responsibility of the offspring's mother. However, in any one reproductive cycle, there exists a potential for competition or conflict between mother and offspring for the control and allocation of resources available to support reproduction. It is in the best interest of each offspring to extract for its own use as many of those resources as possible, even at the expense of future reproductive success of its mother. The genetic self-interests of the mother, on the other hand, may be better served if some of her reproductive resources are withheld from current offspring so they can be invested in later offspring to improve the likelihood of her genes being carried into future generations (for a broader review and discussion of these and other genetic conflicts, see Hurst *et al.*, 1996).

Pinnipeds, with their predictable use of ice or land areas when suckling, sometimes in large and dense aggregations, have been more amenable to studies of maternal investment strategies than have other groups of marine mammals. The efficacy of these studies has been improved immensely with the application of several field techniques, including **isotope dilution techniques** to estimate an animal's lipid and lipid-free components and its rate of water intake (e.g., Costa, 1987; Oftedal *et al.* 1993). These techniques involve administering a measured quantity of either a radioisotope (e.g. tritium) or stable isotope (e.g. deuteriumoxide or O_{18}) to an animal and subsequently measuring the concentration of the isotope in the body fluids (usually blood). Measurement of isotopes, when equilibrated with body fluids, provides an estimate of body water pool size, which, when combined with body mass and the concentration of water in lean tissues, can be used to estimate fat and fat-free components in the body (Oftedal *et al.*, 1993).

Three patterns of maternal lactation strategies each with several variations, are apparent in marine mammals: 1) fasting, 2) foraging cycle, and 3) aquatic nursing (Boness and Bowen, 1996, and references cited therein). The fasting strategy, uncommon in nonmarine mammals, characterizes most phocid seals (Table 13.3) and most large mysticetes. The foraging cycle strategy of most otariids (Table 13.3) is similar to that used by terrestrial mammals that leave their young while they forage. The length of time the mothers spend away from their offspring varies between 2–13 days and is likely related to the distance females

Table 13.3. General Differences Between Maternal Strategies in Pinnipeds (based on Boness and Bowen, 1996).

Feature	Fasting (phocids)	Foraging cycle (otariids)	Aquatic nursing (walrus)
1. Durations of fasting	Most or all of lactation period	5–11 days + trips to sea	Few days
2. Duration of lactation	Short (<1–8 weeks)	Long (4 months to 1.3 yrs)	Long (2–3 yrs)
3. Fat content of milk	Very high (50–60%)	High (24–44%)	Low (14–32%)
4. Pups/calves forage during later lactation	No	No/Yes	Yes

Table 13.4. Some Features of Lactation in Marine Mammals

Species	Lactation length (weeks)	Milk % fat	% protein	Source
Pinnipeds				
Phocids				
Hooded seal	<1	61	na	Boness and Bowen, 1996*
Harbor seal	3.4	50	9	Boness and Bowen, 1996*
Harp seal	1.7	57	na	Boness and Bowen, 1996*
Gray seal	2.3	60	7	Boness and Bowen, 1996*
N. elephant seal	4	54	5–12	Boness and Bowen, 1996*
Weddell seal	8	48	na	Boness and Bowen, 1996*
Otariids				
Australian sea lion	60–72	26–37	10	Higgins and Gass (1993); Gales *et al.*, (1996)
CA. sea lion	43	44	na	Boness and Bowen, 1996*
Steller sea lion	47	24	na	Boness and Bowen, 1996*
Antarctic fur seal	17	42	17	Boness and Bowen, 1996*
Galapagos fur seal	77	29	na	Boness and Bowen, 1996*
N. fur seal	18	42	14	Costa and Gentry (1986)
Walrus	100+	14–32	5–11	Riedman (1990)*
Cetaceans				
Odontocetes				
Harbor porpoise	32	46	11	Gaskin *et al.* (1984)*; Oftedal (1997)
Bottlenose dolphin	76	14	12–18	Pilson and Waller (1970); Oftedal (1997)*
Spinner dolphin	60–76	26	7	Pilson and Waller (1970)
Sperm whale	100	15–35	8–10	Lockyer (1981); Oftedal (1997)
Mysticetes				
Fin whale	24–28	17–51	4–13	Lockyer (1984); White (1953)
Minke whale	20–24	24	14	Best (1982)
Gray whale	28–32	53	6	Schwartz (1986); Rice and Wolman (1971); Zenkovich (1938)
Blue whale	24–28	35–50	11–14	Lockyer (1984); Gregory *et al.*, (1955)
Humpback	40–44	33–39	13	Lockyer (1984)*; Glockner-Ferrari and Ferrari (1984)
Sirenians				
Manatee	52	na	na	Reynolds and Odell (1991)
Dugong	78	na	na	Marsh (1995)
Other Marine Mammals				
Sea otter	20–30	21–26	9–12	Jameson and Johnson (1993); Riedman and Estes (1990)
Polar bear	130	17–36	9–13	Oftedal and Gittleman (1989); Derocher *et al.* (1993)

Symbols: *see for original sources listed.

must travel to find adequate prey. The aquatic nursing strategy is most similar to terrestrial mammals and is seen in odontocete cetaceans, sirenians, and the walrus (Table 13.3), in which young remain with their mothers wherever they go and nurse at sea as well as on ice.

13.3.1.1. Fasting Strategy

The fasting strategy of phocids, where females fast completely and remain out of water for the duration of a relatively short lactation, ranges from less than 1 week (four days) in hooded seals to almost 8 weeks in the Weddell seal (Table 13.4). During lactation, lipids are mobilized from maternal body tissues, converted to high-fat milk, and transferred to the large and rapidly growing offspring. Weaning in phocids is usually abrupt, with the mother suddenly abandoning the pup at the end of lactation. It has been suggested that the seasonably unstable nature of pack ice has selected for extremely short lactation periods in ice-breeding seals that use such an environment for pupping; hooded seal pups suckle for only four days, and harp and bearded seals for only 12–18 days (Bowen *et al.*, 1994) before they are abruptly weaned and forced to rely solely on the lipids accumulated while suckling. To compensate for this brevity of lactation, lactating female harp seals transfer milk and energy to pups in the form of very energy-dense milk (4.5–5.9 cal/g) at a high rate (Oftedal *et al.*, 1996). As discussed by Trillmich (1996), however, factors such as body size and correlated fasting ability (implying energetic limits), as well as ecological factors like foraging options during lactation, may be more influential than breeding habitat stability in determining the length of lactation.

For several pinniped species, such as elephant seals (Arnbom, 1994; Costa *et al.*, 1986) and gray seals (Fedak and Anderson, 1982; Iverson *et al.*, 1993; Reilly *et al.*, 1996), multiyear studies have provided clear examples of the fasting approach to lactation and maternal care. Unlike most other pinnipeds, pregnant northern elephant seals come ashore on rookery beaches from December to early March and give birth soon thereafter (See figs. 11.4 and 12.7). The peak of the pupping season occurs in late January (Le Boeuf, 1974), and pups at birth weigh about 8% of their mother's mass. Females fast through their four-week lactation, remaining on the beach near their pups. Bouts of suckling, each lasting several minutes, occur three to four times each day, with the duration of suckling periods increasing throughout lactation. Elephant seal milk is low (about 10% in fat in the early stages of lactation, but increases sharply through the first half of lactation (Fig. 13.14). The gradual substitution of fat for water is probably an adaptation of the mother to conserve water late in her fast (Riedman, 1990); it also contributes to the developing blubber store of the pup prior to weaning. Pups weigh about 40 kg at birth and gain an average of 4 kg each day prior to weaning (Costa *et al.*, 1986). Most of this growth occurs as an increase in pup adipose tissue, with little increase in lean body mass. Overall, nearly 60% of the total energy expenditure of a lactating elephant seal mother is in the form of milk for her pup.

In elephant seals (and most other phocids) weaning occurs when the pup is forced to transfer its nutritional dependence from milk provided by its mother to its own accumulated lipid reserves. At weaning, most elephant seal pups have quadrupled their birth weights; however, a few may have increased their birth weights as much as seven-fold by sneaking milk from other lactating females after their own mothers have departed to feed at sea (Reiter *et al.*, 1978). Weaned elephant seal pups do not immediately commence foraging for their own food. Rather, they remain on the pupping beaches for a postweaning fast lasting an average of 8–10 weeks. Factors affecting the duration of the postweaning fast likely include body weight at weaning (an indication of the magnitude of the pup's

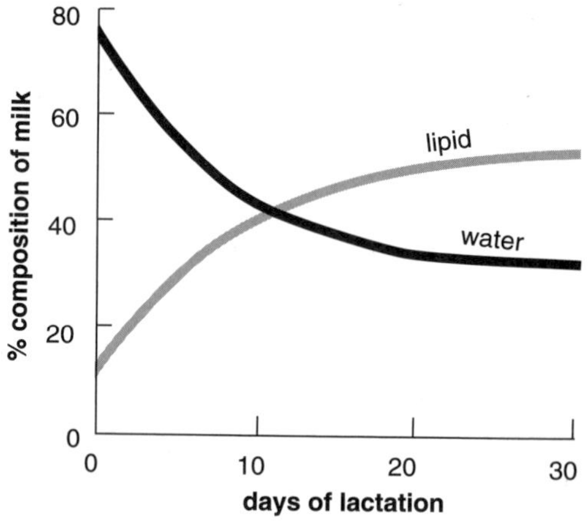

Figure 13.14. Changes in the water and lipid components of northern elephant seal milk through lactation. (Adapted from Riedman, 1990.)

lipid reserves) and availability of appropriate prey in nearshore waters. A study of skeletal development in fasting northern elephant seal pups indicates that despite these unusual conditions they continue development during the fasting period (Patterson-Buckendahl *et al.*, 1994). Only when pups have lost about 30% of their weaned body mass (and are at least three months old) do they go to sea to feed for the first time (Reiter *et al.*, 1978).

As has been already been discussed, most baleen whales are characterized by long migrations between breeding grounds (where they give birth and lactate, but feed little if at all), and high-latitude summer foraging areas. For these migratory mysticetes, the occurrence of winter fasting during reproduction must be evaluated within the framework of the life history of the individual, which would be expected to vary by individual circumstances of age, sex, and reproductive condition. For example, acoustic data indicate that many North Atlantic fin whales migrate south into food-poor waters in winters, yet many others remain in high latitudes through the winter. Adult gray whales clearly commence fasting at the start of their southward winter migration (Rice and Wolman, 1971), but juveniles are thought to forage at least sporadically throughout winter months (Sumich, 1986b). Bowheads offer an interesting exception to the mysticete strategy. They calve at high latitudes in late spring or summer, feed not long afterward, and have a relatively long lactation (Oftedal, 1997). The question remains: if bowhead can successfully do this why do other mysticetes go to such lengths to migrate to low latitudes for birthing?

13.3.1.2. Foraging Cycle Strategy

In the foraging cycle (or attendance) strategy of otariids, mothers fast only for a few days following the birth of relatively small pups. Then the mothers begin foraging trips out to sea, leaving their pups for a few days at a time. The duration of foraging trips largely depends on the distance to foraging areas and on food abundance. Milk intake patterns in otariid pups are intermittent, with a few days of intense suckling followed by several days of fasting until their mothers return. Milk transferred is generally less energy-dense than in phocids but varies in composition with trip duration and time ashore (Trillmich, 1996, and references cited therein). Lactation periods of otariids last from several months to a few years, depending on the species (Table 13.4). Subpolar species such as the northern and Antarctic fur seals have the shortest lactation periods and temperate and tropical species have much longer ones. As the lactation period progresses, most otariid pups begin to enter the water and supplement their milk diet with nearshore prey, and the weaning process is a gradual one. However, this pattern does not follow for two species, the northern fur seal and Antarctic fur seal. In these species weaning is abrupt at about four months of age and shows very little variation. Close observation of the weaning pattern suggests that in these species many of the young wean themselves by leaving the colony while the mothers are still at sea. In general, flexibility in the timing of weaning is typical for temperate and tropical fur seals and sea lions. In this way, mothers are able to buffer pups from unpredictable variation in food availability while pups are gradually increasing their own foraging skills and becoming independent (Trillmich, 1996, and references cited therein).

Multi-year studies of Antarctic fur seals (Costa and Trillmich, 1988; Costa, 1991; Arnould *et al.*, 1996) illustrate the foraging cycle approach to lactation and maternal care. Antarctic fur seals exhibit typical otariid patterns of maternal care and lactation. Pregnant Antarctic fur seals give birth within a week of coming ashore at a breeding rookery (Costa *et al.*, 1985). At parturition, the percentage of body fat of Antarctic fur seal females is about one-half that of elephant seal females (22% vs 40%; Boness and Bowen, 1996). Antarctic fur seals remain with their pups for only one week before returning to forage at sea. These foraging trips, during which the pup remains ashore, last 4–9 days each, and the female will make 15–20 of these trips during lactation. After each trip, the pup is suckled several times a day for the two days that the mother remains at the rookery before her next foraging trip. Antarctic fur seal milk is about 40% fat (Costa *et al.*, 1985), and is among the highest for otariids. Antarctic fur seal pups weigh about 6 kg at birth and grow to 15–17 kg at weaning. This is one of the smallest birth masses of any pinniped, yet the ratio of pup mass to maternal mass is almost twice as great as for elephant seals (15% vs 8%). The pattern of pup growth through the four-month lactation period is intermittent, reflecting the feast-and-fast pattern of milk availability. Unlike most other otariids, Antarctic fur seal pups do not begin to forage during the latter stages of lactation. Instead, the pup initiates weaning when it enters the sea to forage on its own during a foraging trip by its mother. As pups of Antarctic fur seals and other otariids do not experience a postweaning fast as do pups of most phocids, they also avoid the extensive postweaning mass losses characteristic of phocid pups.

13.3.1.3. Aquatic Nursing Strategy

Relatively little information is available for the third maternal care strategy, seen in walruses, and it sometimes is regarded as a variant of the otariid foraging cycle strategy. It is similar in some ways to that strategy except that, soon after birth, walrus pups accompany their mothers on foraging trips into the water. The length of lactation is long, lasting two or three years, although after approximately five months calves begin to feed on benthic organisms. Their dependency on milk decreases as foraging skills are acquired, and most calves are fully weaned by two years of age (Fay, 1982). Mother and pup stay together for 2–3 years and the pup can thus gain considerable foraging experience while still with the mother. Suckling by walruses occurs in the water as well as on shore or on ice (Stirling, 1988).

Odontocete cetaceans, sirenians, sea otters, and polar bears also employ this strategy. Toothed whales have characteristically long lactation periods, averaging between 32 and 100 weeks (Table 13.4). Odontocetes differ from mysticetes in that most female odontocetes feed throughout lactation and weaning is usually at an advanced age of one to three years (Oftedal *et al.* 1996).

The process of suckling in cetaceans involves the tip of the tongue wrapping around the nipple from below and pushing the nipple against the hard palate. The base of the tongue then moves up and down rhythmically, producing suction which pulls the milk toward the throat (Logan and Robson, 1971). It has been suggested that the presence of marginal papillae on the tongues of neonate and juvenile beaked whales may assist the tongue in forming a tight seal while nursing and later in life may assist in holding prey against the palate while letting water escape between the papillae (Kastelein and Dubbledam, 1990; Heyning and Mead, 1996). The retention of marginal papillae, however, appears to be a more general character of odontocetes because they exist for many years after weaning (Kastelein *et al.*, 1997, and references cited therein).

Manatee calves are weaned after one year after birth (Fig. 13.15; Reynolds and Odell, 1991). Data on length of lactation for dugongs are sparse, but the available data indicate that lactation is long, lasting at least 1.5 years, although dugongs start eating sea grass soon after birth (Marsh, 1995). Among sea otters, weaning is gradual and pups remain dependent on their mothers for about six months (Jameson and Johnson, 1993, and references cited therein).

Polar bears have exceptionally long lactation periods (more than 2.5 years) in comparison to other terrestrial carnivores (Oftedal and Gittleman, 1989). Polar bear pups remain in the dens consuming fat-rich milk for two to four months after birth, depending on the lati-

Figure 13.15. Manatee nursing. (Courtesy of U.S. Fish and Wildlife Service.)

tude of the den. By the time they leave their dens, pups have increased their birth weight of less than 1 kg to 10–15 kg. Mean litter size at birth is not known, but is probably close to two in most populations (Amstrup and DeMaster, 1988). Polar bear cubs remain with their mothers for up to 3.5 years (Ramsay and Stirling, 1988) and this may contribute to the species' low reproductive rate (see also Chapter 14).

13.3.1.4. Comparison of Maternal Care Strategies

When one compares the total reproductive energy investments made by pinnipeds, the consequences of the different strategies made by phocid, otariid, and walrus females are clear. Phocid pups are larger at birth than are otariid pups, but only because phocid mothers are larger (62 kg ringed seals to 513 kg northern elephant seals) than otariid mothers (27 kg Galapagos fur seal to 273 kg Steller's sea lion; Costa, 1991; Bowen, 1991). The larger absolute body masses of phocid mothers permit the storage of sufficient lipid reserves to invest heavily in offspring during a short lactation period without supplemental feeding. Otariid females, in contrast, simply lack the body mass necessary to bring ashore their total reproductive investment as stored lipids; therefore, intermittent feeding during lactation supplies an important component of the total amount of energy invested in offspring. Relative to their body masses, otariid females make much larger investments of energy, protein, and time in their offspring than do phocid females (Table 13.5). The cyclical foraging pattern of lactating otariids, however, allows for more flexibility in the duration of lactation than is possible for phocids. Such flexibility may serve as a buffer when food is scarce. The longer lactation period of otariids and the walrus also permits offspring to

Table 13.5. The Relationship between Maternal Mass, Lactation Duration, Pup Growth Rate, and Maternal Investment in Offspring in the Form of Protein and Energy in Some Pinnipeds.

	Maternal	Lactation,	Pup mass	Maternal investment	
Species	(mass, kg.)	(weeks)	gain (kg/day)	Energy, MJ/kg	Protein, g/kg
Phocids					
Harbor seal	84	3.4	0.8	9	na
Harp seal	135	1.7	2.3	6	2
Hooded seal	179	<1	7.1	4	1
Gray seal	207	2.5	2.8	7	37
Weddell seal	447	8	2	7	32
N. elephant seal	504	4	4	5	36
Otariids					
N. fur seal	37	10	0.08	22	150
Ant. fur seal	39	17	0.11	31	192
CA. sea lion	88	43	0.13	36	202
Steller sea lion	273	47	0.38	26	204
Walrus					
Pacific	738	98	0.41	na	na
Atlantic	655	89	0.50	na	na

Original sources listed in Costa, 1991; Boness and Bowen, 1996; Kovacs and Lavigne, 1992.

develop swimming and foraging skills, while still depending on their mothers for energy. It should be noted, however, that classification of maternal care patterns, at least among pinniped families, is probably too simplistic and exceptions can be found. For example, foraging during lactation has been demonstrated in Weddell harp and harbor seals. For harbor seals, Boness and Bowen (1996) suggest that the small maternal body mass of females (about 84 kg vs 504 kg for an adult northern elephant seal female) prohibits them from accumulating sufficient lipid reserves to last the entire duration of their 24 lactation. Therefore, they are forced to forage frequently during lactation, and in doing so, have adopted a typically otariid pattern of pup attendance and suckling. The data listed in Table 13.5 place harbor seals between typical phocids and typical otariids and walruses in their pattern of maternal investment. It is possible that females of another small phocid species, the ringed seal of high northern latitudes, also forage during lactation in a manner similar to that of harbor seals. These otariid-like foraging patterns among phocids suggested to Trillmich (1996) that maternal strategies may be more related to body reserves, distance to foraging areas, and other ecological variables than to phylogenetic constraints, a hypothesis that requires further testing.

In a comparison of pinniped and cetacean lactation strategies Oftedal (1997) suggested that the mysticete-odontocete contrast is similar to that between phocids and otariids. Both phocids and mysticetes have mothers who fast for a part or all of a relatively short lactation period. In otariids and odontocetes, lactation lasts longer and mothers feed throughout lactation. Further study of milk composition reveals that phocids resembled some mysticetes (balaenopterids) in producing high-fat milks whereas otariids resembled odontocetes in producing milk of variable fat content, although some of this variability may be due to combined effects such as sampling error, lactation stage, and environmental conditions (Oftedal, 1997; Table 13.5). The longer lactation of odontocetes coupled with lower predicted rates of energy output confirm a previous suggestion that related this pattern to the learning and predatory skills of odontocetes which feed largely on fish; (whereas mysticetes are largely filter feeders on zooplankton).

13.3.2. Cost of Reproduction

It is obvious that maternal care in pinnipeds is very costly in terms of energy expenditure. Larger mothers transfer significantly larger amounts of resources to their pups. It is very unlikely that they incur greater costs by doing so because the transfer of resources decreases as maternal mass increases (see Fig. 13.16). To get at the true or relative cost of reproduction, changes in fitness must be measured. Fitness costs could, among other possible trade-offs (Stearns, 1989), consist of lowered future fertility or increased risk of mortality of a breeding female. Data on fitness costs of reproduction to phocid females only exist for the northern elephant seal (e.g., Reiter *et al.*, 1981; Le Boeuf and Reiter, 1988; Huber, 1987). The best data exist on the effect of age of reproduction on survival of females. However, the evidence of fitness costs of reproduction is mixed, suggesting that costs exist for Farallon Island seals but not for Año Nuevo populations. Similarly, mortality costs are documented on Año Nuevo but not on the Farallon islands and costs of reproduction in terms of reduced size at birth, growth, or survival to adulthood of pups of mothers having reproduced in the previous year have not been found (Trillmich, 1996).

Data on otariids exist for two species, the Galapagos fur seal and the Antarctic fur seal (Trillmich, 1986; Croxall *et al.*, 1988; Boyd *et al.*, 1995; Arnould *et al.*, 1996). For the Galapagos fur seal, a higher cost of reproduction has been attributed to the fact that females

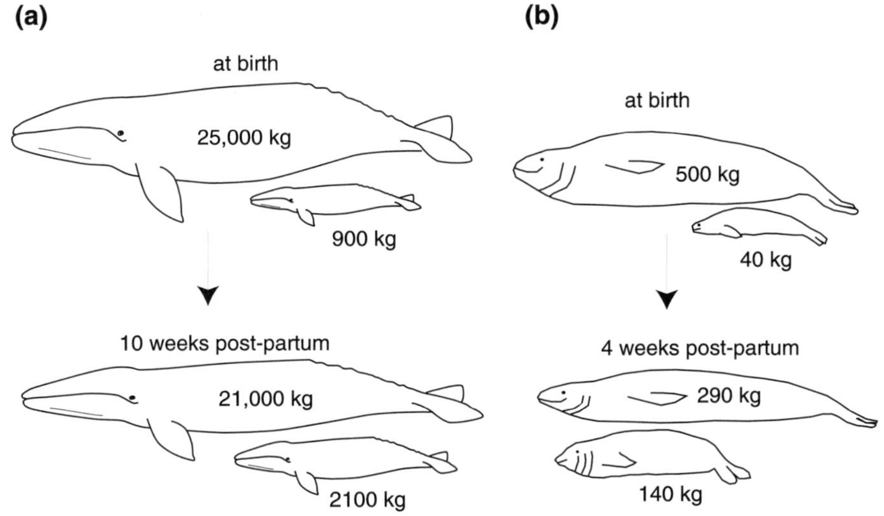

Figure 13.16. A comparison of body masses of female gray whales (a) and northern elephant seals (b) with those of their offspring at birth (top) and at the end of lactation for elephant seals or start of northward migration for gray whales (bottom). (Adapted in part from Riedman, 1990.)

that reproduced in the previous year are still accompanied by a yearling in the next breeding season; they therefore have a much reduced birth rate. This cost is also higher because females that gave birth to a pup when accompanied by the previous year's young were likely to lose the newborn to competition for milk by the older sibling (Trillmich, 1996). However, for the Galapagos fur seal, no mortality cost of reproduction was measured in females, perhaps due to small sample sizes and highly variable years (Trillmich, 1996). Data for the Antarctic fur seal indicate that sustaining high fertility has substantial mortality costs. Boyd *et al.* (1995) suggested that lowered fertility of old Antarctic fur seals may be the result of one of two strategies whereby female seals either reproduce early and nearly continuously every year but die relatively young or reproduce every other year and survive longer. This would lead to an accumulation of low fertility females in old age classes and may explain the apparent decrease in pregnancy rate of older fur seal females without postulating senescence.

The difference in maternal investment between otariids and phocids was briefly explored by Arnould (1997), who noted that the cost of reproduction in Antarctic fur seals is 40–50% of the adult female mortality compared to only 13% in northern elephant seals. Assuming higher juvenile survival in Antarctic fur seals (based on data for the northern fur seal), Arnould (1997) proposed that this species may trade off the cost of high maternal investment for higher offspring survival. Estimates of juvenile survival in the Antarctic fur seal are necessary to test this hypothesis.

13.3.3. Different Investment in Male and Female Offspring

Within the general constraints outlined above that define what can be invested in reproduction, do females preferentially invest more in one gender of offspring? Sexual selection theory predicts that parents (or, in the case of marine mammals, the maternal parent) should either alter sex ratios to produce more offspring of the gender with the least variability in reproductive success, or invest more in the gender whose reproductive success has the greatest variability (Trivers, 1972; Maynard-Smith, 1980). The first option is not available to any marine mammal because sex determination based on male heterogamy limits sex ratios to something very near 1:1. For species with monogynous mating habits and little gender difference in gaining access to mates, such as harp seals, little advantage can be won from investing more heavily in one gender than the other, and no differences in pup weight or growth rate are observed (Kovacs, 1987). In highly polygynous species, females rarely have difficulty securing a mate; if they survive to return to their breeding rookery, they can participate in reproduction. However, most males of the same species never will gain access to receptive females. Only a small percentage of males will succeed in breeding, and a few of these will be spectacular successes (see Chapter 14). To improve their own fitness, mothers can capitalize on this high variability in potential reproductive success of their male offspring to enhance that male's chances of becoming a larger, more competitive, and ultimately more successful breeder when mature.

Although some studies have shown that the most polygynous species of pinnipeds provide evidence of differential investment (Reiter *et al.*, 1978), other studies have found none (Kretzmann *et al.*, 1993). Reiter *et al.* (1978) reported that northern elephant seals suckle male pups an average of one day longer and wean them at larger body masses than female pups. Male pups also are much more likely than female pups to steal milk from other adult females or to be adopted by foster mothers, thereby achieving even greater body mass (especially lipid reserves) before the cessation of suckling. Interestingly, no gender differences in suckling duration were found in northern elephant seals by Kretzmann *et al.* (1993). There also was no difference in the suckling duration of southern elephant seal pups and no differences in growth rate between male and female southern elephant seal pups (Fedak and McCann, 1987). Male southern elephant seal pups consistently weigh more than female pups both at birth and at weaning. This difference, however, has been determined not to be the result of differential maternal investment but rather by female mass at parturition. After birth, expenditure on offspring depends on the mother's mass at parturition and the rate of milk intake by pups, not on pup sex (Arnbom *et al.*, 1997). Other studies have failed to find evidence for male-biased investment. For example, although male gray seal pups are born heavier than female pups, other variables (i.e. growth rates and suckling behavior) indicate that females invest equally in sons and daughters (Siseth and Lorensten, 1995). The same conclusion was reached for several otariid species. In a study of California sea lion pups, Ono and Boness (1996) found that both differential maternal investment and sex differences in pup energy allocation may contribute to larger male pups during their first two months of life. Male pups receive more milk from their mothers, but the difference is not significant when the larger body size of males is considered. Males also contribute to their faster growth by maintaining a lower metabolic rate. For the Antarctic fur seal, no difference in postnatal investment of pups in relation to sex is found because male and female pups consume the same amount of milk or milk energy. Importantly, as shown in this study, mass and mass change may not be appropriate parameters for investigating maternal investment. One difference is that males convert more of their milk consumption into lean tissue whereas females accumulate greater adipose stores (Arnould *et al.*, 1996).

13.3.4. Evolution of Reproductive Patterns in Pinnipeds

Costa (1993) examined the evolution of reproduction and feeding energetics in phocids and otariids. His basic argument is that phocids are adapted to low metabolic expenditures (have low basal metabolic rates) and do not work as hard as otariids while foraging. In contrast, otariids are reported to operate at much higher metabolic rates. He suggested that the otariid breeding pattern (i.e. numerous short duration feeding trips that maximize energy and nutrient delivery to the pup) is ancestral, being most closely linked to their terrestrial common ancestors. According to his model, as ancestral otariids refined their foraging skills they began to increase the duration of their foraging trips and the distance they travelled from shore. Such changes required a greater energy return per trip and an increased reliance on stored maternal reserves. This pattern, he suggested, may have been followed by the extinct desmatophocids, common ancestors of phocids, which evolved large body size. Large body size is a critical factor enabling the separation of feeding from lactation, a characteristic of the phocid pattern. He further suggested that basal phocids, the monachines, which occupied the Hawaiian Islands, were able to pass through the Central American seaway into the Caribbean because they utilized highly dispersed prey with a high energy return per trip. Otariids either could not pass through the seaway or could not reproduce in the Caribbean due to its inherent low productivity. Once in the Atlantic, phocids easily dispersed in the absence of competition from otariids. Upon reaching high latitudes, the short lactation interval may have enabled phocids to breed on unstable substrates such as ice. Once ice breeding was initiated, the lactation interval would be further shortened as phocids extended their range to pack ice. This model, however, as cautioned by Trillmich (1996), will require additional data on the energetics of both phocids and otariids before it is possible to decide whether the suggested lifestyle differences of the two groups are general phenomena.

13.4. Summary and Conclusions

The reproductive structures of marine mammals are similar to those of other mammals. A peculiarity of whales is that the corpora albicans remains for the rest of the animal's life, providing a record of past ovulations in the ovary. This makes it possible to examine the reproductive history of individual whales; each corpus albicans represents one ovulation (although not necessarily a pregnancy). The timing of ovulation and estrus varies among marine mammals. Phocids and otariids have a postpartum estrus which establishes a time frame of nearly one year between copulation in one breeding season and birth in the next. Adjustments to fit gestation periods of less than one year to the one-year cycle are accomplished by seasonal delayed implantation. This reproductive strategy places parturition and mating into a relatively brief period of time and allows the young to be born when conditions are optimal for their survival. Cetaceans show multi-year reproductive cycles with mating and parturition usually separated by at least one, and sometimes two or more, years. Gestation in most marine mammals is approximately one year. Relative to other mammals, pinnipeds (especially phocids) and mysticetes produce high-energy dense milk.

Three maternal strategies characterize marine mammals: fasting (e.g. phocid seals, mysticetes), foraging cycle (e.g. otariid seals), and aquatic nursing (e.g. walruses, odontocetes, sirenians, sea otters, and polar bears). Evidence of the costs of reproduction in female seals is mixed. Similarly, although some studies claim that the most polygynous species of pinnipeds, elephant seals, provide evidence of differential investment in male and female offspring, other studies have found none. A model for the evolution of reproductive patterns in pinnipeds proposes that the otariid breeding pattern (i.e. numerous short duration feeding trips that maximize energy and nutrient delivery to the pup) is ancestral. According to this model, the phocid strategy (i.e. fasting) resulted from an increased body size, seen in their close relatives, the extinct desmatophocids, which enabled a reliance on stored maternal reserves. Further evolution of the phocid strategy involved ice breeding and, as a consequence, a shortened lactation interval.

13.5. Further Reading

For a recent account of the pinniped reproductive system see Laws and Sinha (1993), and references cited therein. The reproductive system of cetaceans is more fully described in Slijper (1966), Harrison (1969), Perrin and Reilly (1984); Lockyer (1984); for sirenians see Hill (1945), Harrison (1969), and O'Shea *et al.* (1995). The evolution of maternal care in pinnipeds is summarized by Boness and Bowen (1966); see also Trillmich (1996). Papers by Oftedal and coworkers summarize lactation in pinnipeds (e.g. Oftedal *et al.*, 1987) and cetaceans (Oftedal, 1997).

References

Amstrup, S. C., and D. P. De Master (1988). Polar bear, *Ursus maritimus. In* "Selected Marine Mammals of Alaska" (J. W. Lentfer, ed.), pp. 39–56. Washington, D.C.

Arnbom, T. (1994). "Maternal Investment in Male and Female Offspring in the Southern Elephant Seal." Stockholm University, Stockholm.

Arnbom, T., M. A. Fedak, and I. L. Boyd (1997). Factors affecting maternal expenditure in southern elephant seals during lactation. *Ecology* **78**(2): 471–483.

Arnould, J. P. Y. (1997). Lactation and the cost of pup-rearing in Antarctic fur seals. *Mar. Mamm. Sci.* **13**(2): 516–526.

Arnould, J. P. Y., I. L. Boyd, and D. G. Socha (1996). Milk consumption and growth efficiency in Antarctic fur seal (*Arctocephalus gazella*) pups. *Can. J. Zool.* **74**: 254–266.

Balcomb, K. C., III (1974). The birth of a gray whale. *Pac. Disc.* **27**: 28–31.

Best, R. C. (1981). The status of right whales (*Eubalaena glacialis*) off South Africa, 1969–1979. *Investl. Rep. Sea Fish. Inst. S. Afr.* **123**: 1–44.

Best, P. B. (1982). Seasonal abundance, feeding, reproduction, age and growth in minke whales off Durban (with incidental observations from the Antarctic). *Rep. Int. Whal. Comm.* **32**: 759–786.

Boness, D. L., and D. W. Bowen (1996). The evolution of maternal care in pinnipeds. *BioScience* **46**: 645–654.

Bowen, W. D. (1991). Behavioral ecology of pinniped neonates. *In* "The Behaviour of Pinnipeds" (D. Renouf, ed.), pp. 66–127. Chapman & Hall, London.

Bowen, W. D., O. T. Oftedal, and D. J. Boness (1985). Birth to weaning in four days: Remarkable growth in the hooded seal, *Cystophora cristata. Can. J. Zool.* **63**: 2841–2846.

Bowen, W. D., O. T. Oftedal, D. J. Boness, and S. J. Iverson (1994). The effect of maternal age and other factors on birth mass in the harbor seal. *Can. J. Zool.* **72**: 8–14.

Boyd, I. L. (1998). Time and energy constraints in pinniped lactation. *Am. Nat.* **152**: 717–728.

Boyd, I. L., K. Reid, and R. M. Bevan (1995). Swimming speed and allocation of time during the dive cycle in Antarctic fur seals. *Anim. Behav.* **50**: 769–784.

Bull, J. J., and E. L. Charnov (1985). On irreversible evolution. *Evolution* **39**: 1149–1155.

Caldwell, D. K., and M. C. Caldwell (1985). Manatees. *In* "Handbook of Marine Mammals" (S. Ridgway, ed.), Vol. 3, pp. 33–66. Academic Press, New York.

Costa, D. P. (1987). Isotopic methods for quantifying material and energy balance of free-ranging marine mammals. *In* A. C. Huntley, D. P. Costa, G. A. J. Worthy, and M. A. Costellini, eds), pp. 43–66. Allen Press, Lawrence, KA.

Costa, D. P. (1991). Reproductive and foraging energetics of pinnipeds; Implications for life history patterns. *In* "The Behaviour of Pinnipeds" (D. Renouf, ed.), pp. 299–344. Chapman & Hall, London.

Costa, D. P. (1993). The relationship between reproductive and foraging energetics and the evolution of the Pinnipedia. *Symp. Zool. Soc. London* **66,** 293–314.

Costa, D. P., and R. L. Gentry (1986). Free-ranging energetics of northern fur seal. *In* "Fur Seals: Maternal Strategies on Land and at Sea" (R. L. Gentry and G. L. Kooyman, eds.), pp. 79–101. Princeton University Press, Princeton, NJ.

Costa, D. P., and F. Trillmich (1988). Mass changes and metabolism during the perinatal fast: Comparison between Antarctic *(Arctocephalus gazella)* and Galapagos fur seals *(Arctocephalus galapagoensis). Physio. Zool.* **61**: 160–169.

Costa, D. P., P. H. Thorson, J. G. Herpolsheimer, and J. P. Croxall (1985). Reproductive bioenergetics of the Antarctic fur seal. *Antarct. J. U.S.* **20**: 176–177.

Costa, D. P., B. J. Le Boeuf, A. C. Huntley, and C. L. Ortiz (1986). The energetics of lactation in the Northern elephant seal, *Mirounga angustirostris. J. Zool.* **201**: 21–33.

Croxall, J. P., T. McCann, P. A. Prince, and P. Rothery (1988). Reproductive performance of seabirds and seals at South Georgia and Signy Island, South Orkney Islands, 1976–1987: Implications for southern ocean monitoring studies. *In* "Antarctic Ocean and Resources Variability" (D. Sahrhage, ed.), pp. 261–285. Springer-Verlag, Heidelberg.

Derocher, A. E. (1990). Supernumerary mammae and nipples in the polar bear *(Ursus maritimus). J. Mammal.* **71**(2): 236–237.

Derocher, A. E., and I. Stirling (1995). Temporal variation in reproduction and body mass of polar bears in western Hudson Bay. *Can. J. Zool.* **73**: 1657–1665.

Derocher, A. E., D. Andriashek, and J. P. Y. Arnould (1993). Aspects of milk composition in polar bears. *Can. J. Zool.* **71**: 561–567.

Estes, J. A. (1980). *Enhydra lutris. Mamm. Species* **133**: 8 pp.

Evans, G. H. P. (1987). "The Natural History of Whales and Dolphins." Facts On File, New York.

Fay, F. H. (1982). Ecology and biology of the Pacific walrus, *Odobenus rosmarus divergens* Illiger. North Am. Fauna Ser., U.S. Dep. Int., Fish Wildl. Serv., No. 74.

Fedak, M. A., and S. S. Anderson (1982). The energetics of lactation: Accurate measurements from a large wild mammal, the gray seal *(Halichoerus grypus). J. Zool.* **198**: 473–479.

Fedak, M. A., and T. S. McCann (1987). Parental investment in southern elephant seals, *Mirounga leonina. Abstr. 7th Bienn. Conf. Biol. Mar. Mamm.,* Miami, FL.

Ford, J. K. B., G. M. Ellis, and K. C. Balcomb (1994). "Killer Whales: The Natural History and Genealogy of *Orcinus orca* in British Columbia and Washington State." University of Washington Press, Seattle.

Fredga, K. (1988). Aberrant chromosomal sex-determining mechanisms in mammals, with special reference to species with XY females. *Phil. Trans. R. Soc. London, Ser. B* **322**: 83–95.

Gales, N. J., D. P. Costa, and M. Kretzmann (1996). Proximate composition of Australian sea lion milk throughout the entire supra-annual lactation period. *Aus. J. Zool.* **44**: 651–657.

Gaskin, D. E., G. J. D. Smith, A. P. Watson, W. Y. Yasui, and D. B. Yurik (1984). *Rep. Int. Whal. Comm. Spec. Issue* **6**: 135–147.

Glockner-Ferrari, D. A., and M. J. Ferrari (1984). Reproduction in humpback whales, *Megaptera novaengliae,* in Hawaiian waters. *Rep. Int. Whal. Comm.* **6**: 237–242.

Gregory, M. E., S. K. Kon, S. J. Rowland, and S. Y. Thompson (1955). The composition of the milk of the blue whale. *J. Dairy Res.* **22**: 108–112.

Harrison, R. J. (1969). Endocrine organs: Hypophysis, thyroid, and adrenal. In "The Biology of Marine Animals" (ed. H. T. Andersen), pp. 349–390. Academic Press, New York.

Harrison, R. J., and J. E. King (1980). "Marine Mammals, 2nd ed." Hutchinson and Co., Ltd. London.

Harrison, R. J., L. H. Matthews, and J. M. Roberts (1952). Reproduction in some Pinnipedia. *Zool. Soc. Lond., Trans.* **27**: 437–541.

Herzing, D. L. (1997). The life history of free-ranging Atlantic spotted dolphins *(Stenella frontalis)*: Age classes, color phases and female reproduction. *Mar. Mamm. Sci.* **13**: 576–595.

Herzing, D. L., and B. R. Mate 1984). Gray whale migrations along the Oregon coast. *In* "The Gray Whale, *Eschrichtius robustus* (Lilljeborg, 1861)" M. L. Jones, S. L. Swartz, and S. Leatherwood, eds.), pp. 289–308. Academic Press, New York.

Heyning, J. E., and J. G. Mead (1996). Suction feeding in beaked whales: Morphological and observational evidence. *Contrib. Sci. Los Angeles Mus. Nat. Hist.* **464**: 1–12.

Higgins, L. V., and L. Gass (1993). Birth to weaning: Parturition, duration of lactation and attendance cycles of Australian sea lions *(Neophoca cinerea). Can. J. Zool.* **71**: 2047–2055.

Hill, W. C. O. (1945). Notes on the dissection of two dugongs. *J. Mammal.* **26**: 153–175.

Huber, H. R. (1987). Natality and weaning success in relation to age of first reproduction in northern elephant seals. *Can. J. Zool.* **65**: 1311–1316.

Hurst, L. D., A. Atlan, and B. O. Bengtson (1996). Genetic conflicts. *Q. Rev. Biol.* **71**: 317–471.
Iverson, S. J., W. D. Bowen, D. J. Boness, and O. T. Oftedal (1993). The effect of maternal size and milk energy output on pup growth in gray seals *(Halichoerus grypus). Physiol. Zool.* **66**: 61–88.
Jameson, R. J., and A. M. Johnson (1993). Reproductive characteristics of female sea otters. *Mar. Mamm. Sci.* **9**(2): 156–167.
Johnson, C. M., and K. S. Norris (1994). Social behavior. *In* "The Hawaiian Spinner Dolphin" (K. S. Norris, B. Würsig, R. S. Wells and M. Würsig, eds, pp. 243–286. University of California Press, Berkeley.
Jones, M. L. and S. L. Swartz (1984). Demography and phenology of gray whales *(Eschrichtius robustus)* in Laguna San Ignacio, Baja California Sur, Mexico. *In* "The Gray Whale Whale, *Eschrichtius robustus* (Lilljeborg, 1861)" M. L. Jones, S. L. Swartz, and S. Leatherwood, eds.), pp. 309–374. Academic Press, New York.
Kastelein, R. A., and J. L. Dubbledam (1990). Marginal papillae on the tongue of the harbour porpoise *(Phocoena phocoena),* bottlenose dolphin *(Tursiops truncatus)* and Commerson's dolphin *(Cephalorhynchus commersonii). Aquatic Mammals* **15**(4): 158–170.
Kastelein, R. A., C. Staal, A. Terlouw, and M. Muller (1997). Pressure changes in the mouth of a feeding harbour porpoise *(Phocoena phocoena).* In "The Biology of the Harbour Porpoise" (A. J. Read, P. R. Wiepkema, and P. E. Nachtigall, eds.), pp. 279–291. De Spil Publishers, Woerden, The Netherlands.
King J. E. (1983). "Seals of the World." Comstock, Ithaca, NY.
Kovacs, K. M. (1987). Maternal behavior and early behavioral ontogeny of harp seals, *Phoca groenlandica. Anim. Behav.* **35**: 844–855.
Kovacs, K. M., and D. M. Lavigne (1992). Maternal investment in otariid seals and walruses. *Can. J. Zool.* **70**: 1953–1964.
Kretzmann, M. B., D. P. Costa, and B. J. Le Boeuf (1993). Maternal energy investment in elephant seal pups: Evidence for sexual equality? *Am. Nat.* **141**: 466–480.
Laws, R. M. (1962). Some effects of whaling on the southern stocks of baleen whales. *In* "The Exploitation of Natural Animal Populations" (R. F. LeCren and M. W. Holdgate, eds.), pp. 137–158. Wiley, New York.
Laws, R. M., and A. A. Sinha (1993). Reproduction. *In* "Antarctic Seals" (R. M. Laws, ed.), pp. 228–267. Cambridge University Press, Cambridge, UK.
Le Boeuf, B. J. (1974). Male-male competition and reproductive success in elephant seals. *Am. Zool.* **14**: 163–176.
Le Boeuf, B. J., and J. Reiter (1988). Lifetime reproductive success in northern elephant seals. *In* "Reproductive Success" (T. H. Clutton-Brock, ed.), pp. 344–362. University of Chicago Press, Chicago.
Lockyer, C. (1981). Growth and energy budgets of large baleen whales from the southern hemisphere. *Mamm. Seas* **3**: 2349–2351.
Lockyer, C. (1984). Review of baleen whale (Mysticeti) reproduction and implications for management. *Rep. Int. Whal. Comm., Spec. Issue* **6**: 27–50.
Logan, F. D., and F. D. Robson (1971). On the birth of a common dolphin *(Delphinus delphinus* L.) in captivity. *Zool. Garten (Leipzig)* **40**(3): 115–124.
Mackintosh, N. A. (1966). The distribution of southern blue and fin whales. *In* "Whales, Dolphins and Porpoises" (K. S. Norris, ed.), pp. 125–144. Univ. Calif. Press, Berkeley.
Marmontel, M. (1995). Age and reproduction in female Florida manatees. *In* "Population Biology of the Manatee" (T. J. O'Shea, B. B. Ackerman, and H. F. Percival, eds.), Inf. Technol. Rep. 1, pp. 98–119. National Biological Service, Washington, DC.
Marsh, H. (1995). The life history, pattern of breeding, and population dynamics of the dugong. *In* "Population Biology of the Manatee" (T. J. O'Shea, B. B. Ackerman, and H. F. Percival, eds.), Inf. Technol. Rep. 1, pp. 56–62. National Biological Service, Washington, DC.
Maynard-Smith, J. (1980). A new theory of sexual investment. *Behav. Ecol. Sociobiol.* **7**: 247–251.
Mills, J. G. and J. E. Mills (1979). Observations of a gray whale birth. *Bull. S. Calif. Acad. Sci.* **78**: 192–196.
Mitchell, E. (1986). Finner whales. *In* "Marine Mammals of Eastern North Pacific and Arctic Waters" (D. Haley, ed.), pp. 49–55. Pacific Search Press, Seattle, Washington.
Nishiwaki, M., and H. Marsh, 1985. Dugong, *Dugong dugon* (Mueller, 1776), *In* "Handbook of Marine Mammals. Volume 3. The Sirenians and Baleen Whales" (S. H. Ridgway and R. Harrison, eds.), pp. 1–31. Academic Press, London.
Norris, K. S., B. Villa-Ramirez, G. Nichols, B. Würsig, and K. Miller (1983). Lagoon entrance and other aggregations of gray whales *(Eschrichtius robustus). In* "Communication and Behavior of Whales" (R. Payne, ed.), pp. 259–293. Westview Press, Boulder, CO.
Oftedal, O. (1997). Lactation in whales and dolphins: Evidence of divergence between baleen-and toothed-species. *J. Mamm Gland Biol. Neoplasia* **2**(3): 205–230.

Oftedal, O. T., and J. L. Gittleman (1989). Patterns of energy output during reproduction in carnivores. *In* "Carnivore Behavior, Ecology, and Evolution" (J. L. Gittleman, ed.), pp. 355–379. Cornell University Press, Ithaca, NY.

Oftedal, O. T., D. J. Boness, and R. A. Tedman (1987). The behavior, physiology and anatomy of lactation in the Pinnipedia. *In* "Current Mammalogy" (H. Genoways, ed.), Vol. 1, pp. 175–245. Plenum, New York.

Oftedal, O. T., W. D. Bowen, and D. J. Boness (1993). Energy transfer by lactating hooded seals and nutrient deposition in their pups during the four days from birth to weaning. *Physiol. Zool.* **66**: 412–436.

Oftedal, O. T., W. D. Bowen, and D. J. Boness (1996). Lactation performance and nutrient deposition in pups of the harp seal, *Phoca groenlandica,* on ice floes off southeast Labrador. *Physiol. Zool.* **69**(3): 635–657.

Ono, K. A., and D. J. Boness (1996). Sexual dimorphism in sea lion pups: differential maternal investment, or sex-specific differences in energy allocation? *Behav. Ecol. Sociobiol.* **38**: 31–41.

O'Shea, T. J., B. B. Ackerman, and H. F. Percival (eds.) (1995). Population Biology of the Florida Manatee, National Biological Service: Information and Technology Report no. 1.

Pabst, D. A., S. A. Rommel, and W. A. McLellan (1998). Evolution of the thermoregulatory function in the cetacean reproductive systems. *In* "The Emergence of Whales: Patterns in the Origin of Cetacea" (J. G. M. Thewissen, ed.), pp. 379–397.) Plenum Press, New York.

Patterson-Buckendahl, P., S. H. Adams, R. Morales, W. S. S. Jee, C. E. Cann, and C. L. Ortiz (1994). Skeletal development in newborn and weanling northern elephant seals. *Am. J. Physiol.* **267**: R726–R734.

Perrin, W. F., and G. P. Donovan (eds.) (1984). Report of the workshop on reproduction of whales, dolphins and porpoises. *Rep. Int. Whal. Comm. (Spec. Issue)* **6**: 1–24.

Perrin, W. F., and S. B. Reilly (1984). Reproductive parameters of dolphins and small whales of the family Delphinidae. *Rep. Int. Whal. Comm. (Spec. Issue)* **6**: 97–125.

Perryman, W. L., M. A. Donahue, J. L. Laake, and T. E. Martin (1999). Diel variation in migration rates of eastern Pacific gray whales measured with thermal imaging sensors. *Mar. Mamm. Sci.* **15**: 426–445.

Pilson, M. E., and D. W. Waller (1970). Composition of milk from spotted and spinner porpoises. *J. Mammal.* **51**: 74–79.

Poole, M. M. (1984). Migration corridors of gray whales along the central California coast, 1980–1982. *In* "The Gray Whale, *Eschrichtius robustus* (Lilljeborg, 1861)" (M. L. Jones, S. L. Swartz, and S. Leatherwood, eds.), pp. 389–408. Academic Press, New York.

Ramsay, M. A., and I. Sterling (1988). Reproductive biology of female polar bears *(Ursus maritimus). J. Zool.* **214**: 601–634.

Reilly, J. J., M. A. Fedak, D. H. Thomas, W. A. A. Coward, and S. S. Anderson (1996). Water balance and the energetics of lactation in gray seals *(Halichoerus grypus)* as studied by isotopically labelled water methods. *J. Zool.* **238**: 157–165.

Reilly, S. B., D. W. Rice, and A. A. Wolman (1983). Population assessment of the gray whale *Eschrichtius robustus,* from California shore censuses, 1967–80. *Fish. Bull.* **81**: 267–279.

Reiter, J., K. J. Panken, and B. J. Le Boeuf (1981). Female competition and reproductive success in Northern Elephant Seals. *Anim, Behav.* **29**: 670–687.

Reiter, J., N. L. Stinson, and B. J. Le Boeuf (1978). Northern elephant seal development: The transition from weaning to nutritional independence. *Behav. Ecol. Sociobiol.* **3**: 337–367.

Reynolds, J. E., III, and D. E. Odell (1991). "Manatees and Dugongs." Facts on File, New York.

Rice, D. W. (1986). Gray whale. *In* "Marine Mammals of Eastern North Pacific and Arctic Waters" (D. Haley, ed.), pp. 62–71. Pacific Search Press, Seattle, Washington.

Rice, D. W., and A. A. Wolman (1971). The life history and ecology of the gray whale *(Eschrichtius robustus). Am. Soc. Mammal., Spec. Publ.* **3**: 1–142.

Riedman, M. (1990). "The Pinnipeds: Seals, Sea Lions, and Walruses." University of California Press, Berkeley.

Riedman, M., and J. Estes (1990). The sea otter *(Enhydra lutris):* Behavior, ecology and natural history, *U.S., Fish Wild., Biol. Rep.* **90**(14): 1–126.

Rugh, D. J. (1984). Census of gray whales at Unimak Pass, Alaska November-December 1977-1979. *In* "The Gray Whale, *Eschrichtius robustus* (Lilljeborg, 1861)" (M. L. Jones, S. L. Swartz, and S. Leatherwood, eds.), pp. 225–248. Academic Press, New York.

Sandell, M. (1990). The evolution of seasonal delayed implantation. *Rev. Biol.* **65**: 23.

Schwartz, S. L. (1986). Gray whale migratory, social and breeding behavior. *Rep. Int. Whal. Comm. Spec. Issue* **8**: 207–229.

Sease, J. L., and D. G. Chapman (1988). Pacific walrus—*Odobenus rosmarus divergens. In* "Selected Marine Mammals of Alaska," pp. 17–38. Mar. Mamm. Comm. Wash., DC.

Sinha, A. A., C. H. Conaway, and K. W. Kenyon (1966). Reproduction in the female sea otter. *J. Wildl. Manage.* **30**: 121–130.

Siseth, P. T., and S.-H. Lorentsen (1995). Evidence of equal maternal investment in the sexes in the polygynous and sexually dimorphic gray seal *(Halichoerus grypus). Behav., Ecol. Sociobiol.* **36**: 145–150.

Slijper, E. J. (1966). Functional morphology of the reproductive system in Cetacea. *In* "Whales, Dolphins and Porpoises (K. Norris, ed.), pp. 277–319. University of California Press, Berkeley.

Spotte, S. (1982). The incidence of twins in pinnipeds. *Can. J. Zool.* **60**: 2226–2233.

Stearns, S. C. (1989). Trade-offs in life history evolution. *Functional Ecology* **3**: 259–268.

Stirling, I. (1988). "Polar Bears." University of Michigan Press, Ann Arbor.

Sumich, J. L. (1986a). Growth in young gray whales *(Eschrichtius robustus). Mar. Mamm. Sci.* **2**: 145–152.

Sumich, J. L. (1986b). Latitudinal distribution, calf growth and metabolism, and reproductive energetics of gray whales, *Eschrichtius robustus.* Ph.D. Dissertation, Oregon State University, Corvallis.

Sumich, J. L. (1996). "An Introduction to the Biology of Marine Life." Wm. C. Brown, Dubuque, IA.

Sumich, J. L., and I. Show (1999). Aerial survey and photogrammetric comparisons of southbound migrating gray whales in the southern California Bight, 1988–1990. *Rep. Int. Whal. Comm. Spec. Issue.*

Temte, J. L. (1994). Photoperiod control of birth timing in the harbour seal. *J. Zool.* **233**: 369–384.

Trillmich, F. (1986). Attendance behavior of Galapagos fur seals. *In* "Fur Seals: Maternal Strategies on Land and at Sea" R. L. and Gentry and G. L. Kooyman, eds.), pp. 168–185. Princeton University Press, Princeton, NJ.

Trillmich, F. (1996). Parental investment in pinnipeds. *In* "Advances in the Study of Behavioral" (J. S. Rosenblatt and C. T. Snowdon, eds.), pp. 533–577. Academic Press, San Diego, CA.

Trivers, R. L. (1972). Parental investment and sexual selection. *In* "Sexual Selection and the Descent of Man, 1871–1971" (B. Campbell, ed.), pp. 136–179. Aldine, Chicago.

Vaughan, T. A. (1986). "Mammalogy." 3rd ed. Saunders College Publ., Philadelphia.

White, J. C. D. (1953). Composition of whale's milk. *Nature* **171**: 612.

Yablokov, A. V., V. M. Bel'kovich, and V. I. Botisov (1972). "Whales and Dolphins." Nauka, Moscow.

Zenkovich, B. A. (1938). Milk of large-sized cetaceans. *Dokl. Akad. Nauk. SSSR* **16**: 203–205.

14

Population Structure and Population Dynamics

14.1. Introduction: Some Population Parameters and Life History Characteristics

A **population** of sexually reproducing animals is usually defined as a discrete part of a species that is interbreeding and that occupies a defined geographical area. In less common instances, a population may consist of all living members of a closely confined species. The reproductive behavior of members of a population creates a gene pool common to them but isolated from the gene pools of other populations. In practice, population geneticists emphasize the genetic character of a population, including patterns of genetic change resulting from emigration, immigration, **genetic drift**, and selection, whereas management agencies often emphasize the geographic distribution of populations in terms of **stocks**, or population units, subject to commercial exploitation. Each of these viewpoints will be addressed in the following discussion.

Descriptions of life history characteristics of individual members of populations represent our attempts to quantify those factors that influence or control the sizes and patterns of change in populations. All populations can be characterized by their size (the number of included individuals), which usually fluctuates over time. Population growth rates (either positive or negative) result from the interplay between factors that promote birth and survival and those that promote mortality. **Natality** is a population parameter used to denote the rate at which offspring are produced, and it is determined by the collective **birth rates** of individual females in a population. **Mortality**, or the rate of death in a population, is age specific and influenced both by average or maximum life spans of individuals and by the age structure of a population. The balance between natality and mortality also establishes patterns of **survivorship** and the **age distribution** of a population.

Essentially all marine mammals have long life spans and large body masses which make them slow to mature and reproduce. Relatively few offspring are produced, and these are intensely nurtured. In population biology terms, marine mammals are classic examples of **k-selected species** (Fig. 14.1), or species whose life history patterns, based on low birth rates and comparably low death rates, have evolved to maintain relatively stable population

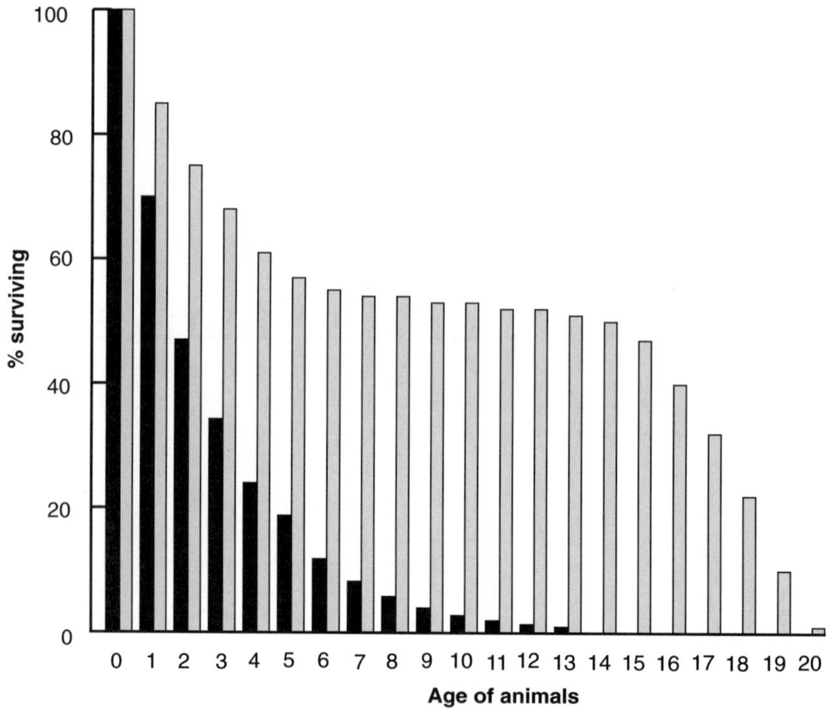

Figure 14.1. Hypothetical age distributions of an r-selected (black bars) and k-selected (gray bars) population. These populations also differ markedly in patterns of mortality, mean age, maximum age, and survivorship.

sizes at or near the **carrying capacity** of their environment (MacArthur and Wilson, 1967). However, when populations of these k-selected species have been reduced by commercial exploitation, as has happened with most species of baleen whales, elephant seals, and sea otters, these populations switch to expressing some **r-selected** life history characteristics, including small and expanding population sizes and relatively youthful age distributions. The capacity of marine mammals to accommodate transformations from k-selected to r-selected conditions (and, in the cases of a few recovered populations, back to k-selected conditions again) is unknown for most species, either because current life history characteristics are unknown or, more commonly, because "normal" life history characteristics of those populations prior to heavy exploitation were never established. Consequently, some of the life history descriptions which follow suffer from one or both of these deficiencies.

Life history characteristics of populations discussed in this chapter include birth and pregnancy rates, growth rates, age determination and longevity, and natural mortality. An understanding of the life history characteristics of a population requires the recognition and identification of individual members. Among the techniques used for monitoring populations reviewed in this chapter are photographic identification, both satellite and radio telemetry technologies, and molecular genetic techniques.

14.1.1. Birth and Pregnancy Rates

The number of offspring a female marine mammal produces is determined by her frequency of pregnancy (which is never more than once per year; Table 13.1), by duration of her reproductive lifetime, and, in polar bears, the number of cubs produced during each pregnancy (all other marine mammals are assumed to normally produce a single offspring per successful pregnancy). In some species, birth rates of individual females are known to change over their lifetimes. Sexual maturity in most marine mammals precedes physical maturity by several years, allowing for substantial body mass increase after a female is capable of her first reproduction. Huber *et al.* (1991) found that younger (and presumably smaller) sexually mature female elephant seals from the Farallon Islands were more likely than older females to "skip" a year by forgoing a pregnancy, and were more likely to "skip" in later years if they had matured early. However, at nearby Año Nuevo Island, no significant age-specific variation in natality was reported by Le Boeuf and Reiter (1988). In species like elephant seals that fast for part or all of their lactation, skipping a year may provide a small female the time necessary to acquire additional body mass between successive pregnancies (Sydeman and Nur, 1994). Similar "skips" may occur in newly mature female gray whales whose body masses are likely near the minimum size capable of supporting the energetic cost of pregnancy and lactation while simultaneously fasting.

A different pattern of changing birth rates over time, consisting of a gradual decline in pregnancy rates in older animals, has been documented in short-finned pilot whales (Marsh and Kasuya, 1991). In this species, killer whales (Ford *et al.*, 1994), and likely in other odontocetes, pregnancy rates decline with increasing age of females. Female short-finned pilot whales are known to live to maximum ages of at least 63 years, yet no individual older than 36 years has been found pregnant; Marsh and Kasuya (1991) proposed that all females in their study population over 40 years of age (about 25% of all females) had ceased to ovulate. Even so, many were found with sperm in their reproductive tracts, indicating a continuation of mating well into their postreproductive years. The functional role of these postreproductive females is unclear. Norris and Pryor (1991) suggest two possible roles that can be viewed as mechanisms to increase these animals' reproductive fitness through the investment of energy, time, or information to their direct descendants or other close kin: 1) in stable, long-duration matrilineal or **matrifocal** (aggregations of matrilines) social groups of odontocetes (i.e. pilot whales, sperm whales, and killer whales), the old members of the group are always females, and these old females may serve as valuable repositories and transmitters of cultural information, 2) nurturing responsibilities such as baby-sitting and fostering (including occasional nursing of other females' young) have been reported for sperm whales (Whitehead, 1996), and, as these species are all deep diving whales, foraging mothers could benefit from the presence of other older and closely related females to tend their calves.

14.1.2. Growth Rates

The growth rates of suckling marine mammal neonates vary tremendously among species. In terms of absolute growth, average rates of mass gain range over several orders of magnitude, from less than 0.1 kg/day in fur seals (Table 14.1) to 5 kg/day during the four-day lactation of hooded seals (Bowen *et al.*, 1985) to more than 100 kg/day in blue whale calves (Rice, 1986). Presumably, absolute rates of mass gain increase even more between weaning and sexual maturity; however, far fewer data on postweaning growth rates are available. Relative rates of growth also can be compared using the time required to double in body mass (Table 14.1). A clear distinction between phocids and otariids is once again apparent, with the doubling time of harbor seal masses being intermediate between typical phocids and typical otariids.

Table 14.1. Birth Mass Doubling Times and Rates of Body Mass Increase for Various Species of Marine Mammals

Species	Approximate time to double birth mass (days)	Rate of birth mass increase (kg/day)	Source
Pinnipeds			
Phocids			
Harbor seal	18	0.6	Costa (1991); Bowen (1991)*
Gray seal	9	2.7	Costa (1991): Bowen (1991)*
N. elephant seal	10	3.2	Costa (1991); Bowen (1991)*
Otariids			
N. fur seal	85	0.07	Costa (1991); Bowen (1991)*
CA sea lion	79	0.13	Costa (1991); Bowen (1991)*
Antarctic fur seal	62	0.08	Costa (1991); Bowen (1991)*
Cetaceans			
Mysticetes			
Gray whale	60	16	Sumich (1986)
Blue whale	25	108	Gambell (1979); Rice (1986)
Other Marine Mammals			
Polar bear	10	0.1	Stirling (1988)

na=not available
*See for original sources.

Although body mass will vary substantially on a seasonal basis in those species which experience prolonged post-weaning or seasonal fasts, body length tends to increase regularly until physical maturity is reached. The pattern of length increase with age usually is sigmoidal in shape and is asymptotic. Several commonly used exponential equations are employed to describe and model the pattern of body length increase with increasing age (Brody, 1968; Richards, 1959).

Two features of individual growth patterns of marine mammals stand out. First, growth to physical maturity continues for several years after reaching sexual maturity, so old sexually mature individuals are often much larger than younger, but still sexually mature, individuals of the same gender. Secondly, in polygynous and sexually dimorphic species of pinnipeds and odontocetes, patterns of male growth exhibit a delay in the age of sexual maturity to accommodate a period of accelerated growth into body sizes much larger than those of females (Fig. 14.2). Before polygynous males can compete successfully for breeding territories or establish a high dominance rank, they must achieve a body size substantially larger than that of females. Males of all polygynous species delay both sexual and physical maturity as compared to females. The longer wait to sexual maturity comes at a substantial cost reflected in overall mortality. For example, in northern elephant seals at Año Nuevo Island, histories of individual males collected between 1967 and 1986 were similar; only 7–14% of males survived to 8–9 years of age, when they could first successfully compete for females. Females, however, must only survive to about four years of age prior to successfully breeding (Le Boeuf and Reiter, 1988; Clinton and Le Boeuf, 1993). The period of accelerated male growth often corresponds to the age at which females of the same species achieve sexual maturity. Although the life history of male northern elephant seals is geared toward high mating success late in life, the chance of living to an age of high

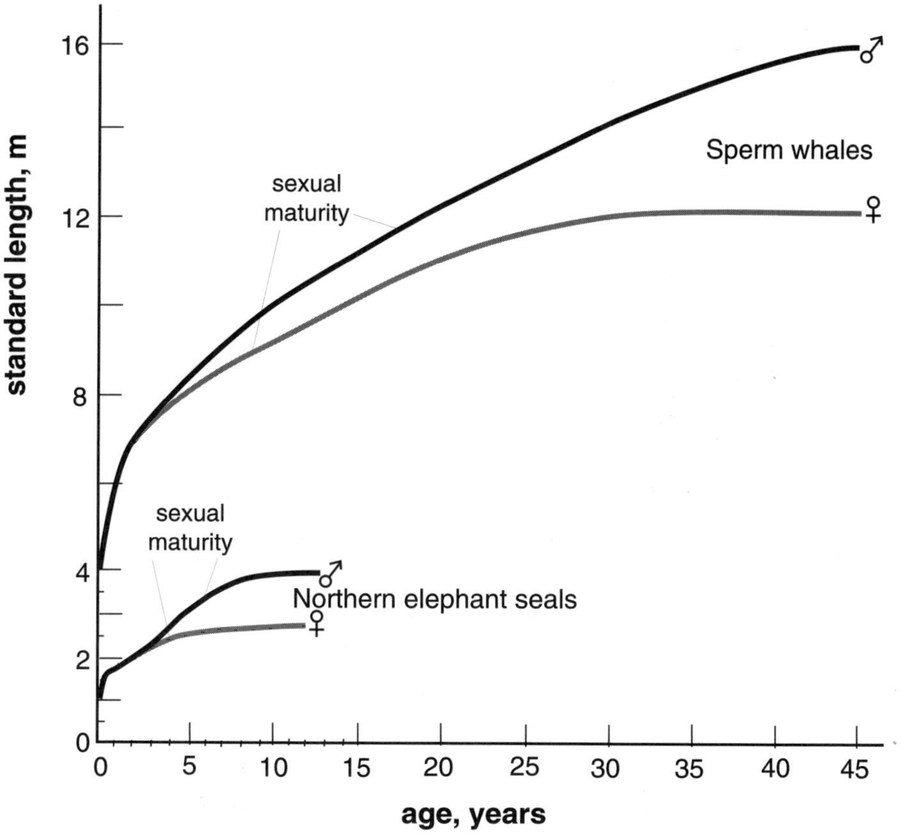

Figure 14.2. Growth curves for male and female sperm whales (top) adapted from Lockyer, 1981 and northern elephant seals (bottom) adapted from Clinton, 1994.

mating success is low because male mortality is relatively high. On average, the highest mating success in males occurs at 12–13 years of age, but male survivorship to this age is approximately 1% of males born (Clinton and Le Boeuf, 1993). In monogamous phocids and mysticetes, growth of both sexes is approximately the same until the age of sexual maturity, when females usually outpace males to achieve a slightly larger body size at sexual maturity (Rice and Wolman, 1971; Lockyer, 1984). Studies of growth rates in mysticetes in particular have been hampered by a scarcity of old and physically mature individuals in heavily exploited species, and by a general lack of any mature animals whose ages are known with certainty.

14.1.3. Age Determination and Longevity

The determination of an individual's age is fundamental to evaluating its reproductive contribution to the population. Techniques for age determination of noncaptive animals vary widely among species and among investigators. Several methods of tagging or marking animals, such as the metal Discovery projectile tags (Fig. 14.3) used widely in the first half of the twentieth century, have provided minimum estimates of the ages of some

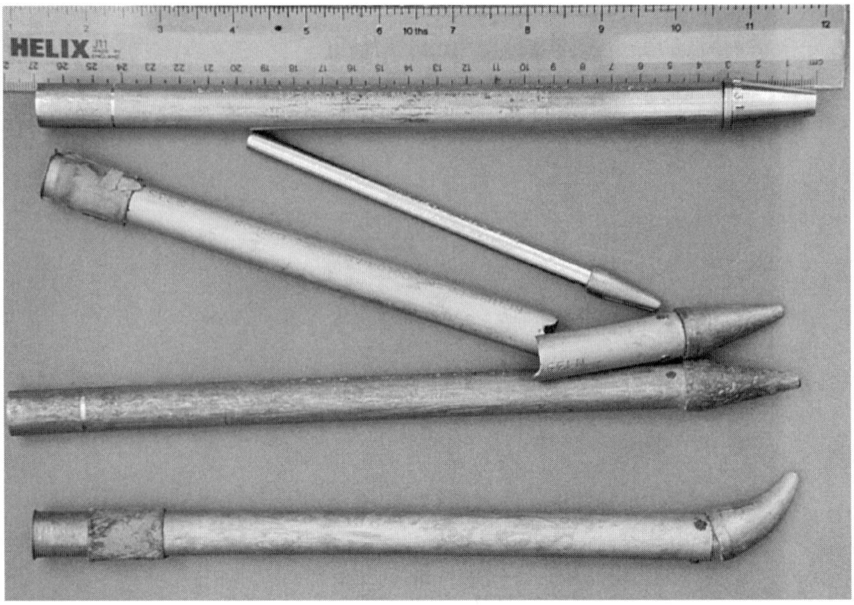

Figure 14.3. Several Discovery-type penetrant tags used for marking large cetaceans. Courtesy G. Donovan, I. W. C.

whales. However, this technique works only if the tagged animal is killed at some later time to recover the embedded tag. Consequently, Discovery tags have been used successfully only with species subject to extensive harvesting and a reasonable likelihood of tag recovery; they are not currently applied to any species.

Another, more reliable method involves determining an individual's age using teeth and bones. As an animal grows, incremental layers accumulate in several hard tissues, especially teeth and bones. These incremental growth layers become a record of the life history of the individual animal, analogous to rings in tree trunks; counting these layers is now widely used to establish ages of individual marine mammals. This technique assumes that teeth or other hard parts can be obtained (teeth are preferred over bone), that incremental growth layers can be discerned, and that the time interval represented by a single growth increment can be independently established. Teeth typically are obtained from dead specimens or from captive or temporarily restrained individuals of all groups of marine mammals except mysticetes. Procedures for enhancing the visibility of the growth increments usually include thinly slicing and polishing teeth, then etching or staining the polished surface to better resolve the growth layers (reviewed in Perrin and Myrick, 1980). Each countable unit of repeating incremental growth layers contains at least one change in tissue density, hardness, or opacity, and is referred to as a **growth layer group (GLG)**; Fig. 14.4. In most species so far examined, each GLG is thought to represent an annual increment (Perrin and Myrick, 1980).

In mysticetes, GLGs of bony tissues such as tympanic bullae and skull bones have been studied with limited success, with the maximum number of GLGs providing only a minimum estimate of age (Klevezal' *et al.*, 1986). More commonly, alternating light and dark zones in the large waxy ear plugs of mysticetes have been used (Fig. 14.5). Several studies have established that one GLG, consisting of one light and one adjacent dark band, repre-

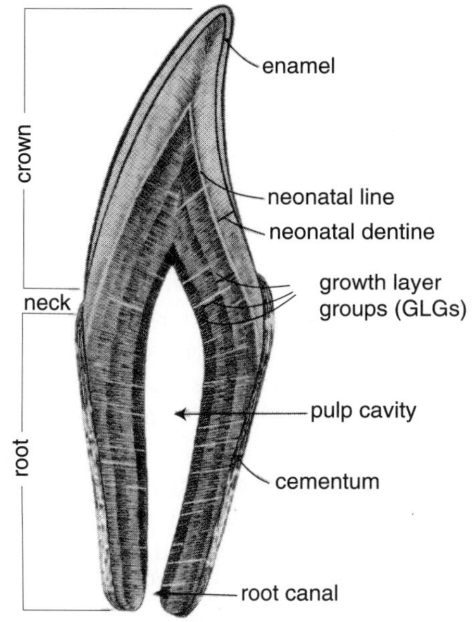

Figure 14.4. Polished cross-section of a dolphin tooth showing major structural features and well-defined growth layer groups. (From Perrin and Myrick, 1980.)

sents an annual increment (Laws and Purves, 1956; Roe, 1967; Rice and Wolman, 1971; Sumich, 1986), although only slightly more than one-half of the ear plugs collected in each of two studies of gray whales by Rice and Wolman (1971) and Blokhin and Tiupeleyev (1987) were considered readable. Additionally, in older animals, there often is some loss of ear plug laminae deposited in an animal's early years, and this technique is usually not considered a reliable estimator of age much beyond the onset of sexual maturity.

For cetacean species that have experienced extended periods of commercial hunting and collection of anatomical specimens (e.g. sperm whales and large mysticetes), reproductive organs can provide some evidence of age as well as of reproductive history. As mentioned

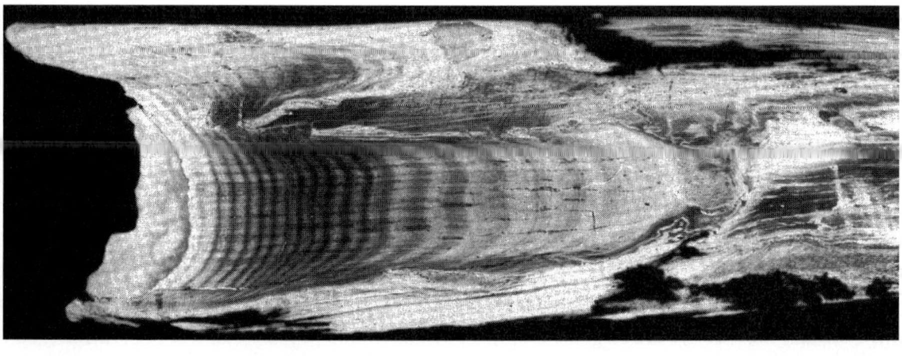

Figure 14.5. Polished cross-section of a fin whale ear plug showing annual growth layers. (From Lockyer, 1984.)

in the previous chapter, the reproductive history of the individual female can be read from an examination of the ovaries and a count of the total number of corpora albicantia. If the time interval between successive pregnancies can be independently established, and the age at sexual maturity is known (see following section), an estimate of age can be derived. For example, a large and physically mature gray whale female reported by Rice and Wolman (1971) to have 34 corpora albicantia is estimated to have been 75–80 years old when she died [(34 corpora) × (2 year interpregnancy interval) + (8–9 years to sexual maturity)], and she was pregnant when she was killed.

For most species of cetaceans, estimates of average or maximum life spans are simply unavailable, either because the species has never experienced intensive commercial exploitation and the tissues needed to establish age have not been available, or because populations of long-lived species with extensive histories of commercial exploitation (including most species of mysticetes) currently express age distributions which have been biased by the harvesting of larger and older animals, leaving a relatively youthful population with few individuals approaching maximum age (Sumich and Harvey, 1986).

A few generalizations concerning pinniped longevity can be made. Females, especially those of polygynous species, tend to live longer than males, most of whom do not survive even to the delayed age of sexual maturity (Bigg, 1981). Southern elephant seal females have been known to pup successfully at 24–25 years, and individual known-age wild female ringed and gray seals have been known to exceed 40 years of age (Bonner, 1971).

14.1.4. Age of Sexual Maturity

Marine mammals are considered sexually mature when they are capable of producing gametes (sperm and eggs). As indicated in Fig. 14.2 and in Table 14.2, there exists a male:female dichotomy in the age of sexual maturity for sexually dimorphic species. In these polygynous species, females typically begin breeding as soon as they are sexually mature, whereas males require several years of social and physical maturation following sexual maturity before they can successfully compete for access to females. Sexual maturity of females occurs around four years of age in northern elephant and gray seals and six years of age in males. Walrus males mature about four years later than females (Table 14.2). The average age of sexual maturity for baleen whales ranges from ten years in the blue whale to 7–14 years in minke whales (Lockyer, 1984; Table 14.2), with no apparent differences between genders. Among odontocetes, estimates of sexual maturity range from 4–5 years in common dolphins to 14 years in killer whales (Table 14.2) with few gender-based age differences. The more dimorphic sperm whale requires about three years longer for males to reach sexual maturity compared to females.

The average age of sexual maturity in some species appears sensitive to density-related competition for space or food. In crowded and commercially unexploited southern elephant seal breeding colonies, females mature at an average age of six years, whereas on recently colonized and uncrowded rookeries, females reach puberty at two years of age (Carrick *et al.*, 1962). Similar reductions in age of maturity have been demonstrated in southern hemisphere fin and sei whales when their populations were reduced by commercial hunting, and in minke whales as the numbers of their larger mysticete food competitors were dramatically reduced during the first half of the twentieth century (Fig. 14.6; Lockyer, 1984; Kato and Sakuramoto, 1991). Lockyer (1984) estimated that by 1970, the overall mysticete whale density was reduced over the entire Antarctic summer feeding area to about 15% of

Table 14.2. Approximate Ages of Sexual Maturity for Several Species of Marine Mammals

Species	Mean age at sexual maturity: Females	Males	Source
Pinnipeds			
Phocids			
Harbor seal	2–7	3–7	Riedman (1990)*
Gray seal	3–5	6	Riedman (1990)*
N. Elephant seal	4	6	Riedman (1990)*
Otariids			
N. fur seal	3–7	5	Riedman (1990)*
CA sea lion	4–5	4–5	Riedman (1990)*
Antarctic fur seal	3–4	3–4	Riedman (1990)*
Walrus	5–6	9–10	Riedman (1990)*
Cetaceans			
Odontocetes			Perrin and Reilly (1984)
Bottlenose dolphin	~12	~11	Perrin and Reilly (1984)
Striped dolphin	9	9	Perrin and Reilly (1984)
Common dolphin	2–6	3–7	Perrin and Reilly (1984)
L.fin pilot whale	6–7	12	Perrin and Reilly (1984)
Killer whale	14	12–14	Ford *et al.* (1994)
Sperm whale	9	12	Lockyer (1981)
Mysticetes			
Gray whale	9	9	Rice and Wolman (1971)
Blue whale	10	10	Rice (1986)
Minke whale	7–14	7–14	Lockyer (1984)
Sirenians			
Manatee	6–10, 12.6	6–10	Reynolds and Odell (1991); Marmontel (1995)
Dugong	9.5	9–10	Marsh (1995)
Other Marine Mammals			
Sea otter	4	6–7	Jameson (1989); Jameson and Johnson (1993)
Polar bear	4	6	Stirling (1988)

*See for original sources.

its pre-1920 level. Whether the effects of these and other whaling-induced changes in resource competition may have influenced inter-pregnancy intervals of these species is discussed by Clapham and Brownell (1996).

Both sexes of manatees typically become sexually mature between six and ten years of age (Reynolds and Odell, 1991), although an average age of 12.6 years for female Florida manatees was reported by Marmontel (1995). In dugongs, the age of sexual maturity reported in a female in one study was 9.5 years and ranged between nine and ten years for males (Marsh, 1995; Table 14.2). Sexual maturity in female Californian and Alaskan sea otters occurred at an average age of four years (Riedman and Estes, 1990; Jameson and

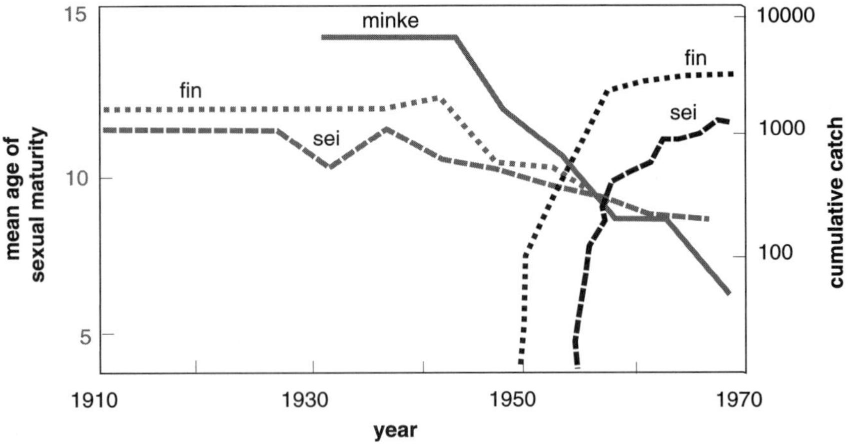

Figure 14.6. Changes in Antarctic balaenopterid ages of sexual maturity over time (thick lines) and cumulative catches in the same whaling areas. (From Lockyer, 1984; and Kato and Sakuramoto, 1991).

Johnson, 1993). Both sexes of polar bears become sexually mature at an average age of 4–6 years and are reproductively senescent by age 20 (Ramsay and Stirling, 1988).

14.1.5. Natural Mortality

Common causes of natural mortality in marine mammal populations include predation, parasites, disease, starvation, and trauma (human-induced mortality is discussed in the following chapter). In general terms, age-specific mortality rates are a function of a population's age distribution and of its age-specific mortality patterns. Most mammalian populations exhibit U-shaped mortality:age curves, with high mortality rates in young age classes followed by several years of low mortality in middle-aged individuals and increasing mortality rates in old-age classes (Caughley, 1966). As noted above, however, several species of large cetaceans which have experienced episodes of population size reduction due to commercial hunting within the last century have yet to recover to their preexploitation population sizes, and these relatively youthful populations exhibit little natural mortality of older animals. Consequently, mortality rates of early year classes are better documented and understood than are rates of older age classes for these animals. First-year mortality rates exceeding 50% are not uncommon and have been documented for several pinnipeds (Barlow and Boveng, 1991; Harcourt, 1992) and cetaceans (Sumich and Harvey, 1986; Aguilar, 1991). Preweaning mortality in pinnipeds is variable and often high because of the physical trauma associated with living in crowded rookery conditions. During early colonization of Año Nuevo Island, northern elephant seal pup mortality averaged 34% while on the rookery, and it increased to 63% by age one. Most (about 60%) of the mortality occurring on these rookeries results from injuries inflicted by adults (Le Boeuf *et al.*, 1994). Postrookery survivorship estimates showed no relation to gender or body mass of pup at weaning. However, in southern sea lions, pups living in colonies had substantially lower preweaning mortality rates than do pups reared by sequestered or isolated mothers (Campagna *et al.*, 1992).

The strong tendency of pinnipeds to haul-out on ice or islands limits the impact of terrestrial predators on these populations. Predation by polar bears on arctic ice seals was discussed in Chapter 11. Other opportunistic terrestrial predators of pinnipeds (especially pups) include wolves, dogs, foxes, jackals, hyenas and pumas (summarized by Riedman, 1990). More serious effects of predators on some pinniped populations are made by marine predators, especially adult male sea lions and leopard seals, killer whales (described in Chapter 11) and several species of large sharks. White sharks have been observed killing and feeding on small odontocetes and scavenging on carcasses of large cetaceans (Long and Jones, 1996, and references cited therein), and at least four other shark species (tiger, white-tip, bull, and gray) have been reported to prey on pinnipeds (Riedman, 1990). Long *et al.* (1996) summarized pinniped records of great white shark bites and provided inferences of annual, seasonal, and geographic trends and variations in shark-pinniped predatory interactions over a 23-year period. Confirmation that white sharks inflict lethal wounds on California sea otters was reported by Ames *et al.* (1996) although they were unable to provide conclusive evidence that white sharks eat sea otters. Hiruki *et al.* (1992, 1993) and Westlake and Gilmartin (1990) have described the impact of wounds inflicted by tiger and white-tip sharks on the reproductive success of female Hawaiian monk seals.

As reviewed by Klimley *et al.* (1996), the predatory behavior of white sharks on young northern elephant seals [described earlier by Tricas and McCosker (1984) and Ainley *et al.* (1985)] involves a stealthy approach along the sea bottom in shallow areas where seals enter the water. White sharks are characterized by strong countershading patterns, and their approach must be difficult for seals to detect while swimming at the surface. When a potential prey is located, the shark swims upward from below and bites the prey to cause profuse bleeding. The bleeding seal is carried underwater where it is held tightly in the shark's jaws until it dies of blood loss. Stomach content analyses indicate that white sharks prefer pinnipeds or whales to other prey such as birds or sea otters. This selective preference for marine mammals with extensive lipid stores may be necessary to satisfy the demands of maintaining elevated muscle temperatures and high growth rates in the cool temperate waters where their attacks on pinnipeds are concentrated (Ainley *et al.*, 1985).

An example of virus-induced mortality in marine mammals is the **morbillivirus** (Fig. 14.7, Hall, 1995, Kennedy, 1998). Morbilliviruses are recognized as serious pathogens of

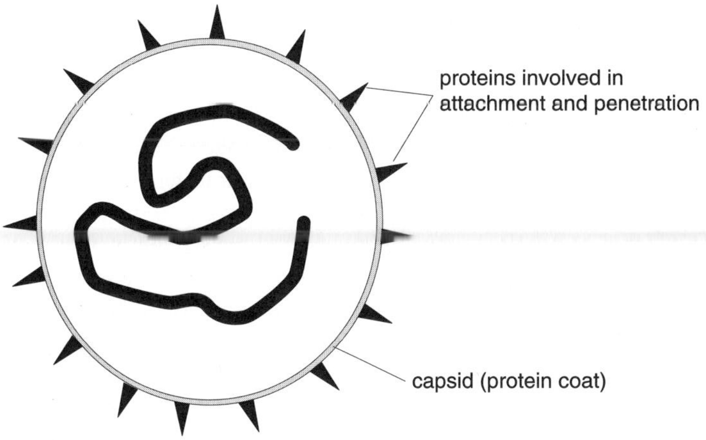

Figure 14.7. Simplified general structure of morbillivirus. (Redrawn from Hall, 1995.)

cetaceans and pinnipeds. In early 1988, harbor seals of the North Sea and adjacent Baltic Sea experienced a massive and abrupt die-off of 17,000–20,000 animals. These deaths accounted for 60–70% of all harbor seals in some local populations. Examination of the dead seals indicated that the ultimate cause of this "seal plague" was a previously unknown virus, which has been christened phocine distemper virus (PDV; Osterhaus and Vedder, 1988; Harwood and Grenfell, 1990). PDV is similar to the virus causing distemper in dogs and measles in humans. In infected seals, the virus suppresses immune system responses, leaving the individual open to secondary bacterial infections. Two other morbilliviruses affecting marine mammals have been recognized, porpoise morbillivirus (PMV) and dolphin morbillivirus (DMV). The latter was responsible for large scale mortalities in striped dolphins in the Mediterranean in 1990 (Duignan *et al.*, 1992). Antibodies to morbilliviruses have been detected in Florida manatees (Duignan *et al.*, 1995a,b), although no infections or clinical problems have been observed. Blood tests have shown that Florida manatees have been infected by a morbillivirus similar to the cetacean virus (PMV and DMV) since 1986, suggesting that the infection is sporadic in this species. A possible explanation is that the Florida manatee is a dead-end host, allowing sufficient viral replication to elicit an antibody response, but not enough to transmit disease. Antillean and Amazon manatees appear not to have been exposed to morbillivirus although sample sizes studied are small (Duignan *et al.*, 1995a).

Massive seal die-offs are not new. Historical records indicate that harbor seal die-offs with symptoms like those seen in 1988 have occurred around Great Britain at least four times in the past 200 years. In 1918, harbor seal populations around Iceland succumbed in large numbers to pneumonia. Another virus-induced die-off of harbor seals occurred in New England in 1979–1980. In 1955, more than 60% of the crabeater seals around the Antarctic died of an unidentified viral infection. Although most of these seal deaths were caused by a virus (possibly the same virus), we do not yet understand what initiates the rapid spread and increased virulence leading to a large-scale die-off of infected individuals. Several hypotheses have been proposed, including crowding and increased resource competition resulting from rapidly increasing population sizes, increasing levels of environmental contaminants in food, toxic dinoflagellate blooms (Boesch *et al.*, 1997), and even gradually increasing water temperatures (Lavigne and Schmitz, 1990). For each of these hypotheses, some evidence exists to support its claim as the factor that caused the seal populations to suddenly become susceptible to the virus in 1988. Other viruses known or suspected to infect marine mammals include those causing papillomas, genital warts, and plaques on penile or vaginal epithelia, conditions that may interfere with successful reproduction.

Several populations of the southern elephant seal have been found to have low genetic variability at immune response loci (i.e. major histocompatibility complex or MHC), as measured by restriction fragment length polymorphisms (see section 14.2.3.3), in comparison to terrestrial mammals (Slade, 1992). Similar observations have been reported previously for fin whales. Together these results have been interpreted as indicating that these marine mammals are exposed to relatively few pathogens and consequently, there is less selection pressure to maintain population-based diversity at immune response loci. Reduced exposure to pathogens which are thought to be diffusely concentrated in the marine environment would also mean that marine mammal populations may be susceptible to occasional pathogen-induced mass mortalities (e.g. morbilliviruses discussed above). Additionally, low levels of genetic variation have been implicated as increasing the vulnerability of a species to infectious diseases (Kretzmann *et al.*, 1997, and references cited therein).

14.2. Techniques for Monitoring Populations

When individual members of populations can be recognized and identified over extended time periods, several life history characteristics of those individuals can be established and some parameters of the populations to which they belong also may be deduced. Currently, the most widely applied techniques for repeated identification of individual noncaptive marine mammals are flipper tagging, photo-identification, radio-tagging, and genetic identification. Individual pinnipeds or sea otters tagged as pups with easily visible plastic tags can be identified repeatedly when hauled out (Fig. 14.8), or even while resting at the sea surface, and movement patterns, home ranges or territories, growth rates, longevity, and reproductive success sometimes can be determined from observations associated with repeated sightings of the same individual.

14.2.1. Photographic Identification

Life history and population information can be established for pinnipeds, cetaceans, and manatees using photographic techniques to identify individuals based on patterns of scars, natural pigmentation, callosities, or barnacle patches on the skin. In its simplest form, the

Figure 14.8. Weaned northern elephant seal pup with flipper tags and a hot brand on the left flank used for long-term identification and to estimate rates of flipper tag loss. Courtesy B. Stewart, Hubbs-Sea World Research Institute.

technique involves photographing a visually unique part of the subject animal, such as its head or flukes, then collecting and cataloging these images so that they may be compared to photographs of the same animal taken at another time and/or place. The complex and separate genealogies of Pacific Northwest killer whale populations (Fig. 10.21) and North Pacific and North Atlantic humpbacks and North Atlantic right whales are based on an extensive collection and cataloging system of photographic images of individual whale pigmentation and scar patterns (Fig. 14.9).

Some of the photographic image collections used for individual identification purposes include up to ten thousand images representing only a few thousand whales. As the extensive collection of images of these whales continues to grow, new and faster methods for digitizing images and computer-based retrieval and matching methods have been developed (Mizroch *et al.*, 1990). High-resolution video or still digital images are beginning to replace film-based photography in the field.

(a)

(b)

Figure 14.9. Individual identification photographs of two killer whales from A pod, northeastern Pacific (a), and a humpback whale near Isla Socorro, eastern North Pacific. Courtesy J. Jacobsen.

14.2.2. Radio and Satellite Telemetry

The location, behavior, and even identity of individual marine mammals are sometimes difficult to monitor because they travel long distances at sea, remain submerged for prolonged periods of time, and are simply difficult to identify individually in crowded groupings. These limitations on individual behavioral studies are being overcome with a variety of electronic monitoring or recording devices, including behavioral and physiological recorders and a variety of very high frequency (VHF) and ultra high frequency (UHF) radio transmitters for data telemetry and position determination. All of these technologies have benefited from advances in earth-orbit satellite communications, electronic miniaturization, information storage, and battery power capacities. These technologies have resulted in improved quality of data, reduced instrument package size, better instrument protection from sea water and hydrostatic pressure, and improved methods of attaching instruments to animals (Stewart *et al.*, 1989).

Attaching recorders and transmitters to free-ranging pinnipeds usually requires their capture and physical restraint or chemical immobilization (DeLong and Stewart, 1991). Substantial progress has been made in the development of immobilizing drugs for terrestrial mammals (including polar bears). However, the use of compounds such as ketamine hydrochloride on pinnipeds is relatively new and is still considered experimental (Erickson and Bester, 1993), and such compounds cannot be used at all on cetaceans or sirenians. Consequently, physical restraint often is preferred for smaller animals (Fig. 14.10) which can be handled safely without chemical immobilization (Gentry and Casanas, 1997).

Once an animal is immobilized or restrained, several methods of attaching instrument packages have been employed successfully, ranging from fast-setting adhesives on pinniped guard hairs (Fig. 14.11; DeLong and Stewart, 1991) to body harnesses on gray whale

Figure 14.10. Temporary net restraint of harbor seals for measuring and tag attachment. Courtesy J. Harvey.

calves (Norris and Gentry, 1974), tail tethers on manatees (Reid *et al.*, 1995), surgical implantation in sea otters (Ralls *et al.*, 1989), and mechanical attachment to dorsal fins of odontocetes (Mate *et al.*, 1995). For radio transmitters, the choice of attachment sites on cetaceans is limited to the dorsal surface, as signal transmission will not occur when the transmitter antenna is submerged. Nontransmitting recorders, such as the time-depth recorders used by Le Boeuf *et al.* (1988) and DeLong and Stewart (1991) have more flexibility in attachment sites but are constrained by the requirement to recapture, or at least precisely relocate, the subject animal at the end of the study period to retrieve the recorder package. Data recorders have been successfully employed on pinniped species that predictably return to the same breathing holes in ice at the completion of a dive (i.e. Weddell seals; Kooyman *et al.*, 1980) or to the same rookery beaches after a foraging trip at sea (fur seals and both species of elephant seals; DeLong *et al.*, 1992; Walker and Boveng, 1995). For other species, transmitting the accumulated data by radio is preferred.

To avoid the complications inherent in capturing or restraining large cetaceans, Watkins and Schevill (1977) pioneered the use of small projectile-fired radio transmitters to track sperm whales. Since those early studies, modifications of delivery and attachment systems for unrestrained animals have led to radio transmitters being attached using skin-penetrating devices (Ray *et al.*, 1978; Mate and Harvey, 1984; Mate *et al.*, 1995) and non-penetrating suction cup attachments (Fig. 14.12; Stone *et al.*, 1994).

Figure 14.11. Harbor seal with microprocessor-based TDR glued to newly molted dorsal pelage. Rear flipper tags are also visible. Courtesy B. Stewart, Hubbs-Sea World Research Institute.

Figure 14.12. Suction cup attachment of a transmitter to a humpback whale. (Courtesy J. Goodyear.)

In general terms, each of these systems is intended to record and either transmit or store information about some aspects of an animal's behavior, physiology, or geographical position (and, if monitored over time, its pattern of dispersal or migration). Some systems, such as the acoustic time-depth transmitters employed by Lydersen (1991) on ringed seals to obtain information on diving and haul-out activities, have a limited range, but are an effective tool to monitor subjects in difficult under-ice conditions. At the other extreme are satellite-linked transmitters and **Global Positioning System (GPS)** navigational receivers for precise, yet global-scale, monitoring and position determination.

Signals from low power and relatively inexpensive VHF transmitters can be monitored with portable directional receiving antennas from shore, ships, or aircraft within line of sight range of the transmitter (usually less than 50 km). Even without specialized sensors, these radio tags can provide useful information regarding the location, foraging and haul-out patterns (of pinnipeds), frequency and duration of dives, and swimming velocities. More powerful UHF transmitters attached to whales have been monitored by satellites such as the polar-orbiting Argos system, to provide coverage over oceanic distances and greatly expand the amount of data that can be collected. For example, Mate *et al.* (1995) obtained data on 63,922 dives over a 25-day period for a single adult bottlenose dolphin equipped with a dorsal fin mounted satellite tag. Satellite monitoring of radio-tagged animals is proving to be an especially valuable technique for monitoring animals in remote or inhospitable (to humans) environments (i.e. Dietz and Heide-Jorgensen, 1995).

14.2.3. Molecular Genetic Techniques

Naturally occurring variations in an organism's DNA, resulting from its tendency to mutate in a regular, or at least predictable, pattern, are being used to establish individual identification, gender, parentage (especially paternity), and also population sizes and boundaries (Dover, 1991). The techniques involved include older, low resolution methods of protein analysis through allozyme electrophoresis, cytogenetics (chromosome studies), and DNA-DNA hybridization, as well as a variety of newer, high resolution techniques for analysis of variation in the DNA including restriction fragment length polymorphisms (RFLPs), multilocus DNA fingerprinting, direct DNA sequencing, and microsatellite analyses (Table 14.3). These methods are discussed in detail elsewhere (e.g., Hillis *et al.*, 1996). In the following discussion we focus on the application of these different techniques to the analysis of the individual identification and population structure in marine mammals and discuss the diversity of issues which may be addressed using molecular techniques. For additional information see reviews of this topic by Hoelzel (1993, 1994).

14.2.3.1. Allozymes

Allozyme electrophoresis, a procedure for separating proteins of different molecular sizes and electrical charges and thus different migration rates in electric fields, is the simplest, most versatile, and least expensive of the techniques for detecting levels of genetic variation within and between populations. The resolution of this technique is low, because only protein-coding regions of DNA may be evaluated and only a small proportion of the changes in those regions will cause a detectable change in the mobility of the protein. Allozymes are visualized by chemical staining the electrophoretic gel after migration. Differences in mobility and the presence of allozyme variants are indicated by different band positions on the gel for **homozygotes** and multiple bands for **heterozygotes**. These different band positions represent the allozymes and thus gene frequencies at the loci being evaluated.

The most extensive analysis of genetic variation based on allozyme variation within and between baleen whale populations to date is that conducted by Wada and Numachi (1991). They surveyed a total of 17,925 whales (including fin, sei, minke, and Bryde's whales) from 15 locations. With the exception of Bryde's whale, which has a tropical/subtropical distribution, the species are distributed in all major oceans and in both hemispheres. Popu-

Table 14.3. Application of Various Molecular Genetic Techniques to Problems in Population Biology

Problem	Population structure	Geographic variation	Paternity testing	Mating systems	Individual relatedness
Allozymes	+	+	m	+	m
Chromosomes	m	m	–	m	–
DNA sequence analysis (mtDNA)	+	+	+	+	+
Restriction analysis (RFLP)	+	m	+	m	m
DNA profiling (mini- and microsatellites, fingerprinting)	+,–	+,m	+,+	+,–	+,m

Symbols: –, inappropriate use of technique; +, appropriate use of technique; m, marginally appropriate or appropriate under limited circumstances.
Based on Hillis *et al.*, 1996.

lations of these species were expected to be isolated to some degree on either side of the equator because seasonal differences between the hemispheres put their breeding seasons out of phase. Surprisingly, the results indicated that fin whales showed very little genetic variation between regions as geographically distant as Antarctica, the North Pacific, and the North Atlantic. However, minke whales showed considerable variation between the Antarctic and the North Pacific. For purposes of conservation and management, cetacean populations usually have been distinguished on the basis of geographic distance and barriers. This study, however, illustrates that geographic distance is not necessarily a good indicator of genetic differentiation in these species.

Another study of genetic variation based on allozymes is that conducted by Lidicker and McCollum (1997) on sea otters. Populations of sea otters from Alaska and California showed levels of genetic variation (i.e. allelic variation and **heterozygosity**) more typical of terrestrial mammals than of marine mammals. Sea otters from California were found to have reduced heterozygosity with local inbreeding proposed as a likely explanation.

14.2.3.2. Chromosomes

Similarities and differences in the size and appearance of chromosomes (chromosome heteromorphisms) have often been used in the study of gene maps, population and species differences, and reproductive isolation. In cetaceans, chromosomes have been used to examine patterns of chromosome variability within and among species. In population studies, chromosome heteromorphism analysis makes it possible to investigate relationships among animals of known associations and to establish patterns of reproductive exchange among marine mammal groups. For example, using this method the parentages of known social groups of bottlenose dolphin have been determined (Duffield and Chamberlin-Lea, 1990).

14.2.3.3. DNA Sequence Analysis

DNA changes over time in a finite number of ways, including substitution of one of the four nucleotides bases for another, deletion of one or more bases, insertion of one or more bases, and the duplication of a segment of DNA. These changes can be quantified through direct analysis of DNA sequences. DNA can be extracted from tissue (e.g. muscle, skin, blood, bone, hair, and internal organs). Once extracted, a specific sequence of DNA can then be amplified (copied). This is done by the polymerase chain reaction method (PCR) by which a highly specific DNA region is simultaneously copied and isolated many times. The capacity of PCR to amplify and isolate DNA means that only very small amounts of tissue are required and can be obtained from small biopsy darts or even from collected patches of shed skin. The rate and pattern of nucleotide substitutions differ among genomic regions, rendering each region more or less appropriate for population genetic analysis. The genomic target region to survey is chosen on this basis. The characteristics or changes in specific genomic regions can then be appropriately matched to a particular technique.

14.2.3.3.1. Mitochondrial DNA (mtDNA) Analysis

Several aspects of population structure and dynamics may be addressed with studies of mtDNA sequence data. Such studies usually begin with an assessment of genetic diversity from which geographic range descriptions can then be mapped. Migration rates between population ranges or their subdivisions can be estimated. Estimates of effective population size also can be made from measures of genetic diversity. But perhaps one of the most powerful uses of mtDNA data has been in the determination of species identity and/or stock structure in many endangered or managed species.

MtDNA evolves 5–10 times faster than nuclear genomic DNA and because of this rapid rate, polymorphisms are more likely to be detectable than in proteins or nuclear DNA. MtDNA is maternally inherited, thus it represents only matriarchial phylogeny, allowing a direct assessment of the dispersal patterns of females. The almost exclusive (though some exceptions are known; see Avise, 1996 for a summary) maternal pattern of inheritance of mtDNA makes it more sensitive to fluctuations in population size. Essentially, if more females are present in a population, more variation in mtDNA should exist. For example, Hoelzel and Dover (1991) estimated the long-term effective population size of minke whales to be 400,000 based on mtDNA variation in three populations.

Analysis of mtDNA variation also can provide information on genetic variation among populations for use in determining stock identifications and management. Results of a study of mtDNA variation in three major humpback whale lineages (i.e. North Atlantic, North Pacific, and Southern Ocean populations) revealed high levels of genetic variation among populations (Baker *et al.*, 1990). Comparable studies of control region (part of the mtDNA genome) diversity in other cetacean species, including killer whales (Hoelzel and Dover, 1991) and harbor porpoises (Rosel *et al.*, 1995), indicate that harbor porpoises have higher levels of nucleotide diversity between populations averaged over three oceanic basins (North Pacific, North Atlantic, and Black Sea) than either the humpback or killer whale populations (Rosel *et al.*, 1995). Moreover, the amount of sequence divergence between North Pacific and North Atlantic harbor porpoise populations is 3.5 times higher than similar comparisons in humpback and killer whales (Rosel *et al.*, 1995). Rosel *et al.* (1995) suggested that lower levels of sequence divergence in humpback and killer whale populations may reflect the greater mobility of these species, resulting in higher levels of genetic exchange among populations.

In pinniped species, patterns of mtDNA variation in the harbor seal revealed that populations in the Pacific and Atlantic Oceans are highly differentiated (Stanley *et al.*, 1996). These data are consistent with an ancient isolation of populations in both oceans due to the development of polar sea ice about 2–3 Ma. In the Atlantic and Pacific, populations appear to have been colonized from west to east, with the European population showing the most recent common ancestry. The results of Stanley *et al.* (1996) were used to define a hierarchy of population units for ranking conservation priorities. In another study, analysis of mtDNA variation in southern hemisphere fur seals revealed distinctly different patterns of molecular evolution and population substructure among four congeneric species (Lento *et al.*, 1994, 1997). These molecular data are inconsistent with current definitions of species and argue for reevaluation of these "species" definitions which, in turn, has important implications for management. Similar studies of mtDNA variation in populations of California sea lions (Maldonado *et al.*, 1995), Steller sea lions (Bickham *et al.*, 1996), Atlantic and Pacific walrus subspecies (Cronin *et al.*, 1994; Anderson *et al.*, 1998), sea otter subspecies (Cronin *et al.*, 1996), and polar bears (Cronin *et al.*, 1991) have concluded that mtDNA is particularly useful in stock identification and conservation management.

Analysis of genetic variation also can provide important information on the demographic history of some species, including the extent of inbreeding within a population. For example, Hoelzel *et al.* (1993) and Halley and Hoelzel (1996) used mtDNA variation and census data to calculate the size and duration of the population bottleneck experienced by the northern elephant seal. Confidence limits of 95% indicated a bottleneck event of fewer than 30 seals for less than 20 years or a single year bottleneck of fewer than 20 seals. Historical evidence, however, supports the later hypothesis of a one-year bottleneck. Calibration of the rate of control region evolution across three families of whales indicates that the three existing clades of humpback whale lineages would have diverged about 5 Ma (Baker *et al.*, 1993; Baker *et al.*, 1998). The current mtDNA variation indicates that humpback whales did not undergo a significant loss of genetic diversity during the recent bottleneck due to the commercial whaling industry.

14.2.3.3.2. Restriction Site Analysis

Restriction enzymes (originally isolated from bacteria) cut double stranded DNA at particular nucleotide sequences, usually four, five, or six nucleotides long. The restriction enzyme will cleave the DNA wherever the particular recognition sequence (or restriction site) of the enzyme occurs. The result is a series of "restriction fragments" of the DNA. Variation in the lengths of these fragments between individuals indicates variation in the presence or absence of the restriction sites, and tests to examine length differences are termed restriction fragment length polymorphisms, or RFLPs. RFLP analyses begin by cutting DNA from each individual with one or more restriction enzymes, then separating the resulting fragments by gel electrophoresis, and scoring the visualized bands of size-sorted fragments. The frequency distribution of RFLP bands among individuals in a population is then used to describe the population structure. This method can be used with great efficiency to screen populations or species for specific changes in sequence. Dizon *et al.* (1991) compared mtDNA RFLP data among different populations of spinner dolphins (i.e. eastern, whitebelly, and pantropical). Results of this study showed high levels of variation within and between populations of eastern and whitebelly forms, indicating significant genetic interchange between them despite large differences in morphology. In another study, Dowling and Brown (1993) investigated mtDNA RFLP variation among bottlenose dolphins from the eastern Pacific and western North Atlantic. Isolation of Atlantic versus Pacific populations and possibly the existence of two or more populations in the western North Atlantic were the principal conclusions of this study.

14.2.3.3.3. DNA Fingerprinting and Microsatellite Analysis

DNA profiling, a commonly used technique, is based on a very high rate of change seen in repetitive DNA regions such as **microsatellites** and **minisatellites**. Researchers employ DNA profiling to investigate variation in minisatellite loci using single locus or multilocus probes which measure variability at one or more locations in the nuclear genome. The resulting bar-code like bands which constitute a DNA profile or fingerprint can be used to determine three major things: 1) identity, 2) parentage, and 3) relatedness. DNA profiles can be used to determine identity in the same way that traditional fingerprints are used to identify individuals uniquely. DNA fingerprints can be used to determine parentage since approximately 50% of the bands in the offspring come from the mother and the remaining bands come from the father. Thus, it is possible to exclude individuals as parents if bands in offspring are not present in the profiles of either parent (Fig. 14.13). Alternatively, a probabilistic statement may be made regarding the likelihood of parentage. This is done by determining a band-sharing coefficient for all possible pairs of sires and offspring and dams and offspring. Pairs with the highest band-sharing coefficients are the most likely to be primary relatives. It is this capability that gives DNA fingerprinting its greatest potential. DNA fingerprinting also can be used to determine nonparental relatedness. In many

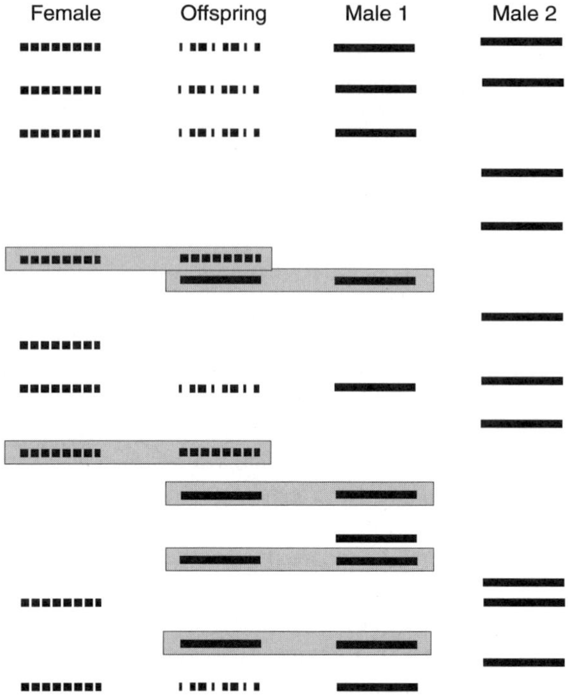

Figure 14.13. Representation of paternity testing by DNA fingerprinting. Offspring bands were derived from the mother (even dashes), the father (solid lines), or both (uneven dashes). Male 2 may be eliminated as the father since he and the offspring share no bands. (Redrawn from Hoelzel, 1993.)

species, the band-sharing coefficient between two siblings, like that between a parent and offspring, is greater than 50%. The proportion of band-sharing between two unrelated individuals can be as low as 20–30%. Thus the degree of relatedness between two individuals can be estimated by their degree of band-sharing based on a survey of band-sharing in individuals of known relatedness.

The use of DNA profiling to study population structure, mating systems, and reproductive behavior has largely involved cetaceans. The use of DNA profiling to test paternity can be especially time consuming when many pairwise comparisons have to be made. Such is the case in the study of paternity among polygynous species. To test paternity, it is usually necessary to collect samples from both mother and offspring, as well as the set of potential sires. However, even the identification of potential sires requires the long-term recognition of individuals and observations of associations between the female and potential mates at the time of conception. One example where the field observation data are this detailed is for a bottlenose dolphin study on the Gulf coast of Florida (Duffield and Wells, 1991). Results from this study indicate that males moving through the home ranges of matrifocal (female related) groups achieve matings through temporary associations. Exclusive male access to females or groups within the community was not observed.

In a related study of paternity in pods of long-finned pilot whales captured in the Faroese drive fishery, Amos *et al.* (1991) found that for only four out of 34 paternity tests were the sires members of the pod. It was assumed in most cases that the entire pod had been captured and sampled. Paternal exclusions were achieved using the multilocus DNA fingerprint probe. A pair of bands apparently representing a single locus within the multilocus pattern was used to assess the probability that mating was random. Amos *et al.* (1991) concluded that males often successfully mate with two or more females, and generally not with females within their own pod.

There are several reasons why DNA profiling has not been as widely used to study pinnipeds as it has to study cetaceans. The reproductive behavior of many pinnipeds can be observed directly, whereas in cetaceans direct observation is difficult. Pinnipeds do not form small social groups or exhibit obvious cooperative behavior as is often found in cetacean social groups. DNA profiling has, however, revealed important information about pinniped social structure, as reviewed by Boness *et al.* (1993). For example, two studies suggest that female harbor seals may be choosing mates and that males positioned in the water just off the beach do not simply have exclusive mating rights to females that move through their territories (Harris *et al.*, 1991; Perry, 1993). Using DNA fingerprinting, McRae and Kovacs (1994) excluded the possibility that attending males within hooded seal trios (consisting of an adult female, her pup, and an attending adult male) were the fathers of the pups, establishing either that they did not remain paired from one breeding season to the next or that, like gray seals, attending males do not necessarily fertilize the females they are attending.

Several other pinniped researchers have used analysis of hypervariable minisatellite loci to investigate general questions of inherent levels of genetic variability. Minisatellites are among the most variable DNA sequences yet discovered and are best suited for indicating individual relatedness. Additionally, in populations with reduced genetic variability, minisatellites often are the only markers able to detect useful polymorphisms (Burke *et al.*, 1996). DNA profiles were examined in the northern elephant seal and compared to the harbor seal (Lehman *et al.*, 1993). Results indicated that this species lacks genetic variability, with roughly 90% of alleles being shared among all individuals tested. In contrast, harbor seals from the eastern Pacific possess much greater levels of variation at these loci. In other studies, Amos (1993) and Amos *et al.* (1995) used analysis of multi- and single-locus profiles to assign paternity in colonies of gray seals on North Rona Island, Scotland. Long-term mate fidelity in gray seals was also studied (Amos *et al.*, 1995), with results indicating a surprisingly high degree of mate fidelity for this polygynous species (discussed in Chapter 12).

In addition to minisatellites, another class of repetitive DNA, microsatellite loci, has been used as an alternative to traditional methods of individual recognition because these loci are permanent and exist in all individuals. The frequency distribution of microsatellite alleles at a single or a few loci can be used to characterize population substructure. Statistical analysis of allelic combinations at several loci can be used to make individual identifications. In a study of humpback whales, analysis of microsatellite loci allowed the unequivocal identification of individuals (Palsbøll *et al.*, 1997). In addition to revealing local and migratory movements of humpbacks, genetic tagging allowed the first estimates of animal abundance based on genotypic data (Palsbøll *et al.*, 1997). Microsatellite markers were used to determine paternity in humpback whales, confirming observations of a promiscuous mating system (Clapham and Palsbøll, 1997). In a study of long-finned pilot whale pod structure, Amos (1993) used microsatellite loci to confirm results of an earlier study (Amos *et al.*, 1991) reporting that pilot whales travel in matrifocal kin groups. Microsatellite data also were used to study the genetic relationship between four Canadian polar bear populations (Paetkau *et al.*, 1995). Considerable genetic variation was detected among all populations, indicating that despite the long-distance seasonal movements undertaken by polar bears, gene flow among local populations is restricted. In another study, the genetic variation in sperm whales measured by analysis of microsatellite markers offered insight into the patterns of kinship, suggesting that females form permanent social units based on one or several matrilines (Richard *et al.*, 1996). This example also illustrates how combining molecular genetic data with analysis of field sightings has increased our understanding of sperm whale social organization.

14.3. Summary and Conclusions

Marine mammals are k-selected species with life history patterns based on low birth and death rates that have evolved to maintain relatively stable population sizes at or near carrying capacity. Growth rates vary considerably between species over several orders of magnitude. Sexual maturity in most marine mammals precedes physical maturity. In polygynous species of pinnipeds and odontocetes, males exhibit a delay in the age of sexual maturity to accommodate accelerated growth into body sizes much larger than those of females. Among common causes of natural mortality in marine mammal populations are predators (especially sharks and killer whales), parasites, diseases (e.g. morbilliviruses, toxic dinoflagellate blooms), and trauma.

Techniques for the repeated identification of marine mammals include flipper tagging, photo-identification, radio and satellite telemetry, and a variety of molecular genetic methods (i.e. analysis of chromosomes, allozymes, and DNA sequences). Molecular genetic techniques are now widely used to establish individual identification and gender, parentage (especially paternity), and population sizes and boundaries. This genetic information has proven particularly useful in stock identification and management.

14.4. Further Reading

For a review of pinniped life history characteristics see Costa (1991), and for cetaceans see Perrin and Reilly (1984) and Lockyer (1984). The population dynamics of sirenians are summarized in O'Shea *et al.* (1995). A collection of edited papers on the application of molecular genetics to problems of marine mammal population biology are in Boyd (1993) and Dizon *et al.* (1997).

References

Aguilar, A. (1991). Calving and early mortality in the western Mediterranean striped dolphin, *Stenella coeruleoalba*. *Can. J. Zool.* **69**: 1408–1412.

Ainley, D. G., R. P. Henderson, H. R. Huber, R. J. Boekekheide, S. G. Allen, and T. L. McElroy (1985). Dynamics of white shark/pinniped interactions in the Gulf of the Farallones. *South. Calif. Acad. Sci. Mem.* **9**: 109–122.

Ames, J. A., J. J. Geibel, F. E. Wendell, and C. A. Pattison (1996). White shark-inflicted wounds of sea otters in California, 1968–1992. *In* "Great White Sharks: The Biology of *Carcharodon carcharias*" (A. P. Klimley and D. G. Ainley, eds.), pp. 309–319. Academic Press, San Diego, CA.

Amos, B. (1993). Use of molecular probes to analyze pilot whale pod structure: Two novel approaches. *Symp. Zool. Soc. London* **66**: 33–48.

Amos, B., J. Barrett, and G. A. Dover (1991). Breeding behaviour of pilot whales revealed by DNA fingerprinting. *Heredity* **67**: 49–55.

Amos, B., S. Twiss, P. P. Pomeroy, and S. Anderson (1995). Evidence for mate fidelity in the gray seal. *Science* **268**: 1897–1899.

Andersen, L. W., E. W. Born, I. Gjertz, O. Wiig, L. E. Holm, and C. Bendixen (1998). Population structure and gene flow of the Atlantic walrus (*Odobenus rosmarus rosmarus*) in the eastern Atlantic Arctic based on mitochondrial DNA and microsatellite variation. *Mol. Ecol.* **7**: 1323–1336.

Baker, C. S., S. R. Palumbi. R. H. Lambertsen, M. T. Weinrich, J. Calambokidis, and S. O'Brien (1990). Influence of seasonal migration on geographic distribution of mitochondrial DNA haplotypes in humpback whales. *Nature* **344**: 238–240.

Baker, C. S., L. Flrez-Gonzalez, B. Abernethy, H. C. Rosenbaum, R. W. Slade, J. Capella, and J. L. Bannister (1998). Mitochondrial DNA variation and maternal gene flow among humpback whales of the Southern Hemisphere. *Mar. Mamm. Sci.* **14**: 721–737.

Baker, C. S., A. Perry, J. L. Bannister, M. T. Weinrich, R. B. Abernathy, J. Calambokidis, J. Lien, R. H. Lambertsen, J. Urban Ramirez, O. Vasquez, P. J. Clapham, A. Alling, S. J. O'Brien, and R. S. Palumbi (1993). Abundant mitochondrial DNA variation and world-wide population structure in humpback whales. *Proc. Natl. Acad. Sci. U.S.A.* **90**: 8239–8243.

Barlow, J., and P. Boveng (1991). Modeling age-specific mortality for marine mammal populations. *Mar. Mamm. Sci.* **7**: 50–65.

Bickham, J. W., J. C. Patton, and T. R. Loughlin (1996). High variability for control-region sequences in a marine mammal: Implications for conservation and biogeography of Steller sea lions. *J. Mammal.* **77**(1): 95–108.

Bigg, M. (1981). Harbour seal- *Phoca vitulina* and *P. largha*. *In* "Handbook of Marine Mammals" (S. H. Ridgway and R. J. Harrison, eds.), Vol. 2, pp. 1–27. Academic Press, London.

Blokhin, S. A., and P. A. Tiupeleyev (1987). Morphological study of the earplugs of gray whales and the possibility of their use in age determination (SC/38/PS18). *Rep. Int. Whal. Comm.* **37**: 341–345.

Boesch, D. F., D. M. Anderson, R. A. Horner, S. E. Shumway, P. A. Tester, and T. E. Whitledge (1997). Harmful algal blooms in coastal waters: options for prevention, control, and mitigation. NOAA Coastal Ocean Program Decision Analysis Series No. 10.

Boness, D. J., W. D. Bown, and J. M. Francis (1993). Implications of DNA fingerprinting for mating systems and reproductive strategies of pinnipeds. *Symp. Zool. Soc. London* **66**: 61–93.

Bonner, W. N. (1971). An aged seal *(Halichoerus grypus)*. *J. Zool.* **164**: 261–262.

Bowen, W. D. (1991). Behavioural ecology of pinniped neonates. *In* "The Behaviour of Pinnipeds" (D. Renouf, ed.), pp. 66–127. Chapman & Hall, London.

Bowen, W. D., O. T. Oftedal, and D. J. Boness (1985). Birth to weaning in four days: Remarkable growth in the hooded seal, *Cystophora cristata*. *Can. J. Zool.* **63**: 2841–2846.

Boyd, I. L. (ed.) (1993). Marine Mammals: Advances in Behavioural and Population Biology. *Symp. Zool. Soc. London* 66, Clarendon Press, Oxford.

Brody, S. (1968). "Bioenergetics and Growth." Hafner, New York.

Burke, T., O. Hanotte, and I. Van Pijlen (1996). Minisatellite analysis in conservation genetics. *In* "Molecular Genetic Approaches in Conservation" (T. B. Smith and R. K. Wayne, eds.), pp. 251–277. Oxford University Press, Oxford.

Campagna, C., B. J. Le Boeuf, M. Lewis, and C. Bisoli (1992). The Fisherian seal: Equal investment in male and female pups in southern elephant seals. *J. Zool.* **226**: 551–561.

Caughley, G. (1966). Mortality patterns in mammals. *Ecology* **47**: 906–918.

Clapham, P. J., and R. L. J. Brownell (1996). The potential for interspecfic competition in baleen whales. *Rep. Int. Whal. Comm.* **46**: 361–367.

Clapham, P. J., and P. J. Palsbøll (1997). Molecular analysis of paternity shows promiscuous mating in female humpback whales *(Megaptera novaeangliae,* Borowski). *Proc. R. Soc. London, Ser. B* **264**: 95–98.

Clinton, W. L. (1994). Sexual selection and growth in male Northern elephant seals. *In* "Elephant Seals" (B. J. Le Boeuf and R. M. Laws, eds.), pp. 154–168. University of California Press, Berkeley.

Clinton, W. L., and B. J. Le Boeuf (1993). Sexual selection's effects on male life history and the pattern of male mortality. *Ecology* **74**: 1884–1892.

Costa, D. P. (1991). Reproductive and foraging energetics of pinnipeds; implications for life history patterns. *In* "The Behavior of Pinnipeds" (D. Renouf, ed.), pp. 299–344. Chapman & Hall, London.

Cronin, M. A., S. C. Amstrup, G. Garner, and E. R. Vyse (1991). Intra- and interspecific mitochondrial DNA variation in North American bears *(Ursus)*. *Can. J. Zool.* **69**: 2985–2992.

Cronin, M. A., S. Hills, E. W. Born, and J. C. Patton (1994). Mitochondrial DNA variation in Atlantic and Pacific walruses. *Can. J. Zool.* **72**: 1035–1043.

Cronin, M. A., J. Bodkin, B. Ballachey, J. Estes, and J. C. Patton (1996). Mitochondrial variation among subspecies and populations of sea otters (*Enhydra lutris*). *J. Mammal.* **77**(2): 546–557.

DeLong, R. L., and B. S. Stewart (1991). Diving patterns of Northern elephant seal bulls. *Mar. Mamm. Sci.* **7**: 369–384.

DeLong, R. L., B. S. Stewart, and R. D. Hill (1992). Documenting migrations of Northern elephant seals using day length. *Mar. Mamm. Sci.* **8**(2): 155–159.

Dietz, R., and M. P. Heide-Jorgensen (1995). Movements and swimming speed of narwhals, *Monodon monoceros,* equipped with satellite transmitters in Melville Bay, northwest Greenland. *Can. J. Zool.* **73**: 2106–2119.

Dizon, A. E., S. J. Chivers, and W. F. Perrin (eds.) (1997). Molecular Genetics of Marine Mammals, *Special Publication 3, Society of Marine Mammalogy,* Allen Press, Kansas.

Dizon, A. E., S. O. Southern, and W. F. Perrin (eds.) (1991). Molecular analysis of mtDNA types in exploited populations of spinner dolphins *(Stenella longirostris). Rep. Int. Whal. Comm., Spec. Issue* **13**: 183–202.

Dover, G. A. (1991). Understanding whales with molecular probes. *In* "Genetic Ecology of Whales and Dolphins" *Rep. Int. Whal. Comm. Spec. Issue* **13**: 29–38.

Dowling, T. E., and W. M. Brown (1993). Population structure of the bottlenose dolphin as determined by restriction endonuclease analysis of mitochondrial DNA. *Mar. Mamm. Sci.* **9**: 138–155.

Duffield, D. A., and J. Chamberlin-Lea (1990). Use of chromosome heteromorphisms and hemoglobins in studies of bottlenose dolphin populations and paternities. *In* "Bottlenose Dolphin" (S. Leatherwood and R. R. Reeves, eds.), pp. 609–622. Academic Press, San Diego, CA.

Duffield, D. A., and R. Wells (1991). The combined application of chromosome, protein, and molecular data for the investigation of social units structure and dynamics in *Tursiops truncatus. Rep. Int. Whal. Comm., Spec. Issue* **13**: 155–170.

Duignan, P. J., J. R. Geraci, J. A. Raga, and N. Calzada (1992). Pathology of morbillivirus infection in striped dolphins *(Stenella coeruleoalba)* from Valencia and Murcia, Spain. *Canadian Journal of Veterinary Research* **56**: 242–248.

Duignan, P. J., C. House, M. T. Walsh, T. Campbell, G. D. Bossart, N. Duffy, P. J. Fernandes, B. K. Rima, S. Wright, and J. R. Geraci (1995a). Morbillivirus infection in manatees. *Mar. Mamm. Sci.* **11**(4): 441–451.

Duignan, P. J., C. House, J. R. Geraci, N. Duffy, B. K. Rima, M. T. Walsh, G. Early, D. J. St. Aubin, S. Sadove, H. Koopman, *et al.* (1995b). Morbillivirus infection in cetaceans of the western Atlantic. *Vet. Microbiol.* **44**: 241–249.

Erickson, A. W., and M. N. Bester (1993). Immobilization and capture. *In* "Antarctic Seals" (R. M. Laws, ed.), pp. 46–88. Cambridge University Press, New York.

Ford, J. K. B., G. M. Ellis, and K. C. Balcomb (1994). "Killer Whales: The Natural History and Genealogy of *Orcinus orca* in British Columbia and Washington State." University of Washington Press, Seattle.

Gambell, R. (1979). The blue whale. *Biologist* **26**: 209–215.

Gentry, R. L., and V. R. Casanas (1997). A new method for immobilizing otariid neonates. *Mar. Mamm. Sci.* **13**: 155–156.

Hall, A. J. (1995). Morbilliviruses in marine mammals. *Trends Microbiol.*, **7**(3): ??

Halley, J., and A. R. Hoelzel (1996). Simulation models of bottleneck events in natural populations. *In* "Molecular Genetic Approaches in Conservation" (T. B. Wayne and R. K. Wayne), eds., pp. 347–364. Oxford University Press, Oxford.

Harcourt, R. (1992). Factors affecting early mortality in the South American fur seal *(Arctocephalus australis)* in Peru: Density-related effects and predation. *J. Zool.* **226**: 259–270.

Harris, A. S., J. S. F. Young, and J. M. Wright (1991). DNA fingerprinting of harbour seals (*Phoca vitulina concolor*): male mating behavior may not be a reliable indicator of reproductive success. *Can. J. Zool.* **69**: 1862–1866.

Harwood, J., and B. Grenfell (1990). Long term risks of recurrent seal plagues. *Mar. Pollut. Bull.* **21**: 284–287.

Hillis, D. M., C. Moritz, and B. K. Mable (1996). "Molecular Systematics," 2nd ed. Sinauer Associates, Sunderland, MA.

Hiruki, L. M., I. Stirling, W. G. Gilmartin, T. C. Johanos, and B. L. Becker (1992). Significance of wounding to female reproductive success in Hawaiian monk seals *(Monachus schauinslandi)* at Laysan Island. *Can. J. Zool.* **71**: 469–474.

Hiruki, L. M., W. G. Gilmartin, B. L. Becker, and I. Stirling (1993). Wounding in Hawaiian monk seals *(Monachus schauinslandi). Can. J. Zool.* **71**: 458–468.

Hoelzel, A. R. (1993). Genetic ecology of marine mammals. *Symp. Zool. Soc. London* **66**: 15–29.

Hoelzel, A. R. (1994). Genetics and ecology of whales and dolphins. *Annu. Rev. Ecol. Syst.* **25**: 377–399.

Hoelzel, A. R., and G. A. Dover (1991). Mitochondrial d-loop DNA variation within and between populations of the minke whale *(Balaenoptera acutorostrata). Rep. Int. Whal. Comm., Spec. Issue* **13**: 171–183.

Hoelzel, A. R., J. Halley, C. Campagna, T. Arnbom, B. Le Boeuf, S. J. O'Brien, K. Ralls, and G. A. Dover (1993). Elephant seal genetic variation and the use of simulation models to investigate historical population bottlenecks. *J. Hered.* **84**: 443–449.

Huber, H. R., A. C. Rovetta, L. A. Fry, and S. Johnston (1991). Age-specific natality of northern elephant seals at the South Farallon Islands, California. *J. Mammal.* **72**: 525–534.

Jameson, R. J. (1989). Movements, home range, and territories of male sea otters off central California. *Mar. Mamm. Sci.* **5**: 159–172.

Jameson, R. J., and A. M. Johnson (1993). Reproductive characteristics of female sea otters. *Mar. Mamm. Sci.* **9**(2): 156–167.

Kannan, K., K. Guruge, N. J. Thomas, S. Tanabe, and J. P. Giesy (1997). Elevated accumulation of tributyltin and its breakdown products in bottlenose dolphins (*Tursiops truncatus*) found stranded along the U.S. Atlantic and Gulf Coasts. *Envir. Sci. and Technol.* **31**: 296–301.

Kato, H., and K. Sakuramoto (1991). Age at sexual maturity of Southern Minke Whales: A review and some additional analyses. *Rep. Int. Whal. Comm.* **41**: 331–337.

Kennedy, S. (1998). Morbillivirus infections in aquatic mammals. *Jour. Comp. Path.* **119**: 201–225.

Klevezal', G. A., L. I. Sukhovskaya, and S. A. Blokhin (1986). Age determination of baleen whales from bone layers. [OT: Opredelenie vozrasta usatykh kitov po godovym sloyam v kosti]. *Zool. Zh.* **65**: 1722–1730.

Klimley, A. P., P. Pyle, and S. D. Anderson (1996). The behavior of white sharks and their pinniped prey during predatory attacks. *In* "Great White Sharks: The Biology of *Carcharodon carcharias,* (A. P. Klimley and D. G. Ainley, eds.), pp. 175–192. Academic Press, San Diego, CA.

Kooyman, G. L., E. A. Wahrenbrock, M. A. Castellini, R. W. Davis, and E. E. Sinnett (1980). Aerobic and anaerobic metabolism during voluntary diving in Weddell seals: Evidence of preferred pathways from blood chemistry and behavior. *J. Comp. Physiol.* **138**: 335–346.

Kretzmann, M., W. G. Gilmartin, A. Meyer, G. P. Zegers, S. R. Fain, B. F. Taylor, and D. P. Costa (1997). Low genetic variability in the Hawaiian monk seal. *Conserv. Biol.* **11**(2): 482–490.

Lavigne, D. M., and O. J. Schmitz (1990). Global warming and increasing population densities: A prescription for seal plagues. *Mar. Pollut. Bull.* **21**: 280–284.

Laws, R. M., and P. E. Purves (1956). The ear plug of the Mysticeti as an indication of age with special reference to the North Atlantic fin whale *(Balaenoptera physalus* Linn.). *Nor. Hvalfangst-Tid.* **45**: 413–425.

Le Boeuf, B. J. (1986). Sexual strategies of seals and walruses. *New Sci.* **1491**: 36–39.

Le Boeuf, B. J., and J. Reiter (1988). Lifetime reproductive success in northern elephant seals. *In* "Reproductive Success" (T. H. Clutton-Brock, ed.), pp. 344–362. University of Chicago Press, Chicago.

Le Boeuf, B. J., D. P. Costa, A. C. Huntley, and S. D. Feldkamp (1988). Continuous, deep diving in female northern elephant seals, *Mirounga angustirostris. Can. J. Zool* **66**: 416–458.

Le Boeuf, B. J., P. Morris, and J. Reiter (1994). Juvenile survivorship of Northern elephant seals. *In* "Elephant Seals" (B. Le Boeuf and R. M. Laws, eds.), pp. 121–136. University of California Press, Berkeley.

Lehman, N., R. K. Wayne, and B. S. Stewart (1993). Comparative levels of genetic variability in harbor seals and northern elephant seals as determined by genetic fingerprinting. *Symp. Zool. Soc. London* **66**: 49–60.

Lento, G. M., R. H. Mattlin, G. K. Chambers, and C. S. Baker (1994). Geographic distribution of mitochondrial cytochrome b DNA haplotypes in New Zealand fur seals *(Arctocephalus forsteri). Can. J. Zool.* **72**: 293–299.

Lento, G., M. Hadden, G. K. Chambers, and C. S. Baker (1997). Genetic variation of southern hemisphere fur seals: *Arctocephalus* spp.: Investigation of population structure and species identity. *J. Hered.* **88**: 202–208.

Lidicker, W. Z., and F. C. McCollum (1997). Allozyme variation in sea otters. *J. Mammal.* **78**(2): 417–425.

Lockyer, C. (1981). Estimates of growth and energy budget for the sperm whale, *Physeter catodon. Mamm. Seas* **3**: 489–504.

Lockyer, C. (1984). Review of baleen whale (Mysticeti) reproduction and implications for management. *Rep. Int. Whal. Comm., Spec. Issue* **6**: 27–50.

Long, D. J., and R. E. Jones (1996). White shark predation and scavenging on cetaceans in the eastern North Pacific Ocean. *In* "Great White Sharks: The Biology of *Carcharodon carcharias*" (A. P. Klimley and D. G. Ainley, eds.), pp. 293–308. Academic Press, San Diego, CA.

Long, D. J., K. D. Hanni, P. Pyle, J. Roletto, R. E. Jones, P. Pyle, and R. Bandar (1996). White shark predation on four pinniped species in central California waters: Geographic and temporal patterns inferred from wounded carcasses. *In* "Great White Sharks: The Biology of *Carcharodon carcharias*" (A. P. Klimley and D. G. Ainley, eds.), pp. 263–291. Academic Press, San Diego, CA.

Lydersen, C. (1991). Monitoring ringed seal *(Phoca hispida)* activity by means of acoustic telemetry. *Can J. Zool.* **69**: 1178–1182.

MacArthur, R. H., and E. O. Wilson (1967). "The Theory of Island Biogeography." Princeton Univ. Press. Princeton.

Maldonado, J. E., F. Orta Davila, B. S. Stewart, E. Geffen, and R. K. Wayne (1995). Intraspecific genetic differentiation in California sea lions *(Zalophus californianus)* from southern California and the Gulf of California. *Mar. Mamm. Sci.* **11**(1): 46–58.

Marmontel, M. (1995). Age and reproduction in female Florida manatees. *In* "Population Biology of the Florida Manatee" (T. J. O'Shea, B. B. Ackerman, and H. F. Percival, eds.), *Inf. Technol. Rep. 1*, pp. 98–119. National Biological Service, Washington, DC.

Marsh, H. (1995). The life history, pattern of breeding, and population dynamics of the dugong. *In* "Population Biology of the Florida Manatee" (T. J. O'Shea, B. B. Ackerman, and H. F. Percival, eds.), pp. 56–62. *Inf. Technol. Rep. 1.* National Biological Service, Washington, DC.

Marsh, H., and T. Kasuya (1991). An overview of the changes in the role of a female pilot whale with age. *In* "Dolphin Societies: Discoveries and Puzzles" (K. Pryor and K. S. Norris eds.), pp. 281–285. University of California Press, Berkeley.

Mate, B. R., and J. L. Harvey (1984). Ocean movements of radio-tagged whales. *In* "The Gray Whale, *Eschrichtius robustus* (Lilljeborg, 1861)" (M. L. Jones, S. Leatherwood, and S. L. Swartz, eds.), pp. 577–589. Academic Press, New York.

Mate, B. R., K. A. Rossbach, S. L. Nieukirk, R. S. Wells, A. B. Irvine, M. D. Scott, and A. J. Read (1995). Satellite-monitored movements and dive behavior of a bottlenose dolphin *(Tursiops truncatus)* in Tampa Bay, Florida. *Mar. Mamm. Sci.* **11**: 452–463.

McRae, S. B., and K. M. Kovacs (1994). Paternity exclusion by DNA fingerprinting, and mate guarding in the hooded seal, *Cystophora cristata. Mol. Ecol.* **3**: 101–107.

Mizroch, S. A. J. A. Beard, and M. Lynde (1990). Computer assisted photo-identification of humpback whales. *IWC Spec. Iss.* **12**: 63–70.

Norris, K. S., and R. L. Gentry (1974). Capture and harnessing of young California gray whales, *Eschrichtius robustus. Mar. Fish. Rev.* **36**: 58–64.

Norris, K. S., and K. Pryor (1991). Some thoughts on grandmothers. *In* "Dolphin Societies: Discoveries and Puzzles" (K. Pryor and K. S. Norris, eds.), pp. 287–289. University of California Press, Berkeley.

O'Shea, T. J., and W. C. Hartley (1995). Reproduction and early-age survival of manatees at Blue Spring, upper St. Johns River, Florida. *In* "Population Biology of the Florida Manatee" (T. J. O'Shea, B. B. Ackerman, H. F. Percival, eds.), pp. 157–170. National Biological Service: Information and Technology Report No. 1.

Osterhaus, A. D. M. E., and E. J. Vedder (1988). Identification of virus causing recent seal deaths. *Nature* **335**: 20.

Paetkau, D., W. Calvert, I. Stirling, C. Strobeck (1995). Microsatellite analysis of population structure in Canadian polar bears. *Molecular Ecology* **4**: 347–354.

Palsbøll, P. J., J. Allen, M. Bérubé, P. J. Clapham, T. P. Feddersen, P. S. Hammond, R. R. Hudson, H. Jørgensen, S. Katona, A. Holm Larsen, F. Larsen, J. Lein, D. K. Mattlla, J. Sigurjónsson, R. Sears, T. Smith, R. Sponer, P. Stevick, and N. Ølen (1997). Genetic tagging of humpback whales. *Nature* **388**: 767–769.

Perrin, W. F., and A. C. Myrick (1980). Growth of odontocetes and sirenians. Problems in age determination. *Rep. Int. Whal. Comm., Spec. Issue* **3**: 1–229.

Perrin, W. F., and S. B. Reilly (1984). Reproductive parameters of dolphins and small whales of the family Delphinidae. *Rep. Int. Whal. Comm., Spec. Issue* **6**: 97–134.

Perry, E. A. (1993). Mating system of harbour seals. Ph.D. thesis, Memorial University, Newfoundland.

Ralls, K., D. B. Siniff, T. D. Williams, and V. B. Kuechle (1989). An intraperitoneal radio transmitter for sea otters. *Mar. Mamm. Sci.* **5**: 376–381.

Ramsay, M. A., and I. Stirling (1988). Reproductive biology of female polar bears *(Ursus maritimus). J. Zool.* **214**: 601–634.

Ray, G. C., E. D. Mitchell, D. Wartzok, V. M. Kozicki, and R. Maiefski (1978). Radio tracking of a fin whale *(Balaenoptera physalus). Science* **202**: 521–524.

Reynolds, J. E., III, and D. K. Odell (1991). "Manatees and Dugongs." Facts on File, New York.

Reid, J. P., R. K. Bonde, and T. J. O'Shea (1995). Reproduction and mortality of radio-tagged and recognizable manatees on the Atlantic coast of Florida. *In* "Population Biology of the Florida Manatee" (T. J. O'Shea, B. B. Ackerman, H. F. Percival, eds.), pp. 171–190. *Inf. Technol. Rep. 1.* National Biological Service, Washington, D.C.

Reynolds, E., III, and J. D. E Odell (1991). "Manatees and Dugongs." Facts on File, New York.

Rice, D. W. (1986). Gray whale. *In* "Marine Mammals of Eastern North Pacific and Arctic Waters" (D. Haley, ed.), pp. 62–71. Pacific Search Press, Seattle, Washington.

Rice, D. W., and A. Wolman (1971). The life history and ecology of the gray whale *(Eschrichtius robustus). Am. Soc. Mammal., Spec. Pub.* **3**: 1–142.

Rice, D. W., A. A. Wolman, B. R. Mate, and J. T. Harvey (1986). A mass stranding of sperm whales in Oregon: Sex and age composition of the school. *Mar. Mamm. Sci.* **2**: 64–69.

Richard, K. R., M. C. Dillon, H. Whitehead, and J. M. Wright (1996). Patterns of kinship in groups of free-living sperm whales *(Physeter macrocephalus)* revealed by multiple molecular genetic analyses. *Proc. Natl. Acad. Sci. U.S.A.* **93**: 8792–8795.

Richards, F. J. (1959). A flexible growth function for empirical use. *Journal of Experimental Botany* **10**: 290–300.

Riedman, M. (1990). "The Pinnipeds: Seals, Sea Lions, and Walruses." University of California Press, Berkeley.

Riedman, M. L., and J. A. Estes (1990). The sea otter *(Enhydra lutris)*: Behavior, ecology and natural history. Biological Report 90(14). U.S. Fish and Wildlife Service, Washington, DC.

Roe, H. S. J. (1967). Rate of lamina formation in the ear plug of the fin whale. *Nor. Hvalfangst-Tid.* **56**: 41–45.

Rosel, P. E., A. E. Dizon, and M. G. Haygood (1995). Variability in the mitochondrial control region in populations of the harbor porpoises, *Phocoena phocoena,* on interoceanic and regional scales. *Can. J. Fish. Aquat. Sci.* **52**: 1210–1219.

Slade, T. W. (1992). Limited MHC polymorphism in the southern elephant seal: Implications for MHC evolution and marine mammal population biology. *Proc. R. Soc. London B* **249**: 163–171.

Stanley, H. F., S. Casey, J. M. Carnahan, S. Goodman, J. Harwood, and R. K. Wayne (1996). Worldwide patterns of mitochondrial DNA differentiation in the harbor seal *(Phoca vitulina). Mol. Biol. Evol.* **13**(2): 368–382.

Stewart, B. S., S. Leatherwood, P. K. Yochem, and M.-P. Heide-Joergensen (1989). Harbor seal tracking and telemetry by satellite. *Mar. Mamm. Sci.* **5**: 361–375.

Stirling, I. (1988). "Polar Bears." University of Michigan Press, Ann Arbor.

Stone, G., J. Goodyear, A. Hutt, and A. Yoshinaga (1994). A new non-invasive tagging method for studying wild dolphins. *Mar. Technol. Soc. J.* **28**: 11–16.

Sumich, J. L. (1986). Growth in young gray whales *(Eschrichtius robustus). Mar. Mamm. Sci.* **2**: 145–152.

Sumich, J. L., and J. T. Harvey (1986). Juvenile mortality in gray whales *(Eschrichtius robustus). J. Mammal.* **67**: 179–182.

Sydeman, W., and J. N. Nur (1994). Life history strategies of female Northern elephant seals. *In* "Elephant Seals" (B. J. Le Boeuf and R. M. Laws, eds.), pp. 137–153. University of California Press, Berkeley.

Tricas, T. C., and J. E. Mc Cosker (1984). Predatory behavior of the white shark *(Carcharodon carcharias). South. Calif. Acad. Sci. Mem.* **9**: 81–91.

Wada, S., and K. I. Numachi (1991). Allozyme analysis of genetic differentiation among the populations and species of the *Balaenoptera. Rep. Int. Whal. Comm. Spec. Issue* **13**: 125–154.

Walker, B. G., and P. L. Boveng (1995). Effects of time-depth recorders on maternal foraging and attendance behavior of Antarctic fur seals *(Arctocephalus gazella). Can. J. Zool.* **73**: 1538–1544.

Watkins, W. A., and W. E. Schevill (1977). "The Development and Testing of a Radio Whale Tag," Ref. No. 77-58. WHOI, Woods Hole, MA.

Westlake, R. L., and W. G. Gilmartin (1990). Hawaiian monk seal pupping locations in the northwestern Hawaiian Islands. *Pac. Sci.* **44**: 366–383.

Whitehead, H. (1996). Babysitting, dive synchrony, and indications of alloparental care. *Behav. Evol. Sociobiol.* **38**: 237–244.

15

Exploitation and Conservation

15.1. Introduction

In this final chapter we consider both the commercial exploitation and conservation of marine mammals. The overexploitation of whales, seals, sea cows, and sea otters has resulted in seriously reduced population sizes, the extinction of several species, and the endangered status of several others. Fortunately, recognition of marine mammals as crucial natural resources to be protected has resulted in the establishment of an international legal framework for their conservation. This framework monitors many human-induced marine mammal mortalities, such as those resulting from net entanglements, incidental fisheries takes, and environmental contaminants. Also considered is the effect of ecotourism activities on marine mammals. Finally, we evaluate our progress at conserving and protecting marine mammals and set goals for the future.

15.2. Commercial Exploitation of Marine Mammals

Marine mammals probably have been exploited for centuries for subsistence purposes by coastal aboriginal human populations on all continents except Antarctica. Pinnipeds at rookery or haul-out sites have been especially vulnerable to hunters foraging for food, clothing, and housing materials. Midden remains of seals, sea lions, and nearshore cetaceans date back as far as 8500 years (Beland, 1996; Krupnik, 1984; O'Leary, 1984). Historical evidence indicates that cetaceans were abundant in the North Sea and in the English Channel during the Middle Ages and earlier. Right whales and perhaps gray whales probably were hunted regularly in this area from at least the ninth century onward; harbor porpoises and other small cetaceans were hunted in this area before the sixteenth century (Smet, 1981).

The impact of aboriginal hunting pressure on marine mammal populations apparently was localized and small in scale in comparison to later industrialized commercial hunting.

15.2.1. Historical Practices

The history of the commercial exploitation of marine mammal populations, under the banner of whaling, sealing, or ottering, has been a long and tragic example of how not to manage renewable living resources in a sustainable manner. Beginning with Basques from the twelfth century, who took North Atlantic right whales, and late sixteenth century Japanese, who took coastal gray whales (Omura, 1984), the story of "commercial" exploitation of marine mammals has been one of repeated overharvesting and serious reductions in preexploitation population sizes. Overexploitation is in part responsible for the extinction of the Steller's sea cow, the Caribbean monk seal, and the Atlantic gray whale, and for the endangered status of several other species including the northern right whale and nearly all populations of manatees (Hofman, 1995).

Sea otters, all species of fur seals, hooded seals, both species of elephant seals, and walruses were heavily harvested for skins and oil beginning in the early nineteenth century (Scammon, 1874; Busch, 1985; Fig. 15.1), but these hunters left few records of the numbers of animals taken. By the late nineteenth century, California sea otters and northern elephant seals were thought to be extinct. Other species, including southern hemisphere fur seals, were depleted but have recovered to preexploitation numbers (Shaughnessy, 1982; Riedman, 1990). Baltic Sea harbor seal numbers also have increased exponentially after protection was introduced for them in the 1960s and 1970s, and as of 1986 exceeded 5000 individuals (Heide-Koergensen and Haerkoenen, 1988).

Also in the early nineteenth century, "Yankee" whalers from New England were extending their reach into the Pacific and Indian Oceans in a widening search for sperm, right, bowhead, and gray whales that swam slowly and could be killed with hand harpoons and lances (Fig. 15.2). By the end of the nineteenth century, right whales in both hemispheres, as well as bowhead and gray whales, had been severely depleted. The northern right whale remains the most endangered of the great whales, numbering fewer than 300 animals, despite almost complete protection for over a hundred years (Donovan, 1995). In 1851 in *Moby Dick,* Herman Melville questioned the future that all whales faced

> ". . . the thousand harpoons and lances darting along all the continental coasts; the moot point is, whether Leviathan can long endure so wide a chase, and so remorseless a havoc" (Melville, 1851).

Figure 15.1. Eighteenth century Aleutian Island hunters chasing sea otters. (From Scammon, 1874.)

Figure 15.2. Nineteenth century whaling scene with bowhead whales being taken with shoulder-fired bomb lance gun. (From Scammon, 1874.)

15.2.2. Current Practices

The era of modern commercial whaling was initiated in the 1860s with the invention of the cannon-fired, explosive-head harpoon. In combination with the development of fast steam-powered catcher boats, whalers for the first time could take large numbers of the faster swimming rorqual whales (initially blue and fin whales). These whales previously had been ignored by whalers with hand harpoons, for they were too fast to be overtaken in sail- or oar-powered boats. At first, whaling for rorquals was conducted from land stations and the number that could be exploited was limited. The first Antarctic whaling station was established in 1904 on South Georgia and 195 whales were taken. By 1913, there were six land stations and 21 floating factories and the total catch was 10,760 whales (Donovan, 1995).

The invention of the stern slipway in 1925 allowed pelagic factory ships to haul harpooned whales aboard for processing at sea (Fig. 15.3) rather than depending on shore stations, and the kill of large rorquals rose dramatically. From 176 blue whales in 1910, the annual take climbed to over 37,000 whales (mostly blues) in 1931, when 41 factory ships were working in Antarctic waters (Fig. 15.4). After the peak year of 1931, blue whales became increasingly scarce. Blue whale catches declined steadily until the catch was commercially insignificant by the mid-1950s. In 1966, only 70 blue whales were killed in the entire world's oceans. Only then, when substantial numbers could no longer turn a profit, was the hunting of blue whales banned in the southern hemisphere.

Whaling operations effectively ceased during World War II. The war caused a world shortage in the supply of whale oil, and the end of World War II encouraged several nations

Figure 15.3. Stern view of an Antarctic whaling factory ship (*Southern Venturer*) showing slipway for pulling harpooned whales to the processing deck. Courtesy Southhampton Oceanography Centre.

to renew their pelagic whaling activities. It was in this immediate postwar setting that discussions were held in London in 1945 and in Washington in 1946 on the international regulation of whaling (the results of these discussions are outlined in the next section). Meanwhile, without large populations of blue whales to exploit, pelagic whalers switched to the smaller, more numerous fin whales, catches of which skyrocketed to over 25,000 whales each year for most of the 1950s (Fig. 15.4; Laws, 1962). By 1960, the fin whale catch also began to plummet, and whaling pressure was diverted to even smaller sei whales. The total southern hemisphere sei whale population probably never exceeded 60,000; one-third of that population was killed in 1965 alone. By the late 1960s, sei whales had followed their larger relatives to commercial extinction, and the whaling effort shifted to even smaller minke whales. Minke whales remained the principal target species of pelagic whalers until pelagic harvesting of baleen whales ceased completely during a moratorium initiated in 1986 (discussed below).

Other harvests of cetaceans, such as the Faroe Island drive fisheries of pilot whales and Japanese harvests of other small coastal odontocetes, continue at present. Pinnipeds are not immune from commercial pressures either. The Namibian government continues to award quotas to harvest Cape fur seals, primarily as a fisheries protection measure (Wickens, 1995). As recently as 1995, the Canadian government authorized personal use hunting of harp, hooded, and gray seals along its Atlantic coast. A subsidy for landed seal meat was established to encourage the expansion of this harvest. For harp seals, the total commercial quota was raised from 186,000 to 250,000 and was justified by the dubious assumption that harp seals are a significant factor impeding the recovery of cod stocks in the western North Atlantic.

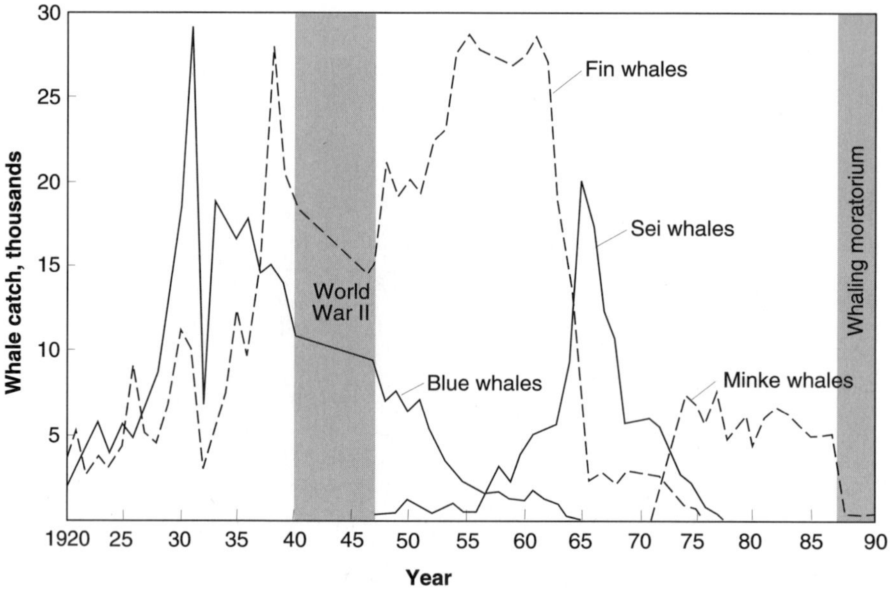

Figure 15.4. Commercial catches of Antarctic baleen whales, 1920–1990. (Data from FAO Fisheries Catch and Landing Statistics.)

15.3. Legal Framework for Marine Mammal Conservation and Protection

15.3.1. International

The United States has entered into agreements regarding the conservation or protection of marine mammals with more than 30 countries. Additionally, several international agreements and conventions have been established. Some of the more important ones are listed with their date of enactment in Table 15.1.

Before 1900, several agreements were made to govern the taking of seals and fur seals, mostly regarding land-based operations in the Antarctic. In 1911, the International Convention on Pribilof fur seals banned the pelagic harvesting of fur seals, although harvesting of young bachelor males continued on land for much of this century (Gentry and Kooyman, 1986). After the Convention lapsed in 1984, commercial harvesting of northern fur seals effectively ceased (Bonner, 1994).

The post-World War II history of modern whaling is essentially that of the history of the International Whaling Commission (IWC). In 1946, the International Convention for the Regulation of Whaling was signed, and in 1948 ratified, establishing the International Whaling Commission. This convention set precedent for international regulation of natural resources by giving conservation equal billing with the economics of whaling, for its stated aim was "to provide for the proper conservation of whale stocks and thus make possible the orderly development of the whaling industry." The IWC originally was established to regulate Antarctic whaling, to make recommendations on quotas and minimum sizes, and to ban the taking of females with calves. It has since been extended to cover all commercial pelagic whaling activities of member nations. The IWC recognized the need for scientific

Table 15.1. A Partial List of U.S.-Related International Agreements and Treaties Affecting Marine Mammals, with Their Date of Inception or Ratification (Wallace, 1994).

1911	International Convention on Pribilof fur seals
1935	League of Nations Convention for the Regulation of Whaling
1940	Convention on Nature Protection and Wild Life Preservation in the Western Hemisphere
1946	International Convention for the Regulation of Whaling
1949	Convention for the Establishment of an Inter-American Tropical Tuna Commission
1957	Interim Convention on Conservation of North Pacific Fur Seals
1958	Convention on the High Seas
	Convention on the Territorial Sea and the Contiguous Zone
	Convention on Fishing and Conservation of the Living Resources of the High Seas
	Convention on the Continental Shelf
1959	The Antarctic Treaty
1964	Convention for the International Council for the Exploration of the Sea
1969	International Convention on Civil Liability for Oil Pollution Damage
1972	Convention for the Conservation of Antarctic Seals
1973	Convention on International Trade in Endangered Species of Wild Fauna and Flora—CITES
	International Convention for the Prevention of Pollution from Ships
	Agreement on the Conservation of Polar Bears
1979	Convention on the Conservation of Migratory Species of Wild Animals
1980	Convention on the Conservation of Antarctic Marine Living Resources
1982	United Nations Convention on the Law of the Sea
1983	Eastern Pacific Ocean Tuna Fishing Agreement
1989	Convention on the Prohibition of Fishing with Long Driftnets in the South Pacific
1989–1991	United Nations General Assembly Resolutions on Large-Scale Pelagic Driftnet Fishing and Its Impacts on the Living Marine Resources of the World's Oceans and Seas (Non-binding)
1990	Agreement on the Conservation of Seals in the Wadden Sea
	International Convention on Oil Pollution Preparedness, Response and Co-operation
1992	Convention on Biological Diversity
	Agreement on the Conservation of Small Cetaceans of the Baltic and North Seas
	Agreement on Cooperation in Research, Conservation and Management of Marine Mammals in the North Atlantic
	Agreement to Reduce Dolphin Mortality in the Eastern Tropical Pacific Tuna Fishery

advice and established an advisory Scientific Committee nominated by member governments. The IWC was intended to "encourage, recommend, organize" studies and to "collect, analyze, study, appraise, and disseminate" information (Article IV), yet specifically lacked both inspection and enforcement powers (Wallace, 1994). Any member government could "object" to any decision with which it did not agree and excuse itself from the limitations of that decision. This, along with the right of member nations to unilaterally issue permits to catch whales for scientific purposes, has severely limited the authority of the IWC to enforce its own regulations. Without the objection procedure, however, it was unlikely the Convention would have been ratified (Donovan, 1995).

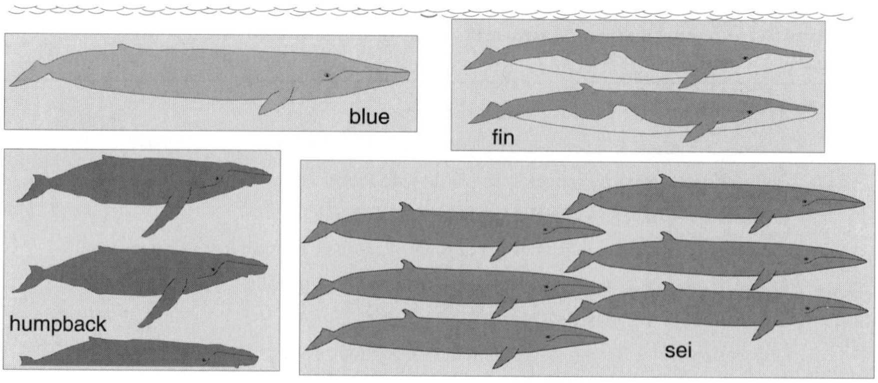

Figure 15.5. BWU equivalents for four species of baleen whales: 1 BWU = 1 blue whale = 2 fin whales = 2.6 humpback whales = 6 sei whales.

Early IWC management procedures were based on the use of the **Blue Whale Unit** (BWU) as a means of setting catch quotas. In terms of oil yield, it was considered that one blue whale was equal to 2 fin, 2.5 humpback, or 6 sei whales (based on their relative oil yields; Fig 15.5; Andresen, 1993), with no distinction given to the actual species being harvested. In 1962–1963, a call from the Scientific Committee for quotas by species was rejected but the total quota was reduced to 10,000 BWUs and humpback whales were protected throughout the southern hemisphere. In 1964–1965, blue and humpback whales were given complete protection and Norway, the Netherlands, and the UK ceased their Antarctic whaling operations, leaving only Japan and the Soviet Union actively engaged in the pelagic harvesting of baleen and sperm whales (Tonnessen and Johnsen, 1982).

Reductions in target population sizes, new national and international regulations, and changing market demands, as well as changing attitudes concerning the ethics of killing large whales for profit, all have contributed to the demise of large-scale pelagic whaling. A new IWC management procedure was instituted in 1974, based on the recognition that management procedures should apply to geographically localized stocks rather than to species. This new procedure also recognized a protection stock category on which no harvesting is allowed. In 1979, a proposal to end pelagic whaling for all species except minke whales was adopted and a sanctuary was declared for the Indian Ocean outside the Antarctic. By 1982, the IWC had agreed to a deferred pause (a "moratorium") in all commercial whaling beginning in 1986, with a responsibility for conducting a comprehensive assessment of large whale stocks by 1990. Norway objected to the moratorium and resumed commercial exploitation of minke whales in the North Atlantic in 1994, even though the moratorium had not and has not been lifted (Hofman, 1995). Japan and Norway have authorized the killing of whales for scientific purposes even though the IWC has questioned the value of such research. In 1994, the IWC accepted a revised procedure for estimating the number of whales that could be taken without causing the affected population to be reduced below its maximum net productivity. This **revised management procedure (RMP)** has been evaluated using computer simulations, but if commercial whaling is resumed it is clear that independent monitoring of the affected population will be required to verify that RMP is working (Hofman, 1995).

The 1973 Convention on International Trade in Endangered Species of Wild Fauna and Flora (CITES) created a mechanism to regulate the international trade of endangered plant and animal species, including numerous species of marine mammals. Species listed in CITES Appendix I include all species deemed to be threatened with extinction which are or may be affected by international trade policies or activities. Species listed in CITES Appendix II include species which, although not currently threatened with extinction, may become so unless international trade is restricted or regulated by participating governments (Wallace, 1994). Marine mammal species currently listed on either CITES Appendix I or II are listed in Table 15.2. Despite cooperation that has resulted from resolutions adopted by CITES and the IWC, incidents of illegal trade in whale products (i.e. meat and blubber) have continued. Among techniques recently developed to allow fast and reliable identification of commercial whale products for sale in retail markets is liquid chromatographic analysis of water-soluble proteins in skeletal muscles (Ukishima *et al.*, 1995, and references cited therein). The best known of these techniques, molecular genetic analyses of whale products in Japan and Korea, has revealed a surprising diversity of whale and dolphin species currently for sale in markets (Baker and Palumbi, 1994; Baker *et al.*, 1996). These same molecular techniques have been used to make species identifications of beaked whales incidentally taken in the California drift gillnet fishery (Henshaw *et al.*, 1997).

The Convention for the Conservation of Antarctic Marine Living Resources, ratified in 1980, was the first international agreement to approach the management of marine resources from an ecosystem perspective. Commercial ventures there, including either whale or krill harvesting, must be consistent with the goals of the Convention, namely the "maintenance of the ecological relationships between harvested, dependent, and related populations of Antarctic marine living resources and the restoration of depleted populations" (Beddington and May, 1982). This was the first in a slowly growing trend of national and international efforts to recognize the integrity of large marine ecosystems (LMEs). To date, about fifty LMEs have been identified, mostly in coastal waters, as ecological systems that respond to external stresses (such as overexploitation), environmental fluctuations (such as ENSO), or large-scale pollution problems (Alexander, 1993).

In 1982, the United Nations Conference on the Law of the Sea adopted a draft "Law of the Sea (LOS) Treaty" that was to go into effect 12 months after ratification (Craven and Schneiden, 1989). Over a decade later, ratification of the treaty was still short of the 60 nations required to enter it into force. However, many nations have unilaterally adopted major elements of the LOS Treaty. The LOS treaty includes many of the key features found in the United States Fisheries Conservation and Management Act. In particular, it internationalizes the concept of 200-mile-wide (324 km) exclusive economic zones (EEZs), granting coastal nations sovereign rights with respect to natural resources (including fishing), scientific research, and environmental preservation. Additionally, the LOS Treaty obliges nations to prevent or control marine pollution, to promote the development and transfer of marine technology to developing nations, and to settle peacefully disputes arising from the exploitation of marine resources.

The imposition of 200-mile-wide EEZs by essentially all coastal nations of the world since 1982 has dramatically changed the assumption of responsibility for management and conservation of marine mammals because most species of marine mammals spend all, or at least a critical portion of their life cycles (either for feeding or for reproduction) within 200 miles of some nation's shoreline (Fig. 15.6). The LOS Treaty is notably silent regarding the Antarctic upwelling area, for national claims to territory on the Antarctic continent are not recognized. Consequently, the Convention for the Conservation of Antarctic Marine Living Resources provides the fundamental legal framework for management issues regarding Antarctic marine mammal species.

Table 15.2. Current Status of Marine Mammal Species Listed as Endangered or Threatened by the U.S. Endangered Species Act (ESA), the U.S. Marine Mammal Protection Act (MMPA), or the Convention on International Trade in Endangered Species of Wild Fauna and Flora (CITES). Braham (1992); Marine Mammal Commission, 1997.

	Pop. size	% of initial trend	Legal status
Pinnipeds			
Hawaiian monk seal	1200–1800	decr.	App. I (CITES)
Mediterranean monk seal	(300–500)	na	App. I (CITES)
Southern elephant seal	na	na	App. II (CITES)
Steller sea lion	87,000	25% decr.	Threatened (ESA); App. I (CITES)
N. fur seal	1,020,000	decr.	Depleted-MMPA
Guadalupe fur seal	na	na	App. I (CITES)
All other fur seals	na	na	App. II (CITES)
Cetaceans			
Right whale	>2000	2%	Endangered (ESA); App. I (CITES)
Bowhead whale	8000	<15%	Endangered (ESA); App. I (CITES)
Pygmy right whale	na	na	App. I (CITES)
Blue whale	<9000	<5%	Endangered (ESA); App. I (CITES)
N. Atlantic Ocean	100–555	<50%	
N. Pacific Ocean	1600	33%	
N. Indian Ocean	na	na	
S. Indian Ocean	5000	50%	
Antarctic	450–1900	<1%	
Humpback whale	>10,000	8%	Endangered (ESA); App. I (CITES)
Sei whale	25,000	<24%	Endangered (ESA); App. I (CITES)
Fin whale	119,000	<26%	Endangered (ESA); App. I (CITES)
Minke whale	725,000	na	App. I (CITES)
Bryde's whale	90,000	na	App. I (CITES)
Gray whale	22,000	100%incr.	removed ESA; App. I (CITES)
Sperm whale	1,810,000	65%	Endangered (ESA); App. I (CITES)
N. Atlantic Ocean	190,000	58%	
N. Pacific Ocean	930,000	74%	
S. Oceans	780,000	66%	
Chinese R. dolphin	100–300		App. I (CITES)
Indus and Ganges Susu	na	na	App. I (CITES)
Beaked whales	na	na	App. I (CITES)
Bottlenose whale	na	na	App. I (CITES)
Tucuxi	na	na	App. I (CITES)
Humpbacked dolphins	na	na	App. I (CITES)
Finless porpoise	na	na	App. I (CITES)
Vaquita	<500	na	App. I (CITES)
Sirenians	na	na	App. II (CITES)
Dugong	na	na	App. I (CITES)
Amazonian manatee	na	na	App. I (CITES)
West Indian manatee	2,300 (U.S. pop.)		App. I (CITES)
West African manatee	na	na	App. II (CITES)
Other marine mammals			
Polar bear	na	na	App. I (CITES)
California sea otter	2,200	na	App. I (CITES)

Symbols: na=not available, decr.=decreasing, incr.= increasing. Population figures in parentheses are rough estimates.

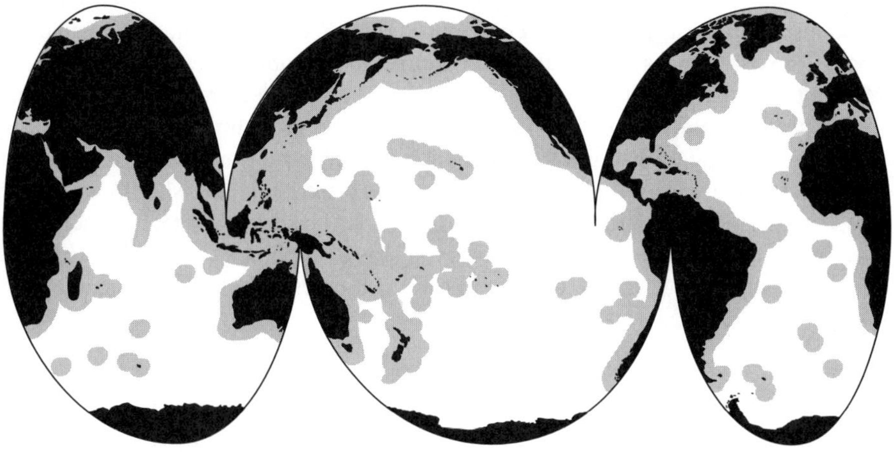

Figure 15.6. Global extent of 200 mile EEZ limits. Compare to the species distribution maps presented earlier in the text.

15.3.2. United States

The **Marine Mammal Protection Act** (MMPA) of 1972 established a moratorium on the taking of marine mammals in U.S. waters and on importing marine mammals and marine mammal products into the United States. It applies to the activities of U.S. citizens and U.S. flagged vessels in U.S. territorial seas or its EEZ. The moratorium does not apply to Indians, Aleuts, or Inuits in coastal Alaska who hunt marine mammals for subsistence (see below) or for making and selling handicrafts. Under a permit system, the act also allows the taking and importing of marine mammals for scientific research, for education and public display, and for incidental catches occurring in the course of commercial fishing operations, such as the purse-seine tuna fishery (Hofman, 1989).

In addition to its regulatory aspects, the MMPA established the Marine Mammal Commission, consisting of three scientists appointed by the President, a Committee of Scientific Advisors on Marine Mammals (appointed by the Commission), and a Marine Mammal Health and Stranding Response Program, which includes the marine mammal stranding networks discussed below.

The MMPA and the U.S. Endangered Species Act (ESA) of 1973 were the first U.S. legislative acts of this type to recognize the values of nonconsumptive uses of protected species. Protected species were listed as either *endangered* (in danger of becoming extinct over a significant portion of its range) or *threatened* (likely to become endangered). A threatened population is automatically considered *depleted* under the MMPA. A depleted population is defined as one that contains fewer individuals than its **optimum sustainable population (OSP)** level, where OSP has been subsequently interpreted as a population level between 60% of carrying capacity and carrying capacity (Gerrodette and DeMaster, 1990). Criteria were established by the ESA for protection of threatened and endangered species and included the effects of overutilization, habitat modification or destruction, disease or predation, inadequate regulations, or other natural or man-made factors. All large commercially hunted whale species were initially assigned endangered status (Braham, 1992). Only one, the Northeast Pacific gray whale population, has been removed from the list because of subsequent population recovery (Federal Register, 1994).

The development of criteria to be used for delisting threatened species is a topic of considerable current interest (e.g., Ralls *et al.*, 1996). The ESA specifies that the recovery plan developed for each species shall include "objective, measurable criteria which, when met, would result in a determination . . . that the species be removed from the list." Although there have been several proposals to improve the ESA by providing quantitative guidance in the form of specific probabilities of extinction within some time frame, experiences of the Southern Sea Otter Recovery Team indicated that these guidelines should not be overly rigid and should allow flexibility for specific situations. This recovery team concluded that the most important consideration in a recovery plan is to appoint a team of individuals that is both technically well qualified and unconstrained by pressures from management agencies (Ralls *et al.*, 1996).

15.3.2.1. Aboriginal Subsistence Harvesting

As authorized by the MMPA, northern fur seals are harvested for subsistence purposes by Aleut residents on the Pribilof Islands. Harbor seals, Steller sea lions, and the Pacific walrus also continue to be harvested by Alaska natives for subsistence (Marine Mammal Commission, 1997).

The IWC establishes catch limits for aboriginal subsistence whaling. In 1997, the IWC agreed to 1998–2002 catch limits for several whale stocks subject to aboriginal subsistence whaling: 280 from the Bering-Chukchi-Beaufort Sea stock of bowhead whales (taken by Alaskan Inuit and native peoples of Chukotka), a total of 620 northeastern Pacific gray whales (taken by those whose traditional, aboriginal and subsistence needs have been recognized), and a total of 175 West Greenland minke whales (taken by Greenlanders). Additionally, annual catches of up to 19 West Greenland fin whales and 12 East Greenland minke whales (taken by Greenlanders) and two humpback whales (taken by natives of St. Vincent and the Grenadines) were authorized. The gray whale total included the newly proposed take of up to 5 whales by the Makah Indian tribe of northwestern Washington State for subsistence and ceremonial purposes. A new aboriginal subsistence management scheme will likely be formulated in the future to review existing quotas once comprehensive assessment of whale stocks subject to subsistence are available.

15.4. Incidental Taking of Marine Mammals

15.4.1. Entanglements

The incidental or passive unintentional capture of cetaceans and pinnipeds in gill nets, both set and drift types, is a global problem, occurring wherever marine mammals and nets occur together. Entanglement in trap or pot lines also is common (Perrin *et al.*, 1994). Very little behavioral information exists regarding when and how entanglement in nets occurs, but it probably includes components of nondetection, curiosity, and possibly social organization.

Available evidence indicates that several stocks of small cetaceans likely cannot sustain the mortality rates occurring due to trap and passive net entanglement. These include (with estimates of the number killed annually) the vaquita in the Gulf of California (30–40), the baiji in the Yangtze River, the Indo-Pacific hump-backed (7–8), bottlenose dolphins (30–40) of the South African Natal coast, Mediterranean Sea striped dolphins (5000–

10,000), harbor porpoises of the western North Atlantic (5000–8600), eastern South Pacific dusky dolphins (1800–1900), North Pacific northern right whale dolphins (19,000), Mediterranean Sea sperm whales (20–30), and several thousand smaller Mediterranean Sea odontocetes (Perrin *et al.*, 1994).

In addition to entanglement in actively tended nets, an unknown (and probably unknowable) number of marine mammals are also killed by discarded or lost fishing gear (Fig. 15.7). The shift since 1940 from the use of natural to synthetic fibers for the construction of nets, lines, and other fishing gear has led to a large increase in the quantity of lost and discarded fishing gear. Gill net fisheries for squid in the central North Pacific Ocean, with over a million kilometers of nets set annually, constitute a large potential source of derelict gear. These nets, if lost, often continue to drift for years, taking a continuing toll on populations of marine mammals and birds that must surface frequently to breathe.

Even after it drifts ashore, derelict net fabric and other synthetic debris can continue to kill. One survey of Antarctic fur seals on Bird Island, South Georgia, indicated that even on that remote island, nearly 1% of the seals were entangled in synthetic debris (Croxall *et al.*, 1990). Most of the seals entangled were wearing "neck collars" made of plastic strapping (59%) or fishing line and net material (29%). A large proportion of these seals exhibited signs of physical injury, and an unknown number of animals presumably died after such entanglement. Between 1985 and 1995, the Marine Entanglement Research Program in the U.S. supported work to assess marine debris, including ways to monitor debris levels, inform the public about problems and solutions, reduce derelict fishing gear, and encourage international efforts to address marine debris pollution (Marine Mammal Commission, 1997; Walsh, 1998).

Figure 15.7. Net entangled gray whale beached on the Oregon coast.

15.4.2. Tuna–Dolphin Interactions

The behavioral association between yellowfin tuna and several species of dolphins (particularly *Stenella attenuata, S. longirostris,* and *Delphinus delphis*) in the Eastern Tropical Pacific Ocean is not well understood, yet it has long been used by the tuna purse seine fishery to locate and catch yellowfin tuna (Lennert and Hall, 1996), although small quantities of skipjack and bigeye tuna are also taken in this way. When tuna seiners sight dolphin schools and yellowfin tuna, nets are set around all of the animals and the net circle tightened and closed, trapping both tuna and dolphins (Fig. 15.8).

Figure 15.8. Modern tuna purse seine, with dolphins escaping (bottom of image) during backdown procedure. (Courtesy W. Perryman.)

Although it was commercial whaling that initially brought about the enactment of the MMPA in the U.S., it was the incidental take of dolphins in the Eastern Tropical Pacific tuna purse seine fishery that became symbolic of the problems confronting marine mammals. In the 1970s, approximately 200,000–300,000 dolphins were killed each year in tuna purse seine operations. Throughout the 1960s and into the early 1970s, the U.S. fleet dominated this fishery and was responsible for more than 80% of the dolphin mortality (Young *et al.*, 1993).

Reduction of incidental mortality of dolphins in this fishery has been a primary focus of the MMPA since it was enacted in 1972. To address the problem of incidental take in fisheries generally, and the tuna purse seine fishery in particular, Congress included in the MMPA a "general permit" requirement. Initially, the MMPA gave commercial fisheries a two-year exemption from the general permit system. During this period, U.S. and foreign vessels in the tuna purse seine fishery killed 424,000 dolphins in 1972 and 265,000 in 1973 (Marine Mammal Commission, 1991). In 1974, the National Marine Fisheries Service (NMFS), which is responsible for administering the MMPA for these species, allowed the U.S. tuna purse seine fleet to take an unlimited number of dolphins until December 31, 1975. Although this permit was invalidated by litigation, the annual kill exceeded 108,000 (NMFS, 1980).

In 1977, the NMFS issued a three-year general permit with annual quotas set to decline from 52,000 in 1978 to 31,000 in 1980. Accompanying this quota were requirements for onboard observers and several fishing gear modifications and procedural restrictions such as the use of fine-mesh net panels and new backdown procedures to release dolphins captured within nets (National Research Council, 1992). During these years, dolphin mortality dropped to less than 50% of the quota allotment (Marine Mammal Commission, 1991).

In 1980, NMFS issued another general permit through 1984 including a total annual quota of 20,500. The permit also imposed additional observer requirements and other regulations governing fishing gear and techniques. By 1984 the U.S. tuna purse seine fleet had declined from 94 vessels in 1980 to approximately 42 vessels (IATTC, 1981). This decline was due, in part, to U.S. vessels moving to and fishing under the flags of other nations to evade MMPA regulations and to avoid the high operating and labor costs in the U.S. The international tuna fleet, now larger than the U.S. fleet, began to contribute heavily to dolphin mortality in the Eastern Tropical Pacific. In fact, the combined U.S. and foreign estimated kill levels for most of the 1980s exceeded the combined kill estimates of the late 1970s (Marine Mammal Commission, 1992). In 1986, for example, 133,174 dolphins were killed in the combined U.S./foreign tuna fishery (Young *et al.*, 1993).

To address foreign take, Congress in 1984 amended the MMPA to require that each nation exporting tuna to the U.S. had to adopt a regulatory program governing the incidental taking of marine mammals in the course of tuna fishing that is comparable to that of the U.S. fleet. The nations also had to assure that the average rate of that incidental taking by the vessels of a fishing nation is comparable to the average rate of the incidental take of marine mammals by U.S. vessels in the course of tuna purse seining. These amendments also required intermediary nations exporting tuna to the U.S. to provide proof that they have acted to prohibit the importation of tuna from those nations prohibited from exporting tuna directly to the U.S., and to establish an onboard observer program that would give reliable estimates of the average rate of incidental take (Young *et al.*, 1993; Hall, 1998).

Another area has focused on identifying new methods of catching yellowfin tuna without the incidental capture of dolphins. In addition, the Secretary of Commerce was instructed to have the National Academy of Sciences (NAS) perform an independent review of these alternatives. The NAS recommendations included (Young *et al.*, 1993):

- Research into incentives to improve captain performance
- Research on tracking flotsam-associated yellowfin, fish aggregating devices, and monitoring of radiotagged dolphins
- Research on the nocturnal behavior of tuna and dolphins
- Use of satellites to locate aggregations of tuna
- Assessment of the impact on tuna populations if purse seining for tuna associated with dolphin is discontinued.

The U.S. Dolphin Protection Consumer Information Act (DPCIA) was passed in 1990, legislating the "Dolphin Safe" certification program for tuna not caught by intentionally deploying purse seine nets around dolphins. At the same time, the three major U.S. tuna canners announced that they would no longer purchase tuna caught by encircling dolphins and that they would develop a tracking and labeling system for their tuna products. This system would enable the federal government to track tuna labeled as "dolphin safe" back to the harvesting vessel to verify whether the product was properly labeled.

The result of the passage of the DPCIA was a decrease in the number of U.S. vessels setting nets on dolphins and a decline in the domestic incidental U.S. kill from 5083 in 1990 to 812 in 1991, to fewer than 500 in 1992 to 0 in 1996 (Marine Mammal Commission, 1997). The International Dolphin Conservation Act of 1992 authorized the Secretary of State to enter into international agreements to establish a global moratorium on the intentional encirclement of dolphins with purse seine nets during tuna fishing operations. The United Nations adopted a resolution in December 1991 calling for a global moratorium on all large-scale driftnet fishing on the high seas. The moratorium became effective at the end of 1992 (Hofman, 1995). Collectively, this agreement and others have reduced Eastern Pacific Ocean dolphin mortality in domestic and foreign tuna purse seining operations from over 130,000 animals in 1986 to about 10,000 by 1993 (Fig. 15.9), and reduced relative annual mortality of all dolphin stocks involved in this fishery to less than 0.2% (Lennert and Hall, 1996). Currently, both the eastern Pacific spinner dolphin and the northeastern Pacific

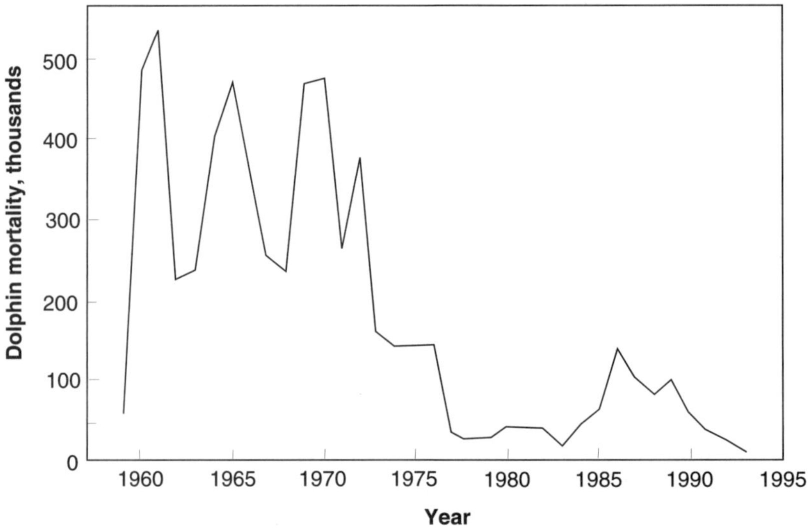

Figure 15.9. Annual dolphin mortality in the tropical Pacific Ocean tuna purse seine fishery. (Redrawn from National Research Council, 1992.)

spotted dolphin population sizes are considered depleted, but stable at about 560,000 and 730,000 animals respectively.

15.4.3. Pinniped–Fishery Interactions

The 1994 amendments to the MMPA added a new section specifically addressing interactions between pinnipeds and fishery resources. A significant feature was its provision allowing states the authority to lethally remove individual pinnipeds identified as affecting certain salmonid stocks provided certain conditions are met (Marine Mammal Commission, 1997). Perhaps the best example of such an interaction is that between California sea lions and spawning steelhead salmon in Seattle, Washington. The number of steelhead running through the Ballard Locks declined from nearly 3000 in the early 1980s to fewer than 100 in the 1993–1994 run. During that time there was an increase in the number of California sea lions congregating near the locks and preying on the steelhead. Because of the ineffectiveness of previous measures taken, in 1995 the Washington Department of Fish and Wildlife was granted authority until 1997 to lethally take individually identifiable California sea lions preying on steelhead migrating through the Ballard locks. To date, no sea lions have been killed: instead, several were marked, transported, and released to a different location (Marine Mammal Commission, 1997).

15.4.4. Acoustic Deterrence

The number of entanglements and deaths of marine mammals may be reduced by the use of active acoustic alarms, or **pingers**, to warn animals about the presence of nets. Field experiments off the New England coast tested the effectiveness of underwater acoustic pingers which emitted a broad-band signal with a frequency of 10 kHz, well within the hearing range of harbor porpoises and harbor seals. Results indicated that acoustic alarms reduced the incidental catch of harbor porpoises by an order of magnitude (Kraus *et al.*, 1997). These results have not yet been fully replicated elsewhere which suggests that pinger effectiveness studies warrant further research (Dawson *et al.*, 1998). Slightly different devices, referred to as acoustic harassment devices, have been used to deter seals from approaching nets and aquaculture sites. It has been discovered, however, that the level of noise pollution associated with these devices may negatively impact marine mammal populations (Johnston and Woodley, 1998).

15.5. Environmental Contaminants

The North Sea, surrounded as it is by many of Europe's industrialized nations, experiences some of the highest levels of marine pollution on earth. The source of the viral epidemic that swept through Baltic, Wadden, and North Sea gray and harbor seals in 1988 has not been established with any certainty, nor has an absolute link between this viral outbreak and any specific pollutant been demonstrated. However, various organochlorides but especially polychlorinated biphenols (PCBs) in the seals' diet are strongly suspected because there is strong experimental evidence that indicates low concentrations of PCBs (and possibly dioxins as well) as leading to suppression of immune system responses of harbor seals

(Kannan *et al.*, 1997). PCBs also interfere with embryo implantation in seals, leading to fewer births and lower birth weights. Seal pups born of PCB-contaminated mothers may still be confronted with higher mortality rates and suppressed immune system problems because these lipid-soluble toxins accumulate in a female's fat reserves and are subsequently transferred via high-fat milk to suckling pups. Marine mammals are thus important global pollution indicators for organochlorides. Comparison of the organochloride levels of marine mammals revealed differences in geographic area and trophic level. For example, marine mammals (seals, odontocetes, and a mysticete) from the western North Atlantic had significantly higher levels of organochloride contamination than marine mammals living in the eastern North Pacific and Bering Sea/Arctic Ocean. In addition seals and odontocetes had higher levels of organochloride contamination in comparison to a mysticete species, a result that was attributed to their higher trophic position in the marine food chain (Mössner and Ballschmiter, 1997; Fromberg *et al.*, 1999).

Studies of stranded beluga whales from a population isolated in the St. Lawrence River system of Canada have revealed high tissue levels of heavy metals, PCBs, DDT, Mirex, and other pesticides (De Guise *et al.*, 1995; Beland, 1996). Unlike Arctic belugas, the St. Lawrence animals exhibited high rates of bacterial and protozoan infections, suggesting compromised immune system responses.

PCBs are a class of industrial chemicals now outlawed in the U.S., but they are still present at toxic levels in many coastal environments. Dioxins are a class of chemicals created as byproducts of incineration, metal smelting, pulp and paper manufacturing, and the manufacture of many pesticides. Dioxins, like DDT, are fat-soluble and stable, and bioaccumulate readily. PCBs and dioxins are carcinogenic and immunotoxic to many animals (including humans); and the most potent dioxin, TCDD, is considered by the World Health Organization to be a Class 1, or known, human carcinogen (Kannan *et al.*, 1997).

Since 1987, large numbers of dolphins, seals, and sea turtles have been killed by disease in the Atlantic Ocean, Gulf of Mexico, North Sea, and Mediterranean. Bottlenose dolphins found dead on Atlantic and Gulf coast beaches in Florida between 1989 and 1994 had elevated levels of tin, a toxic metal that has been used for the past 40 years as an antifouling paint for ships' hulls (Champ and Lowenstein, 1987). Paints with tributyltin (TBT) are more effective and last longer than older copper-based antifouling paints. However, TBT leaches from boat hulls into harbor waters, but in amounts virtually undetectable with present analytical techniques. Concentrations of tin compounds (presumably degradation products of TBT) found in the Florida stranded bottlenose dolphins were much higher than concentrations of tin compounds found in two offshore odontocetes, spotted dolphins and pygmy sperm whales, presumably because bottlenose dolphins spend their lives close to shore, where antifouling paint from boats and ships has contaminated bottom sediments and local food chains. Accumulated tin compounds, combined with PCBs and the pesticide DDT which were also found at high levels, may have deprived the dolphins of their main defense against disease, their immune systems and left them exposed to bacterial and viral infections which they could previously resist. In 1987, the United States Congress passed the Antifouling Paint Control Act that classified TBT as a restricted pesticide and severely limited its use and the amount that could be used in marine paints (Champ and Lowenstein, 1987). Environmental contaminants also have been implicated in congenital skeletal malformations (e.g. reduction of digits or other bones and/or presence of additional digits) in marine mammals (Watson, 1994).

Catastrophic oil spills such as the *Torrey Canyon* (1967), *Santa Barbara* (1969), *Amoco Cadiz* (1978), *Exxon Valdez* (1989), and *Brear* (1993) engender a concern for the marine environment as no invisible contaminant can. Spilled oil floats on seawater providing a constant reminder of its presence until they are washed ashore, sinks or evaporates. Large volumes of oil suffocate benthic organisms by clogging their gills and filtering structures or fouling their digestive tracts. Marine birds and mammals suffer heavily as their feathers or fur become oil-soaked and matted, and they lose insulation and buoyancy. Longer-term detrimental effects result from ingestion of oil while grooming or feeding, and from inhalation of hydrocarbon vapors.

On March 22, 1989, the supertanker *Exxon Valdez* ran aground on Bligh Reef in Alaska's Prince William Sound (Fig. 15.10). The grounding punched holes in eight of the eleven cargo tanks and three of the seven segregated ballast tanks. The result was the largest oil spill to date in United States waters (242,000 barrels or nearly 40,000,000 liters). The spill occurred in an area noted for its rich assemblages of seabirds, marine mammals, fish, and other wildlife. It was one of the most pristine stretches of coastal waters in the United States, with specially designated natural preserves such as the Kenai Fjords and the shoreline of Katmai National Park.

The area of the spill, because of its gravel and cobble beaches, was particularly sensitive to oil. In places, the thick, tarry crude oil penetrated over a meter below the beach surface. High winds, waves, and currents in the days following the accident quickly spread oil over 26,000 km^2. The toll on wildlife was devastating. Over thirty-three thousand dead birds were recovered, and sea otters, seals, sea lions, and other marine mammals, as well as many thousands of commercial and noncommercial fish, were killed. Traditional fishing and cultural activities of the native communities in Prince William Sound were halted for the year, creating enormous social and economic costs. The biological impact of the *Exxon Valdez* oil spill on marine mammal populations has been summarized by Loughlin (1994).

Figure 15.10. The supertanker *Exxon Valdez* spilling crude oil after colliding with Bligh Reef in Prince William Sound, Alaska, 1989. (Courtesy J. Harvey.)

In addition to the direct adverse effects of oil pollution on marine mammals, much concern has been expressed about other possible effects of offshore oil industry operations. Sounds produced by ships, seismic exploration, offshore drilling, and other activities may interfere with communication, breeding, and feeding behaviors causing marine mammals to abandon or avoid these areas (Hofman, 1995). For example, in a comparison of the behavior of bowhead whales in regions of different amounts of human activity, Richardson *et al.* (1995a) noted that the west Arctic bowheads, with greater exposure to human activities, made longer dives, spent a lower percentage of time at the surface, and less frequently raised their flukes; these behaviors made them less conspicuous when at the surface.

15.6. Strandings

15.6.1. Single Beachings vs Mass Strandings

Beached and stranded marine mammals have long been a focus of curiosity and scientific interest. Many of the original descriptions of species included in this book, as well as the establishment of an important and extensive series of base-line measurements of mortality patterns, disease, toxic contamination loads, and other population indicators, have been based on examinations of beached and stranded marine mammals. The terms "beached" and "stranded" often are used interchangeably in regard to marine mammals. However, for the purpose of this discussion, we will follow the definitions of Hofman (1991), using the term "beached" to refer to any dead marine mammal that washes up on shore, and "stranded" to refer more restrictively only to live cetaceans or sirenians that intentionally swim onto or are unintentionally trapped onshore by waves or receding tides. For shorelines with high human usage, a live pinniped, sea otter, or polar bear found ashore may be considered stranded if it is seen as a potential threat to human health or safety. Otherwise, it is considered by the NMFS to be "in its element," even if it is ill or injured, and therefore is not stranded (Dierauf, 1990). Accordingly, because death usually occurs at sea, beached animals almost always occur individually, whereas strandings can occur singly (Fig. 15.11) or as a herd or "**mass stranding**" (Fig. 15.12), defined by Klinowska (1985) as three or more individuals of the same species.

In a study of the causes of beachings and single strandings of marine mammals on the Oregon coast (Stroud and Roffe, 1979), gunshot wounds were deemed the primary cause of death in 30% of the pinnipeds examined, with bacterial infections and parasitism (27% each) accounting for most of the others. Predation, starvation (due to neonatal abandonment), and viral encephalitis were additional primary or contributory causes of stranding. A study of dead beached and stranded animals on the central California coast found that gunshot wounds were the cause of death in 11% of a total of 248 animals (Deiter 1991). Disease accounted for another 10%, and the cause of death for 68% could not be determined, usually because of advanced decomposition of the carcass. Algal biotoxins have been shown to be responsible for strandings of humpback whales in Cape Cod Bay (Geraci *et al.*, 1989) and as a cause of mortality in manatees (O'Shea *et al.*, 1991).

Nearly twenty species of odontocetes have been reported to mass strand, with pilot whales (*Globicephala;* Geraci and St. Aubin, 1977; Dawson *et al.*, 1985; Crespo *et al.*, 1985), false killer whales (*Pseudorca;* Odell *et al.*, 1980), and sperm whales (*Physeter;* Rice *et al.*, 1986) accounting for most mass strandings. Stranding frequency varies geographically as well, as indicated in Table 15.3.

Figure 15.11. Beached minke whale on the Oregon coast.

Figure 15.12. Mass stranding of sperm whales on the Oregon coast, 1979.

15.6.2. Hypotheses Regarding Mass Strandings

Explanations for odontocete mass strandings include the presence of debilitating but non-lethal parasitic infestations of the respiratory tracts, brain, or middle ear; group-wide bacterial or viral infections (e.g. morbillivirus discussed in Chapter 14); panic flight responses to predators (including humans); cohesive social bonds causing the entire herd to follow one intentional strander; and nearshore disorientation of echolocation or geomagnetic signals used for navigation. The latter explanation is based on an assumption that odontocetes are capable of detecting and responding to the earth's magnetic field direction or intensity or both. Biological magnetic detectors (small crystals of the magnetic form of iron oxide, magnetite) have been found in diatoms, intertidal mollusks (Frankel, 1986), sharks and rays (Kalmijn, 1977), and have been suggested for insects and birds (Gould, 1980) and fin whales (Walker *et al.*, 1992). Magnetic material, and possibly magnetite, has been found in the brains, bone, blubber, and muscle of the bottlenose dolphin, Cuvier's beaked whale, Dall's porpoise, and the humpback whale (Bauer, 1986). The magnetite crystals are thought to continually orient themselves in line with the earth's magnetic field, just like a compass. By sensing changes in the orientation of these crystals, the host animal is thought to be able to work out the direction in which it is traveling, a useful ability during extended migrations. Normally, the natural magnetic force fields run north to south at an even intensity. In some places, however, the field is distorted by certain types of geological formations, such as those rich in iron. Such distortions are called geomagnetic anomalies. Because some live strandings of whales occur in areas where geomagnetic anomalies are present, it has been suggested (Klinowska 1985, 1986, 1988) that these strandings may be the result of serious navigational mistakes on the part of whales attempting to use their magnetic sense. Indirect

Table 15.3. Comparison of Cetacean Stranding Occurrences, by Region and Species, on the Continental U.S. Coast. Regions Listed Correspond to Regional Stranding Networks Listed in Appendix 1.

Region	Time period	Source	Species	#
Northeast	1977–1988	Early and McKenzie (1991)	*Globicephala melaena*	334
			Lagenorhynchus acutus	186
			Phocoena phocoena	212
Southeast	1978–1987	Odell (1991)	*Tursiops truncatus*	1472
			Kogia breviceps	224
			Globicephala macrorhynchus	90
Southwest	1982–1987	Seagars and Jozwiak (1991)	*Eschrichtius robustus*	23
			Delphinus delphis	15
			Phocoena phocoena	14
Northwest	1977–1987	Scordino (1991)	*Eschrichtius robustus*	81
			Physeter catodon	48
			Phocoenoides dalli	32
Alaska	1975–1987	Zimmerman (1991)	*Eschrichtius robustus*	81
			Delphinapterus leucas	58
			Mesoplodon stejnegeri	29

and experimental evidence for this hypothetical explanation of mass strandings comes from analyses of cetacean stranding patterns on the United Kingdom (Klinowska, 1985, 1986, 1988) and eastern U.S. coastlines (Kirschvink *et al.*, 1986; Kirschvink, 1990; Walker *et al.*, 1992). This hypothesis, however, has been questioned by a number of workers. Hui (1994) evaluated sightings of free-ranging common dolphins and demonstrated only an association with bottom topography patterns. He found no support for the hypothesis that free-ranging dolphins use magnetic intensity gradients as navigational pathways. An analysis of a comparably sized sample of New Zealand single and mass strandings by Brabyn and Frew (1994) found no apparent relationship between mass stranding locations and either geomagnetic contours or magnetic minima, nor was there evidence that whales appeared to be avoiding magnetic gradients.

Using confusion of echolocation signals or disturbances of geomagnetic patterns to explain mass strandings relies on viewing strandings as accidental consequences of navigational mistakes when animals are near shore. It also requires that potential stranders rely predominantly or exclusively on that single sensory mode for navigational cues, while ignoring contradictory information from other sensory modes such as vision. More information regarding the health status of individual animals involved in strandings that fit the geomagnetic hypothesis may help to clarify this issue.

Necropsies of six false killer whales involved in a mass stranding in Florida indicated heavy parasite loads in the pterygoid sinus complexes, and it was doubted that the animals would have had the ability to function normally had they survived (Odell *et al.*, 1980). In a Florida stranding of 30 pilot whales, Bossart *et al.* (1991) found that of the 17 whales that survived and were returned to sea, all restranded 16 days later. The 13 whales which died after the initial stranding exhibited a wide variety of internal organ lesions and inflammation thought to be consequences of a bacterial or viral infection. These whales also showed light to heavy parasitic nematode infestations of the middle ear. Both the parasite infestations and the lesions and inflammation were indicative of chronic and progressive conditions that had their onset well before the initial stranding occurred; these animals were ill when they came ashore. Currently, all live, mass-stranded cetaceans occurring in Florida are considered to be ill and are not returned to sea until 1) medical examinations of the stranded animals are conducted and 2) the animals are permanently marked or radio-tagged to determine whether subsequent restranding occurs or the release was successful.

15.6.3. Stranding Networks and Strandings as a Source for Study Specimens

The U.S. Marine Mammal Protection Act provided the legal basis to establish six regional stranding networks on the U.S. coastline. These networks, and the states they encompass, are Northeast listed in Table 15.4. Several other countries, including Canada, have set up similar stranding networks for their coastal areas. The MMPA provided each network with appropriate authority and resources to respond to beachings and strandings of marine mammals for the purposes of necropsy and tissue salvage of beached animals and of rescue and/or rehabilitation of live stranded animals (Dierauf, 1990; Hofman, 1991). These networks have become valuable (and sometimes the only) sources of tissues of what are otherwise rare or legally protected marine mammal species.

Table 15.4 U.S. Regional Marine Mammal Stranding Network Contacts (Dierauf, 1990).

Northeast (ME, NH, MA, RI, CT, NY, NJ, DE, MD)
Stranding Coordinator
NOAA, NMFS
One Blackburn Drive
Gloucester, MA 019300
(508) 281-9300

Northwest (OR, WA)
Stranding Coordinator
NOAA, NMFS
7600 Sand Point Way, NE
Seattle, WA 98115
(206) 526-6140

Southeast (VA, NC, SC, GA, FL, AL, MS, LA, TX, VI, PR)
Stranding Coordinator
Sea World of Florida
7007 Sea World Drive
Orlando, FL 32821
(407) 351-3600

Southwest (CA)
Stranding Coordinator
NOAA, NMFS
300 South Ferry Street
Terminal Island, CA 90731
(213) 514-6109

Hawaii
Stranding Coordinator
Pacific Area Office, NMFS
2570 Dole Street
Honolulu, HI 96822-2396
(808) 955-8831

Alaska
Stranding Coordinator
NOAA, NMFS
Box 21668
Juneau, AK 99802
(907) 586-7233

Canada
Stranding Coordinator
P.O. Box 6244
Victoria, British Columbia V8P 5L5
(604) 380-1925

15.7. Ecotourism

15.7.1. Whale Watching

Whale watching is an ancient pastime, but a relatively youthful industry. Only in the past three decades has there been a defined and growing market for allowing large numbers of people very close contact with whales for educational or ecotourist pursuits. These activities range from casual observations of migrating, feeding, or courting whales to intensive and prolonged observations or interactions from boats, aircraft or swimming in the water. In 1991, an estimated four million people worldwide went whale watching. By 1994 this had increased to 5.4 million, with total revenues estimated to be more than $500 million (Hoyt, 1995), and in 1995 over 50 countries and territories offered whale watching tours (IFAW, 1995). Whether it is killer whales in Norway, British Columbia, Puget Sound, and Antarctica; humpback whales in Hawaii, Alaska, Australia, Japan, and New England; gray whales throughout much of their southern winter range along British Columbia, the U.S. west coast and Baja California; or bottlenose dolphins in near-shore waters of the U.S., Australia, and Japan; spinner and spotted dolphins in the Caribbean, Brazil, and Hawaii; all have become the subjects of commercial whale watching activities.

With commercial whale hunting diminishing for most species and ending for others, the International Whaling Commission confronts new responsibilities in overseeing the conservation of whale stocks by providing for the optimum utilization of whale resources in nonconsumptive and nondestructive ways. According to Barstow (1986), these nonconsumptive uses include benign research using remote sensing or noninvasive techniques, habitat protection in the form of sanctuaries or refuges, cultural valuation involving aesthetic appreciation of cetaceans through the arts and emphasizing whales as a unique educational resource, and finally, recreational whale watching.

A basic question facing the IWC and local management agencies of individual stocks exposed to whale watching activities concerns the impact of these activities on the normal behavior of the target animals. Do whale watching activities constitute harassment? In the terminology of the MMPA, harassment is any activity that obviously and substantially disrupts the normal behavior of a protected animal. There is no doubt that some whale watching or seal watching, as well as some benign research activities (Fig. 15.13), result in obvious low-level harassment. Most studies have examined the effects of the presence of boat traffic and noise on baleen whales (reviewed by Richardson *et al.*, 1995b) while only a few have studied influences on smaller odontocetes (reviewed by Janik, 1996). Much less information is available on the effects of tourism on pinnipeds (reviewed by Richardson *et al.*, 1995b; Constantine, 1998). The dominant behavioral reactions of cetaceans reported in these studies were short-term effects such as an increase in swimming speed, spatial avoidance, and changes in diving behavior (Janik, 1996). Such short-term disruptions could cause longer-term changes in the behavior of a population. However, acquiring evidence of harassment is not always clear cut. Salden (1988) noted that Hawaiian humpback cows and calves may be deserting traditional winter resting areas near the Maui shore in favor of waters 3–4 km offshore, presumably in response to increased whale watching activities. However, no evidence has been found of a decline in the relative encounter rate of individual humpbacks, humpback pods, and calves. In the southern California Bight, where whale watching of migrating gray whales is an important winter component of the sportfishing industry, Sumich and Show (1998) demonstrated a definite shift of migratory routes from coastal to offshore locations, even though this population continues to increase in size. For humpback whales in

Figure 15.13. A close encounter with a gray whale (sampling expired lung gases) in its winter breeding lagoon.

Hawaii and gray whales in California, their normal (or at least historical) behavior has changed, but it is not at all certain that those changes are consequences of whale watching activities. As concluded by Janik (1996), behavioral studies need to be carried out alongside more detailed research on individual survival and reproductive rates and movements in order to assess whether boat traffic has a significant impact at the population level. Ultimately, a critical question we need to address is what trade-offs are we willing to accept for the presumed educational, recreational, and commercial benefits of whale watching?

15.7.2. Dolphin Swim and Feeding Programs

Other social interactions between humans and marine mammals include captive and wild dolphin swim and feeding programs. Four facilities in the U.S. conduct swim with dolphin programs in captivity (Marine Mammal Commission, 1994). Quantitative behavioral studies of bottlenose dolphins in these swim with dolphin programs (Samuels and Spradlin, 1995) revealed that human swimmers and dolphins both have risky encounters in some cases. Risky social interactions (e.g. aggressive, submissive, and/or sexual behavior) occurred at higher rates when encounters between dolphins and swimmers were not directly controlled by staff. In controlled situations trainers diminished the potential for dolphin distress and swimmer injury. The long-term effects of swim programs on dolphin behavior are unknown and require tracking the behavior of individual dolphins over several years and analyzing comparative quantitative behavioral data (i.e. Samuels and Spradlin, 1995) with that from non-swim dolphins in zoo and aquarium environments and in the wild.

Although swimming with and feeding wild dolphins is illegal in the U.S. by an amendment to the MMPA (Marine Mammal Commission, 1994), there are a number of opportunities in the U.S. to participate in these activities (e.g. spinner dolphins in Kealakekua Bay in Hawaii; Würsig *et al.*, 1995). A preliminary study of the responses of wild bottlenose and common dolphins to the presence of swimmers in the Bay of Islands, New Zealand revealed that dolphins changed their behavior one-third to one-half of the time that they were approached by the operator's boat. The "line abreast" strategy for placing swimmers in the water resulted in the lowest rate of avoidance by the dolphins but also resulted in no sustained interactions with the swimmer (Constantine and Baker, 1997). It is possible to swim with whales other than dolphins in a few countries (e.g. humpback whales in Tonga, sperm whales in the Galapagos, and pilot whales and beaked whales off the Canary Islands, Constantine, 1998). Among the countries allowing the feeding of wild dolphins is Australia. Monkey Mia in Western Australia is one of the best known areas with a history of human and dolphin interactions (Conner and Smolker, 1985). Significant differences in the behavior of wild and provisioned dolphins have been reported and include an increased mortality rate for calves born to provisioned mothers (references cited in Constantine, 1999). At another feeding program at Tangalooma, Moreton Bay Island, Queensland, forceful contact (e.g. pushy behavior) between humans and wild dolphins during feeding sessions was reported (Orams *et al.*, 1996). The number of dolphins attending a particular feeding significantly increased the pushiness as did the presence of adult males at a feeding.

15.8. Progress and the Future

As the twentieth century nears its end, we can look upon some successes in our attempts to keep populations of marine mammals from the precipice of extinction. Northern elephant seals have made a dramatic recovery in the past century, and to a lesser extent, so have sea otters. The recovery plan for the California sea otter is a case in point. The small size and distribution of the California sea otters and the growing risk of oil spills as a result of increasing tanker traffic in their geographic range resulted in recognition that the best way to minimize the threat from oil spills would be to encourage expansion of the population's range. There was, however, the realization that range expansion of the sea otter could impact commercial and recreational abalone and other fisheries that had developed in the absence of sea otters. Subsequently, the U.S. Fish and Wildlife Service undertook a translocation program to establish a reserve sea otter colony at San Nicholas Island in the California Channel Islands. Although only about 28% of the original number of otters removed from the mainland population and released on the island form the island colony at present (Anonymous, 1995), valuable information was obtained for evaluating whether translocation programs are viable alternatives for conservation.

Populations of most large baleen whales are increasing and the past massive harvests of fur seals have ceased. Marine mammals currently enjoy substantial empathy from the public, yet in spite of this widespread awareness of and concern for the welfare of marine mammals, several species or populations continue to be at risk due to their direct competition with humans for some critical resource. The Steller's sea lion provides a dramatic example of the consequence of this competition for resources. Steller sea lions of the North Pacific numbered about 250,000 animals in 1960 (Loughlin *et al.*, 1992) and were considered important predators of salmon, capelin, pollock, and various rockfish species in the northeastern Pacific Ocean (Fiscus and Baines, 1966). By 1985, the range-wide population was estimated at 135,000, and it continued to decline to 90,000 animals by 1989 (Loughlin *et al.*, 1992). The decline in the late 1980s was especially noticeable in the Aleutian and Kurile Island rookeries (Fig. 15.14).

The proximate cause of the decline was determined to be a reduction in pup and juvenile survival (Merrick *et al.*, 1995), attributable to decreases in the availability of capelin, herring, immature pollock, and other prey of juvenile sea lions. All of these fish species have experienced marked increases in commercial fishing pressure in the past three decades. Although it is difficult to establish the cause of this population decline, it is likely that the numerical reduction and geographical redistribution of appropriate prey species by commercial fishing activities have had detrimental effects on survival rates of juvenile Steller sea lions. Other factors likely contributing to the population decline include entanglement in nets and other debris, disease, and long-term changes in oceanographic conditions (Steller Sea Lion Recovery Team, 1992; Calkins *et al.*, 1999).

The decline of another marine mammal species, the sea otter, may also ultimately be the result of overfishing. Since 1990 a 90% crash in Alaska's Aleutian Island populations of the sea otter has been documented. This decline has been blamed on killer whales which are eating sea otters in response to a decrease of their preferred prey, sea lions and seals. Increased commercial fishing in the Bering Sea may have triggered the chain of events leading to the decline of pinnipeds (Estes *et al.*, 1998). Listed in Appendix 1 are the marine mammal species listed by the MMPA as depleted, by the ESA as endangered, or in CITES Appendix I or II. This tabulation includes species from the large baleen whales, whose pop-

Figure 15.14. Steller sea lion rookery beach photographed on the same day of the year in (a) 1969 and (b) 1987. (Courtesy National Marine Mammal Laboratory, NMFS, NOAA.)

ulations have been reduced by direct harvesting, to small odontocetes such as the vaquita, whose small population continues to decline due to incidental mortality in fishing nets (Hohn *et al.*, 1996), to manatees in Florida, which experience high mortality because of recreational boat activity.

With the human population of the world expected to increase by about 1.3% each year, our future use of the seas as a source of protein, as a disposal site for the unwanted by-products of our civilization, and as a place for recreation and aesthetic pursuits will depend on a better understanding of the consequences of our intrusion on the workings of marine ecosystems. The history of our involvement with marine mammal populations has repeatedly demonstrated a lack of practical awareness of the fundamental disturbances our intervention causes in these natural systems. We have repeatedly violated existing ecological relationships and invented new ones as we intrude into the workings of already heavily exploited marine trophic systems. As we approach the twenty-first century, hopefully we can develop a sense of stewardship towards the world ocean and its inhabitants that is reflected in our personal as well as our political decisions. Only by better understanding the fate we are shaping for the world's ocean can we expect to have healthy populations of marine mammals to be witnessed with fascination and respect by the children of those reading this book.

15.9. Summary and Conclusions

Overexploitation has resulted in the extinction of three marine mammal species: Steller's sea cow, the Atlantic gray whale, and the Caribbean monk seal. Despite establishment of a legal framework to address exploitation, many other species have been and continue to be affected by human activities such as bycatch in commercial fisheries, net entanglements, and environmental contaminants. Information about mortality patterns, disease, and levels of environmental contaminants have been obtained from beached and stranded marine mammals. It is clear that the presence of boat traffic as well as swimming and feeding whales and dolphins alters, at least in the short term, their normal behavior patterns, although the long-term effects of these ecotourism activities are unknown. The recovery of the northern elephant seal and the California sea otter indicates that a few of our conservation efforts have been successful. The future of marine mammal conservation requires better information on the population status and ecological relationships of marine mammals as well as the effects of human-induced activities; these data can only come from further study.

15.10. Further Reading

Marine mammal conservation is the subject of multiauthored volumes by Simmons and Hutchinson (1996), Reeves and Twiss (1999); Clapham *et al.* (1999) and see also Annual Reports of the Marine Mammal Commission especially for U.S. legislation affecting marine mammal conservation. The effects of the *Exxon Valdez* oil spill on marine mammals is reviewed in Loughlin (1994). See Richardson *et al.* (1995a) for a summary of the effects of noise (i.e. boat traffic, offshore drilling, seismic profiling) on marine mammals and O'Shea *et al.* (1999) for a summary of the effects of persistent contaminants on marine mammals.

Among marine mammal conservation groups/agencies with internet addresses are the following:

http://www.nmfs.gov—headquarters of National Marine Fisheries Service (NMFS), the office primarily responsible for marine mammal conservation with links to other NMFS offices.

http://elfi.com/csihome.html—Cetacean Society International, volunteer organization involved in conservation of wild whales and dolphins world-wide.

http://www.eathisland.org—Earth Island Institute, their International Marine Mammal Project is devoted to elimination of commercial whaling, use of dolphins and whales in public display facilities, reduction of incidental dolphin killings within the tuna industry.

http://www.iucn.org—World Conservation Union (IUCN), environmental biologists active in global cetacean conservation.

References

Alexander, L. M. (1993). Large marine ecosystems. *Mar. Policy* **17**: 186–198.

Andresen, S. (1993). The effectiveness of the International Whaling Commission. *Arctic* **46**: 108–115.

Anonymous (1995). Draft of the southern sea otter recovery plan. U.S. Fish and Wildlife Service, Washington, DC.

Baker, S. C., and S. R. Palumbi (1994).Which whales are hunted? A molecular genetic approach to monitoring whaling. *Science* **265**: 1538–1539.

Baker, S. C., F. Cipriano, and S. R. Palumbi (1996). Molecular genetic identification of whale and dolphin products from commercial markets in Korea and Japan. *Mol. Ecol.* **5**: 671–685.

Barstow, R. (1986). Non-consumptive utilization of whales. *Ambio* **15**: 155–163.

Bauer, G. B., M. Fuller, A. Perry, J. R. Dunn, and J. Zoeger (1985). Magnetoreception and biomineralization of magnetite in cetaceans. *In* "Magnetic Biomineralization and Magnetoreception in Organisms." (Kirschvink, J. L., D. S. Jones, and B. J. McFadden, eds.), pp. 489–508. Plenum Press, New York.

Beddington, J. R., and R. M. May (1982). The harvesting of interacting species in a natural ecosystem. *Sci. Am.*, November, pp. 62–69.

Beland, P. (1996). The beluga whales of the St. Lawrence River. *Sci. Am.*, May, pp. 74–81.

Bonner, W. N. (1994). "Seals and Sea Lions of the World." Facts on File, New York.

Bossart, G. D., M. T. Walsh, D. K. Odell, J. D. Lynch, D. O. Beusse, R. Friday, and W. G. Young (1991). Histopathologic findings of a mass stranding of pilot whales *(Globicephala macrorhynchus). In* "Marine Mammal Strandings in the United States" (J. E. Reynolds and D. K. Odell, eds.), pp. 85–90. U. S. Dept. of Commerce, Washington, DC.

Brabyn, M., and R. V. C. Frew (1994). New Zealand herd stranding site do not relate to geomagnetic topography. *Mar. Mamm. Sci.* **10**: 195–207.

Braham, H. (1992). "Endangered Whales: Status Report." *Natl. Mar. Fish. Serv.*

Busch, B. C. (1985). "The War Against the Seals. A History of the North American Seal Fishery." McGill Queen's University Press, Kingston, Ont.

Calkins, D. G., D. C. McAllister, K. W. Pitcher, and G. W. Pendelton (1999). Steller sea lion status and trend in Southeast Alaska: 1979–1997. *Mar. Mamm. Sci.* **15**: 462–477.

Champ, M. A., and F. L. Lowenstein (1987). The dilemma of high-technology antifouling paints. *Oceanus* **30**: 69–77.

Clapham, P. J., S. B. Young, and Brownell, R. L. Jr. (1999). Baleen whales: conservation issues and the status of the most engandered populations. *Mamm. Rev.* **29**: 35–60.

Conner, R. C., and R. Smolker (1985). Habituated dolphins (*Tursiops* sp.) in Western Australia. *J. Mammal.* **66**(2): 398–400.

Constantine, R. (1999). "Effects of tourism on marine mammals." New Zealand Department of Conservation Report, Science for Conservation no. 104, Wellington, NZ.

Constantine, R., and C. S. Baker (1997). Monitoring the commercial swim-with-dolphin operations in the Bay of Islands. *N. Z. Dep. Conserv. Sci. Conserv. Ser.* **56**: 1–59.

Craven, J. P., and J. Schneiden, eds. (1989). The international implication of extended maritime jurisdiction in the Pacific. *Proc., Law of the Sea, 21st Annu. Conf.,* p. 650.

Crespo, E. A., G. Pagnoni, and S. N. Pedraza (1985). Structure of a long-finned pilot whale school stranded in Patagonia. *Sci. Rep. Whales Res. Inst.* **36**: 97–106.

Croxall, J. P., S. Rodwell, and I. L. Boyd (1990). Entanglement in man-made debris of Antarctic fur seals at Bird Island, South Georgia. *Mar. Mamm. Sci.* **6**: 221–233.

Dawson, S. M., A. Read and E. Slooten (1998). Pingers, porpoises and power: uncertainties with using pingers to reduce bycatch of small cetaceans. *Bio. Conserv.* **84**: 141–146.

Dawson, S. M., S. Whitehouse, and M. Williscroft (1985). A mass stranding of pilot whales in Tryphena Harbour, Great Barrier Island. *Invest. Cetacea* **17**: 165–173.

De Guise, S., D. Martineau, P. Beland, and M. Fournier (1995). Possible mechanisms of action of environmental contaminants on St. Lawrence beluga whales *(Delphinapterus leucas). Environ. Health Perspect.* **103**: 73–77.

Deiter, R. L. (1991). Recovery and necropsy of marine mammal carcasses in and near the Point Reyes National Seashore, May 1982-March 1987. *In* "Marine Mammal Strandings in the United States" (J. E. Reynolds and D. K. Odell, eds.), pp. 123–141. U.S. Dept. of Commerce, Washington, DC.

Dierauf, L. A. (1990). Marine mammal stranding networks. *In* "CRC Handbook of Marine Mammal Medicine: Health, Disease, and Rehabilitation," pp. 667–672. CRC Press, Boca Raton, FL.

Donovan, G. P. (1995). "The International Whaling Commission and the Revised Management Procedure. Additional Essays on Whales and Man." High North Alliance, N-8390 Reine i Lofoten, Norway.

Early, G. S., and T. P. McKenzie (1991). The Northeast Regional Marine Mammal Stranding Network. *In* "Marine Mammal Strandings in the United States. Proceedings of the Second Marine Mammal Stranding Workshop, Miami, Florida, December 3-5, 1987." John E. Reynolds III and Daniel K. Odell (eds), pp. 63–68. NTIS number: PB91-173765.

Estes, J. A., M. T. Tinker, T. M. Williams, and D. F. Doak (1998). Killer whale predation on sea otters linking oceanic and nearshore ecosystems. *Science* **282**: 473–476.

Federal Register (1993). Protected species special exception permits. NOAA. **58**: 53320–53364.

Fiscus, C. L., and G. A. Baines (1966). Food and feeding behavior of Steller and California sea lions. *J. Mammal.* **47**: 195–200.

Frankel, R. B. (1986). Magnetic skeletons in Davy Jones' locker. *Nature* **320**: 575.

Fromberg, A., M. Cleemann, and L. Carlsen (1999). Review on persistent organic pollutants in the environment of Greenland and Faroe Islands. *Chemosphere* **38**: 3075–3093.

Gentry, R. L., and G. L. Kooyman (1986). Introduction. *In* "Fur Seals: Maternal Strategies on Land and at Sea" (R. L. Gentry and G. L. Kooyman, eds.), pp. 3–27. Princeton University Press, Princeton, NJ.

Geraci, J. R., and D. J. St. Aubin (1977). Mass stranding of the long-finned pilot whale, *Globicephala melaena,* on Sable Island, Nova Scotia. *J. Fish. Res. Board Can.* **34**: 2196–2199.

Geraci, J. R., D. M. Anderson, R. J. Timperi, D. J. St. Aubin, G. Early, J. H. Prescott, and C. A. Mayo (1989). Humpback whales (*Megaptera novaeangliae*) fatally poisoned by dinoflagellate toxin. *Can. J. Fish. Aquat. Sci.* **46**: 1895–1898.

Gerrodette, T., and D. P. DeMaster (1990). Quantitative determination of optimum sustainable population level. *Mar. Mamm. Sci.* **6**: 1–16.

Gould, J. L. (1980). The case for magnetic sensitivity in birds and bees (such as it is). *Am. Sci.* **68**: 256–267.

Hall, M. A. (1998). An ecological view of the tuna-dolphin problem: impacts and trade-offs. *Rev. Fish Biol. and Fish.* **8**: 1–34.

Heide-Joergensen M. P., and T. J. Haerkoenen (1988). Rebuilding seal stocks in the Kattegat-Skagerrak. *Mar. Mamm. Sci.* **4**: 231–246.

Henshaw, M. D., R. G. Le Duc, S. J. Chivers, and A. E. Dizon (1997). Identifying beaked whales (Family Ziphiidae) using mtDNA sequences. *Mar. Mamm. Sci.* **13**(3): 487–495.

Hofman, R. J. (1989). The Marine Mammal Protection Act: A first of its kind anywhere. *Oceanus* **32**: 21–28.

Hofman, R. J. (1991). History, goals, and achievements of the regional marine mammal stranding networks in the United States. *In* "Marine Mammal Strandings in the United States. Proceedings of the Second Marine Mammal Stranding Workshop, Miami, Florida, December 3-5, 1987." John E. Reynolds III and Daniel K. Odell (eds.), pp. 7–16. NTIS number: PB91-173765.

Hofman, R. J. (1995). The changing focus of marine mammal conservation. *Trends Ecol. Evol.* **10**(11): 462–465.

Hohn, A. A., A. J. Read, S. Fernandez, O. Vidal, and L. T. Findley (1996). Life history of the vaquita, *Phocoena sinus* (Phocoenidae, Cetacea). *J. Zool.* **239**: 235–251.

Hoyt, E. (1995). "The Worldwide Value and Extent of Whale Watching: 1995." Report to the Whale and Dolphin Conservation Society, England.

Hui, C. A. (1994). Lack of association between magnetic patterns and the distribution of free-ranging dolphins. *J. Mammal.* **75**(2): 399–405.

Inter-American Tropical Tuna Commission (1981). Annual Report. La Jolla, CA.

International Fund for Animal Welfare (IFAW) and Tethys European Conservation (1995). "Report of the Workshop on the Scientific Aspects of Managing Whale Watching." IFAW, Tethys and European Conservation, Montecastello de Vibio, Italy.

Janik, V. M. (1996). Changes in surfacing patterns of bottlenose dolphins in response to boat traffic. *Mar. Mamm. Sci.* **12**(4): 597–601.

Johnston, D. W., and T. H. Woodley (1998). A survey of acoustic harassment device (AHD) use in the Bay of Fundy, NB, Canada. *Aqua. Mamm.* **24**(1): 51–61.

Kalmijn, A. J. (1977). The electric and magnetic sense of sharks, skates, and rays. *BioScience* **20**: 45–52.

Kannan, K. *et al.* (1997). Elevated accumulation of tributyltin and its breakdown products in bottlenose dolphins (*Tursiops truncatus*) found stranded along the U.S. Atlantic and Gulf Coasts. *Environ. Sci. Technol.* **31**: 296–301.

Kirschvink, J. L. (1990). Geomagnetic sensitivity in cetaceans: An update with live stranding records in the United States. *Life Sci.* **196**: 639–650.

Kirschvink, J. L., A. E. Dizon, and J. A. Westphal (1986). Evidence from stranding for geomagnetic sensitivity in cetaceans. *J. Exp. Biol.* **120**: 1–24.

Klinowska, M. (1985). Cetacean live stranding dates relate to geomagnetic disturbances. *Aquat. Mamm.* **11**: 109–119.

Klinowska, M. (1986). The cetacean magnetic sense—evidence from strandings. *In* "Research on Dolphins," pp. 401–432. (M. M. Bryden and R. Harrison, eds.), Clarendon Press, Oxford.

Klinowska, M. (1988). Cetacean 'navigation' and the geomagnetic field. *J. Navig.* **41**: 52–71.

Kraus, S. D., A. J. Read, A. Solow, K. Baldwin, T. Spradlin, E. Anderson, and J. Williamson (1997). Acoustic alarms reduce porpoise mortality. *Nature* **388**: 525.

Krupnik, I. I. (1984). Gray whales and the aborigine of the Pacific Northwest: The history of aboriginal whaling. *In* "The Gray Whale, *Eschrichtius robustus* (Lilljeborg, 1861)" (M. L. Jones, S. L. Swartz, and S. Leatherwood, eds.), pp. 103–120. Academic Press, New York.

Laws, R. M. (1962). Some effects of whaling on the southern stocks of baleen whales. *In* "The Exploitation of Natural Animal Populations" (R. F. LeCren and M. W. Holdgate, eds.), pp. 137–158. Wiley, New York.

Lennert, C., and M. A. Hall (1996). Estimates of incidental mortality of dolphins in the eastern Pacific Ocean tuna fishery in 1994. *Rep. Int. Whal. Comm.* **46**: 555–557.

Loughlin, T. R., ed. (1994). "Impacts of the Exxon Valdez Oil Spill on Marine Mammals." Academic Press, San Diego, CA.

Loughlin, T. R., A. S. Perlov, and V. A. Vladimirov (1992). Range-wide survey and estimation of total number of Steller sea lions in 1989. *Mar. Mamm. Sci.* **8**: 220–239.

Marine Mammal Commission (1991). "Annual Report to Congress." Marine Mammal Commission, Washington, DC.

Marine Mammal Commission (1992). "Annual Report to Congress." Marine Mammal Commission, Washington, DC.

Marine Mammal Commission (1994). "Annual Report to Congress." Marine Mammal Commission, Washington, DC.

Marine Mammal Commission (1997). "Annual Report to Congress." Marine Mammal Commission, Washington, DC.

Melville, H. (1851). "Moby Dick." Dutton, New York.

Merrick, R. L., R. Brown, D. G. Calkins, and T. R. Loughlin (1995). A comparison of Steller sea lion pup masses between rookeries with increasing and decreasing populations. *Fish. Bull.* **93**: 753–758.

Mössner, S., and K. Ballschmiter (1997). Marine mammals as global pollution indicators for organochlorides. *Chemosphere* **34**(5–7): 1285–1296.

National Research Council (1992). "Dolphins and the Tuna Industry." Natl. Acad. Press, Washington, DC.

Odell, D. K. (1991). A review of the Southeastern United States Marine Mammal Stranding Network: 1978–1987. *In* "Marine Mammal Strandings in the United States. Proceedings of the Second Marine Mammal Stranding Workshop, Miami, Florida, December 3-5, 1987." (John E. Reynolds III and Daniel K. Odell, eds.), pp. 19–24. NTIS number: PB91–173765.

Odell, D. K., E. D. Asper, J. Baucom, and L. H. Cornell (1980). A recurrent mass stranding of the false killer whale, *Pseudorca crassidens*, in Florida. *Fish. Bull.* **78**: 171–177.

O'Leary, (1984). Aboriginal whaling from the Aleutian Islands to Washington State. *In* "The Gray Whale, *Eschrichtius robustus* (Lilljeborg, 1861)" (M. L. Jones, S. L. Swartz, and S. Leatherwood, eds.), pp. 79–102. Academic Press, New York.

Omura, H. (1984). History of gray whales in Japan. "The Gray Whale, *Eschrichtius robustus* (Lilljeborg, 1861)" (M. L. Jones, S. L. Swartz, and S. Leatherwood, eds.), pp. 27–77. Academic Press, New York.

Orams, M. B., G. J. E. Hill, and A. J. Baglioni, Jr. (1996). "Pushy" behavior in a wild dolphin feeding program at Tangalooma, Australia. *Mar. Mamm. Sci.* **12**(1): 107–117.

O'Shea, T. J., R. R. Reeves and A. K. Long (eds.) (1999). Marine mammals and persistent ocean contaminants. Marine Mammal Commission. Bethesda, MD 150 pp.

O'Shea, T. J., G. A. Rathbun, R. K. Bonde, C. D. Buergelt, and D. K. Odell (1991). An epizootic of Florida manatees associated with a dinoflagellate bloom. *Mar. Mamm. Sci.* **7**: 165–179.

Perrin, W. F., G. P. Donovan, and J. Barlow (eds.) (1994). Gillnets and cetaceans. *Rep. Int. Whal. Comm.* (Special Issue) **15,** Cambridge, United Kingdom.

Ralls, K., D. P. DeMaster, and J. A. Estes (1996). Developing a criterion for delisting the southern sea otter under the U.S. Endangered Species Act. *Conserv. Biol.* **10**(6): 1528–1537.

Reeves, R. R. and J. R. Twiss (eds.) (1999). "Conservation and Management of Marine Mammals." Smithsonian Institution Press, Washington, D.C.

Rice, D. W., A. A. Wolman, B. R. Mate, and J. T. Harvey (1986). A mass stranding of sperm whales in Oregon: Sex and age composition of the school. *Mar. Mamm. Sci.* **2**: 64–69.

Richardson, W. J., K. Finley, G. W. Miller, R. A. Davis, and W. R. Koski (1995a). Feeding, social and migration behavior of bowhead whales, *Balaena mysticetus,* in Baffin Bay vs. the Beaufort Sea-regions with different amounts of human activity. *Mar. Mamm. Sci.* **11**(1): 1–45.

Richardson, W. J., C. R. Greene, C. I. Malme, D. H. Thompson, S. E. Moore, and B. Wursig (1995b). "Marine Mammals and Noise." Academic Press, San Diego, CA.

Riedman, M. (1990). "The Pinnipeds: Seals, Sea Lions, and Walruses." University of California Press, Berkeley.

Salden, D. R. (1988). Humpback whale encounter rates offshore of Maui, Hawaii. *J. Wildl. Manage.* **52**: 301–304.

Samuels, A., and T. R. Spradlin (1995). Quantitative behavioral study of bottlenose dolphins in swim-with-dolphin programs in the United States. *Mar. Mamm. Sci.* **11**(4): 520–544.

Scammon, C. M. (1874) "The Marine Mammals of the Northwestern Coast of North America." Dover, New York (republished in 1968).

Scordino, J. (1991). Overview of the Northwest Region Marine Mammal Stranding Network, 1977–1987. *In* "Marine Mammal Strandings in the United States. Proceedings of the Second Marine Mammal Stranding Workshop, Miami, Florida, December 3-5, 1987." (John E. Reynolds III and Daniel K. Odell, eds.), pp. 35–42. NTIS number: PB91-173765.

Seagars, D. J., and E. A. Jozwiak (1991). The California Marine Mammal Stranding Network, 1972–1987: Implementation, status, recent events, and goals. *In* "Marine Mammal Strandings in the United States. Proceedings of the Second Marine Mammal Stranding Workshop, Miami, Florida, December 3-5, 1987." (John E. Reynolds III and Daniel K. Odell, eds.), pp. 25–34. NTIS number: PB91-173765.

Shaughnessy, P. D. (1982). The status of the Amsterdam Island fur seal. *Mamm. Seas* **4**: 411–421.

Simmonds, M. P., and J. D. Hutchinson (1996). "The Conservation of Whales and Dolphins." John Wiley and Sons, New York.

Smet. W. M. A. D. (1981). Evidence of whaling in the North Sea and English Channel during the Middle Ages. *Mamm. Seas* **3**: 301–309.

Steller Sea Lion Recovery Team (1994). "Recovery plan for the Steller Sea Lion *(Eumetopias jubatus).*" Report to the Office of Protected Resources, NOAA/National Marine Fisheries Service.

Stroud, R. K., and T. J. Roffe (1979). Causes of death in marine mammals stranded along the Oregon coast. *J. Wildl. Dis.* **15**: 91–97.

Sumich, J., and L. T. Show (1999). Aerial survey and photogrammetric comparisons of southbound migrating gray whales in the southern California Bight, 1988–1990. *Rep. Int. Whal. Comm., Spec. Issue.*

Tonnessen, J. N., and A. O. Johnsen (1982). "The History of Modern Whaling." [Translated from the Norwegian by R. I. Christophersen.] C. Hurst & Company, London; Australian National University Press, Canberra. 798 pp.

Ukishima, Y., Y. Sakane, A. Fukuda, S. Wada, and S. Okada (1995). Identification of whale species by liquid chromatographic analysis of sarcoplasmic proteins. *Mar. Mamm. Sci.* **11**(3): 344–361.

Walker, M. M., J. L. Kirschvink, G. Ahmed, and A. E. Dizon (1992). Evidence that fin whales respond to the geomagnetic field during migration. *J. Exp. Biol.* **171**: 67–78.

Wallace, R. L. (1994). "The Marine Mammal Commission Compendium of Selected Treaties, International Agreements, and Other Relevant Documents on Marine Resources, Wildlife, and the Environment," Vols. 1–3. Marine Mammal Commission, Washington, DC.

Walsh, V. M. (1998). Eliminating driftnets from the North Pacific Ocean: U.S.–Japanese cooperation in the International North Pacific Fisheries Commission, 1953–1993. *Ocean Development and International Law* **29**: 295–322.

Watson, A. (1994). Polydactyly in a bottlenose dolphin, *Tursiops truncatus. Mar. Mamm. Sci.* **10**(1): 93–100.
Wickens, P. (1995). Namibian sealing debacle: An environmental disaster and managerial blunder. *Afr. Wildl.* **49**: 6–7.
Würsig, B., K. Barr, R. Constantine, K. Dudzinski, A. Forest, and S. Yin (1995). Swim-with-dolphin programs: Monitoring results and needs. *Abstr. 11th Bienn. Conf. Biol. Mar. Mamm.,* Orlando, FL.
Young, N. M., S. Iudecello, K. Evans, and D. Baur (1993). "The Incidental Capture of Marine Mammals in U.S. Fisheries." Center for Marine Conservation.
Zimmerman, S. T. (1991). A history of marine mammal stranding networks in Alaska, with notes on the distribution of the most commonly stranded cetacean species, 1975–1987. *In* "Marine Mammal Strandings in the United States. Proceedings of the Second Marine Mammal Stranding Workshop, Miami, Florida, December 3-5, 1987." (John E. Reynolds III and Daniel K. Odell, eds.), pp. 43–54. NTIS number: PB91-173765.

APPENDIX

Classification of Marine Mammals

The classification schemes used here follow those proposed by Berta and Wyss (1994) for pinnipeds, Fordyce and Barnes (1994) for cetaceans, and Domning (1994) for sirenians and desmostylians. For the sea otter and polar bear refer to the text. An additional important reference is a review of the taxonomy and distribution of marine mammals provided by Rice (1998). Certain higher taxonomic categories and ranks are not used although hierarchical levels are conveyed by indentation. Phylogenetic systematic studies of marine mammals published in recent years have altered our traditional concepts of included groups and taxa. There continues to be disagreement regarding specific phylogenetic relationships, the validity of particular taxa, and the name and rank of higher taxonomic categories. The higher level classification of various marine mammal taxa proposed by McKenna and Bell (1997) as part of a larger classification system for mammals incorporates both fossil and recent taxa. Detailed review of this scheme, particularly as it relates to marine mammals, is beyond the scope of this book and will require further examination. The most significant changes to traditional higher taxonomic arrangements advocated by McKenna and Bell (1997) are provided under remarks. Emphasis is placed on providing definitions, diagnoses, content (included genera and species), distributional and fossil record data for monophyletic groups at the "family" level. The definition of a taxon is based on ancestry and taxonomic membership and diagnosis is a list of shared derived characters for a particular taxon. The geographic distributions of extant taxa are based on Reeves et al. (1992) and Riedman (1990) for pinnipeds and sirenians, and Leatherwood and Reeves (1983) for cetaceans. Quotation marks are used for taxa whose monophyly is questioned, and an asterisk designates extinct taxa. The time scale used (Fig. 1.1.) follows Harland et al. (1990) and Berggren *et al.* (1995) and the geographic coverage scheme (Fig. 1.) and age correlations for fossil taxa follows Deméré (1994b).

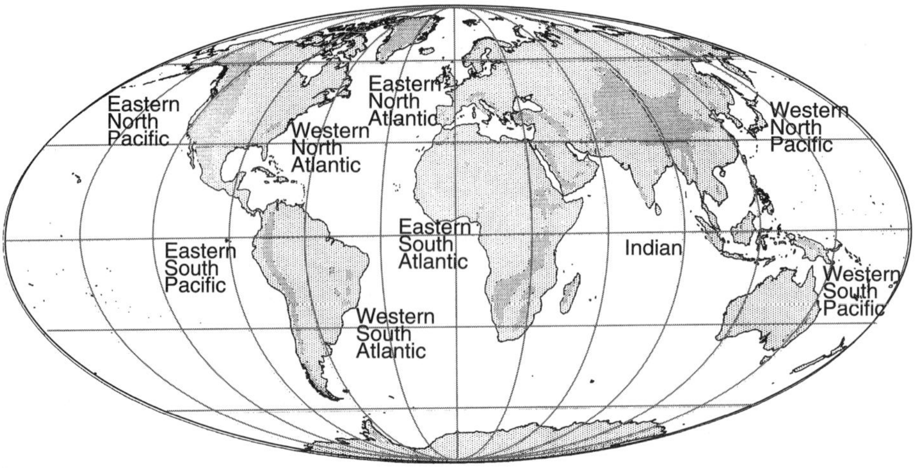

Figure 1. Present day world map with ocean basins discussed in text. From Smith *et al.,* 1994.

CARNIVORA

PINNIPEDIA Illiger, 1811

Diagnosis—Exclusive of fossil taxa *Enaliarctos** and *Pteronarctos**: large infraorbital foramen; anterior palatine foramina anterior of maxilla-palatine suture; round window large with round window fossula; postglenoid foramen vestigial or absent; enlarged jugular foramen; basal whorl of cochlea enlarged; processus gracilis and anterior lamina of malleus reduced; M^{1-2} reduced in size relative to premolars; M^{1-2} cingulum reduced or absent; M_1 metaconid reduced or absent; greater and lesser humeral tuberosities enlarged; short robust humerus; shallow olecranon fossa; digit I on manus emphasized; digit I and V on the pes emphasized; short ilium; strong medial inclination of femoral condyles; large cochlear aqueduct; middle ear cavity and external auditory meatus with distensible cavernous tissue; deciduous dentition reduced; number of lower incisors reduced; foreflipper claws short; manus, digit V intermediate phalanx strongly reduced; embrasure pit P^4-M^1 shallow or absent; mastoid process close to paroccipital process, the two connected by a high continuous ridge; maxilla makes significant contribution to the orbital wall, lacrimal fuses early and does not contact jugal; pit for tensor tympani absent; I^3 lingual cingulum absent; M_{1-2} trigonid suppressed; supinator ridge on humerus absent; olecranon process laterally flattened, expanded distal half; metacarpal heads smooth with flat phalanges, hinge-like articulations; pes long and flattened, metatarsal shafts with flattened heads, hinge-like articulations; pubic symphysis unfused; five lumbar vertebrae; fovea for teres femoris ligament strongly reduced or absent; greater femoral trochanter large and flattened.
Definition—The monophyletic group including the common ancestor of the Otariidae and all of its descendants including the Odobenidae, Phocidae, and *Pinnarctidion**, *Desmatophoca**, and *Allodesmus**.
Distribution—Pinnipeds occur in all of the world's oceans (Figs. 2–6).

Fossil history—Pinnipeds are recognized in the fossil record beginning in the early early Miocene (23 Ma)-Pleistocene, North Pacific (North America, Japan); late Miocene-Pleistocene, eastern South Pacific (South America); late middle Miocene-Pleistocene, North Atlantic (western Europe, North America); latest Miocene-early Pliocene, western South Pacific (Australasia); early Pliocene, eastern South Atlantic (South Africa).

The earlier diverging pinnipedimorphs *Enaliarctos** and *Pteronarctos** are known from the late Oligocene through the early Miocene (27–16 Ma), North Pacific (North America, Japan; Deméré, 1994b). Basal pinnipedimorphs are reviewed by Berta (1991, 1994).

Remarks—McKenna and Bell (1997) divide pinnipeds into two families, the Otariidae and the Phocidae; the latter includes walruses as a subfamily. These families together with a number of extinct taxa (i.e. *Pachycynodon**, *Kolponomos**, *Allocyon**, *Enaliarctos** and *Pteronarctos**) are grouped in the superfamily Phocoidea.

Content—Composed of three families containing all living pinnipeds. A number of fossil genera are included, among which are several not belonging to modern families (i.e. *Pinnarctidion**, *Allodesmus** and *Desmatophoca**).

OTARIIDAE Gill, 1866

Diagnosis—Supraorbital processes large and shelf-like, particularly among adult males; secondary spine on the scapula; uniformly spaced pelage units; trachea with anterior bifurcation of bronchi (Berta and Wyss, 1994).

Definition—The monophyletic group including the common ancestor of *Pithanotaria** and all of its descendants including: "*Thalassoleon*"*, *Hydrarctos**, *Arctocephalus, Callorhinus, Otaria, Zalophus, Eumetopias, Neophoca,* and *Phocarctos.*

Distribution—Otariids are distributed throughout the world except for the extreme polar regions.

Fossil history—Otariids have a fossil record beginning in the early late Miocene (11 Ma)-Pleistocene, eastern North Pacific; Pleistocene, eastern South Pacific (Peru).

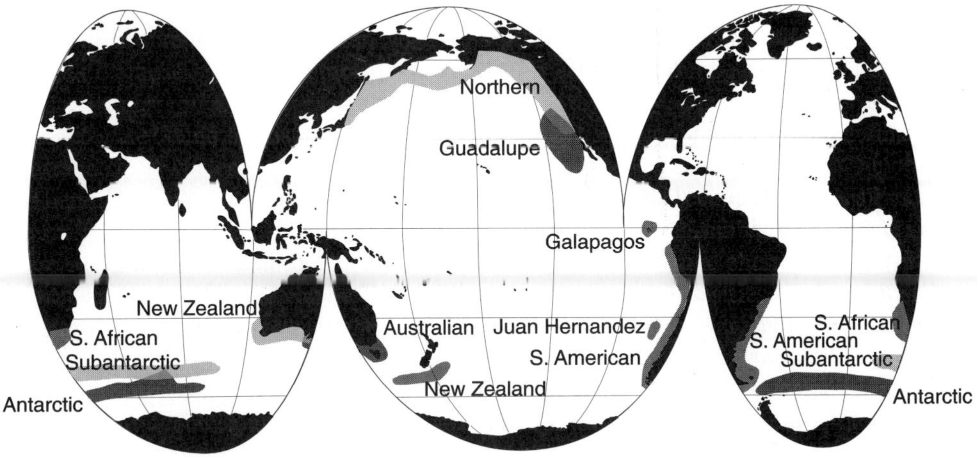

Figure 2. Distribution of fur seals. Based on Riedman, 1990.

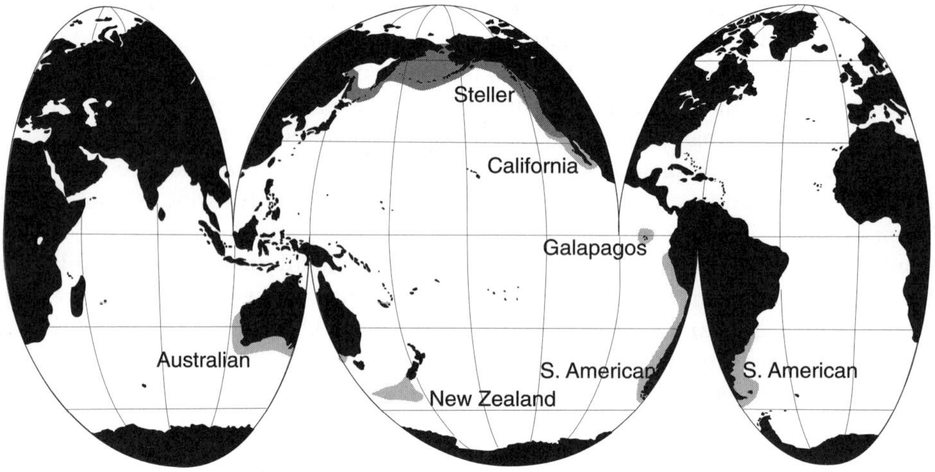

Figure 3. Distribution of sea lions. Based on Riedman, 1990.

Extant genera with a fossil record include *Neophoca,* early Pleistocene, South Pacific (New Zealand); *Arctocephalus,* late Pleistocene, South Pacific (Africa) and late Pleistocene, South America; *Callorhinus,* late Pliocene, eastern North Pacific (California, Japan); *Eumetopias,* Pleistocene, eastern North Pacific (Japan) and eastern South Pacific (South America).

Extinct genera are reviewed by Repenning and Tedford (1977).

Content—Seven genera containing 14 Recent species.

Arctocephalus australis (Zimmerman, 1783)—South American fur seal
Arctocephalus forsteri (Lesson, 1828)—New Zealand fur seal
Arctocephalus galapagoensis (Heller, 1904)—Galapagos fur seal
Arctocephalus gazella (Peters, 1875)—Antarctic fur seal
Arctocephalus philippii (Peters, 1866)—Juan Fernandez fur seal
Arctocephalus pusillus pusillus (Schreber, 1776)—South African fur seal
Arctocephalus pusillus doriferus Wood Jones, 1925—Australian fur seal
Arctocephalus townsendi Merriam, 1897—Guadalupe fur seal
Arctocephalus tropicalis (Gray, 1872)—subantarctic fur seal
Callorhinus ursinus (Linnaeus, 1758)—northern fur seal
Eumetopias jubatus (Schreber, 1776)—Steller's sea lion
Neophoca cinerea (Péron, 1816)—Australian sea lion
Otaria byronia (Blainville, 1820)—southern sea lion
Phocarctos hookeri (Gray, 1844)—Hooker's sea lion or New Zealand sea lion
Zalophus californianus californianus (Lesson, 1828)—California sea lion
Zalophus californianus wollebacki (Sivertsen, 1953)—Galapagos sea lion
Zalophus californianus japonicus (Peters, 1866)—Japanese sea lion

ODOBENIDAE Allen, 1880

Diagnosis—Antorbital process constructed of both frontal and maxilla; distal humerus with diameter of medial lip greater than diameter of capitulum; distal portion of radius with

enlarged radial process; insertion for pollicle extensor muscle on first metacarpal developed as a pit or rugosity; scapholunar with distinct pit for magnum (Deméré, 1994).
Definition—The monophyletic group containing the common ancestor of *Neotherium** and all of its descendants including: *Aivukus**, *Alachtherium**, *Dusignathus**, *Gomphotaria**, *Imagotaria**, *Odobenus*, *Pliopedia**, *Pontolis**, *Proneotherium**, *Prorosmarus**, *Protodobenus**, *Prototaria** and *Valenictus** (Deméré, 1994a).
Distribution—Modern walruses inhabit the shallow, circumpolar Arctic coasts. (see Figure 3.14)
Fossil history—Walruses are known as far back as the early middle Miocene (16 Ma)-Pleistocene, eastern North Pacific (North America); early Pliocene-Pleistocene, North Atlantic (western Europe); late Pleistocene, eastern North Pacific (Japan) (Deméré, 1994b).
Extinct genera are reviewed by Deméré (1994a) and Kohno *et al.* (1995).
Content—One genus and species (2 subspecies) are recognized.

PHOCIDAE Gray, 1821

Diagnosis—Lack of the ability to draw the hind limbs forward under the body due to a massively developed astragalar process and greatly reduced calcaneal tuber; lack of an alisphenoid canal; lack of an auditory meatus and prefacial commissure; pachyostotic mastoid region; pit for insertion of tympanohyal anterior to stylomastoid foramen; greatly inflated heavily ossified caudal entotympanic; transversely directed basilar cochlear whorl; opening of cochlear fenestra outside the tympanic cavity to form a cochlear foramen; strongly everted ilia; insertion for the ilial psoas major muscle.
Definition—The monophyletic group containing the common ancestor of *Leptophoca**, and all of its descendants including *Acrophoca**, *Homiphoca**, *Piscophoca**, "*Monachus*", *Mirounga, Hydrurga, Leptonychotes, Lobodon, Ommatophoca, Erignathus, Cystophora, Halichoerus, Histriophoca, Pagophilus, Phoca,* and *Pusa.*
Distribution—Phocids are distributed throughout the world. (see Figures 4–6)
Fossil history—A record of phocids from the late Oligocene (29–23 Ma) has recently been reported (Koretsky, 1997). However, the stratigraphic provenance of the specimen

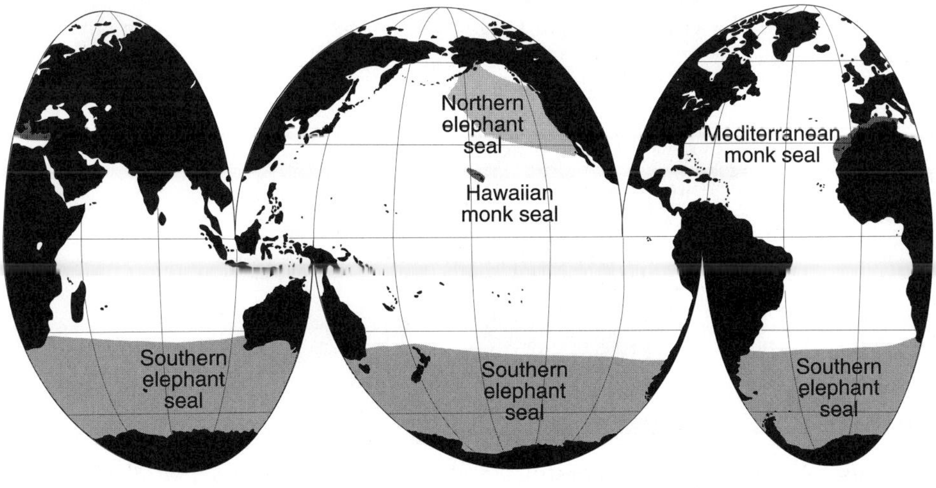

Figure 4. Distribution of "monachines" (monk and elephant seals). Based on Riedman, 1990.

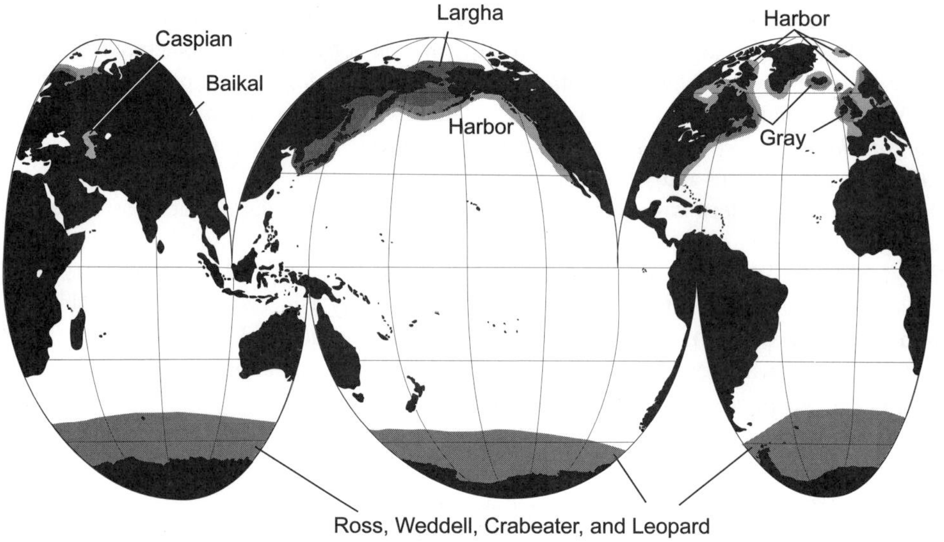

Figure 5. Distribution of some phocine seals. Based on Riedman, 1990.

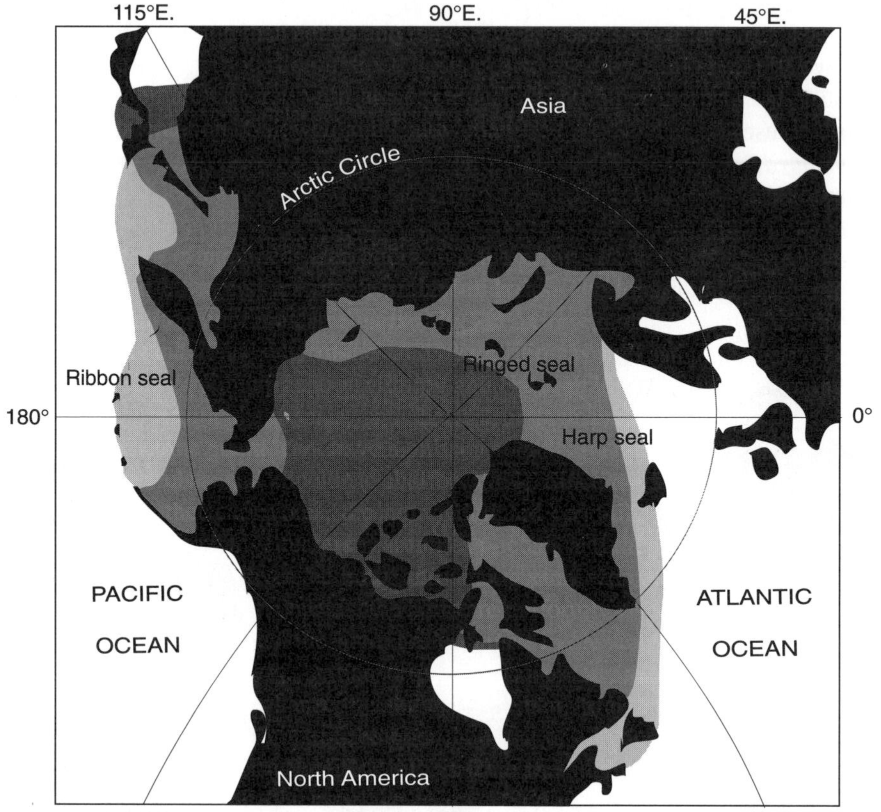

Figure 6. Distribution of Antarctic phocine seals (ringed, harp and ribbon seals). Based on Riedman, 1990.

is uncertain. Phocids are well documented from the middle Miocene-Pleistocene, western North Atlantic (western Europe), eastern North Atlantic (Maryland and Virginia); early Pliocene-Pleistocene, South Pacific (Africa); middle Miocene-Pleistocene, South America.

Extinct genera are reviewed by Muizon (1981, 1982, 1984), Hendey and Repenning (1972), and Cozzuol (1996).

Content—13 genera and 19 Recent species.
Cystophora cristata (Nilsson, 1841)—Hooded seal
Erignathus barbatus (Erxleben, 1777)—Bearded seal
Halichoerus grypus (Fabricus, 1791)—grey or Atlantic seal
Histriophoca fasciata (Zimmermann, 1783)—ribbon seal
Hydruga leptonyx (Blainville, 1820)—leopard seal
Leptonychotes weddelli (Lesson, 1826)—Weddell seal
Lobodon carcinophagus Hombron and Jacquinot, 1842—crabeater seal
Mirounga angustirostris (Gill, 1866)—northern elephant seal
Mirounga leonina (Linnaeus, 1758)—southern elephant seal
Monachus monachus (Hermann, 1779)—Mediterranean monk seal
Monachus schauinslandi Matschie, 1905—Hawaiian monk seal
Monachus tropicalis (Gray, 1950)—West Indian monk seal
Ommatophoca rossi Gray, 1844–Ross seal
Pagophilus groenlandicus (Erxleben, 1777)—harp seal
Phoca caspica (Gmelin, 1788)—Caspian seal
Phoca hispida botnica (Gmelin, 1788)
Phoca hispida hispida (Schreber, 1775)—ringed seal
Phoca hispida ladogensis (Nordquist, 1899)
Phoca hispida ochotensis (Pallas, 1811)
Phoca hispida saimensis (Nordquist, 1899)
Phoca largha Pallas, 1811—spotted seal
Phoca sibirica (Gmelin, 1788)—Baikal seal
Phoca vitulina concolor De Kay, 1842
Phoca vitulina mellonae—freshwater harbor seal
Phoca vitulina richardsi (Gray, 1864)—Pacific harbor seal
Phoca vitulina stejnegeri (Allen, 1902)
Phoca vitulina vitulina Linnaeus, 1758—harbor seal

CETACEA Brisson, 1762

Diagnosis—presence of sigmoid process on tympanic; pachyosteosclerotic ectotympanic and incus; rotation of ossicles; incisors set anteroposteriorly; P^4 paracone height twice that of M^1; hypoglossal foramen opens close to the jugular foramen (Thewissen, 1994).
Definition—The monophyletic group including the common ancestor of *Pakicetus** and all of its descendants including *Ambulocetus**, other archaeocetes, Odontoceti, and Mysticeti (Thewissen, 1994).
Distribution—Cetaceans are distributed throughout the world's oceans.
Fossil history—Cetaceans are recognized in the fossil record beginning in the early Eocene (about 53–54 Ma) in the eastern Tethys (India and Pakistan); middle Eocene, central Tethys (Egypt); late Eocene, western Tethys (southeastern U.S., Australasia); and extending through the Pleistocene.

Remarks–McKenna and Bell (1997) recognize the Cetacea as a suborder in the Order Cete (including Mesonychidae and two other families).
Content—Composed of two suborders containing all living cetaceans and fossil taxa including *Pakicetus**, *Ambulocetus**, and other archaeocetes (see text).

ODONTOCETI Flower, 1867

Diagnosis—concave facial plane (sagittal); asymmetric cranial vertex; asymmetric premaxillae; presence of premaxillary foramen; maxillae overlay supraorbital process; maxillae with the maxillonasolabialis muscle insertion; presence of antorbital notch; nasals anteroposteriorly compressed; pterygoids meet at midline; lateral plates of pterygoids absent; pterygoid hamulae meet at midline; mesethmoid exposed dorsally; absence of ethmoturbinal bones; ligamentous anterior process of periotic/cranium attachment; ligamentous process of periotic/squamosal-occipital attachment; small posterior process of the periotic; presence of panbone in mandible; presence of proximal sacs of the nasal passages; absence of nucleus of lateral olfactory nerve tract; tympanic membrane reduced to "glove finger"; tympanic bulla/ramus attached with band of fibrous tissue; middle ear ossicle/bulla fused (joints stiffened) (Messenger and McGuire, 1998).
Definition—The monophyletic group including the common ancestor of the extinct Agorphidae* and all of its descendants including the archaic families Albeirodontidae*, Dalpiazinindae*, Eurhinodelphidae*, Kentriodontidae*, Squalodelphidae*, Squalodontidae*, and Odobenocetopsidae* and modern families Delphinidae, Iniidae, Kogiidae, Lipotidae, Monodontidae, Phocoenidae, Physeteridae, Platanistidae, Pontoporiidae, and Ziphiidae.
Fossil history—The earliest odontocetes are known from the late Oligocene (29.3–23 Ma)-Pleistocene of western North Atlantic (southeastern U.S.), Paratethys (Europe, Asia), eastern North Pacific (Japan), and western South Pacific (New Zealand); early early Miocene-Pleistocene, western South Atlantic (South America), and eastern North Pacific (Oregon and Washington) (Deméré, 1994b).

DELPHINIDAE Gray, 1821 (incl. Holodontidae Brandt, 1873; Hemisyntrachelidae Slijper, 1936)

Definition—The monophyletic group including the common ancestor of *Albireo** and all of its descendants including *Cephalorhynchus, Delphinus, Feresa, Globicephala, Grampus, Lagenorhynchus, Lissodelphis, Orcaella, Orcinus, Pepenocephala, Pseudorca, Sotalia, Sousa, Stenella,* and *Tursiops.*
Distribution—Widely distributed in all oceans of the world.
Fossil history—The oldest delphinids known are from the latest Miocene (11–7 Ma)-Pleistocene, western North Atlantic (Virginia and North Carolina); late Miocene-Pleistocene, western North Pacific (New Zealand, Japan); early Pliocene, eastern South Pacific (Peru); late Pleistocene, eastern North Atlantic (western Europe) (Deméré, 1994b).

Globicephala and *Pseudorca* are known from the late Pleistocene (790–10,000 yrs.), eastern North Atlantic (Florida; Morgan, 1994); *Delphinus* and *Tursiops* are known from late Pleistocene, eastern North Atlantic (western Europe; Van der Feen, 1968); *Delphinus* is known from the late Pliocene, New Zealand (Fordyce, 1991; McKee, 1994).

Extinct genera are reviewed by Fordyce and Barnes (1994) and Cozzuol (1996; South American record).
Content—17 genera and 36 Recent species are recognized. Heyning and Perrin (1994) review the taxonomy of *Delphinus.*

Cephalorhynchus commersonii (Lacépède, 1804)—Commerson's dolphin
Cephalorhynchus eutropia (Gray, 1846)—black dolphin
Cephalorhynchus heavisidii (Gray, 1828)—Heaviside's dolphin
Cephalorhynchus hectori (van Beneden, 1881)—Hector's dolphin
Delphinus capensis Gray, 1828—long-beaked common dolphin
Delphinus delphis Linnaeus, 1758—common dolphin
Delphinus tropicalis van Bree, 1971—Arabian common dolphin
Feresa attenuata Gray, 1874—pygmy killer whale
Globicephala macrorhynchus Gray, 1846—short-finned pilot whale
Globicephala melaena (Traill, 1809)—long-finned pilot whale
Grampus griseus (G. Cuvier, 1812)—Risso's dolphin
Lagenodelphis hosei Fraser, 1956—Fraser's dolphin
Lagenorhynchus acutus (Gray, 1828)—Atlantic white-sided dolphin
Lagenorhynchus albirostris (Gray, 1846)—white-beaked dolphin
Lagenorhynchus australis (Peale, 1848)—Peale's dolphin
Lagenorhynchus cruciger (Quoy and Gaimard, 1824)—hourglass dolphin
Lagenorhynchus obliquidens Gill, 1865—Pacific white-sided dolphin
Lagenorhynchus obscurus (Gray, 1828)—dusky dolphin
Lissodelphis borealis (Peale, 1848)—northern right whale dolphin
Lissodelphis peronii (Lacépède, 1804)—southern right whale dolphin
Orcaella brevirostris (Gray, 1866)—Irrawaddy dolphin
Orcinus orca (Linnaeus, 1758)—killer whale
Peponocephala electra (Gray, 1846)—melon-headed whale
Pseudorca crassidens (Owen, 1846)—false killer whale
Sotalia fluviatilis (Gervais, 1853)—tucuxi
Sousa chinensis (Kukenthal, 1892)—Indo-Pacific hump-backed dolphin
Sousa plumbea (Cuvier, 1829)—Indian humpback dolphin
Sousa teuszii (Kukenthal, 1892)—Atlantic hump-backed dolphin
Stenella attenuata (Gray, 1846)—spotted dolphin
Stenella clymene (Gray, 1850)—short-snouted spinner dolphin
Stenella coeruleoalba (Meyen, 1833)—striped dolphin
Stenella frontalis (Curier, 1829)—Atlantic spotted dolphin
Stenella longirostris (Gray, 1828)—long-snouted spinner dolphin
Steno bredanensis (Lesson, 1828)—rough-toothed dolphin
Tursiops aduncus (Ehrenberg, 1833)—Indian Ocean bottlenose dolphin
Tursiops truncatus (Montagu, 1821)—bottlenose dolphin

PHYSETERIDAE Gray, 1821

Definition—The monophyletic group including the common ancestor of *Apenophyseter**, "*Aulophyseter*"*, *Diaphorocetus**, *Helvicetus**, *Idiorophus**, *Orycterocetus**, *Physeterula**, *Placoziphius**, *Preaulophyseter**, *Prophyseter**, *Scaldicetus**, *Thalassocetus** and all of its descendants including *Physeter.*
Distribution—Widely distributed in all oceans of the world, avoiding only the polar pack ice in both hemispheres.
Fossil history—The record of physeterids goes back at least to the early early Miocene (23.3–21.5 Ma), Mediterranean (Italy), Paratethys (Europe), and western South Atlantic (Argentina); late early Miocene, western South Pacific (Australasia), eastern North Pacific (central California), and western North Pacific (Japan); early middle Miocene, western

North Atlantic (Maryland and Virginia); late middle Miocene-late Miocene, eastern North Atlantic (western Europe); late middle Miocene-late Pliocene, eastern North Atlantic (Florida); late late Miocene, eastern South Pacific (Peru); late Pliocene, eastern North Pacific (California), and perhaps earlier if *Ferecetotherium** is included from the late Oligocene (29–23 Ma; Deméré, 1994b).

Extinct genera are reviewed by Fordyce and Barnes (1994) and Cozzuol (1996; South American record).

Remarks—McKenna and Bell (1997) include the pygmy sperm whale as a subfamily.
Content—One genus and species are recognized.
Physeter macrocephalus Linnaeus, 1758 (syn. *Physeter catadon*)—sperm whale

KOGIIDAE (Gill, 1871) Miller, 1923

Definition—The monophyletic group including the common ancestor of *Kogiopsis**, *Scaphokogia** and all of its descendants including *Kogia*.
Distribution—Distributed in all oceans of the world (temperate, subtropical and tropical waters), with the range of *Kogia breviceps* recorded as in warmer seas (Handley, 1966).
Fossil History—The fossil record of kogiids goes back to the early late Miocene (8.5–5.2 Ma), eastern South Pacific (Peru); early Pliocene, western North Atlantic (Florida); late Pliocene, Mediterranean (Italy).

Extinct genera are reviewed by Fordyce and Barnes (1994).

Remarks—see Physeteridae.
Content—One genus and two Recent species are recognized.
Kogia breviceps (de Blainville, 1838)—pygmy sperm whale
Kogia simus Owen, 1866—dwarf sperm whale

ZIPHIIDAE Gray, 1865 (including Choneziphiidae Cope, 1895; Hyperoodontidae Gray, 1866)

Definition—The monophyletic group including the common ancestor of *Choneziphius**, *Cetorhynchus**, *Ninoziphius**, *Paleoziphius**, *Squaloziphius**, *Ziphiorostrum** and all of its descendants including *Berardius, Hyperoodon, Mesoplodon, Tasmacetus* and *Ziphius*.
Distribution—Temperate and tropical waters of all oceans, some species located far offshore in deep waters (exceptions *Berardius bairdii* from North Pacific and *Mesoplodon bidens* from cold temperature to subarctic North Atlantic).
Fossil history—The record of ziphiids extends back to the early early Miocene (23.3–21.5 Ma), eastern North Pacific (Oregon and Washington); later middle Miocene (14.6–11 Ma), eastern North Atlantic (western Europe); early Pliocene, North America; middle-late Miocene, western North Pacific (Japan); latest Miocene-early Pliocene, Australasia, western North Atlantic (Virginia and North Carolina, Florida), and eastern South Pacific (Peru); late Pliocene, Mediterranean (Italy), and Australasia (Deméré, 1994b).

Mesoplodon is known from the late middle Miocene (14.6–11 Ma), eastern North Atlantic (western Europe) and late Pleistocene-Holocene (western South Pacific, Argentina).

Extinct genera are reviewed by Fordyce and Barnes (1994) and Cozzuol (1996; South American record).

Remarks—As noted by McKenna and Bell (1997) although the name Hyperoodontidae has priority over Ziphiidae, the latter has been in universal use for more than a century.
Content—Five genera and 19 Recent species.

Beradius arnuxii Duvernoy, 1851—Arnoux's beaked whale
Beradius bairdii Stejneger, 1883—Baird's beaked whale
Hyperoodon ampullatus (Forster, 1770)—northern bottlenose whale
Hyperoodon planifrons Flower, 1862—southern bottlenose whale
Mesoplodon bahamondi Reyes et al., 1995—beaked whale
Mesoplodon bidens (Sowerby, 1804)—Sowerby's beaked whale
Mesoplodon bowdoini Andrews, 1908—Andrews' beaked whale
Mesoplodon carlhubbsi Moore, 1963—Hubb's beaked whale
Mesoplodon denisrostris (de Blainville, 1817)—Blainville's beaked whale
Mesoplodon europaeus Gervais, 1855—Gervais' beaked whale
Mesoplodon ginkgodensis Nishiwaki and Kamiya, 1958—ginkgo-toothed beaked whale
Mesoplodon grayi von Haast, 1896—Gray's beaked whale
Mesoplodon hectori (Gray, 1871)—Hector's beaked whale
Mesoplodon layardii (Gray, 1865)—strap-toothed beaked whale
Mesoplodon mirus True, 1913—True's beaked whale
Mesoplodon pacificus Longman, 1926—Longman's beaked whale
Mesoplodon peruvianus Reyes *et al.*, 1991—Peruvian beaked whale
Mesoplodon stejnegeri True, 1885—Stejneger's beaked whale
Tasmacetus shepardi Oliver, 1937—Tasman beaked whale
Ziphius cavirostris Cuvier, 1823—Cuvier's beaked whale

PLATANISTIDAE Gray, 1863

Definition—The monophyletic group including the common ancestor of *Pomatodelphis**, *Zarachis**, and all of its descendants including *Platanista.*
Distribution—Indus and Ganges River drainages of Pakistan and India.
Fossil history—Fossil plantanistids are known from the late early Miocene (21.5–16.3 Ma), western North Atlantic (Florida); early middle Miocene, western North Atlantic (Maryland and Virginia, Florida).

The stratigraphic occurrence of platanistids is further discussed in Gottfried et al. (1994); Morgan (1994).
Content—A single genus and two Recent species (or subspecies of a single species) are recognized.
Platanista gangetica (Roxburgh, 1801)—Ganges susu
Platanista minor Owen, 1853—Indus susu

INIIDAE Flower, 1867 (incl. Pontplanodidae Ameghino, 1894; Saurocetidae Ameghino, 1891; Saurodelphidae, Abel, 1905).

Definition—The monophyletic group including the common ancestor of *Goniodelphis**, *Ischyrorhynchus**, *Saurocetes** and all of its descendants including *Inia.*
Distribution—Amazon and Orinoco River drainages in central and northern South America.
Fossil history—Iniids are known from early late Miocene (10.4–6.7 Ma), western South Atlantic (Argentina, Uruguay); early Pliocene, western North Atlantic (Florida).

Fossil iniids are reviewed in Fordyce and Barnes (1994) and Cozzuol (1996; South American record).
Content—A single genus and two Recent species (or three subspecies of a single species) are recognized.

Inia geoffrenesis de Blainville, 1817—boto; Amazon river dolphin
I. geoffrensis humboldtiana Pilleri and Gihr, 1977
I. geoffrensis geoffrensis Van Bree and Robineau, 1973
Inia bolivienis D'Orbigny, 1834

LIPOTIDAE Zhou Qian and Li, 1979

Definition—The monophyletic group including the common ancestor of *Prolipotes** and all of its descendants including *Lipotes.*
Distribution—Confined to Yangtze (Changjiang) River drainage on the Chinese mainland.
Fossil history—A single extinct genus, *Prolipotes,* is reported from the Neogene of China (Zhou et al., 1984).
Content—A single genus and species is recognized.
Lipotes vexillifer Miller, 1918—baiji, Yangtse river dolphin.

PONTOPORIIDAE Gill, 1871; Kasuya, 1973
(=Stenodelphinae True, 1908)

Definition—The monophyletic group including the common ancestor of *Brachydelphis*, Parapontoporia*, Piscorhynchus*, Pliopontes*, Pontistes** and all of its descendants including *Pontoporia.*
Distribution—Restricted to coastal central Atlantic waters of South America.
Fossil history—Fossil record of pontoporiids extends back to the late Miocene (10.4–6.7 Ma), western South Atlantic (Argentina); late late Miocene, eastern North Pacific (California, Baja California), and eastern South Pacific (Peru); early Pliocene, western North Atlantic (Virginia and North Carolina), eastern North Pacific (California), and eastern South Pacific (Peru).

Pontoporia is reported from the early late Miocene (10.4–6.4 Ma), western South Atlantic (Argentina).

Extinct genera are reviewed by Fordyce and Barnes (1994); Cozzuol (1996; South American record).
Content—A single genus and species is recognized.
Pontoporia blainvillei Gervais and d'Orbigny, 1844—franciscana, La Plata dolphin

MONODONTIDAE Gray, 1821; Miller and Kellogg, 1955

Definition—The monophyletic group including the common ancestor of *Denebola** and all of its descendants including *Monodon* and *Delphinapterus.*
Distribution—The beluga and narwhal are confined to Arctic and subarctic waters.
Fossil history—Monodontids are known in the fossil record as far back as early late Miocene (10.4-6.7 Ma); late late Miocene, eastern North Pacific (California); late late Miocene, eastern North Pacific (Baja California); latest Miocene-early Pliocene, western North Atlantic (Virginia and North Carolina) and eastern North Pacific (California); late Pliocene, eastern North Pacific (California); late Pleistocene, eastern North Atlantic (western Europe) and Arctic Ocean (northern Alaska).

Extinct genera are reviewed by Fordyce and Barnes (1994).

The extant genus *Delphinapterus* is known from the western North Atlantic (Virginia and North Carolina; Whitmore, 1994). Extant species include *Monodon monoceras* and *Delphinaptereus leucas* late Pleistocene, western North Atlantic (Canada; Harrington, 1977).

Content—Two genera and two species are recognized.
Delphinapterus leucas (Pallas, 1776)—white whale or beluga
Monodon monoceros Linnaeus, 1758—narwhal

PHOCOENIDAE Gray, 1825; Bravard, 1885

Definition—The monophyletic group including the common ancestor of *Australithax*, Lomacetus*, Piscolithax*, Piscorhynchus*, Salumiphocoena**, and all of its descendants including *Neophocoena, Phocoena,* and *Phocoenoides.*
Distribution—Phocoenids are distributed throughout the world.
Fossil history—Phocoenids are known in the fossil record from early late Miocene-late late Miocene (10.4–6.7 Ma), eastern North Pacific (California); late late Miocene, eastern North Pacific (Baja California), and eastern South Pacific (Peru); early Pliocene, western North Atlantic (Virginia and North Carolina); early-late Pliocene, eastern North Pacific (California); late Pleistocene, eastern North Atlantic (western Europe), and western North Atlantic (Canada).

Extinct genera are reviewed by Fordyce and Barnes (1994) and Cozzuol (1996; South American record).

The extant species *Phocoena phocoena* is known from the late Pleistocene, eastern North Atlantic (western Europe; Van der Feen, 1968) and western North Atlantic (Canada; Harrington, 1977).
Content—Three genera and six species are recognized.
Neophocaena phocaenoides Cuvier, 1829—finless porpoise
Phocoena (Austraphocoena) dioptrica (Lahille, 1912), Barnes, 1985—spectacled porpoise
Phocoena phocoena (Linnaeus, 1758)—harbour porpoise
Phocoena sinus Norris and McFarland, 1958—vaquita
Phocoena spinipinnis Burmeister, 1865—Burmeister's porpoise
Phocoenoides dalli (True, 1885)—Dall's porpoise

MYSTICETI Flower, 1864

Diagnosis—telescoped skull in which the maxilla extends posteriorly under the orbit to form a plate-like infraorbital process; antorbital process of maxilla present; mandibular symphysis unfused, with ligamentous or connective tissue attachment.
Definition—The monophyletic group including the common ancestor of the extinct Aetiocetidae* and all of its descendants including the archaic families Llanocetidae*, Mammalodontidae*, Kekenodontidae*, "Cethotheriidae"* and modern families Balaenidae, Balaenopteridae, Eschrichtiidae, and Neobalenidae.
Fossil history—The earliest mysticetes are known from the late Eocene-early Oligocene (34–33 Ma), Antarctica; late Oligocene-Pleistocene, eastern North Pacific (California), western North Pacific (Japan, Australasia); early early Miocene-Pleistocene, western South Atlantic; early middle Miocene, western North Atlantic; late middle Miocene-Pleistocene, eastern North Atlantic (western Europe) (Deméré, 1994b).

BALAENIDAE Gray, 1825

Diagnosis—lack of dorsal fin, rostrum greatly arched, baleen plates numerous and greatly elongated (Barnes and McLeod, 1984; McLeod *et al.,* 1993).
Definition—The monophyletic group including the common ancestor of *Balaenula** and all of its descendants including *Balaena* and *Eubalaena.*

Distribution—Bowheads are circumpolar in the Arctic and right whales are known in temperate waters of both hemispheres.
Fossil history—Balaenids are known in the fossil record from early late Miocene (23 Ma), western North Atlantic (Florida); late late Miocene, eastern North Pacific (California); late Miocene-early Pliocene, western South Pacific (Australasia); early Pliocene, western North Atlantic (Virginia and North Carolina), eastern North Pacific (California), and western North Pacific (Japan); late Pliocene, eastern North Pacific (California), eastern North Pacific (Florida), and Mediterranean (Italy) (Deméré, 1994b).

The genus *Balaena* is reported from the early Pliocene (5.2–3.4 Ma), western North Atlantic (Virginia and North Carolina); late Pliocene, Mediterranean (Italy); early Pleistocene, eastern North Pacific (Oregon).

Extant species *Balaena mysticetus* is reported from the late Pleistocene, North Atlantic (Canada); *Eubalaena glacialis,* late Pleistocene, western North Atlantic (Florida).
Remarks—The taxonomic history of fossil balaenids has been reviewed by McLeod *et al.* (1993).
Content—Two genera and three Recent species are recognized.
Balaena mysticetus Linnaeus, 1758—bowhead whale
Eubalaena (=Balaena) glacialis Müller, 1776—northern right whale
E. (= Balaena) australis Desmoulins, 1822—southern right whale

ESCHRICHTIIDAE Ellerman and Morrison-Scott, 1951 (=Rhachianectidae Weber, 1904).

Diagnosis—knob-like serrations along dorsal ridge; 2–4 ventral throat grooves that do not extend past the throat region (Barnes and McLeod, 1984).
Definition—The monophyletic group including the common ancestor of *Eschrichtius* and all of its descendants.
Distribution—Three or more stocks of gray whales are recognized: North Atlantic stock (or stocks), apparently exterminated in recent historical times (perhaps as late as the seventeenth or eighteenth century); a Korean or western Pacific stock hunted at least until 1966, and now close to extinction; and a California or eastern Pacific stock (Leatherwood and Reeves, 1983).
Fossil history—The genus *Eschrichtius* is known from the late Pleistocene, western North Atlantic (Florida), eastern North Pacific (California; Deméré, 1994b).
Remarks—see Balaenopteridae.
Content—One genus and Recent species.
Eschrichtius robustus Lilljeborg, 1861—gray whale

BALAENOPTERIDAE Gray, 1864

Diagnosis—numerous throat grooves that extend past the throat region (Barnes and McLeod, 1984).
Definition—The monophyletic group including the common ancestor of *Idiocetus** and all of its descendants including *Balaenoptera* and *Megaptera.*
Distribution—Humpback, minke, fin, and blue whales are widely distributed in all oceans. Sei whales and Bryde's whales are usually found in tropical and warm temperate waters and not in polar regions as are other rorquals.
Fossil history—Balaenopterids are known from the early late Miocene (12 Ma), eastern North Pacific (California); late late Miocene, western North Atlantic (Maryland and Vir-

ginia), eastern North Pacific (southern California, Baja California), western North Pacific (Japan), and eastern South Pacific (Peru); latest Miocene-early Pliocene, Australasia; early Pliocene, eastern North Atlantic (western Europe), western North Atlantic (Virginia and North Carolina), western North Atlantic (Florida), eastern North Pacific (California), western North Pacific (Japan), and eastern South Pacific (Peru); late Pliocene, Mediterranean (Italy), western North Atlantic (Florida), and eastern North Pacific (California, western South Pacific, Australasia); early Pleistocene, western North Atlantic (western Europe); late Pleistocene, western North Atlantic (Canada) and eastern North Pacific (California).

The genus *Megaptera* is known from the early late Miocene, eastern North Pacific (central California); late Miocene-early Pliocene (Australasia); early Pliocene, western North Atlantic (Virginia and North Carolina); late Pliocene, western North Atlantic (Florida); late Pleistocene, western North Atlantic (Florida) and western North Atlantic (Canada).

Sei whale (*Balaenoptera borealis*) is reported from the late Pleistocene, western North Pacific (Japan). The humpback whale (*Megaptera novaeangliae*) is known from the late Pleistocene, western North Atlantic (Florida) and western North Atlantic (Canada) (Deméré, 1994b).

Extinct genera are reviewed by Fordyce and Barnes (1994) and Cozzuol (1996; South American record). For additions to the record from Japan see Oishi and Hasegawa (1995).

Remarks—McKenna and Bell (1997) include the gray whale as a subfamily.

Content—Two genera containing six or seven species are recognized.

Balaenoptera acutorostrata Lacépède, 1804—minke whale
Balaenoptera bonaerensis Burmeister, 1867—Antarctic minke whale
Balaenoptera borealis Lesson, 1828—sei whale
Balaenoptera edeni Anderson, 1878—Bryde's whale
Balaenoptera musculus (Linnaeus 1758)—blue whale
Balaenoptera physalus (Linnaeus, 1758)—fin whale
Megaptera novaeangliae (Borowski, 1781)—humpback whale

NEOBALAENIDAE (Gray, 1874) Miller, 1923

Diagnosis—parallel depressions (incipient throat grooves?) in the throat region (Barnes and McLeod, 1984).

Definition—The monophyletic group including the common ancestor of *Caperea* and all of its descendants.

Distribution—Known only in temperate waters of southern hemisphere (including Tasmania, coasts of South Australia, New Zealand, and South Africa).

Fossil history—No fossil species are known.

Content—One genus and species is recognized.

Caperea marginata (Gray, 1846)—pygmy right whale

SIRENIA Illiger, 1811

Diagnosis—External nares retracted and enlarged, reaching to or beyond the level of the anterior margin of the orbit; premaxilla contacts frontal; sagittal crest absent; P^{1-5}, M^{1-3}, or secondarily reduced from this condition by loss of anterior premolars; mastoid inflated and exposed through orbital fenestra; ectotympanic inflated and drop-like; pachyostosis and osteosclerosis present in skeleton (Domning, 1994).

Definition—The monophyletic group including the last common ancestor of "*Prorastomus*"* and all of its descendants including "*Protosiren*"*, the Trichechidae, and the "Dugongidae" (Domning, 1994).
Distribution—Sirenians occur in the Indo-Pacific (dugongs) and the southeastern U.S., Caribbean, and the Amazon drainage of South America (manatees).
Fossil history—Sirenians are recognized in the fossil record beginning in the early Eocene (56.5-50 Ma), western Tethys (Jamaica); middle Eocene, eastern Tethys (Pakistan and India), central Tethys (Egypt), and western Tethys (southeastern U.S.), late Eocene, central Tethys (Egypt, Europe); and extending through to the Recent.
Remarks.—McKenna and Bell (1997) include sirenians in the suborder Tethytheria along with desmostylians and elephants. They propose the Order Uranotheria to include the suborders Hyracoidea, Embrithopoda (extinct rhinoceros-like mammals) and Tethytheria.
Content—Composed of two families containing all living sirenians.

DUGONGIDAE Gray, 1821

Diagnosis—Ventral extremity of jugal lies approximately under posterior edge of orbit, but forward of jugal's postorbital process (if present); ventral border of horizontal ramus of mandible not tangent to angle; development of triangular flukes (Domning, 1994).
Definition—Paraphyletic family includes *Bharatisiren**, *Caribosiren**, *Crenatosiren**, *Corytosiren**, *Dioplotherium**, *Dusisiren**, *Eosiren**, *Eotheroides**, *"Halitherium"**, *Hydrodamalis**, *Metaxytherium**, *Prototherium**, *Rytiodus**, and *Xenosiren**.
Distribution—The dugong is widely distributed in shallow coastal bays of the Indo-Pacific region.
Fossil history—Dugongids are reported from middle Eocene (50–38.6 Ma), central Tethys; late Eocene, central Tethys (Egypt); late Oligocene, Paratethys (Caucasia) and central Tethys (Europe); early early Miocene, western South Atlantic (Argentina); late early Miocene, Paratethys (Austria and Switzerland), western North Atlantic (Florida), and western South Atlantic (Brazil); early middle Miocene, western North Atlantic (Maryland and Virginia); late middle Miocene, Mediterranean (Italy), eastern North Atlantic (western Europe), western North Atlantic (Florida), and eastern North Pacific (California, Baja California); early late Miocene, western North Atlantic (Florida), eastern North Pacific (California), and western North Pacific (Japan); late late Miocene, eastern North Pacific (southern California), and western North Pacific (Japan); early Pliocene, western North Atlantic (Florida), eastern North Pacific (California), and western North Pacific (Japan); late Pliocene, Mediterranean (Italy), western North Atlantic (Florida), and eastern North Pacific (California); early Pleistocene, western South Pacific (Australasia); late Pleistocene, eastern North Pacific (Alaska to central California) and western North Pacific (Japan; Deméré, 1994b).

The extant species *Dugong dugon,* may also occur in the Pleistocene (Domning, 1996).
Content—One extant genus and Recent species is recognized. Taxonomic history of dugongids is reviewed by Domning, 1996.
Dugong dugon (Müller, 1776)—dugong

TRICHECHIDAE Gill, 1872 (1821)

Diagnosis—External auditory meatus very broad and shallow, wider anteroposteriorly than high, reduction of neural spines; possibly tendency to enlargement and (at least in *Trichechus*) anteroposterior elongation of thoracic centra (Domning, 1994).

Definition—Most recent common ancestor of *Miosiren** and all of its descendants including *Anomotherium*, Potamosiren*, Ribodon**, and *Trichechus* (Domning, 1994).
Distribution—Members of this family inhabit the Gulf coast of Florida (*T. manatus manctus)*, the Caribbean and South American coast (*T. manatus latirostris*), the Amazon Basin (*T. inunguis*) and West Africa (*T. senegalensis*).
Fossil history—Trichechids are reported from the late Miocene, western South Pacific (Argentina), and eastern South Pacific (Brazil and Peru); early Pliocene, western North Atlantic (Virginia and North Carolina); late Pleistocene, western North Atlantic (Virginia, Florida (Deméré, 1994b); (Cozzuol, 1996; South American record).

The Antillean manatee *Trichechus manatus* is reported from the late Pleistocene, western North Atlantic (Florida); Deméré, 1994b).
Content—One extant genus and three species are recognized. Domning and Hayek (1986) describe morphologic distinction of subspecies.
Trichechus inunguis Natterer in von Pelzeln, 1883—Amazonian manatee
T. manatus manatus Linnaeus, 1758—Antillean manatee
T. manatus latirostris (Harlan, 1824) Hatt, 1934—Florida manatee
Trichechus senegalensis Link, 1795—West African manatee

DESMOSTYLIA Reinhart, 1953

Diagnosis—Lower incisors transversely aligned; enlarged passage present through squamosal from external auditory meatus to roof of skull; roots of P_1 fuse; paroccipital process enlarged (Ray *et al.,* 1994).
Definition—The monophyletic group containing the common ancestor of *Behemotops** and all of its descendants including: *Paleoparadoxia*, Cornwallius** and *Desmostylus** (Ray *et al.,* 1994).
Distribution—late Oligocene-Miocene of North America and Japan.
Fossil history—Desmostylians are known from late Oligocene, North America; late Oligocene or early Miocene, North America; late early and early middle Miocene, Japan; late Oligocene, North America; middle Miocene, North America (Domning, 1996).
Content—Contains no living genera.

References

Barnes, L. G., and S. A. McLeod (1984). The fossil record and phyletic relationships of gray whales, pp. 3–32. *In* "The Gray Whale *Eschrichtius robustus*" (Jones, M. L., S. L. Schwartz and S. Leatherwood, eds.), Academic Press, New York.

Berggren, W. A., D. V. Kent, C. C. Swisher, Jr., and M. P. Aubry (1995). A Revised Cenozoic Geochronology and Chronostratigraphy. *In* "Geochronology, Time Scales and Global Stratigraphic Correlations" (W. A. Berggren *et al.*, eds.), pp. 129–212. SEPM Special Publication, No. 54.

Berta, A. (1991). New *Enaliarctos** (Pinnipedimorpha) from the Oligocene and Miocene of Oregon and the role of "enaliarctids" in pinniped phylogeny. *Smithson. Contrib. Paleobiol.* **69**: 1–33.

Berta, A. (1994). New specimens of the pinnipediform *Pteronarctos* from the Miocene of Oregon. *Smithson. Contrib. Paleobiol.* **78**: 1–30.

Berta, A., and A. R. Wyss, (1994). Pinniped phylogeny. *Proc. San Diego Soc. Natl. Hist.* **29**: 33–56.

Cozzuol, M. A. (1996). The record of the aquatic mammals in southern South America. *Münchner Geowiss. Abh.* **30**: 321–342.

Deméré, T. A. (1994a). The Family Odobenidae: A phylogenetic analysis of fossil and living taxa. *Proc. San Diego Soc. Natl. Hist.* **29**: 99–123.

Deméré, T. A. (1994b). Phylogenetic systematics of the Family Odobenidae (Mammalia; Carnivora) with description of two new species from the Pliocene of California and a review of marine mammal paleofaunas of the world. Unpublished Ph.D dissertation, University of California, Los Angeles.

Domning, D. P. (1994). A phylogenetic analysis of the Sirenia. *Proc. San Diego Soc. Natl. Hist.* **29**: 177–190.

Domning, D. P. (1996). Bibliography and index of the Sirenia and Desmostylia. *Smithson. Contrib. Paleobiol.* **80**: 1–611.

Domning, D. P., and L. C. Hayek (1986). Interspecific and intraspecific morphological variation in manatees (Sirenia: *Trichechus*). *Mar. Mamm. Sci.* **2**(2): 87–144.

Fordyce, E. (1991). The fossil vertebrate record of New Zealand, pp. 1191–1314. *In* "Vertebrate Paleontology of Australasia" (P. Vickers-Rich, J. M. Monaghan, R. F. Baird, and T. Rich, eds.), Pioneer Design Studio, Melbourne, Australia.

Fordyce, E., and L. G. Barnes (1994). The evolutionary history of whales and dolphins. *Annu. Rev. Earth Planet. Sci.* **22**: 419–455.

Gottfried, M. D., D. J. Bohaska, and F. C. Whitmore, Jr. (1994). Miocene cetaceans of the Chesapeake group. *Proc. San Diego Soc. Natl. Hist.* **29**: 229–238.

Handley, C. O. Jr. (1966). A synopsis of the genus *kogia* (pygmy sperm whales), pp. 62–69. *In* "Whales, Dolphins and Porpoises" (K. S. Norris, ed.). University of California Press, Berkeley.

Harland, W. B., R. L. Armstong, A. V. Cox, L. E. Craig, A. G. Smith, and D. G. Smith (1990). "A Geologic Time Scale–1989." Cambridge University Press, 263 pp.

Harrington, C. R. (1977). Marine mammals from the Champlain Sea and the Great Lakes. *Ann. New York Acad. Sci.* **288**: 508–537.

Hendey, Q. B., and C. A. Repenning (1972). A Pliocene phocid from South Africa. *Ann. So. Afri. Mus.* **59**(4): 71–98.

Heyning, J. E., and W. F. Perrin (1994). Evidence for two species of common dolphin (Genus *Delphinus*) from the eastern North Pacific. *Contrib. Sci. Natl. Hist. Mus. Los Angeles Co.* **442**.

Kohno, N., L. G. Barnes, and K. Hirota (1995). Miocene fossil pinnipeds of the genus *Prototaria* and *Neotherium* (Carnivora: Otariidae): Imagotariinae in the North Pacific Ocean: evolution, relationship and distribution. *Island Arc* **3**: 285–308.

Koretsky, I. (1997). Pinniped bones from the late Oligocene of South Carolina: the oldest known true seal (Carnivora: Phocidae). *Abstr. 57th Ann. Meet. Soc. Vert. Paleo.,* Chicago, p. 58A.

Leatherwood, S., and R. R. Reeves (1983). "The Sierra Club Handbook of Whales and Dolphins." Sierra Club Books, San Francisco.

McKee, J. W. A. (1994). Geology and vertebrate paleontology of the Tangahoe Formation, South Taranaki Coast, New Zealand. *Geol. Soc. New Zealand Misc. Publ.* 80B: 63–91.

McKenna, M. C., and S. K. Bell (1997). "Classification of Mammals above the Species Level." Columbia University Press, N.Y.

McLeod, S. A., F. C. Whitmore, and L. G. Barnes (1993). Evolutionary relationships and classification. pp. 45–70. *In* "The Bowhead Whale" (J. J. Burns, J. J. Montague, and C. J. Cowles, eds), *Special Publication 2, Society of Marine Mammalogy,* Allen Press, Kansas.

Messenger, S. L., and J. McGuire (1998). Morphology, molecules, and the phylogenetics of cetaceans. *Syst. Biol.* **47**(1): 90–124.

Morgan, G. S. (1994). Miocene and Pliocene marine mammal faunas from the Bone Valley Formation of central Florida. *Proc. San Diego Soc. Natl. Hist.* **29**: 239–268.

Muizon, C. de (1981). Les vertébrés fossiles de la formation Pisco (Pérou). "Recherche sur les grandes civilisations." Mémoire no. 6, Instituts Francais d'etudes andines, editions A.D.P.F., Paris, 150 pp.

Muizon, C. de (1982). Phocid phylogeny and dispersal. *Ann. So. Afri. Mus.* **89** (2): 175–213.

Muizon, C. de (1984). Les vertébrés fossiles de la Formation Pisco (Pérou). "Deuxieme partie, les odontocees (Cetacea, Mammalia) du Pliocene inferieur de Sud-Sacaco." "Recherche sur les grandes civilisations." Institut Francais d'Etudes Andines, Mémoire 50: 1–188.

Oishi, M., and Y. Hasegawa (1995). Diversity of Pliocene mysticetes from eastern Japan. *Island Arc* 3(4): 436–452.

Ray, C. E., D. P. Domning, and M. C. McKenna (1994). A new specimen of *Behemotops proteus* (Order Desmostylia) from the marine Oligocene of Washington. *Proc. San Diego Soc. Natl. Hist.* **29**: 205–222.

Reeves, R. R., B. S. Stewart, and S. Leatherwood (1992). "The Sierra Club Handbook of Seals and Sirenians." Sierra Club Books, San Francisco, California.

Repenning, C. A., and R. H. Tedford (1977). Otarioid seals of the Neogene. *Geol. Surv. Prof. Pap.* (U.S.) **992**: 93 pp.

Rice, D. W. (1998). Marine Mammals of the World *Special Publications* 4, *Society of Marine Mammalogy.* Allen Press, Kansas.

Riedman, M. (1990). "The Pinnipeds." University of California Press, Berkeley.

Smith, A. G., D. G. Smith, and B. Funnell (1994). "Atlas of Mesozoic and Cenozoic Coastlines." Cambridge Univ. Press, Cambridge.

Thewissen, J. G. M. (1994). Phylogenetic aspects of cetacean origins: a morphological perspective. *Jour. Mamm. Evol.* **2**(3): 157–183.

Van der Feen, P. J. (1968). A fossil skull fragment of a walrus from the mouth of the River Scheldt (Netherlands). *Bhdragen Tot de Dierkunde* **38**: 23–30.

Whitmore, F. (1994). Neogene climactic change and the emergence of the modern whale fauna of the North Atlantic Ocean. *Proc. San Diego Soc. Nat. Hist.* **29**: 223–227.

GLOSSARY

Acoustic Thermometry of Ocean Climate Program (ATOC) A project that involved the installation of low frequency sound generators off the Hawaiian and California coasts to determine the effect of these sound transmissions on marine mammals

Adaptation A particular biological structure, physiological process, or behavior that results from natural selection

Aerobic dive limit (ADL) The length of time that an animal can remain underwater without accumulating lactate in the blood

Age distribution The relative number of individuals of each age in a population.

Allometry The variation in the relative rates of growth of various parts of the body in relation to the entire animal

Alloparenting A male or female that takes care of an offspring other than its own

Allozyme One of two or more alternate forms of a gene of an enzyme

Anaerobic Lacking oxygen

Ancestral A preexisting character or condition; also referred to as primitive

Antitropical Species pairs in which one member occupies the northern hemisphere and the other occupies the southern hemisphere

Apnea Breath holding

Apomorphic A condition of a character that is derived relative to a preexisting character of that condition; also referred to as derived

Archaeocetes An archaic group of whales

Area cladogram A hypothesized reconstruction of the geographic distribution of related organisms

Baculum Bone in the penis of some marine mammals (sea otter, polar bear, and pinnipeds)

Baleen Plates of cornified epithelial tissue suspended from the upper jaw of mysticete whales, also known as whalebone

Bends A serious condition that results when a diver breathing pressurized air ascends too rapidly after spending a period of time at depth; occurs when nitrogen under high pressure escapes into the blood, joints, and nerve tissue causing pain, paralysis, and death unless treated by gradual decompression

Birth rates The ratio between births and individuals in a specified population

Blastocyst An embryonic stage in mammals consisting of a hollow ball of cells

Blow Exhaled air mixed with water and oil emitted by whales from the blowhole

Blubber A thick layer of fat that occurs in the deep layer of the skin in whales and other marine mammals

Blue Whale Unit An early management procedure for estimating catch quotas using one blue whale in terms of oil yield as a standard equal to 2 fin, 2.5 humpback, or 6 sei whales

Brachyodont Low crowned teeth

Bradycardia A slow heart rate

Brown fat Specialized internal fat with a capacity for a high rate of oxygen consumption and heat production; allows newborn seals to generate heat efficiently; also known as brown adipose tissue (BAT)

Bubble-cloud feeding A strategy employed by humpback and other whales that involves emitting a train of air bubbles underwater which form a circular net; the whale surfaces in the center with mouth open to scoop up entrapped prey

Callosities Hard, thick, raised patches of skin found on the head of right whales; distributed near the mouth; the arrangement of these patches often is used to identify specific individuals

Carnivora An order of mammals that includes pinnipeds

Carrying capacity The maximum population that can be supported by existing resources

Cavum ventrale A hollow sac-like structure formed by the tongue which invaginates forming a ventral pouch in balanopterid whales; expansion of this pouch enlarges the capacity of the mouth and is used to engulf prey

Cenozoic era The last 65 million years of geologic time; marked by the diversification of mammals

Center of origin/dispersalist explanation Biogeographic origin of a group of organisms from a small area or center from which they dispersed

Cetacea An order of mammals that contains the whales, dolphins, and porpoises and their relatives

Cetology The study of cetaceans or whales

Character states Alternate forms of a character

Characterization A list of distinguishing characters that includes shared derived and shared primitive characters and their taxonomic distributions

Characters Heritable morphologic, molecular, physiologic, or behavioral attributes of organisms

Chevron bones Ventral processes on the posterior vertebrae that mark the beginning of the tail in cetaceans

Circumpolar Having a distribution around the poles

Clades Monophyletic groups of organisms

Cladistics A method of reconstructing the evolutionary history of organisms based on the shared possession of derived characters which provide evidence of a shared common ancestry

Cladogram A branching diagram that depicts relationships among organisms based upon cladistic methods

Classification The arrangement of taxa into a hierarchy

Click A broad frequency sound of short duration

Codas Rhythmic patterns of clicks used by sperm whales for communication

Commensalism A relationship between species in which one species benefits and the other is unharmed

Connecting stomach The third of four compartments of the cetacean stomach between the main stomach and the pyloric stomach

Convergence A similarity between organisms that is not the result of inheritance

Corpus albicans A permanent visible scar on the ovary that results from individual ovulations; a peculiarity of whales is that these scars are visible as rounded protuberances that remain for the rest of the animal's life

Corpus luteum The mass of tissue that is left after ovulation when a mature follicle ruptures from the ovary

Corridor A route of dispersal followed by organisms

Cosmopolitan Having a broad, wide-ranging distribution

Cost of transport The power required to move a given body mass at some velocity

Countercurrent heat exchange systems The opposite flow of adjacent fluids that maximize heat transfer rates

Cutaneous ridges Ridges located on the surface of the skin of many cetaceans that play a role in streamlining or tactile sensing

Deep scattering layer Concentrations of zooplankton that are found at depth during the day and that migrate upward to shallower water at night

Defined Recognizing a taxon based on its ancestry and taxonomic membership

Dental formula A convenient way of designating the number and arrangement of mammalian teeth (for example, I3/3, C1/1, P4/4, M3/3). The letters indicate incisors, canines, premolars, and molars. The numbers above the line indicate the number of teeth on one side of the upper jaw; those below the line indicate the number of teeth on one side of the lower jaw

Derived A character or condition that is changed from a preexisting character or condition

Desmostylians The only known extinct group of marine mammals; their close relatives are sirenians

Diagnosed The listing of shared derived characters and their taxonomic distribution for a group of organisms

Dialects Repetitions or calls that are characteristic of a particular geographic region

Diatoms A phylum of algae with glass-like walls that are important constituents of the base of the marine food chain

Digitigrade Walking on the digits (fingers and toes)

Diphyletic Having two separate ancestries

Disjunct The distribution of a species pair in which they are separated by a geographic barrier

Echelon formation A staggered arrangement of animals (e.g., spinner dolphin societies) that may serve a signaling function

Echolocation The production of high frequency sound and its reception by reflected echoes; used by toothed whales to navigate and locate prey

El Niño-Southern Oscillation Oceanographic events that occur in the eastern Pacific Ocean every few years in which prevailing current patterns change, water temperature increases, and upwelling declines; results in reduced food resources for marine mammals

Embolism The obstruction of a blood vessel by a foreign object (e.g., air bubble)

Encephalization quotient A numeric comparison that considers brain size relative to body size

Endemic Confined to a particular geographic region

Eocene An epoch of geologic time beginning approximately 55 Ma that marks the earliest record of cetaceans and sirenians

Escort One of several male humpbacks that attend a female. The principal escort usually is the one involved in mating; often secondary escorts are present that do not play an active role in mating

Estrus The period of sexual receptivity in females

Exaptation A different function for a structure than its original function

Extant Refers to living as opposed to extinct organisms

Facial and cranial asymmetry Bones and soft tissue in the odontocete skull that are of differing sizes; those on the right side are larger than those on the left side

Fast ice Sea ice attached to land

Female or harem defense polygyny Mating strategy in which males establish dominance hierarchies that confer priority access to females

Flukes Horizontally flattened tail of cetaceans and sirenians

Forestomach The first compartment of a multichambered stomach; characteristic of whales and some ungulate mammals

Frequency (power) spectrum A graphic representation of sound pressure levels with frequency

Frictional drag Resistant component to force that results from interaction of the animal's surface with surrounding water

Frontomandibular stay Portion of the temporalis (jaw closing) muscle that optimizes the angle at which the mouth can be opened during engulfment feeding by balaenopterid whales

Fundic chamber The second of four compartments of the cetacean stomach; also referred to as the main stomach

Genetic drift Changes in the gene pool of a population due to chance

Geographic location dive time and depth recorders (GLTDRs) Instruments that record geographic location, duration, and depth of dive

Gestation The period between fertilization and birth

Global Positioning System (GPS) An instrument that is used to locate precise geographic position using satellite data while the user is in the field

Glove finger A hardened plug of tissue in the external ear canal of baleen whales

Growth layer group (GLG) A layer of tissue in bone or teeth that represents a regular interval of time (usually one year)

Guard hairs Outer coat of coarse protective hair found on most mammals

Hematocrit The percentage of red blood cells to total blood volume

Hemoglobin An iron-containing protein in red blood that transports oxygen

Heterodont A dentition in which teeth are differentiated into several types, such as incisors, canines, premolars, and molars, with different functions

Heterogamy Having different gametes (e.g., males have XY sex chromosomes)

Heterozygosity Containing two different alleles for a given trait

Homodont A dentition with all teeth very similar in form and function

Homogamy Having the same gametes (e.g., females have XX sex chromosomes)

Homology A similarity that is the result of inheritance

Homoplasy A similarity that is not the result of inheritance

Homozygotes Containing two identical alleles for a given trait

Hybridization An offspring of two different species

Hyperosmotic Having a higher osmotic pressure than the surrounding environment

Hyperphalangy An increase in number of digits, seen in whales

Hypoosmotic Having a lower osmotic pressure than the surrounding environment

Hypoxia An oxygen deficiency that reaches the body's tissues

Induced ovulators In female polar bears the release of a mature follicle from the ovary (i.e., ovulation) occurs only when she is stimulated by the presence and activity of a male

Infrasonic Low frequency sounds below 18 Hz

Ingroup The group of organisms whose evolutionary relationships are the subject of investigation (see outgroup)

Introgression The transplantation of genes between species resulting from fertile hybrids mating successfully with one of the parent species

Ischemia A local decrease in blood flow resulting from its obstruction

Isotope dilution techniques Field method used to estimate the fat and fat-free components and rate of water intake in an animal. It involves administering a concentration of an isotope to an animal and subsequently measuring the concentration of this isotope in body tissues (e.g., blood).

junk The region of the sperm whale head, below the spermaceti organ, filled with oil and connective tissue; called junk by whalers because of its lesser quantity of oil

K-selected species Characterized by long life spans, low mortality rates, large body size, and production of few offspring that are intensively nurtured (see r-selected species)

Kolponomos An extinct bear-like carnivore that may have filled the sea otter niche during the middle Miocene.

Krill Shrimp-like crustaceans of the family Euphausidae that form the primary food resource for baleen whales and certain pinnipeds (e.g. crabeater seal)

Lactate Metabolic end product produced during anaerobic metabolism

Lek A mating strategy or courtship display in which males display to females

Lineages Ancestor–descendant populations of organisms through time

Lobtail feeding Strategy observed in humpbacks in which feeding is followed by a tail slap which may serve to aggregate prey

Main stomach The second compartment in the multichambered stomach of cetaceans

Mapping Placing the distributions of nonheritable characters (e.g., geographic distribution, ecological association) on a particular tree topology

Marine Mammal Protection Act Federal regulation enacted by legislature in 1972 to protect marine mammals in U.S. waters

Marine mammals Those species of mammals that spend all or most of their existence in the water

Mariposia The practice of drinking seawater

Mass stranding Three or more individuals of the same species that intentionally swim or are unintentionally trapped ashore by waves or receding tides

Mate guarding Mating strategy that involves males displacing one another while attending nursing females

Mating Reproductive activity in animals; also referred to as breeding

Matrifocal Aggregations of matrilines

Matrilineal Descendants of a single female

Melon Fat-filled structure on the forehead of odontocetes that functions to focus sound

Mesonychids Group of extinct ungulates; they are hypothesized to be the closest relatives of whales

Microsatellites Very short repeated DNA sequences

Minisatellites Short repeated DNA sequences

Miocene An epoch of geologic time beginning approximately 23 Ma and ending 5 Ma

Monestrous Having only one estrus cycle each year

Monkey lips/dorsal bursa (MLDB complex) Soft tissue structures located in the nasal passages of odontocetes hypothesized as the mechanisms of sound production

Monogamous A mating strategy in which adult males mate with only one female

Monophyletic group A group of organisms that includes a common ancestor and all of its descendants

Morbillivirus Serious pathogen that affects marine mammals by suppressing immune system responses

Mortality The proportion of deaths in a population

Museau de singe Valve-like slit that opens into the right nasal passage of the sperm whale, homologous to the nasal plugs of other odontocetes

Mutualists Two species which both benefit from the relationship between them

Myoglobin Hemoglobin in the muscles

Nasal plugs Masses of connective tissue that when retracted open the nasal passages of odontocetes

Natality Birth rate

Nitrogen narcosis A state of euphoria and exhilaration that occurs when air is breathed under increased pressure that occurs with depth

Nodes Branching points on a cladogram

Nomenclature The formal system of naming taxa

Nonshivering thermogenesis Process by which an animal keeps warm by metabolizing brown fat to produce heat

Oligocene An epoch of geologic time beginning approximately 35 Ma and ending 23 Ma

Optimization *A posteriori* arguments as to how particular characters should be polarized given a particular tree topology

Optimum sustainable population (OSP) Population level between 60% of its carrying capacity and carrying capacity

Osmotic The flow of solvent through a semipermeable membrane

Osteosclerotic Containing compact bone

Otarioid Non-monophyletic group of pinnipeds that includes walruses, otariids, and their extinct relatives

Outgroup Taxon or group of organisms that is closely related but outside the group whose relationships are the subject of investigation

Outgroup comparison Procedure for determining the polarity (ancestral or derived) condition of a character; assumes that the character found in the outgroup is the ancestral condition for the group in question (ingroup)

Pachyostosis Thick dense bone

Pack ice Sea ice that is unattached to land

Paedomorphism A change in developmental timing such that adults retain juvenile characteristics

Pagophilic Seals that inhabit ice

Paleolithic That period of the Stone Age characterized by stone implements

Pan bone Thin area of bone in the lower jaw of odontocetes filled with a fat channel that is hypothesized as the sound receiver

Parallelism Characters that have evolved independently in two groups

Paraphyletic group A group of organisms that does not include the common ancestor and all of its descendants

Paraxonic An arrangement of digits in which the plane of symmetry passes between the third and fourth digits

Parsimony The principle that prefers the hypothesis with the fewest number of steps

Parturition Giving birth; calving in whales and pupping in pinnipeds and sea otters

Peripheral vasoconstriction Redistribution of blood such that some tissues receive more blood than other tissues

Peritympanic sinuses Air-filled sinuses surrounding the tympanic region of cetaceans

Pharyngeal pouches Air-filled sacs located in the throat of walruses which when struck with the front flippers produce distinctive sounds

Phenetic A method of classification based on overall similarity of the taxa

Pheromones Chemical signals that function in communication between organisms

Photic zone The uppermost zone in the water where sunlight permits photosynthesis

Phylogenetic systematics Method of determining evolutionary relationships among taxa based on shared possession of derived characters; also referred to as cladistics

Phylogenetic tree Branching diagram that represents the relationships of a group of organisms; sometimes distinguished from cladogram as an ecological reconstruction rather than a genealogical reconstruction

Phylogeny Evolutionary history of a group of organisms

Phytoplankton Microscopic algae floating near the surface that forms the base of the food chain

Pingers Acoustic sound devices that are used to prevent marine mammals from net entanglement

Pinnae External ear; reduced or absent in many marine mammals

Pinnipeds Monophyletic group that includes seals, sea lions, and walruses

Pleistocene An epoch of geologic time beginning approximately 1.6 Ma

Plesiomorphic Ancestral or primitive character

Pliocene An epoch of geologic time beginning approximately 5 Ma and ending 1.6 Ma

Pods Social units of certain cetaceans, particularly killer whales

Polychlorinated biphenols Industrial chemicals (i.e., organochlorides) that are toxic to many animals including marine mammals and are identified as pollutants in many coastal environments.

Polydactyly Possession of several or many additional digits

Polygynous A mating strategy in which one male mates with more than one female during a breeding season

Polyestrous Having more than one estrus cycle each year

Polynya A large area of water in pack ice that remains open throughout the year

Polyovular Producing numerous corpora lutea each pregnancy

Polytomy A pattern of unresolved relationships among taxa

Population A group of organisms of the same species occupying a specific geographic region

Porpoising Leaping locomotion; an animal partially avoids the drag associated with surfacing by leaping above the water

Postpartum estrus Female sexual receptivity that occurs immediately following birth and is a characteristic of phocids and otariids

Precocious Born in an advanced state of development (i.e., able to walk and swim); in contrast to altricial which refers to birth in an undeveloped state

Pressure drag Resistant force created by the need to displace an amount of water equal to an animal's largest cross-sectional diameter

Primary production Organisms such as plants able to produce their own food and which support other levels

Primitive The ancestral form of a character (see derived).

Promiscuous Mating system of many cetaceans and sirenians in which adult males randomly associate with females for variable periods of time

Pyloric stomach The final compartment in the multichambered stomach of cetaceans

R-selected species Characterized by rapid population increase (often in unpredictable, fluctuating environments) and production of many offspring with little parental investment

Reniculate Refers to a kidney that is made up of small lobes or reniculi that is characteristic of pinnipeds, cetaceans, polar bears, and sea otters

Resident One of two populations of killer whales occupying coastal waters of the Pacific Northwest. Resident populations are distinguished from transient populations by a number of foraging-related differences

Resource defense polygyny Type of mating system in which males exclude other males from access to females by defending breeding territories

Rete ridges Flap-like projections between the epidermis and dermis of the skin of cetaceans

Retia mirabilia Groups of blood vessels that form blocks of tissue on the dorsal wall of the thoracic cavity, extremities, or body periphery; they function as reservoirs for blood and as countercurrent heat exchange systems

Reversal Loss of a derived feature and reestablishment of an ancestral feature

Revised management procedure (RMP) Estimations of the number of whales that can be taken with low risk of causing the affected population to be reduced below its maximum net productivity

Reynolds number A widely used indicator of the forces acting on submerged bodies, approximated by the equation (body length)× (swimming velocity)/(water viscosity)/(water density)

Rorquals Whales of the family Balaenopteridae; includes humpbacks, sei, minke, and fin whales

Rostral or oral disc Upper lip and mouth of manatees and dugongs; covered with vibrissae and used in feeding

Rostrum Anterior portion or beak region of the skull that is elongated in most cetaceans

Schools Structured social groups observed in odontocetes characterized by long-term association among individuals

Seasonal delayed implantation Suspension of development of the embryo in some marine mammals (pinnipeds and sea otters) for several months

Sexual dimorphism External differences between males and females of a particular species

Signature whistles Narrow band frequency modulated sound produced by dolphins and hypothesized to function for individual recognition as well as communication among group members

Sirenia The only herbivorous order of marine mammals; includes manatees and dugongs

Sister group The closest relative to the ingroup

Sonogram A graphic representation of sound frequency with time

Speciation Splitting of a lineage resulting in the formation of two species from a single common ancestor

Speciation events Those factors such as emergence of geographic barriers that cause lineage splitting

Sperm competition Mating strategy seen in some mysticetes in which copulating males attempt to displace or dilute the sperm of other males in an attempt to increase the probability of being the male to fertilize the female

Spermaceti Waxy fluid that fills the spermaceti organ; this is the sperm whale oil that was sought after by whalers

Spermaceti organ Elongate connective tissue sac in the forehead of sperm whales that contains spermaceti

Stocks Subdivision of a population of animals that is subject to commercial exploitation; term often used by management agencies

Subdermal connective tissue sheath Collagenous tissue layer that envelops the lateral surfaces of cetaceans and serves as an important anchor for muscles of the tail

Surfactants Substances lining lung surfaces that reduce surface tension

Survivorship The number of individuals of a group that are alive at each age

Synapomorphy Shared derived character, used as evidence of a shared common ancestry between taxa

Systematics Study of biological diversity that has as its emphasis the reconstruction of evolutionary histories among organisms

Tapetum lucidum A specialized layer behind the retina that reflects light and enables an animal to see better in darkness

Taphonomic Processes that affect an organism after death

Taxon A particular taxonomic group at a given rank

Taxonomy A branch of systematics that deals with the description, identification, and classification of species

Telemetry Techniques for measuring the distance of an object (e.g., animal) from an observer

Telescoping Change in the relationship of bones of the cetacean skull in response to the migration of the nasal opening to the top of the skull

Tethytheria The monophyletic group that includes proboscideans (elephants), sirenians, and extinct desmostylians

Thalassocnus Extinct aquatic sloth that lived during the early Pliocene

Throat grooves Furrows in the throat region of balaenopterids that can open up like pleats during feeding to expand the mouth cavity

Time depth recorders Instruments that record the duration and depth of dives

Transient One of two populations of Pacific Northwest killer whales that usually do not reside in an area for an extended period of time (i.e., nonresidents) and that can be distinguished from resident populations by a number of foraging-related differences

Trophic levels The division of species in an ecological community based on their main food source

Tusks Enlarged incisor or canine teeth

Tympano-periotic complex Bones of the skull that make up the auditory bulla

Ultrasonic High frequency sounds

Underfur hairs Short fine hairs that serve primarily for insulation

Units Social groups of females and immature sperm whales

Upwelling Areas off continental margins where circulation patterns bring nutrient rich water to the surface

Vicariance explanation An hypothesis to explain patterns of distribution among organisms which argues that organisms occur in an area because they evolved there

Wave riding Behavior seen in dolphins in which they ride the waves of a boat's wake

Whalebone Another name for baleen; term used by whalers

Whale lice Amphipod crustaceans (cyamids) found on the skin of large cetaceans

INDEX

Page numbers followed by f or t denote figures and tables, respectively